College Writing with Readings

Elizabeth Cloninger Long
Sacramento City College

PEARSON
Longman

New York San Francisco Boston
London Toronto Sydney Tokyo Singapore Madrid
Mexico City Munich Paris Cape Town Hong Kong Montreal

Acquisitions Editor: Melanie Craig
Director of Development: Mary Ellen Curley
Development Editor: Katharine Glynn
Marketing Manager: Thomas DeMarco
Senior Supplements Editor: Donna Campion
Media Supplements Editor: Jenna Egan
Production Manager: Ellen MacElree
Project Coordination, Text Design, and Electronic Page Makeup: Electronic Publishing
    Services Inc., NYC
Cover Design Manager: Wendy Ann Fredericks
Cover Designer: Nancy Sabato
Photo Research: Clare Maxwell
Senior Manufacturing Manager: Alfred C. Dorsey
Printer and Binder: Quebecor World—Taunton
Cover Printer: Coral Graphic Services

For permission to use copyrighted material, grateful acknowledgment is made to the copyright holders on pp. 855–856, which are hereby made part of this copyright page.

Library of Congress Cataloging-in-Publication Data
Long, Elizabeth Cloninger.
    College writing resources with readings / Elizabeth Cloninger Long.
        p. cm.
    Includes bibliographical references and index.
    ISBN 0-321-17223-X (pbk.)
    1. English language—Rhetoric—Problems, exercises, etc. 2. Report writing—
    Problems, exercises, etc. 3. College readers. I. Title.
    PE1413.L655 2006
808'.042—dc22   2006004391

Please visit our Web site at http://www.ablongman.com/long

ISBN 0-321-17223-X (Student's Edition)
ISBN 0-321-17225-6 (Instructor's Edition)

1 2 3 4 5 6 7 8 9 10—DOC—09 08 07 06

Contents

iii

PART FOUR
Strategies for Essay Development   233

PART FIVE
Writing for Different Purposes　445

PART EIGHT
Readings for Informed Writing   733

Our Identities

Our World

Our Values

Preface

Students must learn to write clearly and knowledgeably. Despite the availability of hundreds of writing texts and writing courses, students still struggle to master the skills that allow them to produce effective, informed, correct writing. A balance between formulaic grammar and documentation lessons and "nurturing" process-oriented books has yet to be attained in academia. Further, even as they are bombarded by information from online sources, few students are able to sift through irrelevant, unhelpful sources to find credible information. *Sentence Resources for Writers*, *Resources for Writers*, and *College Writing Resources*—a three-book series designed to take students from simple paragraph construction through essay writing—offers students opportunities to practice their writing-process skills while simultaneously eliminating sentence-level errors and learning how to research a topic.

A crucial consideration in writing the *Resources* series is that many students have been academically sheltered and, thus, are lacking basic cultural literacy. Current textbooks do little to assist these students, instead offering examples and assignments based on fictitious situations or popular culture alone. The *Resources* series, however, offers easily digestible information beneficial to instructors and students both in college and in contemporary society. From sample paragraphs and essays on the U.S. Supreme Court and poverty in America to mini-biographies of Albert Einstein and Rosa Parks, the *Resources* books provide students with a cultural foundation upon which to build further writing skills.

Today's increasingly diverse student population gains an additional benefit from material based on American icons and experiences. The broad range of topics for model paragraphs and exercises pique students' interest in American culture and their own writing, and, in turn, makes for more thoughtful, informed prose.

Finally, *College Writing Resources* departs from its essay-level counterparts in clarifying the role that simple research plays in student writing. While many students and instructors alike fear the research essay as a source of excessive stress, learning to write informed, thoughtful essays—using more than one's own experiences for support—is critical to success both in academia and in employment. *College Writing Resources* offers essays in nearly every chapter that illustrate how consulting just one or two sources can greatly improve students' knowledge, credibility, and powers of persuasion. Providing students with a generally documented format (and a formal list of Works Cited available online at www.ablongman.com/long), the essays demonstrate the benefits of integrating others' ideas into one's own for the purposes of being convincing. The essays demonstrate the benefits of integrating others' ideas into one's own work for the purposes of illustration and persuasion. Students learn how a quick search of databases available at many college and public libraries can provide them with details that more solidly support their positions, thus leading to convincing prose.

Goals and Themes

While the pedagogical goal of *College Writing Resources* is to help students develop their writing skills, an all-encompassing goal involves expanding students' body of knowledge in order to help them become better informed students and people. *College Writing Resources* further strives to both instruct and empower students in the development of writing skills though its many varied exercises in every chapter. Additionally, the text encourages students to develop their own writing processes through the multi-faceted writing assignments designed to focus attention on what works for them as writers. Last, *College Writing Resources* encourages students to learn about their topics before completing their writing process; thus, students practice the skill of using others' ideas for support.

Overview of Organization and Content

Part One, "Getting Started," shows students that they already possess and practice key thinking skills. Demonstrating those skills in writing is simply one more step in a process they've already begun. Part One also introduces the four cornerstones of good writing, which serve as four bases for evaluation. The Four Cs—concise, credible, clear, and correct writing—provide students with the foundation to understand and practice the elements of good writing.

Part Two, "The Writing Process," introduces the concepts of prewriting, drafting, revising, and editing, while modeling each concept and providing practice opportunities.

Part Three, "Writing Essays," links key writing skills to the Four Cs, showing students how practicing each skill also leads to the mastery of the Four Cs. In addition, chapters devoted to topics such as sensitive language, word choice, spelling, and sentence variety provide specific guidance for students to follow in improving their writing.

Part Four, "Strategies for Essay Development," serves many functions. First, it introduces, explains, and models the nine traditional modes of essay development. In addition, Chapter 26 explains how to combine strategies effectively. The cultural literacy themes in Part Four provide generally "meatier" topics for discussion and writing, giving students opportunities to think and write about such subjects as dictators, opera, and poverty in the United States. Finally, Part Four provides tiered writing assignments so that instructors (or students) can select the amount of research required for a particular topic. Every chapter offers assignments requiring no research as well as others requiring the consultation of written sources.

Part Five, "Writing for Different Purposes," gives explanations, examples, and practice in writing for specific real-life purposes.

Part Six, "Research," teaches students not only how to find, evaluate, and integrate information but also how to persuasively present their ideas.

Part Seven, "Writing Correct Sentences," provides logical, common-sense explanations of grammar with practice and exercises.

Part Eight, "Punctuation," gives helpful explanations and practice in mechanics, with line-by-line exercises and editing practices for each skill being studied.

Part Nine, "Readings for Informed Writing," includes eighteen high-interest readings clustered around three themes that illustrate a range of writing styles, patterns of development, and subject matter. The readings are accompanied by supportive pre- and post-reading questions.

Chapter Features of *College Writing Resources*

Every feature of *College Writing Resources* is specifically designed to support the goal of helping students improve their writing skills through the writing process as they learn about aspects of their culture and world. That is, students learn to write clearly and knowledgeably at the same time.

Modular Text Format

The modular text format provides opportunities for lessons and assignments within a single chapter but allows for connections between chapters as well. Students can read new information, receive tips to help them integrate that new information into what they have already learned, and find cross-references to other chapters that link past and future lessons. Instructors can tailor chapter assignments to the needs of a specific class or an individual student.

Cultural Literacy Theme

The cultural literacy component offers students easily digestible information beneficial to them in college and in contemporary society. For a variety of reasons, many beginning college writers lack basic cultural literacy. In classes that presume a certain knowledge foundation—such as history, political science, or literature—these students find themselves behind. Each chapter of *College Writing Resources* begins with a Culture Note that introduces a cultural theme; some notes are whimsical and some are serious, but all are designed to illuminate a part of the cultural heritage of the United States and, to a certain extent, the world. Sample essays, paragraphs, and exercises revolve around these themes, so students can see concepts illustrated with real subject matter, not just with fictionalized or overly personalized material. In addition, these themes offer students from diverse backgrounds insight into the historical basis of material they read in their classes, and they also offer a broad range of topics students can use in their own writing.

Cultural Literacy Photos
College Writing Resources contains some three dozen full-color photos that reinforce the cultural literacy themes in the chapters. The photos give students additional insight into our complex cultural heritage, and photo captions provide writing prompts to stimulate students' thinking.

Four Cs of Writing
College Writing Resources uses a simple mnemonic device, the Four Cs, to help students remember that their writing must be *concise, credible, clear*, and *correct*. This formula is completely integrated into the text, examples, and exercises so that students learn how to check their work for the elements of good writing at every stage in the writing process. Graphics and checklists reinforce the Four Cs and provide ready reference for students.

Writing Process
College Writing Resources uses a clear, step-by-step writing process approach to guide students through the how-tos of writing a paragraph: prewriting, drafting, revising, and editing. Examples, exercises, graphics, and checklists consistently support and reinforce this paradigm.

Writing Skills
Four basic writing skills—writing an effective thesis statement, using specific details for support and illustrations, organizing and linking ideas, and writing correct sentences—are integrated into the writing process steps. The skills are also keyed to the Four Cs so that students experience a coherent approach to paragraph writing. For example, students learn that writing an effective thesis statement will make their writing concise and that using specific details will make their writing credible.

Rhetorical Modes
College Writing Resources guides students through an understanding of nine strategies of essay development, as well as providing essay examples that employ several development strategies at once. Each strategy is thoroughly defined through explanation, examples, and both student and professional essays. Further, revision through the Four Cs is exemplified and explained in a student essay in every chapter. Tiered writing assignments give instructors and students options in terms of how much research is required for a particular assignment, and checklists provide handy reference for students.

Readings
Eighteen readings in a separate readings section—in addition to ten readings in the modes section—illustrate a range of writing styles, development strategies, and subject matter of interest to students. Each reading is prefaced by a

biographical note and pre-reading questions and followed by additional activities and writing exercises. Instructors can use readings in conjunction with teaching the rhetorical modes they illustrate or as independent assignments.

Grammar and Language

Each chapter addressing grammar, punctuation, mechanics, word use, and other language issues is developed with the same care and creativity featured in the writing chapters. Cultural literacy themes are used so that students can see sentence-level edits in the context of real subject matter. In addition, Chapter 11, "Sensitive Language," addresses the issue of writing for and about diverse groups in nonbiased ways, a subject hardly touched on in other writing texts.

Additional Features

College Writing Resources includes a wide range of features that provide alternatives for practice and instruction.

- **Guided writing assignments** lead students through every step in the writing process to produce essays.
- **Chapter exercises** throughout the text give immediate reinforcement of content.
- A **wide range of writing topics** gives students relevant writing assignments to choose from.
- A **real-life writing** section in each of the modes chapters shows students how particular development strategies are used in educational, personal, and professional situations.
- An **individual goal sheet** template on page 99 allows students to evaluate completed writing assignments and set goals for improvement in future writing assignments.
- A **peer editing worksheet** template on page 95 helps students constructively evaluate each other's writing.
- **Full research and documentation chapters** help students seek, find, evaluate, integrate, and document sources for their writing.
- A **complete plagiarism section** defines plagiarism and explains its consequences, providing help in avoiding illegal use of others' work.
- **Editing exercises** in the grammar and punctuation chapters give students line-by-line and whole-paragraph practice in identifying and correcting sentence-level errors.
- A **guide to reading critically and writing well** provides an overview to general reading and writing skills.
- An **Internet evaluation** section provides guidelines for choosing and using online sources.

■ **Multicultural readings at multiple skill levels** allow students to experience easy-to-follow texts as well as more complex essays by writers of all backgrounds.

■ **Pre-reading exercises in critical thinking and writing** allow students to consider a topic without the pressure of a formal assignment.

■ **Vocabulary activities** as both pre- and post-reading activities enhance students' comprehension and their skill in sentence variation.

■ **Content and structure questions** for every reading give students tools for greater comprehension and analysis.

Supplements

Text-Specific Supplements

Lab manual to accompany *College Writing Resources* (0-321-46222-X). A comprehensive lab manual extends chapter practice. Available at no additional cost when packaged with *College Writing Resources* or available separately. Contact your Longman sales representative to create a valuepack.

Companion Web site. The complete lab manual is available online at **www.ablongman.com/long.**

Instructor's Manual (0-321-7226-4). This supplement offers useful teaching suggestions and includes an introduction to the textbook.

Annotated Instructor's Edition (0-321-17225-6). A replica of the student text with answers to exercises included.

Test Bank (0-321-46708-6). A collection of tests to accompany *College Writing Resources.*

Computerized Test Bank (0-321-17228-0). A collection of tests available on CD to accompany *College Writing Resources.*

The Longman Developmental English Package

Longman is pleased to offer a variety of support materials to help make teaching developmental English easier on teachers and to help students excel in their course work. Many of our student supplements are available at no additional cost or at a greatly reduced price when packaged with *College Writing Resources.* Contact your local Longman sales representative or visit our online catalog at www.ablongman.com for a complete listing of our support materials.

Multimedia Offerings

Interested in incorporating online materials into your course? Longman is happy to help. Our regional technology specialists provide training on all of our multimedia offerings.

MyWritingLab (www.mywritinglab.com). This complete online learning system is the first that will truly help students become successful writers—and, therefore, successful in college and beyond.

Acknowledgments

I wish to acknowledge the contributions of my colleagues and reviewers who provided valuable advice and suggestions. Irene Anders, Indiana University at Fort Wayne; Linda Borla, Cypress College; Barbara Brown, Olive-Harvey College; Sheila Counts, Spartanburg Technical College; John R. Corrigan, Northern Maine Community College; Thomas Eaton, Southeast Missouri State University; Mark Ende, Onondaga Community College; Jason Evans, Prairie State College; Maria M. Flynn, West Kentucky Community and Technical College; Dan Foltz-Gray, Roane State Community College; Ulanda Forbess, North Central Texas College; Gwendolyn James, Columbia Basin College; Debra Matier, College of Southern Idaho; Donna Matsumoto, Leeward Community College; Matthew Murray, Riverside Community College; Mary Nakano, Leeward Community College; Janet K. Porter, Leeward University; Melissa Utsler, Chaffey College; David Ragsdale, Kingwood Community College; Melissa Rayborn, Valencia Community College; Elaine Rush, College of the Sequoias; Constantine Taylor, Cuyahoga Community College

The editorial staff of Longman Publishers deserve special recognition and thanks for the guidance, support, and direction they have provided. Melanie Craig, editor, was a constant source of knowledge, encouragement, and sanity during even the most stressful stages of this text's development. Katharine Glynn's problem-solving abilities were tested more than once over the course of this project, and she never failed to find logical, creative solutions to sticky problems. Susan Messer's careful eye was invaluable in the final stages of editing, and Lindsey Allen was incredibly prompt in providing me with necessary information and texts during this book's development. Outside of Longman, I also wish to thank Steven Rigolosi, novelist, for initially giving me this chance to write textbooks. Further, I wish to thank Kristin Ramsdell and Judy Clarence (both of California State University at Hayward) and Stephen Nagy, M.D. for their assistance with the opera chapter. Paul Cloninger, M.D. was helpful with the fishing chapter, as were Sara Howard and Andy Cloninger. Andy Cloninger also provided relevant information for the credit cards and libraries chapters. Additionally, Harold Hastings and Lydia Hastings provided apt feedback on the music chapter. I thank Annabelle Long for her suggestion of "Hickory Dickory Dock" for the clocks chapter, and I want to say a final thank-you to Noemi Beas, Charlotte Cloninger, Elsbeth Cloninger, and Mareva Brown for their eleventh-hour assistance and support.

ELIZABETH CLONINGER LONG
SACRAMENTO, CALIFORNIA

PART ONE
Getting Started

1 Your Strengths as a Writer

CULTURE NOTE *Education*

Since writing began as pictographic signs nearly six thousand years ago, education has expanded and taken many forms over the centuries. Whereas education was once limited to privileged groups or religious castes, it is now available—in many countries—to anyone who seeks it. From taking night courses at a community college to being apprenticed to a tradesperson or enrolled full time in a university, we may find that the roads to education increase and lengthen as we live.

Students on Campus

FOOD FOR THOUGHT Though colleges seek to educate students, they provide other benefits through social, political, and emotional support programs. Thumb through your college catalogue or talk with classmates about some benefits of being a student besides the educational ones. Write a few sentences summarizing your findings.

Finding Something to Say

If you're like many students, two of the hardest parts of writing are finding something to say, or knowing enough about a subject to offer a thoughtful, informed opinion. Doing research to learn more about your topic can help solve these problems, but even research can be intimidating if your subject is broad or unfamiliar. However, three steps can improve your writing.

First, learn about general topics that have some connection to your life or world. Thus, when you come across these topics in other courses or in writing assignments, you will already have information—and, hopefully, an opinion—to help you write well. Second, learn how to structure your essays so that you can logically organize and communicate your ideas. Third, learn how to find, analyze, and use information to make your ideas relevant and persuasive. With guidance from your instructor, you can practice these three skills and markedly improve your writing.

Learning While You Write

You probably noticed the Culture Note at the beginning of this chapter. Every chapter of this text contains a similar note. That is because each chapter focuses on a key topic in American or world culture. You'll be learning about many of these topics in your college career. Additionally, this book will give you a taste not only of your college studies but also of humanity's rich social, historical, and intellectual achievements. Pay attention to those topics that inspire or interest you; they may serve as your next essay topic or course selection.

You Already Have the Tools to Write Well

Chances are, you're a better writer than you think you are. Many people think they are not, or cannot be, good writers. That's because they don't realize how many essential writing and thinking skills they use on a daily basis. For example, you might have described what happened to make a day at work or school particularly bad, using example to illustrate your point. You might have told friends about a great weekend, or you might have described what a new car looked like. You've probably had to organize parts of your life, grouping homework, clothes, or tools in logical ways.

These everyday tasks require skills you already possess. You'll use these same strategies, listed below, to communicate in writing.

- Illustration and example
- Narration

- Comparison and contrast
- Cause and effect

- Description
- Classification and division
- Process analysis

- Definition
- Argument

These are strategies we employ on a daily basis to make our ideas clear to other people.

We All Have Different Experiences and Perspectives

Even if our ideas are clear to us, they may not always be clear to others. For example, write down the first thoughts that flash into your mind when you read the next two words.

Phone: _____

_____

School: _____

_____

Now, ask two friends or classmates to write down their ideas. Compare their ideas with yours. Have any of you written exactly the same responses? Even if your ideas are similar, they very likely differ in some ways. These differences are important. They show us that while we all most likely agree that *phone* and *school* are not difficult words to define, we all bring our own experiences and interpretations to reading and writing. If we want people to understand and agree with our point of view, we have to learn to communicate convincingly. Since we can't assume that people automatically understand and agree with us, we must anticipate others' ideas and explain ourselves clearly.

Understanding the Essay

Every writing assignment in this book gives you an opportunity to write a paragraph or essay.

An **essay** is a group of paragraphs working together to make a point, called a **thesis**, which often comes in the first paragraph. The point of an essay may be to inform, persuade, or entertain, and an essay's subject matter—called the **topic**—may come from your instructor or your own inspiration. A traditional essay contains an introduction, body, and conclusion, and the information contained in an essay may come from your own personal experience or from outside sources. The most important concept to remember when writing an essay is that everything you write must somehow help develop the **thesis statement.** The essays you will be asked to write for this textbook will be from two to three pages long, or from five hundred to eight hundred words. Full coverage of essay writing is found in Chapters 8 through 27.

Paragraphs: The Building Blocks of Essays

Nearly all essays are organized and divided into smaller units of thought called **paragraphs**. Paragraphs can be any length but are usually made up of five to twelve sentences related to one idea and are around 150 words long. As with essays, paragraphs have topics and a main idea. The main idea is contained in a **topic sentence**, which is often the first sentence of the paragraph. The other sentences in the paragraph should help support the topic sentence. Just as the thesis helps control the direction of an essay, a clear topic sentence helps readers understand what the writer is trying to communicate. Paragraphs can communicate their own ideas, but the paragraphs you will write using this book will generally serve to develop part of an essay.

Ideas that are organized around a single point—such as the thesis or topic sentence—are much easier to understand and believe. However, having a clear topic sentence doesn't guarantee that an essay will win readers to our point of view. Because no two people think alike, we need to explain our points of view through clear examples. In other words, we need to offer proof.

In paragraphs and essays, proof is called **support**. Your support points are the reasons you feel the way you do and thus the reasons people should believe you.

Read the following paragraph to see how the support points make the topic sentence clear.

Lessons Learned

For many people, *education* means "school." However, there are other ways to learn. First, people can learn by watching. As a child, I learned to change a bicycle tire by watching my older brother. He would pry off the punctured tire, patch it, replace it, and pump it up in what seemed to be seconds. He never let me help him, but just by watching I made a decent first attempt when I finally had my own bike. Second, people can learn by listening. I grew up knowing that my mother suffered from rheumatoid arthritis, which caused her constant pain and prevented her from doing things she loved, such as playing the piano. I could not experience her pain for myself, but I paid attention to her comments about her "angry knuckles" and "rusty knees." Thus, I learned to appreciate every pain-free moment I ever experienced. Finally, people can learn through experience. I used to wait for days to return calls, no matter who had left a message. Once, however, my boss asked me to call ASAP—which to me meant whenever I wanted—and I lost a key shift because I didn't get back to him in time. Next time he called, I called back right away, but only experience could have taught me that. Being "educated" to some people may mean having a degree or reading a lot, but for me education comes just from paying attention.

The topic of "Lessons Learned" is learning, specifically, learning by watching, hearing, and experiencing. The topic sentence—"However, there are other ways to learn"—gives the main idea of the paragraph. The writer supports the topic sentence by offering proof that allows the reader to understand why the writer feels as he does. For example, the first support point is "First, people can learn by watching." To strengthen this support point, the writer gives specific details.

Support Point	Specific Details
Learned by watching.	Watched older brother change bicycle tire.
	Made good first attempt at changing own tire.

The writer also uses **transitions,** terms that give us clues about what's coming next. In the paragraph, the transition words *first, second,* and *finally* keep the support points in order.

EXERCISE 1 IDENTIFYING SUPPORT POINTS IN A PARAGRAPH

Reread "Lessons Learned." Write down the points offered to support the topic sentence. Then, list the specific details that illustrate each reason. The first one has been done for you.

Topic: _learning_

Topic sentence: _However, there are other ways to learn._

Support point 1: _People can learn by watching._

Specific details: Watched older brother change bicycle tire.

_____

Made good attempt at changing own tire.

_____

Support point 2:   _____

Specific details: _____

_____

_____

Support point 3:   _____

Specific details: _____

_____

_____

Paragraphs Versus Essays

Essays and paragraphs are similar in that they are both organized around a single idea, they both have support points, and they both present evidence to illustrate those points. The most important differences between a paragraph and an essay, however, are length and development. Where a paragraph might have one or two examples to support a point, an essay can have a whole *paragraph* developing a single example to make a point. And where paragraphs can usually get by with a transition word to make connections clear, essays often use entire *sentences* to help keep the reader on track. Finally, while both paragraphs and essays concentrate on making a point, essays can contain many more subpoints, all of which need development of their own.

The greatest benefit of being a skilled essay writer is being able to more fully communicate your ideas. In college classes—from English and history to science and speech courses—knowing how to craft a persuasive essay will help you learn material and show your instructors how much you've learned. Additionally, essays—written in letter format—can be valuable tools in bringing about change in your life. Knowing how to write a statement that respectfully and accurately complains to the utility company for overbilling you, for example, can save you stress and money.

Essay Form

The most basic form of the essay is the five-paragraph essay. There are many variations on the essay form, but the five-paragraph version is a solid place to start.

Notice how the body paragraphs contain the same type of format while the first and last paragraphs—the introduction and conclusion—are differ-

---

Five-Paragraph Essay Form

Introduction
Opening: Gets reader's attention.
Thesis statement: Gives the writer's main idea, point of view, and purpose; tells the reader what to expect.

↓

Body Paragraphs
Body paragraph 1
Topic sentence
    Specific details

Body paragraph 2
Topic sentence
    Specific details

Body paragraph 3
Topic sentence
    Specific details

↓

Conclusion
Final thoughts: Add something new that is closely related to the essay's main idea.

---

ent. See the figure above titled "Five-Paragraph Essay Form" for a visual representation of the essay.

A Model Essay

The following essay is based on the paragraph "Lessons Learned." Notice that the writer changed her focus from types of learning to types of education.

An Education by Any Name

For my parents—who didn't finish high school—*education* always meant "school," and school was the path to success. However, since my parents had acquired valuable skills—my father as a

Introduction

plumber and my mother as receptionist—I knew that education could take different forms. According to *Merriam-Webster's Collegiate Dictionary,* to educate is "to provide schooling," "to train by ... supervised practice especially in a skill, trade, or profession," or "to develop mentally, morally, or aesthetically." In fact, each type of education—classroom learning, learning through experience, and learning from mentors—has an important function in our lives.

The first type of education, formal education—or what people learn in school—is essential for success in daily life. For instance, every time I go to the grocery store, reading (which I learned in elementary school) helps me recognize different products, brands, and sales. I can learn where something was grown, how it was processed, and whether it costs less than it did last week. Math (also learned in school) comes in handy at the store, too, where I have to add up the cost of my food as I go to make sure I have enough money to pay for everything at the checkout line. I can also do some quick calculations and figure approximately how much I'll have to pay in tax; that way, I'm not surprised at the checkout counter. What I have learned, and still learn, in school helps me daily.

A second type of education, learning through supervision, also has its place. As a longtime athlete, I have had my share of injuries. Because of my experiences, I want to be a sports trainer or physical therapy assistant. One of my jobs is at a physical therapy clinic, where I help the physical therapist by "prepping" patients for treatment. I help them apply ice or heat, and I get the electrical stimulation and ultrasound machines ready. The physical therapist I work for has given me careful instructions about how best to position patients, how long to let them "heat" or "cool," and how to set up the machines. She also lets me observe some treatment sessions with patients, from which I've learned more about how to help patients gain strength and flexibility. If I am accepted into the physical therapy assistant program at my college, I will have the opportunity to observe and learn from other physical therapists and patients; for now, I appreciate the experiences I've had so far.

Finally, learning from mentors—parents, teachers, coaches, and ministers, to name some—is another important type of education. I can't say that my parents taught me much about calculating tax, but they both taught me the value of a dollar. Further, while they may not have taught me about physical therapy, they have taught me qualities valuable in any job: hard work, punctuality, honesty, and responsibility. I remember interviewing for my current job; I showed up ten minutes early, wearing my best shirt and with my pants pressed and shoes polished. Nothing in the job advertisement had said that certain attire

Thesis statement

Body paragraph 1

Body paragraph 2

Body paragraph 3

was necessary, but I remembered my father telling me that if I take myself seriously—and show it through my appearance and actions—others will take me seriously, too. I got the job, and I give my parents credit for teaching me how to make a good impression.

Conclusion   Formal education—finishing high school, college, or even graduate school—seems to get most of the attention. For sure, school is important for learning skills that help people function in society or for gaining special knowledge, such as in going to medical school. However, two other kinds of education—what we learn from being shown by experts or authorities and what we learn from mentors—play equally important roles in helping us develop as people. Just as I can't imagine being able to read without going to school, I can't imagine treating someone for a groin pull without being shown how or knowing how to look someone in the eye and give a firm grip without having had my parents' guidance. Being educated, really, means learning from whoever is around you.

Note that the thesis statement of the essay "An Education by Any Name," which is very similar to the topic sentence of the paragraph "Lessons Learned" (page 6), outlines the three key areas that the essay will cover. Additionally, each of the three points—formal education, learning through supervision, and learning from mentors—is developed through additional details.

EXERCISE 2   IDENTIFYING SUPPORT POINTS AND DETAILS IN AN ESSAY

Reread the essay "An Education by Any Name." Write down the points offered to support the thesis statement. Then list the specific details that illustrate each reason. The first one has been done for you.

Topic: _education_

Thesis statement: _In fact, each type of education—classroom learning, learning through experience, and learning from mentors—has an important function in our lives._

Support point 1: _Formal education is essential for success in daily life._

    Specific details: _Reading helps shoppers recognize products, brands, and sales._

        Math helps add up costs.

        Math helps calculate tax.

Support point 2: _____

   Specific details: _____

   _____

   _____

   _____

Support point 3: _____

   Specific details: _____

   _____

   _____

   _____

Understanding Audience and Purpose

Anything you write will benefit from having a single point, being clearly organized, and including specific details for support. What that point is, how you organize your ideas, and what types of details you use, however, will vary greatly depending upon two factors: your audience and your purpose.

Your **audience**, the person or group for whom you write, will greatly affect every aspect of your writing. For instance, if you write a letter challenging your former landlord's decision not to return your security deposit, your point should be to convince her of your view, not to make her laugh. Similarly, if you want your former landlord to take you seriously, you will most likely choose language and details that make your points clear. Rather than write "It's not my fault some loser trashed the place, so show me the money," you'd probably be more convincing if you wrote "Since I was not responsible for the damage to the apartment, I should get my deposit back." Your audience and purpose are two axes around which your support points and details revolve. For more on audience and purpose, see Chapter 2.

Using a Computer to Write

If you have the option of using a computer to type your papers for class, do so. Using a computer gives you multiple opportunities to change and save your work, and it makes your work appear professional and neat. Regardless of the length or type of written assignment you are completing, some general tips can assist you as you use a computer when you write.

■ **Save your work often.** Probably the only thing worse than the dog eating your writing assignment is losing it because you didn't save it. Word processing programs have a save function that allows you to keep your work just as you left it. Save often to ensure that you always have your most recent draft available.

- **Back up your work in more than one way.** Saving your writing assignments to the hard drive of a computer—if it's your own—can sometimes be all you need to keep track of your work. To be safe, however, be sure to save your work in at least one place in addition to the hard drive. If you're using your school's computers, you can save your work on a flash drive and also e-mail a copy to yourself.

- **Save different versions of your work.** Though it might seem to take up more space than necessary, saving different versions of your work is a good idea. Sometimes a certain sentence or piece of information doesn't seem to fit into your paragraph right away, but later on it seems perfect. Saving your various drafts allows you to refer back to earlier versions and use whatever information you need. Be sure to give each draft a different title. You could include the date of revision ("Lessons Learned 090506" and "Lessons Learned 090606," for instance) to remember which version of your assignment has your most recent changes.

- **Print out your drafts.** The beauty of using a computer is that it doesn't require you to print out each version on paper immediately. Be sure, though, that you print out your work every time you make major changes. A paper copy allows you to see your work in terms of length and detail, and it lets you work on your paragraph when you're not at the computer.

- **Single-space your work.** Since a computer screen allows you to see less of your work than a piece of paper, you should single-space your work. That way, you can see more of your draft at a time and get an idea of how developed different sections of your draft are. Later, when you're ready to print out your assignment, you can double-space the final copy.

- **Plan for your computer time.** If you use your school's computers, make sure you leave enough time to get your work done. There may be significant waits for computers or printers during peak hours and around midterms, so allow enough time to wait your turn *and* get your work done.

For more detailed information on using a computer throughout your writing process, see Chapters 4 through 7.

WRITING PRACTICE **Write About Your Education**

To be studying composition in college, you have most likely taken—and had success in—other courses either in high school or college. You have probably learned from other people and other experiences, such as jobs you've held. What is the most important skill you've learned that you think will help you in this course?

Your assignment is this: *Write a few paragraphs or a short essay about the most important skill you've learned so far in your education.* For instance, you might write about how you've learned to make a clear point or how to use specific details, or you might write about how you've learned to plan ahead so you can approach assignments in an organized fashion. Be sure to make a point, use specific details to illustrate that point, and organize your ideas as well as you can.

Introduction and Orientation to Lab Manual Online (LMO)

If you've thumbed through this text, you may have noticed many opportunities to improve your writing through both exercises and readings. One more way that *College Writing Resources* helps you improve your reading and writing skills is through its Lab Manual Online (LMO). The LMO provides another set of exercises and assignments for you to complete on your own, with or without help from your instructor. Many of these activities can also be done collaboratively (with your peers in a group).

HOW THE LMO WORKS

After you've finished a particular chapter, you can access additional activities through the Internet.

1. Visit the Web site at **http://www.ablongman.com/Long.** Click on **College Writing Resources.**
2. Click on the icon for the exercise that corresponds to the chapter you have just completed.
3. Complete the activity that appears and check your work through the LMO tutor.

Or, if your instructor has ordered the print lab manual packaged with your textbook, you can access the additional activities in the lab manual provided.

Lab Activity 1

For additional practice in beginning to write essays, complete Lab Activity 1 in the lab manual packaged with your textbook. If you did not receive a lab manual, you can complete this activity online at **www.ablongman.com/long.** Click on **College Resources for Writers** and then click on **Activity 1.**

2

Having a Reader and a Reason: Understanding Audience and Purpose

CULTURE NOTE *Tsunami*

Defined by *Britannica Online* as a "catastrophic ocean wave, usually caused by a submarine earthquake," tsunamis attracted the world's attention after the December 26, 2004, wave that devastated Indonesia, Sri Lanka, southern India, and Thailand, among other countries. Tsunamis have been depicted in movies as being great walls of water; however, the length of a tsunami—sometimes hundreds of kilometers—is what makes the wave unusually large.

Tsunami Devastation

SURF THE NET In the aftermath of the 2004 Indonesian tsunami and Hurricane Katrina in 2005, many people found themselves at the mercy of international aid organizations. How effective are these organizations? Surf the net to learn about the Red Cross, UNICEF, or another aid organization, summarizing your findings in a few sentences. A good place to start your search is at: http://www.cnn.com/2004/WORLD/asiapcf/12/28/tsunami.aidsites/.

Writing for a Reader

Though you may not have thought about it, every time you write something, you're writing for *somebody*. Even if you're just doodling before class starts, you're most likely doing that for a certain person, probably yourself.

Recognizing the person you're writing for, or your audience, is essential to effective writing. Writing the right thing for the right person can go a long way toward making sure you get your point across.

Consider the situations described below. Then describe the clothing you would wear in each situation.

You're going to the gym for a workout. _____

_____

_____

You're interviewing for an internship with a large corporation. _____

_____

_____

You're going dancing with friends at a nightclub. _____

_____

_____

Probably you chose different clothing for each situation. Discuss with a friend or classmate what would happen if you wore the nightclub attire for the corporate interview panel or if you wore the interview ensemble to the gym. Would you get the results you wanted from each visit? How comfortable, both physically and emotionally, would you be? What did you consider when you chose your clothing for each situation? Even if you were going to the gym for only a light workout, you probably wouldn't wear nightclub clothing. And unless you wanted your future employers to see your well-defined abdominal muscles, you probably wouldn't wear your gym clothes to an interview.

EXERCISE 1 IDENTIFYING THE AUDIENCE

Read the following paragraphs. For each one, choose the response that you think best describes the probable audience.

1. ### A Wave of Disaster

    Indonesia, Sri Lanka, and other countries bordering the Indian Ocean were hit hard by a tsunami, a tidal wave of seismic origin, on December 26, 2004. Resulting from an undersea earthquake measuring approximately 9.0 on the Richter scale, the tsunami was responsible for hundreds of thousands of deaths. Although humanitarian efforts largely averted the threat of starvation, the devastation in towns and villages was great. Homes and property were washed away, leaving thousands of people with nothing but their lives.

This paragraph was most likely written for a reader who

   a. is an expert on tsunamis.

   b. lives on the coast of Indonesia.

   c. does not know about the tsunami of December 2004.

2. ### A Wave Without a Smile

    Although my hotel was flooded in the tsunami, I was fine, and I had even managed some good scuba diving before the tsunami hit. I lost all my belongings, but since I had my passport and wallet with me on the scuba trip, I was able to get out of the country and make it home safely. The people who live there weren't as lucky. Please don't worry about me; I have gotten over the initial shock and am looking forward to my next trip.

This paragraph was most likely written for a reader who

   a. cares about the writer.

   b. doesn't know the writer.

   c. wants to go on vacation to Sri Lanka.

3.　　　　　　　　　A Wave of Hope?

Please consider sending a sizable donation to us, the people of Indonesia, who were hit by the December 2004 tsunami. Since your association has been successful in helping other disaster victims in the past, my neighbors and I are confident that you will help us, as well. Specifically, the people in our area are in need of blankets, clothing, and portable housing. Any financial contributions your organization could make above and beyond these items so we can begin rebuilding our homes would benefit us greatly.

This paragraph was most likely written for a reader who

a. works for a charitable organization such as the Red Cross.

b. lives in Indonesia.

c. is obsessed with tragic events.

All of the paragraphs in Exercise 1 are based on the same subject matter, but the messages are very different. Your own writing changes, too, depending on who your audience is. When you write for your instructor, your most common audience, you will probably pay more attention to writing with a thesis statement, topic sentences, specific details, and a clear organizational plan. When you write for your friends, however, you can be more casual. You don't have to worry about getting a grade for your notes or e-mail messages to friends. Knowing your audience when you write helps you choose the best way to make your point.

Writing for a Reason

In choosing *clothing* for the situations described earlier in the chapter, you considered two things. First, you thought about your audience. Second, you thought about your goal, what you wanted to accomplish. Your goals might have been to have a good workout, get hired for an internship, or have fun with your friends.

In your writing class, your **purpose**—why you are writing—will usually be to convince your reader that what you say is worth reading. Your purpose will often fall under one of three headings.

- To inform
- To persuade

- To entertain

Writing to Inform

When you write to *inform,* your purpose is to present information clearly and accurately. You will list causes and effects, define unfamiliar terms, and provide facts that make your point clear. For instance, if you were writing to your new doctor to tell her about your current health, you would emphasize details that describe your overall health: your eating, sleeping, and exercise routines; your professional and recreational activities; your family health history; and your current health status. You could make jokes or use slang in your letter, but that would not help your new doctor understand your overall level of health. Thus, you'd be more effective simply informing her of the facts.

EXERCISE 2   WRITING TO INFORM

Imagine that you have to write a letter to a friend who is considering attending college. The subject of your letter is what your college is like. Make a list of details that tell someone what your college is like.

_____

_____

_____

Writing to Entertain

When you write to *entertain,* you want to elicit a certain reaction from your reader: perhaps laughter, anger, surprise, or fascination. Your job, then, is to include details that make your reader *want* to read on. Whereas writing to inform requires that you include just the facts, writing to entertain demands that you focus on the unusual, the trivial, and the unexpected elements of a situation.

For instance, if you are writing to your brother or sister about how wild your new puppy is, you should include details that *show* the puppy's wildness. You could mention the puppy's destruction of your favorite pillow while his own toys remain unchewed, how the puppy's accidents never fail to occur just after you finish cleaning up, or how the only thing that does *not* make the puppy vomit is a package of your favorite cookies. Being specific and personal will more likely be entertaining than a dry list of your puppy's bad acts.

If you were writing to inform, you might simply write that your puppy is messy and energetic, but to entertain, you want to exaggerate the ridiculousness of his actions.

EXERCISE 3 **WRITING TO ENTERTAIN**

Write a letter to someone you know very well. The subject of your letter is an unusual dining experience. Keeping in mind that you want to entertain your reader, make a list of the details describing that experience.

_____

_____

_____

Writing to Persuade

When you write to *persuade,* you write to convince someone to accept your point of view. Writing to persuade, then, requires that you include details that appeal to emotion, reason, or both.

For instance, if you are trying to convince a family friend to give you a job, you can use emotion to appeal to her sense of loyalty to your family. You can also use reason to convince this person that you are responsible and capable and would make an ideal employee. Either way, you want to include details that will convince your reader to think as you do.

Keep in mind that not all persuasive purposes will be the same. In the paragraphs for Exercise 1, for instance, each writer has a distinct goal. What do you think the purpose of each paragraph in Exercise 1 is? To _____

_____

_____

EXERCISE 4 **WRITING TO PERSUADE**

Write a letter to your boss. The subject of your letter is a raise. Include details that will convince your boss to give you a higher salary.

_____

_____

_____

All three of these purposes rely on your reader choosing to read what you have written. Your message needs to match your audience, or you won't have much chance to get your point across.

EXERCISE 5 IDENTIFYING THE PURPOSE

Read the sentences below. Decide whether the purpose of each sentence is probably (a) to inform, (b) to entertain, or (c) to persuade.

_____ **1.** If I'd known a tsunami was coming, I'd have gone swimming!

_____ **2.** Tsunamis have been known to hit some places as often as every fifteen years.

_____ **3.** Those who can afford it should make a donation to tsunami survivors.

_____ **4.** Emergency identification and warning systems should be upgraded in places where tsunamis are likely to hit.

_____ **5.** Tsunamis are difficult to identify in deep ocean waters.

_____ **6.** Few events have resulted in such tragedy as the December 2004 tsunami.

Identifying Your Audience

Ask yourself the following questions to identify your audience.

1. Who will read the document I am writing? My instructor? My friend? My supervisor at work?

2. How can I best appeal to my audience?

3. What does my audience need to know?

Identifying Your Purpose

Ask yourself the following questions to identify your purpose.

1. Do I want to inform, entertain, or persuade?

2. Do I want to explain a situation? Give an opinion? Suggest a course of action?

WRITING PRACTICE **Writing a Letter for Change**

Imagine this situation: You live in a crowded city apartment, and a new restaurant has opened in the building next to yours. As a result, all the parking spaces reserved for residents of your building are taken by restaurant patrons, forcing you and your fellow apartment dwellers to park blocks away. Additionally, the restaurant is noisy and stays open late, so even those residents without cars are disturbed by the coming and going of customers.

Your assignment is this: *Write a letter to one of the following audiences.*

Your neighbor
The restaurant owner
The parking division of your city

Decide what you want your letter to accomplish: to *inform* the reader of the inconvenience, to *entertain* the reader, or to *persuade* the reader to make a change. *Note:* If this were a real-life situation, you probably would not choose to entertain your reader.

If you want to *inform* your reader about the inconvenience, begin with a topic sentence such as "The new restaurant next door to my apartment building has brought about many inconveniences to the residents of our building." Then include details that show your reader the extent of the inconvenience. You might mention details about carrying groceries from blocks away in the pouring rain, trying to sleep through noisy dinner parties, or trying to invite people to your home when there is no place to park.

If you want to *persuade* your reader to make change, begin with a topic sentence such as "As a responsible restaurant owner and member of the downtown community, you should provide parking elsewhere for your patrons." Then include details that show your reader why providing parking elsewhere is a good idea. Some possible details are that you and your fellow apartment dwellers may someday be restaurant customers, the restaurant owner would also be frustrated if customers couldn't find parking due to apartment residents' cars, and the restaurant would not be an ideal place to dine if the apartment dwellers were loud and obnoxious during meals.

When you finish, share your letter with your classmates, and discuss the types of details you included in order to make your point. *Note:* If you have no experience with or strong feelings about parking issues, you may choose to persuade your reader about another topic.

Remember to do the following:

- Identify your audience through the greeting in your letter.
- Write your main idea in your topic sentence.
- Make sure your purpose is clear in your topic sentence.
- Give support points for your topic sentence.
- Offer specific examples for your support points.

Write your letter on a separate piece of paper.

Lab Activity 2

For additional practice with understanding audience and purpose, complete Lab Activity 2 in the lab manual packaged with your textbook. If you did not receive a lab manual, you can complete this activity online at **www.ablongman.com/long.** Click on **College Resources for Writers** and then click on **Activity 2.**

3 The Bases of Good Writing: The Four Cs

CULTURE NOTE *Fairy Tales Revisited*

Written both to entertain and to instruct, early fairy tales were often violent, gruesome, and sad. While moviemakers usually tell the tales in a standard good-versus-evil pattern, many fairy tales have other interpretations.

Modern-Day Fairy Tale

OBSERVE YOUR WORLD What kinds of stories are most popular today? Pay attention to current news stories, television programs, and movies. Then, decide what about them makes them popular. Are they touching? Action-packed? Familiar? Write a few sentences about why you think certain kinds of stories—those with happy endings, for instance—are popular.

Good Writing Is . . .

If you've ever watched a professional basketball team, you've probably noticed the range of skills involved in the team's play. A quick, strategy-oriented point guard can dribble and pass the ball well, while a shooting guard can sink three-pointers from far away. Meanwhile, a forward uses strength to get close to the basket, and the center is able to put the ball in the hoop as well as block opposing players. The point is that even though every player on the team has a different role, they all work together to bring success to the team.

Your writing is similar to such a team. Several different elements combine to make your writing effective. Understanding what these elements are and how they work together is important. Effective writing has four essential characteristics: it is concise, credible, clear, and correct.

- **Concise.** When your writing is *concise,* you have a clear point (your topic sentence) and you include only the information absolutely necessary to communicate that point. Concise writing gets to the point quickly and does not introduce unnecessary information.

- **Credible.** When your writing is *credible,* it is believable. For your reader to believe what you say, you must offer proof—in the form of specific details—to illustrate your topic sentence.

- **Clear.** When your writing is *clear,* it signals to your reader what points are important and how those points fit together under the umbrella of your topic sentence. Transitions are essential to clear writing.

- **Correct.** When your writing is *correct,* it is free of errors in spelling, grammar, and punctuation.

These four qualities serve as the foundation for effective writing, but they are not the only aspects of good writing. In particular, audience awareness is important as you develop your writing for different purposes and readers.

Recognizing Concise Writing

Concise writing simply makes a point as directly as possible, without giving any information that does not support the topic sentence.

Read the following essays. Then decide which one is more concise. Why?

Fairy-Tale Endings

Even though many fairy tales have "happy" endings, this happiness applies only to a chosen few. I think fairy tales are supposed to contain some kind of fairy, but not all the ones I read do. The "villains" from three fairy tales—Rumpelstiltskin, the giant from "Jack and the Beanstalk," and the witch from "Rapunzel"—suffer despite doing nothing wrong.

Rumpelstiltskin is a funny-looking little man who makes a deal with a pretty miller's daughter and is eventually cheated out of his earnings. My boss is like that: she never pays me for my overtime. A woman has to spin straw into gold because her father boasted to the king that she could. When the king threatens to kill her if she can't, she begs the little man for help on three occasions. When the woman has paid all she can for the little man's services, she agrees to give him her firstborn child should she become queen. If people didn't call child protective services about her, they should have! However, when the little man comes to collect his fee, the queen sobs and begs him not to take her child. The man relents, telling her that if she guesses his name in three days' time, she can keep her child. A royal messenger discovers the man's name—Rumpelstiltskin—and tells the queen, who gives his name correctly. In a rage, Rumpelstiltskin pulls his leg so hard that he splits himself in two and dies.

Like Rumpelstiltskin, the giant from "Jack and the Beanstalk" is cheated but is portrayed as the villain. A simple boy, Jack, trades his cow for magic beans and uses the resulting gigantic beanstalk as a means to steal from a giant three times. Although the giant chases Jack only to recover his lost gold, golden-egg-laying hen, and golden singing harp, the giant is made to appear as the villain of the tale. It seems as though once someone is cast as the bad guy, he can never escape that stereotype. When Jack chops down the beanstalk before the giant can climb down, the giant tumbles to his death in the sea.

Last, even though the witch in "Rapunzel" is stolen from initially, she is described as being unfair and evil, and she loses everything in the end. A pregnant woman's cravings lead her husband to steal rapunzel greens from the witch's garden. When he is caught, the man promises the couple's child to the witch in exchange for the greens. When the baby girl is born, the witch arrives to claim her, calling her Rapunzel after the greens, and keeps her locked in a tower. Accessible only by lowering her long hair, Rapunzel sings sweetly from her tower and attracts a wandering prince. I've always wondered how the witch climbed up the tower when Rapunzel was a baby. After many trials, the prince and Rapunzel run off together, leaving the witch with nothing. Despite being the original victim in the story, the witch is portrayed as the villain and loses everything.

Though "happily ever after" implies that everyone is happy, this is not true. The three characters in "Rumpelstiltskin," "Jack and the Beanstalk," and "Rapunzel," who are innocent bystanders in the beginning, are cheated in some way and eventually lose their gains. It's almost like those reality TV shows where someone is voted out just for being on the wrong team. Perhaps being happy is only reserved for tricky maidens or naïve boys.

A Bad Deal for the Bad Guy

"Happily ever after" seems to be the measure of a fairy tale's justice. If someone ends up happy, he or she usually seems to deserve it. However, many of the "villains" in fairy tales suffer terrible fates even though they did nothing to bring misery upon themselves. In three fairy tales, Rumpelstiltskin, the giant from "Jack and the Beanstalk," and the witch from "Rapunzel" end up unhappily through no fault of their own.

In the story of Rumpelstiltskin, a funny-looking little man brings wealth and royalty to a pretty miller's daughter, but he is cheated out of his fee for his services. To spin straw into gold for a demanding king, a young woman pays this little man with her necklace one night and her ring the next. On the third night, because she has nothing left to pay him, the young woman promises the man her firstborn child should she become queen. One year later, the woman—now queen—gives birth to a child, and the little man comes to claim his fee. However, the queen's tears soften his heart, and he gives her three days to guess his name and win her child back. The queen's messenger learns the man's name, Rumpelstiltskin, and tells her. When she guesses his name correctly, Rumpelstiltskin pulls his leg so hard that he splits himself in two and dies. Despite fulfilling all his promises, Rumpelstiltskin is portrayed as the villain of the story.

The giant from "Jack and the Beanstalk" doesn't end up much better than Rumpelstiltskin. Although the giant simply minds his own business, he ends up suffering. After trading his cow for magic beans, the naïve boy Jack climbs an enormous beanstalk grown from the beans. At the top he finds the giant's castle and, on three separate occasions, steals from the giant: his gold, his golden-egg-laying hen, and his golden singing harp. When the giant tries to reclaim what is his by chasing Jack down the beanstalk, Jack cuts down the enormous vine, causing the giant to land in the sea and drown. Though the giant was the victim of Jack's theft on three different occasions, he is depicted as a brute and dies, too.

Finally, in the story of Rapunzel, a witch shows mercy, only to be tricked and cheated later. When a woman becomes pregnant, she craves greens from the plant called rapunzel growing in a witch's garden and says she'll die without them. Fearing for his wife, her husband enters the garden, steals the greens, and gives them to his wife, who feels better but craves more. The husband steals more rapunzel but is caught by the witch. To escape with his own life and the greens for his wife, he promises the witch their baby. When the baby girl is born, the witch takes her, names her Rapunzel after the greens, and keeps her in a tower. The witch can enter it only through a high window by climbing Rapunzel's long hair, but Rapunzel's sweet singing leads a prince to see her, fall in love with her, and try to rescue her. Despite the witch's attempts to keep Rapunzel to herself, the girl and the prince run away together and leave the witch with nothing. Once again, someone who has been a victim of theft—the witch—is portrayed as evil and is left unhappily ever after.

Many fairy tales end with the lovely princess or handsome prince getting exactly what she or he wants, regardless of who suffers. In "Rumpelstiltskin," "Jack and the Beanstalk," and "Rapunzel," the three characters who eventually suffer or die do nothing to lead themselves into harm. However, when they are stolen from or cheated and try to retaliate or collect their due, Rumpelstiltskin, the giant, and the witch either die or at least lose their prize. I guess that saying a tale has a happy ending depends upon whose happiness matters to you.

The second essay, "A Bad Deal for the Bad Guy," is more *concise* and therefore more effective. It offers no information other than those details that support the thesis statement: "In three fairy tales, Rumpelstiltskin, the giant from 'Jack and the Beanstalk,' and the witch from 'Rapunzel' end up unhappily through no fault of their own." Even the title, "A Bad Deal for the Bad Guy," offers a clue as to what the essay will contain. In contrast, "Fairy-Tale Endings" contains many details that do not directly support the topic sentence: "The 'villains' from three fairy tales—Rumpelstiltskin, the giant from 'Jack and the Beanstalk,' and the witch from 'Rapunzel'—suffer despite doing nothing wrong." For instance, one unnecessary detail is this:

I think fairy tales are supposed to contain some kind of fairy, but not all the ones I read do.

This detail tells explains what fairy tales are supposed to contain, but it says nothing about the topic of how alleged fairy-tale villains are misrepresented.

EXERCISE 1 CONCISE WRITING

Use a pen or pencil to cross out any sections of "Fairy-Tale Endings" that do not support the topic sentence.

How many sentences did you cross out? _____

You should have crossed out the following sentences.

My boss is like that: she never pays me for my overtime.

If people didn't call child protective services about her, they should have!

It seems as though once someone is cast as the bad guy, he can never escape that stereotype.

I've always wondered how the witch climbed up the tower when Rapunzel was a baby.

It's almost like those reality TV shows where someone is voted out just for being on the wrong team.

These details, while they might be interesting, do not help to develop the main idea, "The 'villains' from three fairy tales . . . suffer despite doing nothing wrong." Thus, they need to be removed from the paragraph.

Concise Writing Leads to Unity

One important aspect of good writing is **unity.** In unified writing, all elements of a paragraph work together to communicate a single idea. By making your writing concise—and, thus, free of ideas that do not contribute to the overall message of your paragraph—you ensure that your writing will also be unified.

In Your Own Writing   To write concisely, remember to

1. Have a clear thesis statement that states exactly what your essay is about.

2. Have topic sentences in each body paragraph that directly support the thesis.

3. Make sure every detail you use supports the thesis statement.

After deciding on your thesis statement, make sure you include support points that directly support that thesis. Even if those points are interesting to you, omit them if they do not help you develop the thesis in some way. If you were writing an essay about television programs worth watching, for example, a paragraph on how television programming has changed recently—while possibly interesting—would not help you support your thesis.

Similarly, as you add details to your essay, ask yourself whether they help to explain or clarify your thesis statement. If they do not, take them out. For instance, suppose you are writing an essay on your favorite television program. Describing your television set would distract your readers from your point.

Making Sure Your Writing Is Concise

Ask yourself the following questions in order to determine whether your paragraphs are concise.

1. Do I have a clear thesis statement?
2. Does each paragraph have a topic sentence that directly supports the thesis statement?
3. Does *every single detail* support my thesis statement?

Recognizing Credible Writing

Credible writing gives your readers reason to believe you. Credible paragraphs include specific details that help convince your readers that they should believe you.

Read the essays below. Then decide which is more credible. Why?

Silly Snow White

[1]Many fairy tales contain lessons that are designed to help readers better their lives. [2]Virtue is rewarded, evil is punished, and there isn't much in between. [3]However, while beauty and goodness are

often the means to a happy ending, intelligence isn't. ⁴The tale of Snow White is an example of how brains are not necessary to end up happily ever after. ⁵Although Snow White had a lovely face and a sweet nature, she never showed much common sense.

⁶One way that Snow White didn't show much common sense was in her departure from home. ⁷Snow White lived in a castle with her stepmother, the queen, who was also very beautiful. ⁸Every day a magic mirror in her bedroom told the queen that she was "the fairest of them all." ⁹However, the queen was also evil, and on the day that Snow White's beauty became greater than her own, the queen ordered her huntsman to kill Snow White. ¹⁰The queen's huntsman took pity on Snow White and let her escape, but Snow White just ran into the dark woods. ¹¹She didn't bring any supplies or gear or even a servant. ¹²At the very least, she could have asked to borrow the huntsman's knife, but she didn't use her head at all. ¹³Fortunately, this lack of wisdom didn't hurt Snow White, and she remained unhurt.

¹⁴Another way that Snow White didn't show much sense was in her approach to the Seven Dwarfs' cottage. ¹⁵All alone, Snow White almost died in the woods, but she was lucky and found her way to the cottage of the Seven Dwarfs. ¹⁶When no one answered the door, Snow White went in and made herself at home. ¹⁷She didn't know who lived there—maybe someone who worked for the queen—but she went in anyway. ¹⁸She even let her guard down and took a nap on one of the beds rather than grabbing a weapon and keeping watch in case someone unfriendly came back. ¹⁹Luckily, the dwarfs were kind to her and let her stay despite her unwise decision.

²⁰One final way in which Snow White showed herself lacking in common sense is in her repeated opening of the door to danger. ²¹After the dwarfs heard Snow White's story, they warned her that the queen would try to kill her again, so she shouldn't open the door to anyone but them. ²²Sure enough, the queen's magic mirror told the queen that Snow White was still alive, so the queen disguised herself and went to the dwarfs' cottage. ²³When the queen knocked on the dwarfs' door, Snow White opened it. ²⁴She even bought and sampled harmful goods: a poisoned hair comb, a corset that nearly suffocated her, and a poisoned apple. ²⁵The dwarfs saved her from the first two dangers, but it took a kiss from a prince to save her from that apple. ²⁶Once again, Snow White's lack of good judgment failed to prevent her from ending up happy.

²⁷Beauty and goodness, especially when combined, are almost always rewarded in fairy tales. ²⁸Similarly, evil is nearly always

punished. [29]The tale of Snow White illustrates again and again how an absence of intelligence is not necessarily a vice. [30]Snow White might have saved herself some worry in the woods if she had used her head, but overall, she is rewarded.

Better Lucky Than Smart

[1]In the tale of Snow White, several factors work together to bring about a happy ending for the princess. [2]Snow White's loveliness, her goodness, and her good fortune in finding the dwarfs all combine to lead her to joy. [3]One factor that does not play a role in her happy ending is intelligence. [4]Despite repeated poor judgment, Snow White lives happily ever after.

[5]First, Snow White goes into the dark woods completely unprepared. [6]Since the beautiful evil queen—Snow White's stepmother—has been asking her magic mirror daily if she is the "fairest of them all," you'd think that Snow White would understand her danger if she should become too pretty. [7]Snow White never thinks of this at all and is not nearly ready when the queen tries to kill her. [8]A lack of common sense, however, don't work against Snow White; she's fine in the woods.

[9]Next, Snow White uses poor judgment in approaching the cottage of the Seven Dwarfs. [10]Fortunately, the dwarfs are kind to her and let her stay, so her poor decisions don't harm her here, either.

[11]Finally, Snow White displays a remarkable absence of intelligence by repeatedly opening the cottage door to the wicked queen. [12]Even though the dwarfs warn her that the queen will try to kill her again, it never occurs to Snow White that the queen might actually show up at her door. [13]Once again, however, brainpower is not required for happiness, and Snow White is revived by a prince and led to eternal happiness.

[14]The only person who shows any real intelligence in the tale of Snow White is the queen, who at least comes up with clever ploys to do away with the beautiful Snow White. [15]The dwarfs manage to communicate some common sense in warning the princess of the evil queen. [16]However, it is the person who shows little or no understanding of danger—Snow White—who ends up happily ever after. [17]Ignorance, or at least lack of good judgment, seems to be bliss in fairy tales.

The first essay, "Silly Snow White," is more *credible* and therefore more effective. Both essays are concise and relatively easy to follow. They both have clear thesis statements, topic sentences, and support points. The first essay, however, includes specific examples as proof of the writer's points. For instance, in "Silly Snow White," the writer makes the point that Snow White uses poor judgment in running into the dark woods. Then he offers specific details—the example of Snow White failing to take supplies, gear, a servant, or a knife with her—to show that Snow White does, indeed, use poor judgment.

EXERCISE 2 CREDIBLE WRITING

Listed below are the other support points offered in "Silly Snow White." Read the essay again, paying close attention to the topic sentences in the body paragraphs. Then, underline the sentences containing specific details for the support points developed in those paragraphs.

Support point 2:   Snow White used poor judgment in her approach to the dwarfs' cottage.

Support point 3:   Snow White showed a lack of common sense in opening the dwarfs' door to danger.

Here are the specific details you should have found.

Specific details for support point 2:   Snow White went in the cottage without knowing who lived there; she let her guard down and took a nap; she didn't think to arm herself and wait for someone to return.

Specific details for support point 3:   Snow White opens the door to the evil queen despite being warned against it; Snow White accepts and samples harmful goods.

In "Better Lucky Than Smart," the writer makes these points: Snow White "goes into the dark woods completely unprepared"; Snow White "uses poor judgment in approaching the cottage of the Seven Dwarfs"; Snow White "displays a remarkable absence of intelligence by repeatedly opening the cottage door to the wicked queen." However, the points are not supported by any details. How is Snow White unprepared for the dark woods? In what ways does Snow White use poor judgment at the dwarfs' cottage? How is Snow White's opening of the cottage door to the queen unintelligent? The writer answers none of these questions through examples. Thus, we are left doubting whether the writer knows much about the topic.

In Your Own Writing   To write credibly, offer specific details to show that you have reasons to back up your topic sentence. Specific examples can be

1. Actual examples from your life.
2. Incidents that you've seen happen to someone else.
3. Incidents that you've heard or read about, as long as you can give the source, such as a newspaper or magazine.

For instance, suppose you are writing an essay on your least favorite movie or television program. You could include comments describing how poor computer graphics blurred scenes or failed to show buildings burning even when on fire, or how the actors kept smiling during scenes that were supposed to be sad.

Making Sure Your Writing Is Credible

Ask yourself the following questions to determine whether your essays are credible.

1. Do I provide enough information so that my reader will believe me?
2. Have I made sure my reader knows what I mean?

Recognizing Clear Writing

Clear writing lets your readers easily follow and understand your ideas. In clear writing, information follows a logical order. Information is often ordered either chronologically or emphatically.

In **chronological order**, also called **time sequence order**, events or steps are given in the order or sequence in which they occur. For example, suppose you are telling some friends about your frustrating experience watching an important game such as the Super Bowl. If you were following chronological order, your description of your viewing experience might go something like this:

First, my buddy's neighbor was so noisy that we could hear everything through the apartment wall and had to turn up the TV volume to the highest level to hear the game. **Then,** the satellite signal went out, so I missed some key plays, even a touchdown! **Next,**

Paragraph in Chronological Order

Topic sentence...
....

↓

First event or step..
..............................Specific details...........................
Second event or step...
..............................Specific details...........................
Third event or step...
..............................Specific details...........................
Last event or step...
..............................Specific details...........................

---

my buddy kept switching channels in the second half to check out the NBA scores, so the only things I never missed were the **Super Bowl** commercials. **Finally,** my buddy's team was losing, so he said he wanted to go work out after the third quarter; I had to leave without seeing the rest of the game.

In this example, you're telling your friends what happened *in the order they happened.*

See the diagram above for a clear idea of how a paragraph that is chronologically organized works.

In **emphatic order**, support points are given in order of importance. You as the writer decide which points are least interesting or important and which are the most important ones. Using emphatic order, you place the points that *you think* are less important first, and you end with the points that *you think* are most important. Placing examples later in an essay often sends the message that those points are the most important, so you need to decide which points should come last. For instance, if you are offering safety tips to someone walking, you might begin with a specific tip, such as walking with someone, and end with an all-encompassing tip, such as following your instincts.

According to the National Crime Prevention Council, several tips can help you stay safe when you're walking. **First,** try to walk places with your friends rather than alone. **Also,** stick to well-lighted, well-traveled streets, and know where to go for help if you need it. **Further,** keep any cash or expensive jewelry hidden. **Additionally,** have your car or house key in your hand before you reach the door. **Most**

Paragraph in Emphatic Order

Topic sentence...
....

↓

Least important support point.............................
.........................Specific details.........................
Important support point....................................
.........................Specific details.........................
Important support point....................................
.........................Specific details.........................
Most important support point.............................
.........................Specific details.........................

---

important, be alert. If you think someone is following you, change directions or cross the street. If necessary, move quickly toward an open store or a lighted house. Don't be afraid to yell for help.

In this example, you're placing your safety tips *in order of least to most important.*

See the diagram above for a clear idea of how an emphatically organized paragraph works.

In **spatial order**, the writer organizes the ideas in such a way as to make the reader see things exactly as the writer does. Front to back, inside to outside, bottom to top: these are just three possibilities for spatial organization. Consider the following paragraph on reuniting with a friend the writer hasn't seen for years.

From **across the soccer field,** Hank appeared to be just another fan: normal size, normal weight, and normal soccer-fan clothing. As he started walking **toward** me at halftime, however, I could see vestiges of the old Hank. His shirt was untucked, his belt buckle was off-center, and he walked with the slight limp I remembered. By the time he was **halfway across** the field, I could see that one of his shoes was untied as usual and that he needed a haircut. This was definitely my old buddy. Finally, **just before he reached me,** the spark of mischief in his eyes and the crooked half-grin told me that very little had changed about him in the last ten years.

The far-to-near method of spatial organization helps the reader experience the suspense and happiness the writer felt in seeing an old friend.

Clear writing also includes transition words that reinforce the order of the points. In chronological order, words like *first, then, next,* and *finally* tell your reader what comes next in the sequence. In emphatic order, terms like *in addition, also,* and *most important* tell your reader that your points are becoming more important as you go on. In the preceding paragraph, spatial transitional expressions such as *from across the soccer field, toward, halfway across,* and *just before he reached me* give the reader a sense of the subject's progress as he comes into view for the writer.

Transitions That Signal Chronological Order

finally	last
first (second, third)	last of all
in the first place	next
then	

Transitions That Signal Emphasis

above all	most important
finally	most significantly
most of all	

Words and Terms That Signal Space

above	nearby
across	next to
before	on the other side
behind	opposite
below	there
elsewhere	to the east (north, etc.)
here	to the left
in back of	to the right
in front of	

For a more complete list of transitional words and phrases, see Chapter 11.

Read the essays below. Then, decide which one communicates more clearly. Why?

A Tale with a Real Twist

At the end of most fairy tales, the hero and heroine live happily ever after. Despite all the troubles which they undoubtedly faced in finding and committing to each other, the happy pair—once together—are pretty much guaranteed a trouble-free life. The 2004 movie *Shrek 2* manages to show how even the road after the wedding can be bumpy. *Shrek 2* incorporates reality into its fairy-tale script in a number of ways.

Reality comes in the movie when Shrek meets Fiona's parents. Shrek and Fiona's father Harold immediately feel uncomfortable around each other, and King Harold goes so far as to hire an assassin to kill Shrek. Fiona's parents are unhappy not only that Fiona has married an ogre, but also that she has permanently become one. Having laid plans early in Fiona's life for her to marry Prince Charming and break the part-time-ogre curse, King Harold and Queen Lillian are dismayed when they meet her husband. Despite the fairy-tale setting of *Shrek 2*, the movie explores the very real conflicts among inlaws.

One final dose of reality comes throughout the movie, as references to contemporary culture surround Shrek and his bride. The Fairy Godmother's unsuccessful diets make reference to society's fascination with the latest weight-loss crazes. From an enormous billboard advertising the services of the Fairy Godmother to the reality television series *Knights* (imitating *Cops*), commercialism abounds. Ads for "Gap Queen" and "Burger Prince" make their way into the movie, as does a modern-day red-carpet introduction for "stars" attending the reception for Princess Fiona and her husband. Through still very much a fairy tale, *Shrek 2* never lets us forget the superficial component of our lives.

By showing the early-marriage arguments and the length and frustration of the trip to visit Fiona's parents, *Shrek 2* successfully punctures the fairy-tale bubble. Aspects of reality for Shrek and Princess Fiona come when they receive a summons to meet her parents in the kingdom of Far Far Away. The drive itself is long and frustrating, especially as their friend Donkey repeatedly asks, "Are we there yet?" After initially refusing to go, Shrek relents and makes the trip.

In keeping with traditional fairy tales, *Shrek 2* contains a princess, a fairy godmother, a castle, and a quest. In the midst of all these expected elements *Shrek 2* delivers an unexpected message: reality can intrude upon love even after the wedding. By including details from everyday life, *Shrek 2* manages to make a magic-filled story seem very much like real life.

An Ogre of a Tale

While fairy tales often feature characters who are not physically appealing, such a character is rarely portrayed as the hero. Even when an important character—such as the Beast in "Beauty and the Beast" or the frog in "The Frog Prince"—does end up happily, it's only after he has been transformed into an attractive human. The movie based on the contemporary fairy tale *Shrek* breaks these stereotypes in several ways.

First, the character Shrek is an ogre, a creature that is usually a villain in stories. Physically ugly, Shrek enjoys the effect of his appearance on strangers and uses his scary looks to his advantage in living a peaceful life alone in his swamp. Despite his unattractive appearance, however, Shrek displays noble qualities. He is tolerant of a pushy talking donkey, brave in rescuing a princess, and honest about who he is, comparing himself to an onion—something not everyone likes—rather than something more favorable. Even at his physical ugliest, Shrek is an inwardly good being.

A second way the movie *Shrek* breaks stereotypes is by having the ogre, not the prince, get the girl. Accepting a quest to reclaim his swamp from squatters, Shrek rescues the lovely Princess Fiona for the vertically challenged Lord Farquaad. As the ogre and the princess come to know each other, they begin to care for one another. However, because Shrek believes that Fiona loathes his looks, he nearly misses his chance to confess his love. Luckily, immediately following the wedding ceremony, Shrek declares his love for Fiona just as Lord Farquaad is eaten by a dragon. Thus, even though Shrek is not a handsome prince, he wins the love of a princess.

Most important, the movie *Shrek* breaks stereotypes in its depiction of Princess Fiona. Exceedingly lovely but keeping a secret, Fiona hides herself every day at nightfall. Cursed to be an ogre by dark, Fiona fears that she will never find true love and break the spell. In a traditional fairy tale, just loving Shrek would be enough to transform both herself and her true love from ogres into gorgeous humans. In the movie *Shrek*, though, true love's kiss causes both Shrek and Fiona to remain ogres permanently.

Although fair faces and happy endings seem to go hand in hand, the contemporary fairy-tale movie *Shrek* shows viewers that this does not necessarily have to be so. Having the hero be an ogre who wins the princess who is, herself, an ogre flips the traditional fairy tale on its head but entertains us just the same.

The second essay, "An Ogre of a Tale," is clearer than the first one and therefore more effective. The paragraphs are organized in emphatic order from least to most important. The writer also clearly signals the order of the points through the use of transition words such as *first*. Additionally, the details within each paragraph are organized in a logical manner.

In "A Tale with a Real Twist," the writer places the "final" example in the second body paragraph. Since he includes no other transition words in the other body paragraphs, the writer doesn't show why the paragraphs are ordered in the way they are. Does the writer use emphatic order? Do the essay's examples follow chronological order, in terms of how the events in the movie happen? Neither organizational strategy is clear. Further, within each paragraph, the details are not organized in a logical way. In the third body paragraph, the writer begins by describing the trip to meet Fiona's parents and *then* discusses how Shrek initially refused to go. The reader is left wondering which details are important, when they occurred, and why the writer placed them in this order.

EXERCISE 3 CLEAR WRITING

Use your pen or pencil to underline at least three other transitional expressions in "An Ogre of a Tale." For a more complete list of transitional expressions, see Chapter 11.

Transitional expressions: _____, _____, and

_____.

The first essay, "A Tale with a Real Twist," is both concise and credible, but it lacks any directions for the reader to follow. The writer does not include transitional expressions or logical order of support points or details. Consequently, the reader can't easily distinguish the support points or details or understand the reason for the order in which they are given.

In Your Own Writing   To write clearly, you must do the following:

1. Organize your ideas effectively and logically. For instance, if your topic is "earning my promotion one day at a time," you should use chronological order rather than emphatic order to make your case.

2. Use transitional expressions to let your reader know when important points or details are coming and how important those points or details are.

Making Sure Your Writing Is Clear

Ask yourself the following questions to determine whether your paragraphs are clear.

1. Do I have a logical organizational format that my reader can easily follow? What is it?

2. Do I use transitional expressions to communicate what my points are and which ones are most important?

3. Do I use transitional expressions to signal the order and importance of my specific details?

Recognizing Correct Writing

Correct writing tells your readers that you take yourself seriously and that you care about your work. In correct writing, sentences are free of errors in grammar, punctuation, and spelling.

Read the two essay openings below. Then, decide which version communicates correctly. Why?

Different Ellas: Draft

¹Perhaps the best-known fairy tail is that of Cinderella. ²The story of the lovely, kind daughter who is mistreated by her step-mother and stepsisters only to win the love of a prince continue to inspire generations. ³The movie industry it has been inspired by Cinderella, too. ⁴The names, places, and even plots of some movies may seem far removed from the original fairy tale, Cinderella makes her appearance in many movies. ⁵Including *Pretty Woman, Ella Enchanted,* and *Ever After.*

⁶Cinderellas 1989 imitator, *Pretty Woman,* tells a version of Cinderella on the street. ⁷In *Pretty Woman,* there is no wicked step-mother or stepsisters but the Cinderella character—a prostitute named Vivian—lives a hard life. ⁸Vivian spends the early scenes of the movie trying to earn enough to pay rent, dodging pimps who want her in their employ, and she also tries to keep her drug-addict

friend Kit clean. [9]Hiring her for a week, Vivian's luck appears to be changing when she meets the hardened corporate raider Edward Lewis. [10]Who learns to enjoy his life through Vivan's efforts.

Different Ellas: Final Version

Perhaps the best-known fairy tale is "Cinderella." The story of the lovely, kind daughter who is mistreated by her stepmother and stepsisters only to win the love of a prince continues to inspire generations. The movie industry has been inspired by Cinderella, too. Although the names, places, and even plots of some movies may seem far removed from the original fairy tale, Cinderella makes her appearance in *Pretty Woman, Ella Enchanted,* and *Ever After.*

In *Pretty Woman,* the Cinderella character—a prostitute named Vivian—has no wicked stepmother or stepsisters, but she lives a hard life. Trying to earn enough to pay rent, dodging pimps who want her in their employ, and keeping her drug-addict friend Kit clean are some of the challenges that this Cinderella faces. Vivian's luck appears to be changing when she meets the hardened corporate raider Edward Lewis, who hires her for a week and learns to enjoy his life through Vivian's efforts.

The final version of "Different Ellas" is *correct.* It has no errors in grammar, punctuation, or spelling; therefore, it is more convincing.

EXERCISE 4 CORRECT WRITING

Identify the types of errors in the numbered items in the draft of "Different Ellas." Circle the letter of the type of error you see in each group of words. *Note:* Do not worry if you're unable to answer these questions. By the end of the term, you will be answering questions like these with ease.

1. In item 1, the type of error is

    a. Run-on sentence

    b. Spelling error

    c. Sentence fragment

    d. Pronoun error

2. In item 2, the type of error is

    a. Run-on sentence

    b. Dangling modifier

   c. Sentence fragment

   d. Subject-verb agreement mistake

3. In item 3, the type of error is

   a. Run-on sentence

   b. Pronoun error

   c. Nonstandard usage

   d. Verb tense error

4. In item 4, the type of error is

   a. Sentence fragment

   b. Spelling error

   c. Misplaced modifier

   d. Run-on sentence

5. In item 5, the type of error is

   a. Subject-verb agreement mistake

   b. Run-on sentence

   c. Sentence fragment

   d. Dangling modifier

6. In item 6, the type of error is

   a. Verb form error

   b. Apostrophe error

   c. Nonstandard usage

   d. Run-on sentence

7. In item 7, the type of error is

   a. Run-on sentence

   b. Sentence fragment

   c. Missing apostrophe

   d. Subject-verb agreement mistake

8. In item 8, the type of error is

   a. Subject-verb agreement mistake

   b. Parallelism error

   c. Comma error

   d. Misplaced modifier

9. In item 9, the type of error is

   a. Pronoun error

   b. Spelling error

   c. Misplaced modifier

   d. Sentence fragment

10. In item 10, the type of error is

   a. Sentence fragment

   b. Run-on sentence

   c. Spelling error

   d. Nonstandard usage

You should have chosen the following answers.

1. b	**3.** c	**5.** c	**7.** a	**9.** c
2. c	**4.** d	**6.** b	**8.** b	**10.** a

In Your Own Writing   To write correctly, you must do the following:

1. Review sentence skills to avoid making errors.
2. Proofread to find and correct mistakes.

For a review of sentence-level writing, refer to Chapters 33 through 54.

Making Sure Your Writing Is Correct

Ask yourself the following questions to determine whether your paragraphs are correct.

1. Have I reviewed grammar, punctuation, and spelling guidelines (Chapters 32–52)?
2. Have I proofread to find and correct errors?

EXERCISE 5 REVISING AN ESSAY TO ACHIEVE CONCISE WRITING

When you read the following essay, cross out any details that do not directly support the thesis statement (underlined). *Note:* You may have to cross out entire paragraphs to achieve *concise* writing.

A Grimm Telling

Watching any Disney version of a fairy tale gives viewers the impression that death with a minimum of bloodshed for the villain is a typical ending. This, however, is not the case. If you're willing to do some searching, it's possible to find a lot of blood and guts in stories. As told by the brothers Grimm, many fairy tales originally contained violence and gore. <u>Early versions of three familiar fairy tales—"Cinderella," "Snow White," and "Little Red Riding Hood"—reveal that blood and guts were as much a part of fairy tales as the happy ending.</u>

The gore in "Cinderella" affects her stepsisters directly. In the Grimm version of the tale, not only are the stepsisters punished for their unkindness to Cinderella, but they maim themselves as well. Once my sister pierced her own ears with a needle and a cork, and that seemed painful enough. When the prince himself brings Cinderella's slipper to her home, the stepsisters actually cut off parts of their feet—the big toe for one sister and the heel for another—to make the shoe fit. As if this weren't punishment enough, while going to and from Cinderella's wedding, the stepsisters have their eyes pecked out by white doves as penalty for their cruelty. Even though the fairy tale has a happy ending for Cinderella, the story contains its share of blood and gore.

Nearly every time I turn on the television set, there's something with graphic violence on. Just last week, I watched an episode of *Lost,* and I saw a man brutally beat another man, all because their boss was "displeased." That seems to be a pretty extreme punishment, and I couldn't watch the rest of the program after that. Another time, I watched an episode of a program called *Monk* in which a little kid finds someone's severed pinky finger. There's definitely too much blood and gore on television.

"Snow White" is another story whose modern version is less violent than its original. While the wicked queen dies in the Disney version, her death in the Grimm version is much more unpleasant. After Snow White has been awakened by the prince, she marries him. This seems a bit unrealistic, to marry someone you just met, but I guess it's OK in fairy tales. The wicked queen attends the wedding, only to find that a pair of iron shoes has been placed in the fire for her. As punishment for her cruelty to Snow White, the queen is forced to wear the shoes and dance until she dies. Maybe that could be an alternative for the "money dance," especially if you don't like your in-laws. Though death often involves pain, a death by red-hot shoes would be more painful than most. I can hardly stand wearing shoes that don't fit properly, so wearing red-hot iron shoes would be a nightmare.

Finally, the story of Little Red Riding Hood serves as one last example of a fairy tale that has been toned down in terms of violence. In the Grimm rendition, not only Little Red Riding Hood but also her grandmother is eaten by the wolf. These fairy-tale animals are apparently much smarter than real-life animals; my dog could never manage to disguise himself. However, they are saved by the huntsman, who slices open the wolf's stomach and frees the girl and grandmother. Even though Red Riding Hood and the grandmother are "saved," having been inside a wolf's stomach seems fairly unpleasant. Though the wolf fares poorly in modern versions of the story, being eviscerated before death seems worse than plain old death.

Since the bad guys usually get what they deserve, readers do not often have a problem with their punishment. Even on reality shows, people are punished by being eliminated or having to eat disgusting food. However, it's important to note that, while the villains have almost always been punished, they suffered more in early versions of fairy tales than they do in later ones. "Cinderella," "Snow White," and "Little Red Riding Hood" all show how wicked characters not only die but suffer in stories.

EXERCISE 6 PROVIDING DETAILS FOR CREDIBILITY IN AN ESSAY

The following outline contains a thesis statement and topic sentences identifying support points, but it does not contain specific details that support the topic sentences. Fill in the supporting details. The first detail under every support point has been filled in for you.

Thesis statement: _Fairy tales would be more interesting to me if they_

had more modern plots, characters, and endings.

A. _Fairy-tale plots have little to do with my life._

   1. Detail: _I've never been cursed or affected by magic, so the idea of_

   someone's life being changed through enchantment seems impossible.

   _____

2. Detail: _____

_____

_____

3. Detail: _____

_____

_____

B. Few fairy-tale characters seem to have "real" problems like mine.

1. Detail: The Frog Prince is under an enchantment that keeps him from

being human, but this is a problem that none of my friends have.

_____

2. Detail: _____

_____

_____

3. Detail: _____

_____

_____

C. Fairy-tale endings rarely seem realistic to me.

1. Detail: To be awakened by a prince and live happily ever after seems a

pretty simple and highly unlikely fate for most of the people I know.

_____

2. Detail: _____

_____

_____

3. Detail: _____

_____

_____

EXERCISE 7   ORGANIZING SUPPORT POINTS AND DETAILS IN AN ESSAY

The following essay contains support points and details that are out of order. Read the essay. Then, rewrite it, placing the points and details in a logical order. Add transitional words or phrases where appropriate.

The Magic of Three

Magic plays an important role in fairy tales; indeed, someone is often being punished or rewarded via a poisoned apple or fairy godmother. However, even as some types of magic in fairy tales are obvious, other types are more subtle. The number three, for instance, is important in fairy tales. The number three often represents the number of people, the number of tasks required, or the number of wishes.

The number three is significant in fairy tales is in the number of times something occurs. In "Rumpelstiltskin," for example, the miller's daughter spends three different nights trying to spin straw into gold. Similarly, Jack makes three trips up the beanstalk, the wicked queen tries three times to murder Snow White, and the princess must "pay" the frog in three different ways to earn back her golden ball.

The number three is important because it comes in the form of wishes. In numerous fairy tales, a wisher is given three wishes, which he or she (but usually a man) most likely uses foolishly. In different versions of the story "The Three Wishes," a man wastes his wishes and ends up no better off than he started. Though not technically a fairy tale, the story "Aladdin and the Magic Lamp" makes use of the number three. Thus, three seems to indicate a come-full-circle circumstance in fairy tales.

Three is important is in the number of people involved. In "Cinderella," three people persecute Cinderella: the wicked stepmother and her two stepdaughters. The number three is also important in "The Three Little Pigs," "Goldilocks and the Three Bears," and "The Three Billy Goats Gruff." Finally, several less familiar fairy tales revolve around three main characters: "The Three Spinners," "The Three Snake-Leaves," "The Three Languages," "The Three Feathers," and "The Three Sons of Fortune," for example. One character may be more important than the other two, but having three characters seems necessary for many fairy tales.

While different types of characters, occurrences, and timelines exist in fairy tales, the number three often represents the number of people, tasks, or wishes in a story. Perhaps because three is the least number of points required to make any geometric shape, or perhaps because the number three has significance in different religions, it

remains an important figure in fairy tales.

EXERCISE 8 MAKING AN ESSAY CONCISE, CREDIBLE, CLEAR, AND CORRECT

The following essay contains areas that require rewriting according to each of the four Cs. After each paragraph, identify the areas that need to be rewritten in order to be concise, credible, clear, and correct.

Sci-Fi Cinderella

Because it is the world's most familiar fairy tale, "Cinderella" has appeared in many forms over the centuries and throughout the world. Sometimes I get so sick of this fairy tale that I don't even want to see another movie, but I always go because I love popcorn. Most of these tales include a downtrodden maiden, evil family or community members, a prince of some sort, and a happy ending for the maiden. I heard about a movie with a man as the main character—*Cinderfella,* I think—but I never saw it. One version, however, differs from the traditional Cinderella story. "When the Clock Strikes" by Tanith Lee contains witchcraft, revenge, and an evil Cinderella character.

This paragraph should be revised to be more _____.

Witchcraft is one way that "When the Clock Strikes" veers away from the well-known fairy tale. The maiden in Lee's story looses her mother, as does the original Cinderella, Lee's maiden pays tribute to her mother by takeing up her mother's craft: witchcraft. While the Cinderella figures stepfamily asumes her to be grieving in the ashes, Lees Cinderella character she is practicing witchcraft, growing more powerful and more evil as the story progresses. Voodoo dolls, curses, and enchanted objects all play a role in Lee's tale.

This paragraph should be revised to be more _____.

Revenge is not found in the traditional Cinderella stories. Even in tales where the stepsisters are punished, something besides Cinderella—such as white doves—does the punishing. In "When the Clock Strikes," Ashella's only goal once her mother dies is to punish those—in this case the Duke and his son the prince—she believes to be responsible for her mother's death. At the ball, Ashella casts a spell to bind the prince to her and curse him. The prince in the original Cinderella story also seeks the wearer of the slipper; Lee's prince is destined never to find her. Using her significant magical powers to emerge from her ashes mystically lovely, Ashella attends the ball. As part of her curse, Ashella bewitches the shoe never to fit any but herself; though the prince tries desperately to find Ashella, he loses his mind during the search and dies in the streets.

This paragraph should be revised to be more _____.

Finally, Lee's Cinderalla character, Ashella, is anything but the sweet, simple maiden in traditional tales. Clever, focused, and furious, Ashella rejects the life her father gives her and pursues dark arts. Though her father and stepfamily attempt to draw her out of her ash-bound life, Ashella plots her vengeance. When the story ends, Ashella has gained exactly what she set out to gain. However, Ashella is far from finding peace in a "happily ever after" ending.

This paragraph should be revised to be more _____.

WRITING PRACTICE Write Your Own Essay

In this chapter, you've had the chance to view fairy tales from a slightly different point of view. While fairy tales remain a part of many people's experiences, the tales have been criticized for overemphasizing the importance of beauty. Similarly, many television programs have been denounced for featuring stars that bear little resemblance to everyday people.

Your assignment is this: *Write a few paragraphs or short essay explaining how either fairy tales or contemporary television programs do or do not feature "average-looking" people.* In illustrating your ideas, you may choose characters from this chapter—such as Shrek, Snow White, or Rapunzel— or you may choose a character from another fairy tale or from a television show. At this point, don't worry about producing a perfectly organized, illustrated, and edited essay. Just do your best to make a point and support it in the most logical way you can.

Write your essay on a separate piece of paper.

Lab Activity 3

For additional practice with the four Cs, complete Lab Activity 3 in the lab manual packaged with your textbook. If you did not receive a lab manual, you can complete this activity online at **www.ablongman.com/long.** Click on **College Resources for Writers** and then click on **Activity 3.**

PART TWO
The Writing Process

4 Prewriting: Preparing to Write

CULTURE NOTE *The Internet*

A publicly accessible computer network connecting smaller networks around the world, the Internet blossomed from a U.S. Defense Department project known as ARPANET (Advanced Research Projects Agency Network). ARPANET was established in 1969 with connections between computers at several western U.S. universities. Although ARPANET's purpose was to provide a safe communications system in case of war, the network piqued the interest of academics and researchers. Now a means by which people can research, communicate, and collaborate, the Internet continues to change lives around the globe.

Getting Googled

JOURNAL ENTRY Whereas finding out about people you didn't know was once difficult, it can now be very easy, thanks to search engines such as Google. How has the Internet changed your life, or the lives of people you know? Write a few sentences explaining how the Internet has had an influence on your life or on the life of someone you know.

55

What's Important: The Product or The Process?

For many people, following a process—or routine—makes writing paragraphs and essays much less stressful. The **writing process** consists of the steps you can follow to get from the beginning of a writing assignment to the end. The writing process offers ways to make decisions about your audience and purpose, strategies to help you begin writing your ideas, and guidelines to help you develop your writing.

Eventually, you will adapt the process to your own needs, using some steps over and over, and even eliminating steps depending on your audience, your topic, and your reason for writing. For now, all you have to do is practice following the steps to find out which ones help you the most. Keep in mind, too, that the steps in the writing process do not need to be followed in a certain order every time. As you develop as a writer, you will learn what steps—or parts of steps—in the writing process work best for you. Think about how you might use, or discard, the following strategies in your personal writing process.

The Writing Process

The writing process consists of four basic steps.

1. Prewriting (coming up with ideas)
2. Drafting (writing a rough draft)
3. Revising (making changes in your draft)
4. Editing (checking for correctness)

As you work through the steps, your writing becomes clearer and clearer. Keep in mind that, with the exception of editing, you will use these steps throughout the development of your essays. For instance, if you know the main point you want to make about a topic, you may need only to prewrite to find sources or discover gaps in your support. If you know a lot about your topic but don't know what point to make, though, drafting may help you find your focus. In nearly any type of writing, revising will help you sharpen your focus to help you communicate to your intended audience for your specific purpose.

Step 1: Prewriting—Coming Up with Ideas

This step combines the easy task of writing whatever comes to mind with the important goal of developing a thesis statement, support points, and specific details, which help you achieve the first two of the four Cs: concise writing and credible writing. A number of strategies can help you get started writing and fill up that blank page. These techniques are

- Freewriting
- Questioning
- Clustering

- Listing
- Keeping a journal
- Outlining

Though these activities vary in their degrees of structure, they all can help you find focus and details for your paragraph.

The Role of Audience in Prewriting

Perhaps the most encouraging aspect of prewriting is that it's forgiving. Errors and lack of organization don't matter, and neither do gaps in information. Similarly, since prewriting is an activity you do primarily for *yourself,* you don't have to worry about answering every question a reader might have about your ideas.

It's a good idea, however, to use prewriting as an opportunity to anticipate your readers' needs. Good writing is like good manners: you're always considering someone else first. Keeping questions in the back of your mind—such as "What can I assume that my reader already knows about my topic?" "How much research, if any, should I plan to do to provide the necessary details to make my writing convincing to my reader?" "What is the most convincing way to present this information?"—will help you plan, research, organize, and write your essay from prewriting through editing.

Freewriting

The easiest way to get started is simply to start writing, even if you feel you have nothing to say. This technique of "dumping" anything in your brain onto the paper is called **freewriting**. In freewriting you write as much as you can, as fast as you can, without stopping. Mimi had to come up with ideas for an essay in her composition course, so she used freewriting to get started. Her freewriting looked like this:

> We're supposed to write about the Internet, but—hello!—could there be a broader topic? I don't even know where to start. My folks use the Net for their banking, and my sister uses it mostly for research, but all I really use it for is e-mail. I guess I could write about how the Internet has many useful functions, but that seems so generic, and I'm not that interested in the banking stuff. Maybe I could talk about chat rooms; I've never actually chatted before, but I've thought about it, and this would give me an excuse to check them out. Maybe I could do a pro/con type of essay ... this is getting good.

Mimi clearly needs to do some research to narrow her focus, but she's off to a good start. Her freewriting has helped her eliminate topics such as online banking, online research, and e-mail, and now she can concentrate on learning about what interests her.

EXERCISE 1 FOCUSED FREEWRITING

For ten minutes, write without stopping on the topic of the Internet. Write whatever comes to mind, as fast as you can, and don't worry about making mistakes. Some questions to consider are these: How has the Internet affected you? What do you already know about it? What aspects of the Internet interest you?

Listing

Sometimes freewriting can leave you with what seems like a mass of words that don't make sense. If freewriting doesn't work for a particular paragraph, another type of prewriting can help. **Listing** allows you the freedom of freewriting without the sense of disorganization. When you make a list, you simply write down everything you know about a topic, but you do this in a list form rather than a paragraph form.

Fausto used listing to put his ideas on paper.

The Internet

The Internet	Shopping
E-mail	Video games
Chat rooms	MP3 files (cool music)
Online databases	Photographs
Identity theft	

In this list, Fausto has concentrated on gathering as many ideas and details as possible on his topic in general. Later on, Fausto will sort through his list to eliminate ideas, write a rough thesis statement, and start developing his essay.

Choose one aspect of the Internet—e-mail, research, shopping, or video games, for example—and make a list of ideas relating to that topic.

Questioning

Sometimes the best place to start is with the information you *don't* have. Many times writers are unable to organize their ideas because they don't have enough specific details to use in their writing. A helpful strategy here is a technique called **questioning**. Using a T-chart to ask questions on one side and answer them on the other can help you identify areas where you need more information and organize the information you do have.

Internet Chat Rooms

What are chat rooms?	Actually, I'm not sure of their formal definition. I think they're like private e-mail in real time, but I don't know for certain.
Who visits chat rooms?	I guess all different kinds of people, but I'm not sure.
To what extent do people meet new friends?	My friend Margie met her boyfriend online, and he seems normal.
What are the dangers of chat rooms?	People can lie.
Why do people go to chat rooms?	Because they're shy? Because they're busy? I need to find out.

In this T-chart, Mimi has asked key questions that she needs to answer to write an informed, thoughtful essay about Internet chat rooms. When she first began her chart, she had even less information under the

"Answers" heading. Mimi still needs quite a bit of information, but now she has some questions which can focus her research.

EXERCISE 3 USING A T-CHART FOR QUESTIONS

Make a T-chart about one aspect of the Internet that you are somewhat, but not extremely, familiar with. Write your questions on the left side of the chart, and fill in any answers you have on the right.

Keeping a Journal

The best way to improve your writing skills is to write as often as possible. Keeping a journal offers you one way to write every day in a low-pressure setting. Your journal can help you work through your ideas before you have to produce a final piece of writing. Keeping a journal is like freewriting a little bit every day. Some writers have a special book or notebook that serves as their journal. Others use a computer to record their thoughts. The main point is to do some writing every day.

Simon was interested in learning about the early stages of the Internet, so he wrote in a journal to develop his ideas as he learned more about his topic.

> Monday
>
>   The Internet seems to have something for everyone, but I'm really interested in its early military uses. I read in an essay for class that the people who started the Net were somewhat unhappy that their cool, secret communications network was discovered by mass society. I wonder how true that is, and I wonder if the Net came out of the Pentagon, or secret labs, or someplace else. I also wonder whether or not the military uses the Internet today, though it seems as though it wouldn't be very safe.
>
> Wednesday
>
>   I've changed my mind about military Internet use. My dad read an article in a business magazine about how hospitals are using high-tech information systems—including patient-accessed Internet research sites—to save people. I need to get a copy of the article, but from what my dad told me, the Net can save people's lives by giving their doctors

information they might not otherwise have. Since I'm thinking about medicine as a career, this sounds very cool.

<u>Friday</u>

I think I'm onto something with the medical Internet search. At the health clinic near my house, doctors want to get equipment that lets them enter all their notes about a patient into a computer account, read past information, and send a prescription over the Net to a pharmacy. I think I heard that some pharmacies already have a system where pharmacy records are somehow all connected, so people can't cheat and have different doctors give them prescriptions for the same thing at different pharmacies without getting caught.

Notice how Simon's focus changed as he learned about an article relating to medical Internet use. Because it takes place over different days or times, keeping a journal gives you flexibility in developing your ideas. Simon may, when he reads his journal, remember how interested he was initially in military aspects of the Internet, and he may change his mind again. However, keeping a journal gives you a record of your thought process so you can see the course of your idea's development.

EXERCISE 4 KEEPING A JOURNAL FOR ESSAY PLANNING

Over the next week, set up your own journal. Write for five minutes each day about a topic of your choice. Some possible topics are

- A project in another course
- An upcoming campus event
- An upcoming election
- Your experiences at work, home, or school

Clustering

Another prewriting technique is **clustering**, also called **diagramming** or **mapping**. Clustering helps you organize your ideas visually, and it offers more structure than freewriting. It also helps you see what ideas might be off-topic when you are ready to write your draft. In clustering, write your ideas on paper and then use circles and arrows to connect your ideas.

Dean made a cluster diagram around the topic of "Internet entertainment."

In this example, most of the ideas stem from some aspect of Internet entertainment. Dean has written down other ideas as well—gambling, online dating, and information about fantasy sports—although he doesn't seem to have much information about them. He'd do better focusing on the topics he does have information about: music, video games, and chat rooms.

EXERCISE 5 CLUSTERING TO PLAN AN ESSAY

Make a cluster diagram on the topic of "best prime-time television shows." Concentrate on using arrows and circles to clarify connections between your ideas.

Outlining

Possibly the most helpful prewriting tool is outlining. **Outlining** is an effective means of organizing your ideas without actually writing sentences. Outlining also helps you see any gaps in your support because an outline lays out your whole argument on paper before you begin to write. In general, to outline, begin with your main point and then include supporting ideas and specific details. Outlining is often especially effective in combination with another prewriting strategy, such as freewriting. Once you write your ideas on paper in a less structured format, making an outline can help you see how to use those ideas in your whole writing assignment.

Keep in mind that because outlining demands a higher degree of structure and organization than other prewriting strategies, you may need more practice before it becomes a comfortable prewriting method for you.

Writing on the topic of online dating, Evelyn used an outline to plan her paragraph before she began writing.

Topic: Online Dating

A. Benefits

   1. Convenience of in-home first impression

   2. Possibility of meeting many more people than in daily life

   3. Shy people can warm up before meeting face-to-face

B. Drawbacks

   1. Some services charge fees for initial contact

   2. People lie

   3. Stigma of desperation

C. Popular online dating services

   1. eHarmony.com

   2. Matchmaker.com

   3. PerfectMatch.com

Evelyn's outline is a rough sketch of the material on the topic of online dating. An effective outline presents information in a clear, organized pattern that can easily be turned into an essay. Notice how Evelyn's outline lends itself to a mapped thesis. After writing her ideas in outline form, Evelyn was able to craft a thesis that worked well for her essay: "Successful online dating comes from understanding the benefits, risks, and types of online dating services available."

EXERCISE 6 OUTLINING AN ASSIGNED TOPIC

Use the following template to prepare an outline based on one of these topics: "typical meals of a college student," "challenges of a college student," "ways for college students to relax," "best pets for college students," "survival tips for college students." If you choose the topic "challenges of a college student," simply complete the outline below. If you choose another topic, start your outline on a separate piece of paper.

Topic: _Challenges of a college student_ _____

A. _Finding enough time for school_ _____

    1. _____

    2. _____

    3. _____

    4. _____

B. _Finding enough time for work_ _____

    1. _____

    2. _____

    3. _____

C. _Other priorities take time._ _____

    1. _____

    2. _____

    3. _____

EXERCISE 7 OUTLINING TO PLAN AN ESSAY

Using a separate piece of paper, make an outline of a topic you plan to write about for a class. Do as much as you can in ten to fifteen minutes. Then, check your outline to make sure it develops the idea set forth in your thesis statement.

Using a Computer for Prewriting

If you're a fast typist, a computer is great for prewriting. Just follow these guidelines. For general information on writing with a computer, see the tips for using computers in writing on page 12.

- Type as fast as you can to record every idea that enters your head.
- Don't stop to correct sentence-level errors.
- Try **invisible writing**: turn off the computer monitor (screen) and just type. You'll make progress, but you won't be distracted by how much you've written. Once you're off to a good start, turn the monitor back on.
- Turn your freewriting into a list, a question-and-answer item, or an outline. When lists and outlines look neat and organized, you feel good about your work in progress.
- Use your prewriting file when you're ready for drafting, Step 2 in the writing process.

    A computer can also help you keep a journal.

- Create a file for each month.
- Name your files so that they appear in chronological order in the directory menu: "Journal 0107" (for January 2007) or "Journal 0808" (for August 2008). That way, your computer directory will list your journal files in chronological order, and it will be easy to find specific files.
- When you write in your journal, date each entry.

WRITING PRACTICE 1 Write an Essay Based on an Outline

Write an essay based on the outline you made for either Exercise 6 or Exercise 7. If you did not complete the outline for either of those exercises, do so before you begin writing. Make sure your essay has a clear thesis statement, support points, and specific details.

WRITING PRACTICE 2 Write an Essay Based on a New Outline

Option A. Over the course of this chapter, you've had the chance to read a bit about the Internet. Now, it's time to write about it.

Your assignment is this: *Choose one aspect of the Internet mentioned in this chapter, and make an outline on it in preparation for writing an essay.* You may need to do some research (surfing the Net, for instance) to learn enough about your topic to complete an intelligent outline and essay. Some possible topics are chat rooms, online video games, Internet music options, online dating, or online fantasy sports.

Option B: Using Sources. Write the assignment outlined in Option A, but be sure to read at least two articles on your topic to learn more about it. Consider reading articles from online databases such as ProQuest or EBSCO, or visit your school's library for articles in periodicals. At this point, don't worry about using quotations or making a list of works cited. Just be sure to mention where you learned any specific facts or details you use in your essay.

Lab Activity 4

For additional practice with prewriting, complete Lab Activity 4 in the lab manual packaged with your textbook. If you did not receive a lab manual, you can complete this activity online at **www.ablongman.com/long.** Click on **College Resources for Writers** and then click on **Activity 4.**

5 Drafting: Writing a Rough Draft

CULTURE NOTE *Acupuncture*

The practice of inserting needles at certain body points to stimulate specific nerve fibers, acupuncture has been recognized as a treatment for pain relief since the second century BC. Simultaneously releasing nerve impulses to counter pain impulses and releasing painkilling endorphins, acupuncture has steadily gained credibility in the United States since the 1970s.

Acupuncture Treatment

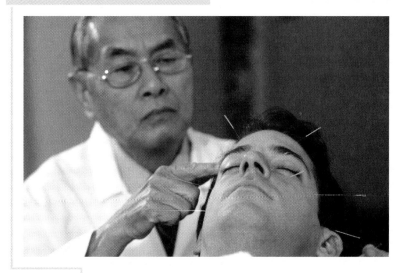

CONDUCT AN INTERVIEW Though such treatments as acupuncture are not always considered traditional, they can provide effective alternatives to health problems. What are some non-traditional health practices of people you know? Interview two or three people, focusing on their family's treatments or procedures. Write a few sentences explaining your findings.

Beginning a Draft

Now that you've spent some time prewriting, you're ready to move on to drafting, the next step in the writing process. **Drafting** is simply writing a rough draft of your essay. In drafting, you use the information you discovered during prewriting to write sentences that work together to convey your ideas.

Rough Drafts Are Not Perfect

Some people think that they should be able to crank out a perfect essay on the first try, but very few writers work this way. Sometimes writing does come easily, but often it just takes time and practice. All that work has a benefit, though: the more you write, the better a writer you will become.

Some professional writers describe their writing experiences in different ways.

Perry James Pitre compares writing to an agonizing roller coaster ride.

The Writer steps into the roller-coaster car and straps himself in. . . . Slowly, agonizingly slowly, the car pulls out onto the track, with the huge first hill before it, seemingly an unconquerable mountain.

Barbara Michaels writes that the only way to write is by writing.

The only way to do it is to do it: by writing, writing, writing.

Donald M. Murray discusses the how the role of revision differs between students and professional writers.

When students complete a first draft, they consider the job of writing done—and their teachers too often agree. When professional writers complete a first draft, they usually feel that they are at the start of the writing process. When a draft is completed, the job of writing can begin.

It's important to remember that the rough version, or **rough draft**, of your essay will not be perfect or finished.

- *A rough draft is not usually concise.* It may contain too many irrelevant details.
- *A rough draft is not usually credible.* It may not have enough specific details to support its topic thesis statement.
- *A rough draft is not usually clear.* Its support points may not be organized logically, and it may have few or no transitional words.

■ *A rough draft is not usually correct.* It may contain many errors in grammar, punctuation, and spelling.

As you work through the writing process, you'll get the chance to correct the flaws in your draft and make your essay more concise, credible, clear, and correct. When writing a rough draft, your goal should simply be to *get your ideas on paper.* Once they're on paper, you can change them, but you can't revise something you haven't written.

Writing a Rough Draft

When you're ready to start drafting, allow yourself plenty of time. Gather your prewriting materials and any other notes, and have your writing assignment handy. Then clear your mind of outside worries as best you can, and start writing.

Your Prewriting Material   You've collected a lot of ideas and details from prewriting: freewriting, listing, questioning, keeping a journal, clustering, or outlining. You may also have taken some notes while doing some reading or other research. Reread these sources to refresh your memory and spark ideas. If you need help with prewriting, see Chapter 4.

Your Thesis Statement   The key to writing an effective essay is having a clear thesis statement. The thesis statement controls the direction of your entire essay and represents the most important idea that you want to communicate. For more on writing thesis statements, see Chapter 8.

Jamal's writing instructor gave his students an assignment to write about a medical treatment they have tried or have thought about trying. Because Jamal was pretty healthy and tried to stay *away* from doctors and medicine, this assignment seemed particularly dull. However, he remembered hearing about acupuncture treatments from a co-worker. Because the treatments worked on the spot and didn't involve lab tests or x-rays, Jamal was mildly interested in the topic.

Your Support Points and Specific Details   After you write a working thesis, you're ready to begin drafting. At this point, it's helpful to review your prewriting to identify potential support points or details. Your prewriting is an important source for support points and details for your essay.

The Rough Draft   The primary difference between prewriting and drafting is that drafting is focused around a thesis statement, while

prewriting is not. During both activities, however, you may feel as though your writing is not as focused or specific as you'd like. Don't worry; just write. Using your working thesis and your prewriting as the foundation for your essay, begin writing. At this point, your support, organization, and sentence-level writing will still be rough, but hopefully you'll be able to see your essay take shape.

In terms of the physical act of drafting, if you are using a pen, skip lines as you write. Leaving space now will help you in Step 3 (revising) and Step 4 (editing) of the writing process. If you are using a computer, see "Using a Computer for Drafting" (page 71).

Jamal's draft follows.

Whenever I've had an injury or health problem throughout my life, my mom has always sent me to the doctor. Sometimes I'd get x-rays, sometimes I'd get a prescription, and sometimes I'd get nothing. However, I always felt my mom was doing everything possible to help me get well. Recently, a co-worker mentioned that nothing seemed to help her back pain until she tried acupuncture. Acupuncture works.

Acupuncture helps control or eliminate pain and insomnia. Knee pain, back pain, and arthritis pain are all gone after less than an hour under the needles. My buddy Neil couldn't fall asleep during finals week, so he'd walk around like a zombie. He tried herbal teas and soothing music, but nothing worked. Finally, a doctor at Neil's job at the med center suggested that he try acupuncture. Neil had health insurance that covered acupuncture treatments, so he gave it a try. Sure enough, he was able to fall asleep more easily after going to acupuncture just twice.

People have many reasons for not trying acupuncture. One fear that people have is that acupuncture will hurt. Other people worry that acupuncture won't work for them. Some people worry that acupuncture is too expensive. After calling several acupuncturists in my area, I learned that the average cost per session for acupuncture treatment is between $50 and $60. When accompanied by other traditional Chinese treatments, such as herbs, the treatment can be more expensive. As to the pain, my buddy Neil said that after feeling a tiny prick—less than the prick of the needle at a dentist's office when anesthetic is being administered—he felt nothing. When a needle's placement bothered him, he told the acupuncturist, who then readjusted the needle until it was comfortable. Even though Neil tried acupuncture only because it was cheap and easy for him, it worked.

Acupuncture doesn't cure everything, however. It can help people feel better and, possibly, even live longer, but some acupuncture procedures—such as eye treatments—don't appear to work as well as others. Need more details!

Notice that not only does Jamal have far too many ideas to develop in an essay, but he also has large gaps in support, incomplete organization, and numerous sentence-level errors (not shown here). However, this draft serves as a starting point for Jamal's writing, which he will develop and fine-tune through revision.

Using a Computer for Drafting

Using a computer can help you greatly by letting you see your whole work, typed out, on the screen. Probably the greatest benefit of using a word processor is *flexibility*. You can type, move, save, and generally manipulate your information before you ever print out your document. Following some specific guidelines can make computer drafting easier.

1. Use your prewriting to type out more than one version of your thesis statement if you're not sure what your main idea is initially.

2. If you are thinking about using emphatic order, move your support points to different places in your draft by using the cut and paste functions. You can decide later how to order the support points.

3. Add illustrations or examples as you write your essay. Or, if ideas come to you when you're working on something else, type those examples in a separate file (or even at the very end of your draft) and then come back and insert them into your essay later.

4. Don't delete anything at this point. If you're not sure whether to keep a support point or specific detail, cut and paste it to the end of your document. Later, when you finish your draft, you can delete it. Until then, you have information that may come in handy at other points in your work.

See also "Using a Computer to Write" (page 12).

WRITING PRACTICE 1 **Using a Computer for Drafting**

Now you need to practice your drafting skills.

Your assignment is this: *Spend ten minutes writing on the computer.* If possible, use the computer to complete a writing assignment for a class. If you do not have a course assignment you can complete using a computer, choose one of the following topics to write about.

- A nontraditional health treatment you've heard about
- A form of entertainment you think you'd enjoy but haven't tried
- Strategies for balancing work, school, and a personal life
- Reasons to take composition courses
- Reasons not to live with your parents after high school

After you finish writing, read what you've written to see whether your writing has any recognizable direction. Then, on a separate piece of paper, answer these questions.

- What ideas might turn into a workable thesis statement?
- What ideas could be used as support points?
- What areas, if any, do you have specific details for?
- What areas do you think you will need to research later?

WRITING PRACTICE 2 Writing an Essay

Now that you've read about and practiced the first two steps in the writing process, it's time to put them together. Throughout this chapter, you've read about different aspects of acupuncture.

Your assignment is this: *Write about a health remedy that you're familiar with.* The remedy you choose may be a well-known treatment from Western medicine, such as aspirin, or it may be a remedy specific to your culture.

Here are some questions to ask to help you get started.

- How does my family react when one of us is sick?
- Has this reaction changed over the years?
- What role, if any, do doctors play in my health?
- What role, if any, do other health practitioners—chiropractors, acupuncturists, and massage therapists, to name three—play in my health?

Follow these steps to write your essay.

1. Use at least two prewriting techniques to come up with ideas for your essay.
2. From your prewriting, do your best to craft a working thesis statement.

3. Use your notes from prewriting and your working thesis to write a rough draft of your essay. Don't worry about making your rough draft perfect; just do your best to write down your ideas.

When you're finished, your essay should include

■ A clear thesis statement
■ Support points that relate to the thesis statement
■ Specific details that give proof of your support points
■ Transitions that connect your support points and examples

Lab Activity 5

For additional practice with drafting, complete Lab Activity 5 in the lab manual packaged with your textbook. If you did not receive a lab manual, you can complete this activity online at **www.ablongman.com/long.** Click on **College Resources for Writers** and then click on **Activity 5.**

6   Revision: Making Changes

Though the Hawaiian Islands are familiar to most people as the fiftieth state, many other American islands, despite their national importance, remain less recognized to all but their local inhabitants. From Ellis Island in New York Harbor to Alcatraz Island in San Francisco Bay, these small pieces of land have played large roles in history.

Ellis Island

JOURNAL ENTRY Known as "The Golden Door," Ellis Island served both to admit and deny immigrants entrance into the United States. As more people leave their homes in hopes of a better life in the U.S., the topic of immigration becomes increasingly heated. What are your thoughts about immigration? Write a few sentences explaining your attitude toward immigration.

Think You're Done? Take Another Look

If you're like many people, you'd prefer writing to be more like a short-answer test: you respond with your first instincts, answer the questions, and you're done. However, good writing most often results from rewriting your essay until the finished product is polished. Once you've finished Step 2 of the writing process, drafting, you get many chances to improve what you've done in Step 3, revising.

Revising is the process of "re-seeing" or "re-looking-at" what you've already written. When you revise, you step back and try to look objectively at what you've written. The best revision is the result of many read-throughs on your part. Each time you read your essay, you focus on one of the first three of the four Cs—concise, credible, and clear writing—until each one is present. You will address the fourth C, correct writing, during the editing stage, explained in Chapter 7.

Step-by-Step Revision

Read your essay at least one time for each characteristic of good writing listed below. As you read your essay, concentrate only on one area at a time. Take breaks between readings to clear your mind and help you refocus your attention. *Hint:* After making changes by hand, you can insert the changes into your computer file. Save this second draft and print it out for further revising.

Making Sure Your Writing Is Concise

Check the length requirement for your assignment (if there is one) to make sure that you're not trying to do too much in your essay. Identify any support points that you think will need extra time and effort, and make sure that you have room to develop each point. If the topic is so broad that you can't cover it thoroughly, refer to your prewriting to determine what parts of the subject interest you the most. Then focus your essay accordingly. Very often, when you've made changes to your draft after the first reading, the new version of your essay will be *shorter* than your original. Don't be alarmed. The shorter length comes from eliminating unnecessary details and repetitive sections. When you read your draft to check that it's credible and clear, you may add new information.

For instance, Zach wrote the following essay. Then, he read through the draft to make sure his writing was concise. He crossed out every detail that did not support his topic sentence.

Three Types of Islands (First Draft)

Islands have played important roles in U.S. history in terms of immigration, correctional facilities, and pleasure.

Perhaps the two most important islands in the history of the United States are Ellis Island and Angel Island. ~~The names of these places don't say anything about the anxiety immigrants felt at first arriving there.~~ From 1892 to 1952, Ellis Island served as the Immigration Processing Station in New York Harbor. Angel Island also served as an immigration center, but it quickly became known for its harsh treatment of immigrants, particularly the Chinese. ~~I heard a rumor that Angel Island was going to be made into a theme park years ago, but it never happened.~~

Islands have also played important roles in U.S. history as places for correctional facilities (jails and prisons). Alcatraz and Rikers Island are sites of famous detention centers. Famous for its security, Alcatraz closed its doors in 1963 because it was too expensive to keep open. ~~I love that movie with Clint Eastwood, when he plays a brilliant inmate who actually makes it off of "the Rock."~~ Rikers Island currently serves as a sort of clearinghouse for people waiting to be freed, tried, or moved to a prison. ~~Until I started watching *Law and Order*, I never knew that Rikers Island was actually an island.~~

Islands such as Catalina on the West Coast and Nantucket on the East Coast offer people escapes from their lives elsewhere. ~~I wonder if Catalina salad dressing got its name from that island.~~ People do live on these islands year-round. These places are most famous for their vacation offerings.

The details that Zach crossed out do not help support the thesis statement, "Islands have played important roles in U.S. history in terms of immigration, prison, and pleasure." Thus, he deleted them.

Is Your Essay Concise?

Ask yourself the following questions to determine whether your essay is concise.
- Do I have a clear thesis statement?
- Does each paragraph directly support the thesis statement?
- Does *every single detail* support my thesis statement?
- Are there any points that do not support my thesis statement?
- Are there any details that are irrelevant to my thesis statement?

EXERCISE 1   REVISING TO MAKE AN ESSAY CONCISE

Read the following draft of an essay about historically significant American islands. Then, cross out any paragraphs or sentences that don't directly support the thesis statement. You may be tempted to make other changes in the essay—such as reorganizing or adding support—but *change the essay only to make each sentence support the thesis.*

Islands Significant in History (First Draft)

[1]If an island makes the news today, it's usually because it's been swamped or bombed or because some new great vacation places have been discovered. [2]While islands have long been strategic sites for military placement, however, they have also been historically interesting. [3]Of course, to me, "interesting" really means "fun," but I guess my future vacation islands can't be considered "historically" significant yet. [4]Three islands, or groups of islands—Roanoke Island, Fort Sumter, and the San Juan Islands—have played significant roles in American history.

[5]Roanoke Island, off the coast of what is now North Carolina (originally Virginia) is imporant. [6]In 1585, a group of Englishmen—following an 1584 expedition financed by Sir Walter Raleigh—landed and attempted to settle Roanoke Island. [7]Sir Walter Raleigh was known for his gentlemanly manners; he once laid his cloak over a mud puddle so that Queen Elizabeth wouldn't muddy her feet. [8]Called "the lost colony," Roanoke Island remains one of the great mysteries in American history.

[9]So many parts of history seem to be "lost." No one knows exactly went on; everything just depends on who wrote things down [10]For instance, I'm sure that we'd know a lot less about the California Gold Rush if someone hadn't actually sent a letter home talking about the discovery.

[11]The island site of Fort Sumter, located in the harbor of Charleston, South Carolina, is historically significant as the place where the first shots of the American Civil War were fired. [12]Inspiring Southerners to continue in their secession efforts, the Confederates' shots at Fort Sumter started the Civil War, making it symbolic of the South's cause. [13]The novel *Gone With the Wind* portrays Southerners as celebrating the South's efforts almost right up until Atlanta burned. [14]Their upbeat attitude didn't help them in their efforts.

[15]The San Juan Islands, located near what is now Washington state, are significant. [16]These islands were the site of the Pig War, also called the Pig Episode, because a pig was said to be the catalyst for the dispute as well as the only death. [17]Pigs can be really dangerous. [18]My great grandfather was attacked by a huge sow and

nearly died. [19]Both countries retain joint minimal military occupation of the island. [20]Though the "British Camp" sits technically on American soil, the Union Jack still flies over it, making it one of very few American sites that routinely flies another country's flag.

[21]The word *island* often brings to mind relaxing vacations on sandy beaches, or even the site of a drowning person's rescue. [22] Three island groups, however, mean much to Americans. [23]Roanoke Island, while its settlement wasn't permanent, gave the British an early toehold in the New World, and Fort Sumter showed the Union just how seriously the Confederacy took its plans to be its own country. [24]Finally, the San Juan Islands made clear how important clear boundaries are between even friendly countries. [25]Even the smallest parcels of land can have large impacts on history. [26]We may never visit any of these islands, but understanding their role in American history is important in understanding the attitudes and actions which helped form the United States.

The sentences that are off-topic are: _____, _____, _____,

_____,_____, _____, _____, _____, _____, and _____.

Making Sure Your Writing Is Credible

On your second pass through your essay, look for gaps in your support. Check your support points, and make sure that you have included specific details to illustrate your points. If necessary, look back at your prewriting exercises to find additional examples you can use.

Reading his first draft, Zach noticed that he needed specific details to illustrate his support points. The specific details that Zach added are in bold print. Note that Zach altered his introduction to lead more smoothly into his thesis statement. He also made other changes and added a conclusion to signal to his reader that he is completing his discussion.

Three Types of Islands (Draft 2)

Though reality TV and the 2004 Indonesian tsunami brought islands into millions of people's living rooms, many people still think of islands as vacation spots or sites of some disaster. In the United States, islands have played important roles in terms of immigration, correctional facilities, and pleasure.

Two islands in the history of the United States are Ellis Island and Angel Island, according to historychannel.com. From 1892 to 1952, Ellis Island served as the Immigration Processing Station in New York Harbor. **Known as the Golden Door, Ellis Island admit-**

ted more than a million immigrants in its peak year of 1907. In 1924, Congress began limiting the numbers of immigrants, so Ellis Island was used primarily used as a detention center for illegal immigrants or those facing deportation. Publicly billed as the Ellis Island of the West, the Angel Island Immigration Station served to admit immigrants. **Its real role was as Guardian of the Western Gate, and** it quickly became known for its harsh treatment of immigrants, particularly the Chinese. **After World War I, the Immigration Station was abandoned and fell into disrepair.**

Islands have played important roles in U.S. history as places for correctional facilities (jails and prisons). Alcatraz and Rikers Island are sites of famous detention centers. **The subject of many movies and books, Alcatraz Island served first as a military prison in the 1850s and later became a maximum-security prison. Famous for its "celebrity" inmates such as Al Capone,** Alcatraz closed its doors in 1963 because it was too expensive to keep open. Rikers Island currently serves as a sort of clearinghouse for people waiting to be freed, tried, or moved to a prison. **Though people refer to the Rikers Island Jail, there are actually ten jails housing approximately 15,000 inmates daily, according to "Beyond Manhattan" on the Columbia University Web site.**

Islands such as Catalina on the West Coast and Nantucket on the East Coast offer people escapes from their lives elsewhere. **Off the coast of southern California, Catalina Island offers visitors wonderful scuba diving opportunities. Catalina offers a botanical garden and an Art Deco Casino building for evening movie viewing. Once a booming whaling station, the island of Nantucket—off the coast of Massachusetts—now offers people beautiful beaches, lovely plant life, and challenging surfcasting (fishing) opportunities.** People do live on these islands year-round. These places are most famous for their vacation offerings.

The same qualities that make islands difficult to inhabit—distance from the mainland, difficulty obtaining supplies, isolation—make them perfect for several functions. In the course of U.S. history, islands have been used to facilitate immigration, contain people who broke or who have been accused of breaking the law, and provide relaxation for vacationers. Whether they are used for processing, prison, or paradise, American islands have played significant roles in history.

Now Zach's paragraph has plenty of examples, and they all support both his thesis statement and the topic sentences of their respective paragraphs. Don't worry if you don't think of all your examples right away. As you read through your draft, just keep thinking about the best way to explain your ideas to your reader. Then, add examples as they come to you.

Is Your Paragraph Credible?

Ask yourself the following questions to determine whether your essay is credible.

- Do I provide enough information so that my reader will believe me?
- Have I made sure my reader knows what I mean?
- Do I need to review my prewriting notes to find more support for my topic sentence?
- Do I need to add more examples or specific details?

EXERCISE 2 REVISING TO MAKE A PARAGRAPH CREDIBLE

Below is the corrected version of the essay you revised in Exercise 1. In this exercise, you need to add specific details to make the essay more credible. Read Specific Details A, B, and C following the essay. Decide in which paragraph they belong. Then write the number of the sentence that each specific detail should follow. You may want to make other changes in the essay, but don't. *Pay attention only to adding more information for support.*

Islands Significant in History (Draft 2)

[1]While islands have long been strategic sites for military placement, they have also been historically interesting. [2]Three islands, or groups of islands—Roanoke Island, Fort Sumter, and the San Juan Islands—have played significant roles in American history.

[3]Roanoke Island, off the coast of what is now North Carolina (originally Virginia) is important. [4]In 1585, a group of Englishmen—following an 1584 expedition financed by Sir Walter Raleigh—landed and attempted to settle Roanoke Island. [5]Called "the lost colony," Roanoke Island remains one of the great mysteries in American history.

[6]The island site of Fort Sumter, located in the harbor of Charleston, South Carolina, is historically significant as the place where the first shots of the American Civil War were fired. [7]Inspiring Southerners to continue in their secession efforts, the Confederates' shots at Fort Sumter started the Civil War, making it symbolic of the South's cause.

[8]The San Juan Islands, located near what is now Washington state, are significant. [9]These islands were the site of the Pig War, also called the Pig Episode, because a pig was said to be the catalyst for the dispute as well as the only death. [10]Both countries retain joint minimal military occupation of the island. [11]Though the "British

Camp" sits technically on American soil, the Union Jack still flies over it, making it one of very few American sites that routinely flies a nother country's flag.

[12]The word *island* often brings to mind relaxing vacations on sandy beaches, or even the site of a drowning person's rescue. [13]Three island groups mean much to Americans. [14]Roanoke Island, while its settlement wasn't permanent, gave the British an early toe-hold in the New World, and Fort Sumter showed the Union just how seriously the Confederacy took its plans to be its own country. [15]Finally, the San Juan Islands made clear how important clear boundaries are between even friendly countries. [16]We may never visit any of these islands, but understanding their role in American history is important in understanding the attitudes and actions which helped form the United States.

Specific Details

a. According to Deborah Franklin's article, "Boar War," the Oregon Treaty of June 15, 1846 unclearly determined the boundary between Canada and the United States. This "gray area" led to a problem when an American farmer shot and killed a pig—owned by a British company employee—in his garden. When British authorities threatened to arrest the farmer, Americans called in the military, which led to a standoff. Both sides were given orders to defend themselves but not to fire the first shot. Though British and American soliders jeered at each other, no one actually fired.

This information belongs after sentence _____.

b. According to Ellen Bailey's essay, "The Lost Colony of Roanoke," several factors led to the failure of the settlement effort. A lack of food and drought doomed this settlement attempt to fail, and so did a bad relationship with the natives. Aid eventually arrived from England; the initial settlers had already returned to England. Fifteen men from the aid ship stayed behind to continue English occupation, but the fate of those fifteen is unknown, and a subsequent effort to settle Roanoke Island was unsuccessful.

This information belongs after sentence _____.

c. South Carolina's secession came in December 1860; Confederate forces fired on the Union-held fort on April 12, 1861, according to "Sieges of Charleston," on Encarta.com. Accounts of the attack tell of Charleston residents sitting on balconies, watching the battle enthusiastically before the fort surrendered on April 13. Union forces tried to reclaim Fort Sumter as it represented a hole in the Federal naval defense. Only when General Sherman's army advanced northward out of Savannah, Georgia, on February 17, 1865, did Confederate forces evacuate the fort.

This information belongs after sentence _____.

Making Sure Your Writing Is Clear

On your third pass through your essay, check that your support points are arranged in a logical, effective order. Decide where your support points should go, and then move them around, if necessary, to create a sense of progress and balance for your reader. Make sure, too, that you signal the order of your points by using transition words like *first, second,* and *finally* in each paragraph of your essay.

During his third pass through his essay about islands, Zach added transitions, words that communicate the writer's direction to the reader. The transitions that Zach added are in bold print. He made other changes as well.

Three Types of Islands (Draft 3)

Though reality TV and the 2004 Indonesian tsunami brought islands into millions of people's living rooms, many people still think of islands as vacation spots or sites of some disaster. In the United States, **however,** islands have played important roles in terms of immigration, correctional facilities, and pleasure.

Perhaps the **two most important** islands in the history of the United States are Ellis Island and Angel Island, according to historychannel.com. From 1892 to 1952, Ellis Island served as the Immigration Processing Station in New York Harbor. Known as the Golden Door, Ellis Island admitted more than a million immigrants in its peak year of 1907. In 1924, **however,** Congress began limiting the numbers of immigrants, so Ellis Island was primarily used as a detention center for illegal immigrants or those facing deportation. Publicly billed as the Ellis Island of the West, the Angel Island Immigration Station **also** served to admit immigrants. **However,** its real role was as Guardian of the Western Gate, and it quickly became known for its harsh treatment of immigrants, particularly the Chinese. After World War I, the Immigration Station was abandoned and fell into disrepair.

Another way in which islands have played important roles in U.S. history is as places for correctional facilities (jails and prisons). **Two islands in particular,** Alcatraz and Rikers Island, are sites of famous detention centers. The subject of many movies and books, Alcatraz Island served first as a military prison in the 1850s and later became a maximum-security prison. Famous for its "celebrity" inmates such as Al Capone, Alcatraz closed its doors in 1963 because it was too expensive to keep open. **On the other side of the continent,** Rikers Island currently serves as a sort of clearinghouse for people waiting to be freed, tried, or moved to a prison. Though people refer to the Rikers Island Jail, there are actually ten jails housing approximately 15,000 inmates daily.

Finally, islands such as Catalina on the West Coast and Nantucket on the East Coast offer people escapes from their lives elsewhere. Off the coast of southern California, Catalina Island offers visitors wonderful scuba diving opportunities, **as well as** a botanical garden and an Art Deco Casino building for evening movie viewing. Once a booming whaling station, the island of Nantucket—off the coast of Massachusetts—now offers people beautiful beaches, lovely plant life, and challenging surfcasting (fishing) opportunities. **Although** people live on these islands year-round, these places are most famous for their vacation offerings.

The same qualities that make islands difficult to inhabit—distance from the mainland, difficulty obtaining supplies, isolation—make them perfect for several functions. In the course of history, islands have been used to facilitate immigration, contain people who broke or who have been accused of breaking the law, and provide relaxation for vacationers. Whether they are used for processing, prison, or paradise, American islands have played significant roles in history.

Although a reader may have been able to figure out which details illustrated certain support points, the transitions that Zach added make the connections extremely clear. Now there is no doubt as to what his support points are, what order they take, or how they relate to each other.

As a result of his three passes, Zach's essay has become concise, credible, and clear.

Is Your Paragraph Clear?

Ask yourself the following questions to determine whether your essay is clear.

- Do I have a logical organizational format that my reader can easily follow? What is it?
- Do I use transitional expressions to communicate what my points are, and which ones are most important?
- Do I need to explain any points more fully?
- Do I need to move or rearrange sentences to make my writing clearer?

EXERCISE 3 REVISING TO MAKE AN ESSAY CLEAR

Below is the corrected version of the essay you revised in Exercise 2. You need to make sure the essay is clear. Answer the questions about clear writing that follow the essay.

Islands Significant in History (Draft 3)

[1] If an island makes the news today, it's usually because it's been swamped or bombed or because some new great vacation place has been discovered. [2] While islands have long been strategic sites for military placement, they have also been historically interesting. [3] Three groups of islands—Roanoke Island, Fort Sumter, and the San Juan Islands—have played significant roles in American history.

[4] Roanoke Island, off the coast of what is now North Carolina (originally Virginia), is important. [5] In 1585, a group of Englishmen—following an 1584 expedition financed by Sir Walter Raleigh—landed and attempted to settle Roanoke Island. [6] According to Ellen Bailey's essay, "The Lost Colony of Roanoke," factors led to the failure of the settlement effort. [7] a to lack of food and drought, a bad relationship with the natives doomed this settlement attempt to fail. [8] Aid eventually arrived from England, the initial settlers had already returned to England. [9] Fifteen men from the aid ship stayed behind to continue English occupation, but the fate of those fifteen is unknown, and a subsequent effort to settle Roanoke Island was unsuccessful. [10] Called "the lost colony," Roanoke Island remains one of the great mysteries in American history.

[11]The island site of Fort Sumter, located in the harbor of Charleston, South Carolina, is historically significant as the place where the first shots of the American civil war were fired. [12]South Carolina's secession in December 1860, Confederate forces fired on the Union-held fort on April 12, 1861, according to "Sieges of Charleston" on Encarta.com. [13]Accounts of the attack tell of Charleston residents sitting on balconies, watching the battle enthusiastically before the fort surrendered on April 13. [14] The Civil War, Union forces tried to reclaim Fort Sumter as it represented a hole in the Federal naval defense. [15] Only when General Sherman's army advance northward out of Savannah, Georgia, on February 17, 1865, did Confederate forces evacuate the fort. [16] Inspiring Southerners to continue in their secession efforts, the Confederates' shots at Fort Sumter started the Civil War, making it symbolic of the South's cause.

[17] A group of islands significant in American history is the San Juan islands, located near what is now Washington state. [18]These islands were the site of the Pig War, also called the Pig Episode, because a pig was said to be the catalyst for the dispute as well as the only death. [19]According to "Boar War" by Deborah Franklin, the Oregon Treaty of June 15, 1846 unclearly determined the boundary between Canada and the United States. [20]This "gray area" led to a problem when an American farmer shot and killed a pig—owned by

a British company employee—in his garden. [21]When British authorities threatened to arrest the farmer, Americans called in the military, which led to a standoff. [22]Both sides were given orders to defend themselves but not to fire the first shot. [23] Though British and American soldiers jeered at each other, no one actually fired. [24] Both countries retain joint minimal military occupation of the island. [25]Though the "British Camp" sits technically on American soil, the Union Jack still flies over it, making it one of very few American sites that routinely flies another country's flag.

[26]The word *island* often brings to mind relaxing vacations on sandy beaches, or even the site of a drowning person's rescue. [27]Three islands groups, however, mean much to Americans. [28]Roanoke Island, while its settlement wasn't permanent, gave the British an early toehold in the New World, and Fort Sumter showed the Union just how seriously the Confederacy took its plans to be its own country. [29]Finally, the San Juan Islands made clear how important clear boundaries are between even friendly countries. [30]We may never visit any of these islands, but understanding their role in American history is important in understanding the attitudes and actions which helped form the United States.

1. How is the essay organized overall? _____
2. How are the support paragraphs organized? _____
3. Which support point would most likely include the words "possibly the most comical of island-related incidents"? _____

4. Which words show cause-and-effect reasoning in paragraph 4?

_____

5. How many times does some form of the word *island* appear?_____

6. Which words show contrast, or a change of direction, in paragraph 8? _____

7. List two words or terms that indicate chronological order in paragragh 3. _____

The Difference Between Revising and Editing

The terms of revision and editing are often used—incorrectly—interchangeably. While this confusion may not seem overly important, it can lead to unnecessary time, effort, and frustration if not caught early.

Essentially, revision comes when you read your essay critically and realize it doesn't meet the Four Cs. Revision encompasses changes that affect an essay's focus, content, and organization—or the first three of the Four Cs (concise, credible, and clear writing)—to make your development of your thesis statement clearer. Cutting, adding, and moving paragraphs, for instance, are all fairly major undertakings. These "big" jobs come during revision, the most important step in the writing process.

Editing, on the other hand, comes when you feel that you've effectively made your case and you're just checking to be sure nothing interferes with that message. At this stage, choosing the best possible words and expressions as well as correcting sentence-level errors is important.

It would be possible to edit before you revise, but it would be a waste of effort. Think of revision as the process of building a house and editing as the process of painting it. Just as you wouldn't paint every board and nail before assembling them, you don't want to polish something that might not end up in your final draft.

Using a Computer to Revise Your Draft

Revision is the part of the writing process where computers really help you.

- Computers are wonderful for deleting information that doesn't help you develop your topic sentence. Since your draft on the computer looks more finished than a handwritten one, you can more easily tell what information is off-topic or unnecessary.

- You can use the cut and paste functions to move examples—or even whole paragraphs—from one part of your draft to another without having to retype your whole draft.

- Word processing programs let you easily insert transitional words and phrases, so your draft becomes much more finished without a lot of effort.

- Computers give you an early sense of how your finished product will look. Instead of messy papers with scribbled-out passages and lines with arrows pointing every which way, your writing will automatically be lined up at the margin, equally spaced, and evenly printed.

The following paragraphs have gone through all the necessary revisions and are now ready to be edited and handed in. For information on editing, see Chapter 7.

All through the writing process, Zach used the working title "Three Types of Islands." For the final draft of his essay, Zach decided on the title "American Islands," which gives the reader a good idea of what to expect.

American Islands (Final Draft)

Though reality TV and the 2004 Indonesian tsunami brought islands into millions of people's living rooms, many people still think of islands only as vacation spots or sites of some disaster. In the United States, however, islands have played important roles in terms of immigration, correctional facilities, and pleasure.

Perhaps the two most important islands in the history of the United States are Ellis Island and Angel Island, according to historychannel.com. From 1892 to 1952, Ellis Island served as the Immigration Processing Station in New York Harbor. Known as the Golden Door, Ellis Island admitted more than one million immigrants in its peak year of 1907. In 1924, however, Congress began limiting the numbers of immigrants, so Ellis Island was primarily used as a detention center for illegal immigrants or those facing deportation. Publicly billed as the Ellis Island of the West, the Angel Island Immigration Station also served to admit immigrants. However, its real role was as Guardian of the Western Gate, and it quickly became known for its harsh treatment of immigrants, particularly the Chinese, according to "Immigration Station" by the Angel Island Association. After World War I, the Immigration Station was abandoned and fell into disrepair.

Another way in which islands have played important roles in U.S. history is as places for correctional facilities (jails and prisons). Two islands in particular, Alcatraz and Rikers Island, are sites of famous detention centers. The subject of many movies and books, Alcatraz Island served first as a military prison in the 1850s and later became a maximum-security prison. Famous for its celebrity inmates, such as Al Capone, Alcatraz closed its doors in 1963 because it was too expensive to keep open, according to Britannica Online. On the other side of the continent, Rikers Island currently serves as a sort of clearinghouse for people waiting to be freed, tried, or moved to a prison. Though people refer to the Rikers Island Jail, there are actually ten jails housing approximately 15,000 inmates daily, according to "A City of Jails" by Kodi Barth.

Finally, islands such as Catalina on the West Coast and Nantucket on the East Coast offer people escapes from their lives elsewhere. Off the coast of southern California, Catalina Island offers visitors wonderful scuba diving opportunities, as well as a botanical garden and an Art Deco Casino building for evening movie viewing. Once a booming whaling station, the island of Nantucket—off the coast of Massachusetts—now offers people beautiful beaches, lovely plant life, and challenging surfcasting (fishing) opportunities. Although people live on these islands year-round, these places are most famous for their vacation offerings.

The same qualities that make islands difficult to inhabit—distance from the mainland, difficulty obtaining supplies, isolation—make them perfect for several functions. In the course of history, islands have been used to facilitate immigration, contain people who broke or who have been accused of breaking the law, and provide relaxation for vacationers. Whether they are used for processing, prison, or paradise, American islands have played significant roles in history.

Following the Four Cs Through Revision

The more you write, the more important revision becomes. For now, follow the four Cs through revision in the order they are introduced in the text—revise for concise writing, credible writing, clear writing, and correct writing. However, depending on your subject and style, you may choose to revise your draft in a completely different order from the one presented. Whatever pattern you choose to follow in terms of revision, be sure to read your drafts with an eye for concise, credible, clear, and correct writing.

EXERCISE 4 REVISING FOR THE FOUR CS

The essay on the following page requires revision in terms of one or more of the first three—concise, credible, and clear writing—of the Four Cs. Read each paragraph, identify the area or areas in which it needs revision, and revise accordingly. You may need to consult another source to add relevant details.

Hawaiian Rainbow of Purposes

The fiftieth state added to the United States of America, Hawaii was once just an exotic destination made famous by explorers. Now, however, Hawaii has come into its own. Known for its vacation get-aways, its native products, and its role in history, tiny Hawaii is a multifaceted state.

One famous aspect of Hawaii is that of vacation paradise. The islands of Maui and Oahu offer many activities to cater to any traveler's whim. Additionally, other activities give people on the go many options. Anyone interested in sports also has choices. Whatever your vacation pleasure, Hawaii probably has it.

Another aspect of Hawaii is its exports. When many people think of products from Hawaii, they think of pinapple, sugar, and coffee. However, according to enterprisehonolulu.com, transportation equipment accounted for 25%, or $93 million of Hawaii's total merchandise exports. Transportation equipment seems a logical way for Hawaii to make a profit since getting to Hawaii requires such equipment. Other top exports were petroleum and coal products (2003 exports of $75 million) computers and electronic products ($29 million) processed foods ($24 million) and machinery manufactures ($22 million). I've heard from friends who have been to Hawaii that everything is incredibly expensive there, so I'm not sure why exporting goods is even necessary. Though Hawaii is a small state in terms of square mileage, it has big earning potential.

Finally, Hawaii's educational aspect may be its most significant. The state was the site of the critical incident that propelled the United States unwillingly into World War II. Early on the morning of December 7, 1941, Japanese planes attacked the United States Navy base in Pearl Harbor, Oahu. After Pearl Harbor was devastated by the attacks, the United States declared war on Japan and was soon fully involved in the second World War. The state was a home for explorer James Cook, whose travels helped map the world. The state's famous volcanoes have provided valuable information in the area of geology. The tiny state has huge historical significance.

Although Hawaii may be best known for its luaus and surfers, its offerings go far beyond vacation pleasures. In addition to its resorts, Hawaii provides the world with important goods. Most importantly, Hawaii's place in American—indeed, in world—history make it a significant state.

Exchanging Help with Your Peers

Working with classmates, or **peer editing,** is one of the best ways to improve your writing. Working with classmates allows you to

- Receive feedback without receiving a grade.
- Receive feedback from someone who shares your experiences, at least in the classroom.
- Gain ideas for your own writing by seeing how your classmates have illustrated or organized their ideas in their writing.
- Ask questions about your writing in front of a few people, not the teacher or your whole class.
- Talk about strategies that can help you improve your writing before you try them out in your paper.

Remembering the Writer's Feelings

Working with classmates lets you give your paper a test run before your instructor sees it. Consider the following questions before beginning your peer editing workshop.

- How do you feel when someone is reading something you've written?
- How much do you value another student's opinion about your writing? Would you rather just have the instructor's comments? Explain.
- If a friend asks you to read something he or she has written, what kind of feedback do you supply? Does your feedback change if the friend is a co-worker or classmate? Explain.

These questions should help you remember that writing is a form of personal expression. When you comment on other people's writing, you need to be polite and careful about their feelings.

Writing as a Response

Writing is such a personal experience that sometimes it's hard to open up and let other people read what you've written. However, allowing your classmates to help you—learning about gaps in support, weak connections, and overall strengths—will ultimately make your writing more effective.

Guidelines for Peer Editing

The following guidelines can help you give constructive feedback to your classmates. Ideally, you will work in pairs or in small groups of three or four students. Each member of your group should have a copy of every group member's draft as well as a Peer Editing Worksheet for each paper. *Note:* Since some classes last longer than others, focus only on the guidelines you have time to cover. Your instructor may tell you which ones to include or ignore for a particular assignment. Additionally, the Peer Editing Worksheet includes space for comments on topic sentence, support points, and details. Other comments should be written in the last section of the worksheet.

Follow these guidelines in evaluating your classmates' writing.

1. **Be kind.** Keep in mind that your classmates may feel nervous about letting you read their work, let alone comment on it. Therefore, do your best to be direct but polite in the comments you make to your peers. Criticism delivered with courtesy is much more likely to be implemented.

2. **Read the draft aloud.** Someone besides the writer should read the draft aloud to force everyone to slow down and focus on every word. That way, people will not be confused because they skipped a word or line by trying to read too quickly. Since the writers know what they mean to say, they might add words or emphasis that they think *should* be there even if these elements are not clear from the writing. To best understand where the writer needs help, someone *not* familiar with the text should do the reading aloud.

3. **Tell the writer what you think the biggest strength of the draft is.** *Every* piece of writing has something positive about it, so work hard to find something nice to say to the writer, even if it's only a compliment on the topic. If you think the writer has some good examples or a solid title, mention that. You may think that the essay is well organized, or even that it has the potential to be well organized.

4. **Write down the thesis statement on the peer review worksheet.** If you copy the sentence that the writer says is the thesis statement, then the writer is on the right track. If you copy another sentence, or if you're not sure which sentence is the thesis statement, talk to the writer about what his or her main idea is.

5. **If the writing lacks a clear thesis statement, help the writer to revise or write one.** (If the writing does have a clear thesis statement, move on to the next guideline.) Discuss what the writer wants to say, and find the best way to say it. Talk about the best way to incorporate the support points and examples the writer has already written.

6. **Write down the support points for the thesis statement.** If the support points you chose are the same as what the writer thinks they are, then the writer is probably on the right track. If you're not sure what the support points are, or if your idea of what the support points are differs from the writer's, talk about what the writer wants to communicate and how certain points will best help support the topic sentence.

7. **Make sure that the writer has included specific details that illustrate every support point.** If the writer needs to offer proof for the support points, tell him or her to do so. You may offer suggestions as to what kinds of examples might work, but the writer should come up with the specific details so that they support the thesis statement and support points.

8. **Make sure the writer uses a strategy (such as chronological or emphatic order) to organize the ideas in the essay.** The essay may already be organized, or partially organized, according to one of the organizational strategies. In this case, help the writer put the support points into a logical order, discussing which points should go first or last and why.

9. **Make sure the writer uses transitions to signal the order of the support points and their level of importance.** Refer to the list of transitions in Chapter 10 for words that help make the connections between ideas clear.

10. **Offer any comments not covered by the earlier guidelines.** These comments may include discussion of details that seem off-topic, places where the writer needs more detail, or places where sentence-level errors make understanding the essay difficult.

Use the worksheet on the following page to help you in peer editing. An example of a partially filled in worksheet appears on page 97.

Peer Editing Worksheet

Reviewer's name: _____ **Date:** _____

Writer's name: _____

1. One strength of this essay is _____

_____

_____

2. The thesis statement for this essay is _____

_____

_____

3. The support points for this essay are _____

_____

_____

_____

4. Write down the specific details the writer uses to illustrate each support point:

Details for support point 1: _____

_____

_____

Details for support point 2: _____

_____

_____

Details for support point 3: _____

_____

_____

5. Overall comments on this essay: _____

_____

_____

Using Feedback

Once we get someone's opinion of our writing, the trick becomes making good use of that opinion. The following is a list of guidelines designed to help you make the most of other people's feedback.

- **Don't expect other people to fix everything.** No one knows everything, and even if you get very good feedback on your writing, that still doesn't guarantee that you will improve your writing enough, say, to raise your grade from a C to an A. The most you can expect from other people is their honest response. Then it's your job to revise your writing accordingly.

- **Don't feel as though you have to take everyone's advice.** Even though almost everyone has room for improvement in writing, don't make changes just because someone says you should. If the suggestions make sense to you—or if *everyone* in your group says the same thing— then you should probably consider revising your draft.

- **Ask your readers to be specific.** If you're not sure what people mean, ask them to explain further. The worst thing you can do in a peer editing situation is try to revise your draft when you're not sure how to go about it. If your group doesn't make its ideas clear, ask your instructor for further clarification.

- **Remember: Your peer editors are trying to help.** Even if you're disappointed that your classmates don't find your ideas as clear as you'd hoped, don't get mad. Accepting criticism from people is often difficult, so do your best to listen and learn from your peers.

Setting Your Goals as a Writer

As you begin writing more frequently and through different assignments, you will discover your strengths as a writer. You may learn that you have wonderful description skills, sharp comparison and contrast skills, or powerful argument skills. You will also learn what areas of your writing you need to focus your attention on.

One tool that can help you improve your writing one step at a time is a goal sheet (see page 99). A goal sheet allows you to keep your topic sentence in mind at all times, emphasize what you're already doing well in

Peer Editing Worksheet

Reviewer's name: Mai   **Date:** 10/6/06

Writer's name: Zach

1. **One strength of this essay is** The topic choice (American islands) is creative and original; I would never have thought of it.

2. **The thesis statement for this essay is** American islands have played important roles in terms of immigration, correctional facilities, and pleasure.

3. **The support points for this essay are** American islands have been used as immigration centers.
American islands have been used as correctional facilities.
American islands have been used for pleasure.

4. **Write down the specific details the writer uses to illustrate each support point:**

   Details for support point 1: Ellis Island and Angel Island; brief histories and functions

   Details for support point 2:

   Details for support point 3:

5. **Overall comments on this essay:** I thought Zach did a good job finding information on his topic.

your writing, and set specific goals for improvement. The goal sheet also allows you to tell your instructor and classmates—or peer editors—what you need from them.

The goal sheet works best if you use it right before you hand in your paper—when your ideas are fresh in your mind—and then review it when you begin another assignment. You may even want to attach it to your final draft so that your instructor can see what your goals for improvement are. Do your best to write well on your goal sheet, but don't worry if you have mistakes.

On page 100 is a sample of a completed goal sheet. The student, Cecilia Chavez, has written an essay on her experience as the daughter of immigrant parents.

Notice that Cecilia isn't always looking for hard-and-fast answers in her goal sheet. Sometimes she simply wants suggestions. Also, she isn't afraid to ask her instructor to look at something she feels good about, in this case, her ability to stay on track in her essay.

WRITING PRACTICE **Write and Revise Your Own Essay**

In this chapter you learned something about different places that had something in common: they were all American islands.

Your assignment is this: *Write an essay about a place you are familiar with or would like to be familiar with.* You may use an island named in this chapter or one related to the theme of American islands, or you may choose a completely different place. Just find some place that interests you in some way. If you choose a place that is less familiar to you, you may want to do some reading or surf the Internet to learn more about your topic before writing about it.

Follow these steps to write your essay.

1. Use at least two prewriting techniques to come up with ideas for your essay.

2. Use your notes from prewriting to write a rough draft of your essay.

3. Revise your essay, reading through it to check for the first three of the four Cs: concise, credible, and clear writing.

Goal Sheet

Name: _____

Class: _____

1. My thesis statement for this assignment is _____

_____

_____

2. The skill I think I've improved in this assignment is _____

_____

_____

   The way I improved this skill is_____

_____

_____

3. The skill I think I still need to work on is _____

_____

_____

   I plan to improve this skill by_____

_____

_____

4. The aspect of my writing that I want my classmates to pay attention to is _____

_____

_____

5. What I really want my instructor to notice or comment on in my writing is _____

_____

_____

_____

Goal Sheet

Name: _Cecilia Chavez_

Class: _English 102, Section C_

1. **My thesis statement for this assignment is** _Although being the daughter of immigrants can be difficult, it has many benefits._

2. **The skill I think I've improved in this assignment is** _the first C, concise writing. I think I've stayed on track better in this essay than in earlier ones._

   The way I improved this skill is _I tried three things. First, I read my instructor's comments and made sure I understood what she meant when she said I was off-topic. Then, I wrote my thesis statement on a 3 by 5 card and held it next to each essay paragraph to make sure the paragraph connected to the thesis. If it didn't, I cut or revised it. Third, I asked my peer editing group to help me find places where I was off-topic. They only found two, so I'm getting better!_

3. **The skill I think I still need to work on is** _the second C, credible writing. Even when I think I have lots of specific details to support my thesis, my instructor still writes "Show me" all over my essay._

   I plan to improve this skill by _I'm going to try to learn more about my topics—by reading, talking to people, and even watching relevant television programs—while I'm writing my drafts. Hopefully I'll get better ideas about what kinds of details to include and how many details I need._

4. **The aspect of my writing that I want my classmates to pay attention to is** _my specific details. Maybe they can tell me if I'm supporting my thesis or if I need additional examples._

5. **What I really want my instructor to notice or comment on in my writing is** _I want my instructor to notice two things. First, I want her to tell me if I'm on track better, and I want her to help me recognize where I need more details._

When you're finished, your essay should include

- A clear thesis statement
- Support points that relate to the thesis statement
- Specific details that give proof for your support points
- Transitions that connect your support points and examples

Lab Activity 6

For additional practice with revision, complete Lab Activity 6 in the lab manual packaged with your textbook. If you did not receive a lab manual, you can complete this activity online at **www.ablongman.com/long.** Click on **College Resources for Writers** and then click on **Activity 6.**

7 Editing: Checking for Correctness

 CULTURE NOTE *Boxing*

Originating when someone raised fists to strike someone else, boxing has had a rich and controversial history. First recognized with bare-knuckle bouts by the ancient Greeks, boxing has become a celebrated but still largely unregulated sport worldwide.

The Greatest

SURF THE NET Known not only for his excellence in boxing, Muhammad Ali became famous for his good looks, charisma, and political activism. Surf the Internet to learn about Ali—born Cassius Clay—and write a few sentences summarizing your findings.

The Importance of Editing

You've moved around, filled in, and shored up different patches of your essay in Step 3 of the writing process, revising. Now you're ready to polish your work. Editing your writing is a painstaking, but very important, part of the writing process. So don't rush! It is during this stage of the writing process that you address the fourth C, correct writing, and make your writing error-free.

Think of editing as the last mirror-check before going to an important job interview. You wouldn't show up to the interview—after carefully preparing and dressing for success—with a piece of spinach between your teeth. Similarly, you shouldn't forget to edit your work after you've spent much time and effort writing and revising it. Well-edited, error-free writing shows your reader you care about your work. It makes you look smart, professional, and prepared.

Editing is changing your writing to make it more effective and to correct errors. There are two parts to editing.

1. Careful examination of your writing to see if you can make it smoother, more interesting, and more effective
2. Careful proofreading to catch and correct errors in grammar, punctuation, and spelling

Notice that both steps begin with the word *careful*. Taking care at this stage—to catch, delete, and correct errors—will go a long way toward making a good impression on your reader.

Editing for Smooth, Effective Writing

Once your essay is concise, credible, and clear, you need to make sure that your reader will enjoy your writing. You want your audience to read all the way to the end of the essay. That won't happen unless your writing is interesting and progresses smoothly. As you read your essay, answer the following questions.

- **Pronoun and verb agreement and consistency.** Do I use the same pronoun throughout? If I start with *you,* for example, do I unexpectedly switch to *we?* Do I use correct verb tenses throughout? (For more on using consistent pronouns and verbs, see Chapters 40–43.)
- **Appropriate language.** Do I use language that is appropriate for an academic assignment? Is my language too casual or too formal? Do I use unbiased, respectful language? (For more on sensitive language and word choice, see Chapters 11 and 13.)

- **Word use.** Have I chosen the best words I can? Are the words colorful, precise, and interesting—or bland, vague, and boring? Is the writing too wordy? Are certain words repeated too often? (For more on using vivid examples and language, see Chapter 9.)

- **Sentence variety.** Have I used different kinds of sentences to keep my writing interesting? Have I made sure that each sentence flows logically and smoothly into the next? (For more on sentence variety and connecting sentences, see Chapter 15.)

- **Punctuation and mechanics.** Do I follow the rules of grammar? Are my sentences punctuated correctly? Is my essay formatted properly? (For more on punctuation and mechanics, study the chapters in Part 7 of this book.)

You address these concerns first during the drafting and revising process. When you reach the editing stage of the writing process, you check to make sure your sentences make sense all by themselves and that they logically connect with each other.

Proofreading for Sentence-Level Errors

You have changed your essay to make it smoother, more interesting, and more effective. Now it's time for **proofreading**—checking your writing for errors in grammar, punctuation, and spelling. Proofreader's marks, shown on the following page, are a standard set of symbols used by instructors, editors, and printers to show changes in written work. Become familiar with these symbols, and use them as you proofread.

By now, you are so familiar with your essay that you probably skip right over any errors without noticing them. That's not surprising. When you use the following three proofreading techniques, you force yourself to read slowly. That way, you have a better chance of spotting mistakes.

Proofreading Sentence by Sentence   Reading your essay one sentence at a time allows you to check for grammar errors such as run-on sentences, sentence fragments, and mistakes in subject-verb agreement and pronoun agreement. It also helps you identify awkward sentences or word choices and other grammar errors. Use a piece of paper to cover up all but one sentence so that you can focus on that sentence alone.

The first pass can be difficult because many errors, not just the ones you're trying to correct at that point, are present. Nevertheless, concentrate on finding the errors at the sentence level. Since you might be changing

Mark	Meaning	Example
∧	Insert	hve
ℓ	Delete	some some cultural
◡	Close up space	t he
⊓	Transpose	some of sort
#	Insert space	inthe
/ℓc	Make lowercase	Origins
≡ Cap	Capitalize	New year's Day
___	Underline (or put in italics)	all
¶	Indent paragraph beginning	¶ Though

Example

¶ Though pretty much everyone in the United States are aware of
Christmas and New year's Day, many other holidays occur during
t he winter months. Other holidays hve many different Origins—
some some cultural, some religious, some societal—but they all
include some of sort celebration) two of these festivals are
Boxing Day and Kwanzaa.

words during this step, you don't want to bother correcting things before
you're sure that you'll keep them.

Proofreading Word by Word   Slowing down and reading your essay
word by word will allow you to find other errors—such as apostrophe or
capitalization errors—that you didn't change when reading each sentence
separately. Further, reading your paper aloud can help you listen to the
voice of your writing and determine whether you've repeated a word too
often or have used too many long words when you could do with shorter
ones. Use a pencil or your finger to point out each word as you read it.

Reading Your Work Backwards   Reading your essay backwards
helps you find spelling errors. Because your essay won't make sense that

way, you won't be able to anticipate—and thus skip—the upcoming words in a sentence. Because you must read every single word closely, this step is very effective.

Using a Computer for Editing

Computers offer you many tools that can help you edit your work. These tools can give you a false sense of security, though, so use them with caution.

- The spelling checker will help you find spelling errors. It will not help you find mistakes in word choice, however. For instance, the following sentence makes no sense: "Were Shirley going to bee insight when the mosque eaters or out." The computer won't catch any of the word choice errors because all the words are spelled correctly. The correct sentence should be "We're surely going to be inside when the mosquitoes are out."

- Grammar checkers, too, can be helpful. However, they should be used carefully as well. Sometimes a computer will point out an error but not explain it. Other times the computer will be wrong. For instance, the following sentence is correct: "If you keep writing in it, it may change into something you like better." However, the sentence originally ran onto a second line. The grammar check marked the sentence wrong, saying that the first word on the second line—in this case *into*—should be capitalized. To be safe, do your own proofreading when you've printed out your final draft.

Follow these guidelines to make the best use of your spelling and grammar checkers.

1. Set the font on your computer to 12 point, which is large enough to make finding errors easier.
2. Set the margins to at least one inch. (Check to see what your instructor recommends.) Leaving yourself room to add questions or comments will come in handy when you're proofreading your draft.
3. Double-space your draft. Setting up your computer so that it automatically double-spaces the lines makes finding errors easier both on the computer screen and on the paper when you print your draft out. Additionally, double spacing leaves you room to write comments on the printed draft.

4. Before you print out your draft, place the computer cursor (the blinking line that appears on the screen) at the very start of your document. Read the line that the cursor is marking. Then, move the cursor down a line using the arrow keys. Continue to use the cursor to focus your attention on one line at a time, and make changes as you go rather than changing everything at once.

EXERCISE 1 READING EACH SENTENCE SEPARATELY

The following paragraph contains many sentence-level errors. Read the paragraph and focus on finding errors in sentence structure and punctuation. In the blanks at the end of the paragraph, write the numbers of the sentences that contain errors. Then, make corrections in the paragraph. There are five errors in all.

A Sport with Some Punch

[1]Although boxing seems to be a sport executed by punching someone. [2]Several different types of punches give the sport its skill and strategy. [3]The most important punch being the jab. [4]The jab is delivered with the hand of the foot which is forward. [5]A right-handed fighter must throw the left hand toward the target in a straight line from the chin. [6]The second and most powerful punch is the straight right (or left). The straight punch, also called a "cross," involves the hand going out in a straight line. [7]However, the straight punch requires weight transfer, which allows a more powerful hit and, unfortunately, a split-second of being off-balance after the punch. [8]Uppercuts are the third type of punch; they are used for fighting very close to an opponent (inside fighting) to deliver a left uppercut, the elbow dips towards the hips, bringing the head somewhat forward and down before the fist lands in the sternum (center of the chest). [9]A last important punch in boxing is the hook. [10]The tricky hook is an inside power punch. [11]Which is initiated and delivered by an entire side of the body, causing the powerful but dangerous weight transfer. [12]While many boxers have a specialty punch, the best fighters excel at all four types.

The sentences containing errors are _____, _____, _____, _____ and _____.

EXERCISE 2 **READ EACH WORD SEPARATELY**

In the following paragraph, look for errors in capitalization, apostrophes, and redundancy. Then, correct the errors you find, and answer the questions at the end of the paragraph. Errors appear in five sentences.

The Greatest

[1]Many people strive to be successful in their given areas, but very few succeed to the level where they can be considered "the greatest." [2]Self-titled "the greatest," heavyweight boxer Muhammed Ali (born Cassius Clay) showed his greatness through his charisma, religious faith, and boxing prowess. [3]Breaking the boxers stereotype as thugs or tough guys, Muhammed Ali was great as an intelligent, articulate representative of his sport. [4]With Alis good looks, impenetrable confidence, and glib lines (such as "I float like a butterfly, sting like a bee"), Ali quickly became known for his "greatness" in public speaking. [5]A second way Ali showed his greatness was through his religion. [6]Joining the Black Muslims, Ali refused to be drafted on religious grounds, and he was stripped of his title and prohibited from Boxing. [7]Though he angered many of his fans, he showed his greatness by never backing down. [8]Finally, Muhammed Ali demonstrated his greatness as one of the best boxers' of all time. [9]With his quick jab and footwork, Ali was the only man to win the world heavyweight title three times. [10] his professional career record was 56 wins, five losses, and 31 knockouts. [11]In many ways, Muhammed Ali was, as he claimed, the greatest.

The sentences containing errors are _____, _____, _____, _____ and _____.

How many times is some form of the word *great* used? _____

What are some words or expressions the writer could use in place of

greatest? _____

EXERCISE 3 **READ THE PARAGRAPH BACKWARDS**

Read the following paragraph backwards, focusing on looking for spelling errors. In the blanks after the paragraph, write the number of the sentences containing errors and the correct spellings of the words. There are five errors in all.

Million-Dollar Movie

[1]In real life, the winners of boxing matches get all the atention; people root for the champs and forget their opponents. [2]In the movies, though, the brightest stars are sometimes the losers of the big fight. [3]Rocky Balboa, the fighter featured in the 1976 movie *Rocky,* looses the least of the three movie fighters. [4]Lucky enough to get a shot at the championship, Rocky fights the match of his life but still loses. [5]However, he still wins respect and the girl he loves. [6]In the 1980 movie *Raging Bull,* boxer Jake La Motta has greater wins than his *Rocky* counterpart, but he ends up losing more, too. [7]La Motta does become middleweight champion, but his personal jelosy and violent nature eventually lead him to lose his love and his freedom. [8]Finally, the character who loses the most is Maggie Fitzgerald, the aspiring woman boxer in the 2004 movie *Million Dollar Baby.* [9]Altho Maggie does distinguish herself as a boxer, she not only loses the big fight, but she ends up losing her mobility, her leg, and her life. [10]Despite being the stars of their films, Rocky Balboa, Jake La Motta, and Maggie Fitzgerald all experiance great loss.

The sentences containing errors are _____, _____, _____, _____ and _____.

The misspelled words are _____, _____, _____,

_____and _____.

WRITING PRACTICE **Write Your Own Essay**

This chapter gave you some information on a sport you might not participate in yourself.

Your assignment is this: *Write a few paragraphs or a short essay about a sport that you would or would not like to play.* You may have already tried the sport, or you may have only thought about playing it. (If no sports interest you, write about a physical activity—such as dance or hiking—that does.)

Your thesis statement may be something like "The sport of Greco-Roman wrestling is fascinating because of the strategy and skill successful players need to win their matches."

Follow these steps to write your essay.

1. Use at least two prewriting techniques to come up with ideas for your essay.

2. Use your notes from prewriting to write a rough draft of your essay.

3. Revise your essay, reading through it to check for the first three of the four Cs: concise, credible, and clear writing.

4. Proofread your essay three times, looking for errors in for grammar, punctuation, and spelling.

When you're finished, your essay should include the following:

- A clear thesis statement
- Support points that relate to the thesis
- Specific details that give proof of your thesis
- Transition words that connect your support points and examples

Lab Activity 7

For additional practice with editing, complete Lab Activity 7 in the lab manual packaged with your textbook. If you did not receive a lab manual, you can complete this activity online at **www.ablongman.com/long.** Click on **College Resources for Writers** and then click on **Activity 7.**

PART THREE
Writing Essays

8 Essay Paragraphs and the Thesis Statement

CULTURE NOTE *Alfred Hitchcock*

With so many special effects available to create terror in the minds of movie viewers—massive explosions, realistic bleeding, and horrific natural disasters, to name some—the simplicity of suspense is often overlooked. However, movie director Alfred Hitchcock made a point of making his viewers wait for answers. Unparalleled in his ability to create suspense, Hitchcock set the standard for suspense to which filmmakers aspire.

Psycho

FOOD FOR THOUGHT Alfred Hitchcock created terror through what he did *not* show, such as the mutilated body of Norman Bates' guest in *Psycho*. Consider the most frightening scene you've ever seen, and write a few sentences explaining what about it is so terrifying.

What Is an Essay?

Because writing an effective essay involves the same skills as writing effective paragraphs, you should make a point to keep using the same skills for both. Remember that, just as a paragraph is a group of sentences working together to communicate an idea, an essay is a group of *paragraphs* working together to communicate an idea. An essay's purpose, like a paragraph's, can be to persuade, to inform, or to entertain. An essay's audience—again, like a paragraph's—will usually be your instructor but may change depending on the purpose of your essay.

The most important differences between a paragraph and an essay are length and development. See the following chart for a quick comparison of paragraphs and essays.

	Paragraph	**Essay**
Main point	Topic sentence	Thesis statement
Support points	Sentences supporting topic sentence	Paragraphs supporting thesis
Specific details	Sentences containing details from personal experience or observation	Paragraphs containing details from personal experience or observation but also from research
Organization	Chronological, emphatic, or spatial; marked by transitional words	Chronological, emphatic, or spatial; marked by transitional words or sentences

Writing both essays and paragraphs requires that ideas be supported and organized around a central idea. As your ideas become more sophisticated and better informed, you will find that the length of the essay—several paragraphs instead of several sentences—has great advantages.

Perhaps the single greatest benefit of being a skilled essay writer is being able to more fully communicate your ideas. In college classes—from English and history to science and psychology courses—knowing how to craft a persuasive essay will help you learn material and show your instructors how much you've learned.

Essay Form

This book covers the **five-paragraph essay,** the most basic form. There are many variations on the essay form, but the five-paragraph version includes all the basics—thesis statement, introduction, body paragraphs, conclusion, support, and organization—all in a compact structure. While some of your college writing will require essays with a more sophisticated format, understanding how to write a clear five-paragraph essay will lay the foundation for other work.

Read the following five-paragraph essay analyzing the filmmaking technique of a movie director.

Suspense at Its Best

Anyone interested in movie thrillers has probably seen a movie directed by, or based on a movie directed by, Alfred Hitchcock. From the terrifying *Psycho* to *The Birds* and *North by Northwest,* Hitchcock rivets his audience. Unlike many movie directors today, however, Hitchcock shied away from blood and gore. Instead, he relied on suspense to create terror. Three techniques that Hitchcock used to create suspense—and for which he became famous—are the McGuffin, the bomb theory, and the use of familiar locales.

The first way Hitchcock creates suspense is through a technique called the McGuffin. The McGuffin, named for one of Hitchcock's friends, is an event that occurs in the movie that means very little to the people watching the movie but is responsible for moving the plot along. For instance, in the movie *Psycho,* the beginning of the movie focuses on a woman who stole some money. In reality, her theft is unimportant except as a way to place her in the Bates Motel, where the real story takes place. The woman's act of stealing money served as the McGuffin in this film. It helped create suspense by giving a reason for the woman to choose a hard-to-find, creepy place to stay, the setting for the main action.

A second way Hitchcock creates suspense is through what is known as the bomb theory. The bomb theory draws the audience deeper into the story by giving viewers more information—the ticking of a bomb, say—than the characters in the movie have. Hitchcock was known for saying, "There is no terror in the bang, only in the anticipation of it," which further explains the significance of the bomb theory. For example, in the movie *Rope,* the audience learns that there has been a murder and that the body has been put inside a large wooden trunk. Dinner guests arrive—including the victim's father, friends, and fiancée—and actually use the trunk as a table. While the guests, of course, are wondering why the victim has not shown up, the audience is anxiously thinking, "Look in the trunk! He's right there!" Having more knowledge than the on-screen characters provides great suspense.

A final, but by no means the only other, way that Hitchcock creates suspense is through the use of familiar locales. The movie *North by Northwest* is a key example of this kind of device because the locales give the audience a sense of order. Seeing the New York skyline or the faces of Mount Rushmore, for instance, leads people to feel confident in their expectations of the movie. When the unexpected occurs—Cary Grant running through a cornfield or climbing all over the presidents' faces in *North by Northwest,* for instance—the audience is doubly thrilled by the contrast of familiar settings and unexpected events.

Although Alfred Hitchcock died in 1980, his influence remains strong. Movies such as *Psycho* and *Rear Window* have been remade since Hitchcock's death, but none has managed to surpass, or even rival, the original. Through the use of the McGuffin, the bomb theory, and familiar locales, Hitchcock delivers excitement to his audience every time.

Notice how the body paragraphs of the essay follow the same format while the first and last paragraphs are different.

Writing an Effective Thesis Statement

A **thesis statement** is a sentence that controls the direction of an essay and ties it into one persuasive whole. The thesis statement—which appears in the introductory paragraph—is the most important part of an essay. The essay "Suspense at Its Best," for example, is based on the thesis statement at the end of the first paragraph: "Three techniques that Hitchcock used to create suspense—and for which he became famous—are the McGuffin, the bomb theory, and the use of familiar locales." A good thesis states the main idea of your essay by revealing your topic and your feelings about your topic. Additionally, a good thesis determines how you organize your ideas, what kind of examples you use, and what kind of transitions you use. Everything you write in your essay should start from and return to the thesis.

The thesis statement serves the same purpose in an essay as a topic sentence serves in a paragraph. The thesis usually comes in the first paragraph—the introduction—of an essay, while the topic sentence often serves as the first sentence of a paragraph. Both thesis statements and topic sentences contain narrowed topics that give the writer's point of view on the topic, and both must be at least one complete sentence. (A thesis statement may be more than one sentence.) The most important similarity between a thesis statement and a topic sentence is that they both control the direction of the writing that follows them. A good topic sentence will often lead a writer to produce an effective paragraph, while a solid thesis statement will often lead into an effective essay.

The checklist on writing a thesis statement will help you.

✔ CHECKLIST for Writing a Thesis Statement

_____ **Does my thesis statement give the main idea of my essay?**

_____ **Does my thesis statement give my point of view?**

_____ **Does my thesis statement tell the reader what to expect?**

_____ **Is my thesis statement arguable?**

_____ **Is my thesis statement at least one complete sentence?**

Be Patient

Don't feel compelled to write a perfect thesis statement on the first try. Remember, the thesis statement will determine everything else that comes in your essay, so give yourself time to come up with one that works for you. Use prewriting activities, both for your essay and for your thesis, and see what ideas seem strongest. Trim your ideas down to a sentence or two, and you'll most likely have a rough working thesis that you can use throughout the drafting process.

For instance, Chia, the writer of the Hitchcock essay, tried out different thesis statements before she came up with one that satisfied her.

First try (not so good):   Alfred Hitchcock directed suspenseful movies.

Second try (better):	Alfred Hitchcock used different techniques to create suspense.
Third try (good):	Three techniques that Hitchcock used to create suspense—and for which he became famous—are the McGuffin, the bomb theory, and the use of familiar locales.

In each statement, Chia manages to include her point of view with a narrowed topic. In her first try, her thesis is broad and hard to argue; someone *might* argue that Alfred Hitchcock did not direct suspenseful movies, but probably not. Chia's second try is better, limiting her topic to techniques used to create suspense. In her third try, though, she specifies the three techniques as "the McGuffin," "the bomb theory," and "the use of familiar locales" to further narrow her topic and prepare her reader for the discussion to follow.

Make Sure Your Thesis Statement Is a Complete Sentence

After you've come up with an idea that interests you, make sure to state the idea in the form of at least one complete sentence. A **sentence** is a group of related words having a subject and verb that makes sense all by itself. Thesis statements can be more than one sentence, and they can even be implicit, or unstated. For the essays you'll write using this text, however, it's a good idea to write thesis statements of a single sentence. The example below shows how a phrase fails to communicate a complete idea, which is what you need from a thesis statement.

Not a sentence:	Taking general education courses
Sentence:	College students should be required to take only those courses that would directly benefit them in getting a job.

Writing "Taking general education courses" might tell some readers that you think more general education courses are unnecessary, but it also might send the message that you think more general education courses should be required. Probably, it will leave your readers wondering what your attitude toward general education courses is. On the other hand, if you write, "College students should be required to take only those courses that would directly benefit them in getting a job," your readers might still disagree with you, but at least they will be clear as to what you're arguing.

EXERCISE 1 WRITING A COMPLETE SENTENCE FOR YOUR THESIS

Rewrite each phrase to make it a complete sentence with a subject and a verb. Feel free to reword the phrases to make them fit more easily into sentence form. An example has been done for you.

Example: Learning a second language in elementary school

Complete sentence: _Learning a second language in elementary_

school has many benefits.

1. Reaching one's potential at work

Complete sentence: _____

_____

2. To develop good study habits

Complete sentence: _____

_____

3. Learning time management skills

Complete sentence: _____

_____

Make Sure Your Thesis Statement Is Broad Enough

Sometimes, even if we passionately believe in what we write, the idea we want to communicate doesn't lend itself to an entire essay. For instance, if you write, "My English instructor gave only one A last semester," what are you going to talk about for the next few paragraphs, or even sentences? Choose a topic that has many different directions and perspectives, such as trends in popular culture or politics, in order to give yourself room to expand your ideas. A thesis statement such as "Grading standards should be tougher in honors classes" not only gives you something to argue but also gives you different ways to develop your thesis.

- The benefits of tougher standards
- The downside of easy standards
- The differences between grading standards in regular courses and honors courses

The following thesis statements need to be broadened.

Not broad enough:	The movie *Scarface* has a violent ending.
Better thesis statement:	In some movies, violence is necessary to depict the harsh consequences of the characters' actions.
Not broad enough:	A professional hockey player faced criminal charges for his on-ice behavior.
Better thesis statement:	Professional hockey players who display poor sportsmanship often receive severe punishments.

The "not broad enough" thesis statements above are hard to develop because they state facts. Perhaps you *could* argue that *violent* means different things to different people, but even then, your essay proving that *Scarface* has a violent ending would simply consist of a list of incidents from the end of the movie. Similarly, since the hockey player of the second example either did or did not face criminal charges, there isn't much room for discussion if you start with a thesis statement that simply claims that he did.

EXERCISE 2 IDENTIFYING THESIS STATEMENTS THAT ARE BROAD ENOUGH

Write OK in the blank before each thesis statement that is broad enough for development, and write an X next to statements that are not broad enough.

_____ **1.** Gwyneth Paltrow starred in a remake of the Hitchcock movie *Dial M for Murder.*

_____ **2.** The remake was titled *The Perfect Murder.*

_____ **3.** While the remake used several key details from the original, it was not as compelling.

_____ **4.** Watching Hitchcock movies is a good opportunity to see superior acting, beautiful scenery, and suspense.

_____ **5.** Three actors who starred in the Hitchcock thriller _Charade_ are Audrey Hepburn, Cary Grant, and Walter Matthau.

Make Sure Your Thesis Statement Is Narrow Enough

After you've crafted a thesis statement that can lead you in multiple directions, you face a new task: narrowing your thesis to make it manageable in the space allotted. Just as a thesis allows you to develop many different perspectives well, it can also become unmanageable if you can't decide which particular angle to follow. An easy way to narrow your thesis is to include a point-of-view statement that lets your reader know the scope of your argument. Here's an example that shows how to narrow a thesis.

Not narrow enough: Science is challenging.

This sentence offers almost too many different directions for development. Not only could you discuss the many types of science, but you could discuss the different types of challenges. You could also discuss the scientists who have faced these challenges. Any of these possibilities is too broad in scope to discuss effectively in an essay, and covering all three well would be impossible.

Better thesis statement: To excel in the sciences, students must be logical, methodical, and patient.

Here, you are letting your reader know both _what_ your topic is (excelling in the sciences) and _how_ to reach that goal (through logic, method, and patience).

Another option: Although science is challenging, students can succeed by being logical, methodical, and patient.

This thesis statement lets your reader know, again, that you think science is challenging, but also that your essay will focus on the ways students can succeed in that subject. Here is another thesis that needs to be narrowed.

Not narrow enough: People watch movies for many reasons.

This thesis could be developed, but it would be impossible to discuss all people and every reason people watch movies in a single essay. Thus, the thesis needs to be narrowed.

Better thesis statement: Young adults watch movies to find humor, romance, or excitement.

EXERCISE 3 IDENTIFYING THESIS STATEMENTS THAT ARE NARROW ENOUGH

Write OK in the blank before each thesis statement that is narrow enough to write about in an essay, and write an X by statements that are not narrow enough.

_____ **1.** Several Hitchcock movies make good use of a specific location.

_____ **2.** Mount Rushmore is an effective setting for *North by Northwest* because of its physical beauty, familiarity, and danger.

_____ **3.** Many movies affect people differently.

_____ **4.** Movies depict the range of human emotion.

_____ **5.** Through dialogue, plot, and setting, movies create fantasy worlds.

Make Sure Your Thesis Statement Is Arguable

Just as you take care to limit your thesis to something you believe, so, too, you should be sure that your thesis can be argued. Having a definite opinion about your topic gives you momentum for writing a persuasive essay, and it lets your reader know where you stand on the issue.

Not arguable: The effects of the new tax cuts haven't been seen yet.

Here the writer may mean that taxes shouldn't have been cut but that the ill effects aren't apparent yet—or the writer may be happy about the tax cuts and, thus, may be eagerly anticipating the changes. Either way, the writer doesn't take a firm stance—tax cuts have positive effects *or* tax cuts have negative effects—so the thesis doesn't clearly lead toward developing an idea.

Better thesis statement: Although the tax cuts were supposed to bring relief to working parents, they're clearly a failure.

By including the word *failure,* the writer makes clear that she was not in favor of the tax cuts.

In the next sentence, the writer's stance is also unclear and, thus, difficult to argue.

Not arguable: Alfred Hitchcock's skill as a suspense film director seems unparalleled.

Is the writer arguing that Hitchcock is the best director of suspense films? Or is the point that other directors may also have Hitchcock's skill? Since the writer doesn't make a particular point, the purpose of the thesis statement is unclear.

Better thesis statement: Alfred Hitchcock was the best suspense film director of all time.

Here the writer has a clear point: Alfred Hitchcock was the best. Even if you disagree with the writer's claim, you know what the point of the essay is and that the writer cares about the topic.

Another type of inarguable thesis is one that focuses only on the writer's view.

Not arguable: I loved that new thriller.

In this case, the reader has a nearly impossible time disagreeing with the writer because no one can tell another person what to think. Since the point of an essay is to convince readers of your views, then, you should avoid thesis statements that rely on your personal opinions alone.

Arguable: That new thriller is worth seeing.

This thesis can be argued because it avoids the personal *I.*

Not arguable: In my opinion, advertisements on television take too much time away from scheduled programs.

Arguable: Advertisements on television take too much time away from scheduled programs.

The preceding example presents a similar challenge. Since the writer begins the thesis statement with "In my opinion," a reader has a tough time arguing with *anything* that the writer states. People can believe or think whatever they choose, so unless you're prepared to argue, "It's *not* your opinion that advertisements take too much time away from scheduled programs," you really have nowhere to go in terms of development.

EXERCISE 4 REWRITING THESIS STATEMENTS TO MAKE THEM ARGUABLE

Rewrite the following sentences to give them a clear stance on the issue discussed. In cases where the writer's stance is unclear, choose whichever side you want to argue.

1. Running is my favorite form of exercise.

Revised: _____

_____

2. Some of the best movies last several hours.

Revised: _____

_____

3. I think that people who talk on cell phones in public are rude.

Revised: _____

_____

4. Learning to speak English is a challenge faced by many people who were not born in this country.

Revised: _____

_____

5. My feeling is that the new restaurant is popular because of its menu, atmosphere, and service.

Revised: _____

_____

Make Sure Your Thesis Statement Has a Purpose

Perhaps the most important, yet often unstated, part of your thesis is its purpose. The purpose is the "why" for your essay, the reason you're writing it (other than that you have to because your teacher assigned it). You need to have a sense of why this thesis is worth developing because if there's no reason to develop it, there's no reason for your reader to read your essay, and that situation makes persuasion difficult. Sometimes the purpose of your essay will be explicitly stated in your thesis. For instance, in the thesis statement "People should be careful when they chat online because visiting Internet chat rooms involves several risks," the purpose—to warn people against the risks of online chat rooms—is clearly stated in the thesis itself.

Other topics, however, may not lend themselves to an obvious explanation of why they're important. In these cases, it's up to you to care enough about your topic that your reader understands its significance. Even if you never directly write that your views are important, your reader should understand from your thesis that they are. If you can't put your finger on why a topic is important to discuss, you probably should find another topic that you care more about.

Make Sure Your Thesis Statement Argues a Single Point

When writing your thesis statement, be sure that you give only one argument at a time. The defining characteristic of an essay is *unity,* or the quality of having everything work together to communicate a single idea. If your thesis itself advances two ideas, you're already off to a rough start. For instance, in the following sentence, the writer states more than one idea.

Lacks a single focus: People must work hard to achieve success, but they must leave time for fun, too.

This thesis sends two messages. First, it sends the message that people need to work hard; second, it communicates that people need to have fun. Both points are weighted equally, so discerning the most important idea is difficult. The reader has no way of knowing which idea will be developed in the course of the essay.

Additionally, by stating two points in the thesis, the writer has set up the tasks of having to fully develop *two* ideas *and* connect them to each other throughout the course of the essay. Aside from the fact that most of your assignments won't give you enough time or length to develop two ideas, trying to do so is much harder than developing only one.

Better thesis statement: People must leave time in their lives for fun.

or   People must work hard to achieve success.

or   Even though people must leave time for fun, they must work hard to achieve success.

In the first two revisions of the thesis with two ideas, the writer chooses one point and focuses on it. In the third revision, the writer still focuses on the idea that people need to work hard to achieve success, but he qualifies his statement by saying that people must leave time for fun.

The Argument of Grammar

In the third option for a better thesis statement above, another way to tell which idea is strongest is to look at the sentence structure. The sentence contains both an independent and a dependent clause (see Chapter 34 for more on clauses). Since the dependent clause—in this case "Even though people must leave time for fun"—cannot stand on its own and make sense, it cannot be the main idea of the sentence. Instead, the independent clause—"they must work hard to achieve success"—is the more important idea in the sentence.

EXERCISE 5 WRITING THESIS STATEMENTS THAT CONTAIN A SINGLE POINT

Rewrite each sentence so that it contains only one point.

1. People should turn down their stereos when driving on the freeway, and they should pay attention to road conditions.

Revised: _____

_____

2. Grading systems vary, and students should become familiar with each of their instructors' standards.

Revised: _____

_____

3. Attending a professional sports event is exciting, but it is often very expensive.

Revised: _____

_____

4. Being rude often has serious consequences, yet people do it frequently.

Revised: _____

_____

5. To live a healthy life, people often try fad diets, or they try trendy exercise programs.

Revised: _____

_____

Consider Offering a Map of Your Essay

Some topics are easy to organize into general support points. For such topics, it is useful to mention your **map**—how you plan to organize your essay. For instance, in the essay "Suspense at Its Best" on page 115, Chia, the writer, mentions the three techniques that Alfred Hitchcock used to create suspense—the McGuffin, the bomb theory, and the use of familiar locales. Although Chia's thesis statement would have been fine without this map, telling her readers the specific items she'll discuss lets her readers know exactly what to expect from her essay. Additionally, a map gives her a plan she can refer back to as she writes her essay.

Avoid Making General Statements of What You Plan to Do

Just as you should avoid making an announcement in a topic sentence, you should avoid simply announcing your topic in your thesis statement. Avoid starting your essay with comments such as "The purpose of this essay is to show that . . . " or "This essay will show the differences between. . . " Sentences like these don't provide any information about your topic, and a clear thesis statement will tell your readers all they need to know about what's to come in your essay.

Avoid:	The purpose of this essay is to show that *Rear Window, North by Northwest,* and *Psycho* are Hitchcock films.
Good:	*Rear Window, North by Northwest,* and *Psycho* are three of Hitchcock's most thrilling films.
Avoid:	In this essay, I will discuss how to analyze a movie.
Good:	Analyzing plot, characters, and lighting is an effective way of understanding a movie.

In the first example, the writer simply eliminates the announcement part of the thesis. In the second example, the writer both omits the announcement and rewords the rest of the sentence to create an effective thesis.

EXERCISE 6 ELIMINATING ANNOUNCEMENTS FROM THE THESIS

Rewrite the following sentences to avoid including an announcement in the thesis.

1. In this essay, I will discuss the effects of global warming on the earth.

Revised: _____

_____

2. In the course of this discussion, I will show how people are not always treated as though they are innocent until proven guilty in the United States.

Revised: _____

_____

3. This essay is about how having a mentor can help people achieve success in their lives.

Revised: _____

_____

Developing the Paragraphs in an Essay

In essays, several different kinds of paragraphs are necessary for different functions. Some paragraphs grab your attention while others simply convey information. Still others condense the content of an essay into a few short sentences. In an essay, there are three main types of paragraphs.

- An introductory paragraph
- Body paragraphs
- A concluding paragraph

Introductory Paragraph

Think about a time when you've given someone unexpected news. Did you just plunge into the big surprise, or did you lead up to it in steps? An introductory paragraph, or **introduction,** provides background information and sets the tone for your essay. Good introductions also get the reader's attention and present the thesis in a logical way.

An effective introduction has

- An **opening** that catches the reader's attention.
- A **thesis statement,** which is a sentence that controls the direction of an essay and manages to tie it into one persuasive whole. You learned how to recognize and write thesis statements earlier in this chapter.

An introduction may also contain a map of your essay, or a statement that shows your reader what your essay will cover or how it will be organized. The map may appear in the thesis statement, or it may come in a sentence after the thesis statement. In "Suspense at Its Best," the writer includes a map in her thesis statement.

Three techniques which Hitchcock used to create suspense—and for which he became famous—are the McGuffin, the bomb theory, and the use of familiar locales.

If she chose, Chia could mention the three areas she plans to develop—her map—in the sentence following her thesis statement.

Hitchcock used, and became famous for using, three techniques to create suspense in movies. These techniques are the McGuffin, the bomb theory, and the use of familiar locales.

Strategies for Developing an Introduction

To write an effective opening, you might try one of the following techniques.

Provide Background Information   One of the writer's most important jobs is making the essay relevant, or meaningful, to a reader. In his essay "The Telephone," Anwar Accawi begins with this introduction.

> When I was growing up in Magdaluna, a small Lebanese village in the terraced, rocky mountains east of Sidon, time didn't mean much to anybody, except maybe to those who were dying, or those waiting to appear in court because they had tampered with the boundary markers on their land. In those days, there was no real need for a calendar or a watch to keep track of the hours, days, months, and years . . . We lived and loved and toiled and died without ever need to know what year it was, or even the time of day.

The writer's thesis, later in his essay, makes the point that as technology becomes more prevalent, simple and satisfying ways are lost. In this case, the writer has prepared us for a discussion of the changes in culture—particularly in his culture—by explaining the customs of his village before modern technology reached it. By the time the writer gets to his thesis statement, the reader understands why a simple lifestyle is so important to him; thus, when he states his thesis, we are prepared for his argument.

Use a Personal Anecdote   Telling a story from your personal experience is another good way to catch your reader's attention. **Personal anecdotes** appeal to most people and are good ways to illustrate important ideas from your essay before your reader even gets to your thesis statement. The writer of the essay "The Ways We Lie" begins her essay with an account of the lies she tells in one day.

> The bank called today and I told them my deposit was in the mail, even though I hadn't written a check yet. It'd been a rough day. The baby I'm pregnant with decided to do aerobics on my lungs for two hours, our three-year-old daughter painted the living-room couch with lipstick, the IRS put me on hold for an hour, and I was late to a business meeting because I was tired.
> I told my client the traffic had been bad. When my partner came home, his haggard face told me his day hadn't gone any better than mine, so when he asked, "How was your day?" I said, "Oh, fine," knowing that one more straw might break his back. A friend called and wanted to take me to lunch. I said I was busy. Four lies in the course of a day, none of which I felt the least bit guilty about.

Opening her essay with a description of the kinds of lies she tells and the reasons she tells them lays the foundation for the discussion of lies and their consequences that follows.

Begin with a Quotation   Beginning your essay with a quotation is a good way to focus your reader's attention on a particular aspect of your topic. Read the following paragraph to see how writer Joyce Jarrett uses a quotation to set the tone and focus the topic for her essay on attaining personal freedom in the midst of racial strife.

> Born free, as free as the wind blows, as free as the grass grows, born free to follow your heart.   *—Don Black*

My first illusion of freedom came in 1966, many years following the Supreme Court's decision on school desegregation. Of course to a fifteen-year-old girl, isolated, caged like a rodent in the poverty-stricken plains of the Magnolia State, *Brown vs. The Board of Education* had no meaning. Though many must have thought that my decision to attend the all-white city high school that fall, along with 49 other blacks, was made in protest or had evolved from a sense of commitment for the betterment of my people, nothing could have been further from the truth. Like a rat finding a new passageway, I was propelled to my new liberty more out of curiosity than out of a sense of mission.

The quotation in this paragraph focuses the essay's topic (and the reader's attention) on the issue of freedom. When the reader arrives at the thesis statement later in the essay, the reader understands both the meaning of the quotation and the relationship between the quotation and the thesis statement.

Use Opposites   Using an example that contrasts with the thesis of your essay can be an effective and attention-grabbing way to begin your essay. Readers will assume that the essay is going in one direction and will then be surprised to learn your true argument. Read the following paragraphs to see how the writer Philip Chiu in his essay "The Myth of the Model Minority" uses an opening with a message that is contrary to that of his thesis statement. The thesis statement is in bold print.

For years, Chinese Americans have been labeled a model minority. We read in the newspapers how diligently they have worked and saved. We see on television how quietly they obey the laws and how conscientiously they stay clear of crime. We learn in magazines how they climb the economic ladder and how much better than the Caucasian kids their children do in school.

> **But of late, we have been reading about a different side of Chinese American life.**

The opening above discusses the successes of Chinese Americans, leading the reader to expect an essay focusing on the positive aspects of this culture's place in American society. When the writer switches perspective and begins discussing how Chinese Americans have another side, the reader is captivated by the contrast and wants to read more.

Ask Questions   Beginning your essay with a question is an effective way to involve your reader immediately. Asking questions forces the reader to consider an issue and think about responses to your question. Read the introductory paragraph below from Jamaica Kincaid's essay "Those Words That Echo . . . Echo . . . Echo Through Life" to see how questions can open an essay.

> How do I write? Why do I write? What do I write? This is what I am writing: I am writing: "Mr. Potter was my father; my father's name was Mr. Potter." So much went into that one sentence; much happened before I settled on those eleven words.

Notice that the writer uses a number of questions to work her way into her actual message. By using several short questions, the writer stimulates the reader's interest and readies him or her for the topic to come.

EXERCISE 7 RECOGNIZING INTRODUCTION STRATEGIES

The following paragraphs use different introduction strategies. After reading each one, circle the letter that corresponds to the introduction strategy used.

1. "Show me the money!" This statement, made famous in the 1996 movie *Jerry Maguire,* seems to become increasingly true. From the time people can show preference, they want the right toys, the right clothes, and the right entertainment. Usually, "right" means expensive. The areas of music, sports, and advertising illustrate how money is often the most significant force in people's decisions.

   a. Background information

   b. Personal anecdote

   c. Quotation

   d. Opposites

   e. Questions

2. All my life I've been shy. When my mother dropped me off at kindergarten for the first time fifteen years ago, I wanted to cry and run after her. However, I saw several other kids do that and still have to stay at school, anyway, so I figured right then that I'd have to deal with my situation. As it turns out, I loved kindergarten and every new challenge I undertook through high school. I learned early on that conquering my shyness paid off in school, work, and my personal life.

   a. Background information

   b. Personal anecdote

   c. Quotation

   d. Opposites

   e. Questions

3. Anyone who's watched an NBA game or reruns of the sitcom *Sex and the City* knows the importance of shoes. Flashy metallic-striped basketball shoes signal the movement of the lightening-quick point guard, and feather-trimmed stilettos show to advantage the lovely legs of the latest fashion icon. Even as they offer warmth or comfort, shoes identify people. From their original function as protective coverings for feet, shoes have evolved to become expressions of art, fashion, and athleticism.

   a. Background information

   b. Personal anecdote

   c. Quotation

   d. Opposites

   e. Questions

EXERCISE 8 PRACTICING INTRODUCTORY STRATEGIES

1. Choose a topic from the list below, and write an introduction using one of the strategies covered in this chapter.

   Your first day in a new school/job/neighborhood

   A particularly entertaining or disappointing movie

   A person you admire

   An important skill

   An irritating habit

2. After you write your introduction, write a few sentences explaining why you chose the introduction strategy you chose and why you think it did or did not work well for your topic.

_____

_____

_____

_____

Body Paragraphs

Once you've written a solid introductory paragraph, your job is to provide proof of your thesis statement. You do this is in the body paragraphs of the essay. **Body paragraphs** perform two main functions.

1. They connect support points to the thesis statement.

2. They provide support points and specific details that support the thesis statement.

Connection to the Thesis Statement

All the body paragraphs must connect to and develop some part of the thesis. The easiest place to connect a body paragraph to the thesis is in the paragraph's topic sentence.

In "Suspense at Its Best," the writer uses some of the key terms from the thesis in the topic sentence to tell the reader how the body paragraph relates to the thesis. These key terms are called a **thesis echo,** and they help to connect your body paragraphs to the thesis statement by repeating key words or concepts.

Thesis statement: Three techniques which Hitchcock used to create suspense—and for which he became famous—are the McGuffin, the bomb theory, and the use of familiar locales.

The key ideas in the thesis statement are: techniques and suspense. Thus, to effectively connect the body paragraphs to the thesis, the writer should incorporate these ideas in every body paragraph by means of a thesis echo. The thesis echo in the first body paragraph is underlined on the following page.

The **topic sentence** of the first body paragraph: "The first way Hitchcock creates suspense is through a technique called the McGuffin."

By repeating key words from the thesis statement—*creates, suspense,* and *technique*—in the topic sentence of the first body paragraph, the writer makes a smooth connection from thesis to support point. This tells the reader that the information in that paragraph connects to and supports the thesis.

Echoing Ideas, Not Just Words

Saying the same thing over and over again, regardless of how important it is, can get boring. Keep in mind, then, that the thesis echo reiterates key *ideas* from the thesis but not necessarily the exact words or phrases from the thesis. For instance, instead of saying, "Hitchcock creates suspense through a technique called the McGuffin" in the topic sentence, the writer could have said, "Hitchcock builds tension via a tool named the McGuffin." The words *builds, tension,* and *tool* serve to communicate the same idea as *creates, suspense,* and *technique,* but they do so by adding variety to the writer's essay and, thus, decreasing the chances for boring repetition. For more on connecting ideas, see Chapter 10.

Giving Support Points and Specific Details That Provide the Thesis

All your evidence comes in the body paragraphs. In "Suspense at Its Best," the writer provides different examples to illustrate how Hitchcock creates suspense. The topic sentence of each paragraph echoes a section of the thesis statement, and each paragraph contains an example that supports the topic sentence of that paragraph. In the following paragraph, the topic sentence is in italics. The rest of the paragraph gives an example that supports the topic sentence.

Body Paragraph 1

The first way Hitchcock creates suspense is through a technique called the McGuffin. The McGuffin, named for one of Hitchcock's friends, is an event that occurs in the movie that means very little to the people watching the movie but is responsible for moving the plot along. For instance, in the movie *Psycho,* the beginning of the movie focuses on a woman who stole some money. In reality, her theft is unimportant except as a way to place her in the Bates Motel, where the real story takes place. The woman's act of stealing money served as the McGuffin in this film. It helped create suspense by laying the foundation for the woman choosing a hard-to-find, creepy place to stay, the setting for the main action.

Conclusion

By the time you've made your way to the concluding paragraph of your essay, you've completed the hardest part of writing it. You've made your points, connected them, and supported them. Good job! Now all you have to do is end your essay gracefully. A solid conclusion can do just this.

A **concluding paragraph,** or **conclusion,** ties together everything you've said in your essay. You can conclude your essay in one of several ways.

1. Adding final thoughts
2. Ending with a question
3. Predicting the future
4. Offering a solution or answer
5. Inspiring readers to take action

Adding Final Thoughts

The writer of "Suspense at Its Best" chose to end her essay by adding a few final thoughts. Here is an original version of the conclusion for "Suspense at Its Best."

> Although Alfred Hitchcock died in 1980, his influence remains strong. Movies such as *Psycho, Dial "M" for Murder,* and *Rear Window* have been remade since Hitchcock's death, but none has managed to surpass, or even rival, the original. Through the use of the MacGuffin, the bomb theory, and familiar locales, Hitchcock delivers terror to his audience every time.

In ending her essay with a reminder of Hitchcock's influence, the writer emphasizes the significance of her topic. Including mention of remakes of Hitchcock classics also communicates the ongoing nature of Hitchcock's influence. These ideas tell the reader something new—that the writer is aware of Hitchcock's importance in his field—but the information is closely related to the rest of the essay, so the reader stays on track.

Ending with a Question

Just as starting your essay can be a great way to catch your reader's attention, ending with a question focuses your reader as well. Consider a third version of the conclusion for "Suspense at Its Best."

> Though Alfred Hitchcock made use of three techniques to create suspense, other aspects of his films help build the terrifying tension that is Hitchcock's signature. Would his movies be as suspenseful without dramatic mood music? Would his movies be as effective without creative camera angles? Perhaps. However, since Hitchcock wove every element of his film into a unified whole, it's hard to believe that changing anything would be an improvement.

In this conclusion, the writer ends her essay by asking questions. However, though the writer doesn't directly answer the question, her final comment—"it's hard to believe that changing anything would be an improvement"—satisfies the reader's curiosity.

Predicting the Future

In using the prediction strategy, the writer offers a forecast of events or circumstances related to the event or situation discussed in the essay. For instance, given the range of suspense techniques that the writer of "Suspense at Its Best" covered, she could easily have predicted the future of suspense movies. Consider this version of her conclusion.

> Alfred Hitchcock made an art of the suspense film. Through various techniques, Hitchcock worked to build tension over the course of his movies that broke only in the final scenes. With the tremendous advances in technology today, filmmakers have even greater means of creating suspense at their disposal than Hitchcock did. However, even with all the special effects in the world, Hitchcock will likely remain the master of suspense.

In this conclusion, the writer predicts that Hitchcock's status as the master of suspense will not change, even in the face of technology.

Offering a Solution or Answer

Offering a solution or answer is another effective way to conclude an essay. Since no real problem presents itself in "Suspense at Its Best," the writer would have a more difficult time making this technique work. However, if the focus of the essay were that Hitchcock's films overly relied upon suspense, here's a possible solution-providing conclusion.

> Though suspense has its place in movies—and Alfred Hitchcock certainly has his place in suspense—this quality comes at the expense of other movie characteristics. Toning down the dramatic music, making the plotlines more realistic, and using settings that more people see on a daily basis would help suspense films become a bit more real for all of us.

Inspiring Readers to Take Action

Inspiring readers to take action is especially effective if the argument put forth in the essay deals with a social or political cause. In "Suspense at Its Best," if the writer had argued that too many movie companies were taking advantage of desperate, underpaid actors, this method would have worked well. Consider one last version of the conclusion.

> It's all very well to appreciate the suspense created by director Alfred Hitchcock from the comfort of a cushy chair in an air-conditioned theater. However, if we stop to consider the sacrifices of other, less-known people—underpaid, non-union actors who work terrible hours for terrible wages, for instance—the movie's effects are less pleasurable. Before we enjoy entertainment too much, we must consider at whose expense it comes.

WRITING PRACTICE   **Identifying Effective Thesis Statements**

Read the sentence pairs below. Then circle the letter of the sentence that is an effective thesis statement. Finally, write a brief explanation of why the sentence you chose is the better thesis statement.

Example: (a.) Watching scary movies is a great way to spend Halloween.

  b. I love to watch scary movies.

The first sentence works better as a thesis statement because it gives the reader something to argue. Although you *could* write "You don't love to watch scary movies"—and, thus, argue with the second thesis statement— these kinds of arguments are difficult to make since the person making the claim will know her preferences—scary movies, for instance—better than a reader.

1. a. Alfred Hitchcock was a film director.

   b. Alfred Hitchcock was the master of creating suspense.

_____

_____

_____

2. a. Movie settings are important.

   b. Bodega Bay, California, is an effective setting for the movie *The Birds*.

_____

_____

_____

3. a. The movie *Rear Window* was remade at least twice.

   b. The original version of *Rear Window* was better than its remakes in terms of plot, setting, and characters.

_____

_____

_____

Lab Activity 8

For additional practice with writing essays, complete Lab Activity 8 in the lab manual packaged with your textbook. If you did not receive a lab manual, you can complete this activity online at **www.ablongman.com/long.** Click on **College Resources for Writers** and then click on **Activity 8.**

9   Supporting Your Ideas

Though Italian spaghetti and macaroni are familiar to most people, other types of noodles, such as Japanese udon or soba or Chinese rice noodles, are less recognizable. Other types of pasta—such as couscous from Northern Africa—are gaining popularity throughout the United States.

Elegant Ramen

OBSERVE YOUR WORLD Nearly every culture boasts some type of pasta or noodle, from Moroccan couscous and Italian penne to Japanese udon and German spaetzle. What kinds of pasta are most popular in your neighborhood or city? Observe your local grocery stores and restaurants, noting what kind of noodles—if any—they carry. Write a few sentences explaining how the presence (or absence) of certain noodles does or does not accurately reflect your local population.

Making Your Case

Even the most wonderful, clear thesis statements need help to be convincing. That's where specific details come in. Specific details make people believe you. If you list reasons why you believe something and then offer proof to support your beliefs, your writing will be effective and professional. Using specific details in your writing helps you master the second of the four Cs: credible writing.

EXERCISE 1 RECOGNIZING CREDIBILITY

The following two paragraphs address the topic of making homemade pasta. The writers of both paragraphs draw on their personal experiences to support their ideas. One paragraph, however, is written by someone who has never tried to make pasta. Can you tell which one it is?

Making Pasta

[1]Homemade pasta is more of an undertaking than people realize. [2]The first step is to gather the proper ingredients. [3]Semolina flour, which is a wheat flour more coarsely ground than other flours (or that has had the finer flour sifted out), is the most important ingredient, but you also need eggs, salt, and water. [4]Mix the ingredients by making a pile of flour on your work surface and making a "well" or hole in the center of the flour. [5]Crack the eggs into the well, add the salt, and mix the ingredients into the flour a little at a time. [6]Once the ingredients are well blended, kneading begins. [7]Kneading—a combination of pressing, folding, and turning the dough—is a way to work the dough so that it blends and holds together properly. [8]Now the dough should feel firm, smooth, and dry, wet enough only to stick to itself but nothing else. [9]At this point, divide the dough into tennis-ball-sized portions, wrap them in plastic wrap, and let them sit for an hour before putting them into a pasta machine or making noodles by hand.

Pasta from Scratch

[1]Making pasta from scratch involves a number of key steps. [2]First, you have to get the ingredients together. [3]The ingredients are important because they can affect the pasta. [4]Next, you must mix the ingredients together, but there's a special way you have to do it. [5]If you don't do it the right way, the pasta won't be as good. [6]After

you mix the pasta, you should check the texture. [7]The texture should feel a certain way, and if it doesn't, you'll have trouble making the pasta. [8]Then, divide the dough up into the right amounts. [9]Make sure, next, that the dough is stored properly while it's getting ready. [10]Last, make the noodles themselves.

Which paragraph is written by someone who has actually made pasta?

_____ "Making Pasta"

_____ "Pasta from Scratch"

In Exercise 1, the first paragraph, "Making Pasta," was written by someone who has actually made pasta. The writer uses support points that allow the reader to understand what the process entails, and he then uses specific examples to *show* the reader what he means. In the end, we can believe that this writer knows what he's talking about because he has used enough detail to be credible. This writer of "Making Pasta" uses his experiences effectively to show that he knows his topic well.

The second paragraph, "Pasta from Scratch," offers very few details that let the reader see how difficult the job is. Instead, the writer simply offers vague steps and repeats her ideas, which do little to prove her point. We are left wondering if this person really understands the pasta-making process at all.

EXERCISE 2 ANALYZING SPECIFIC DETAILS IN PARAGRAPHS

Reread the two paragraphs about making pasta in Exercise 1. Then, fill in the blanks below.

1. What kind of flour is necessary to make pasta, according to these

   paragraphs? _____

2. Which paragraph contains information about the type of flour

   necessary to make pasta? _____

3. Does the writer of "Pasta from Scratch" mention any specific

   ingredients? _____

4. Both paragraphs mention that mixing the dough is a step in the pasta-making process. Which paragraph explains what type of mixing is involved?

_____ "Making Pasta"

_____ "Pasta from Scratch"

5. By reading the first five sentences of the paragraph, you can tell that the writer of "Making Pasta" knows something about making

pasta. How? _____

_____

6. In "Pasta from Scratch," the writer would be more convincing if she offered more specific details. What sentences, in particular, would be more effective with additional details? Choose two sentences that require more detail to be convincing, and write some possible details for those sentences.

_____

_____

Three Types of Details

Evidence can take different forms, and your specific details will come from many sources. Keep in mind that specific details should *add* information to support your points, not simply repeat them. To find a broad range of information, you need to use different types of proof. Explanations of three of the most common types of proof follow.

Descriptions of Objects or Events in Your Life

You've already lived at least two decades, and you've had many experiences. Thus, you have a ready-made source of information available to you: your own life. Writing about situations you've encountered, challenges you've faced, people you've known, and conflicts you've overcome will tell your reader that you are an informed, thoughtful person who has credible information to share.

For instance, if you are telling a friend about a new Japanese restaurant that you like, you might say something like this:

I am so excited that we finally have a Fuji restaurant in our neighborhood! The one near us specializes in noodles, so I can get my favorite udon (the thick white noodles similar to spaghetti) or the healthier soba (a brownish noodle made with buckwheat) any time I like. I love how the restaurant serves the noodles submerged in hot broth in big, heavy bowls, and the hot pepper on the tables gives the noodles a little extra zing for when I need more heat than the soup delivers.

In the passage above, the writer establishes credibility by describing different types of Japanese noodles. Since she includes details of how the noodles are served as well as how they look, we believe that she has firsthand knowledge about this restaurant. Drawing on your own experiences can support your ideas, particularly when you have experiences that directly support the point you're making.

Accounts of Events in Other People's Lives

Sometimes the best way to learn is to listen. Your friends, family, co-workers, and classmates have all shared experiences with you at one time or another, and these experiences may have an important place in your writing. For instance, if your assignment is to write about the pros or cons of taking out a student loan, but you haven't applied for a loan yet, you might have a hard time thinking of things to say. In this case, talking to a friend or classmate, preferably one who already knows about the responsibilities of paying back such a loan, can help.

For instance, a writer who is considering applying for student loans might write this:

Student loans sound too good to be true, so they make me nervous. They don't seem to be too hard to get, and the interest rates don't seem unbearable (better than credit card rates, for sure). My buddy Barry can't say enough good things about them, but he hasn't graduated, so he hasn't started paying them back yet. On the other hand, my friend Chuck *has* finished school, and he *is* paying them back. I know he doesn't like making the monthly payments, which started right after he got his degree, but I know he appreciated not having to work full time while he was in school. Even though I'm still nervous about being in debt, the thought of not working so much is great.

In the passage above, the writer is able to use his friends' experiences to support his ideas. Even though the writer admits that he doesn't have firsthand knowledge of the subject—student loans—he is able to use others' experiences to support his point.

Facts That You've Learned from Trusted Sources

Just as your friends have experiences that you haven't had, so have other people. Watching the news or reading a newspaper can provide you with information to support your topic sentence. For instance, suppose your instructor asks you to write about the dangers of being an American in the Middle East in the early twenty-first century. You might have a hard time obtaining first-hand knowledge about this topic. However, reading in a newspaper about people who live there could give you information to support your ideas.

For instance, a writer who had not been in Iraq could still learn about life for Americans there by reading the newspaper.

> Americans are having difficulty living safely in Iraq these days. An article in the *New York Times* describes how resident Americans in Iraq have been kidnapped or killed in protest of the U.S. presence there. According to the article, even Americans who have bodyguards have been the victims of shootings and car bombs.

This student has not been to Iraq and may not know anyone who has been harmed there; however, by citing a prominent newspaper, he can write about the risks of being an American living in a country where some of the population doesn't welcome him.

For more information on doing research, see Chapters 30 and 31.

Possible Sources of Information

Reference books	Internet
Textbooks	Television
Magazines	Radio
Newspapers	Documentary films

Note: When you use information from other people's experiences, be sure to tell your reader where the information comes from. That way, your reader will not think you're trying to take credit for experiences you haven't had. Also, make sure that your source is credible. Stay away from unofficial documents that may not contain genuine information. Particularly on the Internet, be wary of sites that may be unreliable or outdated. For more on evaluating sources, see Chapter 30.

Knowing Which Details to Choose

One of the most important aspects of using specific details is knowing *which* details to use. For instance, if your assignment is to write about a childhood friend, you probably won't find many helpful details in a newspaper. Similarly, if your assignment is to write about a local news issue, your childhood experiences won't do you much good.

In choosing your specific details, then, *let your assignment determine what kinds of details to use.* Since you are familiar with your own experiences, use examples from your own life whenever you can to support your points. If, however, your life experiences don't address the topic or don't offer enough information, seek details from people you know and other trusted sources. Remember, you can always find information—you just have to know where to look!

EXERCISE 3 CHOOSING RELEVANT DETAILS

Below are possible topics for paragraphs. Decide what kind of details would be most helpful in a paragraph on each topic, and write "My life," "Someone I know," or "Trusted sources" in the space after each topic.

Examples: Health benefits of antioxidants _Trusted sources_

Benefits of going to college right after high school
My life; someone I know

1. Review of current book or movie _____

2. High cost of health care for
   seniors   _____

3. Cures for cancer   _____

4. Latest professional sports strikes _____
   or contracts

5. Benefits of taking early morning _____
   classes

EXERCISE 4 FINDING DETAILS FOR AN ESSAY

The following outline contains a thesis statement, topic sentences identifying support points, and clues as to where to find supporting details.

However, the outline does not contain specific details that support the topic sentences. Use the clues to fill in the supporting details. The first detail under every support point has been filled in for you.

Thesis statement: *People have mixed opinions about the new health-food store.*

A. *I think the organic fruits are a great bargain.*

   1. Example from my life: *I can get five pounds of fresh apples for just $5.*

   2. Example from my life: _____

   3. Example from my life: _____

B. *My friends think that the food is bland.*

   1. Example from someone I know: *My friend Hiro, who is vegan, says that he always craves salt after eating the store's bread.*

   2. Example from someone I know: _____

   3. Example from someone I know: _____

C. *The newspapers report that the store has little variety.*

1. Example from trusted sources: _Mick Donne of the Dixon Gazette_

   claims that the store offers little choice for the truly health-conscious,

   selling only one brand of each product.

2. Example from trusted sources: _____

   _____

   _____

3. Example from trusted sources: _____

   _____

   _____

EXERCISE 5 OFFERING SPECIFIC SUPPORT

Below is a list of topic sentences requiring specific details for support. Add three details to support each topic sentence. An example has been done for you.

Example: Superhero movies have become more popular over the past few years.

   After the Spider-Man movies, the little kids on my street

   dressed up as the web-spinning wonder for Halloween.

   Daredevil made blindness seem to be a strength.

   The Incredibles gave middle-aged parents hope for seeming "super" to their kids.

1. After exercising hard, Lindy looked as though she felt completely relaxed.

   _____

   _____

   _____

2. The old computer was frustrating to use.

3. She slept soundly.

4. The television news today was depressing.

5. Knowing how to _____ made my life easier yesterday.

6. Several students displayed strange habits during final exams last term.

Finding and Choosing Support Points

Somewhere in between writing your major point (your thesis statement) and your evidence for your point (your specific details) comes an essay element that is both general and specific: the support point. Support points are more specific than your thesis, but they are not specific enough to prove your ideas. Good support points organize your details into a manageable format and connect them to your thesis. A question arises, then: How does a writer know which support points to choose?

Doing Your Homework

Before deciding on your support points, learn about your topic. If your topic is based on experiences from your own life, you can choose support points without further research, but if you don't know much about your topic, it's dangerous to decide on support points before you've learned more. Reading the newspaper, online news, or magazines can be a good start toward educating yourself on your topic. Or, if you know someone more familiar with your topic than you are, an interview can be a good place to start. Either way, find out about your topic before plunging into your planning.

Doing Some Prewriting

Once you've done some reading about your topic, do some prewriting. For instance, Ray wanted to write about a recent tax increase to raise money for education, but since he had been working and, thus, paying taxes for only a few years, he wasn't sure he knew enough to offer an informed opinion. Ray preferred the prewriting method of listing, so after reading a few newspaper articles about the proposed tax increase, Ray made a list. He noticed that most of his list items relate to the idea of "schools need money," so he decided to focus on that. After crossing out items that didn't relate to the notion of schools needing money, Ray read over his final list.

Schools need repairs.

Schools need more teachers.

No one new hired in five years.

Many teachers face retirement.

~~Already too much money goes for taxes.~~

Schools need better technology options (computers).

~~Money may not be available until I'm done with school.~~

School roof leaks.

Outdated library holdings.

School heater breaks down every winter.

Students need online research access.

~~Too much homework.~~

From this list, three key areas—schools need money for repairs, for hiring teachers, and for improved campus technology—manifested themselves. Thus, Ray decided that these would be his support points for the general idea "Schools need money." After Ray wrote a rough draft, his working thesis read, "Residents of Solano County should pass Proposition 67 because schools are badly in need of funding for facilities repairs, hiring new faculty, and updating on-campus technology." The three areas that made themselves clear to him in prewriting eventually became Ray's support points.

   Note: Three equally important support points will not always emerge from your prewriting. That's OK. Once you decide on one or two reasons for supporting your main idea, you can focus your thinking and writing to come up with more support points.

EXERCISE 6 FINDING AND CHOOSING SUPPORT POINTS

The following thesis statements need support points. Write three possible support points for each one. An example has been done for you. Feel free to do some prewriting to get ideas for support points.

Example: The owners of professional sports teams should pay their athletes generous salaries.

Most athletes have short careers.

Many sports have a high risk of injury to the players.

The "best of the best" in other fields earn high salaries.

1. College students should/should not (choose one) be required to learn a second language.

_____

_____

_____

2. Using a credit card often can have negative consequences.

_____

_____

_____

3. Declaring a major as a first-year college student has many benefits/drawbacks (choose one).

_____

_____

_____

4. People should wait until they have finished school before getting married.

_____

_____

_____

5. The Internet has many benefits/drawbacks (choose one).

_____

_____

_____

Distinguishing Support Points from Specific Details

Very often during prewriting or drafting, you will think of both support points and specific details. This is primarily positive, but it can be confusing if you're not sure which is which. In general, the more specific a piece of information is—the smaller the range of time or behavior it covers, for instance—the more likely it is to be a specific detail. Consider the following items.

Thesis statement:	Focusing on one activity too early in life can have negative consequences.

Support Points	**Specific Details**
Lack of exposure to other activities	Playing competitive soccer at age ten prevented me from trying other sports or pastimes such as playing a musical instrument.
Risk of early burnout	Having to focus on basketball caused local hoops star Romel to lose interest at age fifteen.
Risk of injury	Working too hard to develop one set of muscles for football caused Brett to injure himself in high school.

Notice that each of the support points could apply to a number of people while the specific details cover just one person or situation at a time. When trying to decide whether an idea is a support point or a specific detail, consider whether or not it can apply to more than one case. If it can, then it's probably a support point.

EXERCISE 7 IDENTIFYING SUPPORT POINTS

In the list below, write an X in the blank before each idea that a support point.

Thesis: Local college students have become socially active in a number of ways.

_____ Selling entertainment books to raise money for children's home

_____ Picketing outside the state capitol to protest budget cuts

_____ Publicly voicing their views

_____ Taking steps to encourage people to vote

_____ Working at local polls

_____ Going from door to door to get out the vote

_____ Holding on-campus rallies to discuss issues

_____ Raising money for specific causes

_____ Making phone calls to request donations

Appeal to the Senses

In addition to proving your point, specific details make your writing more interesting. After all, would you want to read about going to bed when you can write about pouring yourself into a soft nest of smooth, cool, lilac-scented linens? Use your words to paint a picture for your reader, and your reader will *want* to read on to find out what juicy detail you offer next.

Additionally, vivid descriptions lend credibility to your writing. If you're writing about your fear of bees, for instance, but all you can say is "I'm afraid of bees," your reader can't *see* how afraid you are. If, on the other hand, you write about your sweaty palms, pounding heart, and dizziness at the sight of a bee, your reader will most likely acknowledge your fear.

Writing Vivid Details

Often the details we use to support a point in writing could be more convincing if they were more specific. For instance, if you're writing about how cold you were one winter, you'll probably make your point better if you mention your blue lips, ice-crusted eyelashes, and numb fingers than if you just say, "I was really cold." By giving specific, vivid details to *show* your reader the extent of your discomfort, you keep your reader from wondering what, exactly, you mean.

One way to make your ideas clear to your reader is to use **specific words.** Specific words offer your reader a clear view of what you are describing. The list below shows the difference between some general and specific words.

General Words	Specific Words
run	jog, trot, gallop, sprint
bread	whole wheat, sourdough, institutional white
noodle	rice noodle, udon, linguine
song	"My Country 'Tis of Thee," "Stacy's Mom"
looked	glanced, peeked, viewed, studied, stared, glared
game	Monopoly, Chutes and Ladders, charades

Using specific words in a sentence can make its meaning clear and powerful.

General Sentence	Specific Sentence
I exercised hard.	I did bench-press exercises until my pectoral muscles burned, and then ran up and down the stadium stairs for an hour.
He looked mean.	His pale blue eyes stared coldly as his mouth twisted itself downward, and the jagged scar along his jawline throbbed with evil purpose.
The movie was funny.	After one scene, my gut hurt from laughing and my cheeks ached from smiling.

EXERCISE 8 WRITING SPECIFIC WORDS

The following list contains details that could be more specific. After each general detail, write a more specific version. An example has been done for you.

Example: injury _gaping, bloody gash_____

1. phone _____

2. cookie _____

3. doctor _____

4. art _____

5. politician _____

6. church _____

Using Specific Verbs

Another way to make your language more vivid is to make your verbs more specific. Rather than write that you "traveled," write that you "roamed the state in search of cheap truck-stop bacon." Or, instead of saying that you "built furniture," write that you "handcrafted a rocking chair, shaping and sanding the wood until it was smooth." The more specific you can make your verbs, the better your reader will understand your meaning.

EXERCISE 9 PRACTICE WRITING SPECIFIC VERBS

The following is a list of verbs that could be more effective if they were more specific. In the space after each word, write *either* a more vivid verb *or* the verb with a modifier. The modifier can be either a word or a group of words. An example has been done for you.

Examples: breathe _snort_____

   drank _sipped daintily_____

1. threw   _____

2. sang _____

3. sat _____

4. hear _____

5. play _____

WRITING PRACTICE Supporting an Assertion

You've read about different types of support as well as different ways to make your language more effective. Now it's time to practice the art of supporting an assertion. Below are ten general statements which can serve as thesis statements. Your assignment is this: *Write a short essay supporting or refuting one of the following statements (or one of your own, if you'd rather). Try to use all three types of specific details—your own experiences, someone else's experiences, information from trusted sources—to support your point. Be as specific as possible.*

The best friendships are/are not relatively the same over the years.

The best friendships do/do not contain an element of competition.

The hardest jobs to work at for long periods of time are those that

_____.

The easiest jobs to get are those that _____.

Having a single focus—such as only school or only work—is the way to
    achieve success.

Having many, varied interests and responsibilities—such as school, work,
    and various relationships—is the best way to achieve success.

The hobby of _____ requires more than just interest.

Playing _____ requires certain specific skills.

Tips for Writing Specific Details

1. **Use specific names.** Instead of simply mentioning "a guy," write about "Carlitos Sanchez." Or if you're writing about your childhood bike, refer to your Trek mountain bike. Using proper nouns narrows your description dramatically.

General	Specific
I hate that song.	Bob Dylan's Song "Blowin' in the Wind" sounds as if a goose somehow got hold of a kazoo.
He eats unusual lunches.	For lunch, Kenny typically eats an entire loaf of San Luis sourdough stuffed with one pound of sliced Tillamook sharp cheddar and washed down with a gallon of lukewarm original-flavor Gatorade.
That woman's voice sounds nice.	Diana Krall's luxuriously supple alto voice complements her soulful torch songs.

2. **Use descriptive words.** Place descriptive words before nouns. Writing about "the crystal-clear lake" gives your reader a much better idea of what you saw than simply referring to "the lake." If you're describing an action, modifiers help, too. Rather than writing that your friend was "in a hurry," write that he "immediately sped away from muggers."

General	Specific
She signed her name.	With a flourish of black ink on white paper, she scrawled her signature in bold script.
He spilled soup.	He accidentally tipped his bowl, causing slimy, steaming noodles to slither onto the table.
Jerry walked heavily.	Jerry stomped across the newly vacuumed carpet, leaving deep impressions of his elephantine feet.

3. **Use words that appeal to the five senses (hearing, taste, smell, touch, sight).** The best way to help someone understand what you've experienced is to make your writing as close to a physical experience as possible. Using words that help your reader hear, taste, smell, feel, and see what you're describing will make your points more vivid for readers. Saying that your shirt is "itchy" is a good start, but saying that your shirt "chafes like coarse sandpaper" is better. Your reader will immediately know that the shirt feels itchy *and* just how uncomfortably itchy it is.

General	Specific
Her singing needed improvement.	The sounds coming from her open mouth resembled my rabbit's scream upon being cornered by a toddler.
Sonny's jeans were tight.	After lying down and inhaling to zip the jeans, Sonny was disheartened to find that he couldn't breathe.
The driver braked in traffic.	With a screech of tires on asphalt, the driver spun the wheel to narrowly avoid missing the minivan in front of him.

Lab Activity 9

For additional practice with supporting your ideas, complete Lab Activity 9 in the lab manual packaged with your textbook. If you did not receive a lab manual, you can complete this activity online at **www.ablongman.com/long.** Click on **College Resources for Writers** and then click on **Activity 9.**

10 Organizing and Linking Ideas

American Outlaws

Not so much famous as infamous, these men and women made their marks through the unfortunate, and sometimes cruel, treatment of their fellow human beings. Driven by visions of freedom, grandeur, and wealth, outlaws wrote themselves into history through extreme means.

Bonnie and Clyde

JOURNAL ENTRY The entertainment media frequently portray outlaws and other lawbreakers as attractive, glamorous people. Additionally, famous athletes are often given lucrative advertising contracts despite their illegal or unethical behavior. Should famous people be glamorized or rewarded, even if their fame comes from negative acts? Write a few sentences explaining your thoughts on this.

Arranging the Pieces

As you've been reading different examples of effective writing in this book, you've seen that the way ideas are put together is important in making the writing clear. Additionally, you've seen how transitional words can link ideas together, creating connections between the topic sentence, support points, and specific details.

Organizing for Clarity

We've all had someone tell us, "Your idea is great, but. . . " When we hear that one little word—*but*—we immediately know that bad news is coming. How do we know? We know because *but* is one of those words that signal a change of direction. If the person talking to you starts with a good point, such as by telling you that your idea is great, using *but* tells you that something bad is coming. *But* is just one of many transition words that indicate the direction we're going in our writing.

Coming up with a solid thesis statement and finding the support points and details to support it is an important writing skill. Next, you need to practice organizing your ideas so that your reader will know just which ones are most important to you. You also need to link your ideas.

Transitions are words, expressions, or sentences that help your reader understand when you're adding to a point, changing directions, or finishing up. Linking your ideas so that your reader can understand their connection to each other and using transition words to signal these connections will help you improve your writing skills to master the third of the Four Cs: clear writing.

Three Types of Order

As long as your reader can follow the logic of your ideas, you don't need to worry about forcing your ideas into a specific order. However, these general strategies for linking your ideas can make logical connections easier.

- Chronological order
- Spatial order
- Emphatic order

Chronological Order   **Chronological order** indicates that events are linked according to the order in which they happened. The chronological, or time sequence, strategy often crops up in topics whose examples occur over a specific period of time. Time sequence is also logical in explaining how something happened or for anything that must be explained in sequence. The ideas in the following paragraph are linked through time sequence order.

Hero or Hellion?

A hero of the Confederacy, William Quantrill made his mark as a guerrilla warrior in the Civil War. Born in 1837, Quantrill led a quiet early life and worked as a schoolteacher for several years. In 1858, Quantrill began showing a predisposition for excitement when he moved to Utah and made a living as a gambler. In late 1860, wanted for murder and horse theft, Quantrill fled to Missouri. Zealously entering the Civil War on the Confederate side, he became the leader of Quantrill's Raiders, a small unit of fewer than a dozen men who used guerilla tactics to harass Union sympathizers along the Kansas-Missouri border. Soon, Quantrill was labeled "outlaw" by Union forces. Quantrill's career peaked on August 21, 1863, when he led 450 raiders into Lawrence, Kansas, to try to kill pro-Union Senator James H. Lane. Though Lane escaped, Quantrill's Raiders killed 183 men—slaughtering them in front of their families—and set fire to the city. Union Jayhawkers, or Northern guerrilla troops, wrought revenge on Confederate supporters for the Lawrence Massacre, and Quantrill retaliated. However, Quantrill eventually fled to Texas and was killed on a raid in Kentucky in 1865. Quantrill's fame outlived him as several former Raiders, including outlaw Jesse James, applied the group's famous hit-and-run tactics to crimes throughout the late 1860s.

EXERCISE 1 RECOGNIZING CHRONOLOGICAL ORDER

Dates mentioned in "Hero or Hellion?"—such as 1858—indicate the start of new support points. What other signals let you know that the examples in the paragraph follow chronological order? *Note:* Not all the signals are years.

————, ————, ————, ————, ————, ————

————

Emphatic Order   **Emphatic order** indicates that ideas are linked according to which ones are most important. Emphatic order allows for more flexibility than time sequence because you as the writer get to decide which points are least or more important. It's possible that two people could organize the same subject matter completely differently using emphatic order because they see different points as being more or less important. The following paragraph demonstrates emphatic order.

Portrait of an Outlaw

According to *Merriam-Webster Online,* an outlaw is "a person excluded from the benefit or protection of the law" or "a lawless person or a fugitive from the law." However, several aspects of a person's behavior make him or her an outlaw. First, the person must be a bit flashy. Horse thief Belle Starr, for instance, showed her flash by dressing in velvet and feathers or buckskin and moccasins, and she participated glibly (and successfully) in her own legal defense. A second characteristic commonly displayed by outlaws is a willingness to commit extreme acts. For example, Bonnie Parker and Clyde Barrow—the infamous Bonnie and Clyde—committed at least thirteen murders while pursuing their goals of bank robbery and avoiding arrest. Probably the most important characteristic of an outlaw is disregard for any law or life other than his or her own. William H. Bonney, commonly known as Billy the Kid, became famous for his apparent thirst for murder. Supposedly killing his first man at age twelve, Bonney killed at least twenty-one men—one for every year of his life—before finally being gunned down. Though outlaws come in different forms, the qualities of flash, extremism, and lawlessness are common in many.

This writer organizes her ideas beginning with the point that is least important to her topic sentence and ending with the one that is most important. What's critical to realize, however, is that though this writer thinks that lawlessness most significantly defines an outlaw, another writer might think that a willingness to commit extreme acts is most important.

As a writer, you are in charge of ranking your support points. Just be sure that your transitions and examples make clear why you've placed your support points in the order you have. Be aware, too, that you may not be certain about the arrangement of your support points and details until you're far into your drafting. The idea you feel most strongly about at the start of your essay may eventually seem less important; thus, you shouldn't feel locked in by a particular order at any point in the writing process.

EXERCISE 2 RECOGNIZING EMPHATIC ORDER

Read "Portrait of an Outlaw" again. Then, answer the questions below.

1. What is the writer's topic sentence? _____

_____

2. What is the writer's first point? _____

_____

3. What is the writer's second point? _____

_____

4. What is the writer's most important point? _____

_____

5. Do you agree with the writer's idea about which point is the most

important? Why or why not? _____

_____

Spatial Order   Some topics lend themselves to spatial organization, where the order of your points lets your reader see a person, object, or setting exactly as you perceive it. For instance, in using **spatial order** to describe a person, you'd most likely begin with the top of his or her head and describe the rest of the body down to the feet. You could jump around in your description and mention how the person's hands appear right after describing the nose, but doing this would make it difficult for your reader to form a mental picture of the subject. Some other methods of spatial order include bottom to top, front to back, back to front, left to right, right to left, near to far, far to near, inside to outside, or outside to inside. See what patterns, if any, emerge from your prewriting, and then use transitions to indicate how your ideas are linked. The following paragraph is organized using spatial order.

The Kid from Top to Toe

To see him stand and look at you, you'd never think he'd be a threat. His dark crumpled hat sits askew on top of his slightly cocked head, and his eyes seem unfocused above a partially open mouth. No words issue from his mouth, so you have a chance to see the poor teeth, crooked and yellow, from between the parted, cracked lips. His clothes don't seem to be anything serious, either, more like a clown get-up than an outlaw's. From underneath a dark jacket appears a lighter vest, covering vast ties hanging around his neck, and a shirt whose color is indistinguishable from all the dust ground into it. The baggy layers hang heavily, giving his body a rounded, bottom-heavy appearance. His seemingly soft waist is encircled by a belt with a silver buckle that gathers his loose-fitting dark trousers before they're stuffed into worn, creased boots. No, from the looks of him, you'd think he was just someone's neglected son or brother. The only thing making him dangerous is the rifle he holds in his left hand, butt touching the ground lightly in front of him, as if providing a rest for its owner's hand. Combined with the comfortable slouch of its handler, even the rifle seems safe. Until you hear him say his name is Billy, you'd never think a thing.

EXERCISE 3 RECOGNIZING SPATIAL ORDER

Answer the questions below.

1. What spatial direction does the writer use to describe her subject?

_____

_____

2. List in order at least four details that illustrate the spatial order the writer uses. _____

_____

3. Write at least three words indicating the spatial order the writer

uses. _____

_____

The box on pages 164–165 lists transitional words and terms. Become familiar with these lists so that you can use these terms effectively in your own writing. Keep in mind that transition words can come in the middle of a sentence and that they can introduce details as well as support points.

Transitional Words and Terms

Words That Signal Time and Time Sequence

after	finally	shortly afterward
at last	first, second, third	soon
at the same time	immediately	subsequently
before	later	then
during	meanwhile	when
earlier	next	while

Words and Terms That Signal Emphatic Order

above all	first	most important
another	in the first place	most significantly
equally important	last	next
especially	least of all	
even more	most of all	

Words and Terms That Signal Addition

additionally	for another thing	next
again	for one thing	second
also	furthermore	then
and	in addition	third
besides	last of all	too
first of all	moreover	

Words and Terms That Signal Space

above	here	on the other side
across	in back of	opposite
before	in front of	there
behind	nearby to the left	to the East (North, etc.)
below	next to	to the right
elsewhere		

Words and Terms That Signal Examples

an illustration of	one example of	such as
for example	particularly	that is
for instance	specifically	

(continued)

Words and Terms That Signal Change of Direction

although	in contrast	regardless
but	nevertheless	still
despite	on the contrary	though
even though	on the other hand	yet
however	otherwise	

Words and Terms That Signal Conclusion

as a result	in conclusion	then
consequently	in summary	therefore
finally	last	thus

EXERCISE 4 CHOOSING EFFECTIVE TRANSITIONS

Write an effective transition in each blank.

Outlaw Aspirations

I've always wanted to be an outlaw because their daring feats and exciting lives appealed to me. _____, I can't stand the thought of hurting anyone or firing a gun, _____ I haven't had much luck in following in outlaws' footsteps despite numerous tries. _____, I saw movies about outlaws, such as *Butch Cassidy and the Sundance Kid* and *Bonnie and Clyde.* I was suspicious about how realistic the movies were when I saw how good-looking Butch, Sundance, Bonnie, and Clyde were, _____ I decided not to let a little thing like my looks interfere with my ambition. _____ in the movies, I realized that all the outlaws died young, _____ I began to rethink my goals. _____, I read the legends of other outlaws such as Jesse

James and Belle Starr. I was amazed at how many outlaws or their relatives served in Quantrill's Raiders, _____ I was also a bit discouraged because it seemed as though some type of guerrilla training was important for outlaw life. _____ I had no such training, I began to see my outlaw dreams evaporate. _____, I tried to dress the part of an outlaw. Unfortunately, my rain boots were a poor substitute for cowboy boots, _____ I didn't enjoy the hot, sweaty feeling of wearing a hat or mask. _____, I gave up my life-long dream.

Combining Organizing Strategies

Sometimes your ideas will lend themselves to more than one organizational strategy at the same time. For example, in "The Kid from Top to Toe" (page 162), the writer uses the spatial method of organization—moving from top to bottom—to describe Billy the Kid. However, the writer saves the rifle—the only potentially dangerous detail in the paragraph—for her last point, and she indicates its importance by writing "The only thing" before introducing it. In neutralizing the potential danger of the rifle by describing its "resting" position, the writer strengthens her position that the subject of the paragraph does not appear threatening. Thus, you can use spatial or chronological order in your paragraph but still save the most important reason—a characteristic of emphatic order—for last.

Using Transitional Sentences

Sometimes, particularly when writing essays, you'll need more than a word or two to connect paragraphs or ideas. In these cases, transitional sentences—sentences that bridge ideas—are helpful. Transitional sentences should link one idea to the next while maintaining a connection to the thesis. The following sentence comes from the essay "Pretty Boy Floyd" in Exercise 5. It links the first body paragraph to the thesis statement.

Charles is probably most famous for his crime.

Notice how the writer uses the words *famous* and *crime* in his transitional sentence to echo the thesis but also focus the support paragraph on one specific aspect of his thesis.

EXERCISE 5 **WRITING TRANSITIONAL SENTENCES**

Write transitional sentences in the spaces provided in the essay below.
The first one has been done for you.

Pretty Boy Floyd

Born in 1904, Charles Arthur Floyd, also known as Pretty Boy
Floyd, was one of seven children in a poor family. Moving from
Georgia to Oklahoma when Charles was small, the family attempted
unsuccessfully to support themselves through farming. Numerous
natural obstacles such as dust storms prevented the family from
prospering, and they turned eventually to bootlegging. Unbe-
knownst to his family or the world at large, Charles would emerge
from poverty to a life of bad deeds, where he became known for his
crime, his personality, and his relentlessness.

Charles is probably most famous for his crime.
_____

Though he tried to earn an honest living, the great Oklahoma
dust bowl ensured that no jobs were available, and Charles bought
his first gun at age eighteen. According to geocities.com, his crimes
ranged from a bank robbery in which he stole $350 in pennies to a
store robbery in which he stole $16,000. Over a twelve-year period,
Charles robbed thirty banks and killed ten people. During this crime
spree, he gained the name "Pretty Boy" from a brothel madam, and
his fame increased.

_____

Folktales refer to Charles as a sagebrush Robin Hood who
robbed from rich banks and gave groceries to the poor. This nickname came in part from his habit of tearing up mortgages during
bank robberies, thus saving debt-burdened landowners from potential ruin. Further, according to Encarta.com, Charles had great style,
even in his crimes. He was unfailingly courteous and well-groomed
during robberies—a true gentleman, according to some victims—
and his fun-loving personality kept him popular with friends.
Though his means of self-support was illegal, Charles maintained a
sense of charity, style, and fun throughout his career.

_____

According to biography.com, upon hearing that a man had threatened his father, Charles tracked down and killed a man accused of
but later acquitted of killing his father. Additionally, though he was
tried, convicted, and sent to prison for his crimes, Charles jumped

out the window of a moving train on his way to prison in an attempt to avoid his penalty. A last exploit that showed his "never say die" mentality came when Charles was cornered by police. Charles leaped from a moving car and ran, only to be shot in the arm. Charles kept moving but was shot again, this time in the shoulder. Stopping only after being shot at by numerous law-enforcement agents, Charles died within minutes, having fallen for good. His perseverance in righting perceived wrongs and staying free added to his fame.

Although he became Public Enemy No. 1 after John Dillinger's capture, Pretty Boy Floyd was well loved. According to geocities.com, as many as ten thousand people came to view his body before it was sent back to Oklahoma, where twenty thousand are said to have attended his funeral, and his life has been immortalized in Woody Guthrie's song "Pretty Boy Floyd." Though Charles is most commonly labeled an outlaw, his style and determination made him something of a folk hero.

EXERCISE 6 PRACTICING PUTTING IDEAS IN ORDER

The following groups of sentences make up short paragraphs. However, the sentences are out of order. Put the sentences in order by writing 1 in the space before the sentence that should come first (the topic sentence), 2 by the next sentence, and so forth.

1. a. _____ Whatever others called him, Jesse James was only human.

   b. _____ For his reputed kindness to women and the poor, James earned the title Robin Hood.

   c. _____ Many labels have been given to Jesse James.

   d. _____ A third title, however, is not as positive: some modern historians call him a terrorist.

   e. _____ One label, outlaw, is probably the most common.

2. a. _____ Other outlaws who died in violence were Bonnie and Clyde, who were betrayed by a friend and killed in a police roadblock in Louisiana.

   b. _____ Billy the Kid, for one, was shot and killed by Sheriff Pat Garrett.

c. _____ Last, Jesse James was murdered by his own gang member, Robert Ford.

d. _____ Most outlaws seem to die violent deaths.

e. _____ Even Ma Barker was killed by the FBI in a bloody gun battle.

3. a. _____ One factor contributing to her reputation came in the form of her love affairs, supposedly with Thomas Coleman Younger, James H. Reed, Sam Starr, and Jim July.

b. _____ Belle Starr died with a colorful reputation.

c. _____ Third, Belle Starr was known to steal horses and harbor outlaws.

d. _____ Finally, even when arrested, Belle's reputation flourished as she eloquently defended herself in court.

e. _____ Her preferred fashion mode, rich velvet and feathers, also contributed to her reputation.

Other Ways to Link Ideas

Aside from using transitions, three other strategies are helpful in linking your ideas.

- Repeating key words
- Using pronouns
- Using synonyms

Repeating Key Words

Repeating key words involves using important words related to your topic again and again throughout your writing. When used in moderation, this can be an effective technique to keep your reader on track.

For instance, read the following paragraph and pay attention to how often a form of the word *outlaw* is used.

The Outlaw Look

[1]Regardless of their crimes, <u>outlaws</u> seem to be portrayed by extremely attractive stars in movies about their lives. [2]For instance,

in the movie *Butch Cassidy and the Sundance Kid,* the two main outlaws are played by Paul Newman and Robert Redford, two of the biggest heartthrobs of their time. [3]Similarly, in *Bonnie and Clyde,* the exquisite Faye Dunaway and hunky Warren Beatty are cast as the outlaws of that film. [4]Outlaw Jesse James isn't neglected in terms of the actors who play him, either. [5]In the 1957 film *The True Story of Jesse James,* Robert Wagner—generally acknowledged as being very handsome—portrays the outlaw, and later the film *American Outlaws* features appealing actor Colin Farrell as the famous outlaw. [6]Probably it's not true that every famous outlaw had supermodel looks, but it sure seems as though Hollywood wants us to think so.

Using Pronouns

Another way to help your reader stay focused on your topic is to use pronouns. In taking the place of nouns, pronouns offer a more efficient and often less boring way to link ideas.

EXERCISE 7 IDENTIFYING PRONOUNS FOR COHERENCE

In the paragraph below, pay attention to how the pronouns *he* and *his* replace the words *Fisher* and *Fisher's.* Circle each pronoun referring to Fisher or his characteristics or property. You will find nine such pronouns.

Fisher's Law

[1]Outlaw, rancher, and lawman John King Fisher was born in Collin County in 1854, the son of Joby and Lucinda (Warren) Fisher. [2]In 1869 Fisher was accused of stealing a horse after he borrowed it without telling the owner. [3]He was arrested by a posse but reportedly escaped. [4]Fisher made his way to Goliad, where he was arrested again, this time for housebreaking, and sent to prison. [5]After being pardoned four months later, he moved to Dimmit County and established a ranch on Pendencia Creek. [6]Fisher, relying on both patronage and intimidation, quickly established himself as one of the leaders of the area, and ranch became a haven for drifters, criminals, and rustlers in the region. [7]In the section where he reigned, Fisher was feared and respected. [8]A certain road

branch bore the sign "This is King Fisher's road. Take the other."
[9]Fisher reportedly placed the sign to distinguish between his private
road and the public road, but many at the time viewed it as evidence
of the extent of his power and control.

Using Synonyms

Using **synonyms,** or words that have the same meaning, can also help your
reader follow your ideas while adding variety to your writing. If you find
you have repeated the same word too many times, think of others you can
use in its place.

EXERCISE 8 USING SYNONYMS

Read the following paragraph, which is another version of "The Outlaw
Look" (page 170). In the original version, forms of the word *outlaw*
appeared eight times; in this version, however, other words replace the
word *outlaw* in some places. Fill in the blanks below.

The Outlaw Look

[1]Regardless of their crimes, outlaws seem to be portrayed by
extremely attractive stars in movies about their lives. [2]For instance,
in the movie *Butch Cassidy and the Sundance Kid,* the two main ban-
dits were played by Paul Newman and Robert Redford, two of the
biggest heartthrobs of their time. [3]Similarly, in *Bonnie and Clyde,*
the exquisite Faye Dunaway and hunky Warren Beatty were cast as
the outlaws. [4]Desperado Jesse James hasn't been neglected in terms
of the actors who play him, either. [5]In the 1957 film *The True Story
of Jesse James,* Robert Wagner—generally acknowledged as being
very handsome—portrayed the gunslinger, and the more recent film
American Outlaws featured the appealing actor Colin Farrell as the
famous robber. [6]Probably it's not true that every famous bandit had
supermodel looks, but it sure seems as though Hollywood wants us
to think so.

1. What word does the writer use to replace *outlaws* in sentence 2?

2. This word is also used to replace *outlaws* in sentence _____.

3. What words does the writer use to replace *outlaws* in sentence 5?

_____

4. What is another word used in place of *outlaw?* _____

5. How many times does a form of the word *outlaw* appear in this

version of the paragraph, including the title? _____

Planning Your Essay

Before you decide on a hard-and-fast organizational strategy for your essay, think about what method your topic lends itself to. For instance, if you were writing about why a particular day was terrible, you could use emphatic order to discuss the reasons why it was so bad. However, a narrative topic—in which events occur over a set period of time—would probably fit more easily into a chronological format. Finally, spatial order would be most effective if the topic under discussion lends itself to description, such as an account of a senior citizens' home to illustrate poor living conditions. There is no rule dictating certain organizational strategies for certain topics, but some strategies are generally easier to use with specific types of topics.

In planning your own essay, first do some prewriting to determine the focus of your topic and identify some support points and details. Adrian wanted to write about the reasons why some people became outlaws. After doing some freewriting, Adrian realized that three primary elements factored into people's decisions or actions toward attaining outlaw status after the Civil War: political discontent (usually against the Union), lack of marketable skills, and an affinity for violence.

While reading to find support for his topic, Adrian learned that nearly every subject he studied had an appreciation, if not an actual thirst, for violence while not every outlaw had his or her start in political rebellion. Thus, he decided to use emphatic order and make "thirst for violence" his last and most important point. An outline of Adrian's essay follows.

Thesis statement: Though each outlaw's story is unique, many outlaws were drawn into their violent lifestyle through political rebellion, a lack of useful skills, or a thirst for excitement or violence.

A. Political rebellion

   1. William Quantrill formed Quantrill's Raiders as a Confederate guerrilla group.

   2. Jesse James joined Quantrill's Raiders.

   3. Belle Starr supported her brothers, who joined Quantrill's Raiders.

B. Lack of marketable skills

   1. Ma Barker needed support after she was widowed.

   2. Bonnie and Clyde didn't hold down "real" jobs.

   3. Butch Cassidy and Sundance bounced from crime to crime.

C. Thirst for excitement or violence

   1. Quantrill could have been a teacher, but he preferred guerrilla warfare and gambling.

   2. Butch Cassidy chose to join the infamous Wild Bunch in his thirties after serving prison time.

   3. Billy the Kid was known for his love of murder.

In using emphatic order, Adrian placed his most important point—thirst for excitement or violence—last. Though his other two support points are important, Adrian saved his strongest point for the end.

WRITING PRACTICE Organize Your Own Essay Topic

You've had a chance to practice recognizing organizational strategies and transitional words. Now it's time to practice using them in your own writing.

Your assignment is this: *Plan an essay arguing that outlaws, or other lawbreakers, should or should not be written about.* Your topic may include movie stars or actors who have broken the law, or it may include serial killers. The key idea to discuss is whether or not people who have broken society's laws should be remembered by journalists or historians.

Follow these steps to plan your essay.

   1. Use one or more of the prewriting techniques you've learned to come up with ideas for your essay.

2. Write a clear thesis statement.

3. Use your notes from prewriting to develop support points and details.

4. Make sure to place your ideas in a logical order—either by time sequence, emphatic, or spatial order.

5. When you're finished, your plan should include

- A clear thesis statement
- Support points that relate to the topic sentence
- Specific details that give proof of your support points
- A solid organizational structure

Lab Activity 10

For additional practice with organizing and linking ideas, complete Lab Activity 10 in the lab manual packaged with your textbook. If you did not receive a lab manual, you can complete this activity online at **www.ablongman.com/long.** Click on **College Resources for Writers** and then click on **Activity 10.**

11 Sensitive Language

Hockey

Though its exact origins are unclear, hockey is believed to have originated in the colder climates of Northern Europe sometime in the 1500s. Played on ice with a stick and a puck—a frozen rubber disk—hockey has become popular worldwide. Particularly in the United States, however, hockey has a darker side: even as players strive to exhibit skill for their teams' sake, they may be the victims—or agents—of the sport's roughness.

Miracle

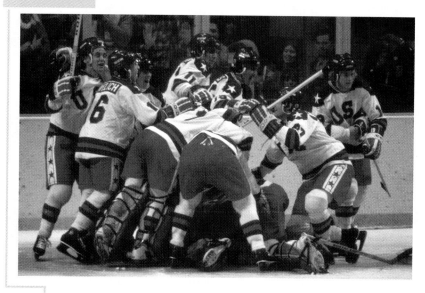

OBSERVE YOUR WORLD The great underdogs of the Lake Placid Olympics, the 1980 U.S. Hockey team shocked the world by beating the mighty USSR team in the semi-finals and the Finland team in the finals. What examples of a victorious "little guy," or underdog, are you familiar with? Observe your neighborhood, city, or state and write a few sentences about a situation where the person or team not favored to succeed does.

175

What Is Sensitive Language?

You probably know that some language—such as profanity or slang—is inappropriate in certain situations. Using a four-letter word during a job interview, for instance, would most likely not make the best impression on most employers. Similarly, saying that women are not as smart as men might offend the people you're speaking to. Using **sensitive language,** or language that is free from stereotypes and ethnic or gender slurs, helps you make your point effectively while keeping your readers open to what you have to say.

Using Sensitive Language

Most people have heard stories about "ditzy blonds" or "dumb jocks," and you have probably used a few generalizations to lump people together in your mind. While these generalizations might seem harmless, they can be hurtful. In general, follow these rules in your writing.

- Don't exclude people.
- Don't make assumptions about groups of people.
- Don't call people by names they do not choose for themselves.
- Don't assume that all members of a group are the same.
- Don't mention a person's race, sex, age, sexual orientation, disability, or religion unnecessarily.

Don't Exclude People

Years ago, people who published articles, stories, and essays used the pronouns *he, his,* and *him* to mean "he or she," his or her," and "him and her." Similarly, writers would write *man* and mean "all humans." While most men had no trouble with these terms, many women came to feel excluded by them. Within the past few decades, both readers and writers have become more sensitive to gender. Now, instead of writing "Man has made great progress in many areas," writers say, "People have made great progress in many areas." Thus, women are represented as well as men.

You can use one of the two following methods to include both genders in your writing.

1. Use *he or she* or *she or he* (and *his or her, her or his, him or her, her or him*).

   Insensitive: The most important piece of equipment for a hockey player is his stick.

This sentence communicates that only men participate in hockey.

Better: The most important piece of equipment for hockey play-
                 ers is their sticks.

This sentence leaves room for both men and women in the game.

2. Use a plural noun such as *people, persons,* or *humans.*

Insensitive: Those who don't enjoy hockey complain of being "hockey
                 widows" when the season starts.

This sentence incorrectly implies that only women don't enjoy hockey;
it also unfairly limits the discussion to married women by using the
term *widows.*

Better: Some people who don't enjoy hockey complain of being
                 abandoned by their friends when the season starts.

By using the plural noun *people,* this sentence includes both genders.

The following terms are generally considered acceptable by the groups they
refer to. Keep in mind that the more specific the term, the better. For instance,
referring to a group of Southeast Asian people as *Vietnamese, Hmong,* or
Laotian is better than simply calling them *Asian.*

African-American or black	disabled (*not* handicapped)
Asian	Indian (for people from India)
Caucasian or white	Latino, Latina
Native American (for people indigenous to the United States)	

Don't Make Assumptions About Groups of People

Even though it's easy to make assumptions about groups or individuals, it's
insensitive and unfair to do so. For instance, assuming that only a man
would want to watch the Stanley Cup finals leaves out the possibility that
a woman would want to watch. With the advent of Title IX, more women
and girls are not only interested in, but participating in, hockey; thus,
assuming that they lack interest in its championship is both insensitive and
incorrect. Always consider that your reader may not feel as you do, and
choose your words accordingly.

To avoid making assumptions, ask yourself the following questions.

1. Does my description really apply to everyone in a group?

2. Could someone whom my description does *not* fit feel offended?

If you can answer "yes" to the first question and "no" to the second, your language is probably safe. Otherwise, think of ways to change it.

Don't Call People by Names They Do Not Choose for Themselves

Giving people nicknames comes naturally to many people. The woman named Elizabeth easily gets called "Liz" while the man named Michael often goes by "Mike." Not all nicknames are insensitive or offensive, but some are. Calling someone named after his father "Junior" instead of his given name, for instance, may offend him if he wishes to establish his own identity. The key to using sensitive language is to let people choose what they wish to be called. Respecting people's right to answer to names of their choosing is an important way to show sensitivity.

Letting people choose their own names applies to groups as well as individuals. For instance, while the term *Oriental* was once commonly used to identify people of Asian descent, it is no longer the term of choice. Instead, the term *Asian* is generally considered to be respectful.

To avoid offending people by using names or group affiliations they may not choose for themselves, do the following:

1. Find out what people prefer to be called. If you're not sure whether to use the term *Hispanic* or *Latino* in one of your papers, do some research or ask your instructor for the preferred term.

2. Pay attention to how people are addressed. Even if you're comfortable calling people by their first names, see how people prefer to be addressed. If everyone calls your boss Ms. Smith, for instance, you should probably call her that, too. In your writing, if you are quoting from a source that identifies someone as Mr. Jones, you should identify him the same way.

Note: Preferences can vary from group to group and from place to place. In addition, sometimes members of a particular group will refer to themselves by a name that they do not wish others to use. A man might talk about going to "boys' night out," but that doesn't mean he wants to be called "boy." Pay attention to what people *prefer* to be called even if that isn't what they call themselves.

Don't Assume That All Members of a Group Are the Same

It's unfair and inaccurate to assume that members of a group are all the same. "Teenagers are emotional and irritable" might apply to some members of that group, but it certainly doesn't apply to everyone from age thirteen to nineteen. Because it's almost impossible to say that all members of a group are a certain way all the time, it's best to avoid generalizations and stereotypes altogether.

To avoid stereotyping, do the following:

1. Look for one exception to the claim you want to make. If even one person doesn't fit the description you offer, don't use it.

2. Avoid using absolute labels such as *all, none, always,* and *never.* These expressions are difficult to support because one exception renders them false.

3. Be especially suspicious of generalizations involving personal characteristics, attitudes, and achievements. Even something that seems complimentary, such as "Asian students are good at math," can prove offensive to the Vietnamese student who writes poetry well or has no interest in math class.

Don't Mention a Person's Race, Sex, Age, Sexual Orientation, Disability, or Religion Unnecessarily

Being specific is important in writing because it helps your readers understand your ideas. However, using discretion when choosing your details is important, too. Sometimes describing someone in terms of race or gender sends an unspoken message of criticism about that person.

If you're writing about someone who cuts you off on the freeway, for instance, the only details you need to pass on are those relevant to the other person's *driving.* Saying that "some jerk" cut you off isn't passing judgment on any particular group of people. Writing that the person who cut you off is a woman, however, would imply that all women are bad drivers. The driver's race, gender, age, disability, religion, and sexual orientation are irrelevant; talking about those factors only serves to communicate bad feelings about a particular group of people.

To avoid using race, gender, or other characteristics unnecessarily, ask yourself the following:

1. In the same situation, would I want someone to describe me in terms of my race, gender, or any other characteristic? If the answer is "no," then omit using such details in your writing.

2. Could my reader think that I am biased against a certain group of people because of the details I include in my writing? If the answer is "yes," then omit such details.

EXERCISE 1 IDENTIFYING INSENSITIVE LANGUAGE

Some of the following sentences contain elements of insensitive language. Read each sentence. Then, decide whether or not it contains insensitive language. Write "OK" by each sentence that isn't offensive, and write "I" by any sentence that contains insensitive language. Rewrite the sentences that contain insensitive language.

_____ **1.** Darla, the black woman, is head of human resources at my company.

_____ **2.** I can't understand why hockey players behave like boys instead of men.

_____ **3.** When I saw Tino watching *Queer Eye for the Straight Guy,* I understood his interest in curtains.

_____ **4.** Isn't it amazing that the softball pitcher Jennie Finch is so feminine?

_____ **5.** Children should be seen and not heard.

_____ **6.** Speakers of other languages often have difficulty learning English.

_____ **7.** When I'm alone at night, I always cross the street if a man is coming toward me.

_____ **8.** Rath is completely obedient, as so many of her people are.

_____ **9.** A secretary or receptionist who polishes her nails during work should be reprimanded.

_____ **10.** If a spousal abuser doesn't receive help, he can never stop his abuse.

EXERCISE 2 FINDING BIAS IN CONTEXT

The following paragraph contains four instances of insensitive language. In the spaces at the end of the paragraph, write the numbers of the sentences containing insensitive language. Then, briefly explain why that language is insensitive. The first item has been completed for you.

Can Hockey Hit Too Hard?

[1]When Canuck Todd Bertuzzi brutally beat Steve Moore in a game in March 2004, he was criticized for his attack. [2]As Moore lay unconscious on the ice, fans and critics alike castigated Bertuzzi for his use of excessive force. [3]Of course, Bertuzzi was only acting as all hockey players act, tough, and Moore was just being a baby. [4]If Moore had sprung to his skates, however, and glided away, Bertuzzi would have received a slap on the wrist from the NHL, rather than the suspension and legal action he faced. [5]The reason for this is that violent, bloody hockey has a firm place in the hearts of its fans. [6]Real men need a masculine outlet, and professional hockey gives it to them. [7]More than any other sport, hockey thrives on intimidation, aggression, and revenge. [8]Testosterone plays a role, too, which is why women hockey players, or chicks with sticks, will never have a place in the game. [9]In fact, animosity can act as a spark which ignites a team and makes the difference between mediocre and top-flight play. [10]Honestly, if a player can't take a hit in good humor—and dole one out in return—he is a pansy and shouldn't even be on the ice. [11]Thus, as long as the hits are legal (and often even if they're not), players and fans alike grin a bit wider when a punch is thrown.

3   It's offensive to say that all hockey players are tough and that

Moore was being a baby.

EDITING PRACTICE

The following sentences contain wording that illustrates each of the five types of insensitive language. Rewrite the sentences to make them free of insensitive language.

1. *Don't exclude people:* Anyone with real sensitivity knows herself well.

_____

2. *Don't make assumptions:* Kim is majoring in child development; she's

trying to get her Mrs degree. _____

_____

3. *Don't call people names they don't choose for themselves:* Since my teeth

are straight, I haven't joined the ranks of the tinsel teeth. _____

_____

4. *Don't assume that all members of a group are the same:* Don't expect P. J.
to be great at expressing himself; those guys who are whizzes at

calculus and physics are the worst communicators. _____

_____

5. *Don't mention a person's race, sex, age, sexual orientation, disability, or
religion unnecessarily:* I wasn't surprised to learn that he had been

arrested because I knew where he grew up. _____

_____

Lab Activity 11

For additional practice with using sensitive language, complete Lab Activity 11 in the lab manual packaged with your textbook. If you did not receive a lab manual, you can complete this activity online at **www.ablongman.com/ long.** Click on **College Resources for Writers** and then click on **Activity 11.**

12 Words That Look Alike and Sound Alike

CULTURE NOTE *Golf*

Banned in Britain in the 1400s for its distracting influence on the military, golf nevertheless gained an early following in Scotland. Though golf was once the game of a privileged few, it is now played by people of all ages, races, genders, and income levels thanks to blockbuster players such as Tiger Woods and Annika Sorenstam.

Tiger Woods

CONDUCT AN INTERVIEW Since Tiger Woods's arrival on the golf scene, younger golfers and those from previously underrepresented groups have embraced the game. What athletes or role models have positively affected an activity? Interview at least two people from a different generation from you about ground-breaking figures and summarize your findings in a few sentences.

Understanding Homonyms

Many words sound like other words but have different spellings and different meanings. These words are called **homonyms.** Read the word groups that follow, paying attention to how the words differ from each other. Then, fill in the blanks with a word from each group.

all ready	totally ready or prepared
already	before; previously

Fill in the blanks: I _____ practiced my golf swing, so I felt

_____ to play.

brake	to stop; device that stops a vehicle
break	to damage or cause to come apart; a pause or rest

Fill in the blanks: Tom needed to put a _____ on his interest in

golf; every lunch _____ cost him money for a
bucket of balls at the driving range.

buy	to purchase
by	near; of; before

Fill in the blanks: When I _____ a titanium driver, I'll improve

my score _____ ten strokes.

coarse	rough
course	school subject; a route; part of a meal

Fill in the blanks: I played a new golf _____, and the

_____ weed patches hurt my game.

hear	to experience sounds
here	in this place

Fill in the blanks: When I _____ about a new golf course

opening, I hope it will be _____.

hole	place where nothing is
whole	complete; entire

Fill in the blanks: The _____ point of golf is to hit a

ball into a _____.

its   belonging to *it*
it's   contraction of *it is* or *it has*

Fill in the blanks: _____ hard to define what makes golf so

difficult; _____ objective is simple.

knew   past tense of *know*
new   fresh, unused; opposite of *old*

Fill in the blanks: I _____ that my _____ neon pink golf

balls would improve my game.

know   to have knowledge about; to understand
no   a negative

Fill in the blanks: However, I had _____ clue how to tee up; I

hope to _____ next time.

pair   set of two
pare   to trim off excess
pear   type of fruit

Fill in the blanks: I hope to _____ down my waistline by
                       playing golf. I've also heard that by eating a

_____ of fruits—such as _____—as a
snack, I can lose unwanted pounds.

passed   past tense of *pass*
past   already happened

Fill in the blanks: In the _____, I lost my temper while playing

golf; I hope those days have _____.

peace   calmness, tranquility
piece   part or section

Fill in the blanks: It's difficult to experience _____ in golf when

a _____ of the course sits on my four iron.

plain   simple, unadorned
plane   aircraft

Fill in the blanks: An overhead _____ can distract a golfer if

_____ old concentration is not part of his or her game.

principal   the head administrator of a school; most important, consequential, or influential; a sum of money that gains interest, dues as a debt, or used as a fund
principle   rule or law

Fill in the blanks: Our school's _____ golfs daily, following the

_____ that all work and no play would make him dull.

right   opposite of *left;* correct; a privilege or power that someone has a just claim to
write   to print or mark words on paper

Fill in the blanks: I _____ out golf instructions to help me

swing the club _____.

cite   to call upon officially or quote by way of example, authority, or proof
sight   something that is seen or worth seeing
site   location of something

Fill in the blanks: I lost _____ of my ball and had to

_____ golf rules to convince my buddies to let

me search the _____ of its disappearance.

than   used to compare
then   at that time

Fill in the blanks: I'd always prefer to play golf now _____ to

wait until after lunch. _____, I'll be too
sleepy.

their   belonging to *them*

there   at that place; word used with verbs like *is, are, was,*
were, had, and *have*

they're   contraction of *they are*

Fill in the blanks: Some golfers ride in golf carts to the clubhouse;

others walk _____. The walkers feel good

about _____ exercise, but _____ careful
not to criticize riders.

threw   past tense of *throw*

through   passing from one side to another; all done

Fill in the blanks: He smiled as his golf ball sailed _____ the

two big trees but then _____ his club in
disgust when the ball landed in a sand trap.

to   toward (They went to the golf course); part of an
infinitive (to try)

too   more than enough (Golf has too many rules); in addition (I'm going to play that course, too)

two   the number 2

Fill in the blanks: I am going _____ tee off in _____

hours. Do you want to play, _____?

wear   to have on

where   in what place

Fill in the blanks: Golf courses are great. _____ else can you

feel good when you _____ golf shoes?

weather   atmospheric conditions

whether   if; in case

Fill in the blanks: True golfers play their game _____ the

_____ is pleasant or not.

whose   belonging to *whom*
who's   contraction of *who is*

Fill in the blanks: _____ that? Is she the one _____
putting is so accurate?

your   belonging to *you*
you're   contraction of *you are*

Fill in the blanks: Bring _____ patience and sense of humor to

the golf course, or _____ in for a long day.

Other Commonly Confused Words

Aside from homonyms, there are a number of other words that look or sound enough alike to be confusing. A list of these words follows. As you did with homonyms, read the word groups that follow, paying attention to how the words are different from each other. Then, fill in the blanks with a word from each group.

a, an   Both *a* and *an* are generally used before other words
to mean "one."

Use *an* before words beginning with a vowel (*a, e, i, o, u*).

an ocean   **an** experience   **an** orange   **an** itch   **an** eyesore

Use *a* before words beginning with consonants (all other letters).

a ball   **a** chip   **a** swing   **a** treat   **a** wasteland

Fill in the blanks: I have always wanted to play golf on _____

island near _____ sandy beach.

accept   to receive; to agree to
except   but; to exclude

Fill in the blanks: _____ for the fact that playing too near sand

is risky, my friends would _____ my invitation to play beach golf.

advice	noun meaning "opinion"
advise	verb meaning "to give advice" or "to counsel"

Fill in the blanks: Our local golf professionals _____ me to give up my sandy dream, but I refuse to heed their

_____.

affect	verb meaning "to influence" or "to change"
effect	noun meaning "result"; verb meaning "to cause"

Fill in the blanks: Even though the pros know more, their disapproval

has little _____ on me; in fact, it doesn't

_____ me at all.

among	implies three or more
between	implies two

Fill in the blanks: The trick is choosing _____ all the sandy courses near the shore; my real decision is to

choose _____ an older and a newer course.

beside	next to
besides	in addition to

Fill in the blanks: _____ their differences in price, they differ in

location; indeed, one course is right _____ the beach.

desert	stretch of dry land; to leave one's job or station
dessert	final course of a meal

Fill in the blanks: The course that's not on the beach has a wonderful

_____ bar for after golf. Of course, the

temptation is that I might _____ my game for pie.

fewer	used to show smaller amount among things that can be counted

less   used to show smaller amount, degree, or value

Fill in the blanks: The _____ I think about the decision, the

_____ my worries will be.

lay   to put or place something (*Note:* the past tense of *lay* is *laid*)

lie   to be prone (*Note:* the past tense of *lie* is *lay*)

Fill in the blanks: No matter which course I choose, I will

_____ down after golf and _____ my clubs gently on the floor.

loose   not tight; not restrained

lose   opposite of *win;* to misplace

Fill in the blanks: At one point, I slept holding my clubs in a

_____ grip; that way, I'd never _____ them.

quiet   free from noise; peaceful

quite   very; completely

Fill in the blanks: However, this strategy didn't _____ work; I still managed to misplace the clubs in the

_____ of the night.

raise   to lift an object; to grow or increase

rise   to get up by one's own power

Fill in the blanks: The worst part was to _____ from bed,

_____ my hand, and discover that my clubs were missing.

though   although; despite

thought   past tense of *think;* an idea

Fill in the blanks: I'd always _____ that playing golf was the hard

part; for me, _____, keeping track of my clubs was.

EXERCISE 1 RECOGNIZING COMMONLY CONFUSED WORDS

For each item below, circle the correct word in each sentence. If you're not sure which word is correct, review the definitions on the previous pages.

Hazards of Golf

(Though, Thought) players claim that golf is relaxing, it can be extremely stressful, particularly if the golfers are not aware of (it's, its) risks or potential losses. One potential loss comes from the risk of (losing, loosing) a ball. On even the most perfectly manicured (courses, coarses), balls can bounce, fly, or roll out of bounds and out of (site, sight). Another hazard is loss of temper. Some players never (rise, raise) (their, there, they're) voices while enjoying golf; others, however, don't (quite, quiet) have complete self-control. Even if the ball is (right, write) (beside, besides) the (hole, whole), an angry player may be (to, too, two) upset to putt. This player, then, is likely to (break, brake) a club when he or she is (through, threw), which comprises a third type of loss. If players (know, no) about the potential losses in golf, perhaps they can avoid them.

EDITING PRACTICE 1

The following paragraph contains ten errors in word choice. Correct the errors.

A Tiger's Tale

Considered one of the best golfers of all time, Eldrick "Tiger" Woods stands out in the game of golf for many reasons. For one thing, Woods's racial mix—black, Chinese, Native American, Thai, and Dutch—is unique between professional golfers. Woods has inspired those who's interest in golf might never have been developed due to an lack of role models. Woods' youth also sets him apart. In 2005, at only twenty-nine, he captured his tenth major golf championship, in which he past all but to people on the all-time list.

Including his three U.S. Amateur Championship wins, he is only the

second golfer to win thirteen majors before age thirty. His first five

USGA Championships put him in the running for the title of great-

est golfer of all time under age twenty. Finally, Woods' success puts

him in a class buy himself. His long drives, accurate short game, and

unwillingness to except anything fewer than his best effort have led

him to more wins on the PGA tour then any other active player.

While Woods has already achieved tremendous success, he strives

to improve, which perhaps will make him even more of a standout

than he all ready is.

EDITING PRACTICE 2   Using Confusing Words Correctly

Choose one word from each pair listed below. Then, on a separate piece of
paper, write a sentence in which you correctly use that word.

its, it's	lose, loose
accept, except	lie, lay
then, than	among, between
there, their	site, sight
knew, new	

Lab Activity 12

For additional practice with words that look alike and sound alike, complete Lab Activity 12 in the lab manual packaged with your textbook. If you
did not receive a lab manual, you can complete this activity online at
www.ablongman.com/long. Click on **College Resources for Writers** and
then click on **Activity 12.**

13 Choosing the Best Words

CULTURE NOTE *Albert Einstein*

Possessing a clear sense of the challenges of physics combined with a desire to unravel their secrets, Albert Einstein was never satisfied with his accomplishments, viewing them only as steps to greater discoveries. For his work, Einstein was awarded the Nobel Prize for Physics in 1921. Though born in Germany and obtaining Swiss citizenship, Einstein eventually immigrated to the United States and became a citizen in 1940.

Albert Einstein

FOOD FOR THOUGHT Albert Einstein's genius in the area of physics is undisputed, yet his IQ (intelligence quotient) was reputedly just over 160 (very high but not unheard-of). What, to you, makes someone a genius? Is intelligence enough, or is accomplishment necessary? Who do you consider geniuses in certain areas? Write a few sentences explaining what the term genius means to you.

Understanding Language Choices

Very few people speak the same way all the time. The words and tone of voice you use when talking to friends probably varies greatly from the language and inflexion you use with your instructors. Many kinds of language help us make ourselves understood to different groups; the key is knowing when to use which type of language.

Choosing Language for Formal Writing Assignments

You probably know someone who understands you so well that he or she seems able to read your mind. No matter what words, expressions, or gestures you use, this person knows *exactly* what you're trying to say. When you talk to this person, you don't need to worry about the language you use because your listener knows you so well.

Chances are, using informal language with someone who knows you well will communicate your ideas every bit as effectively as using formal language, maybe even better. However, it's important to understand that when *speaking* we have certain communication aids that are missing when we write: facial expressions, hand gestures, vocal inflexion. Because these aids can't help us on paper, we must rely on standard, accepted forms of expression. Thus, we must work to make good use of formal written English.

In academic writing, some language isn't as effective as others for getting your ideas across. Additionally, some language is unacceptable in formal writing. Four types of language in particular can interfere with, rather than assist, your communication.

- Slang
- Overly formal language
- Overused expressions
- Wordiness

Slang

Slang is informal language, and it can be very effective in spoken English. In writing, however, slang is unacceptable. In addition, slang can prevent you from communicating clearly. Though some slang expressions—such as "cool"—have stayed popular for decades, most slang loses popularity very quickly. Thus, outdated slang can leave your reader wondering what you really mean. Additionally, slang can take the place of details necessary to communicate important ideas.

Read the following sentences to see how slang can impede communication.

Slang (unclear):	Albert Einstein was <u>tight</u> as a physicist.
Standard English (clear):	Albert Einstein was excellent as a physicist.
Slang (unclear):	Anyone interested in physics should get <u>the 411</u> on Einstein.
Standard English (clear):	Anyone interested in physics should get information on Einstein.

To some readers, the slang used above may be perfectly clear. To others, though, the terms *tight* and *the 411* may be confusing. When you are writing for college or business, use standard English expressions.

EXERCISE 1   RECOGNIZING SLANG

Circle any slang expressions in the following sentences. Then, revise each sentence using standard English expressions. An example has been done for you.

Example: Karwin has the hots for Allyn; he thinks she's phat.

Better: Karwin likes Allyn; he thinks she's great.

1. Because I pulled three all-nighters to study for finals, I'm beat.

Better: _____

_____

2. When my boss promoted Sylvia over me, I was totally bent.

Better: _____

_____

3. Being broke after the holidays really bummed Max out.

Better: _____

_____

4. Before telling her husband that she had totaled his car, Anna told him to mellow out in front of the TV.

Better: _____

_____

5. Tori is too flaky to hold down a full-time job; he always seems to veg out when things get busy.

Better: _____

_____

Overused Expressions

Overused expressions, or **clichés,** are expressions that have been used so much that they have become boring and ineffective. Like slang, overused language often causes writers to omit key details.

Overused Expressions (Clichés)

all work and no play	make ends meet
at a loss for words	one in a million
at this point in time	on top of the world
better late than never	out of this world
break the ice	sad but true
cold, cruel world	saw the light
cry your eyes out	short but sweet
drop in the bucket	sign of relief
easier said than done	singing the blues
free as a bird	taking a big chance
green with envy	time and time again
had a hard time of it	too close for comfort
hustle and bustle	too little, too late
in the nick of time	took a turn for the worse
in this day and age	tried and true
it dawned on me	under the weather
it goes without saying	where he (she) is coming from
last but not least	word to the wise
living hand to mouth	work like a dog

Read the following sentences to see how overused language weakens them. Some clichés must be rewritten to make their meaning more specific; some clichés can be omitted completely.

Overused expression:	In his studies of physics, Einstein was <u>one in a million.</u>
Better:	In his studies of physics, Einstein was exceptional.
Overused expression:	<u>Needless to say,</u> Einstein changed the way we study physics.
Better:	Einstein changed the way we study physics.

The clichés in these sentences may not confuse a reader, but they don't help the writer communicate clearly, either. Changing or omitting them makes the sentences more clear.

EXERCISE 2 RECOGNIZING AND REVISING OVERUSED EXPRESSIONS

Circle any overused expressions in the following sentences. Then, revise each sentence using standard English expressions. An example has been done for you.

Example: Whenever schools starts, Gerard feels ⏝under the weather.⏝

Whenever school starts, Gerard feels unwell.

1. Though Tony explained his feelings to me, I couldn't understand where he was coming from.

_____

2. Angela's new car made Lola green with envy.

_____

3. After working overtime for three days, I needed a break. All work and no play is not healthy.

_____

4. Let Jordan make the speech; he's never at a loss for words.

_____

5. Time and time again, Marya underestimated her own abilities.

_____

Overly Formal Language

Sometimes writers try to make themselves sound knowledgeable or intelligent by using big, impressive-sounding words. Using such words unnecessarily, however, makes the speaker or writer sound artificial. The best writing is as clear and direct as possible.

The following sentences contain examples of overly formal language. Notice how stuffy and pompous they sound.

Overly formal:	For his <u>unsurpassed contributions</u> to physics, Einstein <u>gained numerous awards in recognition of his work</u>.
Better:	For his great work in physics, Einstein won many awards.
Overly formal:	Einstein's <u>mental superiority inevitably</u> resulted in his <u>dwelling much in intellectual solitude</u>.
Better:	Einstein's genius resulted in his spending a lot of time alone.

In almost every case, a simple, direct sentence will be more convincing than an artificial one. Note, too, that overly formal expressions are often wordy. Use the fewest possible words to make your point.

**EXERCISE 3 RECOGNIZING AND REVISING
OVERLY FORMAL LANGUAGE**

Circle any overly formal expressions in the following sentences. Then, revise each sentence using standard English expressions. An example has been done for you.

Example:	Einstein (entered into matrimony) twice: once with Mileva Maric, and later with his cousin, Elsa Löwenthal.
Better:	Einstein was married twice: once to Mileva Maric
	and later to his cousin, Elsa Löwenthal.

1. I was famished by 10 a.m. due to an insubstantial morning repast.

_____

2. To fend off the subzero winter, I donned a multitude of layers.

_____

3. In the midst of a protracted telephone conversation with her loquacious neighbor, Marlene fell asleep.

_____

4. Myron's fury culminated in a deafening verbal assault on his discomposed maternal parent.

_____

5. Feeling parched after his grueling venture into distance running, Richard imbibed a fortified commercial thirst-quencher.

_____

Wordiness

Wordy writing is writing that contains unnecessary words or sentences. Getting to the point quickly saves you and your reader time and energy. The wordy sections are underlined in the following sentences.

Wordy: At the present time, Einstein is respected for his work because of the fact that he made great contributions in the area of physics.

Better: Einstein is currently respected for his work because of his contributions to physics.

At the present time is a longer way to say _currently; because of the fact that_ simply says _because; in the area of_ uses extra words to say _in_.

In the area of can be expressed by saying _in; during the period while_ uses four words to say _while._

Wordy: Unable to find a teaching job, Einstein took a job in the area of a patent office during the period while he was conducting some of his best work.

Better: Unable to find a teaching job, Einstein took a job in a patent office while he was conducting some of his best work.

Each of the wordy sentences above contains unnecessary words or phrases that add length but nothing else. While you don't need to write overly simple sentences that always follow the same pattern, try to use the fewest possible words to get your ideas across.

Wordy Expression	Shorter Expression
a large number of	many
a period of a week	a week
arrive at an agreement	agree
at all times	always
at an earlier point in time	before
at the present time	now
at this point in time	now
because of the fact that	because
big in size	big
by means of	by
circle around	circle
connect together	connect
due to the fact that	because
during the time while	while
for the purpose of	for
for the reason that	because
four in number	four
for the reason that	because
in every instance	always
in my own opinion	I think
in order to	to
in the area of	around
in the nature of	like
in the neighborhood of	around
in the event that	if
in the near future	soon
in this day and age	today
is able to	can
large in size	large
owing to the fact that	because
past history	history
plan ahead for the future	plan
positive benefit	benefit
postponed until later	postponed
return back	return
true fact	fact
until such time as	until
white in color	white

EXERCISE 4 **ELIMINATING WORDINESS**

Circle any overly formal expressions in the following sentences. Then, revise each sentence using standard English expressions. An example has been done for you.

Example: Albert Einstein's (life began in the year of) 1879.

Better: Albert Einstein was born in 1879.

1. When he was at the age of six weeks, his family members made a change by moving from the city of Ulm, Germany, and relocating to the city of Munich.

   Better: _____

   _____

2. Later in his life, Einstein's family moved to the southern European country of Italy, and Albert continued his education at Aarau, Switzerland, before the time at which he entered the Swiss Federal Polytechnic School in Zurich, where he was to be trained as a teacher in physics and mathematics.

   Better: _____

   _____

   _____

3. After holding a series of other jobs in the fields of mathematics and physics, Einstein accepted a job in Berlin, became a citizen of the country of Germany in 1914, and remained in Berlin until 1933, when he renounced his citizenship for reasons of a political nature and left Germany to immigrate to his ultimate destination of the United States.

   Better: _____

   _____

   _____

4. Though Einstein's ideas most likely come across as complicated to a great number of people, his goals were fully and completely clear to him.

Better: _____

_____

_____

5. Moreover and in addition, Einstein never took his accomplishments for granted or became complacent; he constantly strived to reach the next level of achievement and accomplishment.

Better: _____

_____

_____

EDITING PRACTICE

The following paragraph contains slang, overused expressions, and overly formal language. In the spaces following the paragraph, identify the poor language choices: "S" for slang, "O" for overused language, "F" for formal language, or "W" for wordy. Then, rewrite the sentences containing poor word choices to make them more readable. The first item has been completed for you. If a sentence would best be revised by omitting a nonstandard English expression, just write "Omit" after identifying the type of language.

A Quantum Leap for Physics

[1]Historians still call the year 1905 the *annus mirabilis,* the miracle year, because during that year at that point in history Einstein published four remarkable scientific papers addressing fundamental problems about the nature of energy, matter, motion, time, and space. [2]In March 1905, Einstein created the quantum theory of light, the notion or concept that light exists as tiny packets, or particles, which he called photons. [3]Einstein's ideas rocked the physics world: we live in a quantum universe, one built out of tiny, discrete chunks of energy and matter. [4]Next, in April and May, Einstein published two papers that offered proof that atoms actually exist, which topic was still an issue at that time. [5]And then, in June, Einstein really hit his stride with special relativity, which added a twist to the

story: Einstein's March paper treated light as particles, but special relativity sees light as a continuous field of waves. ⁶Such a contradiction took a supremely confident mind to propose, but Einstein just chilled and ignored the critics. ⁷Einstein, at the tender age of 26, saw light as both wave and particle, picking the attribute he needed to confront each problem in turn. ⁸Einstein had not commenced to consummate his most admirable endeavors. ⁹Later in 1905 came an extension of special relativity in which Einstein proved that energy and matter are linked in the most famous relationship in physics in this day and age: $E = mc^2$. ¹⁰That is, the energy content of a body is equal to the mass of the body times the speed of light squared. ¹¹And after 1905, Einstein achieved what no one since has equaled, matched, or met: a twenty-year run at the cutting edge of physics. ¹²It goes without saying that, for all the miracles of his miracle year, his best work was still to come.

Sentence 1: __W___   *during that year at that point in history*

Sentence 2: _____   _____

Sentence 3: _____   _____

Sentence 4: _____   _____

Sentence 5: _____   _____

Sentence 6: _____   _____

Sentence 7: _____   _____

Sentence 8: _____   _____

Sentence 9: _____   _____

Sentence 11: _____   _____

Sentence 12: _____   _____

Lab Activity 13

For additional practice with word choice, complete Lab Activity 13 in the lab manual packaged with your textbook. If you did not receive a lab manual, you can complete this activity online at **www.ablongman.com/long.** Click on **College Resources for Writers** and then click on **Activity 13.**

14 Improving Your Spelling

CULTURE NOTE *Onions*

Known for its flavor and its not always pleasing fragrance, the onion belongs to the lily family. Onions were originally cultivated in Asia but are now grown and enjoyed worldwide. Its name comes from the Latin root *unio*, meaning "union," and the onion was fed to soldiers of great armies to improve their strength and vitality. Even without their fascinating history, onions are a delicious part of many dishes.

Onions

SURF THE NET How are onions commonly eaten? What types of onions are most popular? Who eats onions? Using these questions to guide your search, surf the Internet for information about onions. Write a few sentences summarizing your most interesting—or unexpected—findings.

Understanding Your Spelling Habits

The key to spelling well is *paying attention*—to the words you read, to the words you write, to the words your instructor circles on your papers. Many common spelling errors occur when people rush to write or fail to follow up on the clues they receive through their reading or writing.

A good first step in becoming a better speller is to consider how you figure out how to spell unfamiliar words. Do you guess? Do you ask someone? Do you use a dictionary? Paying attention to your spelling habits—what types of words you typically spell correctly and what types of words you have trouble with—can greatly assist you in making fewer errors and in correcting the errors that do appear in your papers.

Improving Your Spelling

Paying attention to your spelling habits makes for a good start in improving your spelling, but it's only one of many steps you can take to become a better speller. Here are some other tips that can help you improve your spelling.

■ Reading
■ Using a dictionary
■ Creating your own spelling list
■ Understanding basic spelling rules
■ Memorizing the meanings of words that look or sound alike
■ Using a spelling checker

Reading

The easiest way to improve your spelling—without even realizing that you're working—is to read more. Some experts estimate that a person must experience a word forty times before really knowing what that word means and how to spell it. Some words—such as the word *word*—might appear forty times in one chapter of this book! However, other words such as *parallel* or *separate* would not appear forty times in the same amount of reading.

Reading from a variety of sources greatly increases your chances of seeing unfamiliar words. Additionally, reading words in context, as opposed to studying a list or reading a dictionary, can help you learn the meanings of words, which will help you remember their spellings. In addition to your schoolbooks, read publications such as the following:

- Newspapers
- Magazines
- Novels
- Religious works
- Self-improvement books (health, fitness, finance, home improvement)
- Books on child rearing

Even some cookbooks or music books can offer you exposure to different words. Just read as often as possible—for school, work, or pleasure—to give yourself more chances to become familiar with the way words are spelled.

Using a Dictionary

Any time you read or write for college, keep a dictionary at your side. Looking up words in the dictionary takes very little time, and it can bring great rewards.

Creating Your Own Spelling List

To help yourself spell better, create and keep your own spelling list. Every time you misspell a word or read a word that is spelled differently from how you expect, add the correct spelling to your list. This list should include all the words you misspell now and in the future. Once you have identified the words that are most likely to give you trouble, you can review your list regularly, experiencing the word forty times over a period of several days or weeks. Here are some other ways to practice with your word list.

1. **Say the words out loud.** Some people learn better by hearing words and spelling them out. If you fit into this category, you may benefit from pronouncing a word, spelling it out loud to yourself, and pronouncing it again. Hearing the words and letters spoken may help you remember the correct spelling.

2. **Give yourself hints.** Write down any tips or tricks that help you remember the spelling of a word. For instance, suppose that thinking of the word *together* as three short words—*to, get, her*—helps you remember how to spell it; then think of the word that way every time you need to write it. Similarly, breaking down words into individual syllables can help you spell a word one syllable at a time. That isn't as intimidating as spelling the whole word at once.

Here are some other spelling tips to remember.

Three *es* lie in the cem*et*ery.

Sep*a rat*e *a rat* from the cheese.

Attendance is made up of three short words: *at, ten, dance.*

3. **Become an active reader.** Sometimes the best way to remember the correct spelling of a word is to see it in someone else's writing. When you're reading—for pleasure, for research, for class—keep your spelling list handy. Then, whenever you come across a word that's on your list, highlight the word in whatever you're reading (unless it's a borrowed book, of course). Seeing the word in context can help you remember its correct spelling.

4. **Make flash cards.** Making personal spelling flash cards is an easy, compact way to practice your spelling words. Pull out your cards and read through them while you're waiting to see an instructor or at the bus stop, and you'll be well on your way to mastering your list. You can buy blank cards at an office supply store or make your own with index cards.

5. **Be confident!** You may not think you're a "natural" speller, but you *can* become a good speller. All you have to do is take the initiative to improve your spelling.

Understanding Basic Spelling Rules

Remember the three basic spelling rules about adding endings to words. *Tip:* Vowels are the letters *a, e, i, o, u,* and sometimes *y.* Consonants are all other letters.

1. **Doubling the final consonant.** Double the final consonant of a word if these three conditions are met.

   a. The last three letters of a word are a consonant, a vowel, and a consonant (as in *begin* and *omit*);

   b. The accent or stress of the word is on the last syllable (as in *begin* and *omit*) or the word has only one syllable (as in *stun*); and

   c. The ending you add begins with a vowel, such as *-ing, -ed, -er,* or *-es.*

   Examples:

   prefer + ed = preferred

   swim + ing = swimming

big + est = biggest

rob + ed = robbed

2. **Changing the final *y*.** When adding an ending to a word that ends in *y*, change the *y* to *i* if the letter before the *y* is a consonant. However, keep the final *y* if the letter before the *y* is a vowel.

The *y* becomes *i*:   *Fry* + *e s* becomes *fries*.

                          Angry + *er* becomes *angrier*.

The *y* does not change: *enjoy* + *ed* becomes *enjoyed*.

                          Play + *ing* becomes *playing*.

3. **Dropping the final *e*.** In a word that ends with *e*, drop the final *e* if the ending begins with a vowel. Keep the final *e* if the ending begins with a consonant.

The *e* is dropped: *Taste* + *ing* becomes *tasting*.

                         Share + *ing* becomes *sharing*.

The *e* is kept: *Advance* + *ment* becomes *advancement*.

                         polite + *ness* becomes *politeness*.

Memorizing the Meanings of Words That Look Alike or Sound Alike

Recognizing homonyms and other words that look alike or sound alike is one more way to improve your spelling. Review Chapter 12 (pp. 183–192) to have a solid understanding of how different words can be confusing.

Using a Spelling Checker

Most word processors contain a spelling checker. This device is a great help in locating and correcting typing and spelling errors. However, by itself, an electronic spelling checker is not enough to ensure that you will find all your spelling errors because it will find only misspelled words, not misused words. For instance, in the sentence "Their is a knew coat two where on the stares," five words are used incorrectly—*their, knew, two, where,* and *stares*—but none is misspelled. Therefore, an electronic spelling checker would leave this sentence unmarked even though it contains four errors. The sentence should read "There is a new coat to wear on the stairs."

For further assistance, enlist the help of someone who spells better than you do—perhaps a friend, parent, or tutor—and ask that person to proofread your papers. *Do not* let that person make corrections in your papers, however. Instead, ask your proofreader to make a check mark in the margins of the lines that include spelling errors. Then you can go back, locate the errors, and correct them.

Frequently Misspelled Words

The following words are often spelled incorrectly. Study the list below and memorize the words on it. For extra practice, add the words that give you the most trouble to your own spelling list or make flash cards for them.

ache	disappoint	mathematics	ridiculous
address	disapprove	meant	separate
all right	disease	minute	similar
a lot	doesn't	necessary	since
amateur	dozen	nervous	sincerely
among	eighth	occasion	soldier
answer	embarrass	omit	speech
anxious	enough	opinion	strength
argument	environment	opportunity	studying
athlete	exaggerate	optimist	success
August	familiar	original	surprise
autumn	fascinate	ounce	taught
beginning	February	particular	temperature
behavior	finally	people	tenant
brilliant	foreign	perform	thorough
business	government	perhaps	thought
calendar	grammar	personnel	tired
career	height	possess	tongue
careful	hoarse	possible	touch
cereal	illegal	potato	Tuesday
college	immediately	prefer	until
competition	important	prejudice	unusual
condition	integration	prescription	usual
conscience	intelligent	privilege	variety
crowded	interest	probably	vegetable
daughter	interfere	psychology	villain
definite	jewelry	pursue	Wednesday
deposit	knock	quarter	weight
describe	knowledge	reference	window
desperate	library	rhyme	writing
develop	maintain	rhythm	young
different			

EDITING PRACTICE 1

The following paragraph contains twenty-four spelling errors. Cross out the misspelled words, and write the correct spellings above them. Use a dictionary and the list of commonly misspelled words in this chapter to help you determine whether a word is spelled correctly.

Peeling the Layers

Anyone who has eaten French onion soup or some hot, crispy onion rings knows that onions are delishis. They season our meals, provide zing to our appetizers, and—of course—leave behind onion breth. However, despite our familiairety with onions, they have some intresting details beneath their layers. Peel an onion and let the learning begin!

The first interesting onion fact offen moves people to tears. That is, when sliced or cut, onions make pepul cry. However, the reason for this phenominon is less well-known. According to "How Stuff Works" at http://science.howstuffworks.com/question539.htm, onions make people cry becue the enzymes released from the cut onion combine with other substances that escape from onion cells, such as sulfenic acids. The combinashun of these ingredients forms a gas which, when it reaches people's eyes, forms—amung other things—a weak sulfuric acid. Acid in people's eyes, of course, leads to the familiar stinging and tearing that many cooks experience.

Another fasinating onion detail lies in its versetility. Onions are one of the few foods that can be part of any meal. At breakfast, onions compliment eggs as a part of fried potatos or omlettes. At lunch, onions play a large role in sandwiches, as red onions add spice to layers of turkey or cheese and minced onions give a kick to egg, chicken, or tuna salad. Finally dinner brings range of oppertunities for onions: chopped or sliced in salads, sautéed in butter alongside steaks, or pureed in steaming soups. Onions add depth and flavor to every course.

One final detail about onions is that they're entertaining. People may not think of onions when asked what pleases them, but onions show up in many types of amusements. For instance, in the novel *Angela's Ashes,* onions are both a cure and a sourse of stress for the characters. When one of the children is ill, his mother despares when he won't eat his onion boiled in milk, which was sposed to be a healing food. Taking a more heroick role, onions save two teens from deadly lizard bites in the novel (also made into a movie) *Holes.* After the teens eat onions to avoid starvation, they smell so bad that even the feroshus desert lizards won't bite them. Finally, onions serve as a simile for ogers in the movie *Shrek.* When the main character, Shrek, describes his nature, he compares it to an onion, saying that they both have layers even though they might not be pleasing to many people.

While their odor and taste dominate their reputation, onions contane more than meets the eye. From their acidic influense on our eyes to their usefulness in our amusements, onions are anything but boring.

EDITING PRACTICE 2

Write a short paragraph on one of the following topics. Then, check your writing for spelling errors, using the list of frequently misspelled words and a dictionary. Here are some possible topics.

A form of exercise

A form of transportation

A type of television program

A type of food you eat on special occasions

A type of music you enjoy

EDITING PRACTICE 3

Write a paragraph on a topic of your choice. Then, exchange paragraphs with a classmate. Search for spelling errors in each other's writing, using the list of frequently misspelled words and a dictionary.

Lab Activity 14

For additional practice with spelling, complete Lab Activity 14 in the lab manual packaged with your textbook. If you did not receive a lab manual, you can complete this activity online at **www.ablongman.com/long.** Click on **College Resources for Writers** and then click on **Activity 14.**

15 Varying Your Sentences

CULTURE NOTE *Edgar Allan Poe*

Known as the father of modern mystery, Edgar Allan Poe entertained and disturbed readers through both poetry and prose. In famous stories such as "The Fall of the House of Usher" and "The Tell-Tale Heart" and poems such as "Annabelle Lee" and "The Raven," Poe includes elements of doppelgänger (double), despair, and decay. Because his influence is so great, a current NFL team—the Baltimore Ravens—is named in his honor.

Horror in Edgar Allan Poe

OBSERVE YOUR WORLD Critically renowned, Edgar Allan Poe is famous for including elements of the macabre in his work. How popular are terrifying themes today? Pay attention to the subject matter of popular movies, television programs, and top news stories over the next few days. To what extent is horror or violence featured? Write a few sentences about why you think people do or do not enjoy horror.

Recognizing Your Writing Style

You may not realize it, but your writing has a style. Your style may be short, direct, and to the point, or it may be flowery, descriptive, and wandering. Whatever your style is, it's yours alone. The style of writing is what makes people like to read it. If the words flow together seamlessly, and if the words and sentences are balanced between short and long ones, your writing will be more interesting to read. For instance, which of the two short paragraphs below is more enjoyable to read?

Paragraph 1

Known as the father of modern mystery, Edgar Allan Poe entertains and disturbs readers through both poetry and prose. In famous stories such as "The Fall of the House of Usher" and "The Tell-Tale Heart" and poems such as "Annabelle Lee" and "The Raven," Poe includes elements of doppelganger (double), despair, and decay. Because his influence is so great, a current NFL team—the Baltimore Ravens—is named in his honor.

Paragraph 2

Edgar Allan Poe is known as the father of mystery. The mystery is modern. Poe entertains readers through poetry and prose. Poe disturbs readers through poetry and prose. Poe includes elements in famous stories. Poe includes elements in famous poems. The stories are "The Fall of the House of Usher" and "The Tell-Tale Heart." The poems are "Annabelle Lee" and "The Raven." The elements are doppelganger (double), despair, and decay. Poe's influence is great. A current team is named in his honor. The team is an NFL team. The team is the Baltimore Ravens.

Paragraph 1 is more interesting. Even though both paragraphs use the same words, paragraph 1 has greater **sentence variety.** Paragraph 1 also connects ideas with conjunctions and dependent words.

This chapter explores techniques you can use to make your writing more balanced and varied. Specifically, you can use three strategies to make your sentences more interesting.

- Adding an equally important idea (coordination)
- Adding a less important idea (subordination)
- Combining your sentences for brevity and variety

Coordination: Adding an Equally Important Idea

Coordination is joining two complete, equally important ideas to form one sentence. If the sentences in a paragraph are all short, they will sound the same even if their content is different. For instance, the following sentences are variations of sentences from a story by Edgar Allan Poe titled "The Cask of Amontillado."

> Fortunato injured me.
> He insulted me.
> I tried to be patient.
> I vowed revenge.

You probably have no trouble understanding these sentences. Each is a simple, correct sentence that communicates a single idea. Many developing writers actually try to write simple sentences to avoid making errors. While this strategy makes sense, it can lead to boring writing. To make your writing more interesting, you can add a second simple sentence to the first. By doing so, you create a **compound sentence,** which joins two independent clauses.

Notes on Style

Although many styles of writing can be effective, choosing *when* to use certain styles is important. Writing short, simple sentences works very well for children's stories, but it is not the most effective way to communicate in college writing. Similarly, a writer who uses long, difficult sentences to communicate will probably be more effective in reaching an audience of educated adults than in reaching young children or people unfamiliar with his or her subject.

Consider the following revisions of the earlier sentences.

> Fortunato injured me, *but I tried to ignore his harm.*
> He insulted me, *so I decided I would get even with him.*
> I tried to be patient, *or at least I told myself I was patient.*
> I vowed revenge, *and this vow made me happy.*

Each of these sentences contains the original idea expressed in the first simple sentence, but the writer has added another complete idea to each sentence. The result is four sentences that are more interesting to read.

Remember that combining two complete ideas requires a comma and a coordinating conjunction (one of the FANBOYS: *for, and, nor, but, or, yet, so*). For more on Coordinating Conjunctions, see Chapter 35.

EXERCISE 1 COORDINATION: ADDING ANOTHER IDEA TO A SIMPLE SENTENCE

Add a complete idea to each of the simple sentences below using a comma and one of the FANBOYS (*for, and, nor, but, or, yet, so*). An example has been done for you.

Example: You should read some scary stories.

Revision: *You should read some scary stories, or you can see a horror movie.*

1. Studying can be interesting.

   Revision: _____

2. I'm happy to be advancing to the next level.

   Revision: _____

3. Registering for classes can be frustrating.

   Revision: _____

4. Practice helps improve nearly any skill.

   Revision: _____

5. Watching television can be educational.

   Revision: _____

EXERCISE 2 COORDINATION: COMBINING TWO EQUALLY IMPORTANT IDEAS

Each item below contains two simple sentences. Combine the sentences into a single sentence using a comma and a coordinating conjunction (*for, and, nor, but, or, yet, so*). An example has been done for you.

Example: Edgar Allan Poe's life was filled with sadness.

                 His stories reflect his dark outlook on life.

Combined: *Edgar Allan Poe's life was filled with sadness, and*

                 his stories reflect his dark outlook on life.

1. Poe's father abandoned him when he was a baby.

His mother died before he was three.

Combined: _____

_____

2. He was taken in as a foster child by a man named John Allan.
   He quarreled later in life with Allan.

Combined: _____

_____

3. Poe wanted to please his foster father.
   Poe also attended different colleges, including West Point.

Combined: _____

_____

4. Poe let himself be dismissed from West Point.
   He realized he would never be reconciled with his foster father.

Combined: _____

_____

5. Poe went to live with his aunt.
   He married his thirteen-year-old cousin.

Combined: _____

_____

Subordination: Adding
A Less Important Idea

Combining two equally important ideas is a good first step toward making your writing more interesting. Another technique to vary your sentences is **subordination.** Subordination is the process of joining two ideas, but making one of them less important than the other. Specifically, subordination involves making one idea an independent clause and the other a **dependent clause** (a group of words having a subject, verb, and a **dependent word** such as *although, because, since,* or *until.*) Though dependent clauses have a subject and a verb, they do not make sense all by themselves. Thus, they are less important than independent clauses in the same sentence.

Common Dependent Words

after	before	since	until
although	even though	though	when
because	if	unless	while

Let's now use subordination to vary the simple sentences from earlier in the chapter.

Fortunato injured me *until I could stand it no longer.*
He insulted me *although he did not know it.*
I tried to be patient *because I pride myself on my self-control.*
I vowed revenge *when he insulted me the last time.*

In these sentences, the writer has added a dependent clause—a group of words having a subject, verb, and dependent word—to give the sentences variety. The writer could also have arranged the sentences like this:

Until I could stand it no longer, Fortunato injured me.
Although he did not know it, he insulted me.
Because I pride myself on my self-control, I tried to be patient.
When he insulted me the last time, I vowed revenge.

Here, the writer has placed the dependent clause before the independent clause. Either way is correct, but remember to place a comma after the dependent clause if you put it first.

EXERCISE 3 SUBORDINATION: ADDING A LESS IMPORTANT IDEA TO A SIMPLE SENTENCE

Add a dependent clause to each of the following sentences. Remember to put a comma after the dependent clause if it comes first in the sentence. An example has been done for you.

Example: Don't plant poison ivy in your garden.

Revised: Unless you love rashes, don't plant poison ivy in your garden.

1. Do research before buying a car.

Revised: _____

_____

2. Drive away quickly.

Revised: _____

_____

3. The fireworks display was incredible.

Revised: _____

_____

4. Many television stars have had plastic surgery.

Revised: _____

_____

5. Cell phones make life easier.

Revised: _____

_____

EXERCISE 4 **COMBINING TWO IDEAS USING SUBORDINATION**

Each item below contains two simple sentences. Add a dependent word to one sentence to make it a dependent clause. Then, combine the sentences into a single sentence. Be sure to use a comma between the clauses if you place the dependent clause first. An example has been done for you.

Example: Poe's tale "The Pit and the Pendulum" terrifies readers.

The narrator (the one telling the story) is eventually rescued.

Revised: Although the narrator (the one telling the story) is

eventually rescued, Poe's tale "The Pit and the
Pendulum" terrifies readers.

1. A prisoner wakes in unfamiliar surroundings.
He has been sentenced to death by his captors.

Combined: _____

_____

2. The room is completely dark.
The prisoner cannot see anything.

Combined: _____

_____

3. The prisoner seems clumsy and falls down a lot.
One fall saves him from tumbling into a deep, foul-smelling pit.

Combined: _____

_____

4. The prisoner finds himself in danger again.
He wakes to discover himself tied to a large wooden frame.

Combined: _____

_____

5. A sharp blade hanging above him swings back and forth, ever lower.
The prisoner becomes even more terrified.

Combined: _____

_____

Combining Sentences for Brevity and Variety

In addition to simply making short sentences longer, sentence combining can alter the way your sentences flow together. Alternating your short sentences with longer ones or starting a longer sentence with a dependent clause can make your writing more interesting. In addition, combining sentences can accomplish two goals. It can make your writing

■ Less repetitive   ■ More varied

Combining Sentences to
Avoid Repetition

Earlier in this chapter you read two versions of the same paragraph. The less interesting version of the paragraph reads like this:

> Edgar Allan Poe is known as the father of mystery. The mystery is modern. Poe entertains readers through poetry and prose. Poe disturbs readers through poetry and prose. Poe includes elements in famous stories. Poe includes elements in famous poems. The stories are "The Fall of the House of Usher" and "The Tell-Tale Heart." The poems are "Annabelle Lee" and "The Raven." The elements are doppelganger (double), despair, and decay. Poe's influence is great. A current team is named in his honor. The team is an NFL team. The team is the Baltimore Ravens.

This paragraph takes thirteen sentences to say what another version of the paragraph says in three. The paragraph uses so many sentences because it is unnecessarily repetitive. Here are the first two sentences of the paragraph. Circle any words that are used in both sentences.

Edgar Allan Poe is known as the father of mystery. The mystery is modern.

You should have circled *is, the,* and *mystery.* When you see a term like *mystery* repeated in two consecutive sentences, you can often combine those sentences into one. Combining the two sentences above results in this sentence:

Edgar Allan Poe is known as the father of modern mystery.

With that one combination, you've omitted three words: *is, the,* and *mystery.* If you can omit three out of four words from every few sentences, your writing will be more compact.

Sometimes more than two sentences can be combined into a single sentence. Look at the following examples from the same paragraph.

Original:	Edgar Allan Poe is known as the father of mystery. The mystery is modern. Poe entertains readers through poetry and prose. Poe disturbs readers through poetry and prose.
Combined:	Known as the father of modern mystery, Edgar Allan Poe entertains and disturbs readers through both poetry and prose.

Omitted words: *is, mystery, the, Poe, readers, through, poetry, and, prose.*

Original: Poe includes elements in famous stories.

Poe includes elements in famous poems.

The stories are "The Fall of the House of Usher" and "The Tell-Tale Heart."

The poems are "Annabelle Lee" and "The Raven."

The elements are doppelganger (double), despair, and decay.

Combined: In famous stories such as "The Fall of the House of Usher" and "The Tell-Tale Heart" and poems such as "Annabelle Lee" and "The Raven," Poe includes elements of doppelganger (double), despair, and decay.

Omitted words: *Poe, includes, elements, in, famous, the, stories, poems, are*

Original: Poe's influence is great.

A current team is named in his honor.

The team is an NFL team.

The team is the Baltimore Ravens.

Combined: Because his influence is so great, a current NFL team—the Baltimore Ravens—is named in his honor.

Omitted words: *team, is, the*

In the sentence groups above, combining sentences allows the writer to omit almost all the words from one of the sentences. Because the omitted words appear in other sentences, the meaning of the sentence groups is not affected at all.

EXERCISE 5 COMBINING SENTENCES TO AVOID REPETITION

Combine the sentences below to form single sentences. You may need to add words or change some words to combine sentences logically. An example has been done for you.

Example: One of Poe's favorite themes deals with fear.

The fear is of being buried alive.

One of Poe's favorite themes deals with the fear of
Combined: *being buried alive.*

1. In one story, a man buries his twin sister alive.
The story is "The Fall of the House of Usher."

Combined: _____

_____

2. The narrator hears unsettling sounds.
The sounds are made by the sister returning from the grave.

Combined: _____

_____

3. In "The Cask of Amontillado," a character named Montresor tricks his enemy.
The enemy is tricked into following Montresor deep into a damp wine cellar.

Combined: _____

_____

4. Montresor gets full revenge.
The revenge is by building a brick wall to seal his enemy into the cellar alive.

Combined: _____

_____

5. In "The Premature Burial," a man's fear of live burial ends.
The fear ends only when he thinks, mistakenly, that he has been buried alive.

Combined: _____

_____

Combining Sentences for Variety

In addition to purging your sentences of unnecessary words, combining sentences can spice up your writing style. Which of the following two paragraphs is more interesting? Why?

Review of "The Raven"

Unparalleled by any of his other works, Edgar Allan Poe's poem "The Raven" has a solid place in American literature. This extremely popular work, which was incredibly well received by both the public and his contemporary literary critics, is perhaps the work most widely associated with this well-known author. It has won nationwide, as well as trans-Atlantic, praise unceasingly since its first publication, and continues today to be praised and studied as a model of originality and genius. No matter how well or poorly received any of his earlier and later works were, and despite numerous parodies and imitations, "The Raven" never failed to receive the respect and recognition that Poe sought for his work.

"The Raven" Reviewed

Edgar Allan Poe's poem "The Raven" has a solid place in American literature. The work is unparalleled by any of his other works. The work is extremely popular. The work was incredibly well received by the public. The work was incredibly well received by Poe's contemporary literary critics. The work is perhaps the work most widely associated with this author. The author is well-known. The poem won nationwide praise. The poem won trans-Atlantic praise. The praise has been unceasing. The praise has been since its first publication. The poem continues today to be praised. The poem continues to be studied as a model. The model is of originality. The model is also of genius. "The Raven" never failed to receive the respect that Poe sought for his work, no matter how well or poorly received any of his earlier works were. "The Raven" also never failed to receive the recognition that Poe sought for his work, no matter how well or poorly any of his later works were received.

The first paragraph, "Review of 'The Raven,'" is more interesting because its sentences are more varied. The second paragraph is clear and informative, but almost every sentence begins the same way—with a subject followed closely by a verb—and the writing is repetitive. Writing similar sentences is not incorrect, but it does not make for entertaining reading. Look at another example of combining sentences.

Original: The work is extremely popular.

The work was incredibly well received by the public.

The work was incredibly well received by Poe's contemporary literary critics.

The work is perhaps the work most widely associated with this author.

The author is well-known.

Combined: This extremely popular work, which was incredibly well received by both the public and his contemporary literary critics, is perhaps the work most widely associated with this well-known author.

Here the writer made three primary changes. First, he changed *the* to *this* to introduce "the work." Next, he deleted duplicate information such as "incredibly well received" and "author." Finally, he combined the second and third sentences into one clause—a group of words having a subject and verb—that sits in the middle of the main clause, made from the first, fourth, and fifth sentences. Adding information at different points in the sentence— at the beginning, middle, or end—can give you greater variety. For instance, here are the first two sentences of "'The Raven' Reviewed."

Edgar Allan Poe's poem "The Raven" has a solid place in American literature.

The work is unparalleled by any of his other works.

The writer *could* simply join the sentences in sequence to write "Edgar Allan Poe's poem 'The Raven' has a solid place in American literature and is unparalleled by any of his other works." This combination joins the two complete sentences to form one longer, more informative sentence. However, the writer can also vary the writing by inserting the information from the second sentence at the beginning of the first sentence. The information that has been moved has been underlined.

Unparalleled by any of his other works, Edgar Allan Poe's poem "The Raven" has a solid place in American literature.

Here the writer successfully communicates all the information, while at the same time changing the rhythm of the writing. The new, combined sentence has a completely different sound from the two original sentences.

Another possible way to combine the same two sentences places the information from the second sentence *in the middle of* the first sentence.

Edgar Allan Poe's poem "The Raven," unparalleled by any of his other works, has a solid place in American literature.

Again, the sentence includes all the important information.

EXERCISE 6 COMBINING SENTENCES FOR VARIETY

Combine the following pairs of sentences by moving the underlined information from one sentence to the beginning or middle of the other sentence. You may have to change the form of some words to combine the sentences logically. An example has been done for you.

Example: "The Masque of the Red Death" tells the story of a prince who tries to dance away his fears.

The prince is <u>unsuccessful.</u>

Combined: "The Masque of the Red Death" tells the story of a prince who unsuccessfully tries to dance away his fears.

1. In an unknown land, the "Red Death" plagues the people.

   The "Red Death" causes <u>pain, bleeding, and death.</u>

   Combined: _____

   _____

2. Prince Prospero attempts to protect himself from the plague.

   He attempts to protect <u>a thousand of his closest friends, too.</u>

   Combined: _____

   _____

3. He invites these friends to his castle for a great party.

   His castle is <u>completely sealed from those dying outside.</u>

   Combined: _____

   _____

4. The prince and his guests eat, drink, and celebrate for six months.

   After six months, <u>the prince plans an elaborate masque, or ball.</u>

   Combined: _____

   _____

5. Everyone dresses up and dances inside the sealed castle.

   <u>The Red Death finds a way in and kills everyone.</u>

Combined: _____

_____

EDITING PRACTICE

Rewrite the following paragraph, combining sentences to avoid repetition and add variety.

One Heartbeat from Sanity

One of Poe's most renowned characters is the narrator of a story. The story is "The Tell-Tale Heart." In this story, the narrator insists he is sane. The narrator acts like a madman. The narrator cares for a kindly old man. The narrator is frightened of the man's eye. The narrator is unable to stand "the Evil Eye" any longer. The narrator plots to kill the old man. The narrator acts kindly toward the old man. The kind acts disguise the narrator's wicked intentions. The narrator suffocates the old man. The narrator cuts up the body in a tub. The narrator hides the pieces under the floorboards. The floorboards are in the bedroom. The police arrive. Their arrival is in response to a complaint. The complaint is by a neighbor. The narrator is calm. The narrator is confident. The narrator tells the police that the old man has taken a trip. Eventually, the narrator hears beating. The narrator thinks the old man's heart is beating. The beating grows louder and louder. The narrator is certain the police can hear the beating. The narrator confesses to the murder. All the while, the narrator hears a heart. However, the narrator hears his own heart.

Lab Activity 15

For additional practice with sentence combining, complete Lab Activity 15 in the lab manual packaged with your textbook. If you did not receive a lab manual, you can complete this activity online at **www.ablongman.com/long.** Click on **College Resources for Writers** and then click on **Activity 15.**

16 Proper Format

CULTURE NOTE *Swimming*

While swimming has existed since prehistoric times—with references to swimming in works such as *The Odyssey* and *Gilgamesh*—competitive swimming began only around 1800 and primarily included the breaststroke. With the introduction of the trudgen—the style copied from Native Americans by John Arthur Trudgen in 1873 and now known as the crawl—and the acceptance of the butterfly as an event all its own in 1952, swimming has grown to include more than thirty Olympic events, not including diving, synchronized swimming, or triathlon events.

Gold Medalist Michael Phelps

ATHENS 2004

CRITICAL THINKING Many athletic competitions such as swimming, running, and vaulting had their origins in ancient military training. To what extent are newer athletic events—such as rhythmic gymnastics, synchronized swimming, and ice dancing—athletic contests, or sports, as opposed to artistic contests? Write a few sentences about what makes an activity a sport.

229

General Format Guidelines

Your paper's appearance can affect how convincing you are. For the best results in neatness and overall appearance, follow these guidelines.

1. **Use a word processor or computer for your papers whenever possible.** Printed-out pages look neat and professional, and they allow you to make formatting changes easily and effectively.

2. **Use standard-sized typing paper, $8\frac{1}{2}$ by 11 inches.** This size is commonly used in copy machines and printers.

3. **Double-space your paper.** Leaving a blank line after every line of text makes an essay easier to read. It also gives your instructor or peers a place to write comments.

4. **Leave a one-inch margin on all sides of the paper.** Leaving room around the edges of your paper makes your paper more readable and allows space for comments.

5. **If you write your papers by hand, follow these rules.**
   a. **Use a blue or black ink pen.** Pencil and bright colors are more difficult to read.
   b. **Write on every other line.** Writing on every other line looks neat and leaves room for comments.
   c. **Write neatly.** Make your letters clear and easy to read, even if you have to change your writing style.
   d. **Make sure punctuation marks are clear and distinct.** Write firmly when you make a punctuation mark, and leave space after each period.

Title and Heading

Having a clear, direct title and paper heading is an excellent way to make a good impression on paper. Keep in mind that simple, brief titles are often the most effective.

1. **Write a title that tells your reader, in a few words, what your paper is about.** Your title should not be a complete sentence, nor should it be the first sentence of your paper. For instance, if the first sentence of your paper is "Swimming has many benefits," your title could be "A Positive Plunge."

2. **Center your paper title on the first line of the first page.** Your title should be completely plain, with no quotation marks around it, no bold print, and no period at the end. Do not underline your title. Skip a line before you start the text of your paper.

3. **Capitalize the first, last, and main words in your titles.** The following words usually do not require capitalization.

Articles:	*a, an, the*
	Working Out the Wet Way
Prepositions:	*in, of, to,* and so on
	"Crawling to Fitness"
Coordinating conjunctions:	*for, and, nor, but, or, yet, so*
	Splashing for Fun

4. **Include your name, your instructor's name, your course name or number, and the date.** Put these wherever your instructor tells you to write them.

Starting Your Paper

To start your paper properly, use the following guidelines.

1. Indent the first line five spaces from the left-hand margin. Additionally, indent each new paragraph. Indenting signals to your reader that a new paragraph is beginning.
2. Number each page. Set your word processor to insert page numbers in the upper right corner of each page (if your paper is longer than one page) unless your instructor tells you otherwise.

EDITING PRACTICE

Read the paragraph section below. Mark any errors in format as you read. Then, correct any errors.

LEARNING TO "FLY"

of all the strokes in competitive swimming, the butterfly—many would argue—is the trickiest. whereas a swimmer can alternate momentum and upper body strength in other strokes such as the crawl, the butterfly requires that both arms come completely out of the water on every stroke. additionally, keeping the head down is critical to success in the butterfly (except when lifting it to breathe,

of course). Swimmers who lift their heads too often have difficulty

getting their arms out of the water, which makes gaining speed all

but impossible.

Lab Activity 16

For additional practice with proper format, complete Lab Activity 16 in the lab manual packaged with your textbook. If you did not receive a lab manual, you can complete this activity online at **www.ablongman.com/long.** Click on **College Resources for Writers** and then click on **Activity 16.**

PART FOUR
Strategies for Essay Development

17 Providing Illustrations and Examples

The First Reality Series

OBSERVE YOUR WORLD

Confronting participants with ridiculous situations, *Candid Camera* sought to amuse people. What are the purposes of reality TV shows today? Skim your TV listings and write a few sentences explaining what you think reality TV sets out to accomplish.

What Is an Illustration and Example Essay?

Suppose you have an interview for a promising internship that could lead to an excellent job after college. One of the challenges you face is presenting yourself as a motivated, capable prospective intern. To communicate your desire for and potential in the internship, you offer several examples to the interview committee.

- You have simultaneously held down two very different jobs during high school and college.
- You received the Employee of the Month award at one job after just one month of work.
- You regularly read the *Wall Street Journal, Business Week,* and *Forbes* to prepare yourself for a career in business.

These **illustrations,** or **examples,** of your motivation and competence are proof that you are someone worth hiring.

Providing illustrations and examples is one of the simplest and most effective development strategies. In an illustration and example essay, you offer different specific details for your thesis statement. The challenge is to find examples that go together logically. That way, your reader can understand how all the examples fit into the larger picture.

Examples and illustrations are specific details from three sources.

- Descriptions of objects or events in your life
- Accounts of events in other people's lives
- Facts that you've heard about or read in trusted sources

Using Examples in Real-Life Writing

In professional writing, we use examples and illustrations all the time to make a point. Here are some situations in which you might use the strategy of providing illustrations and examples.

For College

- Use illustrations and examples on placement or assessment tests, when you need to make your point immediately, without doing further reading or research.

■ Use illustrations and examples on in-class essay exams—such as in history, English, or art courses—when you need to use written examples to show your instructor that you know certain information rather than through charts, equations, or graphs.

In Your Personal Life

■ Use specific examples to convince someone that a movie or restaurant is worth trying.

■ Use examples and illustrations to your friends that an apartment is a good place to live.

At Work

■ Cite examples from other stores' displays to convince your boss to update your store's window displays.

■ Offer examples of the additional work you've done to persuade your boss to give you more responsibilities—and, thus, a raise.

A Model Student Essay

To use illustration and example, follow the usual basic essay format. Brandi, the writer of the following essay, has developed a thesis statement and support points and then provided illustrations and examples that prove her support points. Read Brandi's essay to see how examples help develop her thesis statement.

Real Learning

Introduction   Though reality TV seems as though it's a fairly new phenomenon, it has been around since the late 1940s. Beginning with programs such as *Candid Camera* and *Kids Say the Darnedest Things*, reality TV has been part of television programming almost from the beginning. Lately, however, reality TV has branched out and taken *Thesis statement* new forms. Instead of simply entertaining people, reality TV teaches them. Three programs in particular—*Trading Spaces, Nanny 911,* and *Queer Eye for the Straight Guy*—offer advice to viewers even as they entertain.

Body paragraph   One example of a program that teaches its viewers practical skills is *Trading Spaces,* broadcast on the Learning Channel, in which two neighbors swap homes in order to remodel one room over two days' time. Interested viewers can learn about space and clutter management as well as building, painting, and decorating skills. For instance, in one episode, two rival designers stripped and then radically changed two rooms in Key West, Florida, homes. Changing wallpaper, flooring, paint, furniture, and room decorations, the two designers transformed dingy rooms into showcases. If viewers paid attention and took notes, they could learn how to manage such a task in their own homes.

Body paragraph

Another illustration of how reality TV can offer practical advice is *Nanny 911,* which airs on the Fox Network. In this show, parents hire a nanny to "tame" their unruly children. In one episode, Nanny Stella spent a week with a family with five children, all under the age of eight. After seeing the children yell at and disrespect each other—largely modeling their parents' behavior toward each other—Nanny Stella provided guidelines in four areas for improving the kids' behavior: (1) no hitting, (2) no foul language, (3) necessary discipline, and (4) consequences (in this case a time-out) for bad behavior. With a promise to attend marriage counseling, the parents thanked Nanny Stella for improving their kids' behavior. Though the program tends to focus on more extreme child-rearing problems, the commonsense advice of the nannies can help almost anyone.

Body paragraph

Finally, the Bravo series *Queer Eye for the Straight Guy* serves as one more example of how reality TV can teach its viewers. In this show, viewers get the chance to learn how to improve themselves—with the advice of five gay men—in terms of fashion, home decor, food, pop culture, and personal appearance. One episode featured a man, Brian, who wished to propose to his girlfriend while still being true to his first love: the New York Jets. Providing a new haircut, home decorating style, menu, clothing, and proposal strategy, the "Fab Five" style gurus helped Brian maintain his devotion to the Jets while simultaneously proposing to, and being accepted by, his girlfriend. Anyone interested in how to romance a woman while still being masculine could learn a lot from this show.

Conclusion

Though some reality series seem only to celebrate the failures of their contestants, others offer insight and information for their viewers. Wading through the reality TV maze, a viewer can actually learn something from the shows. *Trading Spaces, Nanny 911,* and *Queer Eye for the Straight Guy* all offer valuable lessons for home decoration, child rearing, and style, all just a click of the remote away.

The writer's thesis statement is "Instead of simply entertaining people, reality TV teaches them." The following support points show how reality TV teaches people.

1. *Trading Spaces* offers remodeling/decorating tips.
2. *Nanny 911* offers child-rearing tips.
3. *Queer Eye for the Straight Guy* offers style tips.

The writer uses transitional terms to link the support points: *One example, Another illustration, one more example.* The transitions tell the reader to expect examples and illustrations.

EXERCISE 1 FINDING EXAMPLES IN AN ESSAY

Brandi, the writer of "Real Learning," uses examples from her own experience as specific details to support her thesis statement. Some of the details are already filled in below. Read the essay. Fill in the remaining details Brandi uses to illustrate her support points.

Support point 1: *Trading Spaces* teaches remodeling skills.

Examples: Rooms are stripped.

_____

_____

Support point 2: *Nanny 911* gives child-rearing tips.

Examples: _____

_____

_____

Support point 3: *Queer Eye for the Straight Guy* gives style tips.

Examples: _____

_____

_____

A Professional Essay

As important as examples and illustrations are in your writing, they are equally important—and effective—in professional writing. The following essay makes good use of examples to prove its point.

Why Reality TV Is Good for Us

*James Poniewozik, Amy Lennard Goehner,
Jeanne McDowell, and Adam Pitluk*

For eight single professional women gathered in Dallas, it is holy Wednesday—the night each week that they gather in one of their homes for the Traveling Bachelorette Party. Munching snacks and passing a bottle of wine, they cheer, cry and cackle as their spiritual leader, Trista Rehn, braves heartache, indecision and the occasional recitation of bad poetry to choose from among her 25 swains. Yet something is unsettling Leah Hudson's stomach, and it's not just the wine. "I hate that we've been sucked into the Hoover vac of reality TV," says Hudson, 30. "Do we not have anything better to do than to live vicariously through a bunch of 15-minute-fame seekers?"

There you have the essence of reality TV's success: it is the one mass-entertainment category that thrives because of its audience's contempt for it. It makes us feel tawdry, dirty, cheap—if it didn't, we probably wouldn't bother tuning in.

. . .

Well, that ends here. It may ruin reality producers' marketing plans for a TV critic to say it, but reality TV is, in fact, *the best thing to happen to television in several years.* It has given the networks water-cooler buzz again; it has reminded viewers jaded by sitcoms and dramas why TV can be exciting; and at its best, it is teaching TV a new way to tell involving human stories.

. . .

On a sheer ratings level, the latest wave of reality hits has worked a sea change for the networks. And it has put them back on the pop-cultural map after losing the buzz war to cable for years. Reality shows don't just reach tens of millions of viewers but leave them feeling part of a communal experience—what network TV does best, but sitcoms and dramas haven't done since *Seinfeld* and *Twin Peaks.* (When was the last time *CSI* made you call your best friend or holler back at your TV?) "Reality has proven that network television is still relevant," says Mike Fleiss, creator of the *Bachelor* franchise.

. . .

But aesthetics aside, the case against reality TV is mainly moral—and there's a point to it. It's hard to defend the deception of *Joe Mil-*

lionaire—which set up 20 women to court construction worker Evan Marriott by telling them he was a multimillionaire—as hilarious as its fool's-gold chase can be. Even the show's Potemkin Croesus contends that producers hid the show's premise from him until the last minute. "The day before I left for France, I signed confidentiality papers which said what the show was about," Marriott tells *TIME.* "At that point, could I really back out?" Others are concerned about the message of meanness. "There's a premium on the lowest common denominator of human relationships," says James Steyer, author of *The Other Parent: The Inside Story of the Media's Effect on Our Children.* "It's often women degrading themselves. I don't want my 9-year-old thinking that's the way girls should behave."

So *The Bachelorette* is not morally instructive for grade-schoolers. But wallowing in the weaknesses and failings of humanity is a trademark of satire—people accused Jonathan Swift and Mark Twain of being misanthropes too—and much reality TV is really satire boiled down to one extreme gesture. A great reality-TV concept takes some commonplace piety of polite society and gives it a wedgie. Companies value team spirit; *Survivor* says the team will screw you in the end. The cult of self-esteem says everybody is talented; *American Idol*'s Simon Cowell says to sit down and shut your pie hole. Romance and feminism say a man's money shouldn't matter; *Joe Millionaire* wagers $50 million that they're wrong.

The social criticisms of reality TV rest on two assumptions: that millions of other people are being taken in by reality TV's deceptions (which the critic himself—or herself—is able to see through) or are being led astray by its unsavory messages (to which the critic is immune). When a reality show depicts bad behavior, it's immoral, misanthropic, sexist or sick. When *The Sopranos* does the same thing, it's nuanced storytelling. We assume that viewers can empathize with Tony Soprano without wanting to be him; we assume they can maintain critical distance and perceive ironies between his words and the truth. Why? Because we assume that people who like *The Sopranos* are smarter, more mature—better—than people who like *The Bachelorette.*

And aren't they? Isn't there something simply wrong with people who enjoy entertainment that depends on ordinary people getting their hearts broken, being told they can't sing or getting played for fools? That's the question behind the protest of CBS's plans to make a real-life version of *The Beverly Hillbillies* with a poor rural family. Says Dee Davis, president of the Center for Rural Strategies, "If somebody had proposed, 'Let's go into the barrio in L.A. and find a family of immigrants and put them in a mansion, and won't it be funny when they interview maids?' then people could see that's a step too far." It's hard to either defend or attack a show that doesn't exist yet, but it's also true that the original sitcom was far harder on Mr. Drysdale than on the Clampetts. And on *The Osbournes*, Ozzy—another Beverly Hills fish out of water—was "humiliated" into becoming the most beloved dad in America.

Indeed, for all the talk about "humiliation TV," what's striking about most reality shows is how good-humored and resilient most of the participants are: the *American Idol* rejectees stubbornly convinced of their own talent, the *Fear Factor* players walking away from vats of insects like Olympic champions. What finally bothers their detractors is, perhaps, not that these people are humiliated but that they are not. Embarrassment, these shows demonstrate, is survivable, even ignorable, and ignoring embarrassment is a skill we all could use. It is what you risk—like injury in a sport—in order to triumph. "What people are really responding to on these shows is people pursuing their dreams," says *American Candidate* producer R. J. Cutler. A reality show with all humiliation and no triumph would be boring.

And at their best, the shows offer something else entirely. One of the most arresting moments this TV season came on *American Idol*, when a single mom and professional boxer from Detroit flunked her audition. The show went with her backstage, with her adorable young son, as she told her life story. Her husband, a corrections officer, was murdered a few years before. She had taken up boxing—her ring name is "Lady Tiger"—because you can't raise a kid on waitress money. Her monologue went from defiance ("You'll see my album. Lady Tiger don't stop") to despair ("You ain't going nowhere in Detroit. Nowhere") to dignified resolve for her son's sake ("We're never going to quit, are we, angel?"). It was a haunting slice of life, more authentic than any *ER* subplot.

Was Lady Tiger setting a bad example for her son on national TV? Or setting a good example by dreaming, persevering and being proud? *American Idol* didn't say. It didn't nudge us to laugh at her or prod us to cry for her. In about two minutes, it just told a quintessentially American story of ambition and desperation and shrinking options, and it left the judgment to us. That's unsettling. That's heartbreaking. And the reality is, that's great TV.

EXERCISE 2 ANALYZING AN ILLUSTRATION AND EXAMPLE ESSAY

Answer the following questions about the essay "Why Reality TV Is Good for Us."

1. What is the essay's thesis statement? _____

_____

2. What support points do the writers identify?

    a. _____

    b. _____

    c. _____

3. What examples do the writers use to illustrate the support points?

_____

_____

_____

4. According to the essay, what is the biggest objection to reality TV?

_____

5. How do the writers illustrate this objection? _____

_____

_____

Writing an Illustration and Example Essay

Now that you've read and analyzed some illustration and example essays, you're ready to write one of your own. Considering your audience, purpose, topic, thesis, support, and organization can greatly assist you in crafting an illustration and example essay.

Knowing Your Audience and Purpose

Whenever you sit down to write, you need to consider _why_ and _for whom_ you're writing. Even when every essay you write is for the same audience (your instructor) and, seemingly, every purpose is the same (to do well in the class), subtle variations in both audience and purpose can affect how you approach your essay.

    When Brandi started brainstorming for her essay on reality TV, she knew she faced a serious challenge because her instructor had made several disparaging remarks about reality TV programs. Having listened to her instructor, Brandi knew that if she chose to write about how entertaining the shows were, her instructor would be resistant to her arguments. Thus, Brandi decided to modify her purpose in writing about reality shows. Instead of writing to *inform* her instructor about the entertainment value of the shows, Brandi opted to try to *convince* her reader that the shows have some benefits, namely, that the shows can offer helpful tips about real-life situations.

In this case, Brandi's audience was the same as it had been all semester, but she focused on a particular aspect of her audience—the fact that her instructor didn't think highly of reality TV shows—to increase her chances for persuasion.

Choosing a Topic for Development

Sometimes your instructor will give you a topic, but other times you'll choose your own. One way to find a topic that works well for using illustrations and examples is to do some prewriting. For instance, Les wondered if he could write an effective essay about whether reality television had any value since he had never been a huge fan. Les kept a journal for a few nights to help him decide.

Tuesday
  Reality TV seems like a pretty easy topic to write about because all my friends watch at least a couple of shows, and I've even seen some. I checked the TV Guide, and there are at least eight reality shows on every night. There's no way I can watch all these! The ones that seem the least silly are The Amazing Race, Queer Eye for the Straight Guy, and While You Were Out. These at least seem as though they'll teach me something (travel, fashion, home improvement).

Friday
  My eyes are glazed, and I'm totally brain-dead from watching so much TV. I am learning, though. I've figured out that the shows that interest me most are the ones with some sort of competition, such as Survivor or The Apprentice. Other shows, such as While You Were Out or Queer Eye for the Straight Guy, have some interesting or funny parts, but they don't hold my attention the way the competitive shows do. I like how the shows with a single winner become more suspenseful as the show goes on.

Sunday
  I don't think I can fit any more TV info into my brain. However, I think I'm getting hooked on the truly competitive shows; The Contender even makes me want to get in better shape. Even though shows such as American Idol are competitive, too, I think I'm more drawn to the competitive shows that have some relation to my life, such as The Apprentice (I'll need a real job

someday) and even <u>Survivor</u> *(it's interesting to see how people trust each other, or don't).*

Over the course of a few days, Les has discovered his areas of interest within the reality TV topic. He can rule out many of the shows that don't interest him and focus on the strictly competitive shows that do. Because of the abundance of competitive reality shows to choose from, Les began thinking that that providing illustrations and examples might be an effective way to develop his essay.

EXERCISE 3 USING PREWRITING TO NARROW YOUR TOPIC

Keep a journal on one of the topics listed below. Write for at least ten minutes, at least three days this week. Then, read your journal to find any ideas that crop up more than once. Write down a possible narrowed topic and any key ideas after your three days of journal writing. Here are some questions to ask yourself as you write in your journal.

What about this topic interests me?

What about this topic is important in some way?

What experience do I have with this topic?

Note: If journal writing is not helping you come up with ideas, feel free to try another prewriting strategy.

<u>Topics</u>

Cell phones	Fitness programs
Reality television	School registration
Working while in school	General education requirements
Car/home maintenance	The Internet

Writing an Effective Thesis Statement

Les read through his journal, highlighting references to competitive shows. He came up with three ideas that related to reality shows involving direct competition.

Idea 1:   Shows have element of suspense (entertain viewer).

Idea 2:   Shows teach something.

Idea 3:   Shows have relation to my life.

While these three ideas seem very different, Les wanted to find a way to write about all three. Thus, he focused on an overriding idea that would tie all three ideas together into a single thesis. Les decided that all three ideas were connected to the notion of some benefit for the viewer. Thus, Les's thesis statement became "Many reality shows benefit the viewer by providing entertainment, teaching something, or having some relation to the viewer's life."

In this case, Les found three ready-to-use ideas that could serve as support points, or the map element of a thesis. In some cases, you may come up with only one or two ideas that work well as support points, so you may need to do more thinking or prewriting to find a third idea that could serve as another support point. For more on prewriting, see Chapter 4.

Developing Specific Details

Many times you will have experience in the subject you're writing about. In these cases, using examples from your own life will be most effective. However, if your topic is one that you know less about, be sure to rely on examples from other people's experiences or from a trusted source such as a magazine or newspaper.

In Les's case, all his examples came from his own TV viewing experience. However, if he had wanted to include accounts of shows he hadn't watched, he could have read reviews in the newspaper, in magazines, or online. He could also have asked friends which shows they preferred and why. Since he had enough information based on his own experiences, however, Les could craft his examples without further research.

For many of the assignments in this book, examples from your own life or from the lives of people you know will be adequate for support. Just be aware that as you write more complicated assignments, you will need to include examples from additional sources. This is particularly true in many college courses, where you'll be asked to read about a specific event in history or politics, learn about it, and then write what you've learned in an essay or report.

Organizing and Linking Ideas

Writing an illustration and example essay gives you some freedom in organizing your ideas. You don't, for instance, have to show that something definitely came first or caused another event, and you don't have to save your best case for last, as you might in an argumentative essay. Neither are you bound to present your ideas in exactly the way you see them the first time you consider your topic. However, any of these strategies can be effectively used.

The student essays in this chapter—"Real Learning" (page 237) and "Fifteen Minutes of Real Fame" (page 248)—both use emphatic order. Even

Words and Terms That Signal Examples

an illustration of	particularly
for example	specifically
for instance	such as
one example of	that is

though the writers don't use the term *most important* to introduce their final points, placing those points at the conclusion of an essay suggests their importance. Since both writers focus on current reality TV shows, emphatic order works best. If, however, a writer covered progress or changes in reality programming, chronological (time sequence) order would work well. For this topic, spatial order is least desirable, but it could be used in an example to describe a contestant or setting.

Use transitional words and expressions that introduce examples to link ideas. In the sentences that follow, the underlined transitional expressions signal that an example or illustration is introduced.

> <u>For example</u>, *Survivor* and *The Apprentice* give competitors the conflicting challenge of working as a team and working for themselves.
> <u>For instance</u>, in one episode of *The Apprentice,* a boardroom meeting ended with a contestant getting fired for making a flip comment.

✔ CHECKLIST for Developing an Illustration and Example Essay

_____   **Prewriting**

- Choose a topic for which you can find interesting examples and illustrations.
- Use prewriting strategies to get your early ideas on paper.

_____   **Drafting**

- Write a thesis statement that gives the topic, and include words expressing your point of view.

(continued)

- From your prewriting, select convincing support points that prove your thesis statement, and identify specific details that come from your own experience, from the experiences of someone you know, or from other trusted sources.
- Organize your ideas.
- Write a rough draft of your essay. (Feel free to do more prewriting as this point to get more ideas down on paper.)
- Use transitions to connect your support points and ideas.

Revising

- Revise your work, as necessary, according to the first three of the four Cs: *concise, credible,* and *clear* writing.

Editing

- Proofread your work for sentence-level errors.

Following the Four Cs Through Revision

After writing your draft, use the four Cs as a revision plan. In revising his essay, Rob looked at the four Cs to determine where he needed improvement.

Fifteen Minutes of "Real" Fame

Every time we turn on the TV, we are assaulted by a barrage of reality TV programs. Many of these shows help people improve their appearance or living conditions, and some—such as *Extreme Makeover: Home Edition* and *Three Wishes*—make a point of helping people. This is not true of the majority of reality programs, however. ~~Most reality programs celebrate the humiliation of its participants.~~ **Unfortunately, the popularity of reality shows reveals how people will do almost anything to be famous.**

One show that reveals how people will do almost anything for fame is *Fear Factor,* which claims to reward people for successfully facing their fears but really only has people do disgusting things. **For instance, on one episode of "Psycho Fear Factor," three couples who had agreed to stay in the Bates Motel (from the Alfred Hitchcock movie *Psycho*) were startled at the end of the show when thousands of Madagascar hissing cockroaches poured in through the walls. In another episode, the "Home Invasion Fear Factor," families had to drink "shots" of pulverized worms and other disgusting ingredients.** ~~While both of these~~

~~situations contain nasty elements, neither is scary.~~ In both of these cases, the contestants' reactions were neither flattering nor noble; their horrified expressions and muted gagging noises were most likely not their finest means of self-expression. However, the fact that *Fear Factor* has run for seasons *after* these episodes shows that people were not deterred by the contestants' embarrassing reactions to their "fears" and still strive for fame.

Another show which reveals how badly people want to be famous is the *The Swan.* This show takes "ugly ducklings" and makes them into "swans." This program emphasizes beauty above all else, placing women under the knife for major plastic surgery, having them participate in "boot camp" style weight loss programs, and staging them in a beauty pageant at the end of their makeover. While there is nothing wrong with wanting to look one's best, *The Swan* largely disregards the candidates' feelings. **For example, the winner of the program's second season, DeLisa Stiles, was captured receiving divorce papers from her husband of eight years, on camera. Since the point of the show is to beautify women, the producers didn't need to include the traumatic moment when Stiles received the papers. However, the fact that Stiles only vowed to continue in her life with her "new look" indicates that she wasn't horrified at her reactions being captured on television.** ~~That the moment was traumatic for her meant nothing; getting beauty on camera was all that counted. Again, the fact that the program was renewed after Stiles's victory after her traumatic on-camera experience shows that people are interested in contestants' humiliation.~~

One final show in which people are most willing to do anything for fame is *Survivor.* This program, which places a group of contestants in a tropical setting without food, clean water, or modern comforts, places contestants in increasingly difficult contests or "challenges" for rewards or "immunity" against being voted off the island. ~~Since the voting process results in one contestant being shunned, or banned from competition, it is a humiliating experience in itself, not to mention a stressful one.~~ In one series, **not only did the entire remaining group turn against one contestant— who managed to save herself by winning an immunity challenge—they also had to watch as members of their families— flown in for the episode—ate slimy, disgusting food as part of a challenge.** These stunts do not seem to deter people; the show has been running since 2000, and fresh contestants always appear. Money may be part of the motivation for appearing on *Survivor*— the winner takes home a $1 million prize—but since just one person wins, one can only assume that the prospect of fame lures people to compete. <u>Once again, reality TV is proof positive that people will do almost anything to be famous.</u>

A quick click of the remote shows reality shows on nearly every channel, and while the focus of the shows—restoring a home or losing weight—varies somewhat from program to program, these shows all have one thing in common: exposure. If someone participates in a primetime reality series, he or she will most likely be seen by millions of viewers. **If they're lucky, like Colby Donaldson from two *Survivor* shows, they will get work as razor spokespeople or bit-part actors.** ~~Other *Survivor* contestants such as the infamous Richard Hatch or Amber Brkich have gone on to participate in other reality programs, their fame feeding their reality TV careers.~~ And even if they're unlucky and fade into the background after their series ends, they still had their fifteen minutes of fame, regardless of what they had to do to get it.

Revising for the First C: Concise Writing   After reading through his first draft, Rob noticed that several sentences were off-topic. He even had to cross out his original thesis statement—that reality TV humiliated people—when he saw that his examples were leading him elsewhere. He crossed out his off-topic sentences before proceeding to the second of the four Cs.

Revising for the Second C: Credible Writing   After eliminating off-topic ideas from his draft, Rob knew he needed more specific details. His general supporting details—mentioning certain shows in his first and third body paragraphs, for example—gave him a good foundation for support, but he needed details from actual reality shows to illustrate his ideas. The details he added are in bold type.

Revising for the Third C: Clear Writing   Rob revised his essay for clarity three ways. First, he revised the topic sentences for body paragraphs to reflect their connection to the thesis and the weight of the support points. Second, he repeated the words *fame* or *famous* and *show* in the topic sentence of each body paragraph to connect each support point to his thesis. Third, he included transitions such as *one, another,* and *final,* to show his readers which of his support points is most important.

Revising for the Fourth C: Correct Writing   Though Rob's draft now has no errors in it, it did when he first started writing. Rob followed the general proofreading guidelines in Chapter 7 to correct errors in his writing. For more information on correcting sentence-level errors, see Chapters 32 through 53.

WRITING PRACTICE 1 Write an Illustration and Example Essay Step by Step

Now you have a chance to write an essay of your own. Use information on reality TV from this chapter or from your own experiences as a basis for your essay. If you do not watch or have never watched reality TV, watch a few programs to get a sense of how they operate.

Prewriting

1. For your essay, choose a reality TV–oriented topic. Select a reality TV show that includes situations that will allow you to provide illustrations and examples. Here are some possible topics.

- Ridiculous situations
- Competitive situations
- Beautiful scenery
- People with quirky personalities
- People with unpleasant personalities
- Dishonest people
- Difficult physical work
- Difficult decisions
- Great rewards
- Great punishments

2. Freewrite for five to ten minutes on the topic of your choice. Then, use at least one more of the prewriting techniques covered in Chapter 4— listing, questioning, keeping a journal, clustering, or outlining.

   If you need help coming up with a topic and doing prewriting, use the topic "hard work for *Survivor* contestants" and fill in the outline below. Add specific details to complete the outline, but don't feel that you have to fill in every space. If you have only one or two details for a support point, that's fine.

Topic: Hard work for *Survivor* contestants

A. Finding/transporting fresh water and/or food

   1. _____

   2. _____

   3. _____

B. Building shelter

1. _____

2. _____

3. _____

C. Competing in physical contests

1. _____

2. _____

3. _____

Drafting

3. Write a thesis statement. Consider your audience, your purpose for writing, and the points that surfaced during your prewriting. Then, do your best to write a thesis statement that reflects these three elements. For instance, in the outline above, a workable thesis statement could be "Participants on the reality program *Survivor* face difficult physical challenges." Then, choose support points and specific details.

Working with the outline, Mavis identified three areas where contestants faced difficult physical challenges. These are her three support points.

Support point 1: Finding water and food
Support point 2: Building shelter
Support point 3: Facing physical contests

Next, choose details that you think best illustrate your support points and will make your paragraph believable. For instance, for the support points listed above, you might choose the following details.

Support Point	Specific Details
Finding water and food	Contestants had to walk a mile or more to find fresh water. On another series, contestants were afraid to drink nearby water for fear of contamination.
Building shelter	Contestants had to build shelter, cutting trees, dragging them to their campsite, and

| | binding them together. Floods ruined shelters, which had to be rebuilt. |
| Facing physical contests | Contestants had to run obstacle courses, stand with one arm extended overhead, and participate in swimming/diving contests. |

4. Arrange your support points using chronological, emphatic, or spatial order. Decide which order works better by examining your details. If all of Mavis's examples of physical challenges occurred during one series or on one show, she could use emphatic order. However, if her examples occurred over the course of a season or many seasons, she should use chronological order. Finally, if Mavis wanted to describe the physical challenges—the dimensions of the huge trees needed for shelter, for instance—she could use spatial order.

5. Now, write a draft of your essay, including your thesis statement, support points, and specific details. Feel free to go back and do more prewriting if you need more information for specific details.

Revising

6. Revise your essay, checking for three of the four Cs: *concise*, *credible*, and *clear* writing.

Editing

7. Check your essay for the fourth C, *correct* writing. Proofread your essay to make sure you have used correct spelling, punctuation, and grammar.

WRITING PRACTICE 2 Write an Illustration and Example Essay

Now you have the opportunity to choose both the topic and the types of support you will use. Choose Topic A, B, or C for your assignment.

Topic A

Write an essay about a situation in your life. Use only examples from your own life. Here are some topics to consider.

A frustrating experience

A rewarding experience

An experience where hard work paid off

An experience where being _____ was beneficial

An experience where being _____ was detrimental

Possible thesis statement: Taking an advanced English course when I tested at a remedial level was a frustrating experience.

Topic B

Write an essay about a policy (this can be a rule, law, or practice) that you are familiar with. For this essay, use examples from other people's lives as well as your own. You may use examples from written sources such as the newspaper, but you do not have to. Here are some possible topics to write about.

An instructor's policy (homework, attendance, late work, or class participation)

A local traffic situation (speed bumps, hidden stop signs, poorly marked crosswalks)

A school-related policy (adding/dropping classes after a certain date, wait lists, used book buybacks, grading policy, cheating policy)

An employer's policy (overtime, vacation, sick days, meeting deadlines)

A store policy (buying a set number of sale items, return/exchange policy, shoplifting policy)

Possible thesis statement: The R Street speed bumps have proved dangerous to motorists, cyclists, and pedestrians.

Remember to include a thesis statement, support points, and examples in your essay. If you need help, refer to the checklist for developing an illustration and example essay (page 247) and Writing Practice 1 (page 251).

Topic C

Write about someone you don't know but who has influenced you nonetheless. You may use examples from your own or other people's lives, but at least one of your examples must come from a written source—for example, from the Internet, an online database, a newspaper, or a magazine.

Here are some possible topics to write about.

Someone who has inspired you

Someone who has frightened you

Someone who has given you hope

Someone who has surprised you

Someone who has achieved much

Someone who has made decisions that did not turn out well

Someone who came from humble beginnings

Someone who enlightened you

Possible thesis statement: Lakers star Kobe Bryant made some decisions that did not turn out well for him.

WRITING PRACTICE 3 **Write About a Reading**

According to the essay "Why Reality TV Is Good for Us" (page 240), reality
TV has many benefits. The authors offer numerous reasons why reality TV
is beneficial, and they address criticisms against such shows as *Survivor,
The Bachelor,* and *American Idol.* What do you think of reality TV?
    Your assignment is this: *Draw a conclusion about reality TV, and support
it with examples from the essay "Why Reality TV Is Good for Us" as well from
your own experiences and observations.* Your conclusion may be something
like "Reality TV is (entertaining, superficial, artificial)," or you may conclude that reality TV brings out the best (or worst) in its participants (either
contestants or viewers). Follow the steps in Writing Practice 1 to get started.

Lab Activity 17

For additional practice with examples and illustrations, complete
Lab Activity 17 in the lab manual packaged with your textbook. If you did
not receive a lab manual, you can complete this activity online at
www.ablongman.com/long. Click on **College Resources for Writers** and
then click on **Activity 17.**

18 Narrating an Event or a Story

CULTURE NOTE *The Criminal Justice System*

From the time a crime is committed, many steps are involved in the execution of justice. Police reports must be filed, prosecutors must determine whether a case has merit, and the alleged perpetrators must be arrested and arraigned—all before talk of a trial even begins. Understanding how the criminal justice system works in the real world—a far cry from *CSI* or *Law and Order*—requires an open mind and a belief in its effectiveness.

Off the Record

CONDUCT AN INTERVIEW The U.S. criminal justice system is based on the belief that people are innocent until proven guilty. Some feel, however, that simply being accused of or arrested for a crime is proof of guilt. What do your acquaintances think? Interview a few people about the extent to which seeing or hearing of someone's arrest leads them to think that person is guilty. Write a few sentences summarizing what you learn.

What Is a Narrative Essay?

If you've ever sat down after a long day and explained to a friend just what happened to make that day rotten—your alarm clock not going off, your boss getting mad at you, your car breaking down, and your coffee spilling down the front of your white shirt—you've already practiced the art of narration, or of telling a story.

Narration is a method of development in which you write about events in the order they occur (chronological or time sequence order). Narration's purpose is to tell a story, so it works particularly well when our ideas are best supported by events that happen one after another.

Using Narration in Real-Life Writing

In real-life writing, we use narration frequently to provide "the whole story" or to give our readers a context for our arguments. Here are some situations in which you might use the strategy of narrating an event.

For College

■ Use narration in art history or economics exams or papers. Narrating events—especially when they're based on a timeline or outline—can ensure that you include all the necessary details in the correct order.

■ Use narration to summarize an experiment and its results. Recounting various results that occurred over the course of the experiment is often easiest when you narrate them, or tell them in order.

In Your Personal Life

■ Use narration to describe the events leading up to a car crash so that your insurance company will not hold you liable.

■ Use narration to chronicle your family history. Tracking the births, marriages, moves, and deaths of your ancestors is most easily accomplished through narration.

At Work

■ Summarize a meeting in a brief narrative document. Recounting who said what, how people responded, and what was decided will help you keep track of your company's events and decisions.

■ In a job interview, explain your qualifications by offering brief narratives that illustrate your qualifications for a job. For instance, use narrative technique to tell about a problem that you had to solve.

A Model Student Essay

To write a narrative essay, follow the basic essay format. Allen (not his real name), the writer of the essay below, has developed a thesis statement and then included details in chronological order that support his topic sentence.

The Never-Ending Mistake

I guess the nightmare really began when I stupidly agreed to break the law with my cousin. I felt so awful after burglarizing the store that I threw away all the money we stole and thought that was the end of it. Little did I know, that was only the beginning. Being an unwilling participant in the criminal justice system showed me that breaking the law isn't worth anything I might gain from the act.

The knock on my door at 8:05 p.m. three nights after my "mistake" was my first signal that my life had seriously changed for the worse. Two police officers asked me my identity, arrested me while putting on handcuffs, and read me my rights while pushing me into the back of a police car. I told my wife to call my parents to see if they knew a good, affordable lawyer and waited for the ride to end. Since up until the mistake with my cousin I'd been a law-abiding citizen, I had no clue what I was up against. Boy, would I learn.

At the arraignment the next day, I pleaded "not guilty" since I tried to convince myself that the mistake was all my cousin's fault. The judge set my case for trial anyway and set bail at $10,000, which I couldn't afford. At that point, a public defender, Mr. Villareal, was appointed to my case, and he came to see me within a few days. He explained the evidence against me so far, and he explained that unless I "waived time," which meant giving up my right to a speedy trial, my trial would go out in about forty-five days, the norm for misdemeanor cases. Since I was in jail and my wife was pregnant—the reason I decided to take the money—I wanted the trial to move ahead quickly, so I didn't waive time.

Over the next month, Mr. Villareal put together my case, meeting with the assistant district attorney (DA) every week or so to make certain she wasn't going to dismiss the charges (she never was). Eventually, forty-two days after my arrest, my case was "sent out" to trial, and Mr. Villareal and the DA began picking a jury. The judge we were assigned for trial was known for her speediness, so it seemed as though we rushed through the jury selection process, taking only three hours (I'd heard in jail it could several days) to choose all twelve members and two alternates.

The DA's opening statement made me sound completely evil, and I was sweating like crazy listening to her. However, when Mr. Villareal made his opening statement, explaining how stupid—but not evil—I was to be tricked by my cousin, I thought maybe I had a chance for an acquittal (a not-guilty verdict). Over the next two weeks I heard police officers, employees of the store we stole from, eyewitnesses, and my lying cousin testify that they saw me enter the store and take the cash. I took the stand in my own defense and felt good about getting to tell my side. I just couldn't believe that anyone listening to me would think that I was guilty. It wasn't enough, though. The jury found me and my cousin guilty of commercial burglary in less than a day's deliberations. I was now a convict.

The consequences of my actions are many. Even though I'm done with probation, I still hear the unidentifiable noises of jail as I'm trying to fall asleep. The "job experience" section on every job application I fill out has a one-year hole that I constantly hope I'm not asked to explain. My wife gave birth to our son, and I missed it. At some point, I'll have to explain to him why his father went to jail. I wasted a year of my life because I wanted some fast cash for baby furniture. Not only did I not end my financial worries, but I gained many more. I paid my "debt to society," but I'll spend the rest of my life trying to make up for—and trying to forget—the biggest mistake I'll ever make.

EXERCISE 1 IDENTIFYING THE ELEMENTS OF A NARRATIVE PARAGRAPH

Read "The Never-Ending Mistake." Then, fill in the blanks below.

1. What is the starting point for the story? _____

_____

2. What is the end point for the story? _____

_____

3. What steps in the criminal justice system does the writer experience before meeting Mr. Villareal?

   a. _____

   b. _____

4. How does the writer plead at his arraignment? Why?

_____

5. What transitions does the writer use in the following paragraphs that help the reader move from one event to another?

Paragraph 2: _____

Paragraph 3: _____

Paragraph 4: _____

Paragraph 5: _____

Paragraph 6: _____

A Professional Essay

Effective narration includes only those details—in chronological order—that help the writer tell his or her story. In the following professional essay, Luis J. Rodriguez's "Always Running" uses different types of details to develop his ideas.

Always Running
Luis J. Rodriguez

One evening dusk came early in South San Gabriel, with wind and cold spinning to earth. People who had been sitting on porches or on metal chairs near fold-up tables topped with cards and beer bottles collected their things to go inside. Others put on sweaters or jackets. A storm gathered beyond the trees.

Tino and I strolled past the stucco and wood-frame homes of the neighborhood consisting mostly of Mexicans with a sprinkling of poor white families (usually from Oklahoma, Arkansas and Texas). _Ranchera_ music did battle with Country & Western songs as we continued toward the local elementary school, an oil-and-grime stained basketball under my arm.

We stopped in front of a chain-link fence which surrounded the school. An old brick building cast elongated shadows over a basketball court of concrete on the other side of the fence. Leaves and paper swirled in tiny tornadoes.

"Let's go over," Tino proposed.

I looked up and across the fence. A sign above us read: NO ONE ALLOWED AFTER 4:30 PM, BY ORDER OF THE LOS ANGELES COUNTY SHERIFF'S DEPARTMENT. Tino turned toward me, shrugged his shoulders and gave me a who-cares look.

"Help me up, man, then throw the ball over."

I cupped my hands and lifted Tino up while the boy scaled the fence, jumped over and landed on sneakered feet.

"Come on, Luis, let's go," Tino shouted from the other side.

I threw over the basketball, walked back a ways, then ran and jumped on the fence, only to fall back. Although we were both 10 years old, I cut a shorter shadow.

"Forget you, man," Tino said. "I'm going to play without you."

"Wait!" I yelled, while walking further back. I crouched low to the ground, then took off, jumped up and placed torn sneakers in the steel mesh. I made it over with a big thud.

Wiping the grass and dirt from my pants, I casually walked up to the ball on the ground, picked it up, and continued past Tino toward the courts.

"Hey Tino, what are you waiting for?"

The gusts proved no obstacle for a half-court game of B-ball, even as dark clouds smothered the sky.

Boy voices interspersed with ball cracking on asphalt. Tino's lanky figure seemed to float across the court, as if he had wings under his thin arms. Just then, a black-and-white squad car cruised down the street. A searchlight sprayed across the school yard. The vehicle slowed to a halt. The light shone toward the courts and caught Tino in mid-flight of a lay-up.

The dribbling and laughter stopped.

"All right, this is the sheriff's," a voice commanded. Two deputies stood by the fence, batons and flashlights in hand.

"Let's get out of here," Tino responded.

"What do you mean?" I countered. "Why don't we just stay here?"

"You nuts! We trespassing, man," Tino replied. "When they get a hold of us, they going to beat the crap out of us."

"Are you sure?"

"I know, believe me, I know."

"So where do we go?"

By then one of the deputies shouted back: "You boys get over here by the fence—now!"

But Tino dropped the ball and ran. I heard the deputies yell for Tino to stop. One of them began climbing the fence. I decided to take off too.

It never stopped, this running. We were constant prey, and the hunters soon became big blurs: the police, the gangs, the junkies, the dudes on Garvey Boulevard who took our money, all smudged into one. Sometimes they were teachers who jumped on us Mexicans as if we were born with a hideous stain. We were always afraid. Always running.

Tino and I raced toward the dark boxes called classrooms. The rooms lay there, hauntingly still without the voices of children, the commands of irate teachers or the clapping sounds of books as they were closed. The rooms were empty, forbidden places at night. We scurried around the structures toward a courtyard filled with benches next to the cafeteria building.

Tino hopped on a bench, then pulled himself over a high fence. He walked a foot or two on top of it, stopped, and proceeded to climb over to the cafeteria's rooftop. I looked over my shoulder. The deputies weren't far behind, their guns drawn. I grabbed hold of the fence on the side of the cafeteria. I looked up and saw Tino's perspiring face over the roof's edge, his arm extended down toward me.

I tried to climb up, my feet dangling. But then a firm hand seized a foot and pulled at it.

"They got me!" I yelled.

Tino looked below. A deputy spied the boy and called out: "Get down here . . . you *greaser!*"

Tino straightened up and disappeared. I heard a flood of footsteps on the roof—then a crash. Soon an awful calm covered us.

"Tino!" I cried out.

A deputy restrained me as the other one climbed onto the roof. He stopped at a skylight, jagged edges on one of its sides. Shining a flashlight inside the building, the officer spotted Tino's misshapen body on the floor, sprinkled over with shards of glass.

EXERCISE 2 ANALYZING AN ESSAY FOR GOOD NARRATION STRATEGY

Read "Always Running" by Luis J. Rodriguez. Then, answer the questions that follow.

1. Read the section on specific details in a narrative essay (page 266). Then, identify three of each type of detail (background, action, sensory) from Rodriguez's essay.

Background details: _____

_____

_____

_____

Action details: _____

_____

_____

_____

Sensory details: _____

_____

_____

_____

2. What is Rodriguez's thesis?

_____

3. What points does Rodriguez make that support his thesis? (Keep in mind that the points in narrative essays will not usually be clearly identifiable by transitions or explicit links to the thesis.)

_____

_____

_____

_____

4. Over what period of time does Rodriguez's essay take place? _____

_____ How can you tell?

_____

5. Who is Rodriguez's audience? How can you tell? _____

_____

_____

_____

Writing a Narrative Essay

Perhaps the biggest challenge in writing a narrative essay is deciding which details to include. Too few details can prevent your reader from understanding the significance or scope of experience, while too many details can "bog down" your ideas and prevent your reader from understanding the main ideas. By using specific details interspersed with chronological signals, you can effectively tell your story.

Knowing Your Audience and Purpose

Considering your audience and purpose is important when writing a narrative essay because, in the midst of recounting your own experiences, it is easy to lose sight of what you want your story to do. Even though the point of most narratives would seem to be to inform the reader, narration can serve other functions as well. For instance, if you were an eyewitness to a fight and you saw clearly who was at fault, your testimony—your story of the incident—would have the power to *persuade* listeners that one person was more responsible for damages than another. Understanding how your story can affect your reader, and choosing your details and transitions accordingly, goes a long way toward making your narration effective.

Choosing a Topic for Development

Sometimes your instructor will give you a topic, but when you have to choose your own, make sure your topic lends itself to telling a story. Many topics can be organized according to time sequence, but some are easier to write about than others. Some examples of topics that do and do not work well for narrative essays follow.

Topics That Work Well for Narration	Topics That Don't Work for Narration
How you decided to go back to college	The importance of going back to college

(continued)

| The first time you interviewed for a job | Why you dislike your job |
| How you learned an important lesson | Why a certain lesson is important in your life |

Notice that each of the topics that work well is limited to a certain event or time period. The topics that don't work have points that might not necessarily occur in chronological order. For instance, if you think a lesson in life is important because using that lesson keeps you humble *and* motivated, you might have a difficult time deciding which one of those points comes first according to time sequence order. Thus, explaining why a certain lesson is important is not the best choice for a narrative essay.

One way to tell if your topic will work well for narration is to *make a list of all the events that your essay will cover.* Listing will help you keep your facts in order and eliminate facts that are irrelevant.

For instance, in "The Never-Ending Mistake," Allen never mentions other details that surely happened during his ordeal: that he was worried during his stay in jail or that his wife was sad or angry about his arrest. Allen also leaves out details of his stay in jail: who his cellmate was; what happened to him during his "booking," or entrance into jail; or what crimes other inmates were in jail for. While these details are interesting, they don't help Allen develop the idea that his mistake was not worth any possible gain. Thus, he excludes such details.

Notice, too, how Allen hurries through longer periods of time—such as the entire year he spent in jail—so he can focus on the events that matter most.

Wendy was assigned an essay on a particularly instructive event in her life. She began by making a list of events that occurred during her first finals week of college.

<u>Studying for finals</u>

I hadn't done well on midterms.

Finals counted for 50 percent of grade (or more) in each course.

I knew I could get good grades.

Hard metal chair in my apartment

Scent of too-strong coffee brewing

Organized myself by spreading notes for each course on corresponding books.

Eyes felt hot and scratchy

Heart raced from coffee

Studied for history first, which seemed easy to remember

Took breaks by watching MTV

Studied for biology next but left TV on to stay awake

Felt myself growing tired but kept reading for psychology

Almost took a nap but kept studying

Coffee maker turned off by itself

Alternated between biology and psychology

The sun came up.

I was exhausted.

I showered and left for school.

Went to all classes too tired to concentrate.

History went OK, but biology and psychology were a disaster.

Almost got hit by a car crossing the street on the way home (too tired)

Ended up with a B in history and Cs in biology and psychology (not what I wanted)

Vowed to study earlier next term

Most of Wendy's details show a progression from the start of her studying through the end of her finals. Some details—such as the uncomfortable chair and the coffee maker turning itself off—can be omitted because they don't lead to the taking of the final exams.

Writing an Effective Thesis Statement

After making her list, Wendy realized that she mentioned being tired, in some form, several different times. This told her that fatigue was a huge factor in her failure to achieve her goals. Thus, her thesis statement became "Exhausting myself the last night before my finals proved to be a terrible study plan."

Developing Specific Details

Once you've chosen a topic and written a working thesis statement, you may need to work backward from your thesis to decide which details to add, discarding details that don't support your thesis or adding extra details if you need a to emphasize a particular point. To add information and interest to your narrative essays, you can use three types of details.

- Background details
- Sensory details
- Action details

Background Details   **Background details** give information about other events that may have been happening at the same time as the main event of your essay or earlier. Whatever the time in your life, be sure to tell your reader the most significant details that led up to your main event.

The following background details come from Wendy's prewriting list.

I hadn't done well on midterms.

Finals counted for 50 percent of grade (or more) in each course.

I knew I could get good grades.

These details don't tell anything about the actual final exams. However, they provide information that helps the reader understand why *this* round of finals is so important to the writer.

Action Details   **Action details** move your story along from one point to the next. In a narrative essay, the writer doesn't use formal support points. For her essay, Wendy identified the details that served as anchors for her argument, or important place markers for her information. Thus, she knew she would spend equal time on the following parts of her study session.

Preparations for studying

Actual study time

Test-taking experience

Results of all-night study time

Though other actions occurred during her study session, Wendy decided that these were the pivotal action details, the ones she *had* to include to make sure she communicated her point well. Wendy will use other details to develop her thesis statement, but including these points ensures that she will give adequate coverage to the most important parts of her study experience, not just one moment when she felt tired.

Sensory Details   **Sensory details** add information that makes your writing more vivid and thus more interesting. For instance, as Wendy developed her essay, she described her study session using these details.

Scent of too-strong coffee brewing

Eyes felt hot and scratchy

Heart raced from coffee

The details about the "scent of too-strong coffee" and Wendy's "hot and scratchy" eyes all paint a picture for the reader. Even if the reader isn't a student, Wendy is taking care to make sure that the reader *wants* to read her essay.

Wendy uses all three types of details to provide a context for her situation, move the action along, and vividly illustrate the events leading up to her disastrous final exam experience.

Organizing and Linking Ideas

Unlike other essays you've seen in this text so far, narrative essays don't necessarily contain obvious, individual support points. Remember that the purpose of narration is to tell a story. So you need to make sure that each event is clearly connected to the events before and after it. That way, your reader knows that the occurrences in your essay all lead up to the important point that your thesis statement makes.

Because narrative essays are organized according to time sequence, they may seem to have no formal organization at all. It's true that they often don't use transitions like *for one, another point,* and *finally* to introduce individual points. However, narrative essays *are* organized.

One way to organize your ideas before writing them in an essay is to make a timeline. This horizontal list allows you to place events in the order they occurred, along with the times or dates they occurred. That way, you can map out all the events you're writing about before you have to start drafting.

Additionally, *narration requires that you use transitions.* Instead of writing *one example* or *another instance when,* you must use transitions that show time sequence.

Transitions That Show Time Sequence

after	finally	soon
as	first	then
as soon as	later	upon
before	next	when
during	now	while

These transitions will emphasize the chronological order of your paragraph and help keep your reader on track.

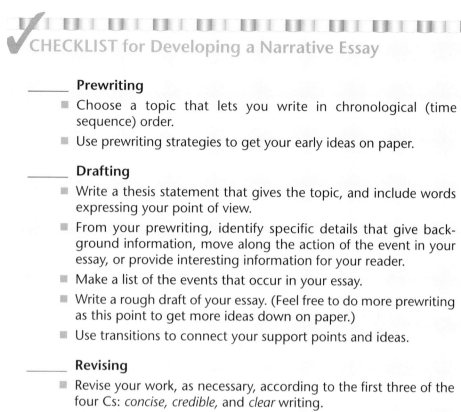

CHECKLIST for Developing a Narrative Essay

_____ **Prewriting**

- Choose a topic that lets you write in chronological (time sequence) order.
- Use prewriting strategies to get your early ideas on paper.

_____ **Drafting**

- Write a thesis statement that gives the topic, and include words expressing your point of view.
- From your prewriting, identify specific details that give background information, move along the action of the event in your essay, or provide interesting information for your reader.
- Make a list of the events that occur in your essay.
- Write a rough draft of your essay. (Feel free to do more prewriting as this point to get more ideas down on paper.)
- Use transitions to connect your support points and ideas.

_____ **Revising**

- Revise your work, as necessary, according to the first three of the four Cs: _concise, credible,_ and _clear_ writing.

_____ **Editing**

- Proofread your work for sentence-level errors.

Following the Four Cs Through Revision

Following the four Cs is especially important during the revision phase of a narrative essay. Since traditional, discrete support points do not usually appear in a narrative essay, every specific detail must count in terms of moving the action along or developing the scene the writer focuses on. The following essay, "Drinking + Driving = End of Life as I Knew It," is the result of revision through all four Cs: concise writing, credible writing, clear writing, and correct writing.

Drinking + Driving = End of Life as I Knew It

If only I had called one more person for a ride, my life would be much simpler now. As it turns out, I was found guilty of driving under the influence, and I'm suffering the consequences now.

My friend Ruthie and I were at an engagement party for our friend Dawn. ~~Dawn had been going out with the same guy since junior high school, and we were beginning to think they'd never tie the knot.~~ Of course, we had to toast the future Mrs. Miller, **so we drank some champagne.** We didn't have that much, <u>but</u> I was glad that Ruthie had agreed to be the designated driver. The trouble was, Ruthie was glad that *I* had agreed (she thought) to be the driver, so when the time came to go home, neither of use was prepared to drive. I figured I was OK—**it had been thirty minutes since my last sip**—so I grabbed my keys, and we left.

<u>After</u> **I barely ran a stop sign,** the red lights of a police car flashed in my rearview mirror. The officer asked to see my driver's license and registration, and, <u>after I provided them</u>, he told me I had run a stop sign and swerved a bit while changing lanes. I smiled and tried not to panic, <u>but</u> something told me I was in trouble. ~~I've had this instinct before, and while it's not always completely accurate, it's often on target.~~ <u>Sure enough</u>, the officer asked me to step out of the car, at which time he gave me a sobriety test. **I could neither stand on one leg without wobbling** nor **walk a straight line,** <u>so</u> he cuffed me and brought me to the jail. Ruthie waited helplessly while the car was towed.

<u>At the jail</u>, I hoped to pass a breathalyzer test, but to my horror, my blood alcohol level was .16, well over the legal limit. <u>Next</u>, I tried to call someone to bail me out, but I was out of luck. ~~Isn't it funny how, once something bad happens, it just snowballs into worse and worse experiences?~~ No one in my family, **and none of my friends,** could afford to bail me out, so I had to wait <u>two days</u> for my arraignment. I was so relieved when I finally was released from custody that I assumed my nightmare was over. <u>Actually, it was only beginning</u>.

<u>Since the night of my DUI</u>, money has become progressively tighter. I hired a lawyer **who gave me a "deal" at $1,200 to negotiate my charge,** but he advised me to plead guilty anyway, saying it was cheaper than a trial. Luckily, I was eligible to serve out my sentence through a work project (my option instead of going to jail), **which turned out to be picking up garbage in city parks with some other, scary people also working off their sentences.** ~~This one guy had tattoos completely covering his face, and I was dying to ask him what they meant, but I just kept picking up candy bar wrappers.~~ <u>However</u>, I had to *pay* the county so that I could pick up

garbage. **I had to pay an additional $1,600 in fines,** and my car insurance premiums skyrocketed. <u>Probably the worst part</u>, though, is that I'm on probation for three years, and if I violate probation, the penalties will be even stiffer.

It's so easy to rationalize getting behind the wheel after a few drinks: "I can handle my alcohol," "I'll take surface streets," "I'll drive slowly." The reality is that even in the best of situations like mine— **where no one was hurt, and my car didn't get a scratch**—getting a DUI is not worth whatever time I might have saved by driving under the influence. Aside from the huge financial cost of the conviction, it was humiliating to do the work project, and now I can never write "no" on a job application that asks me if I've ever been convicted of a misdemeanor. I never tried to get a DUI, but I guess I should have tried harder *not* to get one.

Revising for the First C: Concise Writing   Kat, the writer of the essay on drinking and driving, originally spent much more time describing her fear when the officer pulled her over. After reading through her essay, she concluded that the financial cost of her conviction was the worst consequence; thus, she wanted her details to focus on that. Other details describing the party, her fears, and her fellow community service participants actually detracted from the point of her essay, so Kat eliminated them.

Revising for the Second C: Credible Writing   When Kat first began writing about the consequences of the DUI, she neglected to put in specific details as to the costs of her ordeal. Eventually, because she wanted her reader to know how much she paid in fines and fees, she included details such as her $1,200 lawyer fee and her $1,600 in fines as a result of her misdemeanor. These are shown in bold print.

Revising for the Third C: Clear Writing   Since Kat's essay is narrative, she organized her ideas chronologically. However, once she reached the section about being in jail, she initially included all her information about the financial penalties she paid—fines, money spent for lawyers, insurance premiums—alongside her details of being in jail. Eventually, since all the penalties for the DUI came after the act itself, Kat organized all details of the consequences into a single paragraph at the end of her essay. (This step is not shown.) Throughout her essay, she added transitions (underlined) to tie the events together.

Revising for the Fourth C: Correct Writing   The sentences in this essay are all correct. To check for correctness in your own writing, see Part Seven, "Writing Correct Sentences."

WRITING PRACTICE 1 Writing a Narrative Essay Step by Step

Now you have a chance to write an essay of your own.

Prewriting

1. Choose one of the following topics for a narrative essay.

   - How a new city law or school policy affected you
   - How you discovered that someone was different from what you thought
   - An experience or accomplishment you are proud of
   - An experience or consequence you are ashamed, angry, or embarrassed about
   - An experience that taught you a valuable lesson

2. On a separate sheet of paper, freewrite for five to ten minutes on your topic. Then, use another prewriting technique covered in Chapter 4—listing, questioning, keeping a journal, clustering, or outlining—to see what information you have and where possible gaps are.

   For some essays, the prewriting technique of listing is very helpful because it helps you keep important events in order.

   For example, here is a sample list on the topic "learning to control my temper."

   Controlling my temper at work

   Rumors of layoffs at the office

   Tried extra hard to be pleasant and efficient

   The new guy spilled coffee on my keyboard and all over my inventory forms.

   Inventory forms were due in twenty minutes, so no time to clean them

   Boss yelled at me for handing in messy work

   Tried to defend myself without blaming new guy

   Boss yelled more, accused me of not taking responsibility

   I started getting angry.

   I started thinking about how unfair it was to be getting yelled at.

   I started to say something snide.

   Boss interrupted, asked if I was going to respond.

   A co-worker behind my boss signaled to me to keep cool.

   I took a deep breath and said nothing.

   Boss looked at me, then told me to get back to work.

   New guy was fired when he spilled coffee on the boss's work the next day.

Drafting

3. Write a thesis statement that reflects both your topic and your attitude toward that topic. For example, here is a topic sentence for the listing done above.

Topic:	Controlling my temper at work
Point of view:	Positive results
Possible thesis statement:	Controlling my temper at work proved to have positive results.

4. Since narrative essays often do not have formal support points, choose details around which you want your essay to be organized. For instance, in the list above, the writer has already identified many details he wants to include in his essay.

Some details address the situation leading up to the moment when the writer has to control his temper: rumors of layoffs, extra effort being pleasant, the "new guy" spilling coffee. Other details emphasize the actual situation in which he must exercise self-control: the boss is yelling and accuses him of not taking responsibility. Finally, some details show the results of holding his temper in check: the boss stops yelling, the writer keeps his job, and the new guy gets fired.

5. Organize your details according to when they occurred, getting rid of irrelevant information as you go. Make sure all the details in your list serve some purpose in your essay: background detail, action detail, or sensory detail.

6. Now, write your draft. Do your best to include important details and transitions, but don't worry if they're not perfect the first time around.

Revising

7. Check again to see that your details are in order. Make sure your details are connected through clear transitions.

Editing

8. Proofread your essay to make sure you have used correct spelling, punctuation, and grammar.

WRITING PRACTICE 2 Writing About an Important Day

Now you have the opportunity to choose both the topic and the types of support you use. Your assignment is this: *Choose Topic A, B, or C, and write an essay about a period of time or an event that affected you in some way.* Think about the overall impression you have of that event, and then decide which events helped to make that day stand out.

Topic A

Write a letter about a time or an event in your life that marked some kind of success for you. Choose your tone carefully. For instance, if you wrote to your adolescent nephew about the time you crashed a car, you would probably warn him against doing the same thing. Thus, using a flip, silly tone in your letter wouldn't be the best choice. Use examples from your life alone.

Some times or events that may stand out in your mind are these:

A time or event when you first understood a difficult concept or mastered a skill after many unsuccessful attempts

A time or event when you conquered a fear of something

A time or event when you proved yourself to be the best at something

A time or event when you did the right thing

A time or event when a great effort on your part paid off

A time when you proved yourself at work

A time when you successfully assumed additional responsibilities at work

Possible thesis statement: The day I finally passed geometry marked the end of a long, frustrating battle with math.

Topic B

Write an essay about a time or event that was significant for someone else. For this essay, use examples from other people's lives as well as your own. You don't have to know the person you write about. You may use examples from written sources such as the newspaper, but you do not have to.

Make sure that the time you write about is fairly short—a few hours, a day, or a week. If you choose a topic that focuses on an event that covers a longer span of time, such as a complicated trial, be sure to include only those details most relevant to the event. Also, make sure that the period of time has a definite beginning and end. These are some events that you might consider for this topic.

A time when someone was on trial

A time when someone struggled with substance abuse

A time when someone struggled with academics

A time when someone struggled to balance responsibilities (such as school, work, and family obligations)

A time when someone struggled to make another person's life better

Possible thesis statement: My friend Robert's parents worked for years to give him a chance for a better life.

If you need help, refer to the checklist for developing a narrative essay (page 269) and Writing Practice 1 (page 272). Keep in mind that since you are not writing about your own life, you will need to let your reader know where you learned your details (personal observation, interviews, reading).

Topic C

Write a letter about a significant time or event that you learned about through the media (newspaper, television, Internet). You may choose your purpose—to give advice, to inform, to entertain—but be sure that your audience matches your purpose. If, for instance, you write to your high school mentor about your city's reaction to the 9/11 attacks, you should probably adopt a serious tone. You may use examples from your own or other people's lives—if you or those you know were affected by the event you choose—but at least one example must come from a written source (a credible Internet source, online databases, newspapers, or magazines).

As with Topics A and B, choose an event or a time period that has a definite beginning and end and that spans a set amount of time, such as a month. You may choose to write about an event that lasts longer, but you will need to pay close attention to the details you use, eliminating any that do not help you develop your ideas.

Here are some topics to choose from.

The 9/11 terrorist attacks

An important sports contest (can be an entire series)

An overseas battle or conflict

A celebrity scandal or conflict

A political conflict or election

Possible thesis statement: Martha Stewart's conviction was the result of one little lie that turned into many.

WRITING PRACTICE 3 Writing in Response to a Reading

In his essay "Always Running," Luis J. Rodriguez writes of his childhood, "We were always afraid. Always running." He then develops a narrative essay illustrating the "running"—and its consequences. What feelings do you associate with specific times of your life? For instance, in junior high school, were you always angry? Insecure? When you were a high school senior, were you always confident? Nervous for the future? Choose a time in your life when one feeling—such as fear, anxiety, confidence—dominated others.

Your assignment is this: *Write about a time in your life when one feeling was particularly strong or frequent.* The time you focus on may have occurred twenty years ago, or it may have happened last week. Your thesis statement might be something like this: "Throughout seventh grade, I lived with the hope that I would someday be a professional basketball player." Follow the steps in Writing Practice 1 to help you get started.

Lab Activity 18

For additional practice with narration, complete Lab Activity 18 in the lab manual packaged with your textbook. If you did not receive a lab manual, you can complete this activity online at **www.ablongman.com/long.** Click on **College Resources for Writers** and then click on **Activity 18.**

19 Describing a Scene, a Person, or an Object

CULTURE NOTE *Ansel Adams's Photography*

Famous for his black-and-white landscape photographs of national parks, Ansel Adams used his camera to capture what he considered the truth in the environment. Claiming, "Not everybody trusts paintings but people believe photographs," Adams also pioneered the idea of "pre-visualisation," mentally seeing a completed print and then working through the steps to build that print.

Lake Tenaya

FOOD FOR THOUGHT Ansel Adams reputedly took hundreds of photographs of the same scene before he was satisfied that even one communicated what he saw to his viewers. What, for you, takes many tries before it's perfect? Write a few sentences explaining how some activity or skill—shooting a three-pointer, making a batch of cookies, for instance—is the result of much practice.

What Is a Descriptive Essay?

If you've ever tried to tell someone what an incredible sunset looked like, you know that description is important. Including the different colors, the color changes, and the reflection of the sun on the water are all essential to helping someone else see what you see.

Description is the skill of explaining a person, place, or object so clearly that your reader can form a mental picture from your words. Like using illustrations and examples for support, being able to describe something vividly will come in handy for any type of writing, even when you're not writing a formal "description" assignment.

Using Description in Real-Life Writing

In real-life writing, description helps us make our ideas clear and helps us communicate what we want.

For College

- Use descriptive writing in essays for various courses. Using detailed descriptions of chemical reactions (for your chemistry course) or a person's expression (for your psychology class) will show your reader that you know your subject well.
- Use descriptive language in essays to show your instructors that you care enough about your topics to choose your details carefully.

In Your Personal Life

- Use descriptions for romantic gestures, such as writing poetry about the one you love. Using precise, flattering images will make the object of your affection understand the depth of your attention and feelings.
- Use descriptive language to persuade friends to try a new restaurant or go to a performance by a new band.

At Work

- Be descriptive on order forms and in reports to make your requests clearly understood.
- Describe the nature of a problem in your home—the amount of water leaking from a pipe, the location of the pipe, and the extent of the dam-

age caused by the leak—to help a repair person accurately assess and correct the problem.

A Model Student Essay

As in a narrative essay, details in a descriptive essay may not be grouped into individual support points. Instead, every detail works to support the thesis statement. The key to writing a solid descriptive essay is to make your reader *see* whatever it is you're describing. Read Albert's description of an Ansel Adams photograph in the essay below, paying attention to his use of sensory detail to create a picture for the reader.

At First Sight

Ansel Adams's photograph "Lake Tenaya, Yosemite National Park" does more than reveal a lovely scene. To gaze unhurried at the black-and-white photograph of water, stone, and sky, you could easily imagine what the discoverer of such a place must have experienced. Indeed, resting your eyes on the photographic landscape breeds thoughts quiet and solitary. You couldn't help but think that to be the first person ever to see Yosemite National Park's Lake Tenaya would have been something special.

Imagine yourself walking though the forest, head down, most likely, to keep pine needles from scratching your eyes; it would be easy to think you were just coming to a clearing in the woods, nothing special. Maybe you'd get a glimpse of cloudy sky or sharp granite poking from between the branches, but probably you'd still concentrate on your steps. Emerging from the woods, you might not realize that you could safely look up, and, thus, your first sight would be the slate-colored water, flat and glassy, spanning before you. A slight ripple here or there belies the utter stillness of the scene; it would seem unreal.

Allowing yourself to look slowly up, you'd take in the broad granite bases of the rocks seeming to jut from the water. A rock mountain on the left, a hill on the right, with a valley darkened by cloud shadow in between, would be enough to make you straighten up fully, if you had not already done so. Miniature trees, or so they might seem, sparsely line the shore, growing slightly denser to the right, just below the rocky hill. The rock appears gray and layered, each chiseled stone slab lying atop another as if placed there for specific purpose. Contrasting with the muted water and shadowed valley, the snowy peak in the distance beyond the valley glows bright.

If you lifted your gaze further upward, your attention would be arrested by the clouds resting around and just beyond the rocks. In shades of gray and white, the soft, solid-seeming masses hover silently around rock and water, apparently hushing any cry that might sound. Yet even as they wait soundlessly, these clouds stand sentinel over water, rock, and valley and help you linger in your imagination.

All elements of the photograph—water, rock, shadow, cloud—work together to create a self-contained scene of tranquillity. Only seeing the top edge of the photograph—marked by a darker band of sky—brings your gaze back from your discoverer's dreams and into the black-and-white world of Ansel Adams.

Albert's thesis statement is "Ansel Adams's photograph 'Lake Tenaya, Yosemite National Park' does more than reveal a lovely scene." Albert supports his thesis by identifying three primary aspects of the photograph.

1. The water as seen from just out of the woods
2. The rocks beyond the water
3. The clouds surrounding the rocks

Albert connects his points by using transitions such as *indeed, still, thus, left, in between, in the distance, further upward,* and *around and just beyond.*

EXERCISE 1 IDENTIFYING DESCRIPTIVE DETAILS IN A ESSAY

In "At First Sight," Albert describes various aspects of Ansel Adams's Lake Tenaya photograph. Read the essay to find details that illustrate each of these ideas. Then, answer the questions below.

1. What are three details that describe the water?

   a. _____

   b. _____

   c. _____

2. What are three details that describe the rocks?

    a. _____

    b. _____

    c. _____

3. What are three details that describe the clouds?

    a. _____

    b. _____

    c. _____

A Professional Essay

Description is a particularly useful skill when writing about an object where there is no "action" to move your essay along. Consider how Amy Tan uses detail to "move" her essay forward in "Lost Lives of Women."

Lost Lives of Women
Amy Tan

When I first saw this photo as a child, I thought it was exotic and remote, of a faraway time and place, with people who had no connection to my American life. Look at their bound feet! Look at that funny lady with the plucked forehead!

The solemn little girl is, in fact, my mother. And leaning against the rock is my grandmother, Jingmei. "She called me Baobei," my mother told me. "It means Treasure."

The picture was taken in Hangzhou, and my mother believes the year was 1922, possibly spring or fall, judging by the clothes. At first glance, it appears the women are on a pleasure outing.

But see the white bands on their skirts? The white shoes? They are in mourning. My mother's grandmother, known to the others as Divong, "The Replacement Wife," has recently died. The women have come to this place, a Buddhist retreat, to perform yet another ceremony for Divong. Monks hired for the occasion have chanted the proper words. And the women and little girl have walked in circles clutching smoky sticks of incense. They knelt and prayed, then burned a huge pile of spirit money so that Divong might ascend to a higher position in her new world.

This is also a picture of secrets and tragedies, the reasons that warnings have been passed along in our family like heirlooms. Each of these women suffered a terrible fate, my mother said. And they were not peasant women but big city people, very modern. They went to dance halls and wore stylish clothes. They were supposed to be the lucky ones.

Look at the pretty woman with her finger on her cheek. She is my mother's second cousin, Nunu Aiyi, "Precious Auntie." You cannot see this, but Nunu Aiyi's entire face was scarred from smallpox. Lucky for her, a year or so after this picture was taken, she received marriage proposals from two families. She turned down a lawyer and married another man. Later she divorced her husband, a daring thing for a woman to do. But then, finding no means to support herself or her young daughter, Nunu eventually accepted the lawyer's second proposal—to become his number two concubine. "Where else could she go?" my mother asked. "Some people said she was lucky the lawyer still wanted her."

Now look at the small woman with a sour face. There's a reason that Jyou Ma, "Uncle's Wife," looks this way. Her husband, my great-uncle, often complained that his family had chosen an ugly woman for his wife. To show his displeasure, he often insulted Jyou Ma's cooking. One time Great-Uncle tipped over a pot of boiling soup, which fell all over his niece's four-year-old neck and nearly killed her. My mother was the little niece, and she still has that soup scar on her neck. Great-Uncle's family eventually chose a pretty woman for his second wife. But the complaints about Jyou Ma's cooking did not stop.

Doomma, "Big Mother," is the regal-looking woman seated on a rock. (The woman with the plucked forehead, far left, is a servant, remembered only as someone who cleaned but did not cook.) Doomma was the daughter of my great-grandfather and Nu-pei, "The Original Wife." She was shunned by Divong, "The Replacement Wife," for being "too strong," and loved by Divong's daughter, my grandmother. Doomma's first daughter was born with a hunchback—a sign, some said, of Doomma's own crooked nature. Why else did she remarry, disobeying her family's orders to remain a widow forever? And why did Doomma later kill herself, using some mysterious means that caused her to die slowly over three days? "Doomma died the same way she lived," my mother said, "strong, suffering lots."

Jingmei, my own grandmother, lived only a few more years after this picture was taken. She was the widow of a poor scholar, a man who had the misfortune of dying from influenza when he was about to be appointed a vice-magistrate. In 1924 or so, a rich man, who liked to collect pretty women, raped my grandmother and thereby forced her into becoming one of his concubines. My grandmother, now an outcast, took her young daughter to live with her on an island outside of Shanghai. She left her son behind, to save his face. After she gave birth to another son she killed herself by swallowing raw opium buried in the New Year's rice cakes. The young daughter who wept at her deathbed was my mother.

At my grandmother's funeral, monks tied chains to my mother's ankles so she would not fly away with her mother's ghost. "I tried to take them off," my mother said. "I was her treasure. I was her life."

My mother could never talk about any of this, even with her closest friends. "Don't tell anyone," she once said to me. "People don't understand. A concubine was like some kind of prostitute. My mother was a good woman, high-class. She had no choice."

I told her I understood.

"How can you understand?" she said, suddenly angry. "You did not live in China then. You do not know what it's like to have no position in life. I was her daughter. We had no face! We belonged to nobody! This is a shame I can never push off my back." By the end of the outburst, she was crying.

On a recent trip with my mother to Beijing, I learned that my uncle found a way to push the shame off his back. He was the son my grandmother left behind. In 1936 he joined the Communist party—in large part, he told me, to overthrow the society that forced his mother into concubinage. He published a story about his mother. I told him I had written about my grandmother in a book of fiction. We agreed that my grandmother is the source of strength running through our family. My mother cried to hear this.

My mother believes my grandmother is also my muse, that she helps me write. "Does she still visit you often?" she asked while I was writing my second book. And then she added shyly, "Does she say anything about me?"

"Yes," I told her. "She has lots to say. I am writing it down."

This is the picture I see when I write. These are the secrets I was supposed to keep. These are the women who never let me forget why stories need to be told.

EXERCISE 2 ANALYZING AN ESSAY FOR GOOD DESCRIPTIVE STRATEGY

Read the Amy Tan's essay "Lost Lives of Women." Then, answer the questions that follow.

1. What is Tan's thesis, or main point? _____

_____

2. Rather than use formal support points, how does Tan develop her essay?_____

_____

3. Choose two women from the photograph that Tan describes and summarize their stories. In a few words, explain why these two women's stories are most compelling to you. _____

_____

4. How does Tan organize her essay? How can you tell? _____

_____

5. What types of details does Tan use to differentiate among the

women pictured? _____

_____

Writing a Descriptive Essay

The best aspect of writing descriptive essays is that they let you shine. Depending on the nature of your assignment, you have the opportunity to paint a picture for your reader. A well-known saying goes, "A picture is worth a thousand words." However, your words can not only paint the picture for your reader—through thoughtfully chosen, vivid details—but interpret it as well.

Knowing Your Audience and Purpose

The temptation in writing a descriptive essay is to launch into vivid poetic descriptions of the most minute details of your subject. While these descriptions can be interesting—and while they can, sometimes, advance your ideas—they can also interfere with your communication.

Knowing your purpose in writing a descriptive essay is important because it will help you choose the details that best suit your assignment. For instance, if you were writing about someone who has an upbeat personality, including details about that person's haircut or allergies—unless they had a direct correlation to that person's personality—would most likely lead your reader astray.

Choosing a Topic for Development

Even if your instructor assigns you a specific topic for development, you will have to decide what aspects of the topic work well for you. For a descriptive essay, choose a topic that you find interesting to look at or think about. You don't need to choose a topic that seems "artistic" or complicated as long as you're interested. For instance, Svetlana is interested in a career in retail fashion, and she has noticed that the manager of the department store where she works always appears particularly polished. Svetlana decided to write about the store manager to learn what about her appearance creates this polished impression. She begins by freewriting.

Ms. Mayer always looks so "together." First, her hair and makeup are always perfectly done, so she never seems "thrown together" like I am. She also chooses clothing that suits her. Yesterday her mossy scarf accented the earth tones in her suit, and her brushed gold accessories added the perfect finishing touches. Also, even the way Ms. Mayer stands when she's talking to someone—arms relaxed but still crossed in back (how does she do that?)—is flattering. The way her arms are positioned make the suit coat fall gracefully, as opposed to being bunched up at the elbow. I wish I knew her secrets.

Svetlana has plenty to say about her store manager's appearance, so she decides to use this topic for her essay.

Writing an Effective Thesis Statement

Now Svetlana needs to think about what she conclusion she might draw regarding her store manager's appearance, so she refers to her freewriting. Svetlana recognizes that she is particularly fascinated by how the manager creates her image of being "finished" or "polished." Thus, her thesis statement is "Ms. Mayer, the manager of the Hartline department store, appears polished from head to toe." With that, she identifies three specific aspects of her manager's appearance that she'll develop in her essay.

1. Hairstyle and makeup
2. Clothing and accessories
3. Posture and position

These aspects of Ms. Mayer's appearance will serve as Svetlana's support points throughout her essay. Even though Svetlana could describe other people she knows—her rugged brother, her reggae-loving uncle, or her physically fit best friend—she decides to go with her first instincts and write about her manager in terms of the areas that surfaced during her freewriting.

Keep in mind that in a descriptive essay, the writer still makes a point *in addition* to being descriptive. No matter how lovely your golden sunset is, if you have no point to your writing, your reader will be left wondering "So what?" or "What's the point?"

Developing Specific Details

Specific details are extremely important in descriptive essays because they often comprise the *entire* essay. When choosing details for your essay, consider *what about* the subject of your paragraph makes it worth describing. Is it special or distinctive to you? In what ways? Does it have certain sights or smells that you associate with it? Is there a particular feeling that you're aware of when you're around it? These are the types of questions to ask yourself to find the details to support your topic sentence.

A good way to develop your descriptive paragraph is to use details that appeal to your reader's five senses.

- **Sight.** Use words that help your reader see colors, light, shadow, shapes, and textures. Instead of saying, "The match looked hot," say, "Glowing red in a heap, the coals seemed to be trying to relight themselves before giving up and cooling to gray."

- **Smell.** Use words that let your reader associate what you're describing with specific, familiar scents. For instance, rather than saying, "His cologne was strong," write, "The suffocating fragrance of his aftershave reminded Tasha of the custodian's closet at her elementary school."

- **Taste.** Words that remind your reader of powerful flavors are especially effective in describing taste. Spice up the description of your friend's cooking, for example, by writing, "The spongy white cake beneath the fluffy meringue seemed an island in the midst of milky sweetness." These words are more effective than simply saying, "The traditional South American *tres leches* cake looked yummy."

- **Touch.** Use words that help your reader feel the textures of what you're describing. Instead of saying, "The heat felt good," write, "The warmth from the heating pad soaked into Tito's muscles, loosening their knots and soothing his bruises."

- **Hearing.** Use words that let your reader hear the sounds—and the quality of the sounds—that you hear. Rather than saying, "The faucet dripped," write, "Steadily counting out every hour until dawn, the rhythmic dripping of the faucet seemed to grow louder with every sleepless minute."

Using sensory descriptions in your writing offers two main benefits. First, clear descriptions give you credibility. For instance, suppose you describe running a marathon, but all you say is, "I felt tired." Your reader would have no proof that you completed the race. However, if you use specific details like those listed below, your reader is more likely to believe you.

- The tightening of your stomach as the starter's gun goes off
- The ubiquitous slapping of competitors' shoes on the asphalt
- The dryness of your mouth as you approach an aid station

- The smell of perspiration mingled with sea air as you run along the boardwalk
- The increasing burn of your thigh muscles as the race progresses

The second primary benefit of using sensory details is that they make your writing enjoyable to read. Think about a time when a friend has described a new NBA basketball star to you. If all you hear is that the player is good, you probably won't be able to picture him. However, if your friend describes the fluid motion of the player as he glides down the court, pausing only briefly to gracefully leap toward the rim and lightly lit the ball roll off his fingers, you might be better able to understand the player's skill.

Organizing and Linking Ideas

Emphatic order works well for descriptive paragraphs since many descriptions do not contain events that can be ordered chronologically. Remember that emphatic order lets you organize your ideas from least to most important.

Keep in mind, too, that with descriptive paragraphs, you have the option of describing something in terms of its shape or layout. As Svetlana began her essay describing her store manager, she opted for the "top to toe" approach, and she described Ms. Mayer beginning with her hair and ending with her feet. Svetlana could also have worked her way up from Ms. Mayer's feet; either way works, but having an organizational plan is key. Jumping around from Ms. Mayer's hands to her hair and then her suit, for instance, would be confusing.

If you choose to use spatial signals, be sure you have a plan. For example, you might move your way through the place you're describing, starting on one side and working your way to the other.

Words and Terms That Signal Emphatic Order

above all	first	most important
another	in the first place	most significantly
equally important	last	next
especially	least of all	
even more	most of all	

Words and Terms That Signal Space

above	here	opposite to
across	in back of	there
before	in front of	to the east (north, etc.)
behind	nearby	to the left
below	next to	to the right
elsewhere	on the other side	

✓ CHECKLIST for Developing a Descriptive Essay

_____ **Prewriting**

■ Choose a topic you can describe in detail.

■ Use prewriting strategies to get your early ideas on paper.

_____ **Drafting**

■ Write a thesis statement that gives the topic, and include words expressing your point of view.

■ From your prewriting, select convincing support points, if appropriate, and identify specific details that appeal to the five senses: smell, taste, touch, sight, and hearing.

■ Organize your ideas.

■ Write a rough draft of your essay. (Feel free to do more prewriting as this point to get more ideas down on paper.)

■ Use transitions to connect your support points and ideas.

_____ **Revising**

■ Revise your work, as necessary, according to the first three of the four Cs: _concise, credible,_ and _clear_ writing.

_____ **Editing**

■ Proofread your work for sentence-level errors.

Following the Four Cs Through Revision

Revision is particularly important in writing a descriptive essay because sometimes those details that arise early in prewriting are not the best choices in communicating your main idea. Anna, whose assignment was to describe a person, chose to write about the photographer Ansel Adams. Pay attention to how Anna uses detail to make her points clear.

Portrait of an Artist

Some people observe that pets, after being with their owners for lengthy periods of time, come to resemble them. ~~My aunt, who has very fluffy light hair, has a dog that looks just like her, right down to the fluffy white fur.~~ Perhaps an artist and the subject of his work are no different. **Environmentalist and** photographer Ansel Adams is best known for his black-and-white photographs, particularly those of natural landscapes such as Yosemite National Park. <u>However</u>, in looking at a photograph of the man himself, one can easily see a clear resemblance to those famous sights in Yosemite.

If one begins with a study of the photographer <u>at the top of his head</u>, one can see how the white-fringed dome of his forehead takes on characteristics resembling the Half Dome rock structure. Indeed, just as the back slope of Half Dome curves gently only to drop sharply off, **as if sliced,** so too does Mr. Adams's ~~mug~~ head swell in a curve ~~like a big balloon~~ that ends with the steep descent to his face. ~~I once climbed Half Dome and nearly passed out at the top, only to realize that I still had to hike down.~~ The lines and shadows in the artist's visage resemble so many color variations in the stone wall that marks a rock climber's fantasy.

<u>Working one's way down past the mouth</u>, one continues the comparison between Adams and his beloved photographic model. Images of rushing Bridalveil Falls spring to mind as one sees the **snowy beard cascading** over proud chin. ~~If he ever spilled barbeque sauce down his face, there would be a real cascade.~~ A churning mass of curl, the full beard flows **from near the ears,** <u>descending lower</u> until it peaks in a darkened patch of gray that resembles a quiet pool of water just past the fall's point of impact. Though exhibiting no actual motion, the beard appears alive and energetic in its efforts to adorn its owner.

<u>Peering head-on into Adams's face</u>, one can't help but notice similarities between his expressions and his subjects in nature. His eyes, **bright and clear,** resemble dogwood blossoms arranged delicately on a low, flat stone, and his nose projects proudly <u>from above his</u>

mouth, keeping watch over his face as ~~if it were a living form of~~ El Capitan guards Yosemite Valley. <u>Finally, on his face</u>, Mr. Adams's teeth peek from between curved lips, **serving as small rocks in the stream of his smile.** There can be no doubt that this is the face of one who loved nature.

Most of us may not have the good fortune to resemble something we love as well as Ansel Adams loved Yosemite. Perfecting our skills in specific areas may be the closest we come to emanating art from our persons. Ansel Adams, <u>however</u>, was this lucky. Seeing the artist's face as an expression of his subject gives new depth to the man's **passion and** photography, letting us understand his connection with nature.

Revising for the First C: Concise Writing   When Anna first wrote her draft, she thought she might use humor in her comparison of man to nature. As she progressed in her writing, however, she realized that light-hearted quips might detract from the serious message of her essay, which reflects her great respect for Ansel Adams. Thus, she crossed out off-topic or overly light sentences that did not advance her thesis statement.

Revising for the Second C: Credible Writing   Details are everything in a descriptive essay, so make sure that you have enough details to make your ideas clear. Anna had no problem finding images in nature with which to compare Adams's face, but she did add several details (shown in bold type) for clarification as she revised her essay.

Revising for the Third C: Clear Writing   Anna opted to use spatial organization in describing Ansel Adams. This approach generally works well, but Anna had to make sure that her ideas logically followed each other in her finished essay since, during drafting, her ideas didn't necessarily come to mind in an order that a reader could easily follow. She also added transitions (underlined) to connect her ideas.

Revising for the Fourth C: Correct Writing   The sentences in this essay are all correct. To check for correctness in your own writing, see Part Seven, "Writing Correct Sentences."

WRITING PRACTICE 1 Writing a Descriptive Essay Step by Step

You've had many opportunities to recognize and develop descriptive details in this chapter. Now you can put these skills to use in an essay of your own.

Your assignment is this: *Write an essay describing one of the photographs in this book.* In choosing your topic, try to find a photo that interests you in some way.

Prewriting

1. After you've decided on a photo that is interesting to you, freewrite for five to ten minutes. Then, use at least one more of the prewriting techniques covered in Chapter 4—listing, questioning, keeping a journal, clustering, or outlining.

   In your prewriting, consider details that appeal to the senses.

How do people or objects in the photograph *look?*

How does the setting *look?*

How do you think it *feels* to be in that photograph?

What does the setting in the photograph *smell* like?

What do you think it *sounds* like in the photograph?

What *tastes* do you think you'd experience in the photograph?

For this assignment, not all the senses may be relevant.

When you are writing a descriptive essay, a number of different prewriting techniques can be helpful. Listing can help you see all your details together in one place, and outlining can help you group your details together into a logical sequence.

Here is a sample list on the topic "Janet Leigh in *Psycho*," the photograph on page 111.

<u>Photo of Janet Leigh in Psycho</u>
Black-and-white photo
Terrified expression
Eyebrows bunched together
Eyes glazed
Eyes not focused on the camera
Mouth opened in a scream
Square white tile in the background
Can't see what she's afraid of
~~Norman Bates is bad guy~~
Wet hair matted to head
~~No soap dish visible~~
Water beads on face, neck, shoulders
Body angled away from shower head

Shoulders appear bunched

Neck seems tense

2. Read over your prewriting activity, and eliminate any details that do not seem to help describe your topic. In the list above, the writer has crossed out "Norman Bates is bad guy" and "No soap dish visible" because those details don't directly describe the photograph.

Drafting

3. Write a thesis statement if you haven't done so already.

Possible thesis statement: The photograph of Janet Leigh in the shower scene of the movie *Psycho* is the perfect picture of terror.

4. Choose support points and specific details for your essay, taking care to appeal to the reader's senses. Making an outline from your first list can help you plan your essay.

A possible outline of the Janet Leigh photograph essay follows.

Thesis statement: The photograph of Janet Leigh in the shower scene of the movie *Psycho* is the perfect picture of terror.

A. Facial expression

   1. Bunched eyebrows

   2. Open mouth

   3. Glazed eyes

   4. Wet hair matted to head

   5. Beads of water

B. Physical posture

   1. Angled away from the shower head

   2. Shoulders bunched

   3. Tense neck muscles

C. External details

   1. Black-and-white photo

   2. White tile

   3. Can't see what she's afraid of

5. Arrange your support points and details in a logical order. The outline above groups the writer's details into three main sections, but you don't need to do that. Just make sure that your details have some logical connection to one another.

6. Write a draft of your essay. Do your best to include important details and transitions, but don't worry if they're not perfect the first time around. Make sure all the details in your essay support your thesis statement. If they don't, cross them out.

Revising

7. Revise your essay, checking for the first three of the four Cs: *concise, credible,* and *clear* writing.

Editing

8. Proofread your essay to make sure you have used correct spelling, punctuation, and grammar.

WRITING PRACTICE 2 Describing a Place

Now you have the opportunity to choose both the topic and the types of support you use. Choose Topic A, B, or C, and follow the directions for writing a descriptive essay.

Topic A

Write an essay about a place that you are intimately familiar with. Make sure to choose a place that you can describe without seeing photographs or reading about it, and include details that appeal to the senses. Here are some suggestions:

Your room at home

A room, or rooms, in your parents' home

A room, or rooms, in your grandparents' home

A sports field or arena from your youth

A favorite playground, park, or hangout from your youth

Your place of work

A childhood school

Do some prewriting, as usual, to get your ideas on paper. Then think about your opinion of the place you want to focus on, and write your thesis statement. Remember that your thesis statement controls the direction of your essay.

Here are some possible thesis statements.

My childhood room was a place of perfectly organized chaos.

My father's work shed always seemed to hold secrets.

Grandma's kitchen was the coziest place I've ever known.

The soccer field at Seymour Park came to symbolize the ultimate defeat.

The burger place at our downtown mall was the social center for my high school crowd.

The office building where I worked was the dingiest space imaginable.

My high school resembled a prison.

Topic B

Write an essay describing a place *either* that you can see through a friend's or acquaintance's eyes *or* that you have seen but have no strong feelings about. Have a friend show you a photo of someplace meaningful to him or her, or choose a place in your city that you may have seen (such as City Hall) but have not visited. Consider these questions: What impression does the building itself communicate? What conclusions can you draw about the building, or the establishment it houses, based on its appearance? What mood, if any, does the building bring to mind?

Possible thesis statement: The Department of Motor Vehicles office is a depressing place.

As you begin writing, consider *what about* the place you chose makes it special or distinctive. Are certain smells associated with it? Is there a particular feeling that you're aware of when you enter this place? Does the place have an unusual layout that stands out in your mind? These are the types of questions to ask yourself to find the details to support your topic sentence.

Topic C

Write an essay about a place that you have visited recently for the first time—a new building on campus or a new department at work, for instance. Pay attention to your initial reactions to this place. Do you feel uneasy? Comfortable? How does your reaction to this place differ from your reaction to other places? What about this place contributes to the feelings you're experiencing? Feel free to use these questions as guides to prewriting.

Possible thesis statement: The college stadium is far less imposing up close than it seems from afar.

Be sure to let your reactions—rather than memories of or rumors about the place—be your guide in terms of providing specific details.

Spatial signals are those words that give your reader directions to mentally "look around" the place you're describing. See "Words and Terms That Signal Space" (page 289).

Revise your essay as necessary to make sure it's concise, credible, and clear. Proofread your essay for sentence-level errors.

WRITING PRACTICE 3 Writing in Response to a Reading

Read Amy Tan's essay "Lost Lives of Women" (page 281) and think about her main idea. Then, find a photograph of someone in your family or circle of friends. If you cannot find a photograph, picture a familiar scene from your youth.

Your assignment is this: *Write an essay about a photograph that means something to you, drawing a conclusion based on the picture itself.* For instance, if you choose a photograph of you and your siblings smiling during summer vacation, the conclusion you draw may be that you and your family had fun over the summer. Other possible conclusions are

Appearances can be deceiving.

Our family/friends were _____ to each other.

Our family/friends never thought we'd grow apart.

My childhood was _____.

My family/friends taught me _____.

The key to this assignment is to use the photograph as support of the conclusion you draw. For instance, if you conclude—based on the photograph—that your childhood was stressful, you should choose details from the photograph that illustrate this stress. Mentioning an overly tight grip on your big brother's hand, a forced smile, or an unwillingness to look at the camera are all details that could make clear the stress evidenced in the photograph.

Lab Activity 19

For additional practice writing with description, complete Lab Activity 19 in the lab manual packaged with your textbook. If you did not receive a lab manual, you can complete this activity online at **www.ablongman.com/long.** Click on **College Resources for Writers** and then click on **Activity 19.**

20 Classifying and Dividing

CULTURE NOTE *Opera*

Often intimidating to those unfamiliar with it, opera is simply a musical drama in which most of the words are sung. Although the majority of operas are tragic—such as *La Bohème, Don Giovanni,* and *Madame Butterfly*—comic operas such as *The Magic Flute* and *The Barber of Seville* have also made their mark. Opera purists exclude operetta, or light opera, as part of the opera genre, but composers such as Gilbert and Sullivan and Leonard Bernstein have made this type of musical performance famous.

Brünnhilde

OBSERVE YOUR WORLD Brünnhilde from Richard Wagner's *Gotterdammerrung* or "The Ring" may be opera's most recognizable character. What contemporary stereotypes—the athlete, the diva, the lawyer, to name some—are representative of American culture? Write a few sentences identifying characters who exemplify some aspect of our lives, explaining why you think they, in particular, represent our culture.

What Are Classification and Division Essays?

If you've ever walked into a do-it-yourself home improvement store, it can be overwhelming. With so many different types of projects to consider, people seeking even basic supplies can feel lost. Some steps on the part of store management, however, make the shopping experience easier: having products classified into specific sections; having items grouped according to size and amount; having sale items brightly marked. All of these steps show an awareness of what the customer needs.

In your writing, too, organization is critical. Classification and division skills help you to make your method of organization clear.

Classification means grouping similar items together. On your shopping trip to the home improvement store, you visit the garden section. In this section, you find topsoil, seeds, sprouting plants, and digging tools such as trowels—all garden products. These items have been grouped, or *classified*, as garden products.

Division means breaking down a single, specific thing into its separate parts. The home improvement store itself, for instance, has been *divided* into different sections. "Lighting," "Floors," and "Paint" all have their sections. Similarly, areas like the checkout lanes, the storage area, the employees' area, and the offices represent other examples of the store's division.

For classification, ask: "What idea can I use to group these items together? What do these items have in common?" For division, ask: "What parts can I break this item into? What different pieces is this item made up of?" Classification and division require similar skills, so you can think of them as a single strategy for developing a paragraph. Some additional examples follow.

Classification

Hobbies	**Cars**	**Cuisine**
gardening	hybrids	Japanese
stamp collecting	sedans	Italian
dancing	convertibles	Moroccan
golfing	station wagons	Thai

Division

My School	**A Library**	**An Orchestra**
auditorium	fiction	strings
English building	reference	woodwinds

(continued)

My School	**A Library**	**An Orchestra**
library	audio	brass
administration building	children's books	percussion

Using Classification and Division in Real-Life Writing

In real-life writing, classifying and dividing helps us organize and keep track of our ideas.

For College

■ Make a schedule of your schoolwork, *dividing* the day into time slots for different classes: two hours for history, two hours for English, one hour for music, three hours for math.

■ Under each type of class, *classify* the tasks required for each one. For instance, under "English," list these tasks: complete class readings, prepare for class discussions, work on essay, study grammar.

In Your Personal Life

■ Divide your household chores into different categories: daily chores, weekly chores, monthly chores, seasonal chores.

■ Organize your finances by classifying different expenses in a budget.

At Work

■ Classify different supplies needed during your annual inventory.

■ Divide your job into different components: working the cash register, helping customers, organizing store products.

A Model Student Essay

Read the following essay, written by Danna, to see classification and division at work.

On Opera

For anyone who listens exclusively to pop music, getting lost in the opera section of the music store can be a daunting experience. Browsing over Bizet's *Carmen* when they want Korn can cause contemporary music buffs to quickly grow bleary-eyed. However, in the midst of the classical chaos is a logical way to organize opera. Opera, or musical dramas in which words are primarily sung rather than spoken, can be divided into three categories: grand, comic, and light.

In the first and largest category of opera, grand opera, all the words—even the conversations—are sung. Further, according to Encarta.com, the subjects of grand opera are usually mythological or historical figures who end tragically. One famous operatic composer, Wolfgang Amadeus Mozart, made famous the story *Don Giovanni*. Over the course of the opera, a lecherous military man, Don Giovanni, commits multiple atrocities ranging from rape to murder. Failing to repent for his acts, Don Giovanni dines with a statue of his murder victim, who eventually pulls him down to the underworld. A different opera with an equally tragic ending, Giuseppi Verdi's *Aïda* is the story of an Ethiopian slave who eventually chooses to be buried alive with her lover rather than live without him. Finally, not dying from a statue's revenge or live burial, Mimi is half of another tragic couple in Giacomo Puccini's opera *La Bohème*. In love with a poor poet in Paris, Mimi suffers and then dies of consumption. In grand opera, tragedy is king.

The second category of opera is comic opera, and—unlike its tragic counterparts—it often features everyday people and happy endings. Gioachinno Rossini's opera *The Barber of Seville* features the Count Almaviva, who must disguise himself several times to win the love of the fair Rosina. With the help of the clever barber Figaro, the two lovers end up together. Mozart's opera *The Marriage of Figaro* features the same clever barber as *The Barber of Seville*, but this time Figaro himself is the one to be married. Men disguised as women, women disguised as men, and women disguised as each other all contribute to the confusion—and ultimate happy ending—in *The Marriage of Figaro*. Gaetano Donizetti's comic opera *The Daughter of the Regiment* features a young woman, Marie, who was found and raised by the Twenty-first Regiment of Grenadiers in France. Marie and Tonio love each other and, despite many obstacles to their union, eventually are able to marry. In comic opera, the characters have a good chance at happiness.

Finally, a third category of opera is light opera, or operetta, but this category—which contains spoken dialogue and often frivolous subject matter—is not recognized as opera by opera purists. An example of operetta is *The Merry Widow.* Similar to comic opera, this operetta has a happy ending; it involves both the saving of a country (Pontevedria) and the happy union of two key characters, Anna and Danilo. Several operettas were written and made famous by the team of William Gilbert and Arthur Sullivan. Among these, *The Pirates of Penzance* remains extremely popular because of its humor and music. Finally, the operetta *No No Nanette* with lyrics by Vincent Youmans and music by Irving Caesar and Otto Harbach musically tells the story of wealthy Jimmy Smith and his daughter Nanette, interweaving their stories with tales of how Smith manages his money, much to the dismay of his frugal wife. Never reaching to the heights of grand opera, light opera simply entertains.

Though classic opera may not appeal to everyone, and operettas may not appeal to classical opera fans, these musical productions have many faces. From tearful tragedies to uproarious comedies and lighthearted plots, opera from each of the three categories—grand, comic, and light—is an important expression of drama and music.

EXERCISE 1 ANALYZING A DIVISION ESSAY

Read "On Opera." Then, answer the questions below.

1. What is the thesis statement of "On Opera"? _____

_____

2. What are the three types of opera that the writer describes?

   a. _____

   b. _____

   c. _____

3. What are three examples of each type of opera?

   a. _____

   _____

   _____

   _____

b. _____

_____

_____

_____

c. _____

_____

_____

_____

4. What transitions does the writer use to signal a change from one support point to another?

Paragraph 2: _____

Paragraph 3: _____

Paragraph 4: _____

A Professional Essay

While organization is always important, the *type* of organization is especially vital in a classification or division essay. Classifying her life according to the types of music that match her moods, Brenda Patterson's organization helps her communicate her point.

Life Is a Musical

Brenda Peterson

When the day is too gray, when the typewriter is too loud, after a lovers' quarrel, when a sister calls with another family horror story, when the phone never stops and those unanswered messages blink on my machine like angry, red eyes—I tune out my life and turn up the music. Not my favorite public radio station but my own personal frequency—I have my own soul's station. It is somewhere on the dial between Mozart's *Magic Flute,* the gospel-stomping tiger growl of Miss Aretha Franklin, Motown's deep dance 'n' strut, and the singing story of Broadway musicals.

Whether Katie Webster's Swamp Boogie Queen singing "Try a Little Tenderness" or a South American samba, whether it's the Persuasions crooning "Let It Be" or that throbbing baritone solo "Other Pleasures" from *Aspects of Love,* my musical solace is so complete it surrounds me in a mellifluous bubble like a placenta of sound. To paraphrase the visionary Stevie Wonder, I have learned to survive by making sound tracks in my own particular key of life.

For years now I've made what I call "tapes against terror" to hide me away from the noisy yak and call of the outside world. These homemade productions are dubbed Mermaid Music; sometimes I send them to friends for birthdays and feel the pleasure of playing personal disc jockey to accompany their lives too. Among my siblings, we now exchange music tapes instead of letters. It is particularly gratifying to hear my nieces and nephews singing along to my tapes, as another generation inherits our family frequency.

I trace making my musical escapes to a childhood of moving around. As we packed the cardboard boxes with our every belonging—sometimes we hadn't even bothered to unpack our dresses from those convenient hanging garment containers provided by the last moving company—the singing began. From every corner of the emptying house, we'd hear the harmonies: my father a walking bass as he heaved-ho in the basement; my mother's soprano sometimes shrill and sharp as the breaking glass in the kitchen; my little brother between pure falsetto and a tenor so perfect we knew he'd stopped packing his room simply to sing; my sisters and I weaving between soprano and first and second alto from our bedrooms as we traded and swapped possessions for our next life. At last gathered in the clean, white space that was once our house, we'd hold hands and sing "Auld Lang Syne." Piling into the station wagon, with the cat in a wooden box with slats for air holes, Mother would shift into a rousing hymn, "We'll Leave It All Behind," or sometimes, if she was mutinously happy to hightail it out of some small "burg" as she called them, she'd lead us into "Shuffle Off to Buffalo," substituting wherever we were moving for the last word. "Chattanooga Choo Choo" and "California, Here We Come" were her standard favorites for leave-taking. If, as we drove past our schools and our friends' houses for the last time, the harmonies in the backseat faltered, Mother might remind us that choirs of angels never stayed long in one place singing because the whole world needed music. Father might suggest some slower songs, as long as they weren't sad.

In all the shifting landscapes and faces of my childhood, what stays the same is the music. First, there was my mother's music, which seems now to have entered effortlessly into her children's minds as if we were tiny tape recorders: the mild, sweetly suave Mills Brothers, Mitch Miller's upbeat swing, the close sibling harmonies of the Andrews Sisters, and always the church music, the heartfelt Sunday singing, which is the only thing I ever miss since leaving that tight fellowship of Southern Baptist believers.

Ever since I can remember—certainly I have flashes of being bounced around in the floating dark of my mother's womb as she tap-danced on the church organ pedals, sang at the top of her voice, and boogied across the keys—there has been this music. It is the only counterpoint to, the only salvation from a sermon that paralyzes the soul into submitting to a jealous God. From the beginning, music was an alternative to that hellfire terror. I can still hear it: a preacher's voice, first a boom, then a purr that raises into a hiss and howl to summon that holy hurricane of fire and brimstone. But after enduring the scourge of sins, there came the choir. Cooing and shushing, mercy at last fell upon those of us left on an Earth that this God had long ago abandoned. Listening to the full-bodied harmonies, I could close my eyes and heretically wonder, Wasn't Heaven still here?

Yessss, hallelujah, still here . . . Hush, can't you hear? the choir murmured like so many mammies' lullabies. Then silence as a small woman stepped forward, her rapt vibrato shimmering like humid heat lightning right before rain. Or a baritone dropping his woes and his dulcet voice low as a cello, caressing a whole congregation. If we were blessed that Sunday, there might be a shorter sermon and a "songfest" with harmonies we could hear in our heads, syncopating, counterpointing in a lovely braid of bright sound that beckoned us. *Sing now, brothers and sisters.* And we were many voices making one song. The fundamental fear was gone; weren't we already angels in Heaven?

Now that I am forty and have been what my family pityingly refers to as "settled-down" for ten years, now that I am so far backslid from the fellowship of the Southern Baptist believers, now that I no longer even make top ten on my mother's prayer list, now that the terror of Hell has been replaced by the terror of living, I still find myself calling upon my homemade choirs to accompany me in my car, to surround my study or kitchen and sing back the demons of daily life. Sometimes I've even caught myself slipping another tape against terror into the stereo and singing a distracted riff of my mother's favorite, "We'll Leave It All Behind."

During the recent holy war between the United States and Iraq, with the apocalyptic rhetoric about "Satan" and "infidels" eerily reminiscent of southern revivals—Mermaid Music was working long hours to meet my own and my friends' wartime demands. To offset NPR's daily interviews with military experts commenting on the allied video-war air strikes with the zealous aplomb of sports-casters, I'd surrender to the tender tenor of Aaron Neville singing "With God on Our Side" or "Will the Circle Be Unbroken?" As I drove along freeways where phosphorescent orange bumper stick-ers shouted USA KICKS BUTT! or OPERATION DESERT STORM, as if it were a souvenir banner of a hot vacation spot, I wondered that there was no music for the Gulf War. Where were the songs like "My Buddy" or "It's a Long Way to Tipperary"?

During the last days of the war, I relied upon Bach's Violin Con-certo in D Minor, the fierce longing of Jacqueline DePres's cello, Fauré's Requiem and, as always, Mozart. On a particularly bad day, between the Pentagon press conferences—men with pointers, tar-get maps, smart-bomb videos, and a doublespeak war doggerel that called bombing "servicing a target"—I made a beeline to my public library and checked out every musical from *Oklahoma* to *Miss Saigon*. I made a tape entitled "Life Is a Musical" and divided it into three sections: (1) Love Found in Strange Places, (2) Love Lost Everywhere, and (3) Love Returns. It was astonishing how songs from vastly different time periods and places segued together. My favorite storyline riff is "Empty Chairs at Empty Tables," from *Les Misérables* to "The American Dream," from *Miss Saigon* to "Care-fully Taught" from *South Pacific* to "Don't Cry for Me, Argentina," from *Evita* to "Bring Him Home" from *Les Misérables*. When I sent copies out to a select group of musicals-loving friends, it was as if we were all together at a candlelight mass or cross-continent com-munion, trying to imagine a war where no bombs fell.

Playing my own tapes against terror is a way to document and summon back the necessities that mothered them. For example, "My Funny Valentine," with its Billie Holiday/Sarah Vaughan/Ella Fitzger-ald/Alberta Hunter blues and ebullience is still a favorite, long after that lover has gone. Upon hearing that an old friend had bone can-cer, I made him a tape called "Music to Heal By," which included the Delta Rhythm Boys' version of "Dry Bones." My friend wrote to say it was the first time he'd laughed in a long time. Now he's making his own tapes. After a writer friend of mine drank herself to death, I felt so bereft—since, after all, we'd planned to retire to the Black Hole Nursing Home for Wayward Writers together—that I made a tape called "The Ten Commandments of Love, or Southern Baptists

Beware!" It's every song I ever slow-danced to or memorized in the sweaty backseat of a borrowed car as my date and I broke Sunday school rules on Saturday night. Declared by my siblings and southern pals to have gone into "metal" (their word for platinum or gold), it includes Etta James's soaring "At Last," Sam Cooke's silky "Wonderful World," and a steamy duet of "634–5789" with Robert Cray and Tina Turner. It's a great tape for getting in the mood.

Since ancient times, the Chinese have believed that certain sounds can balance and heal. In acupressure, for example, each organ has a sound. Listening to a healthy heart, an astute healer can hear laughter or, if there is disease, wind. The gallbladder shouts; the stomach speaks in a singsong, sometimes overly sympathetic voice; and the kidney, ever the perfectionist, groans. Sighs can be a sign of liver ailments, and the pitch of a person's voice can tell a story of that body's health just as well as a tongue. In some Taoist practices to enhance longevity, re-creating the sounds of certain organs can strengthen and tone them. For example, the *whuuuh whuuuh* sound of the kidney can revitalize the adrenals, fortifying the immune system. If one cannot take time to sing in the key of every organ, I'd suggest Chinese wind chimes like the ones that grace my back porch. When a strong salt wind blows off the beach, my chimes, which are perfectly pitched to a five-element Chinese scale, play an impromptu arpeggio—a momentary transport to some monastic garden, a Shangri-la of sound. Scientific studies report that the actual sound of nature resonates at the level of eight hertz; by comparison, a refrigerator reverberates at eighty hertz. Is it any wonder some of us need to return to a musical womb to retreat from such technological onslaughts to our nervous systems?

In fact, our time in the womb is not at all quiet; it is a noisy symphony of voices, lower-tract rumbles, whirrings like waterfalls, and white noise. One of my friends found that if she played a tape of the roar of her sturdy Kirby vacuum cleaner, the sound immediately put her boisterous newborn twins to sleep. I have another friend whose entire house is wall-to-wall egg cartons, which absorb sound as well as enhance his audiophilic tendencies. I've visited houses that sound like living inside an aquarium, where pleasant underwater burbles from elaborate tropical fish tanks drown out the world. I've also entered homes where cuckoo clocks, grandfather chimes, and deep gongs count the hours so that I felt I was inside a ticking time bomb. Consciously or unconsciously we all make sound tracks to underscore our lives.

Mermaid Music has allowed me to enter a reverie of song, a backstage "smaller-than-life" sojourn away from all the stresses.

Right now I'm at work on two dance tapes for a summer roll-up-the-rug party. Entitled "Bop till You Drop" and "Bad Girls," the tapes defy all hearers not to kick up their heels with such all-time hits as "Heat Wave" and "I Heard It Through the Grapevine," as well as the ever-popular "R-E-S-P-E-C-T." Of course, I've had request for sequels and am at work on "Life Is a Musical II" divided into (1) "Falling," (2) "Feeling," and (3) "Forever Ruined/Recovery." It flows from "People Will Say We're in Love" to "Happy Talk" to "Just You Wait, Henry Higgins!"

My siblings say I should sell my tapes against terror on late-night TV in the company of such classics as Veg-O-Matics and "Elvis Lives" medleys. The idea fills me with horror. After all, there are copyright violations cops who come like revenuers in the dark of the night to bust local moonshiners and music makers. I'd rather stay strictly small-time and nonprofit, like that long-ago lullaby service I had in college, a trio of nannies against nightmares. But if anyone out there in music land is making his or her own tapes against terror, I'd be open to an exchange. After all, it's better than bombs through the mail or collecting baseball cards.

So tune in, and maybe we'll find ourselves on the same frequency. On this lifelong Freeway of Love, I just want to be an Earth Angel with my Magic Flute. Because after all, Everybody Plays the Fool and Ain't Nobody's Business If I Do.

EXERCISE 2 ANALYZING AN ESSAY FOR GOOD CLASSIFICATION STRATEGY

Read "Life Is a Musical" by Brenda Peterson. Then, answer the following questions.

1. What function does music serve for Peterson? _____

_____

2. What are some categories that music fits into for Peterson? _____

_____

3. What are three examples of specific music serving a specific

function for Peterson? _____

_____

_____

_____

4. Who is Peterson's audience? How can you tell? _____

_____

_____

5. How is Peterson's essay organized? _____

_____

_____

Writing a Classification or Division Essay

Writing a division or classification essay can be a wonderful exercise in organization. To do so, you must focus on the aspects of your subcategories that are most relevant to showing how they can be grouped together or separated. In a discussion of cars, for example, you could probably leave out the types of tires unless they are particularly important to the car's style or performance, as with "monster" trucks or race cars.

Knowing Your Audience and Purpose

Considering your audience's level or interest and expertise in your subject area is essential in writing a classification or division essay. While you should attempt to be clear and specific in your writing, these two aspects of writing development are especially important for this development strategy. For instance, Kim wanted to write about different types of popular music, and she decided upon three subcategories—R & B, rock, and jazz—as her areas for development.

However, once she began writing, she realized that she was using terms such as *fusion, speed metal,* and even *gangsta rap* that she didn't think her instructor would know or be interested in. Knowing her audience also affected Kim's purpose. She had originally decided to go into great detail about specific artists, albums, and songs; however, knowing her instructor's limitations on her subject, Kim revised her purpose and gave more of an overview of popular music. Kim focused her discussion on music that fell under the general headings she selected, choosing mainstream pop artists and well-known musical techniques for her examples instead of little-known musicians with highly specialized styles who illustrated obscure elements of a given music type.

Choosing a Topic for Development

For classification or division essays, make sure you pick a topic that lends itself to being broken down into smaller groups or identified according to an all-inclusive idea. One way to find a topic that works well for using classification or division is to do some prewriting. For instance, Vincent wondered if he could write an effective essay about the different relaxation activities engaged in by his circle of friends. He used listing to help him decide, making a general list first and then making more specific lists for each category he identifies. His first list looks like this:

> Ways my friends relax
>
> Exercise
>
> Reading
>
> Yoga

After coming up with a general way to divide his friends' relaxation strategies, Vincent began thinking of specific examples that illustrated each type of relaxation.

> Cardiovascular exercise
>
> Cindy takes kick-boxing aerobics classes.
>
> Jarrod swims laps.
>
> Alonzo runs for miles.
>
> Reading
>
> Lolo reads murder mysteries late a night.
>
> Dante reads the newspaper between classes.
>
> Shari reads magazines on the bus.
>
> Yoga
>
> Terry takes "hot yoga" classes each week
>
> Malcolm watches yoga videos at home.
>
> Sunny takes hatha yoga courses at the YWCA.

In this case, the connecting idea among all the people Vincent writes about is their relaxation activities. Within that category, three subcategories—cardiovascular exercise, reading, and yoga—provide Vincent with opportunities to develop his essay. Vincent was happy that he had paid attention to his friends' leisure habits, and he felt he had enough information to write an effective classification essay.

Writing an Effective Thesis Statement

Vincent has organized his categories according to how they occurred to him in prewriting.

Category 1: Cardiovascular exercise

Category 2: Reading

Category 3: Yoga

After identifying these categories from listing, Vincent wrote his thesis statement: "My friends' relaxation strategies seem to fall into one of three groups." When he writes his rough draft, Vincent can decide whether he has enough details for each type of relaxation or if he needs to do more prewriting. Vincent's key to writing a clear thesis for his division and classification paragraph is that he identified his topic—relaxation strategies—and wrote that his friends, the source of his specific details, fall into three groups. Thus, his reader knows exactly what to expect from the rest of Vincent's exercise.

Developing Specific Details

Depending on your essay assignment, you may find specific examples primarily from your own life, or you may need to consult outside sources to find support for your topic. In Vincent's case, examples from his own life were adequate for support. Once Vincent began making his lists of the types of relaxation techniques he planned to write about, he only had to think of the friends to ask for specific details. Details such as "Cindy takes kick-boxing aerobics classes" or "Dante reads the newspaper between classes" came directly from Vincent's experience of being friends with them. If Vincent had wanted to write about a relaxation strategy that his friends didn't practice—massage therapy, for instance—he would have had to find articles or experts to interview for information on that technique.

Organizing and Linking Ideas

Classification and division essays can be very easy to write. The key is to have a strong thesis statement that tells your reader how you will categorize your topic into smaller parts, or subcategories. Emphatic order, organizing your ideas from least to most important, is a good way to arrange your support points. Since you get to decide which points are most—or least—important when you're using emphatic order, pay attention to how much detail you derive from your prewriting. Chances are, the points that have the most detail will be the ones that matter the most to you, and they should be the ones you save for last.

To link your ideas, use transitional words and expressions that introduce examples. In the sentences that follow, the underlined transitional expressions signal that an example or illustration is introduced.

> <u>In the first and largest category</u> of opera, grand opera, all the words are sung.
>
> <u>The second category</u> of opera is comic opera.
>
> <u>Finally, a third category</u> of opera is light opera.

Notice that in "On Opera," the writer actually uses a *reverse* emphatic order to introduce her support points. Because grand opera comprises the largest section of opera—and because Danna figured her readers would be more interested if they heard early examples that were familiar to them—Danna chose to present her most important support point first. When writing about a topic that more readers are familiar with, saving the strongest support point for last—in standard emphatic order—is a logical way to go. The ideas for other topics, such as musical time periods, could be linked chronologically, so there's no set way to organize all division and classification essays. Rather, let your ideas and their connections determine the most logical pattern for your essay.

Words and Terms That Signal Emphatic Order

above all	last
another	least of all
equally important	most of all
especially	most important
even more	most significantly
first	next
in the first place	

✓ CHECKLIST for Developing Classification and Division Essays

_____ **Prewriting**

■ Choose a topic that lets you divide your topic into a number of smaller categories.

■ Use prewriting strategies to get your early ideas on paper.

_____ **Drafting**

■ Write a thesis statement that states the general idea and indicates how it will be divided or classified in your essay.

■ Write a rough draft of your essay. (Feel free to do more prewriting at this point to get more ideas down on paper.)

■ Use specific details that illustrate each subcategory.

■ Use transitions to connect your support points and ideas.

_____ **Revising**

■ Revise your work, as necessary, according to the first three of the four Cs: *concise, credible,* and *clear* writing.

_____ **Editing**

■ Proofread your work for sentence-level errors.

Following the Four Cs Through Revision

As with any type of writing, classification writing demands revision. However, your revision in writing such an essay should address balance and transition issues. In the following essay, note how the second support point originally contained far fewer details than the first point. Also notice how the writer, Perry, organized his body paragraphs for clarity, using transitional words as signals for his reader.

Opera's Music: More Than Just a Song

Though Merriam-Webster defines opera as "a drama set to music and made up of vocal pieces with orchestral accompaniment," it is more than just a combination of action and music. In fact, opera manages not only to infuse great action with gorgeous music, but it integrates music and drama at every stage of the performance. ~~The only time I ever saw an opera, it was music from beginning to end.~~ To achieve different purposes in the production, opera's music serves different functions. Thus, operatic music can be classified three ways, according to its purpose.

The first category of operatic music is the recitative. This is the normal, back-and-forth conversation that helps move a story along. **Performers might ask each other how they are, how a battle is going, or what plans they have, depending on the plot of the opera.** What makes recitative different from conversation in a non-musical performance is that it is sung. ~~I think it would be exhausting to have to worry about staying on key when just making a simple comment.~~ Thus, even the most mundane dialogue from *The Marriage of Figaro*—**such as "What are you measuring, my dearest Figaro?" and "I want to see if the bed which the Count has given us will go well in this spot"**—becomes a musical experience. ~~This is the kind of dialogue that many non-opera fans make fun of, probably because they don't understand it.~~ Though non-operagoers may find this musical dialogue hard to follow, recitative is necessary to present key characters and information, and to advance the plot of an opera.

A second category of operatic music is the aria. An aria is a solo for a singer in which the character expresses his or her feelings about a situation. ~~Many people "vent" their feelings through song.~~ One of the most famous arias is "Nessun Dorma," which means "no one sleeps," from Giuseppe Verdi's opera *Turandot*. **In this aria, a prince seeking the hand of the beautiful but cruel princess Turandot sings that no one will sleep until the princess reveals his name. Since he will be executed if the princess does know and tell his name, the aria is filled with emotion: love for the princess, challenge to the night and stars, and hope for the future.** ~~This story has similarities to *Rumpelstiltskin*, though the man whose name is guessed is the hero, not a strange little man.~~ Through extended musical selections such as this aria, operagoers learn of a single character's deepest emotions.

Ensembles, or musical numbers by two or more singers, comprise the last category of operatic music. French for "together," the ensemble allows multiple opera characters to express their views at the same time. ~~If this happened in real life—as when my brothers and sisters and I argue—it would surely not be considered artistic.~~ Ensemble singing is especially helpful in confusing mistaken-identity operas where explaining everyone's confusion could take a long time. Instead, two, three, four, or more singers communicate their feelings and ideas in perfect harmony. **Giuseppe Verdi took the concept of ensembles to the greatest height in his opera *Falstaff*, where ten different singers echo the same musical theme in a fugue (a musical number in which one theme is introduced and then repeated and developed by different characters in sequence). In the fugue—titled "Tutto nel mondo è burla"—the characters sing of how all the world's a joke, man is a jester, and he who laughs last laughs best.** ~~Opera ensembles are very different from pop music, which often has one theme and that's it.~~ Completely interwoven, several characters' parts make perfect sense in an operatic ensemble.

To say that opera is a musical drama is true, but it's insufficient to explain the complexities of music involved in opera. From the musical dialogue of the recitative through single-voiced arias to multi-voiced ensembles, opera's music presents different types of beauty as its types serve different functions. Perhaps hearing one character sing a song might be easier for operagoers, but it's far more interesting to hear composers mix and match their musical talents through various operatic compositions.

Revising for the First C: Concise Writing   Perry wrote this essay for his music appreciation class, and because the subject was unfamiliar to him, he found it easy to get off-track. Reading his essay with an eye for irrelevant details, Perry crossed out the items that did not directly advance his thesis statement.

Revising for the Second C: Credible Writing   Perry's primary challenge in making his essay credible was deciding which details were necessary to illustrate each type of opera. For instance, the detail about Figaro's and Susanna's bed (in bold print) seemed to have little to do with opera. However, it showed exactly how day-to-day topics are covered in a recitative, so Perry decided to include it.

Revising for the Third C: Clear Writing   Perry's ideas didn't seem to be linked in a chronological order, nor did Perry have strong feelings about which point was most important. When he started writing, however, he noticed two things: first, operatic ensembles seemed to potentially involve the most people, and second, ensemble singing seemed to require the most explanation. Thus, Perry saved ensemble for last, reasoning that the discussion of the other two points first would help clarify his last point. Pay attention, too, to how Perry echoed key words (underlined) from the thesis to link his paragraphs to it and each other.

Revising for the Fourth C: Correct Writing   The sentences in this essay are all correct. To check for correctness in your own writing, see Part Seven, "Writing Correct Sentences."

WRITING PRACTICE 1 Writing an Essay Step by Step

Now you have the opportunity to write an essay of your own.

Prewriting

1. From the list below, choose the topic that you think best lends itself to being divided into separate parts or classified according to an overriding principle.

Topics:

Parents	Buying habits	Travel
Cars	People's manners	Movies
Doctors	Entertaining	School courses
Homes	Pets	
Hobbies	Beauty aids	

2. As always, begin by freewriting on the topic of your choice for five to ten minutes. What are your initial ideas about classifying your topic? What details have you written that will work in an essay?

One student, Miranda, chose to freewrite on the topic of "manners."

> My mother always wanted me to have good manners, but sometimes I think I'm the only one who cares. Everyone I know either pays so much attention to manners that it seems phony, or else they ignore manners completely. My friend Janey always wants her manners to be perfect, but then I worry when I'm around her that I'll say the wrong thing or use the wrong fork or something. But then Pete, my brother's buddy, says he doesn't care about manners at all, and he's always belching right when I'm about to start eating. I guess people just have to find manners that work well for them.

In the freewriting above, Miranda already places people into at least two groups according to the kinds of manners they use. One group cares very much about manners, while the other group doesn't care at all. A third group could be people who care just enough about manners, and the connecting idea could be "how much people care" about manners.

After you've finished freewriting, use another prewriting technique covered in Chapter 4—listing, questioning, keeping a journal, clustering, or outlining—to see what information you have and where possible gaps are.

Outlining can be especially effective in planning classification and division paragraphs. Here is Miranda's outline.

Manners

A. People who care too much

    1. Always send thank-you notes

    2. Always know which fork to use

    3. Always say nice things, even if they don't seem to mean them

B. People who care somewhat

    1. Sometimes send thank-you notes, but always call

    2. Sometimes use the right fork, but aren't always sure

    3. Say nice things only if they mean them

C. People who don't care at all

    1. Never send thank-you notes

    2. Never use different forks, just the same one

    3. Never go out of their way to be nice

Miranda has three subcategories for her ideas, and she divides her topic, "manners," based on how much people care about manners.

Drafting

3. Write a topic sentence that clearly divides or classifies your topic. For example, here is a topic sentence for the listing done above.

    Possible topic sentence: People can be classified into three groups according to how much they care about good manners.

4. Choose subcategories and specific details for your topic. For instance, in her outline Miranda identifies three groups of people she will discuss in her essay, and she offers some specific details for each group.

5. Arrange your support points—in this case, your subcategories—using a logical order, mostly likely emphatic order.

6. Now you're ready to write a rough draft of your essay. Use details and transitions as best you can, but don't worry about making your writing perfect at this point. Just get your ideas down in a basic order.

Revising

7. Revise your essay, as necessary, to add details and transitions. Check your essay to make sure that all of your subcategories are classified according to the same connecting idea.

Editing

8. Proofread your essay for sentence-level errors.

WRITING PRACTICE 2 **Using Classification and Division in Real Life**

Classifying and dividing ideas can be helpful in everyday life. Now you have the opportunity to choose both a topic and the types of support you use. Choose one of the real-life topics below and write an essay. Following the directions for Topic A, B, or C.

Topic A

Write an essay in which you explain to a new college student how to budget his or her time. For this particular assignment, knowing your audience is important because your advice will differ depending on several factors. You will need to consider whether or not the following elements play a role in your reader's life.

Course load

Work schedule

Family time

Extracurricular activities (such as school sports teams or student activities)

Leisure time

Goals

Possible thesis statement: New students must carefully divide their time among course work, extracurricular activities, and leisure time.

Topic B

Write an essay classifying the types of challenges new college students are most likely to face. For this essay, use examples from other people's lives (you don't have to know the person you write about) as well as your own life. You may use examples from written sources, such as the newspaper, but you do not have to. Here are some ideas to choose from.

Increased level of difficulty in college work

Balancing school, work, and other activities

Increased level of independence

Increased or decreased number of assignments

Increased cost of attending school (books, lab materials, tuition, among other items)

Increased number of academic choices

Keep in mind that not all of these challenges will apply to every student, so interview a few friends or classmates to best determine the challenges faced by new students at your school. For instance, students who attended a private high school might not notice an increased cost in college.

Possible thesis statement: The challenges that new college students face typically fall into one of three categories: increased level of difficulty in college work, increased level of independence, and increased cost of attending school.

Topic C

Write an essay classifying different articles in one section of your local or college newspaper. For this assignment, you will need to read one section of a recent edition of your local newspaper. In the metro or city section of your newspaper, you may notice that the stories tend to fall under the headings of local politics, local crime, and local color.

Possible thesis statement: The articles in the sports section of *The Fresno Bee* tend to fall into one of three groups: current sports reports/scores, personnel issues (drafts and trades), and personal interest (athletes' community service or legal troubles, for instance).

WRITING PRACTICE 3 **Writing in Response to a Reading**

Brenda Peterson writes in "Life Is a Musical" that the function of her "Mermaid Music" is to "hide [her] away from the noisy yak and call of the outside world." What functions does music perform for you? Your assignment is this: *Write an essay classifying music according to its function or purpose in your life.*

For instance, heavy metal music may help someone "gear up" for a tough job or competition; classical music may help someone else focus while studying; hip-hop may help someone complete a workout less painfully. Your thesis statement may be something like this: "Music in my life can generally be classified into one of four categories: work music, study music, exercise music, and relaxation music."

Lab Activity 20

For additional practice with classification and division, complete Lab Activity 20 in the lab manual packaged with your textbook. If you did not receive a lab manual, you can complete this activity online at **www.ablongman.com/long.** Click on **College Resources for Writers** and then click on **Activity 20.**

21 Explaining a Process

CULTURE NOTE *Fishing*

Although the experience of putting a worm on a hook summarizes the sport of fishing for many people, there are nearly as many different ways to fish as there are people who fish. Additionally, many skills—tying flies, casting, choosing locations, and so on—elevate fishing from simple sport to practiced art. From ice fishing to fly-fishing, the act of luring a fish to one's hook is a challenge not easily mastered.

The Great Outdoors

JOURNAL ENTRY Though camping is praised as a great way to get in touch with nature, it takes a lot of work to have a good camping trip. What other activities require a lot of work before they can be enjoyable? Write a few sentences explaining what skills or efforts are necessary to make a specific activity worthwhile.

What Is a Process Essay?

If you've ever tried to show someone how to do something, you know how important specific instructions are. Suppose you and your roommates agree to combine laundry to save money. Explaining how to separate the colors, add the proper detergent or stain removers, and launder the clothes at the proper temperature will go a long way toward keeping your clothing from turning gray or shrinking three sizes. For success in washing clothes, understanding the laundry process is essential.

Explaining a **process** means describing how to do something or how something works, step by step. This chapter will focus on two kinds of process essays.

- The how-to essay
- The explanation essay

How-to essays tell a reader how to complete some action step by step. For instance, if you are teaching someone how to polish a pair of leather dress shoes, you might write down instructions such as these:

First, put a newspaper down on the polishing surface.

Next, assemble your materials: shoe polish, shoe brush, soft cloths.

Grab the shoes to be polished.

Rub polish evenly over outside of shoes, using a soft cloth.

Let polish dry on shoes for a few minutes.

After polish has dried, use shoe brush to remove excess shoe polish.

Finally, rub shoes with a clean soft cloth until they shine.

In this process, the order is particularly important. Smearing polish over your shoes *after* you completed the other steps would result in still-dull shoes that left dark smudges wherever you went. The process here determines the success of your polishing.

The second kind of process paragraph, the **explanation essay,** explains how something works, such as how a refrigerator operates or how salmon swim upstream. For instance, you can explain the digestive process in the following way.

First, a combination of chewing and salivary enzyme action begins to break down food in the mouth.

Next, food enters the esophagus (the long tube that runs from mouth to stomach).

The esophagus's rhythmic, wave-like muscle movements (called peristalsis) force food into the stomach.

Once in the stomach, the food is churned and bathed in gastric acid.

From the stomach, food enters the small intestine, where bile, pancreatic enzymes, and other digestive enzymes help to further break down food, and fluids and nutrients are absorbed into the blood vessels surrounding the small intestine.

Food then passes into the large intestine, at which point some of the water and electrolytes (chemicals like sodium) are removed from the food.

Finally, leftover elements are excreted as waste.

In this process, while the order is significant, it is important to know that all these steps are going on *continuously*. Thus, even though you must work hard to place the steps in a process in order, some steps in an explanation essay may be ongoing.

Similarly, explanation essays can help explain historical events. In describing an event such as a war or a political movement to your class, your instructor may present this information in terms of a process with one step leading to the next. However, it's possible that this process became apparent only after the end result was achieved. For instance, a writer describing the attack on Pearl Harbor in World War II might detail the steps in the attack as follows:

First, Japan made careful plans to attack Pearl Harbor, including what route to take and what supplies to bring. Next, Japan learned what ships were moored in Pearl Harbor and exactly where they were. Third, Japanese commander Yamamoto meticulously trained his troops for attack. Then, Japanese units—including submarines, aircraft carriers. and escorts—crossed the Pacific to Hawaii. Finally, Japanese forces bombed Pearl Harbor on the morning of December 7, 1941.

Explaining a Process in Real-Life Writing

In real-life writing, we explain processes all the time in order to teach people skills or explain how consequences came about. Here are some situations where explaining a process can be particularly helpful.

For College
- Write about the human circulatory system for a paper in your physiology class.
- Write about how civil rights activists organized the Montgomery bus boycott for a test in your sociology class.

In Your Personal Life

■ Write notes to roommates or repair people about how to perform a task such as cleaning, repair work, or dinner preparation.

■ Write instructions for your parents so they can burn a DVD using a new computer.

At Work

■ Write directions showing how to use a computer program or piece of equipment.

■ Write a detailed explanation of how a proposed program would benefit your department or company.

A Model Student Essay

To explain a process, follow the basic essay format. Jake, a summer fishing guide and the writer of "On the Fly," developed a thesis statement and then explained different steps that explain the process of fly fishing. Notice how Jake integrates fishing terms such as *angler, rod,* and *line* into laymen's, or non-fishing terms, throughout his essay to make his explanations clear to someone who may not be familiar with the sport.

On the Fly

Fishing always sounds great—and easy. Picture three good buddies sitting in a boat on a lake, reminiscing about the old days, and you've got your perfect picture of fishing. What people don't tell you, however, is that fishing has more to it than you'd think. In fact, your best bet is *not* to fish unless you go with someone who can show you how, and even then you should follow some basic steps. Especially in fly-fishing—where the angler, or person fishing, is attempting to trick the fish into biting a fake bug, or fly—knowing the basics can make the difference between a great sport or a great meal and a serious sunburn compounded by a fishless dinner.

First, make your you have the right gear. Whatever you do, don't use a plain, old big stick to fish. It's a nice idea—very back-to-nature and all—but it won't do the job. A stick will most likely be too brittle and too hard to hold so that when you inevitably hook the "big one" that's "this long," the stick will snap, leaving you with no fish, nothing to tempt a fish, and half a lousy stick. Experienced anglers will tell you that a modern rod of graphite or fiberglass is your best bet because of its weight, flexibility, and strength, so you should probably go with one of those. Next, you need to worry about the string. The string, or line, attached to the rod is important because if your line is too thin, it will snap when you try to haul in the big one, and if it's too thick, the fish will get suspicious. The "leader" is another piece of line that connects the regular line to the fake bug, or fly, and it needs to match the type of fly you're casting as well as the type of fish you're trying to catch and the type of weather you're experiencing. If you're into fishing for the tales you can tell, by all means use a stick and your grandma's yarn. If you really want to catch something, though, do what the pros say and get yourself some decent equipment.

After you've taken care of your stuff, make sure you can hold the rod right. Sure, everyone has an idea of what makes for a good hold—thumb on top, baseball grip, whatever—but a good grip will give you flexibility and control. An easy way to practice a workable grip is to think of picking up suitcase so that your thumb is on top of the cork grip. If you want to muscle it and go for something approaching a death squeeze, feel free, but when your thumb's tired and your wrist aches, remember the suitcase. Sure, there's no one "right" way to hold a fishing rod, but the luggage grip—while not macho—works pretty well. Since the motion of the forearm of your fishing hand will be limited to the space between ten o'clock and two o'clock on an imaginary clock, being relaxed in your grip— made easier by the luggage grip—is essential. Just make sure the grip feels relatively comfortable.

Now you're ready for the real thing. Casting is the actual act of fishing, where you send the fly out over the water to where you hope the fish are. Timing is a big deal for good anglers because having a smooth rhythm lets you project how far out you'll send your fly. This may not seem so important, but if you've spent forever making a fly or spent big money on a fly, you want to keep track of it. Also, make sure your casting motion is easy and regular, like the ticking of a metronome (the timekeeper that often torments piano students). Don't "flick" the line out over the water, and work on getting your fly to land gently on the water, just as a real bug would. Remember: the fish are smarter than you think, so unless they're starving, they won't bite a hugely splashed tangle of thread you've just dunked in front of them.

Of course, even if you follow all these steps, you still probably won't catch a lot of fish your first time out. But don't worry: practice makes perfect. Just get yourself a decent rod, a good grip, and a relaxed cast and you're in for some good sport. If the going gets tough, change your spot or your fly, but just do your best to enjoy the day—away from work—in the great outdoors.

EXERCISE 1 ANALYZING A PROCESS ESSAY FOR STEPS AND DETAILS

1. Write down the thesis statement.

_____

_____

_____

2. What main steps are involved in the process above?

Step 1: _____

Step 2: _____

Step 3: _____

3. Within Step 2, what other, smaller steps are involved?

_____

_____

_____

A Professional Essay

Some steps in a process require more development than others. Pay attention to how Hemingway allocates space to his support points in the essay below.

Camping Out

Ernest Hemingway

Thousands of people will go into the bush this summer to cut the high cost of living. A man who gets his two weeks' salary while he is on vacation should be able to put those two weeks in fishing and camping and be able to save one week's salary clear. He ought to be able to sleep comfortably every night, to eat well every day and to return to the city rested and in good condition.

But if he goes into the woods with a frying pan, an ignorance of black flies and mosquitoes, and a great and abiding lack of knowledge about cookery, the chances are that his return will be very different. He will come back with enough mosquito bites to make the back of his neck look like a relief map of the Caucasus. His digestion will be wrecked after a valiant battle to assimilate half-cooked or charred grub. And he won't have had a decent night's sleep while he has been gone.

He will solemnly raise his right hand and inform you that he has joined the grand army of never-agains. The call of the wild may be all right, but it's a dog's life. He's heard the call of the tame with both ears. Waiter, bring him an order of milk toast.

In the first place he overlooked the insects. Black flies, no-see-ums, deer flies, gnats and mosquitoes were instituted by the devil to force people to live in cities where he could get at them better. If it weren't for them everybody would live in the bush and he would be out of work. It was a rather successful invention.

But there are lots of dopes that will counteract the pests. The simplest perhaps is oil of citronella. Two bits' worth of this purchased at any pharmacist's will be enough to last for two weeks in the worst fly- and mosquito-ridden country.

Rub a little on the back of your neck, your forehead and your wrists before you start fishing, and the blacks and skeeters will shun you. The odor of citronella is not offensive to people. It smells like gun oil. But the bugs do hate it.

Oil of pennyroyal and eucalyptol are also much hated by mosquitoes, and with citronella they form the basis for many proprietary preparations. But it is cheaper and better to buy the straight citronella. Put a little on the mosquito netting that covers the front of your pup tent or canoe tent at night, and you won't be bothered.

To be really rested and get any benefit out of a vacation a man must get a good night's sleep every night. The first requisite for this is to have plenty of cover. It is twice as cold as you expect it will be in the bush four nights out of five, and a good plan is to take just double the bedding that you think you will need. An old quilt that you can wrap up in is as warm as two blankets.

Nearly all outdoor writers rhapsodize over the browse bed. It is all right for the man who knows how to make one and has plenty of time. But in a succession of one-night camps on a canoe trip all you need is level ground for your tent floor and you will sleep all right if you have plenty of covers under you. Take twice as much cover as you think that you will need, and then put two-thirds of it under you. You will sleep warm and get your rest.

When it is clear weather you don't need to pitch your tent if you are only stopping for the night. Drive four stakes at the head of your made-up bed and drape your mosquito bar over that, then you can sleep like a log and laugh at the mosquitoes.

Outside of insects and bum sleeping, the rock that wrecks most camping trips is cooking. The average tyro's idea of cooking is to fry everything and fry it good and plenty. Now, a frying pan is a most necessary thing to any trip, but you also need the old stew kettle and the folding reflector baker.

A pan of fried trout can't be bettered and they don't cost any more than ever. But there is a good and bad way of frying them.

The beginner puts his trout and his bacon in and over a brightly burning fire, the bacon curls up and dries into a dry tasteless cinder, and the trout is burned outside while it is still raw inside. He eats them and it is all right if he is only out for the day and going home to a good meal at night. But if he is going to face more trout and bacon the next morning and other equally well-cooked dishes for the remainder of two weeks, he is on the pathway to nervous dyspepsia.

The proper way is to cook over coals. Have several cans of Crisco or Cotosuet or one of the vegetable shortenings along that are as good as lard and excellent for all kinds of shortening. Put the bacon in and when it is about half cooked lay the trout in the hot grease, dipping them in cornmeal first. Then put the bacon on top of the trout and it will baste them as it slowly cooks.

The coffee can be boiling at the same time and in a smaller skillet pancakes being made that are satisfying the other campers while they are waiting for the trout.

With the prepared pancake flours you take a cupful of pancake flour and add a cup of water. Mix the water and flour and as soon as the lumps are out it is ready for cooking. Have the skillet hot and keep it well greased. Drop the batter in and as soon as it is done on one side loosen it in the skillet and flip it over. Apple butter, syrup or cinnamon and sugar go well with the cakes.

While the crowd have taken the edge from their appetites with flapjacks, the trout have been cooked and they and the bacon are ready to serve. The trout are crisp outside and firm and pink inside and the bacon is well done—but not too done. If there is anything better than that combination the writer has yet to taste it in a lifetime devoted largely and studiously to eating.

The stew kettle will cook you dried apricots when they have resumed their predried plumpness after a night of soaking, it will serve to concoct a mulligan in, and it will cook macaroni. When you are not using it, it should be boiling water for the dishes.

In the baker, mere man comes into his own, for he can make a pie that to his bush appetite will have it all over the product that mother used to make, like a tent. Men have always believed that there was something mysterious and difficult about making a pie. Here is a great secret. There is nothing to it. We've been kidded for years. Any man of average office intelligence can make at least as good a pie as his wife.

All there is to a pie is a cup and a half of flour, one-half teaspoonful of salt, one-half cup of lard and cold water. That will make piecrust that will bring tears of joy into your camping partner's eyes.

Mix the salt with the flour, work the lard into the flour, make it up into a good workmanlike dough with cold water. Spread some flour on the back of a box or something flat, and pat the dough around a while. Then roll it out with whatever kind of round bottle you prefer. Put a little more lard on the surface of the sheet of dough and then slosh a little flour on and roll it up and then roll it out again with the bottle.

Cut out a piece of the rolled-out dough big enough to line a pie tin. I like the kind with holes in the bottom. Then put in your dried apples that have soaked all night and been sweetened, or your apricots, or your blueberries, and then take another sheet of the dough and drape it gracefully over the top, soldering it down at the edges with your fingers. Cut a couple of slits in the top dough sheet and prick it a few times with a fork in an artistic manner.

Put it in the baker with a good slow fire for forty-five minutes and then take it out, and if your pals are Frenchmen they will kiss you. The penalty for knowing how to cook is that the others will make you do all the cooking.

It is all right to talk about roughing it in the woods. But the real woodsman is the man who can be really comfortable in the bush.

EXERCISE 2 ANALYZING AN ESSAY FOR GOOD PROCESS EXPLANATION STRATEGY

Read "Camping Out" by Ernest Hemingway. Then, answer the following questions.

1. What three challenges does Hemingway say most campers face?

_____

2. Which challenge does Hemingway spend most of his time explaining?

Why? _____

_____

3. How does Hemingway address the first two challenges? _____

_____

4. Does Hemingway know what he's talking about? How can you tell?

_____

_____

_____

5. Who is Hemingway's audience? How can you tell?   _____

_____

_____

Writing A Process Essay

The best part about writing a process essay is showing off. While an essay gives you the opportunity to reveal your knowledge about a topic and your skill in communicating that knowledge, only the process essay lets you share something specific to your experience and expertise. Thus, choosing your topic and considering your level of detail are especially important. Make sure to choose a topic that interests you and that you know about, and acknowledge your reader's interest and skill relative to your topic.

Knowing Your Audience and Purpose

In writing a process essay, the fastest way to bore your reader is to include too much detail. Depending on your writing style, you may feel comfortable including the most minute steps in explaining a process. This, however, can be a huge mistake. In every process there are steps that are essential—in "On the Fly," for example, it's how to hold a fishing rod—and steps that are extraneous, such as "Squint if the sun gets in your eyes." Your job as a writer is to explain the *essential* steps to your reader and leave out the extras. Understanding your audience (your reader's interest in your topic, level of experience, and general areas of knowledge) and your purpose (giving a general overview, teaching someone a new skill, or teaching someone well enough to enable him or her explain it to someone else) will help you cut out extra steps and focus on the ones that matter most.

Choosing a Topic for Development

It's possible that your instructor will assign a topic that you need to research first, but most likely, you'll get to choose a topic that you're already familiar with. This is your chance to teach your instructor something that you know about or do particularly well. Take advantage of this opportunity and write about something that fascinates you.

Additionally, make sure that your topic has distinct stages or steps that work together as part of a process. Many topics can work well for explaining a process, but some are easier to write about than others. Some examples of topics that do and do not work well for process essays follow.

Good Topics for Explaining a Process	Hard Topics for Explaining a Process
How to run a marathon	The reasons people run marathons
How to execute a "pick and roll" play in basketball	The benefits of a "pick and roll" offensive strategy in basketball
How to make a good impression	Why making a good impression is important

Each of the suitable topics for a process essay deals with a skill or activity. While the topics that do not work as well for process essay are related themes, they do not offer the same opportunities for explaining step by step how to complete a process or how a process works.

One way to tell whether your topic will work well is to *make a list of all the steps that your process involves.* Listing will help you keep your facts in order and eliminate those that are irrelevant.

For instance, in "On the Fly," Jake focuses on the steps that will help a potential angler get started fishing. He does not, however, include such details as how fly-fishing has gained popularity or why some people believe that fly-fishing is superior to bait fishing. While these details are interesting, they do not help explain the *process* of fly-fishing.

Cornel was assigned an essay explaining a process he felt was important. Since he was an assistant coach for his high school football team, he had been required to learn cardiopulmonary resuscitation (CPR). He began by making a list of the basic steps in CPR.

How to perform adult CPR

Make sure the scene is safe for you to help.

~~Don't try to move an injured person.~~

Determine if person is conscious by tapping and shouting, "Are you OK?"

If no response, have someone call 911.

~~Use someone's cell phone, if possible.~~

Position the patient on his or her back.

Open the airway with a head-tilt, chin-lift, or jaw-thrust maneuver.

If airway is blocked, remove objects with your hands.

Look, listen, and feel for breathing (five to ten seconds).

If person isn't breathing, ventilate (blow air into person's mouth) twice.

~~For babies, you'll need to cover both mouth and nose to ventilate.~~

Check for a pulse by palpating (feeling) the carotid artery (artery on side of neck) for ten seconds.

If no pulse, begin chest compressions at a rate of fifteen compressions to two breaths.

~~Don't use your thumb to check pulse.~~

Recheck the pulse after one minute.

Continue steps until help arrives.

Most of Cornel's details show a progression from the start of the CPR process through the end. Some details—such as using a cell phone to call for help or covering a baby's nose and mouth—can be omitted because they don't act as steps in the specific CPR process for adults that Cornel describes.

Writing an Effective Thesis Statement

After looking over his list, Cornel realized he had a fairly complete list telling how to perform adult CPR. After eliminating unnecessary details, Cornel wrote the following thesis statement: "Performing CPR correctly is a simple, though extremely important, process." From there, Cornel was able to start fleshing out items on his list to make them into adequate details.

Developing Specific Details

The details in a process essay come from the steps in the process. Sometimes, a step will include all the detail necessary to communicate a point. For instance, in Cornel's list of CPR steps, he writes, "Begin chest compressions at a rate of fifteen compressions to two breaths." For readers familiar with CPR, this is enough detail. Others, however, might need to know exactly where to compress the chest and approximately how much pressure to apply.

To decide how much detail to include, consider your reader. Cornel knew that his instructor worked as a white-water rafting guide every summer, so he assumed that his instructor was familiar with CPR. If he had been writing for someone not familiar with CPR—a new classmate or one of the players on his football team, for instance—he would have included more details to make the steps in the process clear.

Organizing and Linking Ideas

Process essays, like narrative essays, do not contain specific support points. Instead, the steps in the process act as markers for your readers to know where they are in your process. Thus, one of the most important factors in writing a process essay is *keeping your steps in order.* Using chronological (time sequence) order is a logical way to link your ideas. For example, if you are explaining how to change the oil in a car, you will most likely include the steps of draining the old oil from the car, disposing of the old oil, and adding fresh oil to the car. Forgetting to tell someone to drain the old oil from the car *before* adding the new oil, for instance, could lead to a result you're not happy with.

Sometimes the steps in a process allow for some flexibility. In such a case, grouping the steps logically according to their function or details can help your reader better understand your process. For instance, in "Camping Out" (page 326), Hemingway covers three elements that can ruin camping: bugs, sleeping, and cooking. Depending on when he began his camping trip, he might realistically alternate steps from each of the three areas in preparing his campsite. If he were bitten by a bug while cooking, say, he might interrupt his cooking process to apply the oil of citronella. However, a process essay is most successful if the steps in the process are grouped with details of similar purpose. Thus, Hemingway discusses the steps in dealing with bugs first, in making a comfortable bed second, and in cooking third.

In a process essay, transitions are particularly important. If you don't tell your readers when to perform certain steps, you run the risk of confusing them. See the boxes in this chapter for transition words that are useful in writing a process essay.

Transitions That Signal the Start of a Process

at first	first	initially	begin by

Transitions That Signal That the Process Is Still Going

after	before	meanwhile	until
afterward	during	next	when
as soon as	later	second, third	while

Transitions That Signal the End of a Process

at last   at the end   finally   last

CHECKLIST for Developing a Process Essay

_____ **Prewriting**
- Choose a topic that lends itself to chronological (time sequence) order and that can be explained in individual steps.
- Use prewriting strategies to get your early ideas on paper.

_____ **Drafting**
- Write a thesis statement that identifies your topic as one that can be explained through a series of steps.
- Make a list of the steps involved in the process you are explaining, and decide which steps are most important.
- Organize your ideas.
- Write a rough draft of your essay. (Feel free to do more prewriting at this point to get more ideas down on paper.)
- Use transitions to connect your support points and ideas.

_____ **Revising**
- Revise your work, as necessary, according to the first three of the four Cs: _concise, credible,_ and _clear_ writing. Make sure you haven't left out any important steps.

_____**Editing**
- Proofread your work for sentence-level errors.

Following the Four Cs Through Revision

Topic choice and organization are extremely important in writing a process essay. As you read about the ice fishing process in "On Thin Ice," pay attention to how Rachel has to move details around to group them logically with other details of similar function. Note, too, how Rachel has crossed out several unnecessary details throughout her essay.

On Thin Ice

As a self-proclaimed "girly girl," I can't say I've ever had much interest in ice fishing. It's cold, it's wet, and the warm clothing necessary to make the trip bearable is unflattering. However, I love my father, and since he has always wanted one of his kids to go fishing with him, I've tried to be a good sport. What I've learned, however, is that to stay comfortable during ice fishing, you have to have good preparation.

First, you have to be warm. Even if your fishing hole goes "ballistic" and you have more fish than you can catch and release, you'll be miserable if your fingers are frozen. **Wear layers of clothing, waterproof boots, and a waterproof outer layer.** Don't make the mistake of thinking that you'll "dry" if you get wet; you'll be freeze-dried, which isn't the way to spend a pleasant afternoon with a loved one. ~~Last year I wore this awesome pink snowsuit, complete with faux fur trim, but it only *looked* warm; within five minutes, I was praying we'd leave.~~ Dressing appropriately will guarantee that, even if the temperature is well below freezing, you'll be somewhat comfortable.

Next, you have to be safe. No matter how warm you feel or cute you look in your pink fur-trimmed parka, stepping onto thin ice—**ice that's less than four inches thick**—or "rotten" ice—**ice that's thick enough but may have been weakened by a late winter storm**—will surely ruin your trip. **My father taught me how to check the ice's thickness by grabbing a cut edge of ice between your thumb and forefinger.** Your hand will be freezing—~~and if you don't moisturize later, it will be flaky and dry~~—but it's better to be safe than soggy.

Getting the fishing spot ready is another important step in the process. My father and I first drive out on the ice, ~~which always makes me nervous,~~ and test the ice's thickness. We then pull out the auger, or drill, and drill our holes—one for me, one for dad—in the ice. ~~I like to bring food color to "decorate" my hole. I tell my dad that this helps lure the fish, but really it just makes me feel better about spending a freezing day outside.~~ After we drill the holes, we set up a portable shelter. This is basically a little tent with no bottom that sits on the ice and keeps us from freezing in the wind. We've tried all kinds, **but the one that works best is made of vinyl, has cushioned swivel seats, hammocks, and big storage pockets on the tent itself to hold all our supplies.** It's not as comfortable as a comfy armchair by the fire, but it gets us out of the weather.

<u>Finally, we wait.</u> We talk and watch our lines in the holes, and sometimes we even go check other people's spots to see how they're doing. **Last year we only had to wait about thirty minutes before our lines started straining, but in the past it's taken much longer.** ~~Usually we stay put, though, even if the fish aren't biting, which tells me that Dad likes the trips for the same reason I do: to catch up with each other.~~ When the telltale tug on the line comes, we reel in our catch, unhook them, and throw them back. I've started bringing a camera so that Dad has proof of his fish stories ~~(and I have pictures of my cute outfits)~~, but I don't have to touch the slippery little buggers. Some people stay on the ice for days, but Dad and I usually only manage a few hours ~~(he's sensitive to me, sometimes)~~ before we pack up and go home.

Ice fishing may not be the world's most exciting sport, but it's a good excuse to spend time with someone you care about. That said, even if you're not into the sport for the grand catches, you'll still have a better time if you're prepared. Be warm, be safe, and be sheltered; following these steps will go a long way toward ensuring a decent fishing trip.

Revising for the First C: Concise Writing   Since Rachel admits that ice fishing is not her favorite activity, she has to make sure she doesn't repeat this point too often. Thus, she deletes references to her lack of interest. Rachel also crosses out any sentences that seem to contribute unnecessary detail about keeping warm or visiting with her father.

Revising for the Second C: Credible Writing   Rachel added details about testing the ice, preparing the fishing spot, and waiting (in bold print). Though her terminology is not as specific as one might expect from an expert angler, she explains the process clearly enough, using enough detail—such as in checking the ice and describing the ice shelter—that her reader believes her.

Revising for the Third C: Clear Writing   Rachel's process follows chronological order and her transitions at the start of each paragraph let the reader know how the steps in that paragraph fit with steps from other paragraphs. Other steps—such as drilling holes and reeling in fish—come within the body paragraphs, but Rachel has grouped details logically so that similar steps are listed together.

Revising for the Fourth C: Correct Writing   The sentences in this essay are all correct. To check for correctness in your own writing, go to Part Seven, "Writing Correct Sentences."

WRITING PRACTICE 1 Writing an Essay Step by Step

Now that you've worked through some practice topics to explain a process, it's time to write your own process essay.

Prewriting

1. From the following list of topics for essays that can be developed using the process strategy, choose one that you have experience with.

   Driving in heavy traffic

   Studying for finals

   Getting over an illness

   Making a good first impression

   Telling a joke

   Preparing a typical _____ meal

   Getting something pierced

   Learning to surf the Internet

   Teaching a skill to a younger sibling

   Legally downloading music from the Internet

   Applying for a job

   Falling asleep easily

   Putting someone out of your mind

   Catching someone's attention

   Quitting a bad habit

   Topic of your choice (any task you enjoy or do well)

2. Freewrite for five to ten minutes. In prewriting for a process essay, listing can help you keep steps in order. Below is a sample list on the topic of "falling asleep easily."

   Falling asleep easily

   Don't exercise for at least three hours before bed.

   ~~Don't eat right before bed.~~

   Make your room as dark as possible.

   Make your room cool.

   ~~Don't work in your bedroom.~~

Perform bedtime activities (brush teeth, etc.).

Get into bed.

Turn out light.

Get into comfortable position.

Take deep breaths.

Begin relaxing one body part at a time (work from head to toe or vice versa).

Substitute any stress-causing thoughts with stress-relieving ones.

~~Don't drink alcohol or caffeine within three hours of bedtime.~~

If you're still awake after thirty minutes, get up and read.

Go through the last several steps again as needed.

Drafting

3. Write a thesis statement if you haven't done so already. Don't worry if it's not exactly what you want for now. You can always revise it.

Possible thesis statement: Falling asleep easily is just a matter of having a set routine every night.

4. Choose the steps in the process, and select the details relating to those steps that are the most important to explaining the process.

5. Arrange your steps in chronological (time sequence) order.

6. Write your draft, using transitions to introduce new steps and link your ideas. Include as many details and transitions as you can, but don't spend too much time worrying about making them perfect at this point.

Revising

7. Make sure all the details in your draft directly advance your thesis statement. Eliminate any details do not help explain your process. Check again to see that you've included all the necessary details. Make sure your details are organized and connected through clear transitions that let your reader know where every step in the process comes.

Editing

8. Proofread your essay to make sure you have used correct spelling, punctuation, and grammar.

WRITING PRACTICE 2 Write to Teach Someone

Writing to explain a process can be useful teaching someone how to do something and in describing a series of events. Now you have the opportunity to choose both the topic and the types of support you use.

Topic A

Your college offers a summer program for middle school students aged twelve to fifteen. You have volunteered to act as a mentor to an incoming student in the program. Your assignment is this: *Write an essay explaining to the middle school student how to perform a task from the list below.*

How to buy a hot lunch in the cafeteria

How to buy schoolbooks in the campus bookstore

How to add or drop a class

How to prepare for the first day of class

How to make a good impression on instructors

How to check out a library book

How to get a locker assigned for a physical education class

How to check out lab equipment for a science course

How to take public transportation to and from your campus

How to do online searches at your school's library

Possible thesis statement: By following some specific steps, it's possible to buy all your required course books at the campus bookstore in less than forty minutes.

Topic B

One of the most common reasons students put their education "on hold" is that other aspects of life interfere with their educational goals. Financial worries, child-care responsibilities, and transportation difficulties are just some of the challenges that college students face. Your assignment is this: *Write an essay explaining to a student at your college how best to combat a particular challenge.* For this essay, use examples from other people's lives as well as your own. You may use examples from written sources such as the newspaper, but you do not have to.

Possible thesis statement: Finding timely, affordable transportation to college is possible if you know how to go about it.

Topic C

Many successful businesspeople claim that a key to their success is to have plans—a personal five-year or ten-year plan of achievement, for instance. One way to come up with your own plan is to read what other successful people have done to become successful. For instance, Malcolm X taught himself to read and write by copying a dictionary. For this assignment, you will need to read about or interview (if possible) someone you admire—or someone whose career you aspire to—to have specific details to support your thesis. Your assignment is this: *Write an essay explaining the best way to reach a specific goal after college.* Some possible goals are

To earn a graduate degree by age _____ (you decide)

To have a job that helps people

To have a job that interests you

To own your own business

To own a house by age _____ (you decide)

To earn a specific salary by age _____ (you decide)

To invest or save a specific amount of money by age _____ (you decide)

To be financially independent by age _____ (you decide)

Possible thesis statement: According to my neighbor, owning a bicycle repair business is possible if you use common sense and follow a number of steps.

WRITING PRACTICE 3 Write in Response to a Reading

In "Camping Out" (page 326), Ernest Hemingway writes, "It is all right to talk about roughing it in the woods. But the real woodsman is the man who can be really comfortable in the bush." Thus, he makes the point that having certain knowledge and skills makes a great difference in a camper's level of enjoyment camping. What other activities depend for their enjoyment on the participant's skill or knowledge in some way?

Your assignment is this: *Imitating Hemingway's style of showing negative consequences because of lack of preparation, write an essay explaining how specific preparation makes a particular activity enjoyable or successful.* For instance, if you enjoy singing, you might explain how going to a karaoke club (where people can sing onstage in front of other patrons, accompanied by music) is more fun if you've practiced singing at some time in your life. Some possible topics are

Playing golf

Giving someone a haircut

Planting a garden

Putting together a _____

Taking an exam

Entering an athletic competition

Going skating, skiing, or skateboarding

Going camping today (as opposed to when Hemingway wrote his essay)

Interviewing for a job

Topic of your choice

Lab Activity 21

For additional practice with explaining a process, complete Lab Activity 21 in the lab manual packaged with your textbook. If you did not receive a lab manual, you can complete this activity online at **www.ablongman.com/long.** Click on **College Resources for Writers** and then click on **Activity 21.**

22 Comparison and Contrast

American Poverty

Whereas people living below the poverty line once comprised a minimal percentage of Americans, they now make up about 60 percent of working adults, according to writer Barbara Ehrenreich in "The Shameful Treatment of America's Poor." Even as the government implements welfare-to-work programs, millions of Americans remain impoverished with little hope of raising themselves to reach any sort of comfort or security. The media brings us stories of young moguls and lottery winners, but those living in poverty are largely invisible.

America's Invisible Citizens

CONDUCT AN INTERVIEW Although many agree that the poor are "always with us," deciding what to do to alleviate poverty is not as clear. What are some answers to the poverty question? Talk to at least two other people—preferably who have different backgrounds and experiences—about their views on poverty: its causes, its effects, and its solutions. Write a few sentences summarizing your findings.

341

What Is a Comparison or Contrast Essay?

It's easy to notice the contrast, or difference, that a red shirt makes in a crowd of black-clad people. Yet people also admire the dance group whose dancers are so similar, so in-step, that each seems hardly separate from the others. How much do people really pay attention to differences and similarities? How much should they?

The answers to these questions are important. Comparing and contrasting are skills that help us make well-informed, intelligent decisions. **Comparison** is the development strategy involving finding similarities between two things. The following sentences show comparison between two subjects.

> My neighbor and her pets have very similar personalities.
>
> My co-workers at Haley's department store remind me of soap opera characters.
>
> Despite working from different sides of the courtroom, the prosecutor and the defense attorney employ the same types of professional skills.

Contrast is the development strategy focusing on the differences between two things. Below are examples showing contrast.

> Directors of different Harry Potter movies, Chris Columbus and Alfonso Cuarón brought their own unique styles to the wizard-oriented films.
>
> Early Rolling Stones albums, such as *Sticky Fingers,* make for more interesting listening than later albums, such as *Emotional Rescue.*
>
> Distance running and sprinting require different types of preparation and training for positive results.

The skills of comparison and contrast are important both in school and in life. If you're considering moving to a new place, for instance, you need to consider such aspects of a potential home as monthly rent, parking, public transportation access, and entertainment access. If one apartment is clearly superior to another in most or all of these categories, you'll be more likely to live there. However, if one apartment is superior in all ways to another but is far more expensive, then you'll have to decide which strengths—such as location and public transportation access, say—really matter to you and then make your choice based on those two factors. Whatever you decide, comparing and contrasting will provide you with information to make a good decision.

Using Comparison or Contrast in Real-Life Writing

Comparison and contrast often enter into our daily lives without our awareness. Consider the following instances where we use these development strategies.

For College

- In a history class, compare or contrast two presidents' leadership styles to determine effectiveness while in office.
- In a science class, contrast the results of two experiments to learn about a compound you are testing.

In Your Personal Life

- Contrast two shampoo brands to decide which one is the better product.
- Compare your new contract at work with the contract at your previous job to make sure that you keep the same benefits.

At Work

- Compare your skills with those listed on a job advertisement to show that you are well suited for the position.
- Contrast your company's product to your competitor's to show how yours is superior.

One important point to keep in mind is that often writers compare and contrast to persuade people of another message altogether. For instance, in the essay below, the writer, Corey, contrasts his attitude toward his living situation as a child with his attitude toward it as an adult. However, his point is not simply to say the same thing twice. His essay, while seemingly about contrasting points of view, is really an attempt to show readers that poverty is often inherited or experienced through no fault of the poor. How successful is Corey at making his point?

A Model Student Essay

Read the following essay to see how the writer, Corey, uses contrast to draw a conclusion.

A Sight for Poor Eyes

When my mom told me, at age seven, that she and my dad were getting a divorce, my first question was "Are we going to be poor?" I'd seen too many neighbors leave their homes because divorce had left families—usually the mother and kids—unable to afford to stay in their houses. My mom smiled grimly and replied, "No, honey. We're not going to be poor." And we weren't, at least not that I was aware of. Now that I'm older and supporting myself, my ideas of poverty have changed. In fact, though poverty at a basic level still means "doing without" to me, my ideas of being poor are vastly different now from what they were when I was a kid.

Poverty to my seven-year-old mind meant not having enough stuff: toys, clothes, crayons. Things such as food, clean water, and shelter—the real necessities—were like air to me: they were always there, so I didn't think about them. As long as I had shoes and clothes that fit (who cared if they were hand-me-downs?) when school started and a mostly full stomach, I was OK. We ate my favorite meals—macaroni and cheese, beans and rice, scrambled eggs—often, and my mom's clients (Mom cleaned houses during the day and did alterations at night) often gave us their used but still decent toys and games. My brother and I had fun, but I remember Mom being exhausted pretty much all the time. I knew we weren't rich, but we certainly weren't poor.

Actually, we were. *Poverty* to my adult mind has a different meaning. Whereas my seven-year-old self thought being poor meant not having enough toys, my adult self sees that poverty encompasses other shortages. One shortage is time. When I was a child, my mother never had time to do anything other than work. She'd get up at 5:00 a.m. so she could have our clothes and breakfast laid out for us, she got us up at 6:00 to eat and dress, and we all left at 7:00. Mom worked until 6:00 p.m., cleaning two or three houses each day, and then she came home, picked us up from the neighbors, fed us, and picked up her sewing. I don't know when she went to bed, but it wasn't early enough. Another shortage is rest. My mother worked six days each week—seven, if you count Sunday sewing—and never had so much as a three-day weekend. Even at age thirty, Mom looked old, largely because the blue-black smudges under her eyes added about ten years to her age. One more shortage is space. At age seven, a three-room house was plenty of room, and sleeping in the same bed was no problem. As my brother and I grew, however, we had to find other places to rest—in thrift-store sleeping bags, usually—and there was never any room to stretch out, much less enough room for privacy. Finally, one last shortage that I associate with poverty is health care: our health suffered because we couldn't afford health insurance, prescriptions, or doctor visits. The community health clinic was always crowded, and it was never open late enough. Even when we could see a health-care worker, he or she wouldn't have the right ointment to get rid of a rash or the right cough medicine. As an adult, I see these shortages for what they are: the signs of poverty.

Maybe because Mom did such a good job holding our lives together, I didn't understand how close to the edge we lived. Even though people on TV led lives different from mine, the people around me seemed to be in about the same place. Now I look back and realize that if Mom had gotten seriously sick just once—or if our neighbors hadn't kept an eye on my brother and me for free—we could have been out of our home. My brother and I still live with Mom—and help her with rent—while we're in school, but we both hope to move out eventually. I read somewhere that fewer than five percent of families in which the head of the house has a college degree live in poverty; that motivates me to stay in school until I can graduate. Until then, my family and I work with the goal of not having to work so hard for the basics someday, whenever that day is.

EXERCISE 1 ANALYZING A COMPARISON ESSAY

Read Corey's essay, "A Sight for Poor Eyes." Then, answer the following questions.

1. What is the thesis statement? _____

_____

2. What two things does Corey compare?

a. _____

b. _____

3. What term does Corey's "A Sight for Poor Eyes" use to define

poverty, both as a child and as an adult? _____

4. What details does he use to show differences between his interpretations of his life when he was a child and as he looks back now?

Childhood interpretation:

_____

_____

_____

_____

Adult interpretation:

_____

_____

_____

_____

A Professional Essay

Though the typical comparison or contrast essay focuses on two subjects for discussion, this does not have to be the case. Read the following essay, paying attention to how the writer contrasts the lives of three subjects.

Urban Renaissance Meets the Middle Ages

Steve Lopez

They're yours for the taking: Luxury lofts in downtown Los Angeles, with rooftop pools, swanky cabanas, and views of Porta Potti brothels on skid row. Evelyn, Eduardo and Thomas live within two blocks of each other, caught in the middle of this head-on collision between economic growth and social disintegration. One is on the street, one in recovery, one in a grandly appointed loft overlooking the place he calls Dante's Inferno.

"I wanted to be a part of the downtown renaissance," says Thomas Reid, an RN who moved out of West Hollywood and into his skid-row-adjacent apartment six weeks ago and was immediately "blown away" by the depth of despair at his doorstep. His windows offer "front-row seats to Skid Row Theater," with a soundtrack of screams and sirens. The renaissance he's talking about has brought an influx of people like Reid, thousands of them. In his building, they're paying up to $6,000 a month, which buys them neighbors who sleep on the pavement in rags. "I sit in my loft with the haves and look out at the have-nots—the bottom of the bottom—and I have to rationalize it," says Reid, whose conscience gets to him when he sips a glass of fine wine while watching someone on the street yell for help. "Am I pushing out the homeless?"

. . .

Evelyn, who lives two blocks away, is homeless, depending on your definition. On San Julian Street one night, I notice her makeshift tent because she's given lots of attention to detail, making walls by stretching blankets between two carts. It's a far cry from Thomas Reid's urban contemporary furnishings, but Evelyn's got the lighting perfect and warm, just enough candlelight to let her read James Patterson's "Pop Goes the Weasel." At night, before laying her head down and saying the rosary, she lays out cardboard, Styrofoam, sheets, blankets, and pillows with pillowcases. "Even though I'm on the street, it makes me feel like I'm inside," she says of the place she calls her hookup.

When I ask the East Palo Alto native how long she's been here, she thinks about it a second. "Ten years," she says. Ten years in this one spot? "I started out at the other end of the street," she says.

Evelyn, who says she's epileptic, is a different person when I see her later in the week. The sweet woman with the kind manner and cozy hookup is sprawled on her back, eyes rolling around in her head, zapped by the marijuana she confesses to or maybe the harder stuff she claims to be "backin' off of." She's gone, not even clear-headed enough to weep as she did the other night, when she told me she's 48 and just not ready to move on. When she's 50, she says, she'll have it together. But not yet, 10 years and counting on San Julian Street.

. . .

You see some people out here who just caught a bad break or two, got priced out of the ridiculous real estate market and ended up in the land of soup lines and cardboard condos. But the majority are in a prison with higher walls, trapped by mental illness or devoured by drugs in a place where there isn't enough help for either. Evelyn lives on the street where Nathaniel, my violinist friend, talks to himself. It's the street where I watched paramedics pick up a young woman with needle tracks and only a few breaths left in her.

The stories are so depressing that, after days on skid row, I began looking for some glimmer of hope. I made arrangements to speak to someone in the recovery program at the Midnight Mission. I'm met there by a man in a suit, his tie removed. I ask if he can take me to the gentleman in recovery. You're looking at him, he says. Eduardo Castro is his name. He leads me to a quiet place and tells his story.

It begins in 1992, when Castro was living in Guatemala. He had been trained in the United States as a dental technician and had a happy home and family in Guatemala. One day, on a visit to a farm owned by his in-laws, a relative lost sight of his daughter Laura, who was 2 years, 8 months old. She drowned in a pond and Castro was beyond grief. He couldn't talk about it, couldn't begin to deal with it. Four years later, working for a touring company, he was on an impoverished island in Guatemala when a family asked him for help. Their daughter was desperately ill, and the parents wondered if Castro, with his modest amount of medical training from dental school, could check her. "The little girl died in my arms," he says. She was roughly the same age as his daughter. A stricken Castro decided that in his daughter's name, he would set up a nonprofit clinic on the island where the other girl died. His mission brought him to Los Angeles, where he worked in a dental lab to raise money for his dream. But he was gripped by depression and turned to the bottle, which got the best of him.

"There's a state of addiction where you think you can handle it," Castro says. But he couldn't. He started coming downtown from his Hollywood apartment and ended up on the streets, buying marijuana and cocaine. For four years he was on the skids, too ashamed to ask his family for help or return to Guatemala empty-handed. He slept in shelters and cardboard boxes, dodging muggers but not demons. "I bought drugs on that street," he says, pointing to San Julian. The street where Evelyn lives.

Castro bottomed out just after Christmas last year, when he landed in jail for the second time, at the age of 55, and promised himself he was done. He had known addicts who checked into rehab at the Midnight Mission and walked down the street as if they were new, so that's where Castro went. "I've been sober over 9 months," he says. As part of his recovery, he took a job in public affairs at the Midnight. He gives tours and works with Spanish-language media. Castro takes me upstairs at the mission, where roughly 250 men reside for up to a year and a half, trying to shake the ghost and beat the odds that say only 17% of them will succeed. We walk into Castro's dorm, and the lights are low. The men are bedded down for the night, in this fight together, dreaming of grace and forgiveness. Up on the roof is the big Midnight Mission sign that Thomas Reid can see from his apartment.

. . .

"This is the original mosaic tile and marble," Reid says on a tour of the Pacific Electric Lofts at 6th and Main, once the hub of the Red Car line and a center of downtown culture. The tour takes us to the rotunda library and rooftop pool. New condos are going in next door, and next to that is the Cecil Hotel, where the clients sometimes leave on their backs. "The coroner's van was there the other day."

Friends thought Reid, 35, was out of his mind, trading a rent-controlled apartment in West Hollywood for the hazards and hassles of skid row. But he was captivated by downtown as a boy. His folks would bring him up from Irvine to visit Chinatown or a museum, and the mysteries of the city dazzled and seduced him. "This is an exciting time for downtown Los Angeles," he says, and he wanted to be a part of it. The excitement includes never-ending action at Station 9, the firehouse that was the busiest in the nation in 2003 with almost 21,000 calls. Reid can see the firehouse from his sixth-floor apartment, and the sirens echo off the walls of his high-ceilinged pad, which has concrete floors.

"You wake up to screams and gunshots," he says. He can look out the window, onto Los Angeles Street beneath, and see territorial squabbles among prostitutes. He says he sat in the window while watching the video of the first part in this skid row series and "started to tear up," realizing that a woman had died after being picked up a short Frisbee toss away from his loft. "It's a parade of misery and death all night," he says. "It's like 'Blade Runner.'"

None of this came entirely as a shock. Reid knew he was moving to a work in progress, and he was an emergency room nurse for five years, a job where you see a little of everything. But he's a realist too. For now, when he leaves his apartment, he doesn't head east. Not on foot, anyway. East is too depressing, with all the encampments, and too dangerous. We go outside to walk Amor, Reid's poodle, and cover only the block of Main Street he lives on. North to 6th, across to the west side of the street, down to 7th and back.

On our one lap we pass a woman lying on the sidewalk, two people asking for money, a mentally ill woman, a dive bar, the always-busy doorway of the Cecil, and what appears to be a gathering of drug dealers and customers. I consider suggesting that Reid get a bigger dog. "It's very disturbing," he says of the landscape outside his door, but he's not running back to West Hollywood. Not yet, anyway. "Most people don't want to see this . . . but how can you effect change if you don't do anything?" he asks.

Yuppie lofters like him aren't the problem, he insists after wrestling with his own doubts about their impact. They're part of the solution, so long as a revitalized downtown includes adequate housing and services, and safer streets for merchants and residents of all income levels. "We shouldn't tolerate drugs and prostitution," he says, least of all the way we tolerate it now, with cavalier indifference. Nor should we tolerate the reality that every night, by the thousands, some of the sickest and most helpless human beings among us sleep on our streets. Ragged, anonymous, conveniently invisible to most of us.

EXERCISE 2 ANALYZING AN ESSAY FOR GOOD COMPARISON/CONTRAST STRATEGY

Read "Urban Renaissance Meets the Middle Ages" by Steve Lopez. Then, fill in the blanks below.

   1. What is Lopez's thesis statement? _____

   _____

   _____

   2. Who are the three people under discussion in the essay? _____

   _____ Which technique, comparison or

   contrast, dominates Lopez's essay? _____

   3. What is the purpose of Lopez's side-by-side discussion? _____

   _____

   4. List details that show how the three subjects under discussion are both similar and different.

   Similar: _____

   Different: _____

   _____

5. Who is Lopez's audience? How can you tell? _____

_____

_____

Writing a Comparison or Contrast Essay

Probably what's most important to remember about writing a comparison or contrast essay is that the comparison or contrast itself is really not the point. Comparing or contrasting two things is an important means of weighing information to help you make a decision, but the comparison or contrast is secondary to your own agenda. For instance, if you are trying to decide which summer internship to accept during college, you would want to check the companies' histories, their internship responsibilities and salaries (if applicable), and their interns' track record of gaining employment after the internship. Then, you'd make your decision based on your comparison. The comparison itself is important only in so far as it helps you reach your goal of accepting the best internship.

Knowing Your Audience and Purpose

Writing a comparison or contrast essay raises the challenge of keeping your reader on track throughout your discussion. Since you're covering two ideas in your essay, having a clear sense of organization is even more important than in other essays. Keep in mind that your reader will need extra direction to stay focused on your topic; the transitions you choose will be essential to guide your reader through your essay.

Choosing a Topic for Development

One challenge in writing a comparison or contrast paragraph is finding a topic that will allow you to say something interesting about both subjects you're writing about. For instance, choosing two subjects such as winter clothing and a sports car would present a challenge in terms of finding common areas to discuss for both subjects. Comparing or contrasting winter clothing and summer clothing instead will offer you differences—the times of year to wear certain clothing—along with enough similarities to serve as common ground between the subjects. Thus, you should choose two items that have something in common, such as two friends, two classes, or two desserts.

Once you've decided on your two items for comparison or contrast, you need to decide *what aspects of the two items you wish to focus on.* If you're writing about two types of careers, for example, what about them do you want to compare or contrast? You could mention their job descriptions, necessary qualifications, salaries, advancement opportunities, and benefits. The point is to decide ahead of time, before writing a draft, just what areas you want to discuss.

Some examples of strong and weak topics for comparison and contrast follow.

Strong Topics for Comparison or Contrast	**Weak Topics for Comparison or Contrast**
Comparing *Gone With the Wind* and *Cold Mountain*	Comparing *Gone With the Wind* and *Harry Potter and the Half-Blood Prince*
Contrasting Rosa Parks with Condoleezza Rice	Contrasting Rosa Parks with Rosie O'Donnell
Contrasting hatha yoga with Bikram yoga	Contrasting hatha yoga with watching television

Freewriting on possible comparison or contrast topics is a good way to determine whether you have enough information to develop an essay. Royce was assigned an essay on poverty, a huge topic. To get started, Royce used a T-chart to ask questions about his topic.

Questions	Answers
How is poverty defined?	See Census Bureau Web site, but it's some ratio of income per person in a family unit.
Who lives in poverty?	Anyone can be poor, but women and children seem hardest hit.
How many people are in poverty?	Almost 40 million Americans; 12.9 million kids
	http://money.cnn.com/2004/08/26/ news/economy/poverty
What are some causes of poverty?	I think divorce is a cause, but I don't know others.
	Recession maybe?

Royce has good basic information about the numbers of people in poverty, but he needs to learn more about its causes. His habit of noting his source, when he has one, right next to a specific detail will help him cite sources later.

Writing an Effective Thesis Statement

As usual, you should write your thesis statement after you've done some freewriting and identified some possible areas for development. Ideally, your thesis will identify the two subjects that you are comparing or contrasting, and it will state whether or not you find similarities or differences between these two subjects. For instance, Royce wrote this as a working thesis statement.

> Though some catastrophes affect men and women equally, poverty hits women harder.

Right away, Royce lets his reader know that he will concentrate on the *differences* between two groups of people rather than on the similarities. Here are some other effective thesis statements.

> To your brain, sniffing glue is a lot like drowning.
>
> Playing hockey and playing lacrosse require similar skills.
>
> My friend Ramona and her daughter Leigh couldn't be more different in their means of expression.
>
> Preparing for a job interview is much like studying for an exam.

Developing Specific Details

Many comparison and contrast essays will require details from your own experience and observations. As you write longer, more involved assignments, you will need to consult other sources for information. An important characteristic of comparison and contrast paragraphs is **balance.** Make sure you include approximately the same information about both subjects being discussed. For instance, if Royce spends two full paragraphs discussing the working poor but has only one short paragraph discussing unemployed people in poverty, the reader might conclude that Royce does not understand the problems of women in poverty, and that conclusion won't help Royce in terms of making his point.

One important point to consider in writing a comparison or contrast essay is that you will have *two* areas to research. Be sure to find adequate support for both ideas you write about.

To make sure he included adequate details for both subjects being discussed, Royce referred to his T-chart. Using the prewriting technique of questioning, he was able to see where he needed more information.

From his original chart, Royce could see that he needed more information about poverty's definition and causes. He added some specific details (shown in bold type) to fill out his chart. Eventually, Royce found enough information to write an entire essay.

Questions	Answers
How is poverty defined?	See Census Bureau Web site, but it's some ratio of income per person in a family unit. **The Office of Management and Budget at the Census Bureau defined the poverty threshold in 2003 as $18,810 for a family of four, $14,680 for a family of three, $12,015 for a family of two, and $9,393 for an individual.**
	http://money.cnn.com/2004/08/26/news/economy/poverty
Who lives in poverty?	Anyone can be poor, but women and children seem hardest hit. **Women's poverty rate—especially for single mothers—increased for a third straight year, a jump in child poverty that was the largest in a decade. And the wage gap for men and women widened in 2003 as real median earnings of women 15 and older fell 0.6 percent to $30,724, the first annual decline since 1995.**
	http://www.womensenews.org/article.cfm/dyn/aid/1968/context/archive
How many people are in poverty?	Almost 40 million Americans; 12.9 million kids
	http://money.cnn.com/2004/08/26/news/economy/poverty
What are some causes of poverty?	I think divorce is a cause, but I don't know others. Recession maybe? **Overpopulation, unequal distribution of resources, inability to meet high standards and cost of living, inadequate education and employment opportunities, environmental degradation, economic and demographic trends, welfare incentives.**
	Encarta.msn.com/encyclopedia.761577020_1__135/poverty.html

Organizing and Linking Ideas

Just as you have different options for organizing a narrative essay, you have options for comparison and contrast. Two types of organizational strategies work best.

All-of-One-Side Approach   In using the all-of-one-side approach, as demonstrated in "A Sight for Poor Eyes" (page 344), the writer presents all the details about one item in the essay first, then adds all the details about the other item. The benefit of this type of organization is that it's easier for the writer to remember all the details and examples about each side, since they all go together in the essay. Another plus is that using transitions can be a bit easier because the essay is not jumping back and forth between two separate items. The challenge of this strategy, however, is keeping the reader from forgetting the first item while the essay is discussing the second one. The diagram "All-of-One-Side Approach" shows how this strategy is organized.

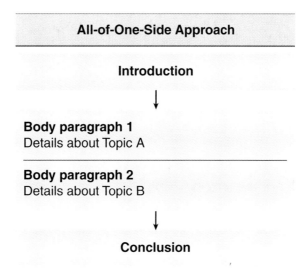

All-of-One-Side Approach

Introduction

↓

Body paragraph 1
Details about Topic A

Body paragraph 2
Details about Topic B

↓

Conclusion

Royce used the all-of-one-side approach to make the following outline.

Though some catastrophes affect men and women equally, poverty hits women harder.

A. Overall poverty statistics

   1. Income

   2. Employment opportunities

   3. Obstacles (affordable housing, health care, child care)

  B. Statistics on women in poverty

   1. Income

   2. Employment opportunities

   3. Obstacles (affordable housing, health care, child care)

Point-by-Point Approach   The point-by-point approach, as illustrated in "No Way to Acceptance" (page 358), alternates details from each item for discussion, offering a detail from one side, then the other side, then back to the first side, and so on. This method integrates both sides throughout each body paragraph of the essay. The benefit of this type of organization is that the reader can see details from both topics side by side and, thus, see the comparison or contrast more easily. One challenge of point-by-point organization is making sure that transitions keep the reader on track at all times. Going back and forth between two ideas can be confusing if the writer doesn't supply good, clear directions by adding transitions. The diagram "Point-by-Point Approach" shows this approach.

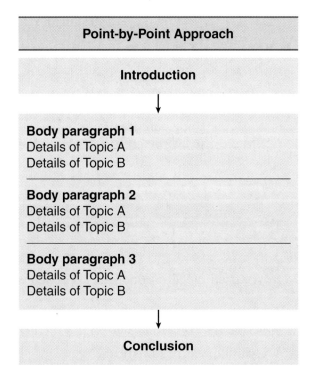

Point-by-Point Approach

Introduction

↓

Body paragraph 1
Details of Topic A
Details of Topic B

Body paragraph 2
Details of Topic A
Details of Topic B

Body paragraph 3
Details of Topic A
Details of Topic B

↓

Conclusion

If Royce had chosen to use the point-by-point method, his outline would have looked like this:

> Though some catastrophes affect men and women equally, poverty hits women harder.

A. Income

    1. Overall population

    2. Women

B. Employment opportunities

    1. Overall population

    2. Women

C. Obstacles

    1. Overall population

    2. Women

Notice that in this form of Royce's outline, he must organize his ideas according to specific factors in poverty rather than by group.

See the following boxes for transitions that work well in comparison and contrast writing.

Transitions That Work Well to Show Comparison

and	in addition	neither
also	in the same way	similarly
both	just as . . . so, too, is . . .	too
each of	like	

Transitions That Work Well to Show Contrast

although	however	whereas
but	in contrast	while
conversely	on the other hand	yet
despite	unlike	

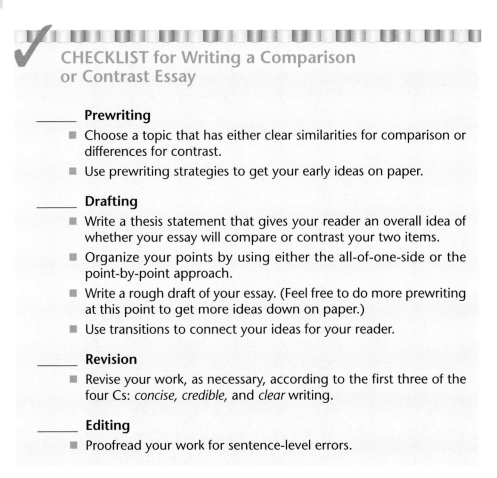

CHECKLIST for Writing a Comparison or Contrast Essay

_____ **Prewriting**

- Choose a topic that has either clear similarities for comparison or differences for contrast.
- Use prewriting strategies to get your early ideas on paper.

_____ **Drafting**

- Write a thesis statement that gives your reader an overall idea of whether your essay will compare or contrast your two items.
- Organize your points by using either the all-of-one-side or the point-by-point approach.
- Write a rough draft of your essay. (Feel free to do more prewriting at this point to get more ideas down on paper.)
- Use transitions to connect your ideas for your reader.

_____ **Revision**

- Revise your work, as necessary, according to the first three of the four Cs: *concise, credible,* and *clear* writing.

_____ **Editing**

- Proofread your work for sentence-level errors.

Following the Four Cs Through Revision

Being specific without being overly wordy or too detailed is important in comparison or contrast essays since you have twice the information to convey. As she wrote her essay "No Way to Acceptance," Miranda continually had to rein herself in because she wanted to add more detail than was necessary to make her points. She also had to make sure she balanced the details from the two situations—death of a parent and poverty—so that her reader couldn't tell that she far preferred discussing poverty to discussing terminal illness.

No Way to Acceptance

When my best friend, Cara, lost her mother to pancreatic cancer, it was awful. Cara went from being desperately hopeful

to being desperately sad over the course of her mother's illness. <u>Later,</u> when I volunteered in a homeless shelter, I realized that many people's reactions to poverty in America—when they're faced with it head-on and can't sidestep the issue—are a lot like the reactions of people going through the five stages of grieving. Except for the last stage, acceptance, people's emotions—from denial to depression—are similar to when they deal with loss.

<u>Denial is many people's first reaction.</u> **When the doctor told Cara and her father that her mother had less than eight weeks to live, Cara couldn't believe it. She went online and searched until all hours of the night, trying to find some expert who'd say what she wanted to believe.** <u>I saw the same reaction at a homeless shelter where I volunteered.</u> When my brother walked into the shelter and saw the women and kids in line for Thanksgiving dinner, he couldn't believe his eyes. "It's the holidays, right? There aren't usually this many people," were his words. Of course, I told him that according to the Census Bureau, half of the families living in poverty were headed by single women, but he still didn't want to believe it. I encouraged him to come back on a "regular" day and see the lines, but since he didn't think that many people are hungry, he didn't see the need to return. Denial was alive and well.

<u>Anger comes, too.</u> **Once Cara saw her mother's suffering— not just the vague pains she'd had for months, but real agony— she became enraged at the doctors, and at her mother. She couldn't believe they couldn't save her, and she couldn't believe her mother would leave her.** <u>I saw anger at the homeless shelter, too.</u> When I initially started volunteering at the homeless shelter as part of a service-learning class, I was full of hope and enthusiasm. I was going to change the world, one hot lunch at a time! I soon saw that the shelter repeatedly ran out of bags of groceries and cooked meals, and even when the hungriest child needed a meal, there wasn't more to give. I couldn't believe that so many people lived like this. Where were their families? Where were the jobs? Where was the health care? Why wasn't somebody *doing* something about this? ~~The sad part is: my anger at seeing people in poverty was nothing compared to the anger I experienced from some of the shelter's residents. No one wanted to ask for help less than they did, and no one felt more resentful than they for having to ask for help.~~ Anger was everywhere, but it didn't change a thing.

<u>Bargaining comes next.</u> **Cara said prayers and promised to go to church every week if only God would make her mom better. She also tried bargaining with the hospital staff for special treatment for her mother, trading some homemade cookies at**

the nurses' station for a few extra checks on Mom. <u>Bargaining when faced with poverty is part of people's reactions, but it's usually a means of helping people to alleviate their own feelings of guilt or shame.</u> "If I volunteer at a homeless shelter one a month, I won't be guilty of allowing 12 million children (according to the Census Bureau) to live below the poverty line," I felt. "If I give a bag of food for the neighborhood church's 'feed the hungry' food drive, I'm not to blame for what Barbara Ehrenreich calls the 'acute distress' of the poor: living in a car, eating chips for a meal, working through major illness. If I donate money in a charity fund-raiser, it won't be my fault that, as stated in Ehrenreich's essay 'The Shameful Treatment of America's Poor,' almost 60 percent of people earn less than a living wage." People faced with poverty often try to deflect feelings of helplessness or guilty by "bargaining" with themselves, but it doesn't change reality.

<u>For months after Cara's mom died, Cara faced depression.</u> **She dropped her classes and cut back her work hours to the bare minimum. She didn't answer her phone, and she left her apartment only to see how her dad was doing. If she didn't have to see her dad, she stayed in bed.** <u>Depression comes, too, for those people who really want to make a change and can't.</u> Unlike me— who volunteered initially as part of a class—many workers at the shelter really wanted and expected to make a dramatic difference in the lives of the people they met. While one or two of the women in the shelter eventually joined job-training program, I don't know if they ever actually got jobs, or jobs that could support them. And that still left the majority of the women without any time, means, or opportunity to support themselves, not to mention the children who moved around so much they never found a permanent school, or home for that matter. For the employees and longtime volunteers at the shelter, just starting a new shift was depressing. ~~Like anger, though, I have to believe that the employees' depression was minor when compared to the hopelessness of those actually in poverty.~~

Cara's mom died two years ago, and with help from her college counselor, Cara is beginning to heal. She still feels cheated by losing her mom so young (at age twenty), but she also appreciates her dad and her friends. If she hasn't accepted her mother's death yet, acceptance will come soon. <u>In relation to poverty, acceptance is the only grieving-related feeling that shouldn't be part of anyone's reactions</u>, but, sadly, it is probably what the majority of nonpoor people feel. As Barbara Ehrenreich points out, the poor are "always with us," a fact which too many people accept too easily. Of course, the same people who "accept" that people live in poverty are those people who never have to take public transportation or work as a maid. Hopefully, by making ourselves aware of those in poverty we can begin to understand the plight of the poor, but awareness is only a beginning.

Revising for the First C: Concise Writing   Miranda felt strongly about her topics for contrast—death of a parent and poverty—so she had to make certain that she didn't include more detail than was necessary. In two support paragraphs, in fact, Miranda found herself wanting to explain the feelings of the people she worked with at the shelter. However, these ideas did not support her thesis, so she crossed them out.

Revising for the Second C: Credible Writing   Miranda's challenge in writing her essay was that she wanted to discuss people's reactions to poverty more than to grief; thus, she initially failed to include any details about the ways her friend Cara dealt with her mother's death. Since comparison involves two subjects, Miranda had to go back and add details about Cara's grief (shown in bold type).

Revising for the Third C: Clear Writing   Never are transitions and a logical order more important than in comparison or contrast essays. Miranda let her ideas follow the pattern established by the five stages of grief, yet she had to make sure that the connections between the two ideas in each paragraph—reactions to grief and reactions to poverty—were well connected. Thus, she included transitional sentences (underlined) in each body paragraph to link the two ideas she was comparing.

Revising for the Fourth C: Correct Writing   The sentences in Miranda's paragraph are all correct. To check for correctness in your own writing, see Part Seven, "Writing Correct Sentences."

WRITING PRACTICE 1 Writing an Essay Step by Step

Now it's time to put what you've learned to use and write your own essay.

Prewriting

1. Below is a list of different topics for essays that compare or contrast two items. Read the list, and think about whether you can find more similarities or differences between the two items in the list. Choose a topic. Then, choose either comparison or contrast.

Two phases in your life, such as childhood versus adolescence

Two different uses of the Internet

Two albums by the same group or singer

Two performers

Two styles—fashion, hair, interview, exercise, for instance

Two role models in your life

Two family members

Two restaurants serving the same kind of food (Mexican, Thai, for example)

A local park at two different times of the day, week, or year

A popular radio station at two different times of the day

Two professional athletes in the same sport

Your goals at two different times of your life

Preparing for two different trips, such as a camping trip versus a weekend with relatives

Your attitude toward school, religion, finances, or some other topic at two different times of your life

2. Questioning is a helpful type of prewriting for comparison and contrast essays because it allows you to focus on the same areas in regard to each item. Look at the sample question-and-answer list below. This writer has chosen to contrast the programming on a major television network during two times of the year.

Question	Answer (May)	Answer (June)
What's on TV?	Season finales, great movies	Reruns, boring movies
What kinds of ads?	Ads for shows' finales, new shows, and network programs	Ads for different products (hair, food, prescriptions)
Attention to schedule?	Programs fall in certain time slots; predictable scheduling	Nothing seems scheduled; shows seem crammed into slots at random
How much does viewer matter?	Very much	Not much

Drafting

3. Write a thesis statement. Make sure that the relationship you're writing about—either comparison or contrast—is clear in your thesis.

Possible thesis statement: Even the channels with the best programming during sweeps or ratings months become boring versions of themselves during other months.

4. Choose support points (the areas of comparison) and specific details.

5. Organize your ideas using an all-of-one-side or point-by-point strategy.

6. Write your draft. Use freewriting to fill in the gaps with details, and keep checking to make sure your organization is consistent throughout your essay.

Revising

7. Make sure all the details in your list directly advance your thesis statement. Eliminate any details that do not show a similarity or difference between your two items. Check again to see that you've included all the necessary details. Additionally, make sure that you have a balanced amount of detail for each item being compared or contrasted. To make sure your details are organized and connected, add clear transitions that let your reader know where every step in the process comes.

Editing

8. Proofread your essay to make sure you have used correct spelling, punctuation, and grammar.

WRITING PRACTICE 2 **Comparing or Contrasting in Real Life**

Now you have an opportunity to choose both the topic and the types of support you use for an essay. Deciding between choices can be very difficult, particularly when many choices exist. The situations below outline real-life situations requiring comparison or contrast as part of a decision-making process.

Your assignment is this: *Choose a topic below, and use your comparing or contrasting skills to help a friend make an important decision.*

Topic A

Your friend plans to rent an apartment and live alone for the first time. Since you've been living on your own for awhile, your friend asks you for advice about where to live. *Write an essay comparing or contrasting two apartment complexes.* Give examples of the two complexes based on your experience and observations, considering such factors as rent, location, size, and miscellaneous restrictions (such as "no pets" rules) for each complex. Use specific details from your own experience and observations. *Note:* If you have never had to find your own place to live, either because you live with your family or you moved in with someone who already had a place, then compare or contrast your living situation with another situation that you're familiar with.

Possible thesis statement: When comparing the Greenhaven Pines and Adobe Court apartment complexes, future renters will learn that Adobe Court proves superior in value, location, and flexibility.

Another option: Despite Mom's great cooking, living on my own is far preferable to living with my parents.

Topic B

Your current cell phone service contract is about to expire, and other companies have been bombarding you with information about their programs. To either cancel or renew your current plan, you must submit a written request to change services. *Write a letter to your former cell phone company comparing or contrasting its services versus those of another cell phone carrier.* Be sure to consider such elements as number of minutes, cost, rollover minutes, and cell coverage. For this assignment, use examples from two different cell phone carriers. *Note:* By typing "cellular phone service" into a search engine on the Internet, you will find numerous side-by-side comparisons for cell phone services.

Possible thesis statement: Although Nextel and Verizon offer similar plans, Nextel's service, coverage, and costs prove to be better.

Topic C

With the cost of education steadily rising, finding ways to pay for classes—as well as books and other supplies—is increasingly difficult. You are trying to decide where to put your time and efforts—aside from school and your job—in terms of financial assistance; scholarships, loans, or a combination. Contact your financial aid office for brochures on various forms of aid or visit your library to learn what your options are. Then, write an essay comparing or contrasting the different types of financial support. Support your ideas with information you gain from your school's financial aid office.

Possible thesis statement: Financial aid, rather than scholarships, is a better way for me to finance my education because it has fewer "strings attached."

Find Scholarships—Free
www.FastWeb.com

Free College Scholarship
www.FreeCollegeScholarships.net

NCAA College Scouting

1700 Colleges in 30 sports looking for qualified student-athletes

www.ncsasports.org

College Scholarships

If You Are Serious About a Scholarship Search, Register Now!

www.findtuition.com

Free—College Money

Search for Your College Scholarship Free- Download Ultimate Scholarship

www.College-Scholarship.us

College Tuition Discounts

Free College Match financial aid, scholarship, waiver

www.TuitionDiscount.com

Free USA College Grants

1000's of Free College Grants, Scholarships for all Students.

www.usagovernmentgrants.org

New Scholarships for 2006

Free Scholarship search worth over $2.5 billion in awards

www.brokescholar.com

Architecture Degree

Master your passion with our MFA Architecture program.

www.academyart.edu/

WRITING PRACTICE 3 Write in Response to a Reading

Steve Lopez writes in his essay "Urban Renaissance Meets the Middle Ages" (page 346) that people deal with the plight of the poor, particularly with those involved in prostitution or drugs, with "cavalier [offhand] indifference." What do you think? Your assignment is this: *Write an essay comparing or contrasting the attitudes toward poverty of two people you know.* For instance, contrast how two people from the same neighborhood or same school have markedly different ideas about poverty. Or, compare your views with the views of someone whose background is very different from yours. Find at least three areas for comparison or contrast, and interview the people (or the person, if you include your own ideas as one point of view) whose ideas you use to learn enough about their habits to write an informed essay.

Lab Activity 22

For additional practice with comparison and contrast, complete Lab Activity 22 in the lab manual packaged with your textbook. If you did not receive a lab manual, you can complete this activity online at **www.ablongman.com/long.** Click on **College Resources for Writers** and then click on **Activity 22.**

23 Developing a Cause-and-Effect Essay

CULTURE NOTE *Civility*

Long associated with high society and formal manners, civility has recently entered the mainstream as a topic of discussion and concern. Among cell phone etiquette rules, consequences of road rage and poor sportsmanship, and online interaction etiquette, questions about civility have emerged for many. The consequences of incivility and the rewards of simple courtesy are widespread.

The Uninvited Guest

CRITICAL THINKING Though many people agree that public cell phone discussions can be uncomfortable for bystanders, people continue to chat away for all to see. To what extent do cell phones make us, or allow us to be, more rude? Write a few sentences explaining your ideas.

What Is a Cause-and-Effect Essay?

Every day we attempt to explain, predict, and control situations in our lives: why we were late, how we'll save enough money to buy holiday presents, how we can lose weight. Though these situations are very different, they all have one thing in common: the element of cause-and-effect reasoning.

In the cause-and-effect essay development strategy, you explain why something occurred by identifying the reasons it happened, or **causes,** and the outcome of certain actions, or **effects,** or even both.

Some sentences focusing on the *causes* of an event follow.

> The combination of many elements can lead a person into extreme debt.
>
> Many factors contribute to an adult student's decision to attend college.
>
> A series of unfortunate events led Lara to lose her job.

Some sentences focusing on the *effects* of an event follow.

> Eating well can have a positive effect on people's health.
>
> Treating people around you with courtesy can reap great rewards.
>
> Achieving success in just one area of life can foster a sense of self-confidence.

Using Cause and Effect in Real-Life Writing

Cause-and-effect reasoning enters into real life daily. Here are some examples of how cause-and-effect thinking plays a significant role in real-life activities.

For College

- In a sociology class, writing about the causes and effects of a social movement can help you understand it better.
- In a sociology class, writing about the causes and effects of a social movement can help you understand it better.

In Your Personal Life

- Explain to a significant other the effects his or her behavior has on your feelings.
- Try to convince a friend that a nonchalant attitude toward you may cause him or her to lose your friendship.

At Work

- Convince an employer to hire you by predicting the positive effects your presence will have at his or her company.
- Explain to your boss the causes for an increase in sales in your division.

A Model Student Essay

Read the sample essay below. It uses cause-and-effect reasoning to explain the role of discourtesy in a postgame altercation.

Deadly Discourtesy

Two years ago, my brother's co-worker Matt had a bad night. After watching his favorite local basketball team lose in the playoffs, he got behind the wheel of his car visibly angry. My brother said that Matt had to slam on his brakes to avoid hitting another motorist, but still drove aggressively, challenging the other driver to a fight. When the two drivers stopped and got out of their cars, Matt charged the other driver, punching him furiously. The other driver responded in self-defense, throwing a punch to Matt's head. A seemingly simple conflict began a series of actions that could never be undone and which led to one man's death. Matt's rudeness brought about a number of negative consequences.

One consequence of his behavior is that his friends and family suffered upon reading about Matt's altercation in the newspapers. His wife and eight-year-old son had to read about how Matt charged and threw the first punches at the other driver. Friends, family, and co-workers also had to read in the newspaper about how someone they knew as an upstanding citizen was making loud, obnoxious comments at the game. Further, Matt's loved ones had to read about how someone they thought was a nondrinker was found to have both alcohol (more than the legal limit) and drugs in his system. Finally, people who respected Matt's calm daily personality had to, again, read about how a loss of temper led to a loss of life. If Matt had not lost his temper and had simply driven home, his family would never have known about his impoliteness, his other indiscretions, or his temper.

Another consequence of Matt's rudeness is a tremendous amount of stress and sadness for the other driver and for the witnesses to the fight. Though no criminal charges were filed against the other driver, he felt compelled to hire an attorney to represent him. Similarly, the passengers in the vehicles driven by the men in the fight hired attorneys in case the truth was somehow not told. Days of interviews, retellings of the story, and negative publicity affected men who simply wanted to see a basketball game. All the men involved, according to the local papers, felt relieved upon hearing that no charges would be filed, but they also felt saddened by one man's death. If Matt had practiced civil behavior, no one would have suffered from this set of circumstances.

Finally, the greatest effect of Matt's rudeness was his own death. Upon inciting the other driver to fight and throwing a number of punches, Matt finally received one punch that the other driver threw in self-defense. The punch, landing on the side of Matt's head, sent him falling backwards, where he cracked his skull on the pavement. Suffering from extreme head wounds, Matt died. If he had simply kept his rage in check—or even if he had vented it at the friend who accompanied him—Matt would most likely be alive today.

Very few people out for a night of entertainment go looking for a fight, and no one wants to lose one. Similarly, very few people set out to be so rude that others feel they have no choice but to defend themselves. Matt's anger most likely had very little to do with the man he attacked, yet by a series of rude, aggressive actions, Matt began a chain of events that led to the end of his life. Though the district attorneys who ultimately decided not to file charges claim that the men involved showed poor judgment, it's hard not to conclude that poor behavior played a role as well.

EXERCISE 1 ANALYZING A CAUSE-AND-EFFECT ESSAY

1. What is the thesis statement in "Deadly Discourtesy"?

_____

2. What effects does the writer say came from the incident?

a. _____

b. _____

c. _____

3. What three transitions does the writer use to introduce the support points?

Paragraph 2: _____

Paragraph 3: _____

Paragraph 4: _____

A Professional Essay

Often situations will have multiple causes or effects. Pay attention to the various effects of cell phone use in the following essay.

Anywhere But Here: More Connected, But More Alone

Anne Taylor Fleming

Cellular telephones are so ever-present now that we somehow no longer bother about them or register the profound changes they have wrought in our culture and our behavior. After all, we've all had telephones forever. The cell phone is just a ready-to-trot wireless version, a gadget of the utmost convenience. So what's the big deal?

The big deal is that the cellular phone has completely changed the way we behave in public and, even more, completely blurred the line between the public sphere and the private without us even realizing it, with wide-reaching implications for how we treat each other—and ourselves. The technology got ahead of any etiquette, any sense we might have had of public decorum, so that we no longer blanch when we overhear people confiding in, yelling at or cooing in the ear of someone else through their cell phones. We've become a nation of compulsive communicators, nonstop babblers airing our most private thoughts in the most public of places—an airport lounge, a restaurant banquette, a city street.

We're now all part of each other's audiences. It's as if we live in a virtual-reality TV talk show, a rolling 12-step public marathon, with complete strangers spewing out intimacies or fighting right in front of us, needful of the validation of our attention. It's as if nothing is real anymore unless it happens in public with an audience, and the cellular phone is the perfect little gizmo to make this possible. You don't have to wangle your way onto Jerry or Oprah, or any of the other confessional TV shows. All you need is a public place and a cellular telephone, and you can be center stage, living one of your life's little or big dramas out loud for all the rest of us to overhear. Look at me, the caller says. I'm somebody. I can't even wait to get back to the office or to a pay phone.

I have to make this call right now. I am needed. I am important. Just listen.

My friends love me. My kids need me. My boss can't breathe without me.

I matter.

In fairness, this isn't just an American addiction. Many of us have had the experience of being in a hillside town in Tuscany or an idyllic, isolated resort and being privy to the same techno-din. In fact, when I was last in Europe, the cellular-phone epidemic seemed even worse than here—all manner of coifed matrons and hip Eurokids strolling down the street barking into their portable phones over the roar of motorbikes.

What's wrong with all of us? Why the desperate need to be vocally tethered to someone else at all times? Can we not stand the downtime, the silence of our own company? Even children are wired up, toting their own phones and beepers, overscheduled to the max—this play date, that soccer game—so that they, too, will learn to be strangers to themselves, unused to stillness, unaware that there is, or should be, a demarcation between public and private. Only in private do we take the measure of our own gifts and failings—no doubt why we avoid it so. Only in private—away from the crowd and the audience—do we do original and creative work and plumb the depths of our consciences. Only in private do we experience the truest and deepest emotions, be they agony or ecstasy.

The rest is posturing: Life as a spectator sport, precisely what we've turned sex into. The accent is no longer on the act itself but on the postcoital play-by-play. Like the tabloid TV shows, the postmodern sitcom is often little else but a titillating talkathon in which groups of friends sit around and dissect their sexual encounters for each other. They cannibalize their meaningful experiences and turn them into cheap anecdotes to be served up on a platter to the rest of their clique.

Cell phones have sped up that process. Jump out of bed and jump on the phone. Guess what I did; guess what he did. These phones have changed the very nature of gossip; they've made it quicker, crueler, more pervasive and instantaneous. There is no time to edit, pull back, savor. Everything is fodder, fair game, grist for the cell-phone mill.

All to say that we seem to have given up on privacy altogether—on the very idea of its virtues. It's as if the entire twentieth century has been about this technologically abetted trend away from privacy, so that we now arrive at a point where nothing is off-limits for public confiding, and where you cannot or need not be alone anywhere. In a car, in a forest, you're reachable and so is your circle of friends. (Friends are the families of the '90s.) You're not alone as long as you have your phone tucked in your purse or pocket, your cellular hedge against loneliness.

No doubt, that's what the phones are ultimately about: loneliness and a frantic attempt to evade it. But the irony is that they make it worse. Think of it: You're walking down a throbbing city street, noise and people all around, human pageantry, but you're busy chatting with a friend or arguing with a spouse via your speed dial. You're cocooned, disconnected from the things and people around you, experiencing that weird nonintimate-intimacy, that weird public-privacy that characterizes so many of our modern interactions, be they via the cellular phone or the Internet. It's not unusual these days to see two people having lunch, forks in hand, talking not to each other but to someone else via their respective cell phones. Clearly we're more hooked up than ever and, on some level, more lonesome. Why else all the manic phoning, the need to be reachable by somebody, anybody, anywhere and everywhere?

There's a little grandiosity in it, too, a sense of self-importance conferred by a ringing phone. Excuse me, somebody needs me right now, this minute. But are any of us that important? Sure, we all have deadlines, personal and professional, but barely a one of us is so vital to some enterprise that the call has to be made this second, in public, no matter where you are or what the circumstances. That's just self-congratulatory folderol. Kids, too, can wait. They don't have to be phoned or fetched at a given instant. After all, we did all get along before we had these things. They provide a false sense of urgency, of faux drama, of life lived to the fullest.

By any measure, cell phones waste more time than they save, like many of our other so-called "timesaving devices." They embroil us in endless, unnecessary chatter that only serves to abbreviate our already overstimulated attention spans.

Yes, there are true emergencies—on the road, in an accident, in a faltering democracy where a coup is imminent. Then a cellular phone can be a lifeline. But that's not what most people are using them for on a daily basis. They're using them to ward off the stillness, the demons, the specter of loneliness. Millions of people around the globe, walking down a jam-packed city street or sunbathing on a beach or lying in bed with a lover, reaching for their cell phones at this very moment, connecting up while simultaneously disconnecting from the time and place and pleasure at hand.

It's a loud, lonesome tableau that speaks to the profound revolution these simple, hand-held devices have brought about in all our lives.

EXERCISE 2 ANALYZING AN ESSAY FOR GOOD CAUSE-AND-EFFECT STRATEGY

Read "Anywhere But Here: More Connected, But More Alone" by Anne Taylor Fleming. Then, answer the following questions.

1. Fleming uses the phenomenon of cell phone popularity to discuss other aspects of people's lives. What effects does Fleming say cell phones have had on people?

a. _____

b. _____

c. _____

2. What examples does Fleming provide that show the effects of cell

phones? _____

_____

3. What causes, or reasons, does Fleming offer for why people are so quick to talk on a cell phone, even in the company of other people?

_____

_____

4. In what situations, if any, does Fleming think that cell phones are

necessary? _____

_____

5. How does Fleming organize her essay? How can you tell? _____

_____

Writing a Cause-and-Effect Essay

The key to writing an effective cause-and-effect essay is to make sure your causes really are the source of the effects you focus on. An insult delivered while an opposing soccer player kicked your shin might be interesting, but it is unlikely to be the *cause* of your fractured bone. Thus, in writing about the causes of your less-than-perfect soccer performance, focus on those details—such as the kick—that show how your performance suffered and whose responsibility the suffering was. It's easy to get bogged down in details that don't develop the cause-and-effect situation in your essay; resist the temptation, however, to add more details than you need.

Knowing Your Audience and Purpose

As always, when you write a cause-and-effect essay, your ideas are clearer to you than they are to a reader, and your job is to clarify your ideas for that reader.

Choosing a Topic for Development

In writing a cause-and-effect essay, choose a topic that allows you to see how one event caused another to happen. For instance, writing about the causes of some types of cancer is tricky because even medical experts don't know this. A better topic, then, would be how smoking causes lung disease since there is a clear, medically supported link between these two.

Once you've chosen a topic, make sure you narrow it down so that you can cover it in an essay. Writing about the causes of World War II, for instance, could lead you to write an entire book! A better topic might be writing about the reasons why a particular soldier chose to enlist in the armed forces to fight in that war, or three effects of the United States' dropping the atom bomb on Hiroshima.

Once you've narrowed your topic to an event that works well for cause-and-effect development, *decide whether the cause or the effect is most significant to write about.* Many topics can be argued from either the cause or the effect viewpoint, but usually one perspective—the cause or the effect—is stronger.

For instance, while exploring the causes of the invention of the automobile—transportation and comfort—could make an interesting paragraph, these concerns applied to horse and train travel, too. However, the *effects* of the invention of the car are so far-reaching that we are seeing them a century later. Thus, writing about the effects of the automobile's invention is a better choice.

James wasn't sure what to write about, but he wanted to find ways to become successful. His stepfather was deeply in debt; worried about his mother and wanting to avoid a similar predicament, James wanted to explore the causes for his stepfather's financial situation. Thus, James decided to learn what brought about—or caused—his stepfather's debt. After reading talking to his family about his stepfather's money habits, James did some freewriting on the subject. He came up with this:

> I can't believe that Len might need to declare bankruptcy. I mean, the guy has a good job with UPS, and he's never done anything illegal, so I can't figure out why he's in such trouble. Mom says he can't say no to his kids, but Len says that's not true. His kids say that he just can't have any extra money around or it "burns a hole in his pocket." Mostly, though, it seems as if his credit cards have gotten him into trouble. Being able to buy something with plastic and not pay for it for six months—like his and Mom's new furniture—keeps coming back to bite him.

In this freewriting sample, James identifies three *causes* of his stepfather's debt: giving money to his kids, not saving money, and buying on credit. Even though he knew he needed more information to write a whole essay, James decided that he had enough ideas to start writing.

Writing an Effective Thesis Statement

After you've chosen your topic, make sure you identify what aspect—cause or effect—you plan to write about. In general, put the area of focus for your paragraph at the end of your thesis statement. For instance, writing "Procrastination can have serious consequences" *could* lead readers to expect a paragraph on the reasons people procrastinate. However, since "serious consequences" comes at the end of the sentence, it's more likely that the writer plans to explain the *effects* of procrastinating. Some other possible topic sentences follow.

> Paul was amazed to see the health benefits of boxing after only six weeks.

In this sentence, the reader expects to learn about the ways Paul's boxing paid off, or the *effects* of his boxing.

> A number of elements play a role in people's insomnia.

Here, the reader expects to learn more about what *causes* insomnia.

> After James finished his freewriting, he identified three possible support points.

Support point 1: Giving money to kids
Support point 2: Not saving money
Support point 3: Buying on credit

Since all three of these points deal with *causes* of being in debt, James came up with this thesis statement.

> Though they might seem harmless at the time, a number of small habits can steadily lead people deeply into debt.

From this thesis statement, a reader expects to learn *causes* of being in debt, which is exactly what James wants to write about.

Different Names for Causes

basis	motive
cause	reason
factor	

Different Names for Effects

consequence	outcome
effect	result

Developing Specific Details

Using prewriting techniques such as freewriting or clustering, make a list of support points for each part of your argument. Then, decide whether focusing on the cause or the effect is better for your topic. After freewriting, James identified "Giving money to kids," "Not saving money," and "Buying on credit" as three causes of being in debt. He knew he needed more information, so he made a cluster diagram to see where he could fill in details.

Words and Terms That Signal Emphatic Order

above all	last
another	least of all
equally important	most of all
especially	most important
even more	most significantly
first	next
in the first place	

Though James already had three support points for his "debt" idea, making a cluster diagram helped him see which ideas were most developed. As he worked on his cluster diagram, James discovered that he had other specific details—ways his stepfather gave money to his kids and bought on credit—that he hadn't originally thought of. Sometimes specific details illustrating causes or effects will come from your own experiences, but if you have trouble thinking of enough detail to support your thesis statement, refer to other sources, such as talking to people or reading trusted publications.

Organizing and Linking Ideas

In writing cause-and-effect essays, your ideas may naturally follow some sort of emphatic order, with your support points linked from least to most important. Pay attention to which ideas seem most or least significant, and save the best point for last. Even though James had an equal number of examples for "Giving money to kids" and "Buying on credit," he felt that buying on credit was a more significant reason for his stepfather's debt. For James, who was trying to support himself and pay for college, the idea of spending money he didn't have was unthinkable. Thus, his stepfather's spending seemed most significant, so he kept that as his last support point.

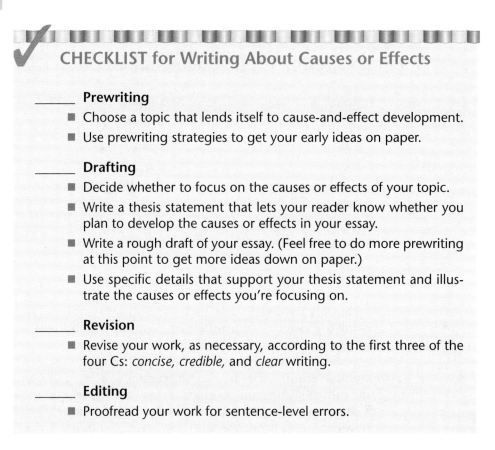

✓ CHECKLIST for Writing About Causes or Effects

_____ **Prewriting**
- ■ Choose a topic that lends itself to cause-and-effect development.
- ■ Use prewriting strategies to get your early ideas on paper.

_____ **Drafting**
- ■ Decide whether to focus on the causes or effects of your topic.
- ■ Write a thesis statement that lets your reader know whether you plan to develop the causes or effects in your essay.
- ■ Write a rough draft of your essay. (Feel free to do more prewriting at this point to get more ideas down on paper.)
- ■ Use specific details that support your thesis statement and illustrate the causes or effects you're focusing on.

_____ **Revision**
- ■ Revise your work, as necessary, according to the first three of the four Cs: _concise, credible,_ and _clear_ writing.

_____ **Editing**
- ■ Proofread your work for sentence-level errors.

Following the Four Cs Through Revision

Because few things in life are caused by just one event or have just one simple effect, writing a cause-and-effect essay—especially one that identifies one cause or effect—can be a challenge. However, by narrowing your focus and your level of detail, you can effectively let your reader know the relationship between an initial act and its results.

Renée wanted to write about how people's actions lead to environmental improvement.

A Little Love for Life

According to civility expert P. M. Forni, the way we treat the environment is a sign of how civil we are. Thirty years ago, many of the world's inhabitants would have received poor marks for their treatment of the earth. Rivers were burning, trees were disappearing, and animals and plants were nearing extinction. In the last three decades, however, the outlook appears brighter. Organizations such as the Sierra Club (founded in 1892) and the Green Belt Movement (GBM) have played a large role in restoring aspects of our natural resources. Because people are treating the environment with respect, the positive effects are many.

One positive effect of people's environmental efforts is the improved water quality across the United States. From burning Lake Erie and desiccated Mono Lake, rivers and lakes were either being polluted so badly or drained so completely that they could hardly be counted as water sources. **According to an article in *Fishing World*, in 1969, Cleveland's polluted Cuyahoga River actually caught fire, and Lake Erie was declared dead.** ~~The Hudson River was another extremely polluted water source, but it has largely been cleaned as well. The source of the Hudson River's pollution stemmed from General Electric's practice of dumping waste into the river.~~ However, the Clean Water Act, passed by Congress in October 1972, which aimed to stop toxic pollution of the nation's waters and make U.S. rivers and lakes safe for fishing and swimming, along with the Great Lakes Water Quality Agreement targeting the health of the Great Lakes, made Lake Erie clean enough for fishing and swimming by the mid-1980s. **Southern California's Mono Lake, slowly being drained to support the human lifestyle in Los Angeles, has also made strides toward achieving original water levels thanks to efforts of the Sierra Club and other organizations dedicated to preserving natural settings.** ~~Because Mono Lake's water levels fell so dramatically, birds that inhabited an island were no longer protected from predators by water and were attacked.~~

Another positive effect of people's environmental efforts is the number of new trees planted and surviving. According to an article in *Mother Earth News,* Kenyan biologist and Green Belt Movement founder Wangari Maathai and the GBM originally attempted to make green those parts of Kenya that faced becoming desert. ~~The GBM acted under the guidance of the National Council of Women in Kenya, and Maathai received the Nobel Peace Prize in 2004.~~ People in Kenya planted seven trees in 1977 to honor women environmentalists. However, **in 2004, after twenty-seven years of consistent planting and nurturing, more than 30 million trees had taken root and survived.** The GBM continues its efforts with great success. ~~Even though new trees are being planted all the time, they still cannot replace the established forests destroyed earlier.~~ Though the movement is concentrated in Maathai's native Kenya, its efforts are recognized worldwide for the positive difference they make.

Finally, animals that have been moved off or "delisted" from the endangered species list mark the third positive effect of people's efforts to improve the environment. **To protect animal and plant species in danger of becoming extinct, the Endangered Species Act (ESA) was passed in 1973.** Since the ESA was passed, animals that were previously endangered or threatened have been nominated for delisting. Among those, the gray wolf of the Upper Midwest has thrived and multiplied to the point where some experts believe it can be safely cut from the endangered species list. ~~Other animals, such as the Chinese alligator, the Brazilian guitarfish, and the Philippine eagle, are on what is known as the red list and are considered critically endangered.~~ **Additionally, according to news.nationalgeographic.com, the bald eagle and the grizzly bear have made such comebacks in numbers of breeding pairs that they are being considered for removal from the list. In all three animals' cases, removal from the Endangered Species List will only occur, if at all, in specific areas where the animals are particularly populous.**

Though the earth is by no means free from environmental threats, not all the nature-oriented news is negative. As some dedicated people have striven to protect waters, lands, and animals, those aspects of nature have recovered. Humans still have great power to harm the environment, but the efforts of the Sierra Club and the Green Belt Movement, among others, ensures a future for plants and animals once thought lost.

Revising for the First C: Concise Writing   Renée's enthusiasm for her topic caused her to include details that didn't necessarily help support her point. Deleting details about the Hudson River, the Green Belt Movement, and endangered species—all of which are related to her topic—proved Renée's greatest challenge. Eventually, she crossed out details that didn't directly support the idea that people's efforts had a positive effect on the environment.

Revising for the Second C: Credible Writing   In terms of credibility, Renée's goal was to let her readers see both how bad aspects of the environment had become and how much they had improved. In her early drafts, she included details that often showed *either* how polluted the environment was *or* the steps taken to improve it, but not both. Thus, at various points in her essay, Renée had to make certain she included both stages of environmental pollution (added in bold type).

Revising for the Third C: Clear Writing   All three areas she covered in her essay were important to Renée, but the only one she had heard about recently was some animals' possible removal from the Endangered Species List. Though she was aware of how polluted lakes and rivers were in the 1970s, she hadn't been born yet. Similarly, though she recognizes the importance of the GBM's contributions, Renée wanted her most important point—the possible delisting of animals—to be a recent one that occurred in her own country. Renée read through her revised draft and added transitions (underlined) to help her readers follow her ideas.

Revising for the Fourth C: Correct Writing   The sentences in this essay are all correct. To check for correctness in your own writing, see Part Seven, "Writing Correct Sentences."

WRITING PRACTICE 1 Writing an Essay Step by Step

Now you have the chance to write an essay of your own.

Prewriting

1. Choose a topic for your essay from the list below.

Causes of heart disease	Effects of working hard
Causes of sibling rivalry	Effects of overeating
Causes of poor student attendance	Effects of exercising regularly
Causes of stress	Effects of treating people rudely
Causes of teen pregnancy	Effects of being a workaholic

2. Freewrite for ten minutes to come up with details for support. Try to think of details that will make your essay believable for your reader. For instance, if your topic is "causes of sibling rivalry," try listing different times when you or someone you know felt competitive toward a brother or sister. A sample list follows about Will's older sister Mira.

Mira was "perfect."

Mira beat me at everything (until age 14).

Mira did everything first.

Mira was bossy to me.

Mira was mean to me.

Drafting

3. Write your thesis statement, making sure to emphasize either the cause or the effect of the situation you're discussing.

4. Choose the support points and details that you think best illustrate your thesis statement.

5. Rearrange your support points and details so that they come in the order you want them. If some details don't fit as well as others, leave them out.

6. Write a draft of your essay using the thesis statement, support points, and details you've chosen.

Revising

7. Make sure all the details in your essay make the causes or effects of the situation being discussed clear. Make sure your details are organized and connected by using clear transitions that let your reader understand the relationship between the causes and effects you discuss.

Editing

8. Proofread your essay to make sure you have used correct spelling, punctuation, and grammar.

WRITING PRACTICE 2 Explaining the Causes or Effects of a Real-Life Situation

Cause-and-effect reasoning often helps us explain, predict, or control situations in our lives. Now you have an the opportunity to choose both the topic and the types of support you will use. Select Topic A, B, or C and follow the directions for writing your essay. Before beginning this assignment, think about how much influence you have over the lives of people you love.

Topic A

You are about to move out of your current apartment. While you're cleaning your current place, you discover a huge stain on the wall in the corner of a room. You fear that your landlord will not return your deposit, so you want to explain the reason for the stain. Your assignment is this: *Write a letter to your landlord explaining the possible cause or causes for the stain on the wall.* Use details from your own experiences and observations to support your ideas. *Note:* If you have never lived in an apartment or other dwelling that required you to pay a deposit, write about a time at your parents' home when you had to explain the causes of some unpleasant event or circumstance to them.

Possible thesis statement: A number of circumstances, all beyond my control, could have caused the stain on the southwest wall of the living room.

Topic B

Cities are affected by innumerable factors, from job layoffs and crime to bad weather and transportation difficulties. A friend of yours is moving to your city, and you want to help him understand the nature of some of your city's challenges. Your assignment is this: *Write a letter to your friend explaining* either *the causes* or *the effects of some city-oriented problem.* For instance, you might explain that because of budget cuts, the local schools (including your college) have suffered. For this essay, use examples from other people's lives as well as your own. You may use examples from written sources such as the newspaper, but you do not have to.

Possible thesis statement: Because of the latest tax cuts, Carter Community College is experiencing negative effects in the areas of course offerings, facilities, and student fees.

Topic C

Although many health conditions remain unexplained by modern medicine, the causes of some diseases are clear. For instance, a clear link between smoking cigarettes and lung disease has been established and documented. Your assignment is this: *Write an essay explaining the causes of a disease.* These are some diseases that have clear-cut causes. *Note:* There are many types of each disease, and not all are easily explained. However, each type of disease listed has a medically established cause.

Type II diabetes   Lung cancer

Heart disease   Skin cancer

Liver disease

For this assignment, you will need to read articles from magazines, newspapers, or Web sites to learn about the disease you are writing about.

Possible thesis statement: Though Type II diabetes can be developed through no fault or habit of the sufferer, some causes of the disease are well-known.

WRITING PRACTICE 3 Writing in Response to a Reading

Anne Taylor Fleming writes that the cellular phone "has completely changed the way we behave in public." To what extent is she right? Your assignment is this: *Write an essay explaining the effects of cell phone use on people's behavior,* citing Fleming's essay (page 371) and your own experiences for support. Your thesis statement may be something like "The cell phone has had a number of effects on the way people behave."

Lab Activity 23

For additional practice with cause-and-effect writing, complete Lab Activity 23 in the lab manual packaged with your textbook. If you did not receive a lab manual, you can complete this activity online at **www.ablongman.com/long.** Click on **College Resources for Writers** and then click on **Activity 23.**

24 Definition

Though the lust for power affects many people, some are more susceptible than others. From Idi Amin and Pol Pot to Josef Stalin and Adolf Hitler, these men have ruled their countries with iron fists. In some cases, dictatorships have brought societal improvements such as better health care and increased literacy to their citizenry; too often, however, a country's population suffers at the hand of a charismatic, all-powerful ruler.

What Is a Definition Essay?

With so many new forms of technology, we are constantly defining terms to better understand others and be understood ourselves. Listening to someone explain how to "download" information from the Internet or "surf" the Net makes understanding current terminology essential.

In the **definition** strategy of essay development, you explain one specific word or idea so that other people can understand it. Definition may be one of the most valuable skills you can master as a writer.

Using Definition in Real-Life Writing

Defining terms is important in everyday communication. Real-life uses of definition follow.

For College

- In a political science class, you define *justice* in terms of your country's legal system.
- In a biology class, you define *stamen* on an exam.

In Your Personal Life

■ You and your partner continually redefine *commitment* in terms of where your relationship is headed.

■ You and your friends define *honesty* and *trust* when you have conflicts.

At Work

■ You may be asked to define yourself in one word at a job interview.

■ You define *progress* for a new employee you're training.

Types of Definitions

You can define terms in a number of ways.

■ Formal definition
■ Definition by class
■ Definition by extended example

Formal Definition   A **formal definition** usually takes no more than two or three sentences. It's similar to what you might find in a dictionary. Some examples of formal definitions follow; note that they are all complete sentences.

> A *s'more is* a dessert consisting usually of toasted marshmallow and pieces of chocolate bar sandwiched between two graham crackers.
>
> A *quadruped* is an animal that has four legs.
>
> *Civility* is an expression of politeness.
>
> *Perfunctory* means "characterized by routine or superficiality."

Formal definitions quickly and accurately tell us what a word means. However, formal definitions are generally not the type of definition required for college writing.

Definition by Class   The type of definition that is more common in college writing is **definition by class.** Definition by class involves two main steps.

Step 1: Place the term you're defining into a general category, or class.

The following examples illustrate the first part of definition by class.

A *bigwig* is a **person** . . .

Loneliness is the **feeling** . . .

A *Reuben* is a **sandwich** . . .

In the above examples, *bigwig* is placed into the general category of *person*, *loneliness* is labeled a *feeling*, and *Reuben* is put in the class of *sandwich*. In all cases, the definition places the term in a broad category before giving any other details.

Step 2: Offer details to further clarify the term.

Simply begin with a topic sentence that includes your general category or class, and then add details to make the meaning of your term clear. Your thesis statement will have two parts: the general category and some details.

To find examples for your definition, ask questions about the term you want to define. For example, for the *bigwig*, ask, *what kind* of person is a bigwig? What makes a bigwig different from other people?

A *bigwig* is a **person** <u>who possesses great influence in any arena in which he or she chooses to exert effort.</u>

For *loneliness*, ask yourself, *what kind* of feeling is loneliness? What about it is different from any other type of feeling?

Loneliness is the **feeling** of <u>being alone when you don't want to be.</u>

For the *Reuben*, ask yourself, *what kind* of sandwich is a Reuben? How is it special or different from other sandwiches?

A *Reuben* is a **sandwich** that <u>contains the perfect blend of richness, substance, and tanginess.</u>

The answers to the questions about the general terms above provide details that help complete the definition by class.

The question "What kind?" is helpful in defining terms. Asking it throughout your definition process will help you find details to illustrate your term.

Definition-by-class essays often contain support points and specific details to support their thesis statements. Victor's essay "The Victim" (page 400) does just this.

Definition by Extended Example   In **definition by extended example,** you use a single example throughout your entire essay. In this case, your essay may begin with a formal definition of the term you're defining, or it may use the same type of thesis as a definition-by-class essay. The key difference between an extended example essay and another kind of definition essay lies in the types of examples you use. In an extended example essay, instead of providing different examples for each support point, you offer aspects of a single, detailed example for each point. This explanation will serve to illustrate the term you're defining. The next essay, "A Dictator," gives a definition by extended example.

A Model Student Essay

Read the essay below to see how definition by extended example works.

A Dictator

According to *Merriam-Webster's Collegiate Dictionary,* a *dictator* is one who rules "absolutely and often oppressively." While this definition is valid, it does not include other relevant characteristics of dictators. A study of the life of Uganda's Idi Amin Dada Oumee (May 17, 1928–August 16, 2003), however, reveals that a dictator is an absolute leader who is charismatic, cunning, and ruthless.

To convince enough people to follow them, dictators must be charismatic, or have great personal appeal. They must be able to persuade people to give up their lives as they know them and follow a new leader. The words and voices of dictators must inspire people and spur them to action in the name of the dictator's cause. Finally, dictators must be able to convince people that whatever atrocities they commit are done for the good of the people. Like so many powerful men, Idi Amin was charismatic. Though he is reputed to have had as many as 300,000 people in his own country murdered, according to an article in the *Irish Times,* and thousands of others exiled, he was initially viewed as flamboyant. Appreciated for his talents—championship boxing and swimming among them—Amin seemed a positive change from the forceful president he replaced, if somewhat preposterous, according to an article in *The Times.* Rather than being ridiculed, Amin was famous also for his many self-given titles, "Last King of Scotland" among them. His seemingly light-hearted, eccentric nature made him a colorful figure that people followed, even as they feared him.

Idi Amin Dada

SURF THE NET Ugandan Dictator Idi Amin Dada was internationally known for his cruelty as well as his ruthlessness. However, Amin also gained fame for idiosyncratic personal behavior. What can you learn about Amin in terms of character and personality? Surf the Internet to learn about Idi Amin Dada and write a few sentences summarizing your findings.

Though dictators are often characterized in terms of their unyielding rule, they must be cunning as well. Dictators must be able to plot and plan their own ascension to power just as they are plotting and planning the current government's downfall. They must be able to see potential conflicts, stamp them out quietly (or violently, as the case may be), and manipulate the details to cast themselves in the best possible light. Again, Amin fits the dictator profile. According to the article in the *Irish Times*, Amin received little formal education. Nevertheless, he managed to gain the confidence of leaders. Upon joining Milton Obote (Uganda's first prime minister, who forced out the previous president), Amin used his political savvy to rise through the ranks and become Obote's chief of staff. Though instrumental in Obote's operation, Amin eventually lost favor and status with him. Upon hearing that Obote was to betray him, Amin staged a coup and overthrew Obote, declaring himself president. Not possessing inexhaustible military power of his own, Amin relied on his keen insight to place himself in power.

Of all qualities that define a dictator, the one that many readily believe is most outstanding is ruthlessness. To rise to power and hold on to that power, dictators must exert unopposable force. On their way to power, they must crush all who thwart them, and once they gain power, they must punish anyone who appears to be a threat. Idi Amin more than fit this description. On his way to power, even as a young solider, Amin was known for his cruelty, according to *The Times* article. Once in a position of power under Obote, Amin used his influence to help Obote force the previous president into exile. Finally, as dictator of Uganda, Amin wiped out hundreds of thousands of his own people, killing and expelling thousands of nonnative residents all in the name of tribalism, a view of society dividing people into subgroups or tribes. Shortly after coming into power, Amin established squads to hunt down and murder Obote's supporters as well as much of the educated Ugandan population, whom he did not trust. Military leaders who had not supported him were killed, many by beheading.

Many qualities define the word *dictator,* and not all of them are negative. Dictatorial leaders such as Idi Amin have often possessed tremendous personal appeal and intelligence. However, whatever positive characteristics a dictator might possess, the one that overshadows all others is ruthlessness. Dictators may individually be remembered for their paranoia, their indulgences, or their idiosyncrasies, but collectively they are remembered as ruthless.

EXERCISE 1 ANALYZING A DEFINITION ESSAY

Read "A Dictator" (page 389). Then, answer the questions below.

1. What is the general class, or category, for *dictator?* _____

2. In the conclusion, what characteristic does the writer say is most

indicative of dictators? _____   _____

3. What are some characteristics of dictators?

  a. _____

  b. _____

  c. _____

4. What are some specific details that illustrate Idi Amin's ruthlessness?

  a. _____

b. _____

c. _____

5. How does the writer organize this essay? How can you tell?

_____

6. What other words does the writer use in place of *dictator?*

_____

Definition by Negative Example   In **definition by negative example**, you state what a term is *not* and then state what the term *is.* An easy way to begin a paragraph that uses definition by extended example is to use a stereotype as the "negative" part of the definition and then add what the term *is* later in the sentence. The following sentences are examples of definition by negation.

Pol Pot was not just a cruel leader.

Dictators are not simply people who lead.

A dictatorship is a type of government that affects not only those people under the dictator's control but also others in countries worldwide.

Each sentence above begins with a statement that the writer considers false and ends with the writer's idea of what the term being defined *is.*

An alternative thesis statement for "A Dictator" that uses definition by negative example could be "A dictator is not simply someone who has gained power but someone who possesses specific traits."

A Professional Essay

Often, definition is important not only to clarify a term but also to convince people of a larger issue surrounding that term. Read "Discrimination Is a Virtue," by Robert Keith Miller, and see how the writer argues his point through definition.

Discrimination Is a Virtue

Robert Keith Miller

When I was a child, my grandmother used to tell me a story about a king who had three daughters and decided to test their love.

He asked each of them "How much do you love me?" The first replied that she loved him as much as all the diamonds and pearls in the world. The second said that she loved him more than life itself. The third replied "I love you as fresh meat loves salt."

This answer enraged the king; he was convinced that his youngest daughter was making fun of him. So he banished her from his realm and left all of his property to her elder sisters.

As the story unfolded it became clear, even to a 6-year-old, that the king had made a terrible mistake. The two older girls were hypocrites, and as soon as they had profited from their father's generosity, they began to treat him very badly. A wiser man would have realized that the youngest daughter was the truest. Without attempting to flatter, she had said, in effect, "We go together naturally; we are a perfect team."

Years later, when I came to read Shakespeare, I realized that my grandmother's story was loosely based upon the story of King Lear, who put his daughters to a similar test and did not know how to judge the results. Attempting to save the king from the consequences of his foolishness, a loyal friend pleads, "Come sir, arise, away! I'll teach you differences." Unfortunately, the lesson comes too late. Because Lear could not tell the difference between true love and false, he loses his kingdom and eventually his life.

We have a word in English which means "the ability to tell differences." That word is *discrimination*. But within the last twenty years, this word has been so frequently misused that an entire generation has grown up believing that "discrimination" means "racism." People are always proclaiming that "discrimination" is something that should be done away with. Should that ever happen, it would prove to be our undoing.

Discrimination means discernment; it means the ability to perceive the truth, to use good judgment and to profit accordingly. The *Oxford English Dictionary* traces this understanding of the word back to 1648 and demonstrates that, for the next 300 years, "discrimination" was a virtue, not a vice. Thus, when a character in a nineteenth-century novel makes a happy marriage, Dickens has another character remark, "It does credit to your discrimination that you should have found such a very excellent young woman."

Of course, "the ability to tell differences" assumes that differences exist, and this is unsettling for a culture obsessed with the notion of equality. The contemporary belief that discrimination is a vice stems from the compound "discriminate against." What we need to remember, however, is that some things deserve to be judged harshly: we should not leave our kingdoms to the selfish and the wicked.

Discrimination is wrong only when someone or something is discriminated against because of prejudice. But to use the word in this sense, as so many people do, is to destroy its true meaning. If you discriminate against something because of general preconceptions rather than particular insights, then you are not discriminating—bias has clouded the clarity of vision which discrimination demands.

One of the great ironies of American life is that we manage to discriminate in the practical decisions of daily life, but usually fail to discriminate when we make public policies. Most people are very discriminating when it comes to buying a car, for example, because they realize that cars have differences. Similarly, an increasing number of people have learned to discriminate in what they eat. Some foods are better than others—and indiscriminate eating can undermine one's health.

Yet in public affairs, good judgment is depressingly rare. In many areas which involve the common good, we see a failure to tell differences.

Consider, for example, some of the thinking behind modern education. On the one hand, there is a refreshing realization that there are differences among children, and some children—be they gifted or handicapped—require special education. On the other hand, we are politically unable to accept the consequences of this perception. The trend in recent years has been to group together students of radically different ability. We call this process "mainstreaming," and it strikes me as a characteristically American response to the discovery of differences: we try to pretend that differences do not matter.

Similarly, we try to pretend that there is little difference between the sane and the insane. A fashionable line of argument has it that "everybody is a little mad" and that few mental patients deserve long-term hospitalization. As a consequence of such reasoning, thousands of seriously ill men and women have been evicted from their hospital beds and returned to what is euphemistically called "the community"—which often means being left to sleep on city streets, where confused and helpless people now live out of paper bags as the direct result of our refusal to discriminate.

Or to choose a final example from a different area: how many recent elections reflect thoughtful consideration of the genuine differences among candidates? Benumbed by television commercials that market aspiring officeholders as if they were a new brand of toothpaste or hair spray, too many Americans vote with only a fuzzy understanding of the issues in question. Like Lear, we seem too eager to leave the responsibility of government to others and too ready to trust those who tell us whatever we want to hear.

So as we look around us, we should recognize that "discrimination" is a virtue which we desperately need. We must try to avoid making unfair and arbitrary distinctions, but we must not go to the other extreme and pretend that there are no distinctions to be made. The ability to make intelligent judgments is essential both for the success of one's personal life and for the functioning of society as a whole. Let us be open-minded by all means, but not so open-minded that our brains fall out.

EXERCISE 2 ANALYZING A PROFESSIONAL ESSAY FOR GOOD DEFINITION STRATEGY

Read "Discrimination Is a Virtue" (page 392). Then, fill in the blanks below.

1. What is Miller's thesis statement? _____

_____

2. How does defining *discrimination* help Miller make his point?

_____

_____

3. What examples of positive discrimination does Miller offer?

_____

_____

4. What examples of failure to discriminate does Miller provide?

_____

_____

5. List three transitions that you think Miller uses particularly well.

_____

_____

_____

Writing a Definition Essay

The beauty of writing a definition essay is that, even though the dictionary may offer one meaning for a term, you can add a completely new interpretation to that term just by providing examples to illustrate your ideas. For instance, the dictionary may say that a brother is "a man who has the same parents," but your experience may lead you to write "A brother is a mentor, coach, and buddy, all rolled into one person." As always, your persuasiveness will depend on the nature of your examples as well as your presentation of them.

Knowing Your Audience and Purpose

The challenge of writing a definition essay is that people will already have an idea of many terms' meanings. Thus, your job is not only to *communicate* your meaning of a term but also to *illustrate* it. For instance, most people could probably offer a simple definition of the word *car:* a four-wheeled vehicle with a gas engine, or something similar. However, if you have a long car commute to work every day, your definition of *car* might be "A car is a small prison on wheels." Since other people might not initially understand your reasons for this definition, your job is to provide details about your car—it has uncomfortable seats, no air conditioning, no stereo—that illustrate your definition.

Choosing a Topic for Development

Choosing a good topic will largely depend on what kind of definition essay you're writing. Much of the time, your instructor will assign you a definition-by-class essay and give you a topic to develop. The only type of term to try to avoid in writing a definition paragraph is one whose meaning pretty much everyone agrees on. Terms like *table, fingernail,* or *mole*—unless they have some special significance that you can demonstrate in your essay—are better left out. Terms that mean different things to different people, however, are better choices. The following common terms are suitable for development in a definition-by-class essay.

Emotions:	love, hate, happiness, loneliness, fear, sadness, joy, excitement
Family:	mother, father, sister, brother, grandmother, grandfather, family, home
Stereotypes:	know-it-all, bad boy, goody two-shoes, nerd, jock, cheerleader, teacher's pet, bully, pest

These represent a very small sample of possible topics your instructor might assign you, but notice that they all allow for a range of explanations. Even terms like *mother* or *father*—terms that most people understand—let you write about *what aspects* of motherhood or fatherhood mean a lot to you. For instance, as an only child, your idea of a mother might be someone who is a parent, counselor, friend, and companion. To someone who was raised in a family with eight siblings, a parent might be a referee, a police officer, an advocate, and a leader. The word *mother* has not changed from writer to writer, but the writers' interpretations of the word differ depending on their experiences.

In preparing to write a definition paragraph, do some prewriting to see what ideas come to mind on your topic. One student, Marina, decided to freewrite for ten minutes on the topic of "bully."

> My neighbor Digol was a bully. Ever since we moved into his neighborhood when I was thirteen, Digol set out to make my life miserable. As the biggest kid on the block and the oldest guy in our class (he had to repeat second grade), Digol had an easy time with those of us who were smaller or younger than he was. At first I believed my mom when she said, "Digol just likes you and doesn't know how to show it," but I was hit, kicked, and pinched too many times to believe that. Digol's bully tendencies weren't just physical; he "messed with my mind," as my brothers say. "Have a boyfriend, Marina?" "Stuff your bra, Marina?" "Nice zits, Marina!" These are all things Digol said to me on the way to the bus. Maybe if I'd been beautiful these things wouldn't bug me, but Digol always seemed to know the things that would hurt most to hear.

Marina's freewriting focused primarily on her neighbor and his actions, so the definition isn't as clear as it will need to be for her essay. However, Marina did identify two possible ways to define the term *bully* through her neighbor: physical abuse and "messing with [her] mind." These two points offer potential for her essay.

Writing an Effective Thesis Statement

As with choosing a topic, writing an effective topic sentence depends on the type of definition paragraph you're writing. Marina's assignment was to define the term *bully*. When she analyzed the two points that surfaced in her freewriting, Marina realized that they all involved her neighbor being unkind to smaller or younger people. Marina's thesis statement was this:

> A bully is someone who exerts force only on those who are weaker in some way.

This statement prepares the reader for examples showing how someone—most likely Marina herself or another younger, smaller kid in her neighborhood—was tormented by Digol.

In Marina's case, her thesis statement is the formal—or dictionary—definition of the term. If she chose, however, Marina could have used her own definition by placing her term in a general class with details: "A bully is a person who torments only those weaker than he or she is."

Developing Specific Details

The details you use will depend on the kind of definition essay you're writing. For instance, the essay "A Dictator" (page 389) gives a definition by extended example. However, the essay "The Victim" (page 400) contains examples of victims of several dictatorships, so it falls under the definition-by-class heading. Whatever kind of details you use, draw from your own experiences, other people's experiences, and trusted sources as necessary in defining your term.

Organizing and Linking Ideas

Since definition essays come in different forms, the ideas found in them follow different patterns of organization. Generally, if your essay uses an extended example, your details will logically follow chronological (time sequence) order since you'll be relating details as they occurred. If you're writing a definition-by-class essay, your topic and examples will dictate the best order to use.

Words That Signal Time and Time Sequence

after	earlier	meanwhile	subsequently
at last	finally	next	then
at the same time	first, second, third	shortly afterward	when
before	immediately	soon	while
during	later		

Words and Terms That Signal Emphatic Order

above all	even more	last	most important
another	first	least of all	most significantly
equally important	in the first place	most of all	next
especially			

✓ CHECKLIST for Writing a Definition Essay

_____ **Prewriting**

■ Write about the topic your instructor assigns you, or choose a topic from the list of common terms for definition on page 403.

■ Use prewriting strategies to get your early ideas on paper.

_____ **Drafting**

■ Write a thesis statement that gives your terms clearly and concisely. If you are writing a definition-by-class essay, make sure your topic sentence places your term in a general category.

■ Write a rough draft of your essay. (Feel free to do more prewriting as this point to get more ideas down on paper.)

■ Use specific details that illustrate different aspects of the term you're defining.

■ Use transitions to connect your ideas for your reader.

_____ **Revision**

■ Revise your work, as necessary, according to the first three of the four Cs: *concise, credible,* and *clear* writing.

_____ **Editing**

■ Proofread your work for sentence-level errors.

Following the Four Cs Through Revision

Few concepts worth writing about can be limited to a single, one-line definition. In fact, dictionaries often offer several simple definitions of a word. Thus, your task is twofold: you have to choose which formal, or dictionary, definition fits your term the best and then expand that explanation through examples. That way, your reader both sees the concise meaning of a word in your thesis statement and has a chance to visualize and understand it by reading your details. In choosing to define *victim*, Victor wanted to show his readers the nonphysical as well as physical suffering that many victims of dictatorships experience.

The Victim

According to *Merriam-Webster's Collegiate Dictionary*, a victim is "one that is subjected to oppression, hardship, or mistreatment." The word *victim* is used to describe beings who suffer any number of ailments: victim of illness, victim of discrimination, victim of poverty. While all these uses reasonably fall under the meaning of *victim*, they take into account only a single malady suffered by the human or animal in question. Victims of dictatorships, however, suffer in many ways.

A victim is someone who suffers political oppression. Victims of dictatorships often lose their property, their livelihood, and their rights. For instance, under Prime Minister Saloth Sar (1976–1979), more commonly known as Pol Pot, Cambodian citizens were forced from cities onto communal farms. These people were forbidden, on penalty of death, to protest the government's actions. ~~The movie *The Killing Fields* shows how Cambodian citizens were kept in check by various violent means.~~ Victims of dictatorships also lose the right to decide where they want to live. **Under Pol Pot, according to an article in *Peace Review*, land mines, which the dictator referred to as "perfect little soldiers," were distributed around the countryside to keep Cambodian people from escaping to Thailand and to prevent potential rescuers from entering.** Suffering with every right that was taken from them, Pol Pot's own citizens were prisoners in their own country, victims of his rule.

A victim is also someone who suffers emotional hardship. Victims of dictatorships suffer from grief over their country's losses and worry that they will be the next target of some hateful act. Victims of Josef Stalin's rule in the former Soviet Union suffered this kind of emotional hardship. Though they were powerful men in their own right, Stalin's political rivals suffered if they even appeared to disagree with him or threaten his rule. **Leaders such as Leon Trotsky were disgraced and exiled for posing even imagined threats to Stalin's power.** ~~The novel *Animal Farm* by George Orwell shows, in the form of a story about animals, how Stalin came to power by getting rid of any potential competition for power.~~ Others suffered as well. **According to Britannica.com, between 1934 and 1938 Stalin began huge purges of the Communist party, government, armed forces, and educated people in which millions of so-called enemies of the people were imprisoned, exiled, or shot.** Of course, being imprisoned, exiled, or shot caused emotional hardship, but those whose turn had not come for punishment suffered as they waited. ~~Some experts claim that the Soviet Union would not have lasted through World War II if it had been led by someone less tough, but victims of Stalin's acts would disagree.~~ Though Stalin's policies and practices caused people to suffer physically and politically, these victims of Stalin's dictatorship also suffered emotionally.

Finally, a victim is someone who suffers physical mistreatment. Victims of dictatorships suffer from illness, starvation, physical abuse, and even death. In one extreme example of this physical mistreatment 6 million Jewish people suffered in the Holocaust (1939–1945) during Adolf Hitler's regime in Germany. **Initially losing rights and property under Hitler's regime, Jews were later herded into concentration camps.** ~~Visiting the concentration camps or seeing photos taken of them adds new meaning to the word *victim*.~~ Forced to perform backbreaking slave labor, Jewish citizens routinely died from overwork, illness, and starvation, according to an article in *USA Today*. **Serving also as the unwilling subjects for cruel "medical" or military experiments, Jews were tortured.** Finally, many of those who escaped death by labor or torture were killed by lethal gas in mass executions at the camps. ~~Though the Holocaust has been over for more than sixty years, the world will never forget its horror.~~ Certainly, political and emotional suffering are unpleasant at best, but the victims of Hitler's dictatorship suffered physically, losing their health and often their lives.

Anyone who suffers can own the label *victim*. The menacing bully, the patronizing employer, or the sneering significant other: all of these can create lasting pain in the people they affect. Many times, however, victims can choose to walk away from being victimized by avoiding the bully, finding a new job, or leaving a loved one. For the victims of Pol Pot, Josef Stalin, and Adolf Hitler, though, their countries became their prisons. To be a victim, then, was to be a prisoner in one's own land.

Perhaps the easiest mistake to make in writing a definition essay is to include details that do not help clarify your term. For instance, in his essay "The Victim," Victor could have included interesting details about the people most affected by Pol Pot's rule. In doing so, however, he would have gotten off-track in terms of defining the term *dictator;* thus, he omitted those details.

Revising for the First C: Concise Writing Victor found that, though the dictionary definition of *victim* was easily understandable, it didn't cover the spectrum of suffering that he wanted to discuss. Thus, Victor defined *victim* in terms of three specific types of suffering, making certain that every word he wrote somehow clarified his definition. Details about *The Killing Fields, Animal Farm,* and concentration camp photos—while fascinating to him—did not help Victor advance his definition of *victim;* thus, he crossed them out.

Revising for the Second C: Credible Writing Victor's challenge in finding and choosing details for his essay lay in deciding which details about suffering to include. In the case of every dictator he discussed, Victor found more than enough information about that leader's cruelty. However, Victor discovered that if he included too much detail, then his definition became lost in a mass of description. Eventually, Victor added specific details (shown in bold type) only if he had a sentence of definition first. For instance, rather than writing about Cambodian citizens' suffering, Victor wrote:

> Victims of dictatorships also lose the right to decide where they want to live. Under Pol Pot, according to an article in *Peace Times,* land mines, which the dictator referred to as "perfect little soldiers," were distributed around the countryside to keep Cambodian people from escaping to Thailand and to prevent potential rescuers from entering.

By including one sentence of definition and one sentence of detail, Victor was able to keep the integrity of his definition while still illustrating it.

Revising for the Third C: Clear Writing For his overall essay structure, Victor used emphatic order. All three of the men he focused on caused innumerable people to suffer, and Victor had originally organized his essay chronologically, placing his discussion of Pol Pot last. However, as he continued writing, Victor discovered that although both Pol Pot and Stalin had acted with extreme ruthlessness and cruelty, neither was as responsible for mass suffering as Hitler. Thus, Victor placed his discussion of Hitler last.

Revising for the Fourth C: Correct Writing   The sentences in this essay are all correct. To check for correctness in your own writing, see Part Seven, "Writing Correct Sentences."

WRITING PRACTICE 1 Writing an Essay Step by Step

Prewriting

1. Choose a topic from the following list of different topics for essays that allow you to use definition to develop your ideas. This list contains slang expressions, some of which are more contemporary than others.

cool	jerk (type of person)
bling-bling	loser
awesome	airhead
the bomb	hip
couch potato	attitude
hot (to describe someone's appearance)	expression of your choice

2. Freewrite for five to ten minutes on your topic. Below is an example of freewriting by a student, Bryn, on the term *cool*.

> For me, _cool_ doesn't mean being popular or in style; it means being confident and secure in nearly all situations. My friend Pete is cool; no matter what happens, Pete always seems under control. Last year, when Pete's girlfriend dumped him and he lost his job, both in one week, he still managed to keep himself together. He didn't lose his temper, he didn't blame anyone, and he started looking for work the same day he was fired.

In writing a definition paragraph, the prewriting technique of questioning can be very helpful. Look at the following question-and-answer list for the term *cool*.

Question	**Answer**
What is the formal definition of *cool?*	A quality marked by steady, dispassionate calmness and self-control

Question	Answer
What is the general category for *cool*?	Quality
What are some examples of cool behavior?	Never sweats or stammers under pressure; takes action when adversity strikes; maintains composure even in difficult situations

Drafting

3. Write your thesis statement, including either a formal definition of the word or a general category and details describing the word.

Possible thesis statement: Being *cool* means being calm, confident, and composed in all situations.

4. Choose support points, if necessary, and specific details to develop your definition. If you want to use a lot of short examples, do more freewriting to come up with them. If you want to use a single extended example, consider making a list or an outline to keep the points of your extended example in order.

5. Organize your ideas using emphatic order or chronological (time sequence) order. Keep in mind that chronological order works very well for an extended example essay.

6. Write your draft. Check to make sure your organization is consistent throughout your essay. Make sure all the details in your list help define your term. If any details do not make your term clearer, remove them.

Revision

7. Revise to make sure your details are organized, and make sure that your ideas are connected through clear transitions.

Editing

8. Proofread your essay to make sure your spelling, punctuation, and grammar are correct.

WRITING PRACTICE 2 Defining an Emotion or Quality

Now you have the opportunity to choose both the topic and the types of support you use. Select Topic A, B, or C for this assignment.

Topic A

Defining a person or activity in one word shows that your thoughts about that person or activity are clear. A common interview question asks a job applicant to define himself or herself in a single word. What word would you choose to describe yourself? Your assignment is this: *Write an essay to a potential employer explaining how you would yourself in one word.* You may choose several different examples from your life to illustrate your definition, or you may develop your definition using a single extended example.

Possible thesis statement: I pride myself on being responsible, which means I make sure the job gets done, no matter whose job it is.

Topic B

Sometimes what a job seems to be and what it is are two different things. Your assignment is this: *Write an essay defining a specific type of worker.* Use this assignment to learn about a career that interests you. Interview someone who holds a job in that field, and think of ways to define that kind of work. For instance, if you interview a firefighter, you might conclude that different kinds of strength are necessary to be successful.

Possible thesis statement: Being a firefighter means being strong in a number of ways.

Topic C

Magazines and newspapers can shape our impressions of different people and activities. Your assignment is this: *Read about a person or an activity. Then, write an essay defining that person or activity.* For instance, if you are interested in investing money, you might conclude that being an effective money manager involves risk. Use examples from your reading to clarify your term.

Possible thesis statement: *Risk* in the world of investing simply means spending, as opposed to saving, money.

WRITING PRACTICE 3 Writing in Response to a Reading

In his essay "Discrimination Is a Virtue" (page 392), Robert Keith Miller argues that being able to recognize differences is important. The dictators described in this chapter conducted much of their cruel behavior in the name of tribal, educational, racial, and social differences. A list of terms related to dictatorships and people's attitudes toward them follows. Your assignment is this: *Choose one of the words below and write an essay defining it.* You may write your essay based on the dictators covered in this chapter, or you may use examples from your experiences and observations to illustrate your ideas.

cruelty	racism	suffering
power	ruler	supremacy
prejudice	tolerance	tribalism
prisoner	safety	

Lab Activity 24

For additional practice with definition, complete Lab Activity 24 in the lab manual packaged with your textbook. If you did not receive a lab manual, you can complete this activity online at **www.ablongman.com/long.** Click on **College Resources for Writers** and then click on **Activity 24.**

25 Arguing a Position

CULTURE NOTE *Privacy*

When George Orwell published his novel *1984* in 1948, his portrayal of futuristic security—in the form of the omnipresent Big Brother—seemed chilling but unrealistic. However, even as we revel in our ability to instantly contact people, quickly find someone's most recent address, or easily learn someone's criminal history, we forget that we, too, are being watched. How much information should people be allowed to have about us? How easy should this information be to obtain? Under what conditions, if any, should our secrets be made public? These are questions that become increasingly difficult to answer.

Big Brother

SURF THE NET George Orwell's novel *1984* detailed lives devoid of privacy as its citizens constantly acted under the watchful eye of Big Brother, brought into their homes by oversize television screens. How much privacy do people have today? Surf the internet for information on Orwell's Big Brother, and write a few sentences explaining how people's lives today are similar to or different from those in Orwell's novel.

407

What Is an Argument Essay?

The term *argument* usually implies something unpleasant: a combative discussion between two people who are tense and upset, or a group of people yelling back and forth without listening.

As a writer, however, to **argue** a position is simply to give reasons to back up your point of view. In a sense, you've been "arguing" throughout this textbook. Every time you state your ideas in a thesis statement and offer support points and examples, you're arguing your point of view.

An **argument** is an exchange of ideas in which two sides attempt to persuade each other. The following sentences represent different sides to arguments.

> Carpool benefits need to be improved.
>
> People who carpool receive enough special treatment as it is.
>
> Eating a high-protein diet is the best way to lose weight.
>
> Eating a balanced diet is the best way to lose weight.
>
> Identity theft is an increasingly serious problem.
>
> The threat of identity theft is exaggerated.

Each of the sentences above expresses one side to an argument. Each sentence also could be a thesis statement that a writer needs to back up with support points and details.

The key to argument is understanding that people do not have to believe you. Thus, your job as a writer is to present enough information and explanation to make your point believable to your reader.

Using Argument in Real-Life Writing

Argument is relevant in many aspects of daily living. Read the examples below to see how argument skills are especially helpful in real-life situations.

For College

- Strong argument skills help you write an essay persuading your history instructor that the United States should or should not have fought in Vietnam.

- Good argument skills help you persuade an instructor to add you to an already crowded section of a course you need.

In Your Personal Life

■ Having solid argument skills can help you dissuade a friend from making a poor choice.

■ Understanding argument can help you decide how biased an article or news report is.

At Work

■ Give examples of your past job performance to convince a potential employer that you are the best candidate for a job.

■ Point out your successful track record on the job to convince your boss to give you more responsibility.

A Model Student Essay

Read the following essay to see how offering support points and examples makes an argument.

Privacy Lost Online

Once upon a time, we had to wait by the phone or the mailbox to hear from someone not physically near us. We could also compose a letter without interruption and make purchases without fear that someone was watching. Things have changed. If we're in line at the mall, our cell phones can ring just as easily as if we were at home, or if we're doing online research, it's just as easy to receive an online message as it is to get a phone call. This effortless communication has a price, however, and we need to be aware of what we're losing before it's gone. What we lose is privacy, every time we go online.

The most common loss of online privacy comes through computer cookies, or information stored on your computer and sent to specific servers when you log on. For instance, if you register at a commercial site such as Amazon.com, the company will store a cookie on your computer to keep track of your personal information and shopping selections. That way, when you return to the site, you'll be greeted by name—"Welcome back, Reggie!"—and given a list of personalized shopping recommendations. According to the Merriam-Webster online dictionary, cookies contain personal information and customized preferences. The danger of cookies comes when they track not only your progress on a given vendor's site but all your activity over the Internet, says Joe Salkowski in his article "Online Ads Can Often Trace Personal Info." Even when we don't know they're there, cookies allow vendors to compile information about us.

A second invasion of privacy online comes in the form of instant messages, which allow people to chat in real time while they are online. They can be very helpful for quick checks or inquiries—such as "Is it OK to call now?"—but their efficiency can be taken too far. According to an article in *PC World,* instant messaging programs can allow people to "spy" on others, providing information about whether or not someone is online or in specific online locations (Thorsberg). Additionally, even if someone isn't trying to snoop, instant messages can be a perpetual interrupter. Computer user Andrew Foster states, "There's nothing worse than trying to meet a deadline and having to keep fending off uninvited chat messages." Of course, there are ways to be unavailable online: you can block certain people from contacting you, or you can use the messaging program's "busy" or "away" feature. However, these precautions require some action on the part of the computer user, and if you're hurrying to get work done and skip the "away" process, instant messages can be a source of irritation and an invasion of privacy.

In the worst cases, a loss of privacy includes other losses as well. If you don't have top-notch blockers, you can be bombarded by "pop-ups," advertisements that appear on your computer screen when you visit particular Web sites. These ads are annoying, but they can also be harmful. A form of online banditry called phishing—also known as carding or spoofing—is an attempt to acquire personal information such as credit card numbers or passwords. Unsuspecting Internet users receive fraudulent e-mails or pop-ups that ask for sensitive information, sometimes even social security numbers. Paul Kerstein writes in "How Can We Stop Phishing and Pharming Scams?" that approximately 1.2 million Americans were victims of phishing scams between May 2004 and May 2005. While scam artists are nothing new, the ease and speed with which they can do serious damage is. In the case of phishing, invasions of privacy can lead to great financial loss.

Perhaps the hardest aspect of the privacy issue to accept is that some loss of privacy is necessary for convenience. If we have to enter personal information on a Web site we visit regularly every time we visit, we waste precious time and energy. If, however, we allow cookies to do their job and fill in the blanks for us, we risk someone tapping into that store of personal information and using it against us. Turning our computers off might slow criminals down temporarily, but only until they found a new way to get to us through other means. For now, people simply need to use good judgment to avoid losing more than just privacy.

Works Cited

Foster, Andrew. Personal interview. 27 Oct. 2005.

Kerstein, Paul. "How Can We Stop Phishing and Pharming Scams?" *CSO.* 19 July 2005 <http://www.csoonline.com/talkback/071905.html>.

Salkowski, Joe. "Online Ads Can Often Trace Personal Info." *Arizona Daily Star.* 23 Dec. 2000. ProQuest. Sacramento City Coll., Learning Resource Center Lib. 27 June 2005 <http://www.proquest.umi.com>.

Thorsberg, Frank. "Instant Messaging Etiquette." 30 May 2002. 26 Oct. 2005 <http://www.pcworld.com/howto/article/0,aid,99405,00.asp>.

EXERCISE 1 ANALYZING AN ARGUMENT PARAGRAPH

Read "Privacy Lost Online." Then, fill in the blanks below.

1. What argument (or point) is the writer making in "Privacy Lost

Online"? _____

_____

2. In which sentence is the argument stated? _____

3. What three examples does the writer give to support her thesis statement?

    a. _____

    b. _____

    c. _____

4. List three sources the writer cites as examples for her support

points. _____

    a. _____

b. _____

c. _____

5. What transitions does the writer use to signal the start of each support point?

Paragraph 2: _____

Paragraph 3: _____

Paragraph 4: _____

6. Does the writer organize her ideas using chronological (time

sequence) or emphatic order? How can you tell? _____

_____

A Professional Essay

In addition to relevant details and logical organization, a writer's tone can prove to be a powerful tool in persuasion. Read Ted Koppel's essay, paying attention to the role his "tone" plays in his argument.

"Take My Privacy, Please!"

Ted Koppel

The Patriot Act—brilliant! Its critics would have preferred a less stirring title, perhaps something along the lines of the Enhanced Snooping, Library and Hospital Database Seizure Act. But then who, even right after 9/11, would have voted for that? Precisely. He who names it and frames it, claims it. The Patriot Act, however, may turn out to be among the lesser threats to our individual and collective privacy.

There is no end to what we will endure, support, pay for and promote if only it makes our lives easier, promises to save us money, appears to enhance our security and comes to us in a warm, cuddly and altogether non-threatening package. To wit: OnStar, the subscription vehicle tracking and assistance system. Part of its mission statement, as found on the OnStar Web site, is the creation of "safety, security and peace of mind for drivers and passengers with

thoughtful wireless services that are always there, always ready."
You've surely seen or heard their commercials, one of which goes
like this:

> **Announcer:** The following is an OnStar conversation. (Ring)
>
> **Onstar:** OnStar emergency, this is Dwight.
>
> **Driver:** (crying) Yes, yes??!
>
> **Onstar:** Are there any injuries, ma'am?
>
> **Driver:** My leg hurts, my arm hurts.
>
> **Onstar:** O.K. I do understand. I will be contacting emergency
> services.
>
> **Announcer:** If your airbags deploy, OnStar receives a signal
> and calls to check on you. (Ring)
>
> **Emergency Services:** Police.
>
> **Onstar:** This is Dwight with OnStar. I'd like to report a vehicle
> crash with airbag deployment on West 106th Street.
>
> **Emergency Services:** We'll send police and E.M.S. out there.
>
> **Driver:** (crying) I'm so scared!
>
> **Onstar:** O.K., I'm here with you, ma'am; you needn't be scared.

Well, maybe just a little scared. Tell us again how Dwight knows
just where the accident took place. Oh, right! It's those thoughtful wireless services that are always there. Always, as in any time a driver gets
into an OnStar-equipped vehicle. OnStar insists that it would disclose
the whereabouts of a subscriber's vehicle only after being presented
with a criminal court order or after the vehicle has been reported
stolen. That's certainly a relief. I wouldn't want to think that anyone
but Dwight knows where I am whenever I'm traveling in my car.

Of course, E-ZPass and most other toll-collecting systems
already know whenever a customer passes through one of their
scanners. That's because of radio frequency identification technology. In return for the convenience of zipping through toll booths,
you need to have in your car a wireless device. This tag contains
information about your account, permitting E-ZPass to deduct the
necessary toll—and to note when your car whisked through that
particular toll booth. They wouldn't share that information with
anyone, either; that is, unless they had to.

The State Department plans to use radio frequency identification
technology in all new American passports by the end of 2005. The
department wants to be sure that we all move through immigration

quickly and efficiently when we return from overseas. Privacy advocates have suggested that hackers could tap into the information stored on these tags, or that terrorists might be able to use them to pinpoint American tourists in a crowd. The State Department assures us that both concerns are unfounded, and that it will allow privacy advocates to review test results this summer.

Radio frequency identification technology has been used for about 15 years now to reunite lost pets with their owners. Applied Digital Solutions, for example, manufactures the VeriChip, a tiny, implantable device that holds a small amount of data. Animal shelters can scan the chip for the name and phone number of the lost pet's owner. The product is now referred to as the HomeAgain Microchip Identification System. Useful? Sure. Indeed, it's not much of a leap to suggest that one day, the VeriChip might be routinely implanted under the skin of, let's say, an Alzheimer's patient. The Food and Drug Administration approved the VeriChip for use in people last October. An Applied Digital Solutions spokesman estimates that about 1,000 people have already had a VeriChip implanted, usually in the right triceps. At the moment, it doesn't carry much information, just an identification number that health care providers can use to tap into a patient's medical history. A Barcelona nightclub also uses it to admit customers with a qualifying code to enter a V.I.P. room where drinks are automatically put on their bill. Possible variations on the theme are staggering.

And how about all the information collected by popular devices like TiVo, the digital video recorder that enables you to watch and store an entire season's worth of favorite programs at your own convenience? It also lets you electronically mark the programs you favor, allowing TiVo to suggest similar programs for your viewing pleasure. In February, TiVo announced the most frequently played and replayed commercial moment during the Super Bowl (it involves a wardrobe malfunction, but believe me, you don't want to know), drawing on aggregated data from a sample of 10,000 anonymous TiVo households. No one is suggesting that TiVo tracks what each subscriber records and replays. But could they, if they needed to? That's unclear, although TiVo does have a privacy policy. "Your privacy," it says in part, "is very important to us. Due to factors beyond our control, however, we cannot fully ensure that your user information will not be disclosed to third parties."

Unexpected and unfortunate things happen, of course, even to the most reputable and best-run organizations. Only last February, the Bank of America Corporation notified federal investigators that it had lost computer backup tapes containing personal information about 1.2 million federal government employees, including some senators. In April, LexisNexis unintentionally gave outsiders access to the personal files (addresses, Social Security numbers, drivers license information) of as many as 310,000 people. In May, Time Warner revealed that an outside storage company had misplaced data stored on computer backup tapes on 600,000 current and former employees. That same month, United Parcel Service picked up a box of computer tapes in New Jersey from CitiFinancial, the consumer finance subsidiary of Citigroup, that contained the names, addresses, Social Security numbers, account numbers, payment histories and other details on small personal loans made to an estimated 3.9 million customers. The box is still missing. Whoops!

CitiFinancial correctly informed its own customers and, inevitably, the rest of the world about the security breach. Would they have done so entirely on their own? That is less clear. In July 2003, California started requiring companies to inform customers living in the state of any breach in security that compromises personally identifiable information. Six other states have passed similar legislation. No such legislation exists on the federal stage, however—only discretionary guidelines for financial institutions about whether and how they should inform their customers with respect to breaches in the security of their personal information. Both the House and Senate are now considering federal legislation similar to the California law. It's a start but not nearly enough. We need mandatory clarity and transparency; not just with regard to the services that these miracles of microchip and satellite technology offer but also the degree to which companies share and exchange their harvest of private data.

We cannot even begin to control the growing army of businesses and industries that monitor what we buy, what we watch on television, where we drive, the debts we pay or fail to pay, our marriages and divorces, our litigations, our health and tax records and all else that may or may not yet exist on some computer tape, if we don't fully understand everything we're signing up for when we avail ourselves of one of these services.

EXERCISE 2 ANALYZING AN ESSAY FOR GOOD ARGUMENT STRATEGY

Read "Take My Privacy, Please!" by Ted Koppel. Then, answer the questions below.

1. What is Koppel's thesis statement? Where is it located? _____

_____

_____

_____

2. What examples does Koppel offer to support his point? _____

_____

3. What is Koppel's attitude toward these technological devices? How

can you tell? _____

_____

_____

4. What expressions does Koppel use that show his feelings about

privacy-invading technology? _____

_____

_____

5. To what extent does Koppel acknowledge the opposition? Does he

do enough to balance his argument? _____

_____

Writing an Argument Essay

In essence, any time you put pen to paper (or fingers to keyboard), you're writing an argument. Even a statement as simple as "Look at those flowers over there" is *arguing* that those flowers, and not some others, are more worth viewing at that moment. Thus, for every assignment you've written so far, you've been practicing your argument skills.

In composition courses, however, *argument* not only means expressing a point of view; it usually means consulting sources beyond your own experiences and observations. For instance, though you may have noticed that people don't seem to be as concerned about privacy as they once were—you've probably overheard someone publicly discussing personal matters on a cell phone, for instance—you will be more persuasive if you can cite other sources that prove your point. Being able to find, cite, and integrate others' views in your writing are key skills in writing an argument essay.

Knowing Your Audience and Purpose

Audience awareness is perhaps more important in writing an argument than in writing any other type of essay because when you take a side on an issue, you risk alienating or boring a reader on the opposite side. While a reader might not describe a shiny new car the same way that you would, your reader will probably not be looking for "loopholes" or gaps in your logic or support as you write a descriptive essay about the vehicle.

If you choose a controversial topic such as motorcycle helmet laws or prayer in schools, and your reader is not on your side, any little weakness in support could render your argument unconvincing. Thus, taking into account your reader's biases and information on a specific issue will go a long way toward making you persuasive. To give yourself the best chance for support, strive for the following characteristics.

- Being diplomatic
- Giving credit where credit is due

Being Diplomatic   Diplomacy simply involves saying something as politely as possible. You may think that people who oppose your views on an issue are ignorant, narrow-minded fools, but saying so won't help your cause. Just as lawmakers and attorneys must use formal titles and expressions even when highly agitated—"My distinguished colleague from North Dakota is sadly mistaken in claiming that . . . ," for instance—so, too, must you make your point delicately.

Giving Credit Where Credit Is Due   Very few issues are so black and white that they have no common ground, and arguing that your opponent is utterly and completely wrong can often harm your case as much as help it. For instance, though advocates for and opponents of "talking while driving" might disagree about how much a driver is distracted by talking on a cell phone, both sides most likely acknowledge the possibility that some emergency situations—reporting that you're being followed, for one—make a cell phone call while driving acceptable. Thus, in arguing for one side or another, disregarding any common points can cause you to lose credibility.

Similarly, even if you disagree with a specific viewpoint, showing that you know and comprehend that viewpoint's strengths—and *still* take the opposite side—will show your reader that you have a thorough knowledge and understanding of your topic. The writer of "Privacy Lost Online" (page 409), for instance, acknowledges that contemporary technology makes communication "effortless" even as she argues that privacy is lost on the Internet. Thus, even if readers disagree with the argument, they cannot fault the writer for failing to consider the good points of online communication.

Choosing a Topic for Development

For the most part, arguments don't occur over topics that people agree on. If people are of one mind about an issue, there isn't much to say about it. Just make sure you believe in your topic.

It's possible to write convincing essays about issues you don't support, but it's much easier to write about topics that you believe in. Think about what's going on in your life right now—such as work, school, parenting, and relationships—and choose a topic that is relevant to your life. For instance, Kalli was frustrated that her city billed residents inconsistently for public utilities such as water use. Kalli did some freewriting to see if she could write an argument in favor of making water meters part of every household.

> Lisa came over last weekend, and while she was here, she asked if she could wash her car since she lives in an apartment and doesn't have a good place to do it. I said yes, but I remembered too late that Lisa's apartment complex isn't on water meters. Basically, Lisa spent fifteen minutes just hosing down her car, left the water on while she soaped it up, and spent another fifteen minutes rinsing it off. My water bill is going to be awful this month, and I didn't take even one long shower! We all use water, and we all pay taxes; it's not fair that some of us have to pay for water while others can use as much as they want without extra fees. I read an article in the *Union* about how, as more people move into the area, water prices will go up. Also, the drought gets worse (the rivers may actually go down) as more people move into the area and use more water. I can deal with that as long as everyone shares the cost.

Kalli was encouraged to research her topic once she saw that she had ideas and some support for her argument for consistent water metering. She decided to search the archives of her local newspaper to learn more about the issue and then develop her point further.

Writing an Effective Thesis Statement

In her freewriting, Kalli identified these points for development.

Point 1:   Taxpayers have equal rights to water, so everyone should pay the same rate.

Point 2:   Paying for water makes people appreciate it—and use less of it.

Point 3:   Metering everyone's water will help ease stress during drought.

At first, Kalli was afraid that she wouldn't be able to find enough information on each support point to write an entire essay. However, as she read more about water metering, she discovered that she had more than enough information. She wrote a thesis statement that tied her support points together.

Putting water meters on everyone's home makes sense.

This thesis statement allows Kalli to use her three points from freewriting as support points in her essay, and she can add details to develop her ideas.

Developing Specific Details

Just by making and supporting a point, you've been sharpening your argument skills. Two additional techniques can help you make your argument even more convincing.

- Making your side stronger
- Making the other side weaker

Making Your Side Stronger   You already know that after you find support points to back up your thesis statement, you need to use specific details to illustrate your support points. Those specific details fall under three headings.

- Descriptions of objects or events in your life
- Accounts of events in other people's lives
- Facts that you've heard or read about from trusted sources

To make your side of an argument stronger, you need to use a variety of examples that support your thesis statement. You can find these examples by interviewing an expert, reading books or articles, or surfing the Internet.

Consulting Experts.   An **expert** is someone who has special skills or knowledge in a certain field. For instance, Elton John is considered an expert in music and music production because he is a pop singer, he has written many popular songs, and he has produced successful Broadway shows. Organizations such as the American Medical Association and the Better Business Bureau are experts, too. Consulting and quoting experts can make your argument stronger because experts can offer support that goes beyond your personal experience.

Getting access to experts, however, is not always easy. It would be great if we could pick up the phone or send an e-mail message to Supreme Court

Justice David Souter every time we had a question about the law, but we don't always have the opportunity to talk face-to-face with experts who can help us. Still, there are ways to get expert opinion for our ideas.

■ Read articles written by experts.

■ Read articles that quote experts.

■ Watch television interviews with experts.

■ Listen to radio interviews with experts.

Seeing, hearing, or reading about experts' ideas can help you make your side stronger. For instance, since Kalli makes the point that water meters will be good for the environment, consulting local environmentalists such as Sierra Club officials can help her make her point.

The following sentence can be made stronger with support from an expert.

Topic sentence:	Paying for water makes people appreciate it—and use less of it.
Expert support:	According to David J. Guy, executive director of the Northern California Water Association, the presence of the meters decreases water consumption by roughly 20 percent because people don't want to pay big water bills.

By incorporating evidence from an expert to offer proof of her claim, Kalli immediately gives herself credibility.

Read About Your Subject.   Reading about your topic is a great way to expand your knowledge and make your side stronger. Suppose you're arguing that a certain car is particularly bad for the environment. Reading reports and reviews about that particular car will give you good information. Newspapers and magazines often carry general information on subjects that the public wants to know about. Books, too, can help, but their information is more quickly outdated, so always check the date of publication.

Topic sentence:	Anonymity, or not knowing who's behind the wheel, makes rudeness on the road easier.
Expert support:	In his book *Choosing Civility*, civility expert P. M. Forni explains that drivers are more likely to be rude if they don't know the person at the wheel of another car.

Again, citing the expert tells your reader that not only do you know your facts, but you care enough about your writing to research them.

Surfing the Internet.   The Internet is a wonderful place to find information. Visiting credible Web sites, such as those operated by schools and respected organizations, can give you reliable information to use in your argument. Online databases can provide a huge amount of credible information as well. Talk to your school librarian about where to search to learn more about the subject of your essay. Your librarian can help you distinguish reliable sources from unreliable ones. For more on unreliable online sources, see the box below. For more on doing research, see Chapter 31.

If you're writing to convince a reader that overexposure to sun can lead to skin cancer, for example, consulting the Food and Drug Administration's Web site can help you make your point.

Topic sentence:	Getting too much sun can cause skin cancer in some people.
Expert support:	According to the Food and Drug Administration's Web site, not only has overexposure to sun caused skin cancer in many people, but skin cancer is becoming increasingly common.

Unreliable Sources

With so many different places to find information—newspapers, television, radio, the Internet—it's unavoidable that some sources are not worth consulting. For instance, if you want to know the negative effects of sports drinks on people's teeth, you probably wouldn't want to consult the Web site of a sports drink manufacturer. Make sure that the sources you use are ones you can trust. Avoid using information from the following types of sources; the information on them is often unreliable.

- **Web pages without any solid credentials.** Established institutions, corporations, and organizations usually consult their own experts before posting information online. However, anyone can post information online, even if he or she is not an expert. If the site you're searching offers no information about studies, degrees, or professional affiliations, you should be wary of citing its contents.

- **Entertainment sources such as cartoons, sitcoms, movies, or comic books.** These entities want to grab your attention, so they may include information that is either untrue or exaggerated.

- **Information from people who don't really know the subject.** Your friends may help you learn about some areas—roommate situations, work experiences, student experiences—but they are probably not experts in all the areas you'll be writing about. They can contribute a personal example now and then, but they shouldn't be your primary source of information.

The online information cited here gives information and credibility to the writer's point.

Making the Other Side Weaker The trick to making the other side weaker is to understand both sides of the argument. That way, you can identify the gaps in the other side's information or logic, and you can target your argument accordingly.

Find Incorrect Information in the Opposition's Argument. For instance, say that you have pulled a muscle while exercising, and you want to regain normal movement and comfort as soon as possible. One friend tells you to simply ignore the pain and "work through it" in order to heal yourself. Other friends continue to give advice, claiming that such treatments as applying heat or ice will make your injury worse or better. If you find an article written by a professional fitness trainer, you can answer your friends' claims. One writer, Diego, researched the results of "working through" injuries. He learned not only that people should *not* continue their normal exercise routines but also that resting after the initial injury and easing back into an exercise routine often prevents further injury. Further, he learned that applying ice to injuries can ease inflammation. Diego's findings are easy to see in a list format.

The Other Side	My Side	Expert Opinion
Exercise normally.	Rest.	Rest and ease back into exercise.
Ice and heat do nothing.	Ice and heat can help.	Ice can prevent inflammation; heat can help head.

Look for Unsupported Claims in the Opposition's Argument. You might think that an argument sounds logical or true, but it's best to research your information to make sure your claims can be verified. For instance, if a friend claims that, despite a pricey menu, "everyone" goes nightly to a trendy new restaurant, you should ask who "everyone" is. Chances are, the number of restaurant patrons are fewer than your friend claims. Or, if a writer claims that green tea cures headaches and prevents cancer, you should make sure that the writer has specific sources to back up such statements before you buy out your local market's supply of green tea.

Organizing and Linking Ideas

Once you've come up with a topic, written a thesis statement and support points, and supported those points with details, you're ready to pay attention to how your ideas are linked. In argumentative essays, ideas often fall in emphatic order, which lets you save your best argument for last.

These are Kalli's three support points for her essay on water metering.

Paying for water makes people appreciate it—and use less of it.

Metering everyone's water will help ease stress during drought.

Taxpayers have equal rights to water, so everyone should pay the same rate.

Even though "Taxpayers have equal rights to water" came to Kalli first in her freewriting, she decided that it was the most important reason for requiring water meters for everyone. Thus, she placed it last.

Words and Terms That Signal Emphatic Order

above all	first	most of all
another	in the first place	most important
equally important	last	most significantly
especially	least of all	next
even more		

CHECKLIST for Writing an Argument Essay

_____ **Prewriting**

▪ Choose a topic that you know something about and feel strongly about.

▪ Use prewriting strategies to get your early ideas on paper.

▪ Do some extra reading to get examples for support. Areas to search for information include newspapers, television news and interview shows, interviews of friends or acquaintances, and trusted Internet sources.

_____ **Drafting**

▪ Write a thesis statement that lets your reader know exactly what your argument is.

▪ Make a list of reasons that support your thesis statement.

▪ Write a rough draft of your essay. (Feel free to do more prewriting as this point to get more ideas down on paper.)

▪ Use specific details from different sources to illustrate each support point you make. Add more details to strengthen your side or weaken the other side, depending on your argument.

▪ Use transitions to connect your ideas.   *(continued)*

_____ **Revision**

- Revise your work, as necessary, according to the first three of the four Cs: *concise, credible,* and *clear* writing.

_____ **Editing**

- Proofread your work for sentence-level errors.

Following the Four Cs Through Revision

If you've ever watched a cartoon in which a character has to make an important decision, you may have seen a little angel and a little devil on the character's shoulders, each trying to persuade him or her to act a certain way. Inevitably, the character's confusion in trying to follow two sets of advice leads to humor but to little resolution.

Writing an argument essay is similar to having two conflicting figures looking over your shoulder: one argues your side, and the other argues the opposite side. The danger—as in the cartoons—is that if you and your reader are overwhelmed with information, your essay will become a chaotic mess. The benefit, though, is that by considering both points of view, you can counter your opposition and write a better essay. As you write, then, keep the opposing viewpoint in mind and continually ask yourself: Am I proving my point? Am I making my point stronger than the opposition's? Adding and deleting information and reorganizing your ideas as you revise your essay will lead you to write an effective argument.

Richard chose to write an argumentative essay addressing the issue of people's willingness to give up privacy; his best information came from online sources.

A Private Concern

At one time, some subjects were better left for private discussion: personal feelings, relationships, and gripes about someone else were all considered inappropriate for public consumption. ~~It was considered especially rude to ignore someone in favor of a phone call.~~ Similarly, personal discussions between two people were generally held behind closed doors, and if someone just wanted to go for a drive to get away from prying eyes, it was possible to do so. However, with the presence of cell phones, reality TV, and global positioning systems, people have willingly tossed aside their privacy in the hope of gain. Whether they seek convenience, safety, or fame, people are willing to pay for it with their privacy.

The first area where people have willingly sacrificed privacy comes in the form of cell phones. Whereas once people were tied to a corded telephone and, thus, forced to talk in the relative privacy of their homes, their offices, or telephone booths, now people can chat anywhere their cell phones have coverage. **According to Anne Taylor Fleming, cell phones have "completely blurred the line between the public sphere and the private." Now, instead of waiting to get home to talk about the jerk in the grocery store, people can whip out their cell phones while still <u>in</u> the grocery store and vent to whoever's available via speed dial.** If someone happens to overhear our conversation, no matter; we're able to say what we want to say right now. Convenience overrides privacy as a priority, and the privilege of intimacy is lost.

Another area that shows how willing people are to give up their privacy is in the use of global positioning systems (GPS). **People install these systems, as auto manufacturers advertise, for "safety and convenience" (Soat).** According to "Privacy and New Technology," cars can be fitted with GPS devices that allow people to know "exactly where you were all the time" you were driving that car. ~~At one time, GPS devices were so expensive that only wealthy people could afford them, but now they're becoming more reasonable.~~ Thus, in trouble with a flat tire or breakdown, you could be easily located by computer access. The downside to GPS, however, is the constant awareness of your actions it gives to anyone with access. Even if you have nothing to hide, just knowing that you could be watched at any given moment can be unsettling. **Further, the devices have been used by spouse abusers, for instance, "so they can keep track of their victim's location" ("Technology's Dark Side").** What began as a safety device has become a threat to privacy, yet people willingly give up their highway anonymity for the sake of potential safety.

One final area where people sacrifice privacy is on reality TV shows. At one time, it was hard to imagine witnessing anyone's first kiss—or flat-out rejection—except our own (or maybe a television or movie character's). With the huge popularity of reality television shows **such as <u>Survivor,</u> <u>American Idol,</u> and <u>The Apprentice,</u>** however, thousands of people eagerly audition to be watched, filmed, edited, and broadcast to the public. **In her article "Reality Bites," Cynthia McVey writes, "Many participants choose to take part because of the potential fame . . . that reality** [programs] **can bring."** Even when they are **"pummeled" by judges, as James Poniewozik and Jeanne McDowell write in their article "The Making of an Idol,"** <u>American Idol</u> contestants willingly perform in front of millions of people (via television) for a shot at being famous. ~~On American Idol, in particular, contestants often endure scathing comments even as they try to control their feelings.~~ On other programs, such as **Big Brother, "ordinary people . . . give up their privacy for the chance to win big" ("Privacy and New Technology"),** usually in the form of widespread recognition. Since reality series winners such as Richard Hatch (<u>Survivor</u>), Trista Rehn (<u>The Bachelorette</u>), and Evan Marriott (<u>Joe Millionaire</u>) have landed on magazine covers and in the company of movie stars and singers, they serve as the ideal to which fame seekers aspire. ~~Other reality TV stars, such as Colby Donaldson from Survivor, claim that they are not taken seriously as actors and that they are not included in "real" stars' gatherings.~~ The cost, however, is a complete surrender of privacy as their every move is photographed and reproduced in the media. They've lost their privacy, but they chose to do it.

With so much new technology on the market, one would expect people to jealously guard their privacy against the threats against it. Knowing that it's possible for someone to watch, listen, or follow them, people—one would think—would be very careful about who they let into their lives. ~~Internet "phishing" is one more area where people are constantly being watched.~~ This does not seem to be the case. **Instead, people rush to their phones—in public—to make that all-important call right now, and contestants rush to auditions in the hope of becoming famous.** If convenience, safety, and fame are worth the loss of privacy, we'll be lucky. If not, we'll just have to find new places to hide.

Works Cited

Fleming, Anne Taylor "Anywhere But Here: More Connected But More Alone." *The Los Angeles Times.* 8 Aug. 1999.

McVey, Cynthia. "Reality Bites." *New Scientist* 31 July 2004: 16. EBSCO host. Belle Coolidge Public Lib., Sacramento. 28 Oct. 2005 <http://0-web6.epnet.com>.

"Privacy and New Technology." *Victoria.* June 2005. Sacramento City Coll. Lib. 29 Oct. 2005 Sacramento City College Lib. 30 Oct. 2005.

Poniewozik, James, and Jeanne McDowell. "The Making of an Idol." *Time.com.* 24 May 2004. 30 Oct. 2005 <http://www.time.com/time>.

Reid, William. Personal interview. 27 Oct. 2005.

Soat, John. "Unfortunately, Big Brother Is Expensive." *Information Week* 14 Jul 2003: 110. Sacramento City Coll. Lib. 28 Oct. 2005 <http://0proquest.umi.com>.

"Technology's Dark Side." *WashingtonPost.com*. 8 June 2003. 28 Oct. 2005 <http://www.washingtonpost.com/>.

Revising for the First C: Concise Writing   Since Richard had done a good deal of reading prior to writing his draft, most of his information helps move his argument forward. However, a few details needed to be deleted, so Richard crossed them out as he revised his draft.

Revising for the Second C: Credible Writing   Even though many of Richard's initial ideas about the loss of privacy issue came from his own experiences, he knew that to be persuasive to a broader audience, he needed to include details from other sources. Thus, he consulted other sources and inserted information (shown in bold type) as needed throughout his essay.

Revising for the Third C: Clear Writing   Richard's ideas followed emphatic order, but what surprised Richard was that he had the most information—and thus, he made the strongest case—about people sacrificing privacy on reality TV. For his final draft, he moved his reality TV example to his last support paragraph.

Revising for the Fourth C: Correct Writing   The sentences in this essay are all correct. To check for correctness in your own writing, see Part Seven, "Writing Correct Sentences."

WRITING PRACTICE 1 Writing an Essay Step by Step

Now you have the chance to write your own essay.

Prewriting

1. Choose a topic from the following list of topic sentences for argument essays. Then, choose one side—for or against the opinion stated—and write an essay arguing that point of view.

   What kind of cars people drive says a lot about them.

Attendance should be mandatory for all college classes.

Any medications that alter energy or attention levels, such as antihistamines or cough medicines, should not be available without a prescription.

No one should ever go on a blind date.

The government should subsidize gasoline when the price rises too high.

Computer courses should be required in elementary school.

Because watching too much television can have negative effects, televisions should be designed not to run more than two hours each day.

The American business workday should include a two-hour rest period after lunch.

School physical fitness classes should be required by law.

Every high school graduate should be required to serve in the military for two years.

Arts and music courses should be a mandatory part of every curriculum.

People who have never broken the law should have to pay less in taxes.

Academic dishonesty (plagiarism, cheating on an exam) should be punishable by law.

All high school students should be required to take a vocational education course such as auto shop.

Learning CPR should be required for graduation from high school or college.

2. Freewrite on your topic for five to ten minutes. In prewriting for an argument essay, outlining in order can helps you keep track of both your supporting reasons and your examples. Below is a sample outline based on the thesis statement "Computer courses should be required in elementary school."

Computer courses should be required in elementary school.

A. Computer use in education

   1. Calculators in math

   2. Word processors and Internet in writing courses

   3. Spreadsheets, databases, tables useful in other courses

B. Computer use for work

   1. Professional-looking documents from word processors

   2. Internet research, e-mail part of many jobs

   3. Internet advertising of jobs

    C. Computer use for recreation

       1. Computerized games increasingly popular

       2. Online chatting, dating

Drafting

3. Write a thesis statement. A possible thesis statement for the topic "Computer courses should be required in elementary school" follows.

> Possible thesis statement: Because computers are becoming part of nearly every aspect of society, computer courses should be required in elementary school.

4. Choose your support points and specific details. For this step, you may need to learn more about your topic. You may have noticed that the outline above lists many reasons that support the thesis statement, but it includes just a few specific details. In writing an argumentative essay, sometimes finding details is easier after you've outlined your general points. Once you've written your first draft, begin putting in specific details that illustrate your reasons.

5. Arrange your points in a logical order, remembering that emphatic order works well for argument essays.

6. Now, write your draft. Do your best to include important details and transitions, but don't worry if they're not perfect the first time around. Make sure all the details in your draft come from trusted sources.

Revising

7. Revise your essay, checking that your details are connected through clear transition words that show your reader how your points are related and why they are important.

Editing

8. Proofread your essay to make sure your spelling, punctuation, and grammar are correct.

WRITING PRACTICE 2 Writing to Effect Change

Now you have the opportunity to choose both the topic and the types of support you use. Having sharp argument skills can be a great benefit in life. Choose one of the real-life situations below, and write an argumentative essay.

Topic A

How important is your privacy? Does privacy matter more in some areas than in others? Your assignment is this: *Write an essay in which you argue that privacy is or is not important in a specific area.* Some possible areas to consider are cell phone conversations, a person's medical history, school report cards, employee evaluations, criminal records, Internet activity, and driving records. For this assignment, use your own experiences and observations to illustrate your ideas.

Possible thesis statement:	Keeping health records private is important because negative results—such as loss of employment or social opportunities—can follow if sensitive health information becomes public.

Topic B

The media feed us a constant stream of information about celebrities, politicians, and other public figures. But do we want to know all of it? Your assignment is this: *Write an essay arguing that the general public does or does not want to know about the private lives of the rich and famous.* For this essay, use examples from other people's lives as well as your own. You may use examples from written sources such as newspapers, magazines, and Web sites, but you do not have to.

Possible thesis statement:	Even though stars' private lives may not improve an ordinary person's personal happiness, many people who are not famous want to learn about celebrities.

Topic C

With so much new information-gathering technology, privacy has been sacrificed in many areas. However, is it possible to have privacy? If so, in what areas is privacy most easily obtained? Your assignment is this: *Write an essay in which you argue that it is or is not possible for people to live private lives.* For this assignment, you will need to read articles from magazines, newspapers, or Web sites to learn about your topic.

Possible thesis statement:	Unless people want to cut themselves off from the world, they cannot live completely private lives.

WRITING PRACTICE 3 Writing in Response to a Reading

In "Take My Privacy, Please!" (page 412), Ted Koppel writes, "There is no end to what we will endure, support, pay for and promote if only it makes our lives easier, promises to save us money, appears to enhance our security and comes to us in a warm, cuddly and altogether non-threatening package." Is he right? Your assignment is this: *Write an essay arguing that people are or are not willing to give up privacy if there is some benefit for themselves.* To support your ideas, use examples from your own experience and observations, interviews of people you know, car advertisements, Koppel's essay, and any other sources you find relevant and credible. Your thesis statement may be something like "No matter how much they may benefit from making their personal information public, people refuse to give up their privacy if they have something to hide."

Lab Activity 25

For additional practice with writing an argument, complete Lab Activity 25 in the lab manual packaged with your textbook. If you did not receive a lab manual, you can complete this activity online at **www.ablongman.com/long.** Click on **College Resources for Writers** and then click on **Activity 25.**

26 Using More Than One Organizational Strategy

Just as all African-American women writers can no more be lumped into a single literary category than all fiction writers or all poets, the three writers in this chapter celebrate a range of styles and subjects. Alice Walker is best known for her Pulitzer Prize–winning novel *The Color Purple,* which explores the lives of two black sisters in the segregated Deep South. Maya Angelou, who read her poem "On the Pulse of Morning" at President Bill Clinton's inauguration in 1993, is an accomplished poet, actor, dancer, and singer. Finally, Jamaica Kincaid, born in Antigua, West Indies, moved to New York City and became a staff writer for *The New Yorker* in 1976.

Maya Angelou

CRITICAL THINKING For ages the dominant voices in American literature belonged to Caucasian men, but with the Civil Rights and women's movements, more voices became heard. How important to you is reading works from different types of writers? How important is reading works from writers with appearances or backgrounds similar to your own? Write a few sentences answering these questions.

Strategies Combined: The Unplanned Miracle

Unless your instructor assigns you to write a comparison/contrast or descriptive essay, most of your writing will employ more than one development strategy, even if you don't intend for it to do so. The reason for this phenomenon is that in writing an essay, you are making a point, and making a point requires support. So you could reasonably argue that, in the midst of writing a narrative or classification essay, you are still writing an argument or an illustration and example essay just by offering support for your points.

The key to successful writing, then, is not to set out to write the perfect *type* of essay, but to communicate your ideas in the clearest possible way using any means available. Thus, in writing about road rage, you will be prepared to come up with a definition and illustrations. Don't worry about trying to include one or more development strategies in your writing; simply make the best case you can. Most likely, when you analyze your writing, you'll find that you've incorporated more than one development strategy without even meaning to.

Analyzing a Professional Essay for Development Strategies

Read Alice Walker's essay "Am I Blue?" and see if you can detect the following development strategies: narration, description, comparison, illustration and example, and argument.

Am I Blue?

Alice Walker

For about three years my companion and I rented a small house in the country that stood on the edge of a large meadow that appeared to run from the end of our deck straight into the mountains. The mountains, however, were quite far away, and between us and them there was, in fact, a town. It was one of the many pleasant aspects of the house that you never really were aware of this.

It was a house of many windows, low, wide, nearly floor to ceiling in the living room, which faced the meadow, and it was from one of these that I first saw our closest neighbor, a large white horse, cropping grass, flipping its mane, and ambling about—not over the entire meadow, which stretched well out of sight of the house, but over the five or so fenced-in acres that were next to the twenty-odd that we had rented. I soon learned that the horse, whose name was Blue, belonged to a man who lived in another town, but was boarded by our neighbors next door. Occasionally, one of the children, usually a stocky teen-ager, but sometimes a much younger girl or boy, could be seen riding Blue. They would appear in the meadow, climb up on his back, ride furiously for ten or fifteen minutes, then get off, slap Blue on the flanks, and not be seen again for a month or more.

There were many apple trees in our yard, and one by the fence that Blue could almost reach. We were soon in the habit of feeding him apples, which he relished, especially because by the middle of summer the meadow grasses—so green and succulent since January—had dried out from lack of rain, and Blue stumbled about munching the dried stalks half-heartedly. Sometimes he would stand very still just by the apple tree, and when one of us came out he would whinny, snort loudly, or stamp the ground. This meant, of course: I want an apple.

It was quite wonderful to pick a few apples, or collect those that had fallen to the ground overnight, and patiently hold them, one by one up to his large, toothy mouth. I remained as thrilled as a child by his flexible dark lips, huge, cubelike teeth that crunched the apples, core and all, with such finality, and his high, broad-breasted *enormity;* beside which, I felt small indeed. When I was a child, I used to ride horses, and was especially friendly with one named Nan until the day I was riding and my brother deliberately spooked her and I was thrown, head first, against the trunk of a tree. When I came to, I was in bed and my mother was bending worriedly over me; we silently agreed that perhaps horseback riding was not the safest sport for me. Since then I have walked, and prefer walking to horseback riding—but I had forgotten the depth of feeling one could see in horses' eyes.

I was therefore unprepared for the expression in Blue's. Blue was lonely. Blue was horribly lonely and bored. I was not shocked that this should be the case; five acres to tramp by yourself, endlessly, even in the most beautiful of meadows—and his was—cannot provide many interesting events, and once rainy season turned to dry that was about it. No, I was shocked that I had forgotten that human animals and nonhuman animals can communicate quite well; if we are brought up around animals as children we take this for granted. By the time we are adults we no longer remember. However, the animals have not changed. They are in fact *completed* creations (at least they seem to be, so much more than we) who are not likely *to* change; it is their nature to express themselves. What else are they going to express? And they do. And, generally speaking, they are ignored.

After giving Blue the apples, I would wander back to the house, aware that he was observing me. Were more apples not forthcoming then? Was that to be his sole entertainment for the day? My partner's small son had decided he wanted to learn how to piece a quilt; we worked in silence on our respective squares as I thought . . .

Well, about slavery: about white children, who were raised by black people, who knew their first all-accepting love from black women, and then, when they were twelve or so, were told they must "forget" the deep levels of communication between themselves and "mammy" that they knew. Later they would be able to relate quite calmly, "My old mammy was sold to another good family." "My old mammy was _____." Fill in the blank. Many more years later a white woman would say: "I can't understand these Negroes, these blacks. What do they want? They're so different from us."

And about the Indians, considered to be "like animals" by the "settlers" (a very benign euphemism for what they actually were), who did not understand their description as a compliment.

And about the thousands of American men who marry Japanese, Korean, Filipina, and other non-English-speaking women and of how happy they report they are, *"blissfully,"* until their brides learn to speak English, at which point the marriages tend to fall apart. What then did the men see, when they looked into the eyes of the women they married, before they could speak English? Apparently only their own reflections.

I thought of society's impatience with the young. "Why are they playing the music so loud?" Perhaps the children have listened to much of the music of oppressed people their parents danced to before they were born, with its passionate but soft cries for acceptance and love, and they have wondered why their parents failed to hear.

I do not know how long Blue had inhabited his five beautiful, boring acres before we moved into our house; a year after we had arrived—and had also traveled to other valleys, other cities, other worlds—he was still there.

But then, in our second year at the house, something happened in Blue's life. One morning, looking out the window at the fog that lay like a ribbon over the meadow, I saw another horse, a brown one, at the other end of Blue's field. Blue appeared to be afraid of it, and for several days made no attempt to go near. We went away for a week. When we returned, Blue had decided to make friends and the two horses ambled or galloped along together, and Blue did not come nearly as often to the fence underneath the apple tree.

When he did, bringing his new friend with him, there was a different look in his eyes. A look of independence, of self-possession, of inalienable *horse*ness. His friend eventually became pregnant. For months and months there was, it seemed to me, a mutual feeling between me and the horses of justice, of peace. I fed apples to them both. The look in Blue's eyes was one of unabashed "this is *it*ness."

It did not, however, last forever. One day, after a visit to the city, I went out to give Blue some apples. He stood waiting, or so I thought, though not beneath the tree. When I shook the tree and jumped back from the shower of apples, he made no move. I carried some over to him. He managed to half-crunch one. The rest he let fall to the ground. I dreaded looking into his eyes—because I had of course noticed that Brown, his partner, had gone—but I did look. If I had been born into slavery, and my partner had been sold or killed, my eyes would have looked like that. The children next door explained that Blue's partner had been "put with him" (the same expression that old people used, I had noticed, when speaking of an ancestor during slavery who had been impregnated by her owner) so that they could mate and she conceive. Since that was accomplished, she had been taken back by her owner, who lived somewhere else.

Will she be back? I asked.

They didn't know.

Blue was like a crazed person. Blue *was*, to me, a crazed person. He galloped furiously, as if he were being ridden, around and around his five beautiful acres. He whinnied until he couldn't. He tore at the ground with his hooves. He butted himself against his single shade tree. He looked always and always toward the road down which his partner had gone. And then, occasionally, when he came up for apples, or I took apples to him, he looked at me. It was a look so piercing, so full of grief, a look so *human* I almost laughed (I felt too sad to cry) to think there are people who do not know that animals suffer. People like me who have forgotten, and daily forget, all that animals try to tell us. "Everything you do to us will happen to you; we are your teachers, as you are ours. We are one lesson" is essentially it, I think. There are those who never once have even considered animals' rights: those who have been taught that animals actually want to be used and abused by us, as small children "love" to be frightened, or women "love" to be mutilated and raped. . . . They are the great-grandchildren of those who honestly thought, because someone taught them this: "Women can't think," and "nigger's can't faint." But most disturbing of all, in Blue's large brown eyes was a new look, more painful than the look of despair: the look of disgust with human beings, with life; the look of hatred. And it was odd what the look of hatred did. It gave him, for the first time, the look of a beast. And what that meant was that he had put up a barrier within to protect himself from further violence; all the apples in the world wouldn't change that fact.

And so Blue remained, a beautiful part of our landscape, very peaceful to look at from the window, white against the grass. Once a friend came to visit and said, looking out on the soothing view: "And it *would* have to be a *white* horse; the very image of freedom." And I thought, yes, the animals are forced to become for us merely "images" of what they once so beautifully expressed. And we are used to drinking milk from containers showing "contented" cows, whose real lives we want to hear nothing about, eating eggs and drumsticks from "happy" hens, and munching hamburgers advertised by bulls of integrity who seem to command their fate.

As we talked of freedom and justice one day for all, we sat down to steaks. I am eating misery, I thought, as I took the first bite. And spit it out.

You may have identified these uses of development strategies in Walker's essay.

- **Use of narration.** Walker's "Am I Blue?" describes a series of events in the order in which they occur, which marks it as a narrative essay. Walker uses the first-person pronoun *I* to communicate the events, and the actions are organized in chronological order. Whatever else Walker might accomplish in her essay, she definitely tells a story.
- **Use of description.** Though Walker tells a story, she includes much description in her essay. These are some of her specific details: "It was a house of many windows, low, wide, nearly floor to ceiling in the living room, which faced the meadow" "by the middle of summer the meadow grasses—so green and succulent since January—had dried out" and "looking out the window at the fog that lay like a ribbon over the meadow." Walker could have written a straightforward argument that animals have feelings that people disregard, but her use of description makes for a more pleasurable—and more powerful—reading experience.
- **Use of comparison.** Walker primarily makes use of comparison in "Am I Blue?" Throughout her essay, Walker compares the horse Blue to many things: humans, human slaves, non-English-speaking brides, "mammies." By comparing Blue to humans, Walker makes the horse's

plight more poignant and portrays his owner's decisions to breed him and then remove his partner as more cruel. Although Walker could have simply told her story without comparing Blue to humans, or simply argued that disregarding animals' feelings is wrong, her comparison of the horse to humans makes her case more relevant and, ultimately, more convincing.

- **Use of illustrations and examples.** Throughout her essay, Walker uses examples to *show* what Blue is feeling. Instead of stopping after she writes, "Blue was lonely," Walker gives examples of other situations that illustrate Blue's feelings: white children whose black mammies had been sold, Indians who were considered to be like animals, non-English-speaking brides. The isolation of the people in her examples communicates clearly the feelings of loneliness that Blue experienced.

- **Use of argument.** Walker's entire essay is an argument for the consideration of animals. Her words, points, and examples work together to communicate that animals have feelings recognizable to humans and that humans need to acknowledge those feelings. Though Walker tells a compelling story, paints a lovely picture, makes apt comparisons, and uses relevant examples, her primary purpose is to convince her reader that animals are much more "human" than many people realize. By incorporating so many other development strategies in addition to argument, she makes her message more powerful.

In All Ways a Woman

Maya Angelou

In my young years I took pride in the fact that luck was called a lady. In fact, there were so few public acknowledgments of the female presence that I felt personally honored whenever nature and large ships were referred to as feminine. But as I matured, I began to resent being considered a sister to a changeling as fickle as luck, as aloof as an ocean, and as frivolous as nature.

The phrase "A woman always has the right to change her mind" played so aptly into the negative image of the female that I made myself a victim to an unwavering decision. Even if I made an inane and stupid choice, I stuck by it rather than "be like a woman and change my mind."

Being a woman is hard work. Not without joy and even ecstasy, but still relentless, unending work. Becoming an old female may require only being born with certain genitalia, inheriting long-living genes and the fortune not to be run over by an out-of-control truck, but to become and remain a woman command the existence and employment of genius.

The woman who survives intact and happy must be at once tender and tough. She must have convinced herself, or be in the unending process of convincing herself, that she, her values, and her choices are important. In a time and world where males hold sway and control, the pressure upon women to yield their rights-of-way is tremendous. And it is under those very circumstances that the woman's toughness must be in evidence.

She must resist considering herself a lesser version of her male counterpart. She is not a sculptress, poetess, authoress, Jewess, Negress, or even (now rare) in university parlance a rectoress. If she is the thing, then for her own sense of self and for the education of the ill-informed she must insist with rectitude in being the thing and in being called the thing.

A rose by any other name may smell as sweet, but a woman called by a devaluing name will only be weakened by the misnomer.

She will need to prize her tenderness and be able to display it at appropriate times in order to prevent toughness from gaining total authority and to avoid becoming a mirror image of those men who value power above life, and control over love.

It is imperative that a woman keep her sense of humor intact and at the ready. She must see, even if only in secret, that she is the funniest, looniest woman in her world, which she should also see as being the most absurd world of all times.

It has been said that laughter is therapeutic and amiability lengthens the life span.

Women should be tough, tender, laugh as much as possible and live long lives. The struggle for equality continues unabated and the woman warrior who is armed with wit and courage will be among the first to celebrate victory.

EXERCISE 1   IDENTIFYING DEVELOPMENT STRATEGIES IN AN ESSAY

Read Maya Angelou's essay "In All Ways a Woman." Then, answer the questions that follow.

1. What is Angelou's main idea? _____

_____

2. Angelou uses the development strategies of argument, comparison, and definition to make her point. List at least one example that shows how each development strategy is used:

Argument: _____

_____

Comparison: _____

_____

Definition: _____

_____

3. Of the three development strategies used, which one do you think is

dominant? Why? _____

_____

The Ugly Tourist

Jamaica Kincaid

The thing you have always suspected about yourself the minute you become a tourist is true: A tourist is an ugly human being. You are not an ugly person all the time; you are not an ugly person ordinarily; you are not an ugly person day to day. From day to day, you are a nice person. From day to day, all the people who are supposed to love you on the whole do. From day to day, as you walk down a busy street in the large and modern and prosperous city in which you work and live, dismayed, puzzled (a cliché, but only a cliché can explain you) at how alone you feel in this crowd, how awful it is to go unnoticed, how awful it is to go unloved, even as you are surrounded by more people than you could possibly get to know in a lifetime that lasted for millennia, and then out of the corner of your eye you see someone looking at you and absolute pleasure is written all over that person's face, and then you realise that you are not as revolting a presence as you think you are (for that look just told you so). And so, ordinarily, you are a nice person, an attractive person, a person capable of drawing to yourself the affection of other people (people just like you), a person at home in your own skin (sort of; I mean, in a way; I mean, your dismay and puzzlement are natural to you, because people like you just seem to be like that and so many of the things people like you find admirable about your-selves—the things you think about, the things you think really define you—seem rooted in these feelings): a person at home in your own house (and all its nice house things), with its nice back yard (and its nice back-yard things), at home on your street, your church, in com-munity activities, your job, at home with your family, your relatives, your friends—you are a whole person. But one day, when you are sitting somewhere, alone in that crowd, and that awful feeling of displacedness comes over you, and really, as an ordinary person you are not well equipped to look too far inward and set yourself aright, because being ordinary is already so taxing, and being ordinary takes all you have out of you, and though the words "I must get away" do not actually pass across your lips, you make a leap from being that nice blob just sitting like a boob in your amniotic sac of the modern experience to being a person visiting heaps of death and ruin and feeling alive and inspired at the sight of it; to being a per-son lying on some faraway beach, your stilled body stinking and glistening in the sand, looking like something first forgotten, then remembered, then not important enough to go back for; to being a person marvelling at the harmony (ordinarily, what you would say is the backwardness) and the union these other people (and they are other people) have with nature. And you look at the things they can do with a piece of ordinary cloth, the things they fashion out of cheap, vulgarly colored (to you) twine, the way they squat down over a hole they have made in the ground, the hole itself is something to marvel at, and since you are being an ugly person this ugly but joy-ful thought will swell inside you: their ancestors were not clever in the way yours were and not ruthless in the way yours were, for then would it not be you who would be in harmony with nature and backwards in that charming way? An ugly thing, that is what you are when you become a tourist, an ugly, empty thing, a stupid thing, a piece of rubbish pausing here and there to gaze at this and taste that, and it will never occur to you that the people who inhabit the place in which you have just passed cannot stand you, that behind their closed doors they laugh at your strangeness (you do not look the way they look); the physical sight of you does not please them; you have bad manners (it is their custom to eat their food with their hands; you try eating their way, you look silly; you try eating the way you always eat, you look silly); they do not like the way you speak (you have an accent); they collapse helpless from laughter, mimick-ing the way they imagine you must look as you carry out some everyday bodily function. They do not like you. *They do not like me!*

That thought never actually occurs to you. Still, you feel a little uneasy. Still, you feel a little foolish. Still, you feel a little out of place. But the banality of your own life is very real to you; it drove you to this extreme, spending your days and your nights in the company of people who despise you, people you do not like really, people you would not want to have as your actual neighbour. And so you must devote yourself to puzzling out how much of what you are told is really, really true (Is ground-up bottle glass in peanut sauce really a delicacy around here, or will it do just what you think ground-up bottle glass will do? Is this rare, multicoloured, snout-mouthed fish really an aphrodisiac, or will it cause you to fall asleep permanently?). Oh, the hard work all of this is, and is it any wonder, then, that on your return home you feel the need of a long rest, so that you can recover from your life as a tourist?

That the native does not like the tourist is not hard to explain. For every native of every place is a potential tourist, and every tourist is a native of somewhere. Every native everywhere lives a life of overwhelming and crushing banality and boredom and desperation and depression and every deed, good and bad, is an attempt to forget this. Every native would like to find a way out, every native would like a rest, every native would like a tour. But some natives—most natives in the world—cannot go anywhere. They are too poor. They are too poor to go anywhere. They are too poor to escape the reality of their lives; and they are too poor to live properly in the place where they live, which is the very place you, the tourist, want to go—so when the natives see you, the tourist, they envy you, they envy your ability to leave your own banality and boredom, they envy your ability to turn their own banality and boredom into a source of pleasure for yourself.

EXERCISE 2 ANALYZING AN ESSAY FOR DEVELOPMENT STRATEGIES

Read Jamaica Kincaid's essay "The Ugly Tourist." Then, answer the questions that follow.

1. What is Kincaid's point? _____

2. Identify at least two development strategies that Kincaid uses, giving examples to show how the strategy is employed.

Description: _____

_____

_____

Contrast: _____

_____

_____

Definition: _____

_____

_____

Argument:_____

_____

_____

3. Which argument strategy is dominant? Support your answer with

examples from the text._____

_____

WRITING PRACTICE 1 **Analyzing Your Own Writing
for Development Strategies**

Read one of your essays written for this class, and identify at least two
development strategies you used, even if you used one strategy unintentionally. Write a few sentences giving examples of the strategies you used.
For instance, if you wrote a descriptive essay, all your details probably
added up to make a point. That point could be considered your "argument."
Show how certain details support the point you make.

WRITING PRACTICE 2 **Adding a Development Strategy
for Specific Effect**

Your assignment is this: *Read one of your essays written for this class, and
choose one support paragraph that you think you could improve. Then, use a
different development strategy to develop that point.* For example, if your essay
is an argument convincing people to carpool with you, use comparison to
make the long drive to work seem similar to the punishment of being
"grounded" or serving detention. Similarly, you could use description to make
the long, hot, lonely drive to work more vivid for your reader, or you could
classify people who don't carpool as "loners," "dictators," or "egomaniacs."

WRITING PRACTICE 3 Write in Response to a Reading

Choose one of the three essays in this chapter to focus on for this assignment. Then, select Topic A, B, or C and follow the directions for writing an essay.

Topic A

Alice Walker writes in "Am I Blue?" (page 433) that "animals are forced to become for us merely 'images' of what they once so beautifully expressed." Is she right? Your assignment is this: *Write an essay arguing that animals are or are not just "images," supporting your ideas with details on how animals are portrayed in movies, advertising, and television.* Use at least two development strategies to make your point.

Topic B

Maya Angelou writes in "In All Ways a Woman" (page 438) that "The woman who survives intact and happy must be at once tender and tough." What does she mean? Your assignment is this: *Write an essay defining what Angelou means by* tender *or* tough, *giving examples from your own experiences and observations to support your point.* Use at least two development strategies to make your point.

Topic C

Jamaica Kincaid writes in "The Ugly Tourist" (page 440) that "every native of every place is a potential tourist, and every tourist is a native of somewhere." How are these two types of people different in the community, city, or region where you live? Your assignment is this: *Write an essay either contrasting natives with tourists* or *classifying different types of natives or tourists you have seen.* Use at least two development strategies to make your point.

🖳 Lab Activity 26

For additional practice with more than one development strategy, complete Lab Activity 26 in the lab manual packaged with your textbook. If you did not receive a lab manual, you can complete this activity online at **www.ablongman.com/long.** Click on **College Resources for Writers** and then click on **Activity 26.**

PART FIVE
Writing for
Different Purposes

27 Writing an In-Class Essay

CULTURE NOTE *The U.S. Supreme Court*

Originally the weakest branch of the U.S. government, the Supreme Court has become an institution of great influence and controversy. Split between justices who seek to interpret the Constitution as the Framers would have done and those who address issues according to today's needs and trends, the highest court is the most stable branch, usually changing one justice at a time.

The United States Supreme Court Justices

SURF THE NET The U.S. Supreme Court makes news almost daily. What sort of decisions is the Supreme Court facing today? How significant, to you, are these decisions? Surf the Internet for information about current Supreme Court cases and write a few sentences about what the most significant ones seem to be.

Taking an Essay Exam

No matter how prepared students are, many still panic at the idea of the essay exam. Somehow, sitting down *in class* and facing a blank page seems like a terrifying experience. Since essay exams become more common as you pass through college classes, knowing how to excel on them is crucial. A bright spot, however, is that essay tests—essays written in your classroom during an allotted amount of time—have many advantages. They allow you to

- Present information in a format *you*, not the instructor, choose.
- Use whatever details and information *you* think best address the exam questions.
- Organize your information in the way *you* think is most effective.
- Add a little style and spice that *you* think makes the essay more interesting.

In short, writing an essay exam gives you power. As long as you've learned the material and become comfortable writing essays, you have an opportunity to show your instructor how much you know and how well you can express that information.

The key to writing a strong essay for an exam is preparation: you need to have a plan. The following guidelines can help you prepare for the challenge of writing an in-class essay.

Before the Exam: Planning

When you know a course will require in-class essays, plan ahead.

Knowing Your Subject Matter   The first step to writing a good in-class essay is to study your subject. Read everything the instructor has assigned, and memorize key people, places, and dates. The more information you know and the better you know it, the better your chances of writing a strong essay exam will be.

Predicting the Future: Preparing for Essay Topics   Wouldn't all tests be easier if we knew the questions in advance? Paying attention can help you figure out what you need to know. Listen to what information the instructor emphasizes, and notice what information your book develops most. Chances are, an essay question will be on a topic that your textbook or instructor has emphasized. Use your analysis of likely topics to plan for your essay exam.

- **Make a list of potential questions.** For instance, Jesse, a student in a political science class, prepared for his essay exam by highlighting the topics in his notes that his instructor had spent the most time talking about. Jesse also made notes on the topics that were covered most thoroughly in his textbook. After reviewing his notes, Jesse figured that the topic of the U.S. Supreme Court—among other topics—had a very good chance of showing up on his test. To prepare for the test, he wrote out every question he could think of that related to the Supreme Court. These are some of his questions.

When and how was the Supreme Court created?

What are its responsibilities, and how are/were they established?

Who sits on the bench, and how are justices chosen?

What Supreme Court decisions prior to 1960 have been particularly significant?

What recent Supreme Court decisions have been significant?

How long is a Supreme Court justice's term?

Through what process, if any, are Supreme Court decisions overturned?

Asking questions gives you a chance to focus your studying and organize the information you learn. Asking and then answering questions before the exam also helps you to make connections between ideas, which will help you explain key concepts on the test.

■ **Answer your questions about the subject.** After you identify possible questions for an essay exam, make sure you know the answers. Some questions are more likely to end up on an essay exam than others. Questions such as "When and how was the Supreme Court created?" don't give students much to write about, but the answers are necessary background information for a response to almost any other question. Other questions—such as "What cases or decisions have been particularly significant?"—could definitely end up as essay topics. Therefore, Jesse made sure he knew the answer to every question he made up. Understanding the subject—not just memorizing it—is essential to preparing for an essay exam. In fact, one skill that essay exams let you show is the skill of *analysis,* the process of breaking down information and making connections where there might not seem to be any.

■ **Make a memory plan.** After you've identified possible test questions and answers, think of a one- or two-word term that helps you remember the information. For instance, Jesse made the following list in response to the question "What Supreme Court cases or decisions prior to 1960 have been particularly significant?"

1. Marbury vs. Madison gave federal government power over states.

2. Plessy vs. Ferguson made "separate but equal" accommodations legal in some cases.

3. Brown vs. Board of Education abolished segregated, "separate but equal" schools.

Jesse decided to memorize the letters *MPB* to represent the names *Marbury, Plessy,* and *Brown.* Those names triggered his full responses to the exam question. Instead of memorizing whole names or words, other students simply remember the first letter of each important term and associate those letters with a saying that is easy to remember. For example, the initials *MPB* could be remembered with the sentence "Mom plans beautifully," which would then evoke the names *Marbury, Plessy,* and *Brown.* The point is to find some technique that helps you remember the information you need for the exam.

M = Marbury

P = Plessy

B = Brown

Mom **P**lans **B**eautifully

Marbury **P**lessy **B**rown

During the Exam: Being Organized

You'll do a better job on an essay exam if you approach your writing task in an organized way.

Reading the Instructions   Before you begin writing, *read the directions on the test.* Some students are so eager to start writing that they ignore this step. Following the directions is important because they tell you *how* the instructor wants you to present the information. For instance, if the directions say to discuss the *effects* of a specific Supreme Court decision, you could make a huge mistake by simply discussing the details of the decision itself.

Jesse's test question was this:

Explain the effects of three Supreme Court decisions.

The key terms for Jesse to pay attention to are *explain* and *effects.* These terms tell him

■ How to approach the topic (*explain* it).

■ What aspects of the topic he needs to focus on (the *effects*)

Here are some other examples of essay questions.

While voting has been a key factor in the U.S. democratic process since this country's formation, people take different views of—and actions toward—voting itself. *Write an essay classifying voters according to how familiar they are with the issues.*

Understanding an Essay Question

Learn the following key terms to better understand the instructions for an essay exam.

- **Analyze** means to break into parts and make connections between those parts. Analysis includes explaining why something happened or why you feel as you do. Other terms indicating analysis include *evaluate, examine,* and *explain.*

- **Argue** means to take a stand on some aspect of the topic (see Chapter 25). Other words indicating that you're taking a stand include *defend, justify,* and *support.*

- **Classify** means to group into subcategories (see Chapter 20).

- **Compare** means to show similarities (see Chapter 22).

- **Contrast** means to show differences (see Chapter 22).

- **Define** means to state the meaning of a term clearly and completely (see Chapter 24).

- **Describe** means to offer details (see Chapter 19). Other instructions with similar meanings are *relate* and *tell about.*

- **Discuss** means to carefully look at and present a subject through examples and illustrations.

- **Discuss causes** means to talk about the causes (see Chapter 23).

- **Discuss effects (results, significance)** means to talk about effects or consequences (see Chapter 23).

- **Divide** means to break down something into its parts (Chapter 20).

- **Evaluate** means to talk about advantages and disadvantages.

- **Follow** means to present each step or action in a sequence. *Trace* also asks you to present steps chronologically.

- **Illustrate** means to give examples and illustrations (see Chapter 17).

- **Narrate** means to tell how something has developed, step by step (see Chapter 18).

- **Summarize** means to give a brief version of events or ideas (see Chapter 28).

Answering Unasked Questions

When an essay exam calls for an explanation of the effects of a situation or decision, it's a good idea to include a brief—perhaps just one-sentence—summary of *what the situation or decision is.* That way, you ensure that your reader understands your answer, and you also give yourself a warm-up by writing information you know before analyzing or interpreting it.

In the example above, the key words to understand are *classifying voters, familiar,* and *issues.* The question asks the writer to group voters according to how much they know about the ballot issues.

> Regardless of who the U.S. president is, he has always been criticized. How much negative attention do today's politicians receive in relation to their predecessors? What is the nature of the criticism? In an essay, *compare or contrast the types of criticism two presidents of your choosing received.* For instance, contrast the amount of negative attention President Abraham Lincoln received with how much President Franklin D. Roosevelt received.

This essay question demands careful reading. The key terms to recognize are *compare or contrast, criticism of two presidents,* and *of your choosing.* This question asks students to find similarities or differences between the criticism of two different U.S. presidents.

> We have all been influenced by different people. *Write an essay describing an influential person in your life.*

The key terms to recognize in this essay question are *describing* and *influential person.* This question asks students to offer details that show how a person was influential in their lives.

Budgeting Your Time   Perhaps students' greatest fear in writing an essay exam is that they'll work hard to learn the material and prepare their ideas only to run out of time during the test itself. Never fear! Once you've read the directions, your next step is to figure out how much time you have to plan, write, and proofread. Suppose you have fifty minutes for the exam. You could decide to spend your time like this:

10 minutes planning

35 minutes writing

5 minutes proofreading

If you're well prepared, you may spend less time planning, but it's better to have a good plan than to forge ahead and write a disorganized essay that may leave out key details. Allotting time for proofreading, even if you don't get to read over your whole essay, gives you options.

Making a Writing Plan   Making a list or an outline is an excellent way to plan your essay. Once you've read the instructions, write out the main concepts you want to include in your response. For instance, when Jesse read that he was to discuss the effects of three significant Supreme Court decisions prior to 1960—a question he had anticipated and prepared for—he quickly wrote out his memory tool:

> MPB for Marbury, Plessy, Brown

These names triggered his memory about the nature and effects of each decision, and he was able to start planning his essay.

Next, Jesse made a brief outline. He wrote a tentative thesis statement and jotted down details that supported the key terms that he had remembered. Jesse's outline looked like this:

> <u>Thesis statement</u>: Though many Supreme Court decisions have proved important, the decisions on <u>Marbury vs. Madison</u>, <u>Plessy vs. Ferguson</u>, and <u>Brown vs. Board of Education</u> have had great significance.
>
> A. <u>Marbury vs. Madison</u>
>
>   1803, Chief Justice John Marshall: Supreme Court established its power to interpret the U.S. Constitution and determine the constitutionality of laws passed by Congress and the state legislatures.
>
> B. <u>Plessy vs. Ferguson</u>
>
>   1892, Chief Justice Melville Fuller: With the exception of dissenter Justice John Harlan, the Supreme Court ruled that "separate but equal" accommodations were legal and met the 14th Amendment's demand for equal protection under the law. Homer Plessy, who was seven-eighths white, was found guilty of refusing to sit in the "colored" car of a train.
>
> C. <u>Brown vs. Board of Education</u>
>
>   1954, Chief Justice Earl Warren: Supreme Court ruled that segregation in public schools is prohibited by the Constitution. This decision abolished "seprate but equal" education offered for black and white students; the Court used sociological arguments to show that "seprate but equal" institutions were not equal. School districts nationwide had to redefine boundaries to include racially diverse student populations.

This rough outline (which is really just an organized list) provides Jesse with the structure he needed to write his essay. Discussion of each decision made up a (body) paragraph in his essay; he needed only to add an introduction and conclusion in order to have a complete essay. Jesse's completed essay appears on page 455.

Note how Jesse's outline contains several sentence-level errors. Jesse will eventually need to proofread his essay, but he doesn't need to worry about the mistakes now.

Writing the Essay   If you're well prepared, you should have no problem writing a clear, organized essay.

- **Relax.** By the time you begin writing, you may be so eager to get your ideas down that you find it hard to relax. Many different techniques can help you remain calm: take a few deep breaths; loosen the muscles in your neck; think a happy thought. All these methods can help you get beyond the heart-pounding first few minutes of the exam and make a strong start to your essay. Then, once you've begun writing, you can concentrate fully on your response.

- **Write neatly, on every other line.** Rarely will you have the time to copy your essay over to make it neat. You'll need to make sure you get everything on paper, and this process may take up most of your time. It's a good idea, then, to write neatly on every other line of your paper or exam booklet. Writing neatly ensures that your instructor can read your writing on your first draft. Writing on every other line gives you the flexibility to go back and insert information or cross out a misspelled word and write it in above the mistake.

- **Write your introduction with a clear thesis statement.** Begin an in-class essay just as you would begin any other essay.

- **Use the specific details** you've learned from your studies to support your ideas. Make sure all your paragraphs logically connect to your thesis statement.

- Do your best to **include transitions and details,** but concentrate on following your plan and getting your information down in essay form as quickly as possible.

Remember that the primary purpose of an essay exam is to draw out your knowledge. Therefore, don't worry about having an attention-getting opening or a dramatic conclusion. While these traits are effective tools (and important ones in out-of-class essays), they are less important than the facts you are writing to show your instructor how much you know.

A Model Student Essay

Here is the essay that Jesse wrote for his political science exam.

Three Supreme Decisions

Though our Constitution established it, the U.S. Supreme Court has no specific duties, powers, or organization according to that document. The Constitution simply placed the judicial power of the country in "one Supreme Court" and any other smaller courts that Congress might establish. Despite this lack of definition, the Supreme Court is extremely powerful. Comprising only nine justices (including one Chief Justice), the Supreme Court is responsible for defining our Constitution and our laws. Though many Supreme Court decisions have proved important, the decisions prior to 1960 in <u>Marbury vs. Madison</u>, <u>Plessy vs. Ferguson</u>, and <u>Brown vs. Board of Education</u> have had particular significance.

One decision with far-reaching effects was <u>Marbury vs. Madison</u> in 1803. This case began as a way to decide who would serve on the Supreme Court when President Thomas Jefferson refused to honor last-minute appointments of his predecessor, John Adams. Chief Justice John

One of the appointees, William Marbury, sued the new Secretary of State, James Madison, so he could serve on the Court.

Marshall decided that while Jefferson should have honored Adams's appointments, the Court could not force him to under the Judiciary Act of 1789, which he declared unconstitutional. This decision gave the Court great power as it now had the power and the precedent to declare other laws unconstitutional. This decision established once and for all that the Constitution is the ultimate law of the land and that the Supreme Court is the interpreter and final authority of the Constitution.

A second decision with significant effects comes from <u>Plessy vs.</u>
separate
<u>Ferguson</u>, which legalized "~~seprate~~ but equal" accommodations for blacks

and whites. When Homer Plessy, a man seven-eighths white and one-eighth

black, sat in the "white" car of a Louisiana train, he was found guilty of
appealed
sitting in the wrong car. Though Plessy ~~apeeled~~ first to the Louisiana

Supreme Court and eventually to the U.S. Supreme Court, he lost both

times. The high court ruled that since the railroad operated only in one

state, and thus was not under federal jurisdiction, the railroad could offer
separate
~~seprate~~ but equal accommodations. Essentially nullifying the effects of
which offered equal protection for all people under the law,
the Fourteenth Amendment, <u>Plessy vs. Ferguson</u> ensured that blacks did

<u>not</u> receive the opportunities given to their white counterparts.

Finally, <u>Brown vs. Board of Education</u> in 1954 marks the third Supreme

Court decision prior to 1960 that had significant effects. This decision
undid the effects of <u>Plessy vs. Ferguson</u> and
established that "~~seprate~~ but equal" education for African-American and
separate
Caucasian students was not equal and, thus, that segregation in the
Not only did this affect school systems that were deliberately trying to be segregated, but it also forced
public schools was unlawful under the Constitution. The Court used

sociological arguments—something quite unusual—to make the decision
separate
by showing that "~~seprate~~ but equal" education was, by its very nature, not

equal for all students.

Since its creation, the U.S. Supreme Court has been responsible for

making critical decisions that affect every aspect of society. From defining

school
system
segrega
reality
the
segrega
was no
intentio
redraw
bounda
include
racially
diverse
studen

government and education to defending them for all people, the Court

certainly has not made everyone happy with its decisions. However, as the

last authority on the Constitution, the Supreme Court defines and

protects the rights and laws that serve as the foundation for this country.

EXERCISE 1 ANALYZING AN ESSAY EXAM

Read Jesse's essay, "Three Supreme Decisions." Then, answer the following questions.

1. What is the thesis statement in Jesse's essay? _____

_____

_____

2. List a major effect of each case the writer identifies.

    a. _____

    b. _____

    c. _____

3. What transitions does the writer use to signal the start of each new point in the body paragraphs?

    a. _____

    b. _____

    c. _____

4. In the topic sentence for each body paragraph, the writer echoes key words from the thesis statement. What are these words?

Body paragraph 1: _____

Body paragraph 2: _____

Body paragraph 3: _____

5. What are three sentence-level revisions the writer makes?

Body paragraph 1: _____

_____

_____

Body paragraph 2: _____

_____

_____

Body paragraph 3: _____

_____

_____

EXERCISE 2 ANALYZING ESSAY EXAM QUESTIONS FOR KEY TERMS

The groups of sentences below are possible essay exam questions. Under-line the key words in the sentences.

Example: In its entire history, the Supreme Court has only had sixteen Chief Justices. Which of these has been the most influential? Write an essay arguing that one Chief Justice has been more influential that the others.

1. Both Stanley Yelnats in *Holes* and Harry Potter in *Harry Potter and the Order of the Phoenix* experience adolescent challenges and frus-trations. Write an essay contrasting these characters.

2. What do ballet and hip-hop dance have in common? Write an essay comparing the two dance styles.

3. How can a person find the best career for his or her abilities? Write an essay explaining what steps a person can take to find the perfect job for himself or herself.

4. Since California recalled its governor in 2003, other states have been considering similar action for various politicians. Should they be able to do the same thing? Write an essay arguing whether or not voters should be able to recall elected officials.

5. Research indicates that preschool-prepared kindergartners are more likely to perform well in elementary school. Should the government require children to attend preschool? Write an essay agreeing or disagreeing with this concept.

CHECKLIST for Developing an Essay Exam

_____ **Before the Exam**

- Study the material you will be tested on.
- Practice asking and answering questions you think may appear on the exam.
- Use memory plans to help you remember important details.

_____ **During the Exam**

_____ **Prewriting**

- Read the exam directions carefully, identifying key words.
- Budget your time to allow for planning, writing, and proofreading.
- Use prewriting strategies to get your ideas on paper.

_____ **Drafting**

- Write a thesis statement that addresses the exam question.
- Select convincing support points and specific details based on your exam preparation.
- Organize your ideas, using transitions to connect your support points for your reader.
- Write neatly on every other line of the paper or exam booklet.

_____ **Revising**

- If time permits, revise your work, as necessary, according to the first three of the four Cs: *concise, credible,* and *clear* writing.

_____ **Editing**

- If time permits, proofread your work for sentence-level errors.

WRITING PRACTICE 1 Preparing for an Essay Exam

Pretend you are taking an essay exam in one of your classes.

1. Make up three questions that your instructor could ask you to write an essay about.

   a. _____

   b. _____

   c. _____

2. Then, study the material to find where you can find answers to your questions.

   Answers

   a. _____

   b. _____

   c. _____

3. Make an outline of your response to one of the questions, complete with a working thesis statement.

   A. _____

      1. _____

      2. _____

      3. _____

WRITING PRACTICE 2 Writing an Essay Exam in Response to a Reading

Follow the guidelines below to write an essay based on one of the readings in this text.

1. Choose any reading from Part Eight of this book.

2. Read the essay of your choice.

3. Follow the steps outlined in this chapter to prepare yourself to write an essay exam on that reading. Be sure to make a list of possible essay questions.

4. Write an essay in response to one of the questions you wrote, following the steps in the checklist on page 459 and allowing yourself only fifty minutes to complete the assignment.

WRITING PRACTICE 3 **Writing an Essay Exam on a General Interest Topic**

Without realizing it, we are often affected by situations and decisions that may seem removed from us. Topics involving some everyday situations are listed below. Choose an essay exam topic from the list, and write an essay. In planning and writing your essay, follow the steps outlined in the checklist on page 459. Give yourself fifty minutes unless your instructor says otherwise.

Essay Exam Topics

Many cities are attempting to revitalize older sections of town in an effort to encourage more people to work, live, and spend their leisure time downtown. Just as large urban areas are making a comeback, however, other people who have long lived downtown and paid cheap rent or mortgages are being forced out of their homes by increased property taxes. *Write an essay discussing whether or not "gentrification," as the improvement process has been labeled, should be allowed.*

Several college football player have recently attempted to be eligible for the NFL draft but have been denied due to their young ages. As a result of attempting to "come out" for the draft, these players have lost their college eligibility. Is this fair? *Write an essay arguing that college players who unsuccessfully try to be drafted in professional sports should, or should not, lose their college eligibility.*

Stereotypes have long been a part of our history and culture, but some new stereotypes, such as the gangsta rapper, have appeared only over the last two decades. *Write an essay describing at least three contemporary stereotypes.*

While public schools through high school require students to take proficiency exams, private schools do not. Should they? *Write an essay explaining why private schools should or should not require their students to take proficiency exams.*

"Guilty by association" is an expression long believed true. To what extent is it accurate? *Write an essay illustrating the truth or untruth of this concept.*

Lab Activity 27

For additional practice with essay exams, complete Lab Activity 27 in the lab manual packaged with your textbook. If you did not receive a lab manual, you can complete this activity online at **www.ablongman.com/long.** Click on **College Resources for Writers** and then click on **Activity 27.**

28 Writing Summaries and Reports

Known for his painfully proud protagonists, Ernest Hemingway made his mark as a writer of human—usually masculine—experience. His trademark minimalist style, which won him a Nobel Prize in 1954, has been imitated widely, though no one else has yet succeeded in capturing the angst of Hemingway heroes. From Jake Barnes in *The Sun Also Rises* to Frederick Henry in *A Farewell to Arms,* Hemingway heroes exhibit what Dorothy Parker identified as "grace under pressure," handling tragedy straight-backed and silently.

A Man's Man

OBSERVE YOUR WORLD Ernest Hemingway wrote about overtly masculine men, men who participated in traditionally "manly" pursuits such as hunting, camping, and fighting. Today, however, some people laud men for their sensitivity and ability to communicate their feelings, something Hemingway detested. To what extent are men stereotyped today? Observe advertising, entertainment, and other media to determine what characteristics comprise a stereotypical man today.

Summaries Are Useful

Imagine a world where no one could get to the point quickly. If you made a visit to a hospital emergency room, a chatty nurse might ask you about all sorts of irrelevant details: what sort of car you drive, where you live, what your hobbies are. While these questions might be interesting, they don't help you get the aid you require. What you need is a nurse who can ask pertinent questions and sort through your answers to determine what kind of help to send.

Summaries act the same way as an effective emergency room nurse. A **summary** concisely restates a longer document such as a lecture, essay, article, or book, emphasizing the key points and eliminating the less important details. When you write a summary, you use your own words, though you may want to borrow key phrases from the original. *Summaries do not contain your opinions or views of the material you're summarizing.* Summaries present only what the original writer had to say. A summary contains the main points of the original but not the specific details unless one or more of them is unusually important. Thus, to write a good summary, you need to be able to tell the difference between what is important in a particular reading and what isn't.

Here are some examples of real-life situations in which summaries are helpful.

- **In meetings or academic group projects.** Summaries are useful where a small group of people needs to understand a lot of material quickly. For instance, if each group member reads just two or three articles and summarizes them, the whole group can learn a great deal of important information without having to read each article. Being accurate, then, is extremely important in summaries.

- **As study tools for students facing essay tests.** Summarizing textbook chapters or class readings is an effective memory aid. Once you've written a summary, producing the same information under pressure (for example, during an essay test) is easier.

Writing an Effective Summary

A good summary must be based on a thorough, thoughtful reading of the original text. A summary presents the main support points without misrepresenting the original. Here's how to proceed.

- **Look over the document for clues about what's most important.** The most important ideas in a reading will stand out in some way: in the title, the thesis statement, the introductory paragraph, the topic sentences of body paragraphs, or the final paragraphs. Important ideas may also be identified through headings, italicized words, or words in bold type.

■ **Read the entire document to get a full understanding of it.** The only way to accurately summarize a reading is to understand it completely. Read the full document slowly and carefully to get a general idea of what the writer is saying.

■ **Reread the document and underline the important ideas.** If you can "connect" with the material you're summarizing, you'll be more likely to understand and remember it. After your first reading of the material, reread it and underline or highlight key ideas. If you're not sure whether to underline a section, mark it and move on. Then, when you're writing your summary, decide how important the questionable details are; you can include or omit them at that time.

■ **Summarize using your own words but keeping the same order as that of the document.** It may be tempting to use the author's style when writing your summary, but resist that temptation. Your job is not to entertain or persuade anyone; all you have to do is present the author's material accurately. Present the information in your summary in the same order that the writer uses in the original document. Do not use expressions like "the author claims" or "the writer points out," which are unnecessary and make the summary longer than it has to be.

■ **Check your summary against the original.** After you've drafted your summary, make sure that you have included the important details and omitted secondary or irrelevant details. Your summary should devote space, proportionately, to key points as the original does. For example, if an article devotes one paragraph to each of two points and three paragraphs to one point, then you should give that same percentage of space to those points in your summary. Additionally, make sure the information in your summary is accurate—don't exaggerate or downplay details. Since a summary will often be used in place of the original, accuracy is essential.

■ **Revise your version for the first three of the four Cs:** *concise, credible,* **and** *clear* **writing.** Check to make sure that your summary has no unnecessary words or phrases. Remember: the benefit of a summary is brevity, so omit anything not absolutely essential to communicating the points of the original. Also, make sure that the connections between ideas are clear and logical.

■ **Proofread your summary.** Correct any errors in spelling, punctuation, and grammar. Follow the tips from Chapter 7 for help with proofreading.

■ **Document your source.** In a note at the end of the summary, include the author's name and the title and publication dates of the book, magazine, journal, or newspaper where you found the original article.

A Model Summary

The following is a summary of an essay that appears in Chapter 21 (page 325). The original is approximately 1,300 words long, but the summary is about 190 words. Note that the writer includes some quotations from the essay but few specific details.

Summary of Ernest Hemingway's "Camping Out"

In the essay "Camping Out," Ernest Hemingway explains how knowledge of bugs, bedding, and cooking is necessary for successful camping. First, you must come prepared to repel insects by bringing, and later rubbing on, oil of citronella and by sleeping under a mosquito net. Otherwise, your neck will resemble "a relief map of the Caucasus." Second, you need to prepare an outdoor bed. To sleep "warm and get your rest," bring "just double the bedding" you think necessary, and then place two-thirds of that bedding under you. Finally, cooking is the most significant skill in terms of making or ruining a camping trip. Hemingway explains the necessary tools and ingredients—from a frying pan and cans of shortening to prepared pancake flour and bacon—to make a tempting meal. He also offers specific cooking details, including how to cook over coals, use bacon to baste trout, and time different dishes to finish cooking together. Hemingway's final cooking instructions give step-by-step instructions for a man to make a pie "as good as his wife." Following these steps, says Hemingway, make "the real woodsman," or someone who can be "really comfortable in the bush."

Hemingway, Ernest. "Camping Out." *Patterns of Reflection.* Ed. Dorothy Seyler. New York: Longman, 2004: 240.

EXERCISE 1 ANALYZING A SUMMARY

Read the summary of Hemingway's essay on camping. Then, answer the questions below.

1. What is the thesis of the summary? _____

_____

_____

2. What three areas does Hemingway organize his essay into? _____

_____

3. What suggestion does Hemingway offer for repelling insects?

_____

4. To which of the three areas of camping does Hemingway give his greatest attention? How can you tell? _____

_____

5. How does Hemingway define the "real woodsman"? _____

_____

EXERCISE 2 SUMMARIZE A READING FOR THIS CLASS

Choose one of the following readings from this book.

"Anywhere But Here: More Connected But More Alone" by Anne Taylor Fleming (page 371)

"Always Running" by Luis J. Rodriguez (page 260)

"Urban Renaissance Meets the Middle Ages" by Steve Lopez (page 346)

Write a one-paragraph summary of the reading. Be sure to follow the guidelines for writing a summary.

EXERCISE 3 SUMMARIZE A READING FOR ANOTHER CLASS

Write a one-paragraph summary of a chapter from a book you are reading for another class. Concentrate on including those ideas that you think you'll need to remember for an exam. Then, follow the guidelines for writing a summary.

Reports Are Relevant

We often find ourselves giving a summary of something that happened—an event at work or school, a situation involving friends or family, or an occurrence on the road, for instance—and then explaining how that event affected us. Telling a friend how the three-lane pileup on the freeway was poorly handled by the highway patrol, causing you to be unnecessarily late to work, makes clear not only what happened but why the occurrence was relevant.

If you are explaining or evaluating a situation or event after you've given a summary of it, you are giving a report. Essentially, **reports** are summaries with an analysis or evaluation added. Reports are useful in everyday situations such as the following:

- **In school.** When you need to write an analysis of a movie, play, concert, display, or book, a report gives your reader the necessary details to understand what the event was and why it was or was not effective or entertaining.

- **At work.** When you need to evaluate a new product, program, or employee, a report is effective. Further, understanding your company's review system can help you prepare for your own employee evaluations.

Writing a Report in Two Steps

Writing a report requires all the same skills as writing a summary plus one more: analysis. While the purpose of writing a summary is to communicate a longer piece of information in a brief format, the purpose of a report is to offer *your view* of the work in addition to the summary. Here are the steps in preparing a report.

- **Write a summary of the piece, including all necessary publication information.** Include the title, author, publisher, and place and date of publication.

- **Write your opinion of the piece.** Be sure to include a thesis statement that makes clear your view of the piece, and support your thesis with examples from the original work. If you claim that a product is ineffective, for instance, you need to show *the ways in which* the product is ineffective. Depending on the type of report you write, you may evaluate the piece based on criteria determined by someone else (an employer or instructor, say) or based on your own criteria: what you look for in this type of piece, product, or film; how this particular piece, product, or film measures up to your expectations and experiences.

A Model Student Report

The report at the top of the next page was written by Brian for an American literature course.

A Review of Ernest Hemingway's

The Old Man and the Sea

While Ernest Hemingway's short novel *The Old Man and the Sea* revitalized his career, it is really a depressing book. The entire story revolves around the old man, Santiago, trying to land a prizewinning marlin, the catch of a lifetime. For eighty-four days, Santiago catches nothing, and the parents of his devoted apprentice force the boy to work for a more productive boat. Santiago, however, never gives up; he remains confident that his luck will change. On the eighty-fifth day, Santiago's luck does change: he hooks a marlin and begins a two-day (and two-night) battle. Eventually, after being dragged in his boat while holding the fishing line, Santiago hauls in the fish. However, the sea reclaims its prize, and Santiago ends up as he began: poor, tired, and luckless.

I can't say I enjoyed the book because it's so sad, but there's a sort of triumph in the way Santiago keeps fighting, even when he's exhausted and bloodied from the battle. However, the victory of the story comes with Santiago's success in battling the fish; even though he is old, tired, and hungry, Santiago "fights the good fight" and catches the fish of a lifetime. Ernest Hemingway is known for writing about people who ultimately lose—their jobs or battles, their loves, their lives—but who are triumphant in simply making a good showing. Santiago certainly puts up a good fight, one I'm sure Hemingway would be proud of, but the fact that he ultimately loses the marlin and returns, beaten and bloodied but without his catch, makes the short novel hard to enjoy.

Notice that Brian's work includes two parts: a summary of the book and Brian's evaluation of it. Brian's opinion—that the book is depressing—does not have to agree with what professional critics would write. As long as he can support his main ideas using examples, which Brian does, his report works.

A Professional Report

Read the following movie review by a professional writer.

Review of *A Farewell to Arms*

Michael W. Phillips

I recently read Ernest Hemingway's *A Farewell to Arms*, which is one of the most beautiful and heartbreaking novels

I've ever read. This early adaptation of it, a prestige picture that was nominated for four Oscars, is an acceptable adaptation. It keeps the main themes of the book, telescopes a lot of events because of time constraints, and puts a censor-acceptable stamp of approval on the relationship at the center of the film. It's not as good as the book, but it succeeds in its own right, which is really all I ask of adaptations.

Gary Cooper stars as Frederick Henry, the American ambulance driver who enlisted with the Italians so that he could fight the good fight in World War I; his own government hadn't gotten around to realizing that Continental affairs affect the United States too. (None of this is explained in the film; he might as well have been an Italian driver who spoke English with a Montana accent.) He spends his time carousing with his best friend and "war buddy" Rinaldi, played with zest and energy by the great Adolphe Menjou, who calls him "baby" and entices him to go on a double date. Rinaldi has his eye on a British nurse, Catherine Barkley (Helen Hayes), and the idea is that Frederick will pair up with the dour Ferguson (Mary Philips), but he has other ideas after he sees Catherine.

I was going to say "luminous Catherine" or "beautiful Catherine," but Helen Hayes was not really either. I wrote in my notes "odd little face," and she certainly has one. She didn't start to be really luminous and beautiful until she was in her forties, when she started to play "mom" and then "grandma" roles; she was most arresting as the little old lady in her Oscar-winning turn in *Airport*. Here, she looks like, well, a young little old lady. It doesn't help that she only comes up to just under Cooper's shoulder. Real-life relationships are often like this—I've dated women a full foot shorter than me—but they look a bit odd onscreen.

Catherine and Frederick quickly become attached to each other. There's a creative diegetic ellipsis the first time they make love: he kisses her, and the camera pans up to the city skyline, where bombs can be seen exploding. The screenplay gets a little hesitant in discussing the consummation of their relationship, which occurs quite early and well before the bonds of matrimony; there are veiled statements about "it" and "last night." Frederick is sent to the front, where he's injured, and Catherine is sent to Madrid, but the two of them are reunited when Rinaldi pulls some strings. There's some odd first-person camera work as Frederick is initially brought into the hospital, where doctors lean down into the camera to talk to "him," and Catherine shoves her face into the lens for a kiss, her cheek squashed onto the glass, as Frederick informs her that she's beautiful.

They share a happy few weeks together, and are even sort of married, until Frederick is sent off to the front again. But nothing can separate true love, especially star-crossed love like this, and both Frederick and Catherine are willing to abandon everything—including their loyalty to the Italian army and the British medical corps—to be together.

Admittedly, the film goes in fits and starts. There are great individual scenes, then extremely rushed transitions as the film runs to catch up with Hemingway's plot. The highlight of the film is a wordless one: a devastating montage illustrating Frederick's desertion from the army explains concisely the statement "war is hell." It is in this montage that the film earns its Oscars for Best Sound Recording and for Charles Lang's cinematography. The melodramatic ending bothered me a bit, but it's because I was expecting the novel's understated resignation. It's still pretty darned good.

Gary Cooper is a little stiff, as he often was; this was one of his first starring roles, and he's listed as second fiddle to Helen Hayes, who was coming off an Oscar-winning performance in *The Sin of Madelon Claudet*. Indeed, she's the real star here. She captures the character's eccentricities very well. There's just enough of a touch of the unstableness that helped define Hemingway's character to come across without having her resort to histrionics. Adolphe Menjou is a delight as Rinaldi, and Jack La Rue is quietly moving as the priest who has grown disillusioned with humanity's prospects in the face of constant war.

In addition to the two Oscars it won, the film was nominated for Best Art Direction and Best Picture, which it lost to *Cavalcade*.

EXERCISE 4 ANALYZING A REPORT

Read the review of the movie *A Farewell to Arms* by Michael W. Phillips. Then, answer the questions below.

1. What is the writer's overall opinion of the movie? _____

_____

2. What areas does the writer discuss in order to support his opinion?

_____

3. What are some of the writer's criticisms of the film? _____

_____

_____

4. What does the writer say are some of the film's strengths? _____

_____

_____

EXERCISE 5 **WRITING A REPORT FOR SCHOOL**

Write a report about a book you've read for school this year. The book may be fiction or nonfiction, and it may be assigned for your writing course or another course.

EXERCISE 6 **WRITING A REPORT FOR WORK**

Write a report about a procedure at your job. (If you do not work, write a report of a procedure—such as registration or adding/dropping a course—at your school.)

WRITING PRACTICE 1 Write a Summary of an Article

Read an article from a magazine or newspaper. Then, write a one-paragraph summary of it. Make sure you include only those details that are necessary to communicate the main point of the article. Include a copy of the article when you hand in your summary.

WRITING PRACTICE 2 Write a Summary of an Oral Presentation

Watch a television program, or listen to an interview on the radio. Then, write a one-paragraph summary of the program or interview. Begin your summary by stating the name and date of the program or interview you're summarizing. For instance, write, "On July 24, 2005, the Discovery Channel's program *Tour de France* showed Lance Armstrong cycling to his seventh consecutive Tour de France France victory."

WRITING PRACTICE 3 Write a Review of a Recorded Performance

Watch a concert, film, or other performance. Then, write a review of the performance. Be sure to include both a summary of the work and your views of the recorded performance.

WRITING PRACTICE 4 Write a Review of a Live Performance

Attend a sporting event, concert, speech, or other performance or event. Then, write a review. Be sure to include both a summary of the material and your views of the live performance.

Lab Activity 28

For additional practice with writing summaries, complete Lab Activity 28 in the lab manual packaged with your textbook. If you did not receive a lab manual, you can complete this activity online at **www.ablongman.com/long.** Click on **College Resources for Writers** and then click on **Activity 28.**

29 Writing to Get a Job

CULTURE NOTE *Job-Finding Tools*

While the saying "It's not what you know—it's who you know" may not be the only important aspect of finding a job, it still holds merit. Getting to the right person—the office manager, the chief executive officer, the human resources administrator—can be a challenge. Today, however, several employment aids can make the job seeker's task of finding work easier. From online services such as monster.com to "headhunters"—people or agencies that find jobs for people and people for jobs—job searchers have never had more help.

The Big Interview

CONDUCT AN INTERVIEW Making a first impression is important in almost every aspect of life, but it is crucial when you're seeking a job. What actions or qualities help a job candidate make a good impression? How important is one's appearance? Interview at least three people you know who have jobs about what it takes to make a good impression. Then, summarize your findings in a few sentences.

Employers Value Good Writing Skills

For many students, learning to write in school is just one step they must take to pass classes and get a diploma. Once they've finished college, they assume they'll never have to write anything else again. The thought of writing outside of school, then, seems out of place.

For most people, though, writing is a necessary skill for many aspects of their lives. Even people whose careers seem to require little writing—artisans, plumbers, and mechanics, for instance—have to do some writing in the form of record keeping, filling out order forms, tracking inventory, and applying for bank or credit accounts in order to keep their businesses running smoothly. In many fields, learning to write clearly can give you an edge in the job market. You may already know what career you want to pursue, but even if you don't, strong writing skills can keep doors open while you're deciding.

Crafting a Résumé

A **résumé** is a brief (usually one-page) summary of your work qualifications. It is a record of your education, training, and job experience. Almost any job you apply for will require you to submit a résumé. The purpose of a résumé is to introduce you to a potential employer and get you an interview. The résumé itself will not usually get you a job, but it's an important first step toward getting hired. The model résumé on page 476 shows what one type of résumé looks like. The following guidelines will help you create a résumé.

- **Make your résumé look professional.** Print your résumé on good-quality paper, leaving a one-inch margin around the edges. Use an easy-to-read format. Always send a clean copy; coffee stains or fingerprints send the message that you do not care how you present yourself.

- **Emphasize your good points.** A résumé is the place to emphasize your qualifications and accomplishments. Mention any relevant extracurricular or volunteer activities you've been involved in; your employer will want to see what you've done in your free time. Don't, however, mention grades (unless they're Bs or better), hobbies, personal interests. Always be honest on your résumé; exaggerating or fibbing about your accomplishments or responsibilities in previous jobs can have negative consequences.

- **Follow a logical format.** It's usual to start with your work experience. If you have no work experience, you can start with your education. List your current school even if you have not yet obtained a degree (see the sample résumé on page 476). Be sure to have some form of organization that's easy for an employer to follow. Also, you should list experiences and educational activities *in reverse order,* starting with your most recent experience and working your way backward in time.

Damon Wong
6138 York Avenue   Edina, MN 55410   (952) 555-1572

Experience: **Sports Director, City of Hopkins, Recreation Department, 8/05–present**
Designed sports-oriented activities, games, and competitions for 96 children aged 7 to 11. Supervised 14 area program leaders.

Program Leader, City of Hopkins, Recreation Department, 6/03–8/05
Executed sports-oriented activities, games, and competitions for 14 children aged 7 to 11.

Education: **Sport/Recreation Management, University of Minnesota Minneapolis, MN 6/2007**

Associate of Arts, Normandale Community College Bloomington, MN 6/2004

Diploma, Edina High School Edina, MN 6/2001

Special Skills: Through my work for the City of Hopkins, I have honed my skills of organization, communication, perseverance, and goal-setting.

Activities: **Assistant Soccer Coach, Edina Whompers, 7/03–present**
I spend two hours per week training ten-year-old boys to play soccer.

References: Available upon request.

A Sample Résumé. Read Damon Wong's résumé to see how he applied the points discussed here to his résumé.

- **Be brief.** A potential employer probably has limited time and many applications to read. Keep your résumé to a single page.

- **Omit unnecessary or negative details.** Don't list your age, marital status, height, weight, health, or other personal details. Additionally, stay away from mentioning your previous salaries or reasons why you left your last job. These details say nothing about your qualifications for the job, and they may unfairly bias an employer against you.

- **Proofread, proofread, proofread!** Everyone makes mistakes, but don't make them on your résumé. A potential employer may interpret errors on your résumé as signs that you are careless or sloppy. Ask a friend to read your résumé, too. Two sets of eyes are better than one.

- **Mention that references are available.** Do not write the names of your references (people who can vouch for you as a responsible employee) on your résumé itself. However, keep a list of names, addresses, and phone numbers that you can provide if a prospective employer asks for references. Make sure you've asked the people you're claiming as references for their permission to do so.

EXERCISE 1 PLANNING YOUR RÉSUMÉ

Use the blank résumé outline format on this and the following page to prepare your résumé. Be sure your information is accurate and clearly stated.

Résumé Outline Format

Name: _____

Address and phone number: _____

_____

Education: _____

_____

_____

_____

(continued)

(continued)   **Experience:** _____

_____

_____

_____

_____

Special Skills: _____

_____

_____

Activities: _____

_____

_____

References: _____

_____

_____

_____

_____

Writing a Letter to Apply for a Job

In addition to preparing a clear, error-free résumé, you must also write a **letter of application,** also called a **cover letter,** to a potential employer. The purpose of this letter is twofold: to introduce you to the employer and to highlight your skills. A good cover letter increases your chances of making a good impression.

In writing your cover letter, follow the same guidelines used in writing a résumé, especially those about being brief and correct. Also follow the additional guidelines below, illustrated in the model cover letter on page 480.

- ■ **Begin with a greeting.** Part of making a good impression, even on paper, is being polite. Offering a correct, courteous greeting will make a good first impression on an employer. If you know the name of the person who will read your application, use it. If not, opening your letter with the greeting "Dear Sir or Madam" is acceptable. Always capitalize your greeting.

- **Clearly state your purpose for writing the letter.** In the first paragraph, tell the employer that you are writing to apply for a job, and explain how you heard about the job. For instance, when Damon wrote a cover letter to apply for a job as a program director in the recreation department where he had worked for several years, he mentioned an advertisement for the job listed in the department newsletter. Note that Damon's first paragraph, shown below, is not indented. This style is recommended for business letters of all kinds.

  I am writing to apply for the position of Program Director for the City of Hopkins Recreation Department that is advertised in the department newsletter.

- **Address the letter correctly.** Though this step may seem obvious, it's very important. Make sure that the inside address (the address of the person you are writing to) appears *exactly* as it does in the advertisement for the job. Double-check the spelling of all names and addresses. Damon sent his letter directly to the office where he was applying. The heading of his letter looked like this:

  Corey Watkins, Senior Program Director
  City of Hopkins Recreation Department
  1640 Minnetonka Boulevard
  Minnetonka, MN 55345

- **Clearly state your qualifications for the job.** In the second paragraph of your letter, briefly state why you are qualified for the job, and direct the reader to your résumé.

- **Clearly state your willingness to be interviewed for the job.** Tell the employer that you are ready and willing to meet for an interview. Emphasize your enthusiasm for the job.

- **End your letter with a closing expression.** Offering an appropriate closing will make a positive final impression on an employer. Be sure to sign your name on the letter in addition to typing it. A polite closing expression is "Sincerely" or "Sincerely yours." Always begin your closing with a capital letter.

Your r
addre

6138 York Avenue
Edina, MN 55410
June 24, 2006

Date

Inside address

Mr. Corey Watkins
Senior Program Director
City of Hopkins Recreation Department
1640 Minnetonka Boulevard
Minnetonka, MN 55345

Greeting

Dear Mr. Watkins:

Your purpose

I am writing to apply for the position of Program Director for the City of Hopkins Recreation Department that is advertised in the department newsletter.

Your
qualifications

In addition to completing my associate of arts degree from Normandale Community College, I am on my way to achieving a bachelor of arts degree in Sport/Recreation Management from the University of Minnesota at Minneapolis. I have learned about recreation program management both through my course work and through my positions as Sports Director and Program Leader for the City of Hopkins Recreation Department. As my résumé indicates, I am well qualified to hold the position of Program Director.

I am committed to the fitness and betterment of children through the Hopkins recreation programs. I am creative and energetic, and I am not afraid of hard work. I know that I can make a positive contribution to the City of Hopkins Recreation Department in a position of greater leadership.

Sincerely,

Damon Wong
Damon Wong

Closir
Your s
and t
name

Enclosure
notation

enc.

A Model Cover Letter. Read Damon Wong's letter to see how he applied the points discussed here to his cover letter.

WRITING PRACTICE 1 **Writing a Cover Letter**

Read the following advertisements for jobs.

> **Accounting—Accounting Assistant.** Westland Homes seeks Accounting Assistant. Responsibilities include A/P processing and maintenance of vendor/subcontractor files. Preferred candidates must possess high-volume A/P experience and familiarity with Timberline and must be fully proficient in all Office 2000 software applications. Interested candidates may submit their résumé information online at www.westlandhomes.com or fax a résumé and cover letter with salary expectations to (954) 782-7775, attn. Vice President of Operations.

> **Alarms/Security—Alarm Technician.** Fast-growing company has excellent opportunity for new and experienced residential and light commercial alarm installers. Serveral openings across the Midwest. Self-starter with clean driving record required. Call Mr. Hall. 1-800-555-4838 8-10 a.m. M-F, or send résumé and cover letter to Haas Security Systems, 78 Sonic Way, Middleton, WI 53562. Position includes benefits.

> **Administrative—Account Executive.** Wiggly-Giggly Preschool Portraits has an Account Executive position available at our office in Augusta, Maine. If you are interested in becoming part of our team, please send your résumé to boss@wigglEgigglE.com. Candidate will be responsible for the routing of district photographers to child-care centers, calling on current customers by phone, and performing administrative duties. Attention to detail and multitasking a must! Required: High school diploma; experience in customer service; two years' experience in position requiring telephone communication; one year experience in routing, scheduling, or related duties. Preferred: Computer skills. Background check will be conducted prior to hiring. Salary begins at $12 per hour.

Pretend that you are applying for one of these jobs. Your assignment is this: *Write the first paragraph of a cover letter, following the guidelines in this chapter.* Since your letter will be for an imaginary job, don't worry about typing a correct address. Instead, concentrate on writing a strong opening paragraph. If possible, ask your instructor or current employer for tips on how to make your opening paragraph more effective.

WRITING PRACTICE 2 Preparing your Résumé

Read the advertisements for jobs in a local newspaper or magazine. Then, prepare your résumé as if you were applying for one of the jobs. Next, write a cover letter with clear opening and closing paragraphs, detailed middle paragraphs, a polite greeting, and an appropriate closing expression. Take care to include the correct contact information in your letter.

Lab Activity 29

For additional practice with writing to get a job, complete Lab Activity 29 in the lab manual packaged with your textbook. If you did not receive a lab manual, you can complete this activity online at **www.ablongman.com/long.** Click on **College Resources for Writers** and then click on **Activity 29.**

PART SIX
Research

30 Finding and Evaluating Information

CULTURE NOTE *Fantasy Fiction*

Differentiated from science fiction by the presence of magic, fantasy fiction has long captivated its readers. Indeed, such fiction is nothing new. Homer's *Odyssey* and Virgil's *Aeneid* gave readers early examples of fantasy fiction, chronicling quests, conflicts of good versus evil, coming-of-age stories, and, of course, magic. Though the Greek epics and the modern plots are perhaps the best-known works in this genre (artistic, musical, or literary category), thousands of other writers contribute to fantasy fiction as well.

Gimli from *The Lord of the Rings*

SURF THE NET Key figures in J.R.R. Tolkein's *The Lord of the Rings* trilogy, Gimli (shown here) and Legolas are admirable characters for different reasons. Similarly, Merry, Pippin, Sam, and Frodo—the four hobbits—earn the respect of great warriors and wizards. Choose one important character from Tolkein's trilogy (you can use the movies as a basis for your decision), surf the Internet to learn about him or her, and write a few sentences discussing that character's personality.

Doing Research: Knowledge Is Power

If you've ever asked friends about or read reviews of a movie or CD before watching it, you've done research. **Research** is the act of performing a careful or diligent search for information, whether the information is for your own personal use—buying a car or looking for a place to live, for instance—or for school or work. You need to do research not only to find information but also to build your case in writing. Imagine, for instance, trying to convince a landlord that the hole in your ceiling is his responsibility if you haven't researched the terms of your lease or your legal options. While writing about what's most familiar is certainly easiest in terms of finding details, it's the rare individual who can go through life without ever consulting another person's opinion.

Fortunately, research has never been easier or faster than it is in the twenty-first century. Your college library and the Internet can provide a wealth of information on nearly any topic; you simply need to know how to manage these resources. With a few keystrokes or mouse clicks, within minutes you'll be well on your way to learning about your assigned or chosen topic.

Using the Library

Your school library is the best place to begin researching your topic. It contains books, periodicals, and online sources to help you find the broadest range of information for your paper. While the traditional concept of a library is a monumental building filled with books, contemporary libraries offer far more. In addition to books, libraries offer access to periodicals (magazines, newspapers, and journals) and to the Internet. Many libraries also allow you to access their resources from your home. Thus, what was once a cumbersome task—thumbing through card catalogs and squinting at books on high shelves—has become markedly easier.

Searching for Books Three Ways

Your library employs an organizational system to help you locate books. This system may be contained in a card catalog, on a computer in the library, or on a Web site. Regardless of where you find your library's book listing, you can locate information about a particular topic three ways: by subject, by author, and by title. Jolie, a student writer, has read several fantasy fiction books, but she has never read any research materials on fantasy fiction and so doesn't know much about that genre beyond what she has read. She knows she needs some of the actual books she has read as well as

Narrowing Your Topic Through Research

Keep in mind that while narrowing your topic and finding information seem to be two different steps, they're interrelated. Just as you may decide to search for information on a topic that interests you, you may also decide to narrow or change your topic based on information you find. Keep an open mind until you're certain you've found an interesting topic that lends itself to research.

other scholarly books about the subject to help her better understand fantasy fiction in general.

Performing a Subject Search   Jolie's first step was to search her library catalog. However, the search term "fantasy fiction" returned ninety-three entries, so she refined her search by adding "history" to "fantasy fiction." Now her search produced just three results: "Fantasy fiction — History and Criticism," "Fantasy fiction — History and Criticism Bibliography," and "Fantasy fiction — History and Criticism Juvenile Literature." The first subcategory, "Fantasy fiction — History and Criticism," gave her ten books, a manageable number. The first book listed was *Fantasy of the Twentieth Century: An Illustrated History* by Randy Broecker. It seemed a good place to start, so Jolie found the book and began her research.

This is the catalog entry for a book Jolie found.

Author	Broecker, Randy.
Title	**Fantasy of the 20th century : an illustrated history / by Randy Broecker.**
Publisher	Portland, Or. : Collectors Press, c2001.

LOCATION	CALL #	STATUS
Central Library	f809.38766 B865 2001	ON SHELF
Fair Oaks Library	f809.38766 B865 2001	ON SHELF

The catalog entry for a book lists not only the author and title but also the publisher and publication date. The book's **call number** tells where the book is located in the library. At Jolie's library, the catalog entry includes the branch where the book is located and also shows whether or not the book is currently available.

Note: The words *a, an,* and *the* are not considered when you are searching by title. Therefore, search for the *second* word if a book's title begins with one of these words.

Performing an Author Search   If Jolie had wanted to find a book under a specific author's name, she could have begun by typing in the author's last name—Broecker, for instance—or even just the first letter of the author's last name.

Performing a Title Search   The third way to locate a book is to search by title. Since Jolie did not know any historical or critical books about fantasy fiction, she typed in "Harry Potter" for a title search. This returned forty-nine books, more than Jolie needed, but since many of the books were translated from other languages, Jolie could narrow her results to those written in English. Since the *Harry Potter* series has been so popular, typing in a partial title was sufficient for Jolie to find fantasy books. Keep in mind, however, that sometimes knowing part of the title is insufficient to find the book; in this case, ask a librarian for help finding the title you seek.

Using a Call Number to Locate a Book

The call number is printed on the spine of every book in the library. Depending on how your library is cataloged, a call number may be a series of numbers and letters (Library of Congress system) or a series of numbers (Dewey decimal system). Either way, you take the same steps to locate your book. *Note:* If your library has closed stacks (ones you are not allowed to search), write the call number on a request slip and give it to library personnel who can find the book for you.

- Locate the call number in the catalog entry of the book you seek. For instance, the call number of Randy Broecker's book *Fantasy of the 20th Century: An Illustrated History* is f809.38766 B865 2001.
- Find the section of the library where books with the same letters as that call number are shelved.
- Find your book by looking at the numerical part of the call number.

Using Commercial Web Sites for Research

Sometimes visiting online bookstores such as Amazon.com or BarnesAnd-Noble.com can give you a good sense of how many books are available on your topic or how your topic can be organized or subdivided. Simply type keywords into the search field, press the Enter key, and view the lists that appear.

One downside of using commercial Web sites for research is that they can be distracting. With many on-screen advertisements and offers, staying on track takes more effort than if you use your library's sources. Additionally, while your search results may help you limit your topic, they will not help you find information about your topic unless you buy the books listed.

Evaluating Books for Currency and Relevance

Make sure that at least some of the books you consult have been published in the past few years. In many fields, research becomes obsolete quickly, so you need to make sure that your sources are up to date. Additionally, remember that one function of a library is to validate sources; in other words, if you find a source at your library, it has a good chance of being credible. Conversely, a local bookstore—whose purpose is to make money and not necessarily to help students—might contain print materials that are not credible.

EXERCISE 1 LOCATING BOOKS IN THE LIBRARY

Visit your college library in person or on its Web site to answer the following questions.

1. Perform a subject search for books about career planning. Write down the titles and call numbers of three books.

_____

_____

_____

2. Perform an author search for books by Jane Smiley. Write down the titles and call numbers of three books.

_____

_____

_____

3. Perform a title search for _That Hideous Strength_. Write down the name of the author.

_____

4. Write down two subject headings for the book _Into the Wild_ by Jon Krakauer.

_____

_____

5. Perform a title search for a book by Piers Anthony, Ray Bradbury, or Ursula K. LeGuin, and write down the catalog information.

Title: _____

Subject: _____

Publication date: _____

Publisher: _____

Call number: _____

Finding Periodicals Two Ways

Periodicals are publications that come out on a set schedule: daily, weekly, monthly, or quarterly. Newspapers, journals, and magazine comprise the periodicals category. Periodicals often provide the most up-to-date research on a given topic; thus, they are valuable sources of information. While magazines and newspapers are easy to spot in coffee shops and waiting rooms, the most helpful sources are found in the library or on the Internet. Periodicals have the advantages of being subject-specific and frequently published. Thus, you can find magazines, newspapers, and journals that not only cover your exact topic but also are up-to-date. Online databases contain access to thousands of periodicals and are easy and fast to search.

Using Printed Indexes   A printed catalog of periodicals, such as the *Readers' Guide to Periodical Literature,* is a good place to begin your research if you don't have access to a computer. The *Readers' Guide* is a multivolume text that lists more than a hundred magazines. Articles are listed alphabetically according to subject and author.

Although the *Readers' Guide* can provide you with many sources, using it can be cumbersome. Your library may not carry the magazines containing the articles you seek, and the search process itself can be slow if you are searching both the printed index and the library archives for your articles. Additionally, even if you find the articles you seek, you must read and take notes from them or make a copy of each article. If your library offers a CD version of the *Readers' Guide,* you can use a computer to locate relevant articles. Simply type in appropriate keywords and let the computer search the index for you.

Using Online Databases   If you have access to a computer, searching online databases for helpful articles is the way to go. Online databases often contain full-text articles that you can print or e-mail to yourself. You simply use keywords, or authors and titles if you know them, to locate articles on your topic. These are some helpful online databases.

- **EBSCO.** This service offers thousands of articles from hundreds of periodicals, so your chances of finding relevant information are good. Many college libraries subscribe to EBSCO, but if yours doesn't, try your local library.

- **InfoTrac.** The InfoTrac database combines a wide range of abstracts, full-text articles, and indexing for scholarly journals and general interest magazines in all academic disciplines.

- **ProQuest General Reference.** This general database offers full-text access and indexing to magazines, scholarly journals, and newspapers in a wide range of subjects, including business, education, literature, and political science.

- **CQ Researcher.** This full-text database from Congressional Quarterly provides detailed "reports" that include background, a chronology, current and future trends, related topics, and a bibliography on current and controversial topics.

- **ProQuest Newspapers.** This database provides full-text access to the *Christian Science Monitor, Los Angeles Times, New York Times, Wall Street Journal,* and *Washington Post.*

- **Britannica Online.** This database provides full-text access to the *Encyclopaedia Britannica Online, Annals of American History Online,* and *Webster's Third New International Dictionary, Unabridged Online.* It is also a subject directory to over 130,000 Web sites that have been "selected, rated and reviewed by Britannica editors."

- **ProQuest Psychology Journals.** This database provides full-text access to 301 psychology journals from 1987 to the present.
- **Country Watch.** This database offers information on specific countries, including an overview of the country, political and economic conditions, and environmental issues. It also includes wire service stories for each country.
- **Ethnic Newswatch.** This ProQuest database offers full text from over 200 newspapers, magazines, and journals from ethnic, minority, and native presses from 1990 to the present, in both English and Spanish.

Another helpful online research source is the Longman Research Navigator, a database giving access to thousands of periodical articles and to the *New York Times* archives. Ask your instructor if this tool has been ordered for your class; if so ask for the password to gain access to the site.

Depending on your topic, you may want to consult one or more of the online databases with a particular focus. These databases are helpful in finding information about a specific topic. Talk to your librarian about which databases might be particularly helpful to you.

Evaluating Periodicals for Currency and Relevance

Just as books can become outdated or obsolete, so too can periodicals. For example, you wouldn't read a 1979 issue of *Sports Illustrated* to get the news on today's football players, teams, and standings. Even though the information in the magazine was most likely relevant and credible at the time it was published, it would have very little bearing on today's football games. Make sure that the periodicals you use have been published in the last few years or even months, particularly if your subject matter is one—such as technology or medicine—that changes constantly.

Additionally, make sure that the magazine is a respected, credible source. With desktop publishing being so easy, people are able to "publish" their own newsletters and magazines easily and inexpensively. Not every source is credible for every purpose; your college librarians have most likely screened out sources with questionable credentials.

EXERCISE 2 SEARCHING ONLINE DATABASES

Search one of the online databases listed above for information on a topic or topics of your choice. Write down the information for three articles. An example has been done for you.

Example: Name of online database: _EBSCO_

    a. Keywords used for search: _Physical therapy_

    b. Author (if listed): _Avery Comarow_

    c. Title: _"Down But Not Out"_

    d. Full text available? Yes _____X_____ No _____

    e. Magazine name: _U.S. News and World Report_

    f. Pages: _3 pages_

    g. Publication date: _Aug. 8, 2005_

1. Name of online database: _____

    a. Keyword used for search: _____

    b. Author (if listed): _____

    c. Title: _____

    d. Full text available? Yes _____ No _____

    e. Magazine name: _____

    f. Pages: _____

    g. Publication date: _____

2. Name of online database: _____

    a. Keyword used for search: _____

    b. Author (if listed): _____

      c. Title: _____

      d. Full text available? Yes _____ No _____

      e. Magazine name: _____

      f. Pages: _____

      g. Publication date: _____

   3. Name of online database: _____

      a. Keyword used for search: _____

      b. Author (if listed): _____

      c. Title: _____

      d. Full text available? Yes _____ No _____

      e. Magazine name: _____

      f. Pages: _____

      g. Publication date: _____

Searching the Internet

If you have online access, the Internet can provide you with quick, easy ways to research your topics. By simply entering a keyword or string of words into the search bar of any search engine, you can find thousands of information sources.

Using Search Engines

A search engine uses words and phrases to sift through Web sites. By using a search engine, you gain access to thousands of sites related to your topic. Getting so many "hits," or matches, to your keyword search creates a problem, however. How do you know which sites will help you the most? Narrowing your search by using other, more specific keywords can help you focus on the Web sites that offer the most relevant information. For instance, Jolie's search on Google for "fantasy fiction" resulted in more than 21 million matches! The

Popular Search Engines

AltaVista	www.altavista.com
America Online Search	http://search.aol.com
Ask Jeeves	www.askjeeves.com
Dogpile	www.dogpile.com
Excite	www.excite.com
*Google	www.google.com
Hotbot	www.hotbot.com
Infoseek	www.infoseek.com
*Teoma	www.teoma.com
*Yahoo	www.yahoo.com
My Virtual Reference Desk	www.refdesk.com
Web Search	http://websearch.about.com

*These sites are recommended by librarians.

results ranged from sites offering specific fantasy fiction titles to possible fantasy-fiction-oriented lesson plans for instructors to use for their classes to online encyclopedias. If an Internet search is your first attempt at finding information, be prepared to limit your searches several times.

Using Search Directories

Sometimes an easier way to find information about your topic through the Internet is to use a search directory. **Search directories** organize links—springboards to other sites—around specific topics.

When you visit the Google home page, click on the "More" arrow and then on the "Directories" tab. You will be presented with a list of categories. To look for "fantasy fiction," Jolie clicked on the "Arts" tab. She was immediately presented with another list of categories that included a "Literature" listing. Jolie clicked on this tab and was presented with an "Authors" heading that gave links to twelve fantasy-fiction-related Web pages, some organized by individuals and some sponsored by better-known Web sites such as geocities.com. Jolie still wasn't sure of her essay's focus, so she clicked on several links.

Evaluating Internet Sources

Since the Internet has put multiple research sources—academic organizations' Web sites, online databases, search engines—literally at our fingertips, quick access to information has never been easier. However, we pay a price for these benefits: sometimes the sources we find are not current or credible, and our research is compromised. How, then, do we determine what sources can help us without leading us astray?

Test your sources according to each of the following four criteria in order to determine whether your source is credible.

- **What type of source are you viewing?** Until recently, a small number of online domain name suffixes made determining the type of source fairly straightforward.

Suffix	Meaning	Example	Dependability
com	Commercial or for-profit site	www.amazon.com (online bookseller)	Depends on site; consider the organization's goals, history, and reputation.

(continued)

Suffix	Meaning	Example	Dependability
org	Organization, often cause-based	www.npr.org (National Public Radio)	Generally dependable
gov	Government	www.senate.gov (U.S. Senate)	Dependable
mil	Military	www.navy.mil (U.S. Navy)	Dependable
net	Internet service provider	www.whitehouse.net (White House)	Depends on site; consider the site's history, purpose, and reputation.
edu	Education	www.csus.edu (California State University, Sacramento)	Generally depend able; consider whether the site is sponsored by the school or by an individual (such as a student).
~ (tilde)	Individual	www.dde.com/ ~Kjohnson/birdcare.htm	

Now, however, we have many more to choose from, thus making the source evaluation process trickier. Look for the following:

aero   Aviation group

biz   Business

coop   Cooperative, such as a farm co-op or credit union

info   Anyone may use this domain name

museum   Museum

name   Family name

pro   Credentialed Professional (such as a certified public accountant or a physician)

After determining the type of Web site you want to use, ask yourself three basic questions.

■ **How current is the information provided?** Information is helpful only if it's timely. Look for a recent revision or posting date at the top or bottom of a Web pages. If the last update was completed two years ago, for instance, chances are this site won't be much help. Evaluate the links provided, if any. Current, functional links are a sign that the site has been recently tended; outdated or nonfunctional links show that a site may not be as recent as you need.

■ **What is the purpose of the site?** For instance, is the site offering just a broad overview of the topic you're researching? If so, the information might not meet your in-depth needs. Make sure, too, that the site's audience includes a broad enough population for your needs. If the information targets only women, for instance, you may need to look elsewhere. Finally, consider any bias or slant; the site at http://forces.org, for instance, strongly advocates smokers' rights, so if you seek to learn about the dangers of smoking, this site is probably not for you.

■ **What credentials does the site offer?** Make sure that the site offers some credible qualifications, such as affiliations with educational or professional organizations. If a Web site is affiliated with a prominent publication or organization (for example, CNN or the American Medical Association) it's probably a safe source of information.

EXERCISE 3 FINDING INTERNET SOURCES

Choose three search engines from the list on page 495. Then, search for information on a topic of your choice. Write down the addresses of the links you would most likely use for a research essay.

Example: Search engine: *Google* _____

    Topic: *Bargain shopping* _____

    Results: *overstock.com* _____

        esmarts.com

        topsitelists.com

1. Search engine: _____

    Topic: _____

    Results: _____

2. Search engine: _____

    Topic: _____

    Results: _____

3. Search engine: _____

Topic: _____

Results: _____

EXERCISE 4 EVALUATING INTERNET SOURCES

Use a search engine or search directory to find three Web sites related to one of the topics below. Fill in the blanks to evaluate each site.

Possible topics

Camping	Martial arts	Solid waste disposal	Solar ovens
Tattoos	Prayer in schools	Sewer history	Overseas adoption
Ropes courses	Hair donation	Home health remedies	Causes of street gangs
PETA (People for the Ethical Treatment of Animals)	Personal credit reports	Home cleaning remedies	Work-related injury or illness
AIDS	Attention deficit disorder	Vegetable gardens	Hybrid vehicles
West Nile virus	Chronic fatigue syndrome	Terrorism	Water pollution
Arthritis	Organic foods	Physical therapy	Endangered fish
Yoga			

Example: Topic: _Physical therapy_____

Address: _www.physicaltherapy.about.com_____

Description: _List of different conditions and different remedies_
(stretching, exercises) as well as advertisements for different
physical therapy products, degree programs, and services

Evaluation: _There's a lot of information in a little bit of space,_
and there aren't too many ads. I like the links that lead to more
information about specific topics as well as the specialized
sections (such as "Abdominal Exercises").

1. Topic: _____

Address: _____

Description: _____

_____

_____

Evaluation: _____

_____

_____

_____

2. Topic: _____

Address: _____

Description: _____

_____

_____

Evaluation: _____

_____

_____

3. Topic: _____

Address: _____

Description: _____

_____

_____

Evaluation: _____

_____

_____

Lab Activity 30

For additional practice with searching, evaluating, and integrating information, complete Lab Activity 30 in the lab manual packaged with your textbook. If you did not receive a lab manual, you can complete this activity online at **www.ablongman.com/long.** Click on **College Resources for Writers** and then click on **Activity 30.**

31 Writing a Research Essay

CULTURE NOTE *The Works of J. R. R. Tolkien and J. K. Rowling*

Fantasy fiction has become increasingly popular as a result of the movies based on J. R. R. Tolkien's *Lord of the Rings* trilogy and J. K. Rowling's Harry Potter series. In these books, seemingly average heroes exhibit extraordinary bravery and power in taking on great evil. From unassuming Frodo Baggins to scar-marked Harry Potter, Tolkien and Rowling integrate ancient fantasy themes into original plots while developing new languages and detailing with exquisite precision every step in each character's dark journey.

Harry Potter

CRITICAL THINKING Though the Harry Potter books and movies have become wildly popular, they are not the only stories involving magic, young heroes, and plots of good versus evil. What makes the Harry Potter stories so popular? Write a few sentences explaining why you think so many people are such huge fans of the stories. If you haven't read the books or seen the movies, ask people about them or read reviews to learn about them.

Why Write a Research Paper?

If you're a college student, knowing how to write a research paper is invaluable. Finding a suitable topic, searching for credible information, and integrating your ideas with someone else's are skills that will serve you well in college and in life. Additionally, writing a research essay provides you an opportunity to learn something about a topic you care about while honing your writing skills.

Fortunately, when broken down into individual steps, writing a research essay is a straightforward process.

Choosing a Topic

Before starting a research project, make sure you're interested in the topic. Particularly when you're writing a research paper, which requires more time and effort than a simple paragraph or an essay, interest in your topic is crucial. Knowing your instructor's requirements—such as how long the paper must be, how many sources you must consult, how many sources you must cite, and when your project is due—will help you determine whether your topic is broad enough, or narrow enough, for your assignment. Jolie decided to research the general topic of "fantasy fiction." Her first step was visiting her library. For more information on using the library and the Internet to find information and narrow your research topic, see Chapter 30.

Writing an Effective Thesis Statement

After you've scoured the library and the Internet for information about your topic, you're ready to plan your research essay. Begin drafting a thesis statement so you have some means of organizing your ideas. Remember, at this early stage, your thesis statement is just a guide; you can always revise it later if you want to write about a different aspect of your topic.

Jolie had noticed that various fantasy-based movies such as *The Lord of the Rings* and the *Harry Potter* series were gaining popularity, and she read a few of the books herself. She also paid attention to similarities between the books she read. Specifically, she identified three aspects of fantasy fiction that seemed to show up frequently: a quest, a growing-up theme, and battle of good versus evil. Jolie wrote a working thesis statement, which read as follows:

> Three themes commonly appear in fantasy fiction novels: a quest, a coming-of-age by a main character, and a battle of good versus evil.

Jolie includes a map of her essay by listing the three areas she intends to focus on.

For more information about how to write a thesis statement, see Chapter 8.

Taking Notes

If you've ever seen a great movie and then e-mailed a friend about the highlights of the movie afterward, you know how to take notes. Note taking is simply the act of writing down the highlights of whatever you've read, seen, or heard. Good notes should do two things.

- Summarize important information.
- Jog your memory.

The important thing to remember about taking notes is that they are *tools* to help you write a paper; they are not fully developed ideas themselves.

Summarizing Important Information   Good notes should be brief summaries of information you've read or heard. Thus, they should include all titles, headings, and key terms from the book, article, lecture, or other work you're referring to. For instance, Jolie checked out a library book on fantasy fiction and made copies of several pages that she found especially useful for her research. She highlighted parts of two paragraphs as follows:

> Fantasy can only satisfactorily be defined negatively: it is fiction which is *not* realistic, fiction which could *not* have taken place in our world as it is in the present, as we know it to have been in the past, or as we might reasonably suppose it to be in the future.
> . . . This fantasy is much narrower in scope; it takes place in an invented world, which may or may not have some doorway to our own, where humans coexist with creatures of myth and legend—giants and dragons and trolls and dwarves and elves—and where heroes with magic talismans save the world from the dark forces of evil.

Jolie also made sure to write down the publication information for her source.

Edwards, Malcolm, and Robert Holdstack. <u>Realms of Fantasy</u>. Garden City: Doubleday, 1983. 4.

As Jolie went through the book, she took notes, being careful to add quotation marks around wording that was copied exactly.

1. Fantasy <u>not</u> realistic
2. "Could <u>not</u> have taken place in our world" now, in past, or in future
3. In fantasy, people "coexist" with mythical creatures, and heroes "save the world."

Jolie's notes include all the important details from the highlighted passage, but they are far shorter. Thus, when Jolie writes her paper, she can easily find the details she needs for support without having to reread the entire book. Eventually, Jolie eliminated this material from her essay as her writing changed direction; consulting the source, however, gave her a better understanding both of her topic and of the aspects of her topic that she had decided not to cover.

For more information on summarizing information, read Chapter 28.

Jogging Your Memory   In addition to providing important information in an easy-to-find format, good notes should also serve to remind you of what else you've read. When Jolie read the term *mythical creatures* in her notes, she was reminded of giants, dragons, trolls, dwarves, and elves. Remembering more of the article than just what she'd written down was helpful to Jolie because later, when she remembered something else she hadn't written down, her notes gave her a general idea where to locate the information she sought.

Note-Taking Methods   Good note taking simply requires time and attention. You can use 3" by 5" cards, separate pieces of paper, or computer

Tips for Note-Taking

As you take notes, remember the following:

- Write on only one side of the paper or card.
- Write the topic, or important terms, at the top of each note.
- Write information from only one article or chapter on each piece of paper or card.
- Write the author's name, source information, and the page number at the bottom of each note.

files for your notes. Just be sure you're comfortable with whatever method you adopt.

Jolie normally carried a three-ring binder, so she opted to use notebook paper to keep her notes. Jolie divided her binder into three sections—quests, battles of good versus evil, and coming-of-age tales—and then filed her notes under each heading as she finished them. When the time came for Jolie to write each section of her essay, she referred to the relevant section of notes.

Integrating Research into Your Writing

After finding the information you need to make your point, you need to find a way to gracefully weave your research into your essay. If you simply "plug in" others' ideas without signaling to your reader that they're from a particular source, you risk losing credibility and, worse, stealing others' ideas.

Developing Specific Details

Now that you've found wonderful information, you need to organize it. The information you find from research serves as the specific details for your research paper. In writing an essay you can use your own experiences and observations to support your ideas, but in writing a research paper you must use others' ideas to back up your own. For more on finding specific details, see Chapter 10. For more on finding information through doing research, see Chapter 30.

Using Quotations

To use a direct quotation, type the words you wish to use *exactly as they appear in the original,* adding quotation marks to indicate that the words enclosed in them belong to someone else. For quotations more than four lines long, indent the material one inch (ten spaces) on the left, and double-space it. Do not use quotation marks when you indent a quotation. For more information on using quotation marks, see Chapter 49.

To use just part of a quotation, add an ellipsis to indicate an omission from the original quotation. Jolie left some words out of the quotation, so she replaced them with an ellipsis as follows:

> This fantasy is much narrower in scope; it takes place in an invented world, which may or may not have some doorway to our

own, where humans coexist with creatures of myth and legend . . .
and where heroes with magic talismans save the world from the
dark forces of evil (Edwards and Holdstack 4).

The ellipsis tells the reader that words from the original quotation are
missing. Notice that Jolie gives the authors' names and the page number
where the quoted material can be found. Because Jolie has documented the
source, her readers can consult the book and read the missing information.

Leading into a Quotation

In using quotations, you need to prepare your reader to read someone else's
information. By leading into a quotation, you give proper credit to the source
you're citing, and you increase your credibility by showing that you've consulted other authorities for information. When Jolie uses a quotation in her
paper, she needs to include the name of the author(s) and the title of the work
she is quoting. Here are three ways to introduce a quotation.

In the introduction to their book <u>Realms of Fantasy</u>, Malcolm

Edwards and Robert Holdstack claim, "This fantasy is much nar-

rower in scope." (source + authors claim + quote)

"This fantasy is much narrower in scope," claim Malcolm

Edwards and Robert Holdstack in the introduction to their book

Realms of Fantasy. (quote + state authors + source)

According to Malcolm Edwards and Robert Holdstack in the intro-

duction to their book <u>Realms of Fantasy</u>, "This fantasy is much nar-

rower in scope." (according to authors + source + quote)

When Jolie wants to refer to this same book later in her paper, she can
simply use the authors' last names to introduce another quotation.

Edwards and Holdstack emphasize their point, stating that "Bilbo
Baggins . . . is an unlikely figure for a hero" (14).

Following Up After a Quotation

The danger of finding a lot of wonderful information to use in your paper is forgetting to include your own views. Remember, your research is *only* supposed to support your ideas; it should never make up the bulk of your argument. A safe way to ensure that you explain your ideas fully in relation to each quotation is to use two lines (or more) of your own writing for every quotation you use. Read how Jolie explains the importance of the quotation by using her own words.

> Edwards and Holdstack argue that fantasy "is fiction which is *not* realistic, fiction which could *not* have taken place in our world as it is in the present, as we know it to have been in the past, or as we might reasonably suppose it to be in the future" (4). As Frodo Baggins and Harry Potter have become more popular, so, too, have the details of their stories which best categorize them as fantasy. Frodo possesses a ring that seems to promise great power but which cannot be controlled by anyone except the dark lord who made it, and Harry's experiences—from his broomstick-riding games of Quidditch to his invisibility cloak—seem to come straight from children's imagination. Real life allows nothing even close to the magical adventures these two heroes experience.

Jolie explains to her reader not only that she has found relevant information to support her views, but also that she understands this information. Thus, the reader is more likely to be persuaded by Jolie's argument. Keep in mind that the more complex your topic is, the more explanation you will need to provide to explain the relevance of your research. Eventually, you should strive to write two lines of explanation for every *line* you quote from someone else's work.

Plagiarism

Passing off someone else's ideas as yours is **plagiarism,** and it's an offense that can result in failure or expulsion.

Intentional Plagiarism

Knowingly using someone else's ideas in your work and not giving credit to that person for the ideas is deliberate or intentional plagiarism. Deliberate plagiarism includes actions such as these:

- Copying an essay from the Internet and handing it in as your own

- Asking or paying another person to write your essay and then turning it in under your name
- Taking another person's ideas—either another student's or a professional writer's—and passing them off as your own

In all three cases, the writer has made a conscious decision to cheat by claiming that someone else's work is his or her own. This type of cheating is not only unethical—it's illegal. Be very careful to provide complete information about the sources you use.

Easy to Cheat, Easy to Catch

With so much pressure on students to succeed, cheating can be tempting. Especially on the Internet, finding something to hand in—a few sentences, a paragraph, or an entire essay—is not difficult. However, since your instructor has been reading your work over the course of the term, he or she will recognize a different writing style or a piece of information that did not come from ordinary class discussions. Additionally, it's as easy for your instructor to search for plagiarized papers online as it is for you to find them. Simply typing in a few key words from an Internet essay can help an instructor locate the same work that a student downloaded. Be very careful to give credit to the sources you consult to avoid the penalties of dishonest writing.

Unintentional Plagiarism

Even if you're careful not to take someone else's ideas, it can happen accidentally. The idea behind research is to learn enough about your topic to write an informed, intelligent essay. However, in the midst of searching for sources, you might find yourself with a "chicken or egg" issue: Did you think of an idea first and then look for information to support it? Or did you read something that rang true and decide, even subconsciously, that it was your own idea?

The best way to avoid plagiarism is to come up with your own ideas to begin with and then use other people's ideas to back up yours. For instance, Jolie initially wanted to write about different fantasy writers, but she was familiar only with J. R. R. Tokien (writer of the *The Lord of the Rings*) and J. K. Rowling (writer of the *Harry Potter* books). When Jolie started reading professional writers' opinions about other fantasy writers such as Piers Anthony and C. S. Lewis, she automatically adopted—and used—the professional writers' views because she had none of her own. Since Jolie didn't have time to read new fantasy fiction for her research essay, she eventually changed her topic to focus on the themes of fantasy fiction, which she could illustrate using examples from books she had read herself.

Always give credit to those people whose work you use, even while you're drafting your essay; this practice will help you avoid even unintentional plagiarism.

Benefits of Documenting Your Sources

Documenting your sources is the best way to give credit to other people for their ideas. Keep track of publication information as you draft your essay, and you'll gain these benefits.

- **Stay organized.** Jotting down the source of a quotation or a piece of information will help you find related material later.
- **Stay aware.** By taking notes and keeping track of your sources, you'll have a record of your support. Thus, you can locate gaps in your support before you even begin writing.
- **Stay honest.** Writing down the source of a piece of information can help you avoid using it as your own.

Showing What You Know Through Documentation

Aside from giving the proper credit to the authors you've cited, documenting your sources allows your reader to see that you have made the effort to incorporate others' ideas into your writing. This increases your credibility and makes you more persuasive.

This chapter shows you how to use a simple version of documentation published by the Modern Language Association (MLA), including parenthetical citations and a list of works cited.

Using Parenthetical Citations

It's easy to use parenthetical citations in your writing. When you use someone else's words or ideas, simply give the author's name and the page number of the publication you cited, placing this information in parentheses at the end of the borrowed material. The parenthetical citation serves to point your readers to your list of works cited, where they can learn more about the source. Notice the parenthetical citations in an excerpt from Jolie's essay. (The full essay begins on page 517.)

Similarly, Harry Potter is not the ideal do-gooder. He breaks rules, fails to show respect to his elders, and loses his temper throughout Rowling's novels. In fact, Harry's popularity is often attributed to the fact that he is "bad and mischievous—i.e., not good" (Abanes 195).

In the citation, Jolie gives the author's last name followed by the page number where she found the borrowed information.

Using Parenthetical Citations

To use parenthetical citations, remember the following:

- Place the parenthetical citation *after* the borrowed information but *before* the period at the end of the sentence.
- Use only the *last* name of the author(s) of the work being cited.
- Do not use a comma to separate the author's last name from the page number.
- When using more than one source by the same author, give an abbreviated form of the title between the author's last name and the page number: (Rowling, *Sorcerer's Stone* 45).

Preparing a List of Works Cited

The greatest benefit you give readers of your research paper is knowledge. At the end of your paper, your readers should know considerably more about your topic than they did before reading it. Hopefully, your work will be interesting enough that some of your readers may want to learn still more about your subject. This is where the **list of works cited** comes in. It gives your readers all the information they need to pursue additional study of your topic through the sources you've identified. Your list of works cited also gives credit to those writers whose articles you used for your paper.

The model Works Cited entries below show how to list commonly occurring types of sources according to Modern Language Association (MLA) style.

Book by One Author

Place the author's last name first, with a comma between the last and first names. Underline the title of the book. List the city of publication, the publisher's name, and the year of publication.

Pilcher, Rosamunde. <u>The Carousel</u>. New York: St. Martin's, 1982.

Preparing a List of Works Cited

When preparing your Works Cited list, follow these guidelines.

- Use a new page to begin your works cited list.
- Number the works cited page consecutively with the rest of your essay.
- Place the title *Works Cited* in the center of the first line, one inch from the top of the page. Do not italicize or use quotation marks.
- Double-space your list of works cited.
- Alphabetize the list according to the authors' last names.
- End most items in an entry with a period.
- Indent the second and subsequent lines of each entry five spaces (one-half inch).

Book by Two Authors

List the second author's first name first.

Child, Julia, and Jacques Pepin. <u>Cooking at Home</u>. New York: Knopf, 1999.

Book by Four or More Authors

You may use *et al.* ("and others") to indicate the second and subsequent authors if there are four or more. List all the authors if there are two or three.

Sklar, S. Jay, et al. <u>NYT Organizing a Company</u>. New York: Lebhar-Friedman, 2000.

Two or More Books by the Same Author

List books in alphabetical order according to title. After the first entry, use three unspaced hyphens instead of the author's name.

Crichton, Michael. <u>Timeline</u>. New York: Random, 1999.

---. <u>A Case of Need</u>. New York: Penguin, 1993.

Edited Book

Sexton, Anne. <u>Anne Sexton: A Portrait in Letters</u>. Ed. Linda Gray Sexton and Lois Ames. Boston: Houghton, 1992.

Translation

Esquivel, Laura. <u>Like Water for Chocolate</u>. Trans. Carol Christensen and Thomas Christensen. New York: Anchor, 1994.

Revised Edition

Warner, J. Sterling, and Judith Hilliard. <u>Visions Across the Americas</u>. 4th ed. New York: Heinle, 2000.

Note: MLA citations require the short forms of publishers' name—"Random" for Random House, for example—and the city, but not state, of publication.

Book Chapter

Alcott, Louisa May. "Grandma." <u>An Old-Fashioned Girl</u>. Reissue edition. New York: Penguin, 1870. 120–136.

Selection from an Anthology or Edited Collection

Martin, Judith. "Manners Matter." <u>A Civil Word: A Contemporary Issues Reader</u>. Ed. Elizabeth Cloninger Long. New York: Longman, 2003. 46–48.

Pamphlet

<u>How to Be a Good Parent</u>. New York: Planned Parenthood, 1996.

Magazine Article

After the title of the magazine, place the day first, then the month, then the year.

Reilly, Rick. "Past Its Peak." <u>Sports Illustrated</u> 5 June 2006: 78.

Newspaper Article

In the following example, the final letter and number indicate the page number of the article, and the plus sign indicates that the article is continued on a nonconsecutive page in the same section. (If it had continued on the next page, the page number would have read *C1-2*). Note that you should omit *The* from a newspaper title: *The Sacramento Bee* is listed simply as *Sacramento Bee*.

McNeal, Martin. "Kings Can Thank Luck This Time." <u>Sacramento Bee</u> 17 Nov. 2003: C1+.

Article from an Online Database

The first date tells when the article was initially published, and the second is the user's access date. Place the URL within angle brackets followed by a period.

Weir, Tom. "Fat-Food Nation." <u>Progressive Grocer</u>. 1 Mar. 2003. 18 Nov. 2003 <http://0-web11.epnet.com.alpha.saclibrarycatalog.org/citation>.

Television Program

"The Good Fight." <u>Sex and the City</u>. HBO. 3 Nov. 2003.

Personal Interview

Byrd, Norwood. Personal interview. 3 Jan. 2005.

Film

<u>March of the Penguins</u>. Dir. Luc Jacquet. Warner Bros. 2005.

Videocassette/DVD

<u>The Civil War</u>. Dir. Ken Burns. Videocassette. PBS Video, 2002.

Music Recording

Vivaldi, Antonio. "Spring." <u>Vivaldi for Dummies</u>. Angel Records, 1996.

EXERCISE 1 PUTTING SOURCES INTO MLA FORMAT

Put the following sources into MLA format according to the guidelines in this chapter. An example has been done for you.

Example: An article titled "In the Frame," published in the August 22–28, 2005, issue of *Variety* magazine on page A4, written by Michaela Boland.

Boland, Michaela. "In the Frame." <u>Variety</u> 22–28 Aug. 2005: A4.

1. A book by Lindsay Porter titled *Car Bodywork Repair Manual: The Complete, Illustrated Step-by-Step Guide,* published by Haynes North America in Newbury Park, California, in 2000.

_____

_____

2. An article entitled "The Reigning Queen of Tech" from the online database ProQuest at http://www.proquest.com written by David Kirkpatrick in the May 16, 2005 issue of *Fortune.* Accessed on Sep-

tember 5, 2005 at the Cosumnes River College Library in Sacramento, California.

_____

_____

3. An article published in the September 2005 issue of *Health* magazine, titled "A Blissful Run," found on page 47. No author is listed.

_____

4. An article written by Rob Stanger, found in *Sports Illustrated* online (SI.com) and titled "First Timers Under Fire," from the September 5, 2005, issue of the magazine; accessed at http://sportsillustrated.cnn.com/preview/siexclusive/2005 on September 7, 2005.

_____

_____

5. An article written by John Heilemann in the March 2000 issue of *Wired,* on page 25, titled "Fear and Trembling in Silicon Valley."

_____

Organizing Your Research

Now that Jolie has a thesis statement, she can begin sorting through her research to find details that will support her thesis. Specifically, Jolie wants to find information showing that the three themes she identifies are, indeed, common in fantasy fiction. Jolie has made an outline to make clear the points she wants to develop.

Thesis statement: Three themes commonly appear in fantasy fiction novels: a quest, a coming-of-age by a main character, and a battle of good versus evil.

A. Introduction

B. Quest

C. Coming of age

D. Battle of good versus evil

E. Conclusion

Jolie began organizing her research by arranging her notes: one stack for information about quests, another for battles of good versus evil, one more for coming-of-age tales, and a last group of notes containing information on more than one support point.

As Jolie read through each pile, she marked important information and highlighted details. She worked on her outline to plan the structure of her essay.

Fantastic Reading

A. Introduction

   1. Fantasy definition

   2. Thesis: three themes in fantasy fiction

B. Quest theme

   1. Quest defined; *Lord of the Rings* example

   2. Quest has "adventurous journey"; *Lord of the Rings* example

C. Growing-up theme

   1. Growing up through passage of time; *Harry Potter* books as example

   2. Growing up through fighting evil "without and within"; *Harry Potter* example

D. Good versus evil theme

   1. All-good and all-evil characters in *LOR* and *HP*

   2. Main characters as combination of good and bad traits

E. Conclusion

This outline gives Jolie a good idea of what points she needs to cover to do her topic justice. She lists not only her general points but also the sources (*Lord of the Rings* and *Harry Potter* books) that will help her support her points.

Jolie's next step is to translate her research into a form that she can use in her paper. For more on organizing ideas, see Chapter 10.

A Model Student Essay

Jolie's completed research essay follows.

Hwang 1

Jolie Hwang
Professor Sanchez
English 360
1 November 2005

Fantastic Reading

We've all heard fairy tales: stories about innocent or disadvantaged people who, usually through the help of magic, triumph over evil and live happily ever after. These stories not only entertain us, but they also bring reason and order to a chaotic world. According to Richard Abanes in his book <u>Fantasy and Your Family</u>, fantasy fiction is part of the overall folklore genre (category), specifically, part of the fairy-tale branch. Fantasy, or fairy tales, explains Abanes, contains "an element of supernaturalism (e.g., magical objects, witches, spells, wizards" (12). Thanks to modern technology, Hollywood has brought contemporary fairy tales to the silver screen; the <u>Lord of the Rings</u> trilogy based on J. R. R. Tolkien's work and the <u>Harry Potter</u> movies based on J. K. Rowling's series have become immensely popular over the past ten years.

Not only are these stories thrilling, but they illustrate the same patterns that fantasy stories as a whole follow. Specifically, three themes commonly appear in fantasy fiction novels: a quest, a coming-of-age by a main character, and a battle of good versus evil.

The quest theme is commonly developed throughout fantasy fiction. The idea of a quest is developed in J. R. R. Tolkien's work The Lord of the Rings. In this work, an unassuming hobbit (a small, human-like creature) named Frodo Baggins finds himself the bearer of an ancient ring of power. In a 1956 review of Tolkien's work, W. H. Auden noted that the "One Ring [is] the absolute physical and psychological weapon which must corrupt any who dares to use it." Knowing this, Frodo is understandably reluctant to embark on the quest to destroy it, but when it becomes clear that no other race is capable of or willing to actually see the task through without giving in to the temptation of using the ring, Frodo volunteers for the job. The journey by which Frodo delivers the ring to the place it was forged serves as the quest in Tolkien's books.

Hwang 3

According to <u>Merriam-Webster's Encyclopedia of Literature</u>, a quest usually involves "an adventurous journey." Frodo's quest in <u>The Lord of the Rings</u> is filled with adventure. From early on, Frodo is pursued by the Nine Ringwraiths—men corrupted by power who have become Sauron's slaves (Abane 84). He is also led (after being followed) by Gollum, the ring's longtime owner, who is completely untrustworthy because he desperately wants the ring back. Additionally, Frodo's quest leads him to be injured or captured by potential enemies—not the least of which is a giant spider—and he must sneak into enemy land to destroy the ring, which uses its own power to control Frodo. Finally, Frodo's fight with Gollum over molten lava at Mount Doom and his rescue by giant eagles mark nothing less than great adventure. By developing a quest, over their course, Tolkien's works fall under the "fantasy" heading.

Another prominent theme in fantasy fiction that shows itself in popular books is the coming-of-age, or growing-up, theme. According to Prof. Richard Schumaker at the University of Maryland University College, J. K. Rowling's <u>Harry Potter</u> books fall into this

Hwang 4

category (Schumaker). Even without his adventures, Harry Potter becomes an adult over the course of the novels, starting at age eleven in Book 1 and becoming an "adult" wizard at age seventeen (the wizarding world's "of age" year) at the start of the final volume. Additionally, Harry begins to see himself as an adult. Introduced as a boy who at eleven was "small and skinny for his age . . . [and] looked even smaller and skinnier than he really was" in Book 1 (Rowling, Sorcercer's Stone 20), Harry survives childhood pangs with his mother's family, the Dursleys, as well as the pain and confusion of adolescence at Hogwarts School of Witchcraft and Wizardry. Eventually, Harry sees himself as "Dumbledore's man, through and through" by the end of Book 6 (Rowling, Half-Blood Prince 649), and, as a part of seeing himself as a man, he has grown up.

The coming-of-age theme, however, usually involves more than the simple passage of time. In Harry Potter's case, he acts as a "young protagonist [facing] evil without and within" (Mooney). At the start of Book 1, Harry Potter and the Sorcerer's Stone, Harry is unaware that he possesses magical powers or that he is

Hwang 5

special in any way. However, over the course
of Rowling's books, Harry learns who he is,
how he is special, and what is expected of
him. By the end of Book 6, <u>Harry Potter and
the Half-Blood Prince</u>, Harry is nearly of age
and ready to face his greatest challenge. This
readiness, however, did not come easily. Only
after twice defeating Voldemort, the most
powerful dark wizard; witnessing the deaths of
a classmate, his godfather, and his mentor;
and accepting the responsibility to kill the
evil Voldemort does Harry accept unpleasant
realities of his life. Michiko Kakutani writes
in her review of Book 5, <u>Harry Potter and the
Order of the Phoenix</u>, that a "disillusionment
charm" at the start of the novel serves as a
symbol for "Harry's loss . . . of his boyish
illusions and for his teenage immersion into
the ambiguities and perils of the grown-up
world." Harry is well on his way to growing
up, placing his stories under the fantasy
fiction umbrella.

One last fantasy fiction theme that
shows itself in popular books—and probably
the most significant one—is the theme of good
versus evil. According to children's book
writer Nicholas Tucker as quoted in <u>Fantasy</u>

Hwang 6

<u>and Your Family</u>, one of the advantages of reading fantasy fiction is that it shows people that they are "born into a world of death, violence, wounds, adventure, heroism and cowardice, good and evil" (Abanes 95). Both Tolkien's <u>Rings</u> books and Rowling's <u>Harry Potter</u> books illustrate this conflict. At one end of the good-versus-evil spectrum are Gandalf, the aging gray-then-white wizard of Tolkien's novels, and Albus Dumbledore, the aging but still powerful headmaster of Hogwarts School of Witchcraft and Wizardry. Both wizards exhibit actions which, though sometimes flawed—as in Gandalf's initial trust in Saruman and Dumbledore's failure to tell Harry of his destiny sooner—are never evil. At the other end of the spectrum are Sauron in the <u>Rings</u> and Lord Voldemort in the <u>Potter</u> books. Neither of these villains started out evil, but Sauron "became so through self-seeking" (Abanes 97), and Voldemort, both in revenge against his muggle (nonmagical) father and in a desire for power, also became corrupt.

In between these extremes of good and evil are the heroes: Frodo Baggins and Harry Potter. Each of these heroes accepts his burden—Frodo to destroy the ring and Harry to face Voldemort—but neither seeks it. Frodo is not completely good: he gives in to the temptation to use the ring, experiences powerful feelings of hatred toward Gollum, and even turns on his friend and companion, Sam. According to Jane Chance of Rice University, "Frodo is a little guy who is called upon to do heroic work against enormous evil" (qtd. in McNamara). Similarly, Harry Potter is not the ideal do-gooder. He breaks rules, fails to show respect to his elders, and loses his temper throughout Rowling's novels. In fact, Harry's popularity is often attributed to the fact that he is "bad and mischievous—i.e., not good" (Abanes 195). However, both make the "right" choices—Frodo to destroy the ring and Harry to face Voldemort—even when their burdens weigh them down. Both Frodo's and Harry's struggles to do right in the face of great evil illustrate the good-versus-evil theme of fantasy fiction.

Fantasy has never been so popular. People wait in line to buy the next <u>Harry Potter</u> books, and movies based on Tolkien's and Rowling's works have grossed hundreds of millions of dollars. Amidst the hype and the special effects, though, <u>The Lord of the Rings</u>

and the <u>Harry Potter</u> series are simply fairy tales, fantastic stories of an unassuming hero who takes on the bad guys. Though Tolkien and Rowling have written very different stories, each manages to illustrate key themes in fantasy fiction. The themes of quests, growing up, and good versus evil ring loudly through some of the most entertaining books of our time.

Works Cited

Abanes, Richard. <u>Fantasy and Your Family</u>. Camp Hill: Christian, 2002.

Auden, W. H. "At the End of the Quest, Victory." <u>New York Times</u> 22 Jan. 1956. 7 Aug. 2005 <http://www.nytimes.com/1956/01/22/books/tolkien-king.html>.

Kakutani, Michiko. "For Famous Young Wizard, a Darker Turn." <u>New York Times</u> 21 June 2003, late ed: A1.

McNamara, Mary. "Lord of Literature: J. R. R. Tolkien's Good-Versus-Evil Theme Still

Hwang 10

Resonates, Especially Now in the Face of
Conflict." <u>Los Angeles Times</u> 21 Oct. 2001:
E1. ProQuest. Learning Resource Center
Lib., Sacramento City Coll. 27 June 2005
<http://www.proquest.umi.com>.

Mooney, Bel. "Writing Through Ages." <u>Times</u>
[London]: 28 Aug. 2002: 17. ProQuest.
Learning Resource Center Lib.,
Sacramento City Coll. 27 June 2005
<http://www.proquest.umi.com>.

"Quest." <u>Merriam-Webster's Encyclopedia of
Literature.</u> 1995.

Rowling, J. K. <u>Harry Potter and the Half-Blood
Prince</u>. New York: Arthur A. Levine Books,
2005.

---. <u>Harry Potter and the Sorcerer's Stone</u>. New
York: Arthur A. Levine Books, 1997.

Schumaker, Richard. Professing Literature.
Home page. Sept. 2001-Dec. 2001. Dept. of
English, U of Maryland U Coll. 29 Jun 2005
<http://faculty.ed.umuc.edu/~rschumak/>.

Lab Activity 31

For additional practice with writing a research essay, complete Lab Activity 31 in the lab manual packaged with your textbook. If you did not receive a lab manual, you can complete this activity online at **www.ablongman.com/long.** Click on **College Resources for Writers** and then click on **Activity 31.**

PART SEVEN
Writing Correct Sentences

32 Prepositional Phrases

Music

Defined in *Merriam-Webster's Collegiate Dictionary* as "the science or art of ordering tones or sounds in succession, in combination . . . to produce a composition having unity and continuity," music is something few people try to define but nearly everyone recognizes. From primitive drumbeats through complex orchestral compositions to contemporary tunes, every type of music begins with the basics: a melody and a beat.

Another Kind of Reading

OBSERVE YOUR WORLD Music plays a role in nearly every aspect of our lives, from childhood learning exercises to symbols of tradition in formal ceremonies. What role does music play in the lives of people you know? Interview someone you know well about the functions music serves in his or her life, summarizing your findings in a few sentences.

Identifying Prepositional Phrases

A **phrase** is a group of related words lacking a subject and a verb. A **prepositional phrase** is a phrase beginning with a preposition. Many prepositional phrases show spatial and time relationships between ideas. Recognizing prepositional phrases can help you identify the subject and verb of a sentence.

The easiest way to identify prepositional phrases is to look for prepositions. A **preposition** relates a noun or pronoun to the rest of a sentence.

<u>in</u> the house   <u>with</u> her sister

<u>after</u> the game   <u>for</u> breakfast

Common Prepositions

aboard	besides	on
about	between	onto
above	beyond	out
according to	by	outside
across	concerning	over
after	despite	through
against	during	throughout
along	except	to
along with	for	toward
among	from	under
around	in	underneath
at	inside	until
before	into	up
behind	like	upon
below	near	with
beneath	of	within
beside	off	without

Note: Some of these words can also be other parts of speech, such as conjunctions.

Read the following sentence.

<u>In</u> music, notes sit <u>on</u> lines or <u>in</u> the spaces <u>of</u> a staff.

The words *in, on,* and *of* appear on the list of common prepositions, so in this sentence they begin four prepositional phrases. To determine the end of a prepositional phrase, remember that *every preposition asks a question.* The noun that answers the question is at the end of the prepositional phrase. For instance, when you see the word *in* or *of,* ask yourself, "In what?" or "Of what?" In the example above, the nouns that answer those two questions—*music* and *staff*—mark the ends of the prepositional phrases.

There is no shortcut to learning the prepositions. You simply need to memorize the list on page 530.

EXERCISE 1 WRITING PREPOSITIONAL PHRASES

Write your own prepositional phrases using the prepositions below, answering the question that each preposition asks.

Example: against *against a brick wall* _____   *against my leg* _____

1. to   **a.** _____   **b.** _____

2. despite   **a.** _____   **b.** _____

3. by   **a.** _____   **b.** _____

4. about   **a.** _____   **b.** _____

5. under   **a.** _____   **b.** _____

Using Prepositional Phrases to Identify the Subject of a Sentence

The prepositional phrases in the following sentence have been crossed out.

~~In music~~, notes ~~on the treble clef~~ are named ~~for letters of the alphabet from A to G~~.

Taking out the prepositional phrases, you're left with *notes are named.* These remaining words include the subject and verb of the sentence. *Notes* is the subject, and *are named* is the verb. By eliminating the prepositional phrases, you've made the job of identifying the subject and verb much easier.

Watch Out for Infinitives

An **infinitive** is a verb form that looks like a prepositional phrase but isn't. Infinitives are made up of the word *to* plus a verb, such as *to dance*. The following phrases begin with infinitives (underlined).

> <u>To feel</u> sleepy
>
> <u>To see</u> clearly
>
> <u>To ask</u> for permission

When you see an infinitive, remind yourself that it's not a prepositional phrase. Note that it's not the verb, either. For instance, each of the following sentences contains an infinitive (underlined).

> Jack wanted <u>to play</u> the Sousaphone, but he was too little.
>
> <u>To become</u> first chair, or the best flutist, Shawna practiced constantly.
>
> I hoped <u>to learn</u> his music secrets, so I paid attention when he performed.

EXERCISE 2 IDENTIFYING PREPOSITIONAL PHRASES

In the following sentences, underline the twenty prepositional phrases and circle the prepositions.

Example: Music is read (from) left (to) right.

1. The notes on the lines of the treble clef are EGBDF.

2. One way for music students to remember these notes is to think: "Every good boy does fine."

3. On the other hand, the notes in the spaces are FACE.

4. For most people, remembering the notes in the spaces is easier because they spell a real word.

5. A written note has an oval-shaped head, a straight stem on one side of the note, and possibly a flag attached to the stem.

6. Notes can be empty or black, depending on their type.

7. For instance, an empty note without a stem is a whole note, and an empty note with a stem is a half note.

8. A black note with a stem but no flag is a quarter note, and a black note with a stem and a flag is an eighth note.

9. The head of the note indicates how high or low it sounds; for example, if a note is higher on the staff, it has a higher pitch.

10. The stems and flags are used for a different purpose; they indicate a note's duration.

EDITING PRACTICE

In the following paragraph, underline the twenty-five prepositional phrases and circle the prepositions. There may not be a prepositional phrase in every sentence.

Melody: The Sound of Music

Melody is one of the most basic elements of music. A note, a sound with a particular pitch and duration, serves as the foundation for melodies. Stringing a series of notes together, one after the other, creates a melody. The melody of a song, however, isn't just any string of notes. Not necessarily coming at the very beginning or very end of a piece, the melody is that combination of notes that catches your ear and sounds most important in a song. In fact, over the course of an arrangement, the melodic line—the string of notes that make up the melody—will often repeat itself in verses. Not all notes in a song are part of the melody. Despite sounding difficult and important, extra notes such as trills or slides are called ornaments or embellishments; these embellishments do not advance the melody. Instead, these embellishments are added to the melody either by the composer or the performer to make the melody more complex and interesting, but they are not part of the melody itself.

Lab Activity 32

For additional practice with prepositions, complete Lab Activity 32 in the lab manual packaged with your textbook. If you did not receive a lab manual, you can complete this activity online at **www.ablongman.com/long.** Click on **College Resources for Writers** and then click on **Activity 32.**

33 Subjects and Verbs

An offshoot of civil rights legislation, Title IX was passed in 1972 to provide equitable scholastic and athletic opportunities for women. While its opponents argued that Title IX would destroy men's sports, it has instead increased the number of scholarships—and, thus, the number of college graduates—among women. Largely responsible for the U.S. women's dominance in major sporting events such as soccer and softball, Title IX ensures that wherever federal funding is received, women are not denied academic or athletic opportunities.

U. S. Women's Goalie Brianna Scurry

CRITICAL THINKING Have girls' and women's opportunities in sports changed over your lifetime? Think about the chances women you know have had to get an education and participate in organized sports, and write about the extent to which these opportunities have changed—for better or worse—over the course of your life.

The Main Parts of a Sentence

Subjects and verbs are the basic units of sentences. In fact, a group of words can't be a sentence unless it includes both a subject and a verb. Some sentences also have **objects,** words that receive the action or direction of another word such as a verb or preposition.

Identifying Verbs

Verbs tell us what's going on in a sentence. They give any action or change in time and condition that takes place. **Main** verbs communicate the primary action or state of being in a sentence, while **helping verbs** let us know when and under what conditions the action of the main verb took place. **Linking verbs** connect the subject to words that identify or modify it. For instance, read the sentences below and ask yourself what is going on in the sentence. The verbs are underlined.

> Title IX <u>ensures</u> gender fairness.
>
> (What's going on? Title IX *ensures* gender fairness.)
>
> Trixie <u>is</u> a successful athlete.
>
> (What's going on? Trixie is *being* a successful athlete.)
>
> Marc <u>succeeds</u> in academics and sports.
>
> (What's going on? Marc is *succeeding* in academics and sports.)

In each sentence there is only one verb, so verb identification is straightforward. Note that for the sentence containing *is,* the explanation is that Trixie "is being" a successful athlete. Some verbs, such as the verb *to be,* do not show overt action so much as a state of being. In these cases, just remember that forms of the verb *to be* (*am, is, are, was, were, be, being, been*) can act as the main verb of a sentence.

Finding the Complete Verb

Helping verbs work with main verbs to communicate when an action took place or the conditions under which it took place. The **complete verb** in a sentence includes helping verbs and main verbs. To fully understand the rules of grammar and punctuation, you need to be able to identify *all parts of the verb.*

The complete verbs are underlined in the following sentences. All of the helping verbs tell *when* the action of the main verb takes place.

Title IX <u>is considered</u> an important piece of legislation.

(*Is* indicates *when* Title IX is being considered: now, not in the past or future.)

Many women <u>have attended</u> college since Title IX's passage.

(*Have* indicates *when* women have attended college: some time before now.)

In the following sentences, the helping verbs indicate *condition.* The helping verbs qualify whether or not the action of the main verb will actually take place. Again, the complete verbs are underlined.

Sarah <u>could play</u> college soccer if she wanted to.

(*Could* indicates the condition under which Sarah might play college soccer. The writer doesn't say Sarah actually *plays* soccer but just offers the possibility.)

Pete <u>may coach</u> the women's softball team.

(In this case *may* indicates a possibility. The writer does not say Pete definitely *coaches* the team but instead uses *may* to offer the possibility.)

Sometimes both types of helping verbs—those indicating time and those indicating condition—are used together. The complete verbs in the following sentences are underlined.

Monty <u>may have overreacted</u> when his sister received a scholarship and he didn't.

(Here *may* casts doubt as to whether Monty overreacted, while *have* indicates that the overreaction occurred sometime before now.)

He <u>should be seeking</u> ways to make himself appealing to college scouts.

(*Should* communicates a recommendation that he make himself appealing while *be* indicates that the action of *seeking* takes place now, not in the past.)

Common Helping Verbs

are	had	must
been	has	shall
can	have	should
could	is	will
do	may	would
does	might	

Linking Verbs

Linking verbs often indicate action that is hard to see. Below are some examples of linking verbs that link the subject to words that identify or modify it.

Liv <u>feels</u> better about her athletic participation.

(Liv is not using her hands to feel something; instead, her feeling is internal.)

Ed <u>looks</u> tired.

(Ed is not looking at anyone; he *seems* as if he might be tired.)

Linking Verbs as Main Verbs

Think of linking verbs as equal signs when they are used as the main verb in a sentence. For instance, think of "Liv feels better" as "Liv = better" and "Ed looks tired" as "Ed = tired." That way, you don't have to worry about looking for an action since the "action" is that of being equal. Other words that act as equal signs are *appear, be (am, is, are, was, were), become, feel, look,* and *seem.*

EXERCISE 1 IDENTIFYING THE COMPLETE VERB

Underline the complete verb in each sentence. *Hint:* Cross out any prepositional phrases first. An example has been done for you.

Example: Many positive changes <u>have occurred</u> since Title IX's passage.

1. Before 1972, fewer than 300,000 girls had participated in high school sports every year.

2. Now, however, nearly 3 million girls will participate every year.

3. Additionally, the number of women on intercollegiate sports team has gone from 30,000 to more than 150,000.

4. In the last twenty years, the number of women's college teams has nearly doubled.

5. Finally, since Title IX's passage, professional leagues for women's soccer, volleyball, bowling, and basketball have been established.

Identifying the Subject

The **subject** of a sentence says what the sentence is about. Finding the verb allows you to find the subject of the sentence. Once you've identified the verb, ask yourself, *who* or *what* is performing the action of the verb? The subject of a sentence is often a **noun**—the name of a person, a place, a thing, or an idea.

Look again at the sentences given at the beginning of the chapter. The subjects shown in bold type.

Title IX ensures gender fairness.
(Who or what ensures fairness? *Title IX* does.)
Trixie is a successful athlete.
(Who or what is a successful athlete? *Trixie* is.*)
Marc succeeds in academics and sports.
(Who or what is succeeding in academics and sports? *Marc* is.)

Finding More Than One Subject or Verb

Part of finding subjects and verbs involves finding *all* subjects and verbs. Sentences must have at least one subject and one verb, but some sentences may have more than one subject and/or verb. Subjects with more than one part are called **compound subjects.**

Siblings **Cheryl** and **Reggie Miller** were both outstanding basketball players.
(*Cheryl* and *Reggie Miller* are the subjects of the sentence.)

Cheryl and Reggie <u>made</u> baskets and <u>guarded</u> opponents well.
(*Made* and *guarded* are the verbs of the sentence.)

EXERCISE 2 **IDENTIFYING SUBJECTS AND VERBS**

Read the following sentences. Underline the subjects once and the verbs twice. Some sentences contain more than one subject or verb. *Hint:* Cross out any prepositional phrases first.

1. Many women have been exceptional athletes and have played on exceptional teams.

2. For instance, Mildred "Babe" Didrikson Zaharias ran track and played golf, both with tremendous success.

3. Babe Didrikson Zaharias once won an entire team track championship by herself and dominated women's golf for years.

4. Perhaps the greatest woman athlete of all time, Babe Didrikson Zaharias is remembered for her Olympic gold medals and is admired for her courage in her losing fight against cancer.

5. Billie Jean King and Bobby Riggs also made history in a "battle of the sexes" tennis match.

6. After publicly boasting of men's superiority in tennis, Riggs emerged from retirement and played King.

7. King rose to the challenge and crushed Riggs in three straight sets.

8. American women soccer players, softball players, and basketball players have also established their dominance in the world.

9. In 1999, the U.S. women's soccer team outscored the Chinese team in penalty kicks and defeated them 5 to 4.

10. Finally, the U.S. women's softball team has won the three consecutive

Olympic gold medals and five consecutive world championships.

What to Watch Out For

Finding subjects and verbs is often an easy process. However, some sentence elements can look like subjects and verbs and, thus, make the identification process more difficult. Some of the most common causes for confusion are discussed below.

Nouns That Follow the Verb

What is the subject of the following sentence?

Some people have protested Title IX.

You might have been tempted to choose *Title IX* as the subject. *Title IX* is not part of prepositional phrases, and it is a noun. However, it is not the subject. Ask yourself, "Who or what has protested?" Now it's clear that the *people,* not Title IX, perform the action of the verb. Thus, *people* is the subject.

The subjects are in bold type in the sentences below, while any nouns following the verb are in italics.

Mom baked me a *cake* for my birthday.
(*Mom,* not *cake,* is doing the baking.)
Bob drove his *car* too fast yesterday.

Understanding Objects

- A direct object is a noun or pronoun that receives the action of the verb.
  Brandi Chastain kicked the *ball.*
- An indirect object is a noun or pronoun that receives the direct object.
  Jennie Finch pitched *me* the ball.
- An object of a preposition is the noun or pronoun introduced by a preposition.
  Title IX has benefited women in many *ways.*

(*Bob,* not the *car,* is doing the driving.)

Tonya found a gold *watch* near her *house.*

(*Tonya,* not *watch* nor *house,* did the finding.)

Pronouns

A **pronoun** is a word that can take the place of a noun. Pronouns as well as nouns can be subjects. Look out for the following pronouns as the subjects of sentences.

I, you, he, she, it, we, they

Treat pronoun subjects exactly the same way that you would treat any other subjects.

I went to the store.

She reads frequently.

They make this course more interesting.

Commands

Sometimes the subject of a sentence is the pronoun *you* even if the word *you* does not appear. For example:

Try to win a scholarship.

The subject of this sentence is actually *you.* Written out completely, the sentence is

(You) try to win a scholarship.

Because the sentence is a **command**—an order to do something—the writer doesn't need to include the subject specifically. Keep in mind that if a sentence appears to be giving an order, the subject is probably *you.*

Each pair of sentences below contains one sentence in which *you* is not written and one sentence with *you* written in parentheses.

Call me as soon as you get there.

(You) call me as soon as you get there.

Stay away from the water!

(You) stay away from the water!

No, Not, and *Always*

Watch out for words such as *no, not, never, always, still, very,* and *just.* These words are **adverbs,** words that describe verbs. They often sit right next to the verbs, but they are *not* part of the verb.

Sam <u>was</u> **not** <u>trying</u> to make you angry.
(*Was trying* is the verb; *not* is not part of the verb.)
Nicole <u>should</u> **just** <u>relax</u> when she takes a free throw.
(*Should relax* is the verb; *just* is not part of the verb.)

Words Ending in *-ing*

A word ending in *-ing* is never the sole verb of a sentence. An *-ing* word can be *part* of the verb, but only if a helping verb precedes it.

Incorrect: Coach <u>pushing</u> us to do our best.
(*Pushing* is not a complete verb; thus, the word group does not form a complete sentence.)
Correct: Coach <u>is pushing</u> us to do our best.
(*Is pushing* is the complete verb; the word group is a sentence.)

Infinitives

A verb with *to* in front of it is never the verb of the sentence.

Erika <u>planned</u> **to attend** the same college as her brother.
(*Planned,* not *attend,* is the verb.)

EDITING PRACTICE **Finding Complete Subjects and Verbs**

In the following sentences, underline the subjects once and the verbs twice. Some sentences contain more than one subject or verb. Be sure to underline all parts of the verb.
Hint: Cross out any prepositional phrases first.

1. Title IX bans sex discrimination from taking place in schools, in both academics and athletics.

2. Title IX was created after Title VI of the Civil Rights Act of 1964, prohibiting discrimination based on race, color, or national origin.

3. Since its passage, much progress has been made in closing the education gap that existed between men and women completing four years of college.

4. For instance, in 1971, twenty-six percent of men and eighteen percent of women high school graduates completed four years of college.

5. Today, that gap does not exist.

6. According to the *Washington Post,* 57 percent of bachelor's degrees are earned by women.

7. Not all people have supported this legislation, however.

8. According to Title IX critics, women's academic and athletic opportunities have weakened men's opportunities.

9. Specifically, detractors of the legislation have accused Title IX of draining men's athletic scholarships.

10. Advocates of Title IX remain strong in the face of such attacks.

Lab Activity 33

For additional practice with subjects and verbs, complete Lab Activity 33 in the lab manual packaged with your textbook. If you did not receive a lab manual, you can complete this activity online at **www.ablongman.com/long.** Click on **College Resources for Writers** and then click on **Activity 33.**

34 Clauses

CULTURE NOTE *Potatoes*

The base ingredient for some of America's favorite snacks such as chips and French fries, potatoes contain large amounts of essential nutrients such as potassium. Additionally, because they were the primary food source for thousands of Irish people in the 1800s, crop failures due to a potato fungus partially caused the Irish potato famine of 1845–1849.

Our Favorite Starch

JOURNAL ENTRY Just about any food can be stripped of its nutritional value if enough fat or sugar is added, and the potato is no exception. What kinds of foods make up your daily diet? Think about your eating habits, writing down everything you eat for a day or two, and write a few sentences explaining how your diet is or is not generally healthy.

Clauses and Sentences

In almost every area of life, some elements of an object or situation are more important than others. For instance, in a car, the fuel injection system is more important than the audio components. Different sections of sentences are more important than others, too. One important aspect to writing well involves knowing how to emphasize the ideas that you think are the most important through their placement in a sentence.

What Is a Clause?

The basic unit of a sentence is the **clause,** which is a group of related words having a subject and a verb that work together to communicate an idea. Clauses can be very long, but they can be very short as well. The following word groups are examples of short clauses.

Plants grow. (*Plants* is the subject; *grow* is the verb.)

Move! (*You* is the subject; *move* is the verb.)

Potatoes are one of the most versatile foods in cooking.
(*Potatoes* is the subject; *are* is the verb.)

When I don't know what I'm in the mood for, I make mashed potatoes.
(*I* is a subject and *do know* is a verb; *I* is a subject and *make* is a verb.)

EXERCISE 1 IDENTIFYING CLAUSES AND PHRASES

In the sentences below, identify the italicized sections as either a phrase (a group of related words without a subject and a verb) or a clause. Write P for a phrase and C for a clause. *Hint:* Crossing out the prepositional phrases and underlining the subjects and verbs may help you determine whether or not a group of words is a clause.

Example: ___C___ *Because people often smother them in sour cream and butter,* potatoes can be fattening.

The group of words has subject (*people*) and a verb (*smother*), so it is a clause.

_____ **1.** However, potatoes are actually *a cholesterol-free, fat-free food.*

_____ **2.** *The average potato contains 100 calories,* 3 grams of fiber, 4 grams of protein, and 720 milligrams of potassium.

_____   **3.** *Since one pat of butter also contains 100 calories* and many people put several pats of butter on a single baked potato, potatoes can be fattening.

_____   **4.** Calories sneak their way into potato dishes *through cheese, bacon, gravy, and other fat-laden toppings.*

_____   **5.** *Those willing to skip rich additions will find potatoes a satisfying, nutritious treat.*

Independent Clauses

A clause that makes sense all by itself is an **independent clause.** An independent clause is a complete sentence. In the sentence *Plants grow,* you may wonder why someone is giving you this piece of information, but you probably understand what the speaker is talking about without further explanation. The following sentences are examples of longer clauses.

The Irish potato famine was at least fifty years in the making.
(*Irish potato famine* is the subject; *was* is the verb.)
Several factors—including British economic policy, destructive farming methods, and a potato fungus—created the famine.
(*Factors* is the subject; *created* is the verb.)
Various sources attribute between 500,000 and more than 1 million deaths to the famine in only five years.
(*Sources* is the subject; *attribute* is the verb.)

Dependent Clauses

A group of words that has a subject and a verb but doesn't make sense all by itself is a **dependent clause.** When a dependent clause is not attached to an independent clause, it is a fragment (see Chapter 36). The dependent clauses are italicized in the sentences below.

Because *they were starving,* nearly 2 million citizens left Ireland.
Although *Irish immigrants sought to live,* many of them died en route to a new country.

Notice that each of the italicized sections above has a subject (*they, Irish immigrants*) and a verb (*were starving, sought*). For a group of words to be a clause of any kind, *it must have a subject and a verb.* A dependent clause, however, also has another element: a dependent word. *A clause with a dependent word cannot be a sentence.* In the preceding dependent clauses, dependent words appear in bold type. Cover up the dependent words with your thumb and read the remaining clauses.

> **Because** they were starving
> **Although** Irish immigrants sought to live

Dependent clauses are so named because they *depend* or *rely* on an independent clause to make sense. Notice that without the dependent words, the clauses are *independent*—they make sense all by themselves. *With* the dependent words, the clauses do not make sense on their own, so they are therefore *dependent* clauses. Memorize the list of dependent words that follows.

after	even though	unless
although	if	until
because	since	when
before	though	while

EXERCISE 2 IDENTIFYING DIFFERENT CLAUSES

Read the clauses below. If a clause is independent, write IC in front of it. If a clause is dependent, write DC in front of it. *Hint:* If you're not sure whether a clause is independent or dependent, read it aloud. If it sounds as if it needs more information to make sense, most likely it's a dependent clause.

Example: __DC__ Until the great famine.

_____ **1.** Potatoes were the Irish citizens' main food crop.

_____ **2.** They were high in food energy and easy to cultivate.

_____ **3.** Because they required little effort in seeding, weeding, and watering.

_____ **4.** After the blight—a potato fungus that made potatoes mushy and inedible—ruined potato crops.

_____ **5.** Widespread famine occurred.

Sentences Built with Clauses

Independent clauses are important to recognize because they serve as the building blocks for longer, more complicated sentences.

Simple Sentences

A single independent clause is also called a **simple sentence.** The following independent clauses are simple sentences.

> Writer Nora Ephron uses potatoes as a relationship barometer in her novel *Heartburn.*
>
> (*Nora Ephron* is the subject; *uses* is the verb.)
>
> Potatoes Anna is the perfect dish for happy people .
>
> (*Potatoes Anna* is the subject; *is* is the verb.)
>
> For someone with a broken heart, mashed potatoes are the answer.
>
> (*Potatoes* is the subject; *are* is the verb.)

Compound Sentences

A sentence containing two or more independent clauses joined together using a semicolon or a comma and a coordinating conjunction is called a **compound sentence.** Because every clause in a compound sentence is an independent clause, every part of the sentence is equally important. The following are examples of compound sentences. Brackets surround each independent clause.

> [Potatoes can be easy to prepare], but [they can also be difficult].
>
> [I can bake a plain potato], or [I can grate, mash, sauté, or top potatoes], depending on my mood.

Notice that the comma and the conjunctions are not part of either clause.

EXERCISE 3   IDENTIFYING CLAUSES IN A COMPOUND SENTENCE

Each of the following sentences is a compound sentence. Add brackets around the independent clauses. *Hint:* Look for the comma and conjunction as a clue to where the clauses are separated.

Example: [People from Norway are familiar with *lefse*], but [not all Americans know about it].

1. *Lefse* is a flat Norwegian potato cake that resembles a tortilla, but its flavor is very different .

2. Making *lefse* is tricky, for you must make a sticky potato dough without initially adding flour.

3. Adding the flour before chilling the dough results in a gray color, and the dough resembles school paste.

4. Proper *lefse* dough should be rolled out on a floury surface, or the dough will stick and tear.

5. Cook the *lefse* in a dry frying pan, and serve it with butter and sugar.

Complex Sentences

A sentence that combines at least one independent clause with at least one dependent clause is a **complex sentence.** Even though the word *complex* can make these sentences seem tricky, they're not difficult to write. The following are examples of complex sentences. Brackets surround each clause. Notice that when the dependent clause comes first, you must use a comma to separate the two clauses. However, if the independent clause comes first, you do not need a comma.

	dependent clause independent clause
	S V S V
Comma needed:	[As long as potato chips are salty], [I will eat them].
	S V S V
	[Although carrot sticks are healthier], [I can't resist
	independent clause
	a fresh, crisp—preferably sour cream and onion fla-
	vored—chip].
	independent clause dependent clause
	V S
No comma:	[I constantly drink water] [whenever I eat chips].
	S independent clause V
	[My desire for good health outweighs my desire for
	dependent clause
	S V
	potato chips] [until my stomach begins its familiar
	late-night growling].

The important part of recognizing and writing compound and complex sentences is being able to identify the clauses in each sentence. Remember to find the subjects and verbs in compound and complex sentences because they will help you identify each clause.

EXERCISE 4 IDENTIFYING CLAUSES IN COMPLEX SENTENCES

In the following complex sentences, place brackets around the clauses.
Write DC above each dependent clause and IC above each independent
clause. *Hint:* Look for the dependent word as a clue to the start of a
dependent clause.

Example:
           IC   DC
[Potatoes can be a plain food], [although they can be prepared in

many interesting ways].

1. For instance, if you're not worried about calories , filling the potato

    skin with butter, bacon, and cheese makes a good meal .

2. Another delicious potato food is French fries unless you don't like

    fried food .

3. When I was growing up , we often ate potato pancakes with apple

    sauce on nights when we didn't have meat .

4. I've also heard of a cold potato soup called Vichyssoise , although

    I've never had it myself .

5. Probably because my mother didn't cook it , I've never had potato

    pasta—called gnocchi—either even though it sounds fantastic .

EDITING PRACTICE

In the following sentences, identify each italicized word group as P for
a phrase, IC for an independent clause, or DC for a dependent clause. *Hint:*
Cross out prepositional phrases and underline subjects and verbs to help
you determine whether or not a word group is a clause.

A Potato for the People

Created in 1952 in Pawtucket, Rhode Island, Mr. Potato Head is

probably the world's most famous potato. ¹However, *although*

Mr. Potato Head achieved fame and fortune as the "spokespud" for the American Cancer Society's Great American Smokeout in 1987, he did not let his celebrity go to his head. _____ [2]Rather, *at the age of 40,* Mr. Potato Head became health-conscious—no couch potato he!—and was given an award from the President's Council for Physical Fitness. _____ [3]His popularity peaked in 1995 *with his supporting role in Disney's animated movie* Toy Story, but he continued to set a good example and helped get out the vote through the League of Women Voters in 1996. _____ [4]*His only signs of succumbing to the pressures of fame came in 1997* when he urged people to "Try the Fry" in Burger King's advertising campaign. _____ [5]*Fans can only hope* that the appearance of a potential enemy, Darth Tater, will not further deter Mr. Potato Head from his chosen path. _____

Lab Activity 34

For additional practice with clauses, complete Lab Activity 34 in the lab manual packaged with your textbook. If you did not receive a lab manual, you can complete this activity online at **www.ablongman.com/long.** Click on **College Resources for Writers** and then click on **Activity 34.**

35 Run-On Sentences

CULTURE NOTE *Rosa Parks and the Montgomery Bus Boycott*

Known to many as only a poor seamstress, Rosa Parks was much more. A longtime civil rights activist, Ms. Parks was chosen to be a test case of segregation ordinances and, as such, willingly endured her removal from a bus and her subsequent arrest for refusing to give her seat to a white man. Known as the midwife or mother of the civil rights revolution, Ms. Parks's actions led to the 381-day bus boycott in Montgomery, Alabama, that desegregated buses throughout the United States.

Rosa Parks

OBSERVE YOUR WORLD Sparking eventual national desegregation, Rosa Parks made history when she began the Montgomery bus boycott by refusing to give up her seat to a white man. Who, if anyone, today is responsible for significant change in some aspect of our culture? Pay attention to our society's heroes and role models and write a few sentences about someone you think is bringing about change.

What Is a Run-On Sentence?

One of the most common mistakes in writing is the run-on sentence. Run-ons take two forms: the fused sentence and the comma splice. Both types of run-on sentence attempt to combine two independent clauses without proper conjunctions or punctuation. The result is a sentence that tries to do too much, thus confusing the reader.

Fused Sentences

A **fused sentence** is one in which the writer tries to join two independent clauses without any connecting words or punctuation.

> **Fused:**   Many versions of the Montgomery bus boycott depict Rosa Parks as a poor seamstress she was much more.

> **Fused:**   Ms. Parks served as secretary to the local chapter of the NAACP she had worked for the Union of Sleeping Car Porters.

Each sentence contains two independent clauses placed one after another without any connecting word or punctuation, thus creating a fused sentence.

Comma Splices

Comma splices are the most common type of run-on sentence. **Comma splices** join two independent clauses with a comma. A comma is not a strong enough punctuation mark to connect two independent clauses.

> **Comma splice:**   The Montgomery bus boycott didn't happen overnight, it was the result of much planning by community leaders.

> **Comma splice:**   In fact, plans for the boycott had been in place for months, the leaders just needed a catalyst.

These sentences both make an attempt to connect the two independent clauses they contain. However, the connections need to be stronger and clearer. The ways to fix run-on sentences are covered in the next section of this chapter.

EXERCISE 1 **IDENTIFYING RUN-ON SENTENCES**

For each item below, write F for a fused sentence, CS for a comma splice, or C for a correct sentence.

_____ **1.** On December 13 a carpool involving three hundred vehicles was created to help supporters of the boycott the Montgomery police took action immediately.

_____ **2.** Carpool participants found themselves the target of further unfair treatment, riders and drivers were arrested for various reasons.

_____ **3.** Carpool riders were arrested for loitering as they waited for their rides.

_____ **4.** Drivers were ticketed frequently they were arrested for overloading their cars.

_____ **5.** This treatment did not deter people from the boycott, bus riders endured inconvenience and even hardship to achieve their goal.

Correcting Run-On Sentences

There are four ways to correct run-on sentences.

Making the Run-On into Two Separate Sentences

To change a run-on into two separate sentences, place a period at the end of the first independent clause and capitalize the first word of the second independent clause.

Correct: Many versions of the Montgomery bus boycott depict Rosa Parks as a poor seamstress. **She** was much more.

The trick to using this method effectively is determining where one clause (or complete idea) ends and the other begins. If you're not sure where to place the period and begin a new sentence, try reading the run-on out loud. Chances are, your voice will drop when you come to the end of the first clause.

EXERCISE 2 CORRECTING RUN-ON SENTENCES

Some of the following run-on sentences are fused sentences, and some are comma splices. In each case, determine where the two clauses meet. Then, correct the run-on using a period and a capital letter.

A Risky Ride

[1]Rosa Parks faced many risks in refusing to give up her seat she lived in a time and place where justice did not often apply to African-Americans. [2]One risk she faced was losing her job, Ms. Parks was employed as a tailor's assistant in a department store. [3]After refusing to give up her seat, she lost her job her husband was fired, too. [4]Another risk Ms. Parks faced was physical harm her husband was afraid for her. [5]He warned her that she could be killed for her actions Ms. Parks felt she had to hold her ground. [6]One last risk Ms. Parks faced was that of further injustice, she had plenty of proof that this could happen. [7]Two months prior to Ms. Parks's refusal, the murderers of a fourteen-year-old African-American boy had been set free, the jury was all-white. [8]Civil rights activists were targets an NAACP activist in Mississippi was killed just two weeks before Ms. Parks said "no." [9]Other than some discomfort, Ms. Parks was not

harmed her actions paved the way for segregation's end. ¹⁰Thanks to

Ms. Parks, many unfair laws have ended , the country has made strides

toward ensuring fair treatment of its citizens.

Using a Comma and a Coordinating Conjunction

The second way to correct a run-on is by using a comma and a coordinating conjunction. **Coordinating conjunctions** are words that join elements of equal importance, such as two independent clauses. The list gives the most common coordinating conjunctions.

Common Coordinating Conjunctions

Word	Meaning	Example
for	because	Rosa Parks is famous, for she played a key role in ending segregation.
and	more of the same; in addition	Ms. Parks acted bravely, and her actions were effective.
nor	an addition of negative ideas	Neither walking to work nor having to carpool deterred boycott participants from their goal.
but	opposition or change; however, except	Ms. Parks was asked to give up her seat, but she refused.
or	indicates a choice	Many African-American bus riders had to find rides to work, or they had to walk.
yet	but	Montgomery endured 381 days of the bus boycott, yet their perseverance was rewarded.
so	therefore; indicates	Not everyone understood Ms. Parks's actions, so she traveled the country and made speeches to explain them.

Remembering the Coordinating Conjunctions

An easy way to remember coordinating conjunctions is to think of FANBOYS, which is made up of the first letters of the words *for, and, nor, but, or, yet,* and *so.*

Although the coordinating conjunctions serve the same function, they mean different things, so choose your conjunction carefully. For instance, the fused sentence below can be corrected in a number of ways.

Fused: Rosa Parks is my favorite civil rights activist Martin Luther King, Jr., was an impressive person, too.

This sentence contains two independent clauses, but the reader can't tell how the two ideas are related. Using a comma and a coordinating conjunction can make this connection clear.

Correct: Rosa Parks is my favorite civil rights activist**, and** Martin Luther King, Jr., was an impressive person, too.

(This combination explains two things: first, Rosa Parks is the writer's favorite civil rights activist; second, Martin Luther King, Jr., was also impressive.)

Correct: Rosa Parks is my favorite civil rights activist**, but** Martin Luther King, Jr., was an impressive person, too.

(This combination explains that although Martin Luther King, Jr., was impressive, Rosa Parks is still the writer's favorite civil rights activist.)

Both corrected sentences above make sense, and both are grammatically correct. However, the simple switch in coordinating conjunction from *and* to *but* radically alters the meaning.

EXERCISE 3 CORRECTING RUN-ONS USING COMMAS AND CONJUNCTIONS

Correct each comma splice by inserting an appropriate coordinating conjunction.

Example: People often think that Rosa Parks was too tired to move from

her seat, *but* she was no more tired than usual.

1. Ms. Parks had been arrested for refusing to give up her seat before, she was willing to be arrested now.

2. Ms. Parks knew the bus driver, James Blake, she did not like him.

3. In fact, Ms. Parks despised Mr. Blake, he had thrown her off his bus ten years earlier.

4. More people entered the bus, Mr. Blake demanded that all African-American riders give up their seats.

5. Ms. Parks knew that this was her chance to test the desegregation laws, she remained seated.

EXERCISE 4 JOINING INDEPENDENT CLAUSES USING COORDINATING CONJUNCTIONS

For each item, add an idea that logically follows from the first independent clause. Use a comma and the coordinating conjunction shown to join the two independent clauses.

Example: *and*   I've always tried to be well informed *, and I've done my best to stay current with the news.*

1. *and*   My courses seem manageable this semester _____

_____

2. *but*   I keep thinking I'd like more hours at work _____

_____

3. *for*   Danny can fix almost anything _____

_____

4. *so*   The Johnsons left early _____

_____

5. *but*   I'd love to help you _____

_____

6. *or*   For dinner, we can make pizza _____

_____

7. *and*   The telephone helps me get work done _____

_____

8. *for*   The *Harry Potter* books are fascinating _____

_____

9. *but*   She took a speech class to conquer her shyness _____

_____

10. *so*   I have some free time tomorrow _____

_____

Using a Semicolon

A third way to correct run-ons is to separate the two independent clauses with a semicolon. Essentially, if you can use a period to separate two clauses, you can a semicolon instead. Using semicolons instead of periods, however, gives your sentences more variety.

Using a Semicolon to Separate Independent Clauses   If you discover a fused sentence or comma splice in your writing, simply place a semicolon between the two clauses. Each of the following sentences would be a run-on if it didn't have a semicolon.

    Run-on: Riding public transportation is a bit different every day I never sit in the same spot or next to the same people.

    Correct: Riding public transportation is a bit different every day; I never sit in the same spot or next to the same people.

Run-on: I'm always exhausted when I get on the bus, I can't imagine
having to give up my seat for no good reason.

Correct: I'm always exhausted when I get on the bus; I can't imagine
having to give up my seat for no good reason.

EXERCISE 5 USING A SEMICOLON TO CORRECT RUN-ONS

Insert a semicolon between the two clauses in the following run-on sentences.

Example: The Montgomery bus boycott was not the first time people

had tried to boycott the buses the Reverend Vernon Johns had tried to

start a boycott earlier.

1. Johns, in his sixties, entered the bus he accidentally dropped his

   dime on the floor.

2. The bus driver rudely demanded that Johns pick up the dime Johns

   refused.

3. The bus driver ordered Johns to pick up the dime or get off the bus

   Johns opted to exit the bus.

4. As he departed the bus, Johns urged his fellow riders to exit the bus

   with him no one else moved from his or her seat.

5. Johns was greatly disappointed his actions show how important

   planning and organization were to the actual boycott later on.

Using Semicolons with Transitions   Another way to use a semi-colon is with a transitional word or phrase. These words can help tell your reader how the two ideas linked by the semicolon are related. The most common transitions (also called **conjunctive adverbs**) used with semi-colons follow. See Chapter 10 for a complete list of transitions.

The following sentences use a transition with a semicolon to link two ideas.

Run-on: My mother wanted me to watch the movie *The Rosa Parks Story* on television I wanted to watch one of the *CSI* programs.

Correct: My mother wanted me to watch the movie *The Rosa Parks Story* on television; **however,** I wanted to watch one of the *CSI* programs.

Common Transitional Phrases (conjunctive adverbs)

Term	Meaning
also	and
furthermore	and
in addition	and
moreover	and
however	but
nevertheless	but
on the other hand	but
in fact	indicates emphasis or gives an example
indeed	in fact
instead	indicates an alternative
meanwhile	during the time mentioned
otherwise	indicates a different outcome
as a result	indicates an effect
thus	indicates an effect
consequently	indicates an effect
therefore	indicates an effect

Run-on: She told me that I'd learn more from the movie she was right.

Correct: She told me that I'd learn more from the movie; **in fact,** she was right.

Notice that you need to place a comma after a transition that follows a semicolon.

EXERCISE 6 USING SEMICOLONS AND TRANSITIONS TO CORRECT RUN-ONS

Join the two clauses below using a semicolon and a transition from the list of common transitional phrases. Make sure to choose a transition that makes sense in your sentence, and remember to include a comma after the transition.

Example: Rosa Parks was not the original selection as a test case *; however,* she proved to be the best choice.

1. Within the twelve months prior to Parks's arrest, four other people had been asked to leave a bus one was fifteen-year-old Claudette Colvin.

2. Colvin protested the bus driver's request she was dragged off the bus.

3. Colvin was arrested by the police she was treated rudely and hand-cuffed.

4. Colvin was charged with violating segregation laws, disorderly conduct, and assault she was convicted and fined only for assault, the most ridiculous of the charges.

5. The ruling was clever and sent a message to African-Americans it avoided a challenge to the unconstitutional segregation laws.

6. The NAACP was prepared to make Colvin its test case in a segregation ordinance test case local NCAAP president E. D. Nixon met with Colvin to discuss the situation.

7. Colvin was indignant at the way she had been treated she might have been willing to help the NAACP's cause.

8. Unfortunately for the NAACP at that time, Colvin had recently become pregnant her youth and habit of using profanity caused Nixon to worry.

9. He desperately wanted to challenge the segregation ordinances he feared that churchgoing African-Americans would not rally around Colvin.

10. When Rosa Parks found herself in the same situation as Colvin, Nixon had his solution there was no doubt that people would support the solid citizen Rosa Parks.

Creating a Dependent Clause

The last way to correct a run-on sentence is to use a dependent word to make one of the clauses subordinate to the other. **Subordination** just means making one idea weaker, or less important, than the other one. That way, your reader can easily tell which one is the focus of the sentence. For more on dependent clauses, see page 547.

   The run-on sentences below have been rewritten so that one idea is less important than the other. Now, each contains a dependent clause and an independent clause. The dependent words are in bold type.

Common Dependent Words

after	even though	unless
although	if	until
because	since	when
before	though	while

Run-on: You learn about history, you can't understand it.

Correct: **Until** you learn about history, you can't understand it.

Run-on: I've tried to make sense of world events I haven't learned about them.

Correct: I've tried to make sense of world events **though** I haven't learned about them.

Run-on: I now know that I must give history a chance I decide whether I like it.

Correct: I now know that I must give history a chance **before** I decide whether I like it.

Note: When the *dependent* clause comes first, a comma comes between the clauses; however, when the *independent* clause comes first, you don't need a comma.

EXERCISE 7 CORRECTING RUN-ONS USING DEPENDENT WORDS

Correct each run-on sentence below by using the indicated dependent word to make one idea less important than the other. Remember to use a comma if the dependent clause comes first.

Example: *when*   When people's
                    People's lives are affected, they are most likely to take

            action.

1. *if*   People sit around, very little changes.

2. *because*   Rosa Parks became the mother of the civil rights

movement she was willing to take a stand.

3. *although*   Her life was disrupted, Rosa Parks took action to

bring about change.

4. *until*   Civil rights leaders felt unable to act they found the

right test situation.

5. *after*   Rosa Parks showed a willingness to take a stand, the

NAACP put the boycott plans into action.

EXERCISE 8 USING DEPENDENT WORDS FOR SUBORDINATION

Fill in each blank with an appropriate dependent word.

1. _____ I've told you before, orange stripes and purple polka dots are not the best combination.

2. Sergio changed his mind _____ he learned that his girlfriend was going, too.

3. Telling someone the brutal truth always seems like a good idea

_____ the time comes to actually say something.

4. _____ my test was difficult, I think I did well.

5. _____ you get into that car, make sure you're OK to drive.

6. Jett practiced his piano lessons _____ he learned of the upcoming performance.

7. Playing fantasy football was the perfect distraction _____ Curt vacuumed.

8. _____ you really think it's a good idea, I'll support you.

9. _____ I broke my right arm, I learned to write left-handed.

10. The backyard has resembled a swamp _____ the rain came yesterday.

EDITING PRACTICE 1

Using the four methods of correcting run-ons, rewrite the fused sentences and comma splices below. Use each correction method at least twice. You do not need to keep the clauses in the order given.

1. Ending segregation was the primary victory of the Montgomery bus boycott, the Montgomery Improvement Association originally had other goals.

_____

_____

_____

_____

2. African-Americans had been treated so rudely by some bus drivers they wanted courteous treatment.

_____

_____

_____

_____

3. Additionally, people requested first-come, first-served seating, the current situation was unfair.

_____

_____

_____

_____

4. Finally, the Montgomery Improvement Association requested African-American drivers the buses covered routes through African-American neighborhoods.

_____

_____

_____

_____

5. The desegregation of buses proved to be the greatest victory of all, it affected the most people.

_____

_____

_____

_____

6. Rosa Parks won a great victory for her country, she also won on a personal level.

_____

_____

_____

_____

7. In 1976, 12th Street in Detroit was renamed Rosa L. Parks Boulevard it could honor her.

_____

_____

_____

_____

8. In 1979, Ms. Parks won the Spingarn Medal for her civil rights work this award is given annually by the NAACP for outstanding achievement by an African-American.

_____

_____

_____

_____

_____

9. Ms. Parks was awarded an honorary doctorate from Shaw College she received a similar degree from Wayne State University.

_____

_____

_____

_____

10. Ms. Parks never sought recognition for her courage, others recognized her for it.

_____

_____

_____

_____

EDITING PRACTICE 2

Correct the five run-on sentences in the paragraph below, using the techniques you learned in this chapter. Use each correction technique at least once.

A Group of Heroes

The incorrect portrayal of Rosa Parks as a poor seamstress too tired to give up her seat has several negative implications. First, portraying Parks as being motivated only by fatigue takes away from the heroism of her actions. We can all relate to wanting to sit after a long day, it's hard to imagine starting a revolution just because of being tired. Second, leaving out Parks's involvement with the NAACP makes the Montgomery bus boycott seem spontaneous, almost miraculous. The boycott was not spontaneous it was the result of months of planning. To characterize the boycott as a spur-of-the-moment act detracts from the long-term investment of the organizers. Further, spontaneous mass organization is difficult to achieve, telling a story of a spontaneous mass action makes the story less inspiring who can really imagine pulling off a feat like that so quickly? Finally, portraying Parks as "just" a seamstress takes away from the fact that Parks was part of a team she did not fight this battle alone. It's hard to imagine being a lone rebel in a hostile environment, it's not difficult to imagine being one of the boycott participants.

Lab Activity 35

For additional practice with run-on sentences, complete Lab Activity 35 in the lab manual packaged with your textbook. If you did not receive a lab manual, you can complete this activity online at **www.ablongman.com/long.** Click on **College Resources for Writers** and then click on **Activity 35.**

36 Fragments

Though little is known about timekeeping in prehistoric cultures, artifacts and records indicate that people have long been fascinated with measuring and registering time. Tracking celestial bodies served as an early way to mark the passage of time while sundials and water clocks emerged later. Today we remain preoccupied with time: from digital time displays on cell phones and computers to great chiming clocks around the world, we are constantly made aware of passing seconds.

Big Ben

CONDUCT AN INTERVIEW Thanks to watches, clocks, and electronic timing devices for competition, nearly every second of our lives is accounted for. Is this a positive phenomenon? To what extent should we keep track of time? Interview someone about the importance of tracking time in an area of life—such as in work or in spare time, as in watching television—and summarize your findings in a few sentences.

What Is a Fragment?

A **fragment** is an incomplete idea that tries to stand alone as a sentence. Because fragments don't communicate a complete idea, they can be very confusing. Even though we use sentence fragments all the time in speaking, fragments are unacceptable in standard written English. There are three major types of fragments.

- Dependent clause fragments
- Phrase fragments
- Missing-information fragments

Recognizing and Correcting Dependent Clause Fragments

A **dependent clause fragment** is a dependent clause that is not attached to an independent clause. These fragments are easy to recognize because they begin with a dependent word or term. A list of dependent words and terms follows.

Dependent Words and Terms

after	in order that	what	whichever
although	since	whatever	while
because	so that	when	who
before	that	whenever	whoever
even though	though	wherever	whose
how	unless	whether	
if	until	which	

Here are some examples of dependent clause fragments. The dependent words are in bold type.

Incorrect: **Although** early timekeeping devices seem simple. They were surprisingly accurate.

Incorrect: Timekeeping devices were developed in different places. **Because** all cultures desired to track and record time.

The fragments above contain a subject and a verb, so at first glance, they look like sentences. However, the presence of the dependent term—

although, because—turns each statement into a dependent clause. (Try reading each dependent clause by itself, and you'll hear that it sounds incomplete.) Because each dependent clause is not attached to an independent clause, it is a fragment.

There are two primary strategies for eliminating dependent word fragments.

- Attach the fragment to another sentence.
- Turn the fragment into a complete sentence.

Attaching the Fragment to Another Sentence

The easiest way to correct a dependent word fragment is to attach it to another sentence. If a dependent clause comes before an independent clause, you must separate the two clauses with a comma. Look at the corrected versions of the dependent clause fragments in the preceding example.

Correct: **Although** early timekeeping devices seem simple, they were surprisingly accurate.

(The fragment has been attached to the sentence that *follows* it.)

Correct: Timekeeping devices were developed in different places **because** all cultures desired to track and record time.

(The fragment has been attached to the sentence that *precedes* it.)

Eliminating the Dependent Word

A second way to correct dependent clause fragments is this: eliminate the dependent word in the dependent clause, and let the clause stand alone as a complete sentence.

~~Although~~ Early timekeeping devices seem simple. They were surprisingly accurate.

Timekeeping devices were developed in different places. ~~because~~ All cultures desired to track and record time.

In each sentence, the fragment has been corrected by simply eliminating the dependent word. While eliminating the dependent word is an effective way to correct fragments, it can make your writing boring, so use this technique sparingly.

Finding Dependent Words

Sometimes the dependent word is not the first word in a dependent clause. This situation can lead to fragments. Consider the following:

I love this watch. The one <u>that</u> my dad gave me.

In this case, the dependent word *that* is the third word in the fragment. The writer can correct this fragment by simply attaching it to the preceding sentence.

I love this watch, the one that my dad gave me.

When looking for fragments, look for the dependent word at or near the start of the clause. It may not be the very first word.

EXERCISE 1 ATTACHING DEPENDENT CLAUSES TO INDEPENDENT CLAUSES

Correct each of the following dependent clause fragments by attaching it to a sentence that you write. You may add a sentence either before or after the dependent clause.

Example: Whenever Thomas gets hungry, *he eats an avocado.*

1. Although she knows better.

_____

_____

2. Where the wind blows fiercely cold.

_____

_____

3. Because he knew the answer.

_____

_____

4. When I get to the end of my patience.

_____

_____

5. Unless Rodrigo changes his mind soon.

_____

_____

EXERCISE 2 **CORRECTING DEPENDENT CLAUSE FRAGMENTS IN A PARAGRAPH**

Correct the five dependent clause fragments in the following paragraph by using a technique you learned in this chapter. Be sure to use each technique at least once.

Dripping Instead of Ticking

[1]Water clocks were among the earliest timekeepers. [2]That did not depend on the observation of celestial bodies. [3]One of the oldest was found around 1500 B.C. [4]Later named *clepsydras* ("water thief") by the Greeks, these were stone vessels with sloping sides. [5]Which allowed water to drip at a nearly constant rate from a small hole near the bottom. [6]Other clepsydras were cylindrical or bowl-shaped containers designed to slowly fill with water coming in at a constant rate. [7]Markings on the inside surfaces measured the passage of time. [8]As the water level reached them. [9]These clocks were used to determine time at night. [10]Although they may have been used in daylight as

well. [11]Another version consisted of a metal bowl with a hole in the bottom. [12]When placed in a container of water. [13]The bowl would fill and sink in a certain amount of time. [14]Such bowls were still used in North Africa in the twentieth century.

The fragments are found in word groups _____, _____, _____, _____, and _____.

Recognizing and Correcting Phrase Fragments

Phrase fragments are the most common type of fragments. Phrase fragments come in three major forms.

- *-ing* word fragments
- *to* fragments
- extra-information fragments

Correcting *-ing* Verb Fragments

An *-ing* fragment is a phrase that begins with the *-ing* form of a verb. Some examples follow.

Incorrect: Built as early as 3500 B.C., obelisks (slender, tapering, four-sided monuments) cast shadows. **Enabling** people to divide the day into morning and afternoon.

Incorrect: To determine day length, obelisks also used the noon shadow. **Telling** which days were shortest or longest.

Incorrect: Egyptian shadow clocks or sundials were used. **Dividing** a sunlit day into ten parts and two "twilight hours" in the morning and evening.

Notice that the phrases that contain the *-ing* words do not make sense all by themselves.

There are two ways to correct fragments beginning with *-ing* words.

- Attach the *-ing* phrase to the sentence before or after it.
- Turn the *-ing* phrase into a sentence by adding a subject and changing the *-ing* word to the correct verb form.

Attaching the *-ing* Phrase to a Sentence   An easy way to correct a phrase fragment is to attach it to a nearby sentence. The phrase can be attached to the beginning or end of the sentence, or it can be built into the sentence, as in the third example below.

> Built as early as 3500 B.C., obelisks (slender, tapering, four-sided monuments) cast shadows, **enabling** people to divide the day into morning and afternoon.
>
> (The fragment has been attached to the sentenced that *precedes* it.)
>
> To determine day length, obelisks also used the noon shadow, **telling** which days were shortest or longest.
>
> (The fragment has been attached to the sentenced that *precedes* it.)
>
> **Dividing** a sunlit day into ten parts and two "twilight hours" in the morning and evening, Egyptian shadow clocks or sundials were used.
>
> (The fragment has been moved and attached to the sentence that *precedes* it. It could also be attached to the end of the preceding sentence.)

Turning the *-ing* Phrase into a Sentence   Another way to correct an *-ing* word fragment is to turn the *-ing* phrase into a sentence. There are two steps: (1) add a subject to the *-ing* phrase, and (2) change the *-ing* word to its proper verb form. In the examples that follow, the added subject is in bold type and the new verb is underlined.

> Built as early as 3500 B.C., obelisks (slender, tapering, four-sided monuments) cast shadows. **They** <u>enabled</u> people to divide the day into morning and afternoon.
>
> (*Enabling* has been changed to *They enabled.*)
>
> To determine day length, obelisks also used the noon shadow. **It** <u>told</u> which days were shortest or longest.
>
> (*Telling* has been changed to *It told.*)
>
> Egyptian shadow clocks or sundials were used. **They** <u>divided</u> a sunlit day into ten parts and two "twilight hours" in the morning and evening.
>
> (*Dividing* has been changed to *they divided.*)

The two methods do not work equally well for all fragment corrections. In particular, it's often more effective to turn a fragment with *being* into a sentence with the verb *is* or *are.*

> **Incorrect:**   People today use timepieces other than sundials. Being less efficient as, say, quartz clocks.
>
> **Correct:**   People today use timepieces other than sundials since they *were* less efficient than, say, quartz clocks.

Correcting *to* Fragments

To fragments, also called **infinitive fragments,** are easy to recognize. They begin with an infinitive—the word *to* followed by a verb. For more on infinitives, see Chapter 33.

Incorrect: A regular, constant or repetitive process or action is necessary in a clock. <u>To mark</u> equal increments of time.

To correct this fragment, attach it to the sentence before or after it, just as you would do to correct an *-ing* fragment.

Correct: A regular, constant or repetitive process or action is necessary in a clock <u>to mark</u> equal increments of time.

EXERCISE 3 CORRECTING *-ING* AND *TO* FRAGMENTS

Correct the *-ing* and *to* fragments in the following paragraph by crossing out the mistakes and writing the corrections above the original wording. You may need to change verbs or other words.

Minute Progress

In Europe during most of the Middle Ages (roughly A.D. 500 to 1500), little was done to improve clocks. Progressing very slowly in terms technology and accuracy. Sundial styles evolved, but they didn't move far from ancient Egyptian principles. During these times, simple sundials placed above doorways were used. To identify midday and four "tides" of the sunlit day. By the tenth century, several types of pocket sundials offered convenience. Being used frequently outside the home. In the fourteenth century, large mechanical clocks arrived, Appearing in the towers of several large Italian cities. These public clocks were fueled by weight and balance. To operate the mechanism. This type of mechanism reigned for more than three hundred years with several variations. However, all had the same basic problem. Being difficult to regulate. In Germany between 1500 and 1510, another advance was the invention of spring-powered clocks. Replacing the heavy drive weights with springs. To permit smaller (and portable) clocks and watches. These timepieces were popular among wealthy individuals. Owing to their size and the fact that they could be set down instead of hung. However, they had only an hour hand, and there was no glass protection. Coming in the seventeenth century. Still, these advances in design were precursors to truly accurate timekeeping.

Correcting Extra-Information Phrases

A third type of phrase that sometimes ends up as a fragment is the **extra-information phrase.** Such phrases contain details that contribute meaning to the subject of another sentence, usually the previous one. Certain words often begin the extra-information phrases.

Words That Often Begin Extra-Information Phrases

also	for instance	like
especially	for one	such as
except	from	
for example	including	

Note: A fragment that begins with *including* is an *-ing* fragment as well as an extra-information fragment. Since you can correct these two types of fragments the same way, don't worry about deciding which type of fragment an *including* fragment is.

In the examples that follow, the terms introducing the extra-information phrases are underlined.

Incorrect: The variety of clocks available is amazing. <u>Especially</u> if you're considering older types that are no longer commonly used.

Incorrect: Because of the multitude of different timepieces, clockmakers must be able to fix many types of clocks. <u>Including</u> grandfather and cuckoo clocks.

The information provided in the fragments is interesting and necessary for specific communication. However, because these details appear in fragments, the reader will have difficulty understanding how they relate to the rest of the information provided.

Two main strategies can help you correct extra-information fragments.

- Attach the fragment to the sentence before or after it.
- Turn the fragment into a sentence by adding a subject and verb.

Attaching the Fragment to the Sentence Before or After It

When attaching an extra-information fragment to the previous sentence, remember to use a comma.

Because of the multitude of timepieces, clock repair businesses must be able to fix many types of clocks, <u>including</u> grandfather and cuckoo clocks.

(The fragment is attached to the previous sentence.)

The variety of clocks available is amazing, <u>especially</u> if you're considering older types that are no longer commonly used.

(The fragment is attached to the previous sentence.)

Turning the Fragment into a Sentence
You can correct an extra-information fragment by turning it into a sentence. There are two ways to do this: (1) add a subject and a verb to the fragment, or (2) revise to make it a sentence.

Because of the multitude of timepieces, clock repair businesses must be able to fix many types of clocks. These **types** <u>include</u> grandfather and cuckoo clocks.

(The writer has added a subject to the fragment and has revised the verb to make a sentence.)

The variety of clocks available is amazing. The variety is especially impressive if you're considering older types that are no longer commonly used.

(The fragment has been revised to be its own sentence.)

EXERCISE 4 CORRECTING EXTRA-INFORMATION FRAGMENTS

Revise the following paragraph by correcting the extra-information fragments. Cross out each error and write the correction above it.

Shaving the Seconds

Many improvements in timekeeping have helped humans measure time more accurately. Including great strides made over the last three hundred years. In 1656 a Dutch scientist used the first pendulum clock to drastically reduce the error factor. From minutes per day to seconds. Eventually, this type of clock became even more accurate. Especially when its error became less than ten seconds per day. The same Dutch scientist developed a balance wheel and spring assembly. That resembled those still found in some clocks today. Additionally, improvements in pendulum clocks in London provided even greater accuracy. In some cases, losing less than a second per day.

Recognizing and Correcting Missing-Information Fragments

The last type of fragment is the **missing-information fragment.** This type of fragment leaves out an essential part of a sentence. The result is an incomplete idea. Missing-information fragments, like the one below, usually lack a subject.

Incorrect: The quartz clock revolutionized timekeeping in the mid-twentieth century. And <u>provided</u> an excellent, inexpensive means of monitoring time.

(The fragment contains no subject for the verb *provided*.)

Sometimes, however, missing-information fragments lack a verb.

Incorrect: Quartz clocks operate by causing a quartz crystal to vibrate to produce an electric signal. And the **electronic clock display's source of power.**

(The fragment is missing a verb for the subject *electronic clock display's source of power.*)

Missing-information fragments are easy to correct. Simply use the same techniques that you've used throughout this chapter to correct other types of fragments.

- Attach the fragment to the sentence before it.
- Add the missing information to the fragment and turn it into a complete sentence.

Attaching the Fragment to the Sentence Before It

Attaching the fragment to the sentence before it brings about the following results:

The quartz clock revolutionized timekeeping in the mid-twentieth century <u>and provided an excellent, inexpensive means of monitoring time</u>.
(The fragment has become part of the preceding sentence.)

Quartz clocks operate by causing a quartz crystal to vibrate to produce an electric signal<u>, which is the electronic clock display's source of power</u>.
(The fragment has become part of the preceding sentence.)

Turning the Fragment into a Sentence

You can also provide the missing information to turn a fragment into a complete sentence.
Note: While this option lets you write correct sentences, it can make your writing less interesting, so be careful not to overuse this technique.

The quartz clock revolutionized timekeeping in the mid-twentieth century. **It** provided an excellent, inexpensive means of monitoring time.
(The writer added the subject *It* to make the sentence complete.)

Quartz clocks operate by causing a quartz crystal to vibrate to produce an electric signal. **This signal** is the electronic clock display's source of power.
(The writer added the subject *This signal* to make the fragment a complete sentence.)

EXERCISE 5 CORRECTING MISSING-INFORMATION FRAGMENTS

Use the techniques you learned in this chapter to correct the missing-information fragments in the following paragraph. Cross out each error and write the correction above it, using each technique at least once. The fragments are in bold type.

The Sound of Time

Although many people today wake to the sound of pop music or loud buzzing, early clock sounds were more pleasant. And had interesting stories. For instance, the famous Westminster chime, though originally fitted for University Church in Cambridge, England, is often associated with London's Big Ben at the Houses of Parliament. And is thought to offer all or part of a prayer with every quarter-hour chime. Another chime comes from one of Beethoven's compositions. And uses the first eight measures of his hymn "Joyful, Joyful, We Adore Thee." Some other popular chimes include "God Bless America." And "America the Beautiful." These chimes provide rich, melodious signs of the passing daytime hours. And comfort during the long nights.

EDITING PRACTICE 1

The following paragraph contains several fragments. Underline each fragment, and then correct it using one of the techniques from this chapter.

Sailing Through Time

Ships' bell clocks are a particular type of nautical clock. Having a rich history. Dating back hundreds of years. The particular chimes, or bell strikes, are specially designed. To let sailors know the start and finish of their shifts. Which are generally four hours in duration. The clock strikes eight times at 4:00, 8:00, and 12:00. And then counts each half hour with bell strikes. For example, striking eight times at 4:00. Which lets sailors know that their shift is over. Then the clock strikes once at 4:30, twice at 5:00, three times at 5:30, four times at 6:00, five times at 6:30, six times at 7:00, and seven times at 7:30. Repeating again at 8:00 with eight strikes. This cycle is followed by the counting of the half hours with bell strikes until 12:00. When another eight strikes are produced. Still used today, this method of time indication is unique. As well as meaningful for those who live by it.

EDITING PRACTICE 2

Using the techniques you learned in this chapter, turn the following fragments into complete sentences.

Example: Beginning the long walk home

Beginning the long walk home, *Maddie wrapped her scarf tightly around her neck.*

1. As well as being intelligent _____

2. Trying his best to make the team _____

3. Before they left the crime scene _____

4. To put himself in her shoes _____

5. When everything improves at school _____

6. Understanding that she had lost the opportunity _____

7. Without even muttering "Good night" _____

8. To be the same person as he was before _____

9. Although Eduardo didn't even try _____

10. And many other people, too _____

EDITING PRACTICE 3

Correct the seven fragments in the paragraph below, using the techniques you learned in this chapter. Do not use the same technique for every correction.

Timely Tales

[1]Clocks are generally regarded as tools to help us. [2]Although they have a rich literary side as well. [3] In the fairy tale "Cinderella," who can forget the clock at midnight. [4]Striking twelve to end Cinderella's night at the ball? [5]Another important clock comes from the science fiction story "When the Clock Strikes" by Tanith Lee. [6]Every hour bringing a different figure to the front of the chiming clock. [7]And ending with the robed form of Death at midnight. [8]In Edgar Allan Poe's story "The Masque of the Red Death," an eerie clock causes discomfort. [9]Among guests at the Prince Prospero's elaborate ball. [10]In poetry, clocks play a central role. [11]As in Henry Wadsworth Longfellow's poem "The Old Clock on the Stairs." [12]Which seems to echo the words *never* and *forever* throughout the verse. [13]Emily Dickinson also used clocks in her poems. [14]Such as the poem

"Consulting Summer's Clock." [15]Finally, the children's nursery rhyme "Hickory Dickory Dock" immortalizes a clock. [16]And the mouse who runs up it. [17]We may never have enough time to read. [18]But we have many opportunities to read about time.

The fragments are found in word groups _____, _____, _____, _____, _____, _____, _____, _____, _____, and _____.

Lab Activity 36

For additional practice with fragments, complete Lab Activity 36 in the lab manual packaged with your textbook. If you did not receive a lab manual, you can complete this activity online at **www.ablongman.com/long.** Click on **College Resources for Writers** and then click on **Activity 36.**

37 Regular Verbs

CULTURE NOTE *Glass*

The product of fire-heated sand containing a high silica content, glass was first produced intentionally by humans in bead form around 1000 B.C. Now found almost everywhere we look, glass protects us from the elements, eases our daily lives, and beautifies our homes and persons.

Man Blowing Glass

SURF THE NET Though we may be aware of many everyday uses for glass, it has other, less-known uses as well. Surf the Internet for other ways glass is used. Some concepts to consider are: fiberglass, fiber-optics, insulation, magnification. Write a few sentences summarizing what you learn.

587

The Principal Parts of Regular Verbs

Most verbs in English are **regular verbs,** which means they follow the same pattern in their principal parts. For instance, the past tense of regu-

Four Principal Parts of Verbs

Present Tense

The **present tense** of a verb is the form seen in the dictionary: *like, kiss, tap.* The present tense allows us to communicate actions that occur *now,* that are ongoing, or that are generally true.

Action occurs now: I <u>like</u> chocolate.
Action is ongoing: I <u>kiss</u> my mom when I see her.
Action is generally true: Nervous people often <u>tap</u> their fingers.

Past Tense

The **past tense** indicates actions that occurred before now. The past tense consists of the present tense plus *-d* or *-ed: liked, kissed, tapped.*

Action that occurred before now: I <u>liked</u> my fifth grade teacher.
Action that occurred before now: As a toddler, Amy <u>kissed</u> her reflection in the mirror.
Action that occurred before now: I <u>tapped</u> the peg into place with my hammer.

Past Participle

The **past participle** is often the same as the past tense form. It consists of the present plus *-d* or *-ed: liked, kissed, tapped.* It works with forms of *have* or *be* or can be used alone as a modifier.

Past participle with a form of *be:*   I <u>was liked</u> by my soccer coach.
Past participle with a form of *have:*   I <u>have kissed</u> many frogs in my search for a prince.
Past participle as a modifier: The <u>tapped</u> phone conversation led to Mick's arrest.

Present Participle

The **present participle** consists of the present tense plus *-ing: loving, jumping, picking.* It works either with forms of *be,* as a modifier, or as a noun.

Present participle with a form of *be:*   I <u>am liking</u> every second of this movie.
Present participle as a modifier: "The <u>kissing</u> disease" is another name for mononucleosis.
Present participle as a noun: <u>Tapping</u> your foot constantly can be annoying.

English Verb Tenses

Verbs in the English language can take twelve forms. Consider the forms of the verb *talk*.

Present:	I <u>talk</u> to Mona daily.
Past:	She <u>talked</u> to Mona yesterday.
Future:	They <u>will talk</u> to Mona tomorrow.
Present perfect:	I <u>have talked</u> to Mona daily since last week.
Past perfect:	He <u>had talked</u> to Mona weekly before that.
Future perfect:	They <u>will have talked</u> to Mona seven days straight tomorrow.
Present progressive:	I <u>am talking</u> to Mona as I write this.
Past progressive:	She <u>was talking</u> to Mona yesterday as I cooked dinner.
Future progressive:	They probably <u>will be talking</u> to Mona the next time you call.
Present perfect progressive:	I <u>have been talking</u> to Mona for the past fifteen minutes.
Past perfect progressive:	He <u>had been talking</u> to Mona until you interrupted them.
Future perfect progressive:	They <u>will have been talking</u> to Mona before you even call.

lar verbs is formed by adding *-d* or *-ed* to the present tense. All verbs have four **principal parts:** present, past, past participle, and present participle. These four parts help us create all the different verb tenses—the forms of the verb—which tell us the time and condition under which the action of the verb takes place. For example, for the verb *to love*, the principal parts are *love, loved, loved,* and *loving.* Here are some more examples of the four verb forms.

Principal Parts of Regular Verbs

Present	Past	Past Participle	Present Participle
burn	burn<u>ed</u>	burn<u>ed</u>	burn<u>ing</u>
try	tri<u>ed</u>	tri<u>ed</u>	try<u>ing</u>
melt	melt<u>ed</u>	melt<u>ed</u>	melt<u>ing</u>
decorate	decorat<u>ed</u>	decorat<u>ed</u>	decorat<u>ing</u>
shape	shap<u>ed</u>	shap<u>ed</u>	shap<u>ing</u>

Forming the Tenses of Regular Verbs

Knowing when things happen is important. If you're explaining to your boss that you need a day off tomorrow for a doctor's appointment but then say, "My appointment *was* Friday," your boss will wonder why you need time off for an appointment that already occurred. The simple switch from *is* (present tense) to *was* (past tense) can radically alter your meaning. Thus, understanding the different verb tenses—and knowing how to form them— is crucial to your success as a writer.

Present Tense

The **present tense** of a verb tells a reader that an action is going on right now, as opposed to sometime in the past or future. Form the present tense of regular verbs like this:

- Use the present form in the principal parts for *I, you,* and *they* and other plural subjects.

    I <u>smile</u> every time I hear that song by the Beastie Boys.

    You <u>watch</u> me to make me nervous.

    They <u>cry</u> to get attention.

- Add *-s* or *-es* to the present form if the subject is *he, she, it,* or any singular name. For instance, the following sentences contain verbs ending in *-s* or *-es.* Each action below is going on right now.

    Ginger <u>smiles</u> when she hears her name.

    (The subject is *Ginger;* the present tense verb ends in *-s.*)

    Tracy <u>watches</u> every movie scary movie that comes out.

    (The subject is *Tracy;* the verb ends in *-s.*)

    It <u>cries</u> just like a real baby.

    (The subject is *It;* the verb ends in *-s.*)

Past Tense

The **past tense** of a verb indicates that an action occurred some time in the past. For regular English verbs, the past form (in the principal parts) ends in *-d* or *-ed.* Look at the verbs in the sentences below. Each verb communicates that the action in the sentence already happened.

Last year, I smile<u>d</u> at each setback.

She watch<u>ed</u> the balloon of hot glass expand.

My coaches cri<u>ed</u> when I quit the team.

To create the past tense verb, the writer added -*d* or -*ed* to the present tense form.

 TIP

Remember that if a participle (a word ending in -*ing* or -*ed*) is not preceded by a helping verb, then it cannot be the verb of the sentence.

Recognizing Participles as Adjectives

Even though the term *participle* refers to a verb form, participles can be used as adjectives.

Past Participles as Adjectives

The past participle verb form can serve as an adjective if it follows a linking verb.

Linda looked <u>amazed</u> when she heard the news.

(The adjective *amazed* describes the subject *Linda.*)

The past participle can also be used as an adjective if it comes before a noun.

The <u>faded</u> jeans looked fabulous on him.

(*Faded* describes the subject *jeans.*)

Remember that a participle acts as a verb only if it is accompanied by a helping verb.

Using Present Participles as Adjectives

Like past participles, present participles—verb forms ending in -*ing*—can be used as adjectives.

The <u>living</u> room was dusty.

(The participle *living* serves as an adjective that modifies the preceding noun, *room.*)

Words with Multiple Personalities

One reason being able to identify verb forms is important is that sometimes a word can *look* like a verb but not act like one. See how the word *moving* can serve as three different parts of speech.

Verb Form Used as a Noun

A **gerund** is a verb form that ends in *-ing* and is used as a noun.

Moving to a new home is stressful.

(*Moving* is a noun used as the subject of a sentence.)

Verb Form Used as an Adjective

A **participle** is a verb form ending in *-ing* or *-ed* that can be used as an adjective.

The moving van was crammed with all my stuff.

(Here the word *moving* is acting as an adjective, modifying the noun *van.*)

Verb Form Used as a Verb

A participle can also act as a verb, but only if a helping verb accompanies it.

My pet gerbil is moving with me.

(Here the word *moving* works as the action verb of the sentence; the word *is* is the helping verb.)

Pay attention to whether or not a helping verb is present to determine whether a word is acting as a verb.

EXERCISE 1 WRITING CORRECT REGULAR VERB FORMS

In each blank, write the correct present or past tense form of the verb given in parentheses. You may need to add *-s, -es, -d,* or *-ed* to make the verb form correct.

Helpful Breakthroughs

Glass (appear) _____ in many places in our lives. For

instance, glass windows (protect) _____ us from extreme

weather conditions in our homes, and windshield glass—actually a piece of laminate sandwiched between two pieces of glass—(prevent) _____ us from getting wind and objects in our eyes as we drive. Specially heated, or tempered, glass shows up in the side and rear windows of vehicles. This glass, if made properly, (fracture) _____ into thousands of small glass beads that don't cut human skin. Eyeglasses, or spectacles, (seem) _____ to contain glass; in fact, the term *glasses* (imply) _____ that eyeglasses are made from glass. However, today's eyewear (start) _____ being made from plastic because of the risk of shattering. Finally, glass (act) _____ as a strengthening agent and an insulator in the form of fiberglass. Many glassmakers (experiment) _____ with fiberglass; when adequate machines were developed, glassmakers effectively (create) _____ workable fiberglass.

EDITING PRACTICE Correcting Regular Verb Tense Errors

Read the paragraph below. Then, edit any incorrect verbs by adding *-s* or *-es* for the present tense or *-d* or *-ed* for the past tense. There are fifteen verb errors in all. *Hint:* A verb following *has, have,* or *had* will require a participle form.

Crystal Clear

In addition to making our daily lives easier, glass makes it more beautiful. The term *stained glass* generally refer to glass that has

been color during its manufacturing process. For instance, adding copper to molten glass create green or blue glass. The molten glass is then anneal (heat and cool) slowly in a furnace; this produce sheets of glass. Artists paint intricate details such as shadows on the cooled glass with paint made from metal oxide. The artist then heat the piece in a kiln (a special oven). Crystal is another form of glass that beautify our lives. Another form of glass, lead crystal, is made with lead oxide during its production; it also provide beauty in our lives. The lead in the glass improve the glass's luster (sheen or radiance) while not interfering with its ability to transmit light. Thus, crystal bottle or glasses often store liquids
                                            ∧
with vivid colors, such as wine, and crystal chandeliers delights people. Manufacturers warn people, though, that alcohol cause the lead to leach out of the crystal and contaminate its contents. Lead crystal remain popular as a sign of luxury, but its health risks detract a bit from its beauty. Glass serve many purposes in our lives.
                                    ∧

🔧 Lab Activity 37

For additional practice with regular verbs, complete Lab Activity 37 in the lab manual packaged with your textbook. If you did not receive a lab manual, you can complete this activity online at **www.ablongman.com/long.** Click on **College Resources for Writers** and then click on **Activity 37.**

38 Irregular Verbs

CULTURE NOTE *Poetry*

Though often associated with hard-to-understand language and romantic messages, poetry takes many forms and has many themes. The ancient Greeks wrote—and spoke—poetry as an expression of art; today, people write poetry for nearly every purpose. From the structured Shakespearean sonnet to the exuberant expressions of Walt Whitman and from Mother Goose to Dr. Seuss, poetry has something for everyone.

"The Tyger"

JOURNAL ENTRY Poetry is often thought inaccessible—or difficult to understand—for many people, yet it appears in many places. What experience do you have with poetry? What do you think of it? To what extent to you enjoy reading or writing it? Write a few sentences considering these questions.

The Principal Parts of Irregular Verbs

Even though most English verbs are regular, English also has many irregular verbs. Unlike regular verbs, whose parts are formed the same way for every verb, **irregular verbs** have unpredictable forms for the different tenses. For example, the past tense of *sing* is *sang,* and the past participle is *sung.*

Below is a list of the most common irregular verbs. If you're not sure what the past or past participle of a verb is, check the list below or look in a dictionary to make sure you have the correct form.

Principal Parts of Irregular Verbs

Present	Past	Past Participle	Present Participle
am (are, is)*	was (were, was)	been	being
arise	arose	arisen	arising
awake	awoke *or* awaked	awoke *or* awaked	awaking
become	became	become	becoming
begin	began	begun	beginning
bend	bent	bent	bending
bid	bid	bid	bidding
bite	bit	bitten	biting
blow	blew	blown	blowing
break	broke	broken	breaking
bring	brought	brought	bringing
build	built	built	building
burst	burst	burst	bursting
buy	bought	bought	buying
catch	caught	caught	catching
choose	chose	chosen	choosing
come	came	come	coming
cost	cost	cost	costing
cut	cut	cut	cutting
dive	dived *or* dove	dived	diving

*The infinitive ("to" form) is *to be.*

Present	Past	Past Participle	Present Participle
do (does)	did	done	doing
draw	drew	drawn	drawing
drink	drank	drunk	drinking
drive	drove	driven	driving
eat	ate	eaten	eating
fall	fell	fallen	falling
feed	fed	fed	feeding
feel	felt	felt	feeling
fight	fought	fought	fighting
find	found	found	finding
flee	fled	fled	fleeing
fly	flew	flown	flying
forget	forgot	forgot *or* forgotten	forgetting
freeze	froze	frozen	freezing
get	got	got *or* gotten	getting
give	gave	given	giving
go (goes)	went	gone	going
grow	grew	grown	growing
hang (suspend)	hung	hung	hanging
have (has)	had	had	having
hear	heard	heard	hearing
hide	hid	hidden	hiding
hold	held	held	holding
hurt	hurt	hurt	hurting
keep	kept	kept	keeping
know	knew	known	knowing
lay	laid	laid	laying
lead	led	led	leading
leave	left	left	leaving
lend	lent	lent	lending
let	let	let	letting
lie	lay	lain	lying

(continued)

Present	Past	Past Participle	Present Participle
lose	lost	lost	losing
make	made	made	making
meet	met	met	meeting
pay	paid	paid	paying
ride	rode	ridden	riding
ring	rang	rung	ringing
rise	rose	risen	rising
run	ran	run	running
say	said	said	saying
see	saw	seen	seeing
sell	sold	sold	selling
set	set	set	setting
send	sent	sent	sending
shake	shook	shaken	shaking
shrink	shrank	shrunk	shrinking
shut	shut	shut	shutting
sing	sang	sung	singing
sink	sank *or* sunk	sunk	sinking
sit	sat	sat	sitting
sleep	slept	slept	sleeping
slide	slid	slid	sliding
speak	spoke	spoken	speaking
spend	spent	spent	spending
spring	sprang *or* sprung	sprung	springing
stand	stood	stood	standing
steal	stole	stolen	stealing
stick	stuck	stuck	sticking
sting	stung	stung	stinging
swear	swore	sworn	swearing
swim	swam	swum	swimming
swing	swung	swung	swinging
take	took	taken	taking
teach	taught	taught	teaching
tear	tore	torn	tearing

Present	Past	Past Participle	Present Participle
tell	told	told	telling
think	thought	thought	thinking
throw	threw	thrown	throwing
wake	woke *or* waked	woken *or* waked	waking
wear	wore	worn	wearing
win	won	won	winning
write	wrote	written	writing

Recognizing Participles as Adjectives

Even though the term *participle* refers to a verb form, participles can be used as adjectives. In the following sentence, the present participle form of an irregular verb is used as an adjective.

The <u>ringing</u> phone woke Sid from his nap.

(The present participle of *ring—ringing*—modifies *phone.*)

In the following sentences, the past participle forms of irregular verbs are used as adjectives.

Walter hid the <u>stolen</u> goods in his backback.

(The past participle of *steal—stolen*—modifies *goods.*)

The <u>worn</u> coat did little to keep her warm.

(The past participle of *wear—worn*—modifies *coat.*)

The Big Three: *To Be, To Do,* and *To Have*

The three irregular verbs that routinely give writers the most trouble are three of the most common verbs: *to be, to do,* and *to have.* The easiest way to avoid errors with these three verbs is to memorize their correct verb forms.

Principal Parts

Once you've memorized the correct verb forms of *to be, to do,* and *to have,* you will be surprised at how often they appear in your writing.

To Be

Present	Past	Past Participle	Present Participle
am, is, are	was, were	been	being

To Do

Present	Past	Past Participle	Present Participle
do, does	did	done	doing

To Have

Present	Past	Past Participle	Present Participle
have, has	had	had	having

Tenses

Since *to be, to do,* and *to have* are irregular verbs, their tenses take unpredictable forms.

Present Tense of *To Be*

Subject	Verb
I	am
you	are
he, she, it	is
we	are
you (plural)	are
they	are

Past Tense of *To Be*

Subject	Verb
I	was
you	were

he, she, it	was
we	were
you (plural)	were
they	were

Notice that for *to be,* the past tense changes depending on the subject.

Present Tense of *To Do*

Subject	Verb
I	do
you	do
he, she, it	does
we	do
you (plural)	do
they	do

Past Tense of *To Do*

Subject	Verb
I	did
you	did
he, she, it	did
we	did
you (plural)	did
they	did

Present Tense of *To Have*

Subject	Verb
I	have
you	have
he, she, it	has
we	have
you (plural)	have
they	have

Past Tense of *To Have*

Subject	Verb
I	had
you	had
he, she, it	had
we	had
you (plural)	had
they	had

Avoiding Common Errors with Irregular Verbs

People often use incorrect verb forms when speaking informally. Be careful not to use the following expressions.

Incorrect	**Correct**
I be	I **am**
He don't	He **doesn't**
She have	She **has**

These expressions are not considered acceptable in standard written English, and they can hurt your credibility as a speaker and a writer.

EXERCISE 1 USING CORRECT IRREGULAR VERB FORMS

In each blank, write the correct form of the irregular verb given in parentheses. The first one has been done for you.

Short and Sweet

During my childhood, my parents (make) _____*made*_____ me

write poetry, and I (find) _____ that I prefer short poems.

In fact, there (be) _____ really only three types of poems I

like: the epigram, the couplet, and haiku. An epigram is a short and

witty poem dealing with a single thought or event and often ending with a clever idea. For instance, the Roman epigrammatist (epigram

writer) Martial (write) _____ the following:

    You're rich and young, as all confess,

    And none denies your loveliness;

    But when we hear your boastful tongue

    You're neither pretty, rich, nor young.

This poem (be) _____ just twenty-five words, and it (send)

_____ a message I understand. Another favorite form of

poetry that (come) _____ to mind is the couplet. This form

(have) _____ two lines of verse that usually rhyme and

communicate a complete thought or unit. The poem "The Night

Before Christmas" is (write) _____ in a series of couplets.

The famous opening lines, for example, (read) _____:

"'Twas the night before Christmas and all through the house, / Not

a creature was stirring, not even a mouse." These nineteen words on

a topic that I can relate to, Christmas, (catch) _____ my

attention years ago. Finally, haiku (be) _____ my favorite

type of poetry. It (have) _____ a Japanese origin, three

lines, and just seventeen syllables in every poem. Here is my latest

effort.

    Cheese after six months

    under my family-room couch

    smells and looks awful.

I have never (think) _____ myself a poet, but even I

(do) _____ haiku.

EDITING PRACTICE

Circle the correct verb forms in parentheses in the paragraph below.

Rhyming from the Start

Poetry (is, are) often very serious, detailing war, pestilence, and
death. However, just as poetry (brings, brought) serious themes to
readers, it also (have, has) a lighter side. Three types of children's
poems—Mother Goose rhymes, Shel Silverstein's poems, and
Theodore Geisel's (Dr. Seuss's) books—(show, shown) readers the
funny side of rhyme. Traditional nursery rhymes, credited to Mother
Goose, often (let, letting), children see silliness in the bedtime routine. For instance, the rhyme "Diddle, Diddle Dumpling" (told, tells)
the story of a boy who (goes, go) to bed wearing his pants and one
shoe. Poet Shel Silverstein also (written, writes) about everyday happenings, but with a silly twist. His poem "Chester" is a good example. In it, a boy (grows, grown) a second head and (have, has) to face
his teacher. Finally, Dr. Seuss has (made, making) an art of writing—
and rhyming—about ridiculous situations. The poem "Too Many
Daves," for instance, tells how Mrs. McCave has (naming, named) all of
her twenty-three sons Dave but (paying, pays) the consequences for
this, wishing she had instead given them different names such as
"Sneepy" and "Soggy Muff." Though lists of great poetry usually
(leaving, leave) out these three groups of rhymes, Mother Goose,
Shel Silverstein, and Dr. Seuss all (give, given) kids a chance to love
poetry from their earliest years.

⬛Lab Activity 38

For additional practice with irregular verbs, complete Lab Activity 38 in the
lab manual packaged with your textbook. If you did not receive a lab manual, you can complete this activity online at **www.ablongman.com/long.**
Click on **College Resources for Writers** and then click on **Activity 38.**

39 Subject-Verb Agreement

Black Holes

Areas in space where the gravitational pull is so strong that even light cannot escape from them, black holes fascinate us. Scientists believe that black holes are formed by large explosions of stars, called supernovas, which force the matter of a star into an extremely small space. Since nothing humans have yet encountered is believed to be able to escape a black hole—not even light—the mysteries of these phenomena remain untested and unexplained.

Stephen Hawking

The Origin of the Universe
Stephen Hawking

FOOD FOR THOUGHT Focusing his energies and attention on understanding black holes, physicist Stephen Hawking has become famous for explaining his theories in everyday language. What mysteries of our earth or universe do you wish to understand better? Write a few sentences about some earthly or space-related phenomenon—volcanoes, earthquakes, solar heat, for instance—that interests you.

Understanding Subject-Verb Agreement

For sentences to make sense, subjects and verbs have to agree with each other. This means that if a subject is **singular** and deals with one person only, then the verb should reflect an action by one person. Also, if the subject is **plural** and deals with more than one person, then the verb must reflect action by more than one person. The subjects and verbs in the following sentences reflect the same numbers. For more on subjects and verbs, see Chapter 33.

> **Einstein** <u>was</u> a great physicist.
>
> (The subject *Einstein* indicates a single person, and the verb *was* indicates action by one person. If the subject were plural, the verb would need to be *were* to reflect more than one person as the subject.)
>
> Experienced **scientists** <u>remain</u> baffled by black holes.
>
> (The plural subject *scientists* matches the plural verb *remain*. If the subject were *A scientist,* the verb would need to be *remains.*)

Subject-verb agreement—meaning that the subject and verb reflect the same number—is one of the most important grammar skills you can master. The good news is, subject-verb agreement is usually simple when the subject and verb are close to each other. However, errors in subject-verb agreement can happen in the following cases.

- Words come between the subject and the verb.
- The verb comes before the subject.
- The subject has two or more parts.
- The sentence contains an indefinite pronoun.

Agreement When Words Come Between the Subject and the Verb

Sometimes when words come between the subject and verb, it's hard to decide what the subject of a sentence is. Remember that a prepositional phrase coming between the subject and verb is *not* the subject. In the sentences below, the subject is in bold type and the verb is underlined.

> Different **aspects** of black holes <u>make</u> them interesting to study.
>
> (The subject *aspects* is plural, so the verb *make* must also be plural.)
>
> Black **holes** featured in fiction <u>inspire</u> readers to learn about them.

Note: When the verb has both a helping verb and a main verb, the helping verb changes to agree with the subject.

Scientists <u>are working</u> to answer as many space questions as they can.

(The subject *Scientists* is plural. Thus, the helping verb *are* must be plural also.)

Some **phenomena,** such as black holes, <u>have inspired</u> interest outside of strictly scientific circles.

(The plural subject *phenomena* agrees with the helping verb *have.*)

When subjects are joined by *either . . . or, neither . . . nor,* or *not only . . . but also,* the verb must agree with the subject that is closest to it.

Not only **other galaxies** *but also* the **Milky Way** <u>has</u> black holes at the center.

(Even though *other galaxies* are part of the subject, *Milky Way* is the one that agrees with the verb since it's closer.)

Neither **astronomy** *nor* **physics** completely <u>explains</u> the mystery of black holes.

(Even though the subject has two parts—*astronomy* and *physics*—the conjunction *nor* makes the subject singular. Thus, the verb *explains* must also be singular.)

EXERCISE 3 **MAKING VERBS AGREE WITH SUBJECTS HAVING MORE THAN ONE PART**

Circle the correct form of each verb in parentheses.

1. Answering questions or explaining a theory (keep, keeps) astronomers busy.

2. For instance, the issues of life span and gravity (surround, surrounds) the topic of black holes.

3. Not only a star but also black holes (have, has) a finite life.

4. However, the incredible length of a black hole's life and its relative lack of threat to the earth (make, makes) it interesting but not frightening.

5. Neither astronomers nor my eighth grade brother (is, are) willing to stop studying black holes, though.

Agreement When the Sentence Contains an Indefinite Pronoun

An **indefinite pronoun** is a pronoun that does not refer to a specific person or thing. Even though the following indefinite pronouns often refer to more than one person, they usually take singular verbs.

Indefinite Pronouns That Take Singular Verbs

anybody	either	neither	none	somebody
anyone	everybody	no one	nothing	someone
anything	everyone	nobody	one	something
each	everything			

Using a Singular Pronoun with *Everyone* and *Everybody*

Do not use the pronoun *they* to agree with *everyone* and *everybody*. Even though these words seem as if they should be plural, they are singular.

Anyone who wants his or her questions answered <u>is</u> welcome to ask me.
(The subject *anyone* takes a singular pronoun such as *his* or *her*.)

Everyone at the lecture wanted his or her program signed.
(The subject *everyone* takes a singular pronoun such as *his* or *her*.)

Some indefinite pronouns require plural verbs.

Indefinite Pronouns That Take Plural Verbs

both
few
many
several

Few classmates <u>share</u> my fascination with black holes.

(The subject *few* requires a plural verb *share*.)

EXERCISE 4 MAKING VERBS AGREE WITH INDEFINITE PRONOUNS

Circle the correct form of each verb in parentheses.

1. Nothing about black holes (is, are) boring to my sister Nicki.

2. Of all her books, none (wear, wears) out faster than her science books.

3. Of course, everyone (knows, know) that she just wants to be like me.

4. Anything Nicki studies (comes, come) from my vast stack of reading materials.

5. Everyone (know, knows) that my personality is worth emulating, especially my humility.

EDITING PRACTICE 1

Circle the correct form of each verb in parentheses.

Suction or Sponge?

(Has, Have) you ever had to vacuum the carpet? You may have noticed that dust and dirt (move, moves) toward the vacuum cleaner. A black hole—similar to a vacuum cleaner—cleans up debris left behind in outer space. What (is, are) the power that causes things to fall into a black hole? Suction is not the factor. Instead, a black hole uses the power of gravity to pull things toward it. When a large star (run, runs) out of fuel, it can no longer support its heavy weight. The pressure from the star's hydrogen layers (forces, force) the star to shrink, becoming smaller and smaller. Eventually the star (shrinks, shrink) to become smaller than an atom. This process—or its results—(is, are) similar to having a sponge fully compressed between your hands. From this "squishing" process (come, comes) increased gravity as the item becomes smaller. A massive star collapsed to a tiny size, then, (has, have) incredible gravity, trapping everything—even light—that gets too close. Even with this simple explanation, black holes and their mysteries (continues, continue) to interest people all over the world.

EDITING PRACTICE 2

The following paragraph contains sixteen errors in subject-verb agreement. Cross out the incorrect verbs, and write in the correct form of each verb.

Gray Matter Takes On Black Holes

A leading theoretical physicist, British scientist Stephen Hawking is a premier scientific expert. Black holes and the Big Bang theory is his specialty. Everything in a black hole, according to Hawking's earlier research, were destroyed. In 2004, however, Hawking admitted that he were mistaken about black holes. Whereas he once believed all matter to be destroyed once inside a black hole, he professed in 2004 that matter escape from a black hole, but in an unrecognizable form. Further, Hawking is one of many theoretical physicists searching for a "theory of everything"— a unified scientific theory that answers such questions as *"How did the universe begin?" "Why is the universe the way it is?"* and *"How will it end?"* Everything are explained in his best-selling book *A Brief History of Time,* which have been translated into thirty-three languages. Why is Hawking's discoveries so remarkable? Aside from the fact that he still make great strides in physics, Hawking has achieved much personally. Diagnosed at age twenty-one with amyotrophic lateral sclerosis (ALS)—a severe nerve disease also known as Lou Gehrig's disease—Hawking continue his work with great success. He get around in a motorized wheelchair, and since losing the use of his vocal chords in 1985, he communicate through a computer. A speech synthesizer speak for him after he punch in what he want to say, selecting words in the computer software by a hand-operated switch. Each of Hawking's discoveries are that much more marvelous considering the physical obstacles he face.

Lab Activity 39

For additional practice with subject-verb agreement, complete Lab Activity 39 in the lab manual packaged with your textbook. If you did not receive a lab manual, you can complete this activity online at **www.ablongman.com/long.** Click on **College Resources for Writers** and then click on **Activity 39.**

40 Verb Tense and Verb Consistency

CULTURE NOTE *Gambling*

Glamorized in entertainment and celebrated as part of recreation, gambling has become a hot topic nationwide with the presence of Native American gambling casinos. What are the games? What are the risks? Is it possible to play a "friendly" game of poker? The myths and the mystique of gambling cloud the issue.

Big Winner?

CONDUCT AN INTERVIEW People gamble for different reasons, some people claiming that betting makes watching various competitions "more interesting." Others say that the lottery is their retirement plan. Why do people gamble? Interview someone you know—preferably someone who gambles or has gambled—about his or her reasons for participating in games of chance. Summarize your findings in a few sentences.

Consistency in Verb Tense

Consistency in verb tense simply means using the same verb tense throughout your writing. If you start a story or example in the past tense, for instance, then you must write your entire paragraph or essay in the past tense.* Otherwise, you send a confusing message to your reader. The following sentences use *inconsistent* verb tense. The verbs are underlined.

Incorrect: Grandma <u>played</u> serious bingo until she <u>loses</u> a round each week.

(The verb *played* is past tense, but the verb *loses* is present tense.)

Incorrect: She <u>tries</u> to win a cuddly pink bear, but it <u>escaped</u> her clutches.

(The verb *tries* is present tense, but the verb *escaped* is past tense.)

These sentences send unclear messages to the reader, who does not know whether the action in the sentences is taking place now or has already taken place. The sentences can be revised two ways.

- Revise to put both verbs in the present tense.

    Grandma <u>plays</u> serious bingo until she <u>loses</u> a round each week.

    She <u>tries</u> to win a cuddly pink bear, but it <u>escapes</u> her clutches.

- Revise to put both verbs in the past tense.

    Grandma <u>played</u> serious bingo until she <u>lost</u> a round each week.

    She <u>tried</u> to win a cuddly pink bear, but it <u>escaped</u> her clutches.

Either revision is fine, but the writer needs to decide on one verb tense and carry that throughout the entire piece of writing.

Note: Inconsistencies in verb tense often occur in pieces of writing that are a paragraph or longer. When proofreading your work for school, be sure to pay close attention to verb tense in your paragraph and essay writing.

*Note: Sometimes longer works require different verb tenses. In these cases, it is important to make sure your verbs are consistent through the specific sections of your work rather than through the whole piece.

Changing Verb Tense

Generally, you should keep your verb tense consistent throughout your sentence, paragraph, or essay. However, there are some instances when you may *need* to switch tenses. When you want to indicate different times in one sentence, use different verb tenses.

> In high school, my buddy <u>gave</u> into gambling; now, however, he <u>is</u> much better at restraining himself.

The verb *gave* indicates that one action took place in the past—in high school—but the verb *is* communicates that the other action is taking place right now.

Another area where you may need to change your verb tense is in discussing the influence of people or events in the past. We often read of people who, though they have died, have current influence on us. For instance, Coach Vince Lombardi still inspires football players to perform well, just as Julia Child inspires chefs. Thus, if we were telling their stories straight through, we would use the past tense to describe their actions that occurred before now. However, even though these actions occurred in the past, their influence on us is *ongoing*. Thus, discussions of people who have died may begin in the present tense to indicate that their stories still have value for us today. For instance, a discussion of Vince Lombardi may begin like this:

> One of the greatest coaching legends in football history, Vince Lombardi <u>continues</u> to affect football coaches and players. Even after he <u>died</u> in 1970, his coaching ideals and philosophy set the standard in football.

The present tense verb *continues* in the first sentence tells us that the influence of Vince Lombardi is still present, while the past tense verb *began* in the second sentence indicates that the beginning of Lombardi's life was in the past.

Verb Tense and Writing About Literature

Writing about literature—poetry, stories, novels—requires that writers use the present tense to discuss the action, even if the works were written years ago. Additionally, writers use the present tense to talk about authors' writing style and technique, even if those authors have died. For instance, we write, "William Shakespeare explores themes of love and revenge in his play *Othello*." Even though Shakespeare wrote this play centuries ago, we still discuss his works as if he were writing them right now.

The reason for this use of present tense comes from the idea that as a story is being read or discovered, its action continues for the readers as they read. No matter how many times we read the same story, it always begins again and follows the same pattern of development. Thus, a story can never be over—and, thus, in the past tense—since to begin the story again requires simply picking it up and reading from the beginning.

EXERCISE 1 USING CONSISTENT VERB TENSE IN A PARAGRAPH

Circle the correct verbs in parentheses in the paragraph below.

A Growing Gamble

In many James Bond movies, Bond appears in an elegant casino, (asks, asked) for a martini, and casually (observes, observed) a villain ruthlessly cheating some unsuspecting soul. When Bond decides to make his presence known, he challenges the bad guy, (used, uses) the cheating mechanism to his own advantage, and wins a fortune he doesn't need. Gambling, however, is not limited to slick secret agents. Wagering (has, had) its roots in the ancient lotteries that first appeared in Burgundy in the fifteenth century. Readily adopted by both the poor, who had little to lose, and the rich, who didn't care if they lost as long as they had fun, gambling (makes, made) a solid start. In time, however, other games came into their own. Poker, blackjack, and craps (rockets, rocketed) to popularity and (inspires, inspired) various forms of entertainment from books to movies. This (occurs, occured) in the United States primarily thanks to Nevada, which made gambling one of its two big industries (divorce was the second) in 1931. Atlantic City (follows, followed), and then reservation casinos brought gambling closer to almost everyone. Now, gambling (was, is) a multibillion-dollar industry and a source of prime-time entertainment. Gambling has indeed come into the mainstream.

EDITING PRACTICE

Rewrite the following paragraph so that the verbs are consistently in present tense throughout. There are twelve errors in verb consistency.

One Lottery You Don't Want to Win

In a small town, a lottery takes place every year. People willingly show up to participate, each family waiting patiently before the process begins. As they wait, the families kept busy, picking up stones and placing them into piles. They chat about the history of the lottery, commenting on the poor towns that gave it up long ago. When the time came for the lottery to begin, a member of each family stepped forward to remove a folded piece of paper from a wooden box. Opening the paper, people visibly sighed with relief if it contains no mark. One man, however, unfolded a piece of paper bearing a black mark, at which point his wife began to complain of the lottery's inherent unfairness. Ignoring her complaints, the organizer placed one piece of paper back into the box for each member of the man's family. Now husband, wife, and children each remove a folded piece of paper. When the wife's paper proved to carry the black mark, she complained ever louder about the lottery. However, her complaints fell on deaf ears as the townspeople picked up stones from the piles, surround her, and killed her. Even this summary of the short story titled "The Lottery" by Shirley Jackson shows that gambling has a downside.

Lab Activity 40

For additional practice with correct and consistent verb tense, complete Lab Activity 40 in the lab manual packaged with your textbook. If you did not receive a lab manual, you can complete this activity online at **www.ablongman.com/long.** Click on **College Resources for Writers** and then click on **Activity 40.**

41 Pronoun Types

Either as part of a police force or as a private investigator, a detective works to solve crimes or find information about people. Many fictitious detectives were made famous through literature, such as Sir Arthur Conan Doyle's ultimately logical Sherlock Holmes or Dashiell Hammett's hardboiled Sam Spade. More recently, television detectives such as quirky Adrian Monk or dry Lennie Briscoe have fed our appetite for crime solvers.

Ageless Sam Spade

OBSERVE YOUR WORLD
Dashiell Hammett's fictional character detective Sam Spade in many ways set the standard for private detectives. Tough, smart, and succinct, Spade not only solved his cases but stayed true to himself as well. What characteristics do contemporary detectives—either in movies, television, or fiction—possess? Pay attention to how detectives are portrayed in entertainment and write a few sentences characterizing them.

Recognizing Pronouns

Pronouns are words that take the place of nouns. They are essential to clear, concise communication because they allow us to substitute a short, easily recognizable word for a longer word or phrase. In this chapter, we focus on the five most common types of pronouns.

- Subject pronouns
- Object pronouns
- Possessive pronouns
- Reflexive pronouns
- Demonstrative pronouns

Subject Pronouns

A **subject pronoun** is the subject of a sentence or clause.

Subject Pronouns

Singular	**Plural**
I, you, he, she, it,	we, you, they

The subject pronouns are underlined in the sentences below.

<u>She</u> completed her police academy training.
(*She* is the subject of the verb *completed*.)
<u>They</u> promoted him early in his career.
(*They* is the subject of the verb *promoted*.)
After Mike took the case, <u>it</u> seemed more complicated than ever.
(*It* is the subject of the verb *seemed*.)

Here are guidelines to help you with correct subject pronoun usage.

- **Use a subject pronoun as part of a compound subject.** (A compound subject has more than one part.)

Incorrect:	Miss Marple and <u>me</u> are interested in crime.
	<u>Us</u> and <u>them</u> need to look at the evidence.

Correct: Miss Marple and <u>I</u> are interested in crime.

                                <u>We</u> and <u>they</u> need to look at the evidence.

If you're not sure which pronoun to use, try reading the sentence using the pronoun by itself as the subject. To say "Me is interested in crime" doesn't sound right, so you know to use the pronoun *I*.

■ Use a subject pronoun after forms of *to be*.

Correct: It was <u>he</u> who committed the murder.

                                It may have been <u>they</u> who witnessed the crime.

                                It was <u>we</u> who discovered the body.

The sentences above may sound strange or artificial, but they are grammatically correct. Even though you can make your point in conversation by using expressions such as "It was him" or "It may have been them," these uses of pronouns are incorrect in standard written English and, thus, should not appear in your writing. If you're not comfortable using subject pronouns after forms of the verb *to be*, simply revise your sentences.

Correct: <u>He</u> committed the murder.

                                <u>They</u> witnessed the crime.

                                <u>We</u> discovered the body.

■ **Use a subject pronoun after *than* or *as*.** When a clause starts with *than* or *as*, a verb is understood to follow the subject pronoun.

Correct: Sherlock Holmes has better logic than <u>I</u>.

                                Miss Marple is less active than <u>she</u>.

                                Joe Friday and Andy Sipowicz act as tough as <u>they</u>.

In these sentences, the same verb is understood to follow the subject pronoun even if it is not written out a second time. To determine what pronoun to use, try silently adding the same verb after the subject pronoun.

Sherlock Holmes has better logic than <u>I</u> *have*.

Miss Marple is less active than <u>she</u> *is*.

Joe Friday and Andy Sipowicz act as tough as <u>they</u> *act*.

If your sentence doesn't make sense when you silently add the verb, you probably need to change your pronoun.

Object Pronouns

An **object pronoun** is the object of a verb or a preposition. (Prepositions are words such as *about, for, behind,* and *to* that relate a noun or pronoun to the rest of a sentence.) An object pronoun can never be the subject of a sentence. A list of object pronouns follows.

Object Pronouns

Singular	**Plural**
me, him, her, you, it	us, them, you

Note that *it* can be either a subject or object pronoun.

In the sentences below, each underlined object pronoun is the object of a preposition.

> After Miss Marple identified Ralph as the killer, the police slapped handcuffs *on* <u>him</u>.
> (*Him* is the object of the preposition *on*.)
> After hearing the family's sad story, we talked *about* <u>it</u>.
> (*It* is the object of the preposition *about*.)

In the following sentences, each underlined object pronoun is the object of a verb.

> The detective *read* <u>me</u> my rights when I was arrested.
> (*Me* is the object of the verb *read*.)
> Philip Marlowe *discovered* <u>him</u> in the shadows.
> (*Him* is the object of the verb *discovered*.)

Mistakes with object pronouns happen when writers aren't sure whether to use a subject pronoun or an object pronoun.

Incorrect: The mayor gave the bravery award to <u>she</u> and <u>I</u>.
The information about the crime came from <u>they</u> and <u>we</u>.
This case provides a great opportunity for <u>you</u> and <u>I</u>.

Correct: The mayor gave the bravery award to <u>her</u> and <u>me</u>.
The information about the crime came from <u>them</u> and <u>us</u>.
This case provides a great opportunity for <u>you</u> and <u>me</u>.

If you can't decide which pronoun to use, try saying the sentence aloud with each pronoun by itself. The pronoun that sounds correct will most likely be the right choice. For instance, "The information about the crime came from *we*" sounds awkward, but "The information about the crime came from *us*" does not.

Identifying Object Pronouns

Because *like* can be a preposition, a pronoun following it should usually be an object pronoun.

I know you want to be like *her*.

Check to see if the pronoun follows a preposition. If so, it's likely to be the object of the preposition.

Can we go camping with *him*?

Check to see if the pronoun follows a verb. If so, it's likely to be an object of the verb.

I haven't seen *her* today.

EXERCISE 1 IDENTIFYING SUBJECT AND OBJECT PRONOUNS

Underline all subject pronouns and circle all object pronouns in the paragraph below. The first sentence has been done for you. You will need to underline sixteen subject pronouns and circle six object pronouns. For the pronoun *it*, see how the word is used and then underline or circle it accordingly.

Life of a Real Private Eye

People often seem impressed when <u>they</u> hear that <u>I</u> am a private investigator or P.I. They imagine me sneaking around after dark, hand on a concealed gun, lying in wait for the bad guys. Actually, I usually work on cases for one particular court-appointed defense attorney, so my job is to find facts for her. This means that I take a lot of photos of crime scenes, talk to family and friends of the accused, and talk to the defendant. The attorney gives me a set of questions to ask, so I follow those. The attorney and I talk about the witnesses and defendant to determine how credible they and he or she seems, as well as who, if anyone, can back up the defendant's story. In addition to finding information about the defendant, I spend time talking to witnesses. I have to ask them questions about their names, occupations, and whereabouts at certain times. People are often disappointed to hear that I don't have to "rough up" people or "tail" witnesses; instead, I just call them, set up a meeting, and take notes in addition to taping all conversations. No, I just do my job with all the routine it offers. Though Lennie Briscoe or Sam Spade might have more glitz in his life, I wouldn't have it any other way.

Possessive Pronouns

A **possessive pronoun** shows possession, that something belongs to someone or something. A list of possessive pronouns follows.

Possessive Pronouns

my	her	your
mine	hers	yours
your	its	their
yours	our	theirs
his	ours	

The possessive pronouns are underlined in the sentences below.

Patrick took great pride in <u>his</u> job.
(*His job* means "the job that belongs to him.")
I thought I'd broken the lamp, but the blame was <u>hers.</u>
(*Hers* means "the blame that belongs to her.")

When you write possessive pronoun, make sure you *never* use an apostrophe. (For more on apostrophes, see page 671.)

Incorrect: The smoking gun was <u>your's</u>.
                     She wants to find a house that's <u>her's</u> alone.

Correct: The smoking gun was <u>yours</u>.
                     She wants to find a house that's <u>hers</u> alone.

EXERCISE 2 USING POSSESSIVE PRONOUNS CORRECTLY

Correct any pronoun errors in the sentences below.

Example: Private investigator movies contain elements that are ~~their's~~ *theirs* alone.

1. For instance, a giant eye on a frosted glass door sends it's own message.

2. Similarly, private investigators' ashtrays filled with lipstick-stained cigarette butts are their's to display.

3. A mystery movie might show the detective's face, but when the distressed woman client enters, we rarely see her's.

4. Instead, we ask ourselves if that gloved hand or hat silhouette are her's.

5. All these elements combine to create a pleasure that is our's.

Pronouns Ending in *-Self* or *-Selves*

Two kinds of pronouns end in *-self* or *-selves*.

- Reflexive pronouns
- Intensive pronouns

Reflexive Pronouns

A **reflexive pronoun** indicates that someone performed an action himself or herself. The reflexive pronouns are underlined in the sentences below.

In serving the public, law enforcement officials are proud of <u>themselves</u>. (*Themselves* refers to *law enforcement officials.*)
The novice detective must prevent <u>herself</u> from making careless mistakes. (*Herself* refers to *novice detective.*)

Avoid using a reflexive pronoun as the subject of a sentence.

Incorrect: My roommate and <u>myself</u> never miss any episode of *Law and Order.*

Correct: My roommate and <u>I</u> never miss any episode of *Law and Order.*

Think of a reflexive pronoun as a *reflection* of the subject. Thus, if the subject is *I*, the correct reflexive pronoun is *myself.* Since you can't have a reflection of an object without the object itself, you shouldn't use a reflexive pronoun—the *reflection* of the subject—without having the subject present.

Intensive Pronouns

An **intensive pronoun** is used for emphasis. It always directly follows the word it refers to.

Adrian Monk <u>himself</u> was pleased when he cracked the case.

(*Himself* emphasizes that Adrian Monk—in addition to others—was pleased with his success.)

We on the police force <u>ourselves</u> have to set a good example. (*Ourselves* emphasizes that *in addition to* other people, we, who are members of the police force, have to set a good example.)

Avoiding Mistakes with Intensive and Reflexive Pronouns

Make sure to form plural intensive pronouns by adding *-selves* rather than *-selfs.*

Incorrect: themselfs, yourselfs, ourselfs
Correct: themselves, yourselves, ourselves

Avoid nonstandard usage of reflexive or intensive pronouns.

Incorrect: hisself, theirselves, meself
Correct: himself, themselves, myself

EXERCISE 3 USING REFLEXIVE AND INTENSIVE PRONOUNS CORRECTLY

Write the correct reflexive or intensive pronoun in each blank below.

1. The suspect _____ did not believe his own story.

2. Thus, the detectives helped _____ by not interrupting him.

3. Interestingly, the district attorney felt obligated to handle the case _____.

Demonstrative Pronouns

A **demonstrative pronoun** singles out a specific item or person. The demonstrative pronouns are *this, that, these,* and *those.*

Demonstrative Pronouns

Singular   Plural
this, that   these, those

In general, use *this* and *these* to indicate something or someone nearby, and use *that* and *those* to indicate something farther away. The demonstrative pronouns, acting as nouns, are underlined in the sentences below.

<u>This</u> was not what I had in mind for vacation.
I'd never do anything as silly as <u>that.</u>
Who would pay more than a few cents for <u>these</u>?
<u>Those</u> are the real thing.

Demonstrative pronouns can be used as adjectives, too. The demonstrative pronouns are underlined in the sentences below.

<u>This</u> case will be hard to solve.
<u>These</u> people don't seem likely suspects.
<u>That</u> activity could get you into trouble.
<u>Those</u> files have been missing for a long time.

Avoid using nonstandard expressions like *this here* and *that there* in your writing. While these sayings may help you effectively communicate your ideas in speech, they not acceptable in standard written English.

EXERCISE 4   USING DEMONSTRATIVE PRONOUNS CORRECTLY

Write the correct demonstrative pronoun in each space provided.

1. _____ old detective stories are the best.

2. For instance, Raymond Chandler's novel *The Simple Art of Murder*

is far more interesting than _____ silly book on my lap.

3. Agatha Christie's works, too, hold my interest more than

_____ mysteries right here.

4. My favorite detective stories, however, are _____ that feature Sherlock Holmes.

5. His inductive and deductive reasoning are stronger than in the

detective's in _____ novel.

EDITING PRACTICE

Circle the correct pronouns in parentheses in the paragraph below.

The Detective's Dance

One of Sherlock Holmes's greatest detective victories comes in the story "The Adventure of the Dancing Men." In (him, it), the following scrawl terrifies Elsie, the young American wife of Mr. Hilton Cubitt. Difficulties arise when Elsie receives a disturbing letter, which (she, her) throws onto the fire. The dancing men then appear, sometimes on a piece of paper left on a sundial overnight, sometimes scrawled in chalk on a wall, a door, even a windowsill. Each time, (theirs, their) appearance has an obvious, terrifying effect on Elsie, but (her, she) will not tell her husband what the letters mean to (she, her). Having promised (his', his) wife never to inquire into a past that is (hers, her's) apart from (he, him), Mr. Cubitt does not ask (she, her) for an explanation. Holmes asks Cubitt for copies of the dancing men message to be sent to (him, he), which Cubitt (him, himself) manages and which provides Holmes with (his, his') most important clue. Only by realizing that (those, that) dancing men are an alphabetical cipher and rushing to the Cubitts' home does Holmes prevent Elsie's death. Eventually, Holmes sends a message of (his, he) own—in dancing-men code, of course—and lures the killer into (he, his) clutches. When Holmes captures (he, him) walking into the Cubitts' home, the killer confesses and gives (his, himself) up. Seeing clues that only (that, he) (hisself, himself) sees, Holmes astounds (this, those) people who are present and saves the day.

Lab Activity 41

For additional practice with pronoun types, complete Lab Activity 41 in the lab manual packaged with your textbook. If you did not receive a lab manual, you can complete this activity online at **www.ablongman.com/long.** Click on **College Resources for Writers** and then click on **Activity 41.**

42 Pronoun Agreement

CULTURE NOTE *Hypnosis*

Widely debated in terms of its existence, purpose, and benefit, hypnosis is generally believed to be a state that resembles sleep but is brought about by another person whose suggestions are readily accepted. Hypnosis is most commonly used for entertainment in shows where the hypnotist places people in a trance and commands them to act uncharacteristically, and it is also used in health fields such as for weight loss or treatment of nicotine addiction. The very fact that hypnosis is used for the disparate purposes of amusement and healing only increases its controversy.

David Copperfield

SURF THE NET What is hypnosis? Who practices or benefits from it? How valid a practice is it? Surf the Internet for information about hypnosis and summarize your findings in a few sentences.

Recognizing Pronoun Agreement

Pronouns must be consistent in number with their **antecedents,** the word or words they replace. Singular antecedents require singular pronouns, just as plural antecedents require plural pronouns. Some examples of correct pronoun usage follow.

Some doctors shake <u>their</u> heads when asked about <u>their</u> practice of hypnotism.

(*Their* refers to *doctors* in both cases.)

The hypnotic process has been questioned nearly <u>its</u> whole life.

(*Its* refers to *process.*)

One physician claims that <u>she</u> willingly practices hypnosis.

(*She* refers to *physician.*)

The next examples show both incorrect and correct pronoun usage.

Incorrect: At the fair, a <u>volunteer</u> can find out if <u>they</u> can be hypnotized.

(*Volunteer* is singular, but the pronoun *they is* plural; the pronoun does not agree with its antecedent.)

Correct: At the fair, a <u>volunteer</u> can find out if <u>he</u> or <u>she</u> can be hypnotized.

(The pronouns *he* and *she* both agree with *volunteer.*)

Incorrect: <u>Everyone</u> in the front row was chosen to try <u>their</u> luck under hypnosis.

(*Everyone* is singular, but *their* is plural.)

Correct: All the <u>people</u> in the front row were chosen to try <u>their</u> luck under hypnosis.

(Note that the verb *were* was changed to match the antecedent *people.*)

Personal Pronouns

A **personal pronoun** refers to a specific person or thing. A list of personal pronouns follows.

Personal Pronouns

I, me, mine, myself

you, your, yours, yourself

he, him, his, himself

she, her, hers, herself

it, its, itself

they, them, their, their, themselves

we, us, our, ours, ourselves

EXERCISE 1 **USING PRONOUNS CORRECTLY**

In each blank, write the correct pronoun from the list on pages 631–632.

Example: Many former smokers credit hypnosis with curing

_____*their*_____ addiction.

1. My roommate Ann never believed that a class could help her quit

   smoking, but she tried _____ anyway.

2. Ann attended a class where _____ listened to a talk and
   received an audio CD.

3. When Ann played _____, she heard a voice telling her that
   she didn't want to smoke.

4. Ann also tried other self-improvement programs, and

   _____ all helped her.

5. Thanks to _____, Ann is nicotine-free and ten pounds
   lighter.

Indefinite Pronouns

The following words, called **indefinite pronouns,** are singular. Indefinite
pronouns do not refer to any specific person or thing.

Common Singular Indefinite Pronouns

anybody	everybody	no one	one
anyone	everyone	nobody	somebody
anything	everything	none	someone
each	neither	nothing	something
either			

Plural Indefinite Pronouns

both	many
few	several

Make sure that when you use an indefinite pronoun as the subject of a sentence, the verb agrees with it. The pronouns that agree with indefinite pronouns must also be singular: *he, him, his, she,* or *her.* If you don't know the gender of *everyone* or *anyone* in a sentence, use the expression *he or she* or *him or her* to include both sexes.

Anyone who thinks hypnosis is harmful has his or her information wrong.

In fact, everyone I know who's tried it thinks he or she is better because of it.

However, neither of my brothers was willing to take his chances with it.

EXERCISE 2 PRACTICE WITH PRONOUN AGREEMENT

Circle the correct pronouns in the sentences below.

1. Everyone undergoing surgery should hear about (his or her, their) options for anesthesia.

2. Often someone chooses chemical painkillers because (they, he or she) doesn't know there are other ways to stop pain.

3. However, during the U.S. Civil War, field doctors had to try something; (they, it) turned out to be hypnosis.

4. Although hypnosis seemed effective in the field, nearly everyone who had access to the anesthetics ether and chloroform found that (he or she, they) could relieve patients' pain more easily than through hypnosis.

5. Currently, someone who has a negative reaction to a chemical pain-killer could have (their, his or her) pain relieved through hypnosis.

Pronoun Reference

Sometimes the antecedent to a pronoun is unclear. The following sentences contain unclear **pronoun references,** pronouns that do not seem to refer to anything in particular.

Unclear: When my brother asked about hypnosis for his insomnia, they told him it could be very effective.

(The pronoun *they* doesn't refer to anyone specific; there is no plural word to act as an antecedent.)

To make the sentence clear, substitute a specific person for *they*.

Clear: When my brother asked a *counselor* about hypnosis, <u>she</u> told him it could be very effective.

Unclear: Troy talked to Vic about <u>his</u> positive experience with hypnosis.

(In this sentence, the reader wonders whose experience— Troy's or Vic's—was positive.)

Clear: Troy talked to Vic about Vic's positive experience with hypnosis.

Clear: Vic told Troy, "I had a positive experience with hypnosis."

Unclear: I tried self-hypnosis for my insomnia, and it is really improving.

(In this case, is self-hypnosis improving? Or is insomnia?)

Clear: I've really improved my self-hypnosis for my insomnia.

Clear: Self-hypnosis has really improved my insomnia.

EXERCISE 3 MAKING CLEAR PRONOUN REFERENCES

Rewrite the following sentences to correct the unclear pronoun references in italics.

1. On the Encyclopedia Britannica Web site, *they* discuss Dave Elman, one of the pioneers of hypnosis in medicine. _____

   _____

2. Elman named the Esdaile state after the work of Dr. James Esdaile. The term describes a state of complete anesthesia, *which* was

   remarkable. _____

   _____

3. Dr. Esdaile had written about instances of this "coma state" in his

   journals. *They* were significant. _____

   _____

4. Elman believed he had found that state that Esdaile had written

about. *He* was fascinated by it. _____

_____

5. Even though the Esdaile state is called the coma state, the patient does not experience unconsciousness, *which* is not actually a coma.

_____

_____

Pronoun Consistency and Point of View

Good writing is clear and consistent in point of view. **Point of view** refers to the perspective of the writer—whether the writer is telling his or her *own* story (first person), telling a story *to* someone (second person), or telling a story *about* someone else (third person).

First person: <u>I</u> wanted to try hypnosis to lose weight.
Second person: <u>You</u> should consider hypnosis to get rid of your headache.
Third person: <u>He</u> seemed more apt to just take an aspirin.

Pronouns should be consistent throughout your writing. For instance, if you start a paragraph using *I*, don't suddenly switch to using *you*. The pronouns determining point of view are as follows:

Point of View	Singular Pronouns	Plural Pronouns
First person	I (me, my, mine, myself)	we (us, our, ourselves)
Second person	you (your, yours, yourself)	you (your, yours, yourselves)
Third person	he (him, his, himself) she (her, hers, herself) it (its, itself) one (one's, oneself)	they (them, their, theirs, themselves)

The pronoun *one* is usually used to mean a single person in general.

Reading through the literature on hypnosis, <u>one</u> could get lost.

(The word *one* refers to no one in particular.)

Here are some examples of shifts in point of view.

Incorrect: When <u>people</u> think about being hypnotized, <u>you</u> imagine a gold watch swinging back and forth before your eyes.

(Shifting to *you* is an easy error to make because we use *you* to mean *one;* however, the shift can be confusing for your reader.)

Revised: When <u>people</u> think about being hypnotized, <u>they</u> imagine a gold watch swinging back and forth before their eyes.

Incorrect: Before <u>I</u> was hypnotized onstage, <u>you</u> could see my husband shrink in his seat.

Revised: Before <u>I</u> was hypnotized onstage, <u>I</u> could see my husband shrink in his seat.

Just as nouns used as subjects must agree in number with the verbs in their sentences, so too must pronouns agree with verbs.

<u>She</u> <u>wants</u> to learn self-hypnosis. (Both *she* and *wants* are singular.)

<u>They</u> <u>think</u> that hypnosis is silly. (Both *they* and *think* are plural.)

Sometimes changing a pronoun requires a change in the verb in a sentence to make it agree with the pronoun. For instance:

<u>They</u> <u>wake</u> at 3:00 a.m. every morning.
(The plural subject *They* requires a plural verb, *wake.*)
<u>He</u> <u>wakes</u> at 3:00 a.m. every morning.
(The singular subject *He* requires a singular verb, *wakes.*)

When the subject of the sentence changes point of view, the verb must reflect that change.

EXERCISE 4 KEEPING POINT OF VIEW CONSISTENT

In the following sentences, correct any problems with inconsistent pronouns. Change the verb form if necessary.

Example: When would-be hypnotists face the parents of neighborhood kids they have tried to hypnotize, ~~you~~ *they* always keep a straight face.

1. Seeing the shiny object used to try to entrance small children, parents lose one's cool.

2. When these pretend hypnotists explain the reasons for the process,

you can easily become flustered.

3. As parents see little Johnny staring at his sister's locket and

muttering "Cookie," you get angry.

EDITING PRACTICE 1

In each sentence below, cross out the incorrect pronoun and write in the correct pronoun. Then, circle the letter before the type of pronoun error made in the sentence. There may be more than one error in a sentence.

Example: One aspect of hypnosis not often discussed is ~~their~~ *its* effect on chickens.

a. pronoun agreement   **b.** pronoun reference   **c.** point of view

1. According to H. B. Gibson in his book *Hypnosis: Its Nature and*

Therapeutic Uses, a chicken can be hypnotized by holding your head down to the ground.

a. pronoun agreement   **b.** pronoun reference   **c.** point of view

2. After holding the chicken's head down, draw a line extending from their

beak out in front of them.

a. pronoun agreement   **b.** pronoun reference   **c.** point of view

3. Staring at the line, the chicken will then enter a trance. Who can be different every time.

a. pronoun agreement   **b.** pronoun reference   **c.** point of view

4. The chicken will remain immobilized, staring at the line, for

anywhere from fifteen seconds to thirty minutes, which is remarkable.

a. pronoun agreement   **b.** pronoun reference   **c.** point of view

5. Chicken hypnosis is useful for people feeding large reptiles. They are too slow to catch a moving chicken.

a. pronoun agreement   **b.** pronoun reference   **c.** point of view

EDITING PRACTICE 2

Circle the correct pronouns in parentheses below.

Fictitious Hypnosis

Hypnosis has been a topic of detective fiction as a tool to help witnesses remember details such as license plate numbers that cannot otherwise be recalled. This tactic appears in television series, and (it, they) has been expanded to the notion of remembering past lives in movies such as *Dead Again*. In real-life cases, experts have used hypnosis in many cases, but (their, its) effectiveness is disputed. Proponents claim that recovered memories have aided in the solving of many crimes, but critics suggest that (they, you) can never be certain that the results are valid. For instance, if someone doing hypnosis makes a suggestion, (he or she, they) might skew the results of the process. The notion of planting suggestions has been explored in movies ranging from comedies such as the *Naked Gun* trilogy and *Zoolander* to dramas such as *The Manchurian Candidate*. Either of the terms *brainwashing* or *mind control* can imply a loss of personal control in (their, its) subjects.

Lab Activity 42

For additional practice with pronoun agreement, complete Lab Activity 42 in the lab manual packaged with your textbook. If you did not receive a lab manual, you can complete this activity online at **www.ablongman.com/long.** Click on **College Resources for Writers** and then click on **Activity 42.**

43 Adjectives and Adverbs

Credit Cards

Begun as a means for car owners to purchase gas conveniently in the 1920s, credit cards have become a way of life for millions. Allowing people to have what they want now while deferring payment, credit cards can greatly simplify life. However, as credit card companies charge higher and higher rates for unpaid balances, these little plastic helpers can become a burden.

Paying with Plastic

CONDUCT AN INTERVIEW Credit cards have become increasingly easy to acquire and use; consequently, more people than ever use them. One downside of paying with credit cards, however, is the interest people must pay on any unpaid balances every month. How often do people use credit cards? For what types of expenses do people use them? How much do people pay in terms of finance charges? Interview at least two people you know about how they, or people they know, use credit cards.

639

What Is an Adjective?

An **adjective** describes a noun (a person, place, or thing) or a pronoun. An adjective answers the question "Which one?" "What kind?" or "How many?"

Adjectives usually come before the word they describe, but they can also come after forms of the verb *to be* (*am, is, are, was, were, have been*). Adjectives can also follow **linking verbs** such as *look, appear, become, feel, seem, smell, sound,* and *taste.* The adjectives are underlined in the following sentences.

A <u>low</u> *balance* on my credit card is easy to pay.

(The adjective *low* describes *which* balance the writer means.)

When the *mall* seems <u>irresistible</u>, I reach for my credit card.

(The adjective *irresistible* describes *what kind* of mall the writer means.)

Paying the bills for <u>three</u> *credit cards* is no fun.

(The adjective *three* describes *how many* credit cards the writer means.)

Types of Adjectives

People often think of adjectives as words that provide details appealing to the five senses—sight, hearing, taste, touch, and smell—and often adjectives do just that. However, adjectives' primary job is to modify, or help identify, nouns or pronouns. Under that definition, four groups of words must be included as adjectives.

- **Articles.** The three articles—*a, an,* and *the*—answer the questions "Which one?" and "How many?" Be sure to identify them as adjectives.
- **Possessive pronouns.** These words, which show ownership or possession, also act as adjectives. These words are possessive pronouns: *my, mine, your, yours, his, her, hers, its, our, ours, your, yours, their, theirs.* These adjectives answer the question "Which one?"
- **Demonstrative pronouns.** These words that introduce a specific person, place, or thing are also adjectives. The demonstrative pronouns are *this, that, these,* and *those.* These adjectives answer the question "Which one?"
- **Numbers.** Numbers answer the question "How many?" and, thus, are adjectives.

Using Adjectives for Comparison

One of the most important uses for adjectives is making **comparisons**—the process of finding similarities or differences between two things.

Comparative adjectives are used to compare *two* things. You can change most one-syllable adjectives and some two-syllable adjectives into a comparative by adding *-er* to the end.

Paying cash is <u>easier</u> for people who live near ATMs.

Using a credit card for payment is often <u>faster</u> than writing a check.

Superlative adjectives are used to compare three or more things. You can change most one- or two-syllable adjectives into a superlative by adding *-est* to the end.

Swiping a credit card at the grocery store was <u>faster</u> than writing a check, but paying cash is the <u>fastest</u> way to pay.

Adjectives ending in *y*, however, must change the *y* to *i* before adding *-er* or *-est*.

I was <u>happier</u> with my finances when I stopped using my credit cards, but I was <u>happiest</u> when I cut them up.

For longer adjectives, add *more* when comparing two things or *most* when comparing three or more things.

Writing a personal check is <u>more</u> convenient than getting a cashier's check, but using a credit card is the <u>most</u> convenient type of credit for me.

To make negative comparisons, use *less* when comparing two items and *least* when comparing three or more items.

The American Express card is <u>less</u> dangerous for me than my Visa because I have to pay my balance every month.

I feel the <u>least</u> guilty when I keep my plastic in my wallet.

Keep this important point in mind when using adjectives: Use only *-er/ -est* or *more/most* in making a comparison. Using both is incorrect.

Incorrect: I am the <u>most stingiest</u> when I've just paid my credit card bill.

Correct: I am the <u>stingiest</u> when I've just paid my credit card bill.

Incorrect: He was <u>more kinder</u> than his sister.

Correct: He was <u>kinder</u> than his sister.

Some adjectives have irregular forms. Learn the forms of the words on the following page.

Adjective	Comparative (comparing two things)	Superlative (comparing three or more things)
bad	worse	worst
good	better	best
little (amount)	less	least
many	more	most
much	more	most
well	better	best

EXERCISE 1 USING THE CORRECT FORMS OF REGULAR ADJECTIVES

Change each adjective in parentheses to the correct form. You may need to add -er or -est or more or most to make the adjective form correct.

1. What I believed to be my (happy) surprise arrived when I received a "free introductory offer" on a credit card.

2. I opened the envelope, feeling (excited) than I'd ever felt at receiving junk mail.

3. Upon returning the application, however, I realized that there was a

   $200 annual fee, the (high) I'd ever heard of for a credit card.

4. Apparently, the "free" offer was good only for the first month, too,

   so my (good) surprise soon became my (bad).

5. Not only would I have to pay the (exorbitant) credit card fee ever, but I was too afraid of debt to use the card at all.

What Is an Adverb?

An **adverb** is a word that describes a verb, an adjective, or another adverb. Many adverbs end in -ly. Adverbs answer these questions: "How?" "When?" "Where?" and "To what extent?" The adverbs in the following sentences are underlined.

I readily open every credit card offer that comes in the mail.
(The adverb *readily* describes *how* the writer reads the offer.)
Yesterday alone, I studied four offers.

(The adverb *yesterday* describes *when* the writer studied the offers.)

Once I have <u>completely</u> read the offers, I shred them and throw them away.

(The adverb *completely* describes *to what extent* the writer reads the offers.)

Note: Never, no, not, and *very* are adverbs.

Using Adverbs

Writers sometimes incorrectly use an adjective when they should use an adverb, especially after a verb.

Incorrect: I spend money <u>quick</u>.

Incorrect: When his credit card was cut up, Tony was <u>real</u> mad.

Incorrect: I'm <u>sure</u> going to stop lending people my credit card.

In each sentence, adding *-ly* makes the underlined adjective an adverb.

Correct: I spend money <u>quickly</u>.

Correct: When his credit card was cut up, Tony was <u>really</u> mad.

Correct: I'm <u>surely</u> going to stop lending people my credit card.

EXERCISE 2   CHOOSING BETWEEN ADJECTIVES AND ADVERBS

Circle the correct adjectives and adverbs in parentheses.

Getting Carded

One (common, commonly) type of criminal is known as a carder. This villain specializes in stealing information from credit cards. Because they often know about digital security, carders are (adeptly, adept) at breaking into security systems. Using computer expertise to hack their way into adminstrative computer panels, carders attempt to steal credit card information from companies' Web sites. Other carders simply purchase stolen credit card numbers and use those numbers for their own purchases. The carder's (primary, primarily) means of making money is to "skim" information from a credit card's magnetic stripe to make a (fake, fakely) credit card. (Ironically, Ironic), many carders know how to commit the crimes but do not (thoroughly, thorough) understand the technology they exploit.

Using *Good* and *Well*

The words *good* and *well* are often confused. While these words seem to have the same meaning, *good* is an adjective used to describe nouns and pronouns while *well* is an adverb used to describe verbs, adjectives, and other adverbs. *Well* can also be used as an adjective to describe someone's health.

            adverb   *adjective*

I try to save money <u>well</u> because I don't have <u>good</u> health insurance;

                  adjective

then I can afford to pay to get <u>well</u> when I am sick.

(The adverb *well* modifies the verb *save;* the *adjective good* modifies the noun *health insurance;* and the adjective *well* modifies the pronoun *I.*)

EXERCISE 3 USING *GOOD* AND *WELL* CORRECTLY

Circle the correct modifier in each sentence below.

   1. If my credit card balance is too high, I can't get a (good, well) night's rest.

   2. Last month, my balance was (good, well) over $500.

   3. Consequently, I lost (good. well) hours of sleep.

   4. I handle other aspects of my life (good, well), but not this one.

   5. Somehow I can't stay (good, well) when I use my credit cards.

EDITING PRACTICE

The following paragraph contains twelve adjective and adverb errors. Cross out the incorrect words and write in the correct modifiers.

Getting Yourself Credit

At some point, you'll probably need to borrow money so you can

buy a house or car or pay for your education. Thus, taking steps to

get a gooder credit rating makes sense. The most big factor in a credit rating is punctuality. According to a financial advisor at a major U.S. financial services firm, 35 percent of a person's credit rating comes from making promptly—or at least not serious late—payments. If you're well at making timely payments, you're on the most best road to good credit. The second significantest factor in a credit rating is the ratio of debt compared to credit limits. Thus, if all your credit cards are "maxed out," your debt ratio will be more high and, thus, won't help your rating. Length of credit history makes up 15 percent of a credit rating, so eighteen-year-olds with real good payment records still have a more harder time getting credit compared to thirty-five-year-olds with the same payment records. Finally, the types of credit you use and the amount of credit sought recent make up 10 percent each in your credit rating. Comprising severally factors, your credit score affects whether or not you are able to get financial assistance when you need it.

Lab Activity 43

For additional practice with adjectives and adverbs, complete Lab Activity 43 in the lab manual packaged with your textbook. If you did not receive a lab manual, you can complete this activity online at **www. ablongman.com/long.** Click on **College Resources for Writers** and then click on **Activity 43.**

44 Misplaced Modifiers

Places where animals are restricted within artificial environments and shown to the public, zoos—short for *zoological gardens*—were originally maintained by royalty for their private pleasure. Zoos became public attractions following the French Revolution and now serve many purposes, including public pleasure, scientific study, and endangered species protection. Though widely enjoyed, most zoos are not financial successes, relying on government grants and individual and corporate donations for solvency.

Animal in Captivity

CRITICAL THINKING Some people argue that since humans have affected animals' habitats, animals should be protected, but others feel that animals have few, if any, rights. What do you think? Should animals be protected? Should they be held in captivity for study? Which ones have greater rights than others? Write a few sentences explaining the extent to which you think animals should be protected or studied.

What Is a Misplaced Modifier?

Modifiers (adjectives and adverbs) help us clarify our ideas and make them more vivid. However, just as a well-placed adverb or adjective can help us communicate our ideas, a misplaced modifier can confuse our readers. A **misplaced modifier** is a word or group of words in the wrong place. (See also Chapter 45, "Dangling Modifiers.") Because of its confusing placement, a misplaced modifier sends an incorrect message to the reader. The misplaced modifiers are underlined in the sentence below.

> **Misplaced modifier:**   The zoo is a favorite destination for my family, <u>which boasts several new species</u>.

(The modifier *which boasts several new species* actually describes the *zoo*. However, the placement of the modifier makes it seem as if the modifier is describing the *family*.)

> **Misplaced modifier:**   The ring-tailed lemur was of particular delight to my small brother <u>with his long striped tail</u>.

(The modifier *with his long striped tail* describes the *lemur*, but the placement of the modifier leads the reader to think that the *brother* has a tail.)

> **Misplaced modifier:**   Many animals drew sympathy from my sister, <u>kept confined in a small space</u>.

(Here *kept confined in a small space* really modifies *animals*, but the placement of the modifier makes it seem as if the *sister* was caged.)

Correcting Misplaced Modifiers

Most misplaced modifiers are simply too far away from what they're describing. Thus, the easiest way to fix such an error is to move the modifier as close as possible to what it's describing.

> **Misplaced:** The zoo is a favorite destination for my family, <u>which boasts several new species</u>.
>
> **Correct:**   The zoo, <u>which boasts several new species,</u> is a favorite destination for my family.
>
> **Misplaced:** The ring-tailed lemur was of particular delight to my small brother <u>with his long striped tail</u>.
>
> **Correct:**   The ring-tailed lemur, <u>with his long striped tail,</u> was of particular delight to my small brother.

Misplaced: Many animals drew sympathy from my sister, <u>kept confined in a small space</u>.

Correct: Many animals, <u>kept confined in a small space,</u> drew sympathy from my sister.

Note: Single-word modifiers such as *almost, even, nearly,* and *only,* should come right before the word they modify.

EXERCISE 1 INTERPRETING MISPLACED MODIFIERS

Underline the misplaced modifier in each of the following sentences. Then, explain both what the sentence actually says and what the writer means.

Example: Domestic animals and some wild animals are housed in petting zoos, <u>which are docile enough to touch and feed</u>.

What the sentence says: *Petting zoos are docile enough to touch and feed.*

What the writer means: *Wild animals are docile enough to touch and feed.*

1. Petting zoos offer special animal food, extremely popular with young children.

   What the sentence says: _____

   _____

   What the writer means:_____

   _____

2. To ensure the health and safety of the animals, the animals' food is provided by the zoos, easily stored in nearby kiosks or vending machines.

   What the sentence says: _____

   _____

   What the writer means:_____

   _____

3. Some risks do accompany petting zoos, which can be avoided by common sense and good personal hygiene.

What the sentence says: _____

_____

What the writer means:_____

_____

4. In fact, a 2002 bill requires hand-washing facilities at animal exhibitions in Pennsylvania, which attempts to control disease outbreaks.

What the sentence says: _____

_____

What the writer means:_____

_____

5. The bill was passed as a result of fifty-five people being infected by *E. coli* bacteria, one of whom required a kidney transplant.

What the sentence says: _____

_____

What the writer means:_____

_____

EDITING PRACTICE 1

Underline the misplaced modifiers in the sentence below. Then, rewrite that sentence so that it makes sense.

Example: A lot of work is involved in keeping zoos functional. First, animals must have homes, much accustomed to wandering free in the wild.

Revised sentence: First, animals, much accustomed to wandering free in

the wild, must have homes.

1. Setting up animal living quarters is a huge job for zoo personnel with a strong resemblance to their natural environs.

   Revised: _____

   _____

2. Of course, even though animals' homes in nature aren't cleaned by humans filled with droppings and uneaten food pellets, their zoo homes must periodically be scoured to be kept sanitary.

   Revised: _____

   _____

3. Appropriate meals must be distributed to animals, a result of careful research and measuring.

   Revised: _____

   _____

4. "Please don't feed the animals" appears on signs designed to protect animals from receiving potentially harmful food, which is common and sometimes humorous.

   Revised: _____

   _____

5. Zoo animals seem to be fed to me continually, but this only seems to be the case because the many animals have different eating schedules.

   Revised: _____

   _____

EDITING PRACTICE 2

Cross out the misplaced modifiers in the paragraph below. Then, revise each sentence so that it makes sense, showing where the modifier should appear.

Modern Zoos

Zoos appear in most large cities, ~~which showcase different ani-mal exhibi~~ts. In some zoos, monkeys are often the star attraction for spectators, ~~who are allowed to roam freely among visitors.~~ Peafowl are also frequently allowed to roam freely among visitors, ~~known for their beautiful feathers~~. Zoos also have benefits for children in school, ~~a common destination for school field trip~~s. However, some zoo signs with animal information provide little relevant knowledge for students, explaining their diet and natural habitat. Modern zoos are a wonder to people, very dynamic, creating new exhibits, and constantly breeding animals. Most zoos are almost open every day of the year since animal care is necessary on a holiday. ~~which includes feeding, cleaning, and medical attention~~. Though zoos vary in size and quality, they all include animals. ~~which range from drive-through parks to small menageries with concrete slabs and iron ba~~rs. Birds are the cause of dismay to visitors, ~~whose wings may be clipped so that they cannot fly~~. However, zookeepers strive to make animals' zoo experience as much like home as possible.

Lab Activity 44

For additional practice with misplaced modifiers, complete Lab Activity 44 in the lab manual packaged with your textbook. If you did not receive a lab manual, you can complete this activity online at **www.ablongman.com/long.** Click on **College Resources for Writers** and then click on **Activity 44.**

45 Dangling Modifiers

Public Libraries

Though libraries are so ubiquitous in the United States that it's easy to take them for granted, public libraries did not always exist. The first libraries open to the public were housed in the dry sections of Roman baths and served few. Allowing visitors to read Greek and Latin scrolls, these libraries were thus limited to the educated population. Today public libraries give those who desire it the opportunity to read, research, and relax.

The New York Public Library

OBSERVE YOUR WORLD   While libraries are often thought to be just collections of reading material, they now serve many functions from research to entertainment and basic literacy. What services does your library provide? Visit your local or college library, examine its offerings, and write a few sentences summarizing its services.

What Is a Dangling Modifier?

A **dangling modifier** is a word or group of words, usually at the beginning of a sentence, that does not modify the word next to it. (See also Chapter 44, "Misplaced Modifiers.") Thus, dangling modifiers can cause confusion. Read the following sentence to see how dangling modifiers can send the wrong message to a reader.

> **Incorrect:**   Containing books, magazines, and computers, my mind reels at the thought of the library.

Read literally, this sentence says that someone's *mind* contains books, magazines, and computers. What the writer means to say is that *the library* contains those things.

Correcting Dangling Modifiers

Since a dangling modifier is too far away from what it describes, it can easily be corrected by revising the sentence to bring the modifier and the word it describes closer together. The writer of the incorrect sentence in the preceding example has three options for revision.

■ **Option 1: Move the word being described closer to the dangling modifier.**

Containing books, magazines, and computers, the library makes my mind reel.

(The verb *makes* has also been added.)

■ **Option 2: Make the word being described part of the modifier.**

Since the library contains books, magazines, and computers, my mind reels at the thought of it.

(Now the reader has no doubt about what the library contains or the writer's reaction to it.)

■ **Option 3: Move the dangling modifier close to the word being described.**

My mind reels at the thought of the library, which contains books, magazines, and computers.

(The writer has added *which* before the moved modifier in order to make the meaning clear.)

EXERCISE 1 INTERPRETING DANGLING MODIFIERS

Each of the following sentences begins with a dangling modifier. Underline the misplaced modifier. Then, write down what the writer means as well as what the sentence actually says.

Example: Never opening early enough, books await me in the library.

What the writer means: *The library never opens early enough.*

What the sentence says: *Books never open early enough.*

1. Giving free Internet access, online databases help me in the college library.

   What the writer means:_____

   What the sentence says: _____

2. Containing current, relevant articles, the library restrooms are located near the computers.

   What the writer means:_____

   What the sentence says: _____

3. Continually crowded with people I don't know, I have learned to study away from the main lobby.

   What the writer means:_____

   What the sentence says: _____

4. Stacked next to each other on long, high shelves, my friends love books as much as I do.

   What the writer means:_____

   What the sentence says: _____

5. Torn, taped, and stained, the librarians have a huge responsibility repairing damaged books.

   What the writer means:_____

   What the sentence says: _____

6. Ripping pages from books, library cards should be taken from people who mistreat library property.

What the writer means:_____

What the sentence says: _____

7. Attracting mice, rats, cockroaches, and silverfish, students who bring food into the library show blatant disregard for its policies.

What the writer means:_____

What the sentence says: _____

8. With a smaller staff, the wait time to speak to a reference librarian increases as a result of library budget cuts.

What the writer means:_____

What the sentence says: _____

9. Diligent about preserving their place of learning, vermin can be eliminated if students follow the library rules.

What the writer means:_____

What the sentence says: _____

10. With their minds on research and learning, library rules improve the academic experience of students and staff alike.

What the writer means:_____

What the sentence says: _____

EDITING PRACTICE 1

Underline the dangling modifier that begins each sentence below. Then, rewrite each sentence so that it makes sense.

Example: Considered essential for having a literate citizenry, many countries boast impressive public libraries.

Revised: Many countries boast impressive public libraries, which are

considered essential for having a literate citizenry.

1. Seen as unnecessary for survival, few people in ancient time benefited from the act of reading.

Revised: _____

_____

2. Written in scholarly languages that common people neither wrote nor spoke, the wealthy and the clergy were among the few people with the education to read what books existed.

Revised: _____

_____

3. Originally consisting of volumes copied by monks, few people were allowed into the stacks of ancient libraries.

Revised: _____

_____

4. Tempted to use books as fuel, books were rarely taken out of the library by even interested readers.

Revised: _____

_____

5. Greatly improved since ancient times, people have far more reading opportunities today.

Revised: _____

_____

EDITING PRACTICE 2

Underline the ten dangling modifiers in the paragraph below. Then, rewrite the paragraph so that it makes sense.

The Ultimate Gift of Literacy

Nearly synonymous with the word *library*, great works of generosity were the life focus of Andrew Carnegie. Operating a spindle on which yarn or thread is wound in a cotton factory, $1.20 a week was the amount Carnegie received in his first job as a bobbin boy.

This makes his ultimate success even more impressive. Having made a fortune with his own steel company, almost 90 percent of Carnegie's $400 million fortune was donated in philanthropic efforts. Believing that the very wealthy had an obligation to give away their money to help others, free libraries became the signature act of Andrew Carnegie. At one time the wealthiest man in the world, the essay "The Gospel of Wealth" explains Mr. Carnegie's reasons for distributing wealth for the betterment of society. Even marrying a woman who believed in using wealth to help people, libraries were Carnegie's pet project. To educate and improve themselves, free libraries numbered very few when Mr. Carnegie began his building mission. Numbering 2,509 in 1881, Carnegie built libraries throughout his life. Also making donations to adult education and fine arts programs, the sum of $350 million from Carnegie's fortune was donated during his lifetime. Carnegie also donated to adult education and education in the fine arts. Benefiting from his great generosity, wealth became a means to change the world.

Lab Activity 45

For additional practice with dangling modifiers, complete Lab Activity 45 in the lab manual packaged with your textbook. If you did not receive a lab manual, you can complete this activity online at **www.ablongman.com/long.** Click on **College Resources for Writers** and then click on **Activity 45.**

46 Commas

CULTURE NOTE *Water*

Part of every aspect of our lives, water serves to clean, entertain, and sustain us. Depending on the region of the country, water also means big money or big trouble. Too much water can result in flooding, which not only destroys homes but takes lives, while a shortage results in drought, which affects food production and, ultimately, the economy. While water itself seems simple enough, formed from a combination of the two elements hydrogen and oxygen, the issues that surround it are many and complex.

Hoover Dam

JOURNAL ENTRY

Aside from being necessary for survival, water provides opportunities for pleasure. Additionally, certain waters have long been thought to possess specific tastes or powers. What role does water play in your life, aside from being necessary for life and hygiene? Write a few sentences considering how water is part of your activities.

Understanding Commas ,

Commas separate items in a sentence. Because commas are so small, it is easy to leave them out of a sentence by mistake or put them in where they don't belong. But a misplaced comma can radically alter the meaning of your sentence. Knowing how to use commas properly is essential to keeping your writing clear and easy to read.

You may have been taught that a comma signals a pause in a sentence. While this may seem like an easy guideline for comma use, it can lead to mistakes, especially in longer sentences. What commas actually do is signal to the reader to *keep reading*. When writers want to signal a pause or a break, they use a semicolon, a colon, or a period. Thus, when you're trying to decide whether to use a comma in your writing, think about whether you want to give your reader a signal to keep reading.

Commas have six main uses:

- Setting apart items in a series
- Setting off introductory material
- Setting off information that interrupts the main ideas in a sentence
- Joining two independent clauses also linked by a coordinating conjunction (one of the FANBOYS: *for, and, nor, but, or, yet, so*)
- Setting off a direct quotation from the rest of a sentence
- Clarifying everyday information (such as dates, addresses, and numbers)

Setting Apart Items in a Series

Use commas to set apart, or separate, items in a series. A **series** is two or more items—two or more adjectives, for example—in a row. Here are some examples of how commas work with a series of items.

Pure water is colorless, odorless, and tasteless.
Water is necessary to humans, animals, and plants for survival.
Water can be drunk as liquid, breathed as vapor, and eaten as ice.
Water's pleasant, soothing qualities can be relaxing.

In a series of three or more items joined by a conjunction, the final comma is optional, but it often helps clarify meaning. Whether or not you decide to include the final comma is up to you, but be consistent in your writing.

Sometimes it's difficult to decide whether you need a comma between two adjectives. Use a comma between adjectives in a two-item series only if the word *and* can logically be substituted for the comma. For instance, in the sentence "Water's pleasant, soothing qualities can be relaxing," you can replace the comma with *and*. The sentence then reads, "Water's pleasant and soothing qualities can be relaxing." When the word *and* sounds strange between two adjectives, you can omit the comma. For example, in the sentence "Swimming in the ocean made Rosa feel that she needed a good long rest," saying "a good *and* long rest" would sound strange, so no comma is needed.

EXERCISE 1 USING COMMAS IN A SERIES

Add commas where necessary in the following sentences.

1. Water's many uses include drinking cleaning and irrigation.

2. Water makes swimming surfing and boating possible.

3. In some countries, clean safe drinking water is not readily available.

4. Resort hotels provide dry comfortable living conditions, even in the rainy season.

5. Water challenges in the United States include flooding in the Southeast drought in the Southwest and rising water levels near the Gulf of Mexico.

Setting Off Introductory Material

Use commas to set off introductory material in a sentence.

Necessary for survival, water is also a source of pleasure.
In fact, relaxing hot tubs are common in health clubs.
Sitting back in a steaming pool, people feel their worries dissolving.
Although heated water can be relaxing, staying in it too long can be harmful.

If an introductory phrase is very short and describes *when* or *where*, the comma is sometimes omitted.

In 2006 I tried my first bottle of flavored water.

EXERCISE 2 USING COMMAS TO SET OFF INTRODUCTORY MATERIAL

Add commas where necessary in the following sentences.

1. Unlike other substances water is found naturally on earth in all three states: solid, gas, and liquid.

2. Constantly in motion the earth's water continually interacts and changes.

3. Called the universal solvent water dissolves more things than any other liquid.

4. If fact it dissolves more substances than sulfuric acid.

5. Freezing at 32 degrees Fahrenheit water boils (at sea level) at 212 degrees.

Setting Off Information That Interrupts the Main Ideas in a Sentence

One of the most important uses of the comma is to set off, or highlight, information that interrupts the main ideas in a sentence. Such information is often interesting and colorful, but it is not essential to communicate the main ideas of the sentence.

Interruptions in the Middle of a Sentence

Use two commas to set off information that comes in the middle of a sentence.

Water's chemical makeup, describing the elements that form its molecules, is written H_2O.

Two ions of hydrogen, each having a positive charge, are attached to one negatively charged oxygen ion.

These charges, since opposites attract, draw other water molecules toward them.

Water molecules, then, actually "stick" together.

Essential and Unessential Information

Commas are needed to separate information from the rest of the sentence *only if that information is unnecessary for the sentence to make sense*. For instance, the sentences on the previous page make sense even if you leave out the information between the commas. Thus, the commas are necessary. In the following sentences, however, the extra information (underlined) is necessary for the sentence to make sense, so no commas should be used.

The atoms <u>that make up a water molecule</u> are hydrogen and oxygen.

In this case, leaving out the information *that make up a water molecule* would make the full meaning of the sentence unclear. Readers would not know *which* atoms the writer is referring to. Similarly, the following sentence requires no commas.

The qualities setting water apart from other liquids are many.

Here, the information *setting water apart from other liquids* is necessary to identify the qualities. Without this information, the reader has no idea *which* qualities the writer means.

Often you can tell whether or not commas are necessary by reading a sentence out loud. This strategy allows you to hear if a piece of information is necessary to the meaning of the sentence. If the information is necessary, do not use commas. If the information is not needed for a full understanding of the meaning of the sentence, then use commas.

Additional Material at the End of a Sentence

Use commas to set off material at the end of a sentence.

Water is extremely versatile, used for survival and amusement.

In this case, the phrase "used for survival and amusement" could also have come at the beginning or in the middle of the sentence.

Used for survival and amusement, water is extremely versatile.
Water, used for survival and amusement, is extremely versatile.

Regardless of where it appears, the phrase provides extra information that is not essential to the meaning of the sentence. Thus, it must be set off from the rest of the sentence by a comma or commas.

Direct Address

When people are being addressed (spoken or written to), their names should be set off from the rest of the sentence.

> Martha, please take your bath now.
>
> Stay away from me, Herman, if you know what's good for you.

EXERCISE 3 **USING COMMAS TO SET OFF EXTRA INFORMATION**

Add commas where necessary in the following sentences.

1. Water one of the most important substances required for survival makes up a large part of us.

2. Water makes up about 60 percent of our bodies. Our brains in fact contain 70 percent water.

3. Eating and drinking activities essential for water replacement are responsible for putting back the 2.4 liters of water we lose daily.

4. Our lungs responsible for the processing of oxygen are about 90 percent water.

5. Finally our blood which helps digest food transport waste and control body temperature is more than 80 percent water.

Joining Two Independent Clauses Also Linked by a Coordinating Conjunction

One of the most important comma uses is joining two independent clauses. (For more on independent clauses, see page 547.) When two independent clauses are joined *without* a comma, the result is a run-on sentence—a very common error. (For more on run-on sentences, see page 554.)

Keep in mind that standard written English requires a coordinating conjunction—one of the FANBOYS (*for, and, nor, but, or, yet, so*)—along with the comma. (For more on coordinating conjunctions, see page 557.)

> Water can be soothing, **and** it is necessary for good health.
>
> Frozen water in the form of icicles can be dangerous, **for** the frozen spears can fall and injure people.
>
> Heavy rains can help farmers, **but** they can also cause disaster.

Each sentence contains two complete ideas in the form of two independent clauses. Thus, each sentence also contains a comma and a conjunction.

A Sentence with One Subject

Do *not* use a comma when a sentence has one subject but more than one complete verb. The verbs below are underlined. Note that each sentence contains only one independent clause.

Water <u>can be</u> soothing and <u>is</u> necessary for good health.

Frozen water in the form of icicles <u>can be</u> dangerous but <u>can fall</u> and <u>injure</u> people.

Heavy rains <u>can rescue</u> farmers but <u>can</u> also <u>cause</u> disaster.

Because each sentence has only one subject (*Water, water, rains*), the writer does not need to use a comma.

EXERCISE 4 USING A COMMA TO JOIN TWO INDEPENDENT CLAUSES

Add commas where necessary in the following sentences.

1. The Dust Bowl of the 1930s was caused by massive drought and it was also caused by harmful farming techniques.

2. Millions of acres of topsoil were removed by the wind for the native sod had been broken up for wheat farming.

3. Additionally, the large buffalo herds that had once grazed the plains were gone and there was nothing, then, to fertilize the land.

4. The Dust Bowl resulted from a series of dust storms but overproduction following World War I also contributed to the disaster.

5. Thousands of families could not make payments on their farms so between 300,000 and 400,000 people from the Great Plains had to leave their homes.

Setting Off a Direct Quotation

Commas are used to signal the start and sometimes the end of a quotation. The following sentences illustrate how commas work to set off quotations. Make sure you place periods and commas *inside* the quotation marks. (For more on quotation marks, see page 680.)

My instructor claims, "Water has inspired many great quotations."

(The comma indicates the start of the quotation.)

"We must build dikes of courage to hold back the flood of fear," said civil rights leader Martin Luther King, Jr.

(The comma indicates the end of the quotation.)

"The four building blocks of the universe," says writer Dave Barry, "are fire, water, gravel, and vinyl."

(The commas signal an interruption in the quotation—in this case, to provide information about the speaker—and its continuation after the interruption.)

EXERCISE 5 USING COMMAS TO SET OFF A DIRECT QUOTATION

In each sentence below, add a comma to set off the quotation from the rest of the sentence.

1. Exiled Emperor of France Napoleon Bonaparte claimed "Water, air, and cleanness are the chief articles in my pharmacy."

2. "I'm an instant star" claimed singer David Bowie. "Just add water and stir."

3. Former NFL star Lynn Swan observed "People drinking bottled water is a good sign they're hydrated, but it doesn't mean they're healthier."

4. "Women are like tea bags" said Eleanor Roosevelt. "We don't know our true strength until we are in hot water!"

5. Comedian W. C. Fields claimed "I never drink water because I'm afraid it may become habit-forming."

Clarifying Everyday Information

Commas help us make sense of and organize everyday information. Use commas in the following ways.

■ **Dates**

Formed on August 27, 1965, Hurricane Betsy was the costliest hurricane up to that date.

■ **Addresses**

Forward my mail to 1152 Dacian Avenue, Durham, NC 27701.

■ **Greetings and closings of letters**

Dear Grandma,

Dear Dr. Simmons,

Yours truly,

Note: In business correspondence, use a colon instead of a comma in the greeting ("Dear Sir:" or "Dear Madam:").

■ **Numbers**

Grace saved her $100,000 lottery winnings in an account that paid 7 percent interest.

EXERCISE 6 USING COMMAS TO ORGANIZE EVERYDAY INFORMATION

Add commas where necessary in the following sentences.

1. The storm on March 30 1943 caused 320461 people to use umbrellas.

2. Little Ruby loves the water park at 874 East Woodward Avenue Manteca California 95337.

3. August 31 2005 was the first day we started giving money to the Red Cross.

4. We plan to give more than $2200 over the course of the next ten years to help flood victims.

5. Thus, our plans to move to 5700 Dartmouth Street Wyckoff New Jersey 07481 are postponed.

EDITING PRACTICE 1

Add commas where necessary in the following paragraph. You will need to add twenty-one commas in all.

Dam Facts

According to the U.S. Department of the Interior Hoover Dam is 726 feet tall and 660 feet thick at its base. Lake Mead the reservoir formed by Hoover Dam when it blocked the Colorado River and flooded the Mojave Desert contains enough water to flood the entire state of New York with a foot of water. On a daily basis as many as 20000 vehicles drive across the 45-foot-wide top of the dam between Nevada and Arizona and there is enough concrete in the dam to build a two-lane lane road from Seattle Washington to Miami Florida or a four-foot-wide sidewalk around the earth at the equator. During periods of peak electricity use enough water runs through the seventeen generators each of which can supply electricity to 100000 households to fill fifteen average-sized swimming pools (holding 20000 gallons) in a single second. The Colorado River supplies water to Los Angeles and San Diego California; Phoenix Arizona; and Las Vegas Nevada. Although not every state uses water or power from Hoover Dam every state in the Union from Alabama to Wyoming furnished supplies and materials for the construction of the dam.

EDITING PRACTICE 2

Add commas where necessary in the following paragraph. You will need to add twenty commas in all.

Watered-Down Entertainment

Many stories use water as an important aspect of setting or plot. In *Moby-Dick* a sea tale "Call me Ishmael" is the first line. In this famous novel by Herman Melville which largely takes place at sea a whaling captain is obsessed with catching the white whale. Another famous ocean story now comes in paperback and on DVD. *Jaws* written by Peter Benchley chronicles the battle of local authorities and shark seekers against a great white shark in the waters off the coast of Amity New York. *Jaws* gained fame for many reasons but one of its most famous quotations comes when Chief Brody sees the shark for the first time and says to fellow fin hunters "You're going to need a bigger boat." On a different note the plot of the science fiction novel *Dune* also the name of the desert planet on which the novel is primarily set pivots around the hoarding of water. If the Fremen people seemingly nomadic folk indigenous to Dune can save up enough water they can restore Dune to a garden planet instead of the sandworm-ridden wasteland it has become. Because water is part of our daily lives we may ignore its possibilities for novels movies and quotations. We are fortunate however that others have not done so.

EDITING PRACTICE 3

Add commas as necessary to the following letter. You will need to add twenty-five commas in all.

Sondra Merrill

5294 Firedance Way

Reno NV 89502

March 4 2006

Dear Ms. Merrill:

I am writing to dispute two charges that recently appeared on my credit card statement. I notice that they both occur in the state of Hawaii. I am a resident of Reno Nevada and I have never been to Hawaii so neither of these items could possibly be mine. First, the charge of $4823.11 from Oscar's Ocean Supply a sports equipment store is not my purchase. While scuba diving snorkeling surfing and boogie boarding all sound wonderful there's not much call for them in Reno. The next charge for $2379.48 comes from Philippe's Friendly Fish located in Lahaina Hawaii. I have never been terribly fond of fish and I can't imagine buying more than $2000 worth of it so my canned tuna from the local supermarket will do just fine without help from Philippe or his fishy friends. Finally if you intend to live up to your company motto "If life gets hard use the card" then you must remove these charges and issue me a new card. Instead of making my life difficult I would like to make things easier by using the credit card. However until this dispute is resolved I will use my debit card.

Sincerely

Ariel Perch

Lab Activity 46

For additional practice with commas, complete Lab Activity 46 in the lab manual packaged with your textbook. If you did not receive a lab manual, you can complete this activity online at **www.ablongman.com/long.** Click on **College Resources for Writers** and then click on **Activity 46.**

47 Apostrophes

CULTURE NOTE *The U.S. Armed Forces*

Employing approximately 1.5 million personnel for active duty and nearly 900,000 others in the seven reserve branches, the U.S. military is unmatched in terms of strength by any single nation or organization. Led by the President of the United States as its commander in chief, the four main branches of the military—Army, Navy, Air Force, and Marines—serve to protect our persons, our borders, and our freedoms.

Be All That You Can Be

CONDUCT AN INTERVIEW Because of the conflict in Iraq, some people argue that the United States should bring back a military draft, where every able citizen would be required to serve in the armed forces. What do people you know think about this? Interview at least two people, preferably of different generations, about whether or not a draft is a good idea. Write a few sentences summarizing your findings.

Understanding Apostrophes '

One of the great time-savers in punctuation, the **apostrophe** allows us to omit letters and even whole words. The apostrophe has two main uses.

- Showing the omission of letters
- Showing possession or ownership

Showing the Omission of Letters

An apostrophe allows us to leave out letters in a contraction. A **contraction** is formed by the combination of two words.

will + not = won't

I + had = I'd

they + are = they're

Here are some common contractions.

I + have = I've   who + is = who's

I + had = I'd   could + not = couldn't

I + will = I'll   did + not = didn't

I + would = I'd   do + not = don't

it + is = it's   is + not = isn't

it + has = it's   will + not = won't

they + are = they're   would + not = wouldn't

you + are = you're

Note: Some contractions can be used for two different word combinations. For example, *I'd* can mean "I had" or "I would." You can tell the meaning of the contraction from its use in the sentence.

I'd planned to join the Air Force since I was three.

(Here, *I'd* means "I had.")

I'd like to fly F-16s.

(In this case, *I'd* means "I would.")

EXERCISE 1 FORMING CONTRACTIONS IN CONTEXT

Combine the word pairs in parentheses into contractions.

More than Toy Soldiers

For as long as I can remember, (I have) wanted to be in the Army. When I was little, I played with G.I. Joe toy soldiers, hoping that (I would) have a chance to do more than play someday. My chance came in high school, when (I had) planned to sign up for the Reserve Officers' Training Corps (ROTC). I (could not) wait for the chance to join, and my buddy Keith even said that (he would) join, too. (We have) been best friends since preschool, so I knew (we would) do this together. We approached the ROTC trailer and saw the other kids milling around, nervous about what (they had) gotten themselves into. (I had) heard that some kids backed out at the last minute, but (I have) never backed out of anything, so I entered the trailer.

Showing Possession or Ownership

Many expressions can show ownership or possession: *owned by, possessed by, belonging to, of.*

the uniform *owned by* the admiral

the desk *possessed by* the general

the training schedule *belonging to* the squadron

However, while these expressions accurately communicate the idea of possession or ownership, there is another, faster way to show the same thing: use an apostrophe.

Singular Nouns

For a singular noun, add an apostrophe and an *s* (*'s*) to show possession or ownership.

the admiral's uniform
the general's desk
the squadron's training schedule

If a singular noun ends in *-s,* follow the same rule: add an apostrophe and an *s* to show possession.

Julius's physical fitness improved greatly after boot camp.

Note: Singular nouns ending in an *s* or *z* sound may not add another *s* to form the possessive.

These nouns include names having more than one *s* sound (*Moses'*), names that sound like plurals (*Banks'*), and names followed by a word starting with *s* (*James' safety*).

**EXERCISE 2 USING APOSTROPHES TO SHOW
POSSESSION OR OWNERSHIP**

Rewrite the underlined portion of each sentence to include an apostrophe and an *s* to show possession or ownership.

Example: The physical fitness of the new recruit is a concern.

The new recruit's physical fitness

1. The times for the run belonging to the soldier were far too slow.

_____

2. Because he was often late, the work habits the recruit possessed seemed to be lacking.

_____

3. However, <u>the leader belonging to the company</u> took a special interest in the recruit.

_____

4. In fact, <u>the training regimen of the leader</u> proved to be a perfect fit for the recruit.

_____

5. Within two weeks, <u>the improvement of the neophyte</u> was marked.

_____

6. <u>The times of the recruit</u> in runs and obstacle courses came down.

_____

7. <u>The progress of the trainee</u> in sit-ups and push-ups was amazing.

_____

8. Even at the <u>office of the sergeant</u>, people noticed.

_____

9. <u>The pride belonging to the newbie</u> infected everyone.

_____

10. <u>The hands possessed by the beginner</u> shook with excitement.

_____

EXERCISE 3 SHOWING POSSESSION OR OWNERSHIP THROUGH APOSTROPHES

Rewrite the underlined portion of each sentence to show possession or ownership.

History of the Navy

Older than the United States itself, the Navy came about as a result of <u>a resolution belonging to the Continental Congress</u> urging the colonies to build and arm fleets. Even <u>the schooner owned</u>

by George Washington was part of this early program to form a

navy. Historically, the forces of the U.S. Navy can be divided into

two major groups. One group is noted for innovation in its use of

ironclad ships during the American Civil War. The name belonging

to this small force is "Old Navy," which was a respected force of sail-

ing ships. The second group is a result of an effort toward modern-

izing the military that began in the 1880s. The name possessed by

this group is the New Navy.

Plural Nouns

For a plural word that already ends in *-s*, add an apostrophe to the word to show possession or ownership. Do not add another *-s*.

The sailors' expressions were serious and confident.
(The expressions belong to more than one sailor.)
The two ships' course was unwavering.
(The course is followed by more than one ship.)

For plural nouns not ending in *-s*, simply add *'s* to show possession or ownership.

the bunks belonging to the women = the women's bunks
the concern of the people = the people's concern

Unnecessary Apostrophes

Be careful not to misuse or overuse apostrophes. Avoid using apostrophes in two areas in particular.

- Do not use apostrophes with possessive pronouns.
- Do not use apostrophes with simple plurals.

Do Not Use Apostrophes with Possessive Pronouns

When you're showing possession or ownership by using a possessive pronoun (*his, hers, theirs,* or *your,* for instance), remember *never* to use an apostrophe. For more on possessive pronouns, see page 624.

Incorrect:	Their's is the uniform with the white hat.
Correct:	**Theirs** is the uniform with the white hat.
Incorrect:	Your's is the face I'll miss most.
Correct:	**Yours** is the face I'll miss most.
Incorrect:	I am more concerned for your safety than for her's.
Correct:	I am more concerned for your safety than for **hers.**

Do Not Use Apostrophes with Simple Plurals

To make most nouns plural, add an *-s* to the end of the word. *Never* add an apostrophe. Plural nouns that end in *-s* are **simple plurals.**

For instance, if you want to discuss more than one soldier, write *soldiers,* not *soldiers'* or *soldier's,* which are incorrect as simple plurals. Instead, keep in mind that the apostrophe shows possession or ownership. Therefore, use an apostrophe only to indicate that something belongs to, or is owned by, someone.

Simple plural:	The **soldiers** wore muddy uniforms.
Possessive plural:	The **soldiers'** uniforms were caked in mud, and their legs and boots were wet.

In the last sentence, the only word requiring an apostrophe is *soldiers'.* The possessive plural shows that the uniforms, legs, and boots all *belong to* the soldiers. The *s* on the words *uniforms, legs,* and *boots* simply shows that there is more than one of each of them.

EXERCISE 4 USING APOSTROPHES CORRECTLY

In the following sentences, add the ten apostrophes that are necessary. Then, at the end of the paragraph, list the simple plural nouns.

The Call of Army Life

¹One of Army lifes interesting aspects is its music. ²Nearly every activitys signal is its own bugle call, from *Reveilles* early morning

notes to *Taps* end-of-day tones. ³Announcing scheduled and certain nonscheduled events, bugle calls are prescribed by the commander. ⁴The calls sequence, at least for daily scheduled events, changes little. ⁵New soldiers impressions of the calls vary. ⁶Some are delighted by the signals musical nature while others are intimidated by the calls formality. ⁷According to Sergeant Jim Williams, "The calls definitely make you feel like you're a part of something." ⁸At first, not everyone understands the signals meanings, but eventually the soldiers ears are trained.

Simple plurals:

Sentence 1: _____   Sentence 5: _____

Sentence 2: _____   Sentence 6: _____

Sentence 3: _____   Sentence 7: _____

Sentence 4: _____   Sentence 8: _____

EDITING PRACTICE

In the following paragraph, rewrite the underlined sections to add apostrophes. The first item has been done for you.

The "D" Doesn't Stand for "Defeat"

Because of ~~the objections of people~~ *people's objections* to many military decisions and the losses that accompany battle, not all military engagements have the blessing of the public. One battle, however, has few critics: the Invasion of Normandy, usually referred to as D-Day, which took place on December 6, 1944. Near the beginning of World War II, the losses of the Allies had led to the control of France by Germany. By 1944, the Germans knew that the Allies, also now including the United States and others, would attempt a liberation of Europe through an invasion of France. The <u>forces of the Allies</u> decided to begin the invasion by landing a huge army at five beaches in the Normandy area. The <u>code names of the beaches</u> were Utah Beach, Omaha Beach, Gold Beach, Juno Beach, and Sword Beach. Prior to the actual amphibious invasion, Allied planes pounded the <u>positions of the Germans.</u> The <u>failure</u> <u>of the Germans</u> to successfully defend Normandy in essence doomed <u>the dream of Hitler</u> of a Nazi-controlled "Fortress Europe" and marked the beginning of the end for Germany.

Lab Activity 47

For additional practice with apostrophes, complete Lab Activity 47 in the lab manual packaged with your textbook. If you did not receive a lab manual, you can complete this activity online at **www.ablongman.com/long.** Click on **College Resources for Writers** and then click on **Activity 47.**

48 Quotation Marks

CULTURE NOTE *Mark Twain*

Writer, journalist, and lecturer Mark Twain (Samuel Langhorne Clemens) had a varied life, part of which included employment as a Mississippi riverboat pilot (1857–61). He adopted his pen name from a call used to sound the river shallows: "mark twain" meant that the water was two fathoms deep. With wry humor and keen insight, Twain addressed social and political issues such as racism. Among his many writings, *The Adventures of Tom Sawyer, The Adventures of Huckleberry Finn,* and *A Connecticut Yankee in King Arthur's Court* are among his most famous.

Huck and Jim

OBSERVE YOUR WORLD The relationship between Huckleberry Finn and Jim was shocking to Mark Twain's first readers, yet it now stands as an example of true friendship. What relationships in today's fiction, television, movies, or other entertainment, if any, do you think shock or surprise people? Why? Pay attention to popular culture and write a few sentences about a friendship or other relationship that breaks barriers in some way. If you think no barriers are left to be broken, explain why not.

Understanding Quotation Marks " "

Quotation marks are used to set off, or in some way identify, specific words, expressions, or titles, signaling that what follows demands special attention. Quotation marks have three major functions.

- Setting off direct quotations
- Setting off titles of short works
- Setting off special words or expressions

Setting Off Direct Quotations

Use quotation marks to indicate that certain words are being spoken by a specific person.

> Mark Twain said, "The man who does not read good books has no advantage over the man who cannot read them."
>
> (Quotation marks set off Mark Twain's words.)
>
> "Forgiveness," said Twain, "is the fragrance that the violet sheds on the heel that has crushed it."
>
> (Since the quotation is split up, two pairs of quotation marks are needed to show exactly what Twain said.)
>
> One of my favorite quotations from Mark Twain says, "Age is an issue of mind over matter. If you don't mind, it doesn't matter."
>
> (The closing quotation marks appear where the entire quotation is completed.)

Keep the following guidelines in mind when you use quotation marks.

- Unless a quotation begins a sentence, it should be introduced by a comma.
- A quotation begins with a capital letter.
- A quotation more than one sentence long needs only one set of quotation marks.
- A comma or period at the end of a sentence goes *inside* the quotation marks.

EXERCISE 1 USING QUOTATION MARKS CORRECTLY

In the following sentences, add quotation marks where necessary to set off someone's exact words.

1. I love to quote Mark Twain to my sister Jeanette, especially when she says, I really need to study.

2. When she claims to need to learn something, I tell her, Don't let schooling interfere with your education.

3. She usually frowns and answers, I don't believe that Mark Twain said that.

4. This is tricky because if I respond, A man is never more truthful than when he acknowledges himself a liar, Jeanette will think I'm lying.

5. However, I can't ignore her, so I say, Grief can take care if itself, but to get the full value of a joy you must have somebody to divide it with.

6. Are you saying that you want to share joy with me? my sister asks.

7. When I don't answer right away, she says, You're a fountain of joy.

8. Thank you, I tell her. Quoting Twain, I continue, I can live for two months on a good compliment.

9. I smile and admit that the compliments people have paid me always embarrass me because, as Twain says, I always feel that they have not said enough.

10. I've had just about enough of Mark Twain and you, fumes my sister.

EXERCISE 2 USING QUOTATION MARKS IN WRITING A CONVERSATION

On a separate piece of paper, write a short conversation. Make sure to use quotation marks to identify who is speaking. Start your paragraph by saying "My mother said, . . . " and continue by writing "I answered her by saying, . . . " Include at least three quotations from each person, and remember to indent each time a different person speaks.

Example: My mother said, "You need to eat less junk food; you're getting chubby."

I answered her by saying, "I'm twenty-three, Mom, and I don't even live here, so don't worry about me."
"I just want you to be healthy," she explained.
"I appreciate that," I responded, "but telling me I'm chubby doesn't inspire me!"
"I know," she said, "but you're too sensitive."
"Thanks, Mom. Can you pass the potatoes?" I asked her.

Using Part of a Quotation

Sometimes you will want to use only part of what someone said instead of quoting the whole statement. In these cases, simply place the quoted part in quotation marks.

Whole quotation: Mark Twain said, "Honesty is the best policy— when there is money in it."

Part of quotation: The clause "when there is money in it" undermines the credibility Twain built in the first part of the sentence by emphasizing the importance of "honesty."

In this example, the writer explains Mark Twain's quotation without giving the whole statement. Since Mark Twain used the words "honesty" and "when there is money in it," the writer places those terms in quotation marks.

Whole quotation: Mark Twain says, "Get your facts first, then you can distort them as you please."

Part of a quotation: In urging people to "get facts" before they "distort them," Twain implies that people's inaccurate use of statistics or details is deliberate. Telling people that they "can distort," Twain essentially gives people permission to be dishonest.

Here again the writer explains Twain's quotation, but she only puts the actual words said by Mark Twain in quotation marks.

Indirect Quotations

Often you may want to communicate what someone meant without quoting his or her exact words. **Indirect quotations** summarize a person's words and are often introduced by *how, if, that, what, whether, who,* or *why.* In these cases, you do not need to use quotation marks.

> **Direct quotation:**   My grandfather said, "No one is more entertaining than Mark Twain."

(The writer is relating the exact words of her grandfather.)

> **Indirect quotation:**   My grandfather said that he knew of no one more entertaining than Mark Twain.

(The writer is summarizing her grandfather's opinion rather than giving a word-for-word quotation. The speaker introduces the indirect quotation with the word *that.*)

> **Direct quotation:**   Sam's note to his roommate said, "I am going to give up smoking like Mark Twain did: thousands of times."

(Here the writer is relating Sam's exact words.)

> **Indirect quotation:**   Sam's note to his roommate said that he wanted to quit smoking the way Mark Twain did: not at all.

(Again, since the writer is not quoting Sam's exact words, no quotation marks are needed.)

EXERCISE 3 USING INDIRECT QUOTATIONS

Revise the following sentences to change the direct quotations into indirect quotations.

Example: I often tell my buddies, "I want to be a riverboat captain."

Revised: *I often tell my buddies that I want to be a riverboat captain.*

1. They always roll their eyes, asking, "Is this another Mark Twain copycat idea?"

2. I pretend to be offended, responding, "If you read as much as I did, you'd want to be like Twain, too."

_____

_____

3. "Yeah, yeah," starts my buddy Jimmy, "but when you change your mind, I'll remind you that you did."

_____

_____

4. I grin and explain, "This time is different."

_____

_____

5. My buddies relent and say, "Even if it's not, your goals make us think about ours."

_____

_____

Setting Off Titles of Short Works

Use quotation marks to indicate the title of a short work, such as the following:

- Book chapters
- Newspaper or magazine articles
- Songs

- Essays
- Poems
- Stories

Magazine article: "A Notable Conundrum" was one of the many newspaper articles Mark Twain wrote.

Song title: Tony Bennet's song "I Left My Heart in San Francisco" gives a more positive impression of that city than many of Mark Twain's statements.

The titles of longer works are indicated by underlining or italics. The examples that follow are underlined. For more information on underlining titles in MLA-style documentation, see page 511.

■ Newspapers

> New York Times, Washington Post, Christian Science Monitor

Note: The word *the* is not underlined or capitalized at the beginning of a newspaper's name.

■ Magazines

> Time, Newsweek, People, Popular Science

■ Books

> Eats, Shoots and Leaves; The Zero Tolerance Approach to Punctuation; Mutiny on the Bounty; The Firm

■ Albums and CDs

> Wiggly Safari; Beauty and the Beat; Songs for Swingin' Lovers

■ Movies

> Pride and Prejudice; King Kong; Batman Begins

Notice how quotation marks and underlining are used in the following examples.

The poem "My Mistress' Eyes Are Nothing Like the Sun" is in The Collected Works of William Shakespeare.
(The poem title is set off by quotation marks; the book title is underlined.)

The chapter "Fever 'n' Ague" in Little House on the Prairie explains how settlers came down with malaria.
(The chapter title is set off by quotation marks while the book title is underlined.)

The newspaper article "Tempting Fate: Seeking Safe Ground" from the Sacramento Bee deals with the issue of potential flooding.
(The article title is set off by quotation marks while the newspaper title is underlined.)

The song "Rock 'N' Roll Lifestyle" from Cake's Motorcade of Generosity seems to be written about my friend Noelle.
(The song title is set off by quotation marks while the book title is underlined.)

Steve Carrell was hilarious in the episode of The Office titled "The Injury." (The episode title is set off by quotation marks while the series title is underlined.)

In professionally published works, titles of longer works are set off by italics (*The Hobbit*) rather than by underlining (<u>The Hobbit</u>). If you use a computer for your writing, you may wish to use an italic font instead of underlining. Before you do so, though, find out what your professor prefers.

EXERCISE 4 USING QUOTATION MARKS AND UNDERLINING FOR TITLES

Add quotation marks or underlining as necessary below.

1. The Adventures of Huckleberry Finn may be Mark Twain's most renowned work.

2. This book is often compared to Twain's novel The Adventures of Tom Sawyer, but the two books are very different.

3. In her review titled Continuation of a Tale, Esther A. Lombardi points out that Huck Finn's story has great depth when compared to Tom Sawyer's.

4. Another of Mark Twain's works is A Connecticut Yankee in King Arthur's Court, which includes the chapter The Boss.

5. Sacramento residents are proud of their newspaper, the Sacramento Daily Union, because Twain once wrote for it.

6. However, despite riveting articles such as The High Chief of Sugardom and Whaling Trade, the Union eventually went out of business.

7. The public radio program Fresh Air featured a discussion titled Rediscovering Mark Twain.

8. I have never heard of any songs featuring Mark Twain, but I can imagine that one entitled Floating on a Raft with Huck Finn would be popular.

9. Hal Holbrook toured the country in his one-man show Mark Twain Tonight.

10. From Huck Finn's comment about kings—It's the way they're raised—to Twain's story titled Advice to Little Girls, it's hard to not find a laugh in Twain's writing.

Setting Off Special Words or Expressions

Quotation marks can be used to set off special words or expressions. For instance:

Mark Twain observed that the term **"truth"** has many interpretations.

Words being used in this way may be italicized instead. Whichever style you choose, be consistent.

Using Single Quotation Marks ' '

Use single quotation marks to indicate a quotation within a quotation. For instance:

> My instructor told us, "Reading Twain's short work 'Italian Without Grammar' will make you appreciate the illogic of English."
>
> My aunt comments frequently on Mark Twain, saying, "I love his saying 'Age is an issue of mind over matter. If you don't mind, it doesn't matter.' "

Both sentences contain items that would require quotation marks even if they were not part of someone's actual words. The regular quotation marks (" ") indicate that someone is speaking, while the single quotation marks (' ') highlight an article title and another speaker's words within the main quotations.

EDITING PRACTICE 1

Add quotation marks and underlining in the eleven places where necessary in the following paragraph.

Samuel Clemens and Dullness:
Never the Twain Shall Meet

Although the term entertainment means something different for everyone, Mark Twain's idea of humor certainly seems to be mine. From his articles for the Sacramento Daily Union to Huck Finn's and Jim's conversations in The Adventures of Huckleberry Finn, the words of Mark Twain speak to me. For instance, when Twain claims in a speech, Always do right; this will gratify some and astonish the rest, I imagine the shocked look on my mother's face when she looks up from her People magazine and sees that I cleaned the house for her, without being asked. Another favorite Twain quote deals with talking. Twain says, The right word may be effective, but no word is as effective as a rightly timed pause. Maybe not everyone would laugh at this, but if people knew how my little sister talks constantly—saying, See how quiet I can be? I am not saying one single word—they would give new credit to the saying. Finally, I love that Twain isn't afraid to be honest about the limits of his knowledge or intellect. When he says, I was gratified to be able to answer quickly and I did. I said I didn't know, I feel as though I have a kindred spirit in literature. I once heard my English instructor say, Mark Twain's idea of truth—that it will not break—gives me hope. I agree wholeheartedly.

EDITING PRACTICE 2 **Using Quotation Marks and Underlining in Real-Life Writing**

To practice using quotation marks and underlining in real-life writing, follow the directions below.

1. Read a paragraph from a book. Then, write down a quotation from it. Be sure to use quotation marks to set off the quotation. Give the source, underlining the book title.

_____

_____

_____

_____

2. Listen to a conversation between two people, either someone you know or actors on television. Then, write down a few sentences of the conversation, being careful to indicate who said what. (See page 682 for a short conversation you can use as a model.)

_____

_____

_____

_____

_____

_____

3. Write down a sentence that you heard someone say on the radio or on television. Make sure you give credit to the person who said the words you quote, and use quotation marks where necessary.

_____

_____

_____

_____

Lab Activity 48

For additional practice with quotation marks, complete Lab Activity 48 in the lab manual packaged with your textbook. If you did not receive a lab manual, you can complete this activity online at **www.ablongman.com/long.** Click on **College Resources for Writers** and then click on **Activity 48.**

49 Other Punctuation Marks

Sandra Day O'Connor

The first woman appointed to the U.S. Supreme Court, Sandra Day O'Connor became known as the swing vote in many controversial decisions. Her pragmatic approach to judicial rulings, which applied to the facts at hand but left room for future jurists' interpretations, made her one of the best-known Supreme Court justices and arguably one of the most influential women in U.S. history. Justice O'Connor retired from the Court in 2006.

Sandra Day O'Connor

SURF THE NET With her retirement from the bench, Sandra Day O'Connor faced scrutiny once more. Her life, her work, and her Supreme Court decisions were widely analyzed as she left her post. Based on what you learn online, what can you conclude about the kind of justice O'Connor was? Surf the Internet for information on her and write a few sentences summarizing what you learn.

Understanding Other Punctuation Marks

Commas, quotation marks, and apostrophes are very common punctuation marks. Some other forms of punctuation that are used less often also serve special functions. These marks are

- Semicolons
- Hyphens
- Parentheses

- Colons
- Dashes

Knowing how to use these forms of punctuation can help you write a variety of sentences.

Semicolons ;

Use a **semicolon** to join independent clauses without a coordinating conjunction.

Sandra Day O'Connor was an attorney; she was also a state senator.

O'Connor served as an assistant attorney general in Arizona; she also raised three children.

O'Connor reputedly lacked a sense of humor on the bench; most people, however, agree that her excellent service more than made up for her seriousness.

Another use of the semicolon is to separate items in a series where the individual items contain commas. A **series** is two or more items in a row.

Sandra Day O'Connor had several roles in life. She was a fledging attorney, trying to find a good job; she was a devoted mother, trying to raise three sons; and she was a dedicated Supreme Court justice, trying to make fair decisions.

Some books about O'Connor are *Sandra Day O'Connor: Supreme Court Justice* by Lisa McElroy; *Sandra Day O'Connor: How the First Woman on the Supreme Court Became Its Most Influential Justice* by John Biskupic; and *The Majesty of the Law: Reflections of a Supreme Court Justice* by O'Connor herself.

EXERCISE 1 **USING SEMICOLONS CORRECTLY**

Add semicolons where necessary in the following sentences.

1. Sandra Day O'Connor made decisions that involved school prayer, a topic of great controversy children's issues, on which she has been considered less conservative and women's issues, another highly controversial arena.

2. O'Connor had several reputations. One was cold and humorless, which applied to her personality another was pragmatic and fair, which applied to her means of making decisions one more was thoughtful and conservative, which applied to her actual rulings.

3. Sandra Day O'Connor is more than a Supreme Court justice: she is a woman, someone who loves her family an attorney, one who has practiced law and a jurist, one who interprets the law.

Colons

Colons tell the reader to pay attention to what's coming. Use a colon for these purposes.

- To introduce a list
- To introduce a lengthy quotation
- To call attention to the words following the colon
- To separate the minutes from the hour in telling time

Three of Sandra Day O'Connor's notable decisions came in the following cases: *McConnell vs. Federal Election Commission, Boy Scouts of America vs. Dale,* and *United States vs. Lopez.*

(The colon introduces the list of cases.)

Sandra Day O'Connor was quoted as saying: "Do the best you can in every task, no matter how unimportant it may seem at the time. No one learns more about a problem than the person at the bottom."

(The colon introduces a quotation that is more than one sentence long.)

Here's your 2006 Tournament of Roses Grand Marshal: Sandra Day O'Connor.

(The colon calls attention to the name that follows.)

Sandra Day O'Connor was known to be at work at 9:00 p.m. on a Tuesday.

(The colon separates the hour from the minutes in an expression of time.)

EXERCISE 2 USING COLONS CORRECTLY

Add colons where necessary in the following sentences.

1. Sandra Day O'Connor has held one title for most of her life woman.

2. I plan to begin my essay about Sandra Day O'Connor's Supreme Court decisions tomorrow at 2 00 p.m.

3. Perhaps my favorite quotation from Sandra Day O'Connor is Yes, I will bring the understanding of a woman to the Court, but I doubt that alone will affect my decisions. I think the important thing about my appointment is not that I will decide cases as a woman, but that I am a woman who will get to decide cases.

Hyphens -

Use a **hyphen** to join two words working together to communicate one concept. For instance:

Concern for her husband's well-being led Sandra Day O'Connor to retire.

(The words *well* and *being* are connected by a hyphen to communicate the idea of happiness or wellness.)

Many words that need hyphens are listed in the dictionary.

Hyphens are also used to split a word at the end of a line. To divide a word at the end of a line, make the break between syllables. *Hint:* If you're not sure of syllable breaks, check a dictionary. One-syllable words should never be hyphenated, and no word should be divided unless absolutely necessary.

Sandra Day O'Connor claimed that she had trouble finding a threat to reli-gious freedom in a room of silent, thoughtful schoolchildren.

(The hyphen tells the reader that the word *religious* continues on the next line.)

Since word processors and computers often contain a "wraparound" feature to keep whole words on a single line, you will rarely need to use hyphens to divide single words.

EXERCISE 3 USING HYPHENS CORRECTLY

Add hyphens where necessary in the following sentences.

1. Several well known Supreme Court rulings gave O'Connor food for thought.

2. Perhaps we can all work together to understand the reasons for the specific decision in this case.

3. O'Connor's sons, daughters in law, and grandchildren are all proud of her accomplishments.

Dashes —

Use **dashes** to set off remarks that interrupt the flow of a sentence. The interruption that a dash signals is longer and more obvious than one set off by two commas. Dashes are made by typing two hyphens in a row. If you are writing a dash by hand, make it as long as two letters.

Some people—those who wanted to undermine O'Connor's credibility—claimed she wasn't tough enough on women's issues.

Because O'Connor was the first woman on the Supreme Court—having been appointed by President Ronald Reagan—she was expected to make a mark for women everywhere.

Parentheses may be used instead in the same places where you might choose a dash; see the examples in the following section.

EXERCISE 4 **USING DASHES CORRECTLY**

Add dashes where appropriate in the following sentences.

1. O'Connor's opinions on life, work, and religion are easy to find online.

2. Many law students ones who also want to be influential in their careers revere O'Connor.

3. Thus, even though she has left the bench, O'Connor remains now and for the future an inspiration in the field of law.

Parentheses ( )

Parentheses set off information that interrupts the flow of a sentence. Usually the information in parentheses is interesting but not essential to understand the sentence. Information commonly set off in parentheses includes dates and page numbers.

As recounted in *Great Justice* (p. 48), O'Connor's initial job search following law school was frustrating.

Sandra Day O'Connor served twenty-four years on the Supreme Court (1981–2005) before announcing her retirement.

John O'Connor III (Sandra Day O'Connor's husband) was proud to have such a powerful wife.

(The writer could also have used dashes to set off the extra information about John O'Connor.)

Note: If a comma follows parentheses, it should go *after* the parentheses, as illustrated in the first sentence.

EXERCISE 5 **USING PARENTHESES CORRECTLY**

Add parentheses where appropriate in the following sentences.

1. Sandra Day O'Connor first woman on the Supreme Court more than made a mark on the bench.

2. Her birth date March 26, 1930 serves as my own personal holiday each year.

3. Her place on the bench which sounds uncomfortable to me will never be filled in same the way that she filled it.

EDITING PRACTICE

Add the correct punctuation marks (colon, semicolon, hyphen, dash, or parentheses) where appropriate in the following paragraph. You will need to add four hyphens, two dashes, two colons, one semicolon, and two parentheses.

A Justice for All

Sandra Day O'Connor born March 26, 1930 was an Associate Justice of the Supreme Court of the United States from 1981 to 2006. Though she was distinguished in many aspects of her career, one accomplishment stands out above the others she was the first woman to serve on the Supreme Court. Due to her case by case approach to jurisprudence and her relatively moderate political views despite Republicans' hope that she would be extremely conservative she was the crucial swing vote on the Court. In 2004, *Forbes* magazine called her the fourth most powerful woman in the United States *Forbes* also named her the sixth most powerful woman in the world. After twenty four years of service, O'Connor announced her retirement from the Supreme Court, effective on the confirmation of her successor. Perhaps an apt summary of her attitudes is her own statement "Do the best you can in every task, no matter how unimportant it may seem at the time. No one learns more about a problem than the person at the bottom."

Lab Activity 49

For additional practice with other punctuation marks, complete Lab Activity 49 in the lab manual packaged with your textbook. If you did not receive a lab manual, you can complete this activity online at **www.ablongman.com/long.** Click on **College Resources for Writers** and then click on **Activity 49.**

50 Capitalization

New Orleans, Louisiana

Known for its wonderful food and music, New Orleans hosts the nation's largest celebration for Mardi Gras (literally "Fat Tuesday," the last day before Lent). In 2005, however, Hurricane Katrina put New Orleans on the map for another reason: fatal flooding. Though many of the city's residents were displaced as a result of the floods, New Orleans remains a cultural hub of the United States.

Mardi Gras in New Orleans

OBSERVE YOUR WORLD Mardi Gras, literally "fat Tuesday," marks the last day before Lent, traditionally a period of deprivation in the Christian Church. However, celebrating Mardi Gras—especially in New Orleans—is not limited to Christians. What other traditions or holidays have grown beyond their original significance to include a broader range of people? Pay attention to the special days your community celebrates, noting the days' origins, and writing a few sentences about them.

697

Primary Uses of Captial Letters

Understanding the rules of capitalization can aid you greatly in your writing courses. Keep in mind, though, that different capitalization conventions apply to various academic disciplines. Certain words may be capitalized in science classes, for instance, that are not capitalized in humanities courses. When in doubt about what should be capitalized, consult a dictionary.

Capital letters are used in many instances; these are the most common.

- Names of persons and the pronoun *I*
- Names of specific places
- Names of holidays, months, and days of the week
- Brand names of products
- Titles of written or performed works
- First word in a sentence or direct quotation

Names of People and the Pronoun *I*   Capitalize people's names and the pronoun *I*.

> **M**arian, **L**uc, and **I** wanted to go to New Orleans last year.
>
> The new mayor, **S**imon **B**eauregard, plans to build a new arena.
>
> My friend **C**hristie loves the beads she and **I** get during Mardi Gras every year.

Names of Specific Places   Capitalize the names of specific places, including institutions, cities, states, countries, regions, lakes, parks, and mountains. Do *not* capitalize directions.

> Tell Spencer to head southeast; he'll eventually find my home in the **D**eep **S**outh.

Institutions:	College of the **S**equoias, **S**acred **H**eart **H**ospital, **D**epartment of the **I**nterior
Cities:	**S**eattle, **S**an **A**ntonio, **H**elena
States:	**I**daho, **M**ichigan, **S**outh **D**akota
Countries:	France, the **D**emocratic **R**epublic of **C**ongo, **V**ietnam
Regions:	**P**acific **C**oast, **S**outhwest

Names of Holidays, Months, and Days of the Week   Capitalize the names of religious and secular holidays. Also capitalize the names of months and days of the week.

> Each **T**hanksgiving, I appreciate getting **T**hursday, **F**riday, and the weekend days off right before the **D**ecember shopping season.

Note: Do not capitalize the names of the seasons of the year: spring, summer, fall, winter.

Brand Names of Products   Capitalize the *name* of a product, but not the *type* of product.

> I prefer **G**hirardelli **c**hocolate for baking.

Capitalizing Brand Names

Brand Name	Product
L. L. Bean	boots
Ivory	soap
Kleenex	tissue
Chevron	gasoline

Titles of Written or Performed Works   Capitalize the first, last, and main words in the titles of articles, books, magazines, newspapers, poems, stories, movies, songs, television shows, and your own papers.

> Kate Chopin's work *The Awakening* is partially set in New Orleans.

The following words usually do not require capitalization.

Articles:	*a, an, the; Harry Potter and the Goblet of Fire*
Prepositions:	*in, of, to,* and so on; "Ode on a Grecian Urn"
Coordinating Conjunctions:	*for, and, nor, but, or, yet, so; Sense and Sensibility*

First Word in a Sentence or a Direct Quotation   Capitalize the first word in a sentence or a direct quotation.

> **G**oing to New Orleans for spring break was the goal of some college students.
>
> Theo asked, "**W**hy don't we just watch *The Big Easy* instead?"

EXERCISE 1 CORRECT CAPITALIZATION

Change lowercase letters to capital letters where necessary in the following sentences. Each item tells you how many words to capitalize.

Example: after reading about new orleans online, i decided to get the fodor's travel guide.

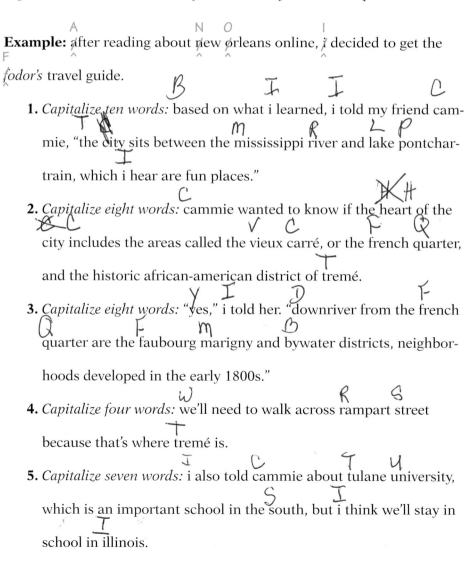

1. *Capitalize ten words:* based on what i learned, i told my friend cammie, "the city sits between the mississippi river and lake pontchartrain, which i hear are fun places."

2. *Capitalize eight words:* cammie wanted to know if the heart of the city includes the areas called the vieux carré, or the french quarter, and the historic african-american district of tremé.

3. *Capitalize eight words:* "yes," i told her. "downriver from the french quarter are the faubourg marigny and bywater districts, neighborhoods developed in the early 1800s."

4. *Capitalize four words:* we'll need to walk across rampart street because that's where tremé is.

5. *Capitalize seven words:* i also told cammie about tulane university, which is an important school in the south, but i think we'll stay in school in illinois.

Additional Uses of Capital Letters

Capital letters are necessary in other areas, too. Use capital letters in the following cases.

- People's titles
- Names showing family relationships
- Names of groups with specific affiliations
- Names of school courses (including languages)
- Historical periods and events

People's Titles   Capitalize the title that comes in front of a person's name.

Everyone says that **J**udge Weingard always rules fairly.
I hope that **D**r. Stabler will remove my cast today.
Last week **S**enator Wilson requested a new driver.

Do not capitalize a title if it does not come before a name.

Everyone says that the judge always rules fairly.
I hope that the doctor will remove my cast today.
Last week the senator requested a new driver.

Common Titles

Mr.	Dr.
Mrs.	Professor
Ms.	

Names Showing Family Relationships   Capitalize any name you might call a family member.

On Sundays **G**randma **G**race goes to church, but **G**rampy prefers to watch football.
When is **A**unt **E**lsbeth making lobster risotto again?
Because **M**other keeps a very formal home, we rarely visit.

If you place a possessive pronoun in front of a family name, do not capitalize the name.

My grandma goes to church, but my grandpa prefers to watch football.
When is our aunt making lobster risotto again?
Because my mother keeps a very formal home, we rarely visit.

Names of Groups   Capitalize names of groups with specific affiliations.
- Races and nationalities
- Political groups
- Unions
- Religions
- Companies
- Clubs and other associations

The **A**merican **R**ed **C**ross and the **N**ew **Z**ion **B**aptist **C**hurch had much to do in New Orleans after Hurricane Katrina hit. Local **G**irl **S**cout troops as well as the **L**ouisiana **M**inority **B**us **C**ouncil all contributed their time and effort. Strategists for the **R**epublican **N**ational **P**arty and the **AFL-CIO** helped spur **S**tate **F**arm **I**nsurance into action.

Names of School Courses   Capitalize the names of specific school courses.

To better understand the New Orleans culture, I am taking **C**reole **S**tudies, **F**rench, **B**ayou **P**reservation **C**hemistry, and **S**outhern **A**merican **L**iterature.

Do not capitalize the names of general subjects, but always capitalize the names of languages.

To better understand the New Orleans culture, I am taking a local studies class, a **F**rench course, a chemistry class, and a literature class.

Historical Periods, Events, and Documents   Capitalize the names of historical events and specific periods in history.

New Orleans was founded by the French in 1718 but was ceded to the Spanish as part of the **T**reaty of **F**ontainebleau in 1762, before the **R**evolutionary **W**ar. France acquired Louisiana again in 1800, but Napoleon sold the city to the United States as part of the **L**ouisiana **P**urchase in 1803.

Names of Historical Events and Periods Requiring Capitalization

the Civil War	World War II
the Vietnam War	the Renaissance
the Romantic Movement	the Middle Ages
the Treaty of Versailles	the Great Depression
the Battle of Bunker Hill	the Constitution

EXERCISE 2 USING CAPITAL LETTERS CORRECTLY

Change lowercase letters to capital letters where necessary. Forty-two words require capitalization.

katrina's effects

New Orleans residents—african-americans, european americans, asians, and latinos alike—suffered from the effects of hurricane katrina on and after august 29, 2005. Three days earlier, indications that the hurricane was heading toward the florida gulf coast changed. In the gulf of mexico, the hurricane grew to a Category 5 storm as it turned north toward new orleans. The city government issued a mandatory evacuation, telling people, "take only what is absolutely necessary," and 80 percent of the population left before the storm. rain, wind, and flooding caused tremendous intitial damage, but the situation worsened when levees of four of the city's canals were breached. as much as 80 percent of the city was flooded, with water reaching a depth of twenty-five feet in some areas. Almost no building—not charity hospital, not the felicity united methodist church, not the snug harbor jazz bistro—was spared from damage. The next day, governor kathleen blanco reported to cnn, "we have an engineering nightmare." The u.s. army corps of engineers and the orleans levee board are working to solve problems so that this situation can be avoided in the future.

Avoiding Unnecessary Capitalization

Do not use capital letters where they are not needed. Words that serve as general labels, such as *city, river, company,* and *airport,* are not capitalized unless they are part of a name. The general terms below are not capitalized.

The painter William Pajaud celebrates his native city, New Orleans. Pajaud paints familiar scenes such as his mother on her way to church. Though his art is not filled with majestic mountains or flowing rivers, Pajaud's work is pleasing.

EXERCISE 3 CORRECTING ERRORS IN CAPITALIZATION

Correct any errors in capitalization in the following sentences by changing the incorrectly capitalized word to a word beginning with a lowercase letter.

1. *Change three letters:* Last Winter, I decided to go to The Big Easy and celebrate Mardi Gras the New Orleans Way.

2. *Change five letters:* In my reading about the City, I learned that Mardi Gras is the most Famous of the Carnival Celebrations with its Parades and Parties.

3. *Change three letters:* The Mardi Gras Parades are sponsored by Krewes, Organizations of varying size and Membership.

4. *Change five letters:* One of the most Famous Krewes, the Zulu Aid Society and Pleasure Club, is Responsible for the Celebration's First parade of Mardi Gras Day, the Last day before Lent begins.

5. *Change five letters:* Another Tradition is king cake, which is a Braided, colorfully iced bread, filled with cream cheese or marzipan, that contains a Trinket. Whoever finds the Trinket gets to be king or queen of the Party where the king cake is served.

EDITING PRACTICE

Change lowercase letters to capital letters where necessary in the following paragraph. Thirty words require capitalization.

"Easy" Reading

Because of its history, culture, and french influence, New Orleans is the backdrop for many significant works of literature. One work, tennessee williams's play *a streetcar named desire,* focuses on the clash between a fading southern belle and an up-and-coming member of the industrial working class. Just as blanche dubois will always be remembered for saying, "i have always depended on the kindness of strangers," stanley kowalski is immortalized in his agonizing cry of "stella!" another famous work set in New Orleans is kate chopin's novel *the awakening.* In this work, a young matron, edna pontellier, experiences personal awakenings on several levels. although many argue that the story ends unhappily, others claim that the ending—in which edna swims too far from shore and can't get back—is apt. finally, Walker Percy's novel *The Moviegoer* is one more respected work set in the Big Easy. featuring handsome, well-to-do stockbroker binx bolling, the novel follows binx on his search to find whatever he's "onto," for, as Binx explains, "not to be onto something is to be in despair." in all three works, New Orleans, louisiana, gives the characters time, space, and opportunity to become more than they already are.

Lab Activity 50

For additional practice with capitalization, complete Lab Activity 50 in the lab manual packaged with your textbook. If you did not receive a lab manual, you can complete this activity online at **www.ablongman.com/long.** Click on **College Resources for Writers** and then click on **Activity 50.**

51 Numbers and Abbreviations

CULTURE NOTE *The Space Race*

An informal competition between the United States and the former Soviet Union, the so-called space race sought to broaden these countries' knowledge and use of satellites. Beginning in 1957 with the launch of the Soviet *Sputnik 1,* the race became an important Cold War issue as military implications became increasingly apparent.

Neil Armstrong

CRITICAL THINKING When Neil Armstrong first set foot on the moon, the world watched in great suspense. How exciting or suspenseful do you think space travel is to people now? Is it as thrilling as it was at the beginning? What factors have influenced people's attitudes toward space travel? Write a few sentences in response to these questions.

Using Numbers

Depending on the nature or discipline of the paper you're writing, different abbreviations can be acceptable. In many courses in math, science, and engineering, for instance, numerals and other abbreviations are used to save time and space.

While this chapter covers some rules for basic usage of abbreviations and numerals, always ask your instructors if they have particular conventions they want you to follow.

Spelling Out Numbers

In general, you should spell out numbers that can be written in one or two words.

thirty-four years	fifty-six corn chips
seventeen kiwi seeds	ninety-nine photographs

Numbers over one hundred should be expressed using numerals.

524 rocks	1,600 paper clips
12,677 miles	103,792 contestants

The space race was between **two** main contestants: the United States and the Soviet Union.

Nearly **500 million** people worldwide watched Neil Armstrong land on the moon.

Using Numerals for Everyday Information

Use numerals to express dates, time, page numbers, book sections, addresses, and percentages.

On **October 4, 1957,** the USSR successfully launched *Sputnik 1,* the first artificial satellite to reach orbit.

Chapter 3 of *The Great Space Race* contains an excellent photo of *Sputnik 1.*

At **10:00 a.m.** I will go to the theater at **3722 Adams Avenue** to see an IMAX film with **50 percent** of the local space nuts.

Using Ordinals

Ordinals are types of numbers that show order.

3rd = third
37th = thirty-seventh
51st = fifty-first

In general, avoid using ordinals in formal writing. Some exceptions:

■ Describing a military unit
   The 1st Infantry Division fought valiantly.
■ Using street names
   The astronauts stopped for coffee mean the **15th Street** bridge.

EXERCISE 1 USING NUMERALS CORRECTLY

Correct the nine errors in numbers in the following sentences. Cross out each mistake and write the correction above it.

1. On July twenty-nine, nineteen fifty-eight, President Dwight Eisen-

hower signed the act establishing the National Aeronautics and

Space Administration (NASA).

2. When it began operations on October 1st nineteen fify-eight,

NASA consisted mainly of 4 laboratories and some eight

thousand employees of the government's 46-year-old research

agency for aeronautics, the National Advisory Committee for

Aeronautics (NACA).

3. While its predecessor, NACA, operated on a five million budget,

NASA's funding rapidly accelerated to five billion per year.

Using Abbreviations

Avoid using abbreviations in formal writing.

Incorrect: I don't have class on Tues. and Fri.
Correct: I don't have class on **Tuesday** and **Friday.**
Incorrect: Sean wants to be a prof.
Correct: Sean wants to be a **professor.**

However, a few types of abbreviations are acceptable.

People's Titles   Always abbreviate these titles when they are used with proper names: *Mr., Ms., Mrs., Dr., Jr.,* and *Sr. Note:* The title *Miss* is not an abbreviation.

> **Ms.** Hastings taught me everything I know about the moon.
> **Dr.** Spacer still reads old Buck Rogers comic books.
> Andy Spacer, **Jr.,** is writing his own comic books.

Note: When commas are used with *Jr.,* or *Sr.,* place them before and after the title.

> Andy Spacer**,** Jr.**,** is a good pilot.

Do not abbreviate *professor* before a name: Professor Lily Strickler.

Initials in a Signature   Sometimes part of a person's name may be abbreviated. Follow the abbreviation with a period.

Neil A**.** Armstrong   Susannah Q**.** Winter
M**.** Donald Cousins   B. J. Banks

Organizations and Items Known by Their Initials   Some companies, government agencies, and other groups are known by their initials. Other common items may also be known by their initials. Do not use periods with these abbreviations.

ATM (automatic teller machine)
NASA (National Aeronautics and Space Administration)
CD (compact disc)
ABC (American Broadcasting Corporation)

References to Time   a.m. *or* A.M.

p.m. *or* P.M.   2,000 B.C.   A.D. 46

Note: Remember to write the year *after* writing A.D.: A.D. 32.

Note: You should spell out *noon* and *midnight* to avoid confusion in expressions of time: 12:00 a.m. is the same as 12:00 midnight.

Note: Using numerals in place of non-numerical words is incorrect. Incorrect: I will always be here 4 you. Correct: I will always be here for you.

EXERCISE 2 ELIMINATING UNNECESSARY ABBREVIATIONS

Correct the eight errors in abbreviations in the following sentences by crossing out the mistake and writing the correction above it.

My buds and I went to our prof's house in Feb. to watch a

TV show about the 1st spacewalk. It lasted about 90 min., which was

long enough for me to get tot. hungry. We went to a fast-food place,

but I had only 73¢, not enough for the cheapest item on the menu.

EDITING PRACTICE

Find thirty errors in numbers and abbreviations in the following paragraph. Cross out each mistake and write the correction above it.

A Man in Flight

Neil Alden Armstrong (born 8/5/30) is a former test pilot and

astronaut who was the 1st man 2 walk on the moon. In nineteen

fifty, he was sent to Korea, where he flew 78 combat missions. He

received the Air Medal with 2 Gold Stars. He attended Purdue U,

through which Northwestern Ave. runs. Armstrong rec'd a

B.S. degree in Aero. Engr. in nineteen fifty-five. Armstrong then became a civilian test pilot at Edwards Air Force Base in CA. Armstrong made a tot. of 7 flts in the N. Am. X-15, reaching an alt. of two hundred seven thousand five hundred feet in the X-15-3 and a speed of Mach five point seven four (three thousand nine hundred eighty-nine miles per hour) in the X-15-1. He ended his career w/ a total of two thousand four hundred fifty flying hrs in more than 50 types of aircraft. In Ch. Five of *First Man: The Life of Neil Armstrong,* the auth. shows some great pics of Armstrong in action.

Lab Activity 51

For additional practice with numbers and abbreviations, complete Lab Activity 51 in the lab manual packaged with your textbook. If you did not receive a lab manual, you can complete this activity online at **www.ablongman.com/ long.** Click on **College Resources for Writers** and then click on **Activity 51**.

52 Tips for Second Language Writers

The U.S. Constitution

The supreme law of the United States of America, the Constitution was completed on September 17, 1787, and was adopted by the Constitutional Convention in Philadelphia, Pennsylvania. Ratified by the original thirteen states, the Constitution created a union of individual states as well as a federal government to run that union. Currently the oldest written constitution in use, the U.S. Constitution took effect in 1789 and has served as a model for the constitutions of numerous other nations.

The United States Constitution

JOURNAL ENTRY As part of their preparation for citizenship, applicants must study the Constitution, among other aspects of U.S. history. What else do you think people must know or do, if anything, to earn United States citizenship? Write a few sentences explaining your ideas.

Understanding ESL Needs

If you learned another language before you learned English, you have a tremendous advantage. Not only can you communicate in two tongues, but you have the choice of using words and expressions from two languages in considering and developing your ideas.

Speaking English as your second language is a great bonus, but writing English presents certain challenges. English grammar is complex, and for many rules, there are exceptions. This chapter focuses on some of the fundamental concerns **English as a Second Language (ESL)** students face in writing. Specifically, this chapter discusses how to use the following elements correctly.

- Subjects
- Articles
- Prepositions

- Verbs
- Adjectives

Using Subjects Correctly

A group of words cannot be a sentence unless it has a subject. When writing English sentences, be sure to follow these rules.

- Include a subject in each clause.
- Make every noun a subject or an object.
- Avoid extra or unnecessary pronoun subjects.

Including a Subject in Every Clause

Every sentence must have a subject and a verb. Leaving out a subject results in a sentence fragment (see Chapter 36). In the example that follows, the underlined word group needs a subject.

People study the Constitution often. <u>Have several interpretations</u>.

In this case, the writer probably means to say, "*They* have several interpretations." However, because the writer has not included a subject, it's hard to understand the meaning of this group of words. Including a subject makes the meaning clear.

They have several interpretations.

Now we know that people who study the Constitution are the ones who have many interpretations.

Here is another example of a sentence requiring a subject.

Incorrect: The Constitution lays out guidelines for our country's government. Includes room for future lawmakers' interpretations.

Correct: The Constitution lays out guidelines for our country's government. **The Constitution** includes room for future lawmakers' interpretations.

Every sentence must have a subject, even if you have to use a place-holder subject such as *here, there,* or *it.*

Incorrect: Is possible to read the original Constitution.

Correct: **It** is possible to read the original Constitution.

Incorrect: Are many ways to study its effects.

Correct: **There** are many ways to study its effects.

Incorrect: Is an interesting way to learn about government.

Correct: **Here** is an interesting way to learn about government.

Sometimes a sentence requires more than one subject. For instance, the following sentence has two **clauses** (groups of related words having a subject and a verb that work together to communicate an idea), so it requires two subjects.

Some **people** love to criticize the United States even if **they** have never been here.

Because this sentence has two clauses, it requires two subjects: *people* and *they.* Omitting one of the subjects would result in a sentence error.

Making Every Noun a Subject or an Object

In some languages, a word or phrase with no grammatical connection to the sentence announces what the sentence is about. This kind of structure is incorrect in English.

Incorrect: Career goal I plan to be a constitutional law professor.

This sentence makes no sense in English because the term *career goal* serves as neither a subject nor an object. Even though *career goal* appears at the beginning of the sentence—a typical place for the subject—it is not the subject because it does not go with the verb, *want.* The sentence subject is *I.* Furthermore, *career goal* is not an object of the verb *want* or of a preposition. It has no grammatical connection to the rest of the sentence. You can revise this sentence two ways.

- **Create a subject.** You can make *career goal* the subject of the sentence above.

  Correct: My **career goal** is to be a constitutional law professor.

- **Create an object.** You can make *career goal* the object of a preposition in a prepositional phrase.

  Correct: For my **career goal,** I plan to be a constitutional law professor.

Notice that the writer had to change other words so the corrected versions would make sense.

Avoiding Unnecessary Pronoun Subjects

English does not permit a sentence to have repeated subjects for the same verb. Don't follow the subject with a pronoun that refers to that subject.

Incorrect: My role model he is George Washington.
Correct: My **role model** is George Washington.
Correct: **He** is George Washington.

Even if the subject is separated from the verb by several words, do not repeat the subject with a pronoun.

Incorrect: My roommate who wants to be a judge she loves to study for her citizenship exam.

(The pronoun *she* is unnecessary.)

Correct: My roommate who wants to be a judge loves to study for her citizenship exam.

EXERCISE 1 USING SUBJECTS CORRECTLY

Circle the correct word groups in parentheses below. The first one has been done for you.

Loving the Law of the Land

(My father he, My father) has become an expert on the U.S. Constitution. (I study. Have learned much from him. *or* I study. I have learned much from him). The (Constitution styles, Constitution it styles) itself the supreme law of the land. (Courts they have, Courts have) interpreted this phrase to mean that when laws conflict with the Constitution, (they have no effect, have no effect). (Decisions by the Supreme Court over the course of two centuries they, Decisions by the Supreme Court over the course of two centuries) have repeatedly confirmed and strengthened the doctrine of constitutional supremacy.

Using Verbs Correctly

Every sentence must have a verb that is right for the sentence. In your writing, make sure to follow these rules.

- Include a verb in every sentence.
- Use the correct verb tense.
- Use the progressive verb tense correctly.
- Use gerunds and infinitives correctly after verbs.

Including a Verb in Every Sentence

Every sentence must have a verb. In particular, be sure not to omit linking verbs (forms of the verb *be: am, is, are, was, were*).

Incorrect: The Constitution's language very effective.
Correct: The Constitution's language <u>is</u> very effective.
Incorrect: I a proud American.
Correct: I <u>am</u> a proud American.

Using the Correct Verb Tense

Verbs tell when the action of the sentence takes place. However, other words can also indicate time. Make sure that the verb tense makes sense with the rest of the sentence.

Incorrect: Yesterday, I view a copy of the Constitution at the library.

Correct: Yesterday, I <u>viewed</u> a copy of the Constitution at the library.

(The past tense verb *viewed* is consistent with the time indicator *yesterday*.)

Incorrect: Tomorrow I understood the document for myself.

Correct: Tomorrow I <u>will understand</u> the document for myself.

(The past tense verb *understood* in the first sentence is not consistent with the word *tomorrow*. Thus, the future tense verb *will understand* is needed for the sentence to make sense.)

Using the Progressive Verb Tense

The **progressive verb tense** consists of forms of the verb *be* and the *-ing* form (present participle) of the main verb. This tense indicates actions still occurring at a certain time.

Many immigrants *will be studying* the Constitution for their citizenship exam.

Verbs that apply to the five senses, mental states, possession, and inclusion are not usually used in the progressive tense.

Incorrect: Shaya is owning a new car.

Correct: Shaya <u>owns</u> a new car.

(The word *owns* refers to posession.)

Verbs Not Usually Used in the Progressive Tense

Mental states:	know, understand, think, agree, believe, hate, imagine, want, like, love, prefer, wish
The five senses:	see, hear, taste, touch, smell, feel
Possession:	belong, have, own, possess
Other verbs:	contain, include, be, have, need, weigh, cost, mean

Using Transitive Verbs for Passive Voice

Make sure that you use transitive verbs in explaining something in the **passive voice** (where the subject does not perform the action of the verb). To make sense, transitive verbs require objects; check your dictionary if you're not certain whether or not a verb is transitive and, thus, requires an object.

Incorrect: Since we are late, the train may be arrived now.

(*Arrived*—an intransitive verb—requires no object, so using it in the passive voice is incorrect.)

Correct: Since we are late, the train <u>may arrive</u> now.

(In this case, *train* is performing the action of the verb and is arriving. Thus, the sentence makes sense.)

> **Incorrect:**   The instructor is imagining the class to be bored.
> **Correct:**   The instructor <u>imagines</u> the class to be bored.

Using Gerunds and Infinitives After Verbs

Verbals are forms of verbs used as other parts of speech. A **gerund,** for instance, is a verb form that serves as a noun, as in "The *building* is very tall." *Building* is a form of the verb *build,* yet it can be used as a noun. **Infinitives,** on the other hand, are made up of the root form of the verb preceded by *to,* as in *to build.* Infinitives can be used as nouns, adverbs, or adjectives.

> <u>To build</u> a skyscraper is Rico's dream. (*To build* is a noun.)
>
> Rico hopes he gets a chance <u>to build</u> one. (*To build* is an adjective modifying *chance.*)
>
> First, he needs to learn <u>to build</u> smaller structures. (*To build* is an adverb modifying the infinitive *to learn.*)

The trick in using these verb forms correctly lies in being aware of what verbs can follow them. The following lists give examples of verbs that can be followed by gerunds only, by infinitives only, or by both.

Verbs Followed by Gerunds but Not Infinitives

admit	deny	keep	resent
adore	describe	keep on	resume
anticipate	detest	look forward to	risk
apologize for	discuss	mention	suggest
appreciate	dislike	mind	suspect of
approve of	enjoy	miss	talk about
avoid	fancy	postpone	thank for
be used to	feel like	practice	think about
believe in	finish	quit	tolerate
can't stand	give up	recall	
carry on	insist on	recommend	
contemplate	justify	report	

Incorrect: He will discuss to read if you are prepared.
Correct: He will discuss <u>reading</u> if you are prepared.
Incorrect: He tolerates to swim, but he doesn't enjoy it.
Correct: He tolerates <u>swimming</u>, but he doesn't enjoy it.

Verbs Followed by Infinitives but Not Gerunds

agree	have	need	refuse
arrange	hesitate	plan	seek
claim	hope	pretend	wait
decide	intend	promise	
expect	manage	propose	

Incorrect: He decided reading the Constitution.
Correct: He decided to read the Constitution.
Incorrect: She promised studying the document.
Correct: She promised to study the document.

Verbs Followed by a Gerund or an Infinitive

attempt	hate	neglect	remember
begin	like	prefer	start
continue	love	regret	try

Correct: Paul continues <u>liking</u> that law program.
Correct: Paul continues <u>to like</u> that law program.

EXERCISE 2   PRACTICE USING CORRECT VERBS

Circle the correct verb forms in parentheses below.

A Quotable Document

Perhaps because the Constitution (is, is being) a document that affects all Americans, many quotations refer to it. For instance, columnist Dave Barry (writing, writes), "The primary function of the government is—and here I am quoting directly from the U.S. Constitution—'to spew out paper.'" Of course, people appreciate (reading, to read) humorous quotations, but they often expect (learning, to learn) something when they read. Benjamin Franklin said, "The Constitution only gives people the right to pursue happiness. You have to catch it yourself." On a more serious note, Abraham Lincoln (said, was saying), "Don't interfere with anything in the Constitution. That must be maintained, for it is the only safeguard of our liberties." Will Rogers (was agreeing, agreed), pointing out, "Our Constitution protects aliens, drunks and U.S. Senators." Secretary of Defense Donald Rumsfeld (is defending, defends) his president's power when he says: "Don't begin to think you're the President. You're not. The Constitution provides for only one." Supreme Court Justice Antonin Scalia justifies (protecting, to protect) the rights of people accused of crimes by saying, "There is nothing new in the realization that the Constitution sometimes insulates the criminality of a few in order to protect the privacy of us all." Even Albert Einstein attempted (to assign, assigning) responsibility for the Constitution by claiming, "The strength of the Constitution lies entirely in the determination of each citizen to defend it." Similarly, Gerald Ford (discussed, was discussing) the role of the Constitution in saying, "Our Constitution works. Our great republic is a government of laws, not of men." Finally, even British novelist Thomas Hardy could not deny (to feel, feeling) that our Constitution works when he said, "Like the British Constitution, she owes her success in practice to her inconsistencies in principle." Not everyone quotes from the Constitution daily, but at least some people have thought about it.

EXERCISE 3 USING CORRECT SUBJECTS AND VERBS

Revise each sentence below, adding either a subject or verb to make it correct.

Example: George Washington was important. Was first to sign Constitution.

Revised: _____

1. The Bill of Rights it is the name given to the first ten amendments to the Constitution.

   Revised:_____

   _____

2. Many of the Constitution's early opponents claimed being upset, saying it was an aristocratic scheme to remove the rights of Americans.

   Revised:_____

   _____

3. The Bill of Rights includes rights. These rights freedom of speech, freedom of the press, freedom of religion, and freedom of assembly.

   Revised:_____

   _____

4. The Second Amendment seeks protecting people's right to bear arms.

   Revised: _____

   _____

5. This Amendment it has come under attack because of increased gun-related violence.

Revised:_____

_____

Using Articles Correctly

An **article** signals that a noun will follow. The **indefinite articles** are *a* and *an*. Indefinite articles introduce a noun that cannot yet be specifically identified.

a pen   **a** seat   **a** desk   **a** soldier   **a** politician

These items could be *any* pen, seat, desk, soldier, or politician. In using *a*, the writer does not identify any one specific pen, seat, desk, soldier, or politician.

Use *an* with a word that begins with a vowel (*a, e, i, o, u*) or a vowel sound.

an opinion   **an** inkwell   **an** injury   **an** accident   **an** hour

Note: Hour begins with a consonant, but it takes *an* because the *h* is silent. *Uniform* begins with a vowel, but it takes an *a* because it begins with a *y* sound.

A **definite article** introduces a noun that refers to a specific, identifiable item. *The* is the only indefinite article.

the pen	**the** seat	**the** desk	**the** soldier
the politician	**the** opinion	**the** injury	**the** hour

In writing <u>*the*</u> *pen,* the writer has in mind a *particular* pen.

An article may come directly in front of a noun, or it can be separated from the noun by modifiers.

a shiny black desk

an obvious mistake

the sweet, humble speaker

Using Articles with Nonspecific Nouns

A noun is **nonspecific** if the reader doesn't know its exact identity. Use *a* or *an* to introduce nonspecific nouns.

A college instructor could read that easily.

(The college instructor could be any instructor, not one in particular.)

Using Articles with Specific Nouns

If a noun is **specific**—referring to something that can be identified in particular—use *the* to refer to it. Using *the* tells the reader that one particular thing is being identified. Here are some ways to identify a specific noun.

- From other information in the sentence

    See that document in **the** center of the room?

    (*The* indicates that the *center* is in the room.)

- From other information in another sentence

    I read a fascinating interpretation of the Fourth Amendment. **The** interpretation incorporated ideas from past and present politicians.

    (Here *the* tells the reader that the interpretation refers to the one mentioned in the previous sentence.)

- From general information

    The ozone layer protects us from **the** sun.

    (Here, *the* refers to *ozone layer* and *sun* because the reader can be expected to know what these are.)

Using Determiners

Determiners, given here, are adjectives that *identify* rather than *modify* nouns.

Articles:	a, an, the
Demonstrative pronouns:	this, that, these, those
Possessive pronouns:	my, our, your, his, her, its, their, mine, yours, hers, ours, theirs
Possessive nouns:	Pat's, my uncle's
Determiners indicating amount:	a few, a little, all, any, both, each, either, enough, every, few, little, many, much, neither, not, several, some, what, which, whose
Numerals:	one, first, etc.

■ Before the superlative form of an adjective

    the tiniest crumb   **the** worst song

■ Before numbers indicating sequence or order

    the first child   **the** last chapter

Using Articles with Count and Noncount Nouns

Understanding count and noncount nouns helps you decide when to use articles and what kind to use. **Count nouns** identify people, places, things, or ideas that can be counted and made plural.

    pen   desk   soldier

You can give a number to all of these nouns and count them: *three* pens, *two* desks, *five* soldiers. For this reason, they are called count nouns.

    Noncount nouns refer to things that cannot be counted.

    hunger   warmth   mucous   energy

You cannot have *two* hungers or *four* warmths, so words like these are called noncount nouns.

    Noncount nouns cannot be given specific numbers to indicate amounts. However, their amounts can be described by using words that indicate non-specific amounts. Here are some common modifiers for noncount nouns.

    a bit   a little   a part of   a piece of   a section of more some

    In the examples that follow, the modifiers are italicized, and the noncount nouns are underlined.

        Sandra handed *a section of* <u>lumber</u> to the foreman.

Examples of Noncount Nouns

Concepts and feelings:	loneliness, fatigue, compassion, sensitivity, persuasiveness
Activities:	planting, loving, peeking, skipping, soccer
Food and drink:	meat, lasagna, milk, chocolate, tea, water
School courses:	history, biology, Spanish
Bulk materials:	iron, oil, fertilizer, alfalfa, sugar
Weather signs:	rain, fog, hail, wind, lightning

After the flood, *some* <u>sleet</u> added frustration to the situation.

Just *a piece of* <u>cake</u> was enough to tempt her.

Note: Some nouns can serve as both count and noncount nouns. For instance, the noun *meat* is used as a count noun in the following sentence.

Five <u>meats</u> top Sammy's famous all-meat pizza.

Meats here refers to individual types of meat; thus, *meats* is a count noun. However, *meat* in the following sentence is a noncount noun.

<u>Meat</u> is the one thing Marissa can't bring herself to give up.

Meat here refers to a general concept; thus, it cannot be counted.

Omitting Articles

Do not use articles with nonspecific plural nouns and nonspecific noncount nouns. Plural nouns and noncount nouns are nonspecific when they indicate something in general.

Nonspecific	Specific
People make <u>changes</u> when they write.	The <u>changes</u> were not improvements.
Keep <u>sugar</u> on hand at all times.	The <u>sugar</u> is all clumped together.
<u>Painters</u> can make a good living.	The <u>painters</u> did a great job.

Using Articles with Proper Nouns

Proper nouns—words referring to specific names of people, places, things, or ideas—are always capitalized. Most proper nouns do not require articles. For those that do, such as the following types of nouns, use *the.*

- Plural proper nouns
  the Hiltons   the Appalachian Mountains
- Names of significant geographic areas
  the Everglades   the Northeast   the Indian Ocean   the Charles River
  Do not use *the* before the following types of nouns.

- Names of people and animals
  Le Bron James   Fluffy
- Names of most places on land
  Asia   Maine   New Jersey   Weller Way   Seymour Park
- Most countries
  Brazil   Ethiopia   Japan
  Exception: the United States
- Most bodies of water
  Lake Mead   Idaho Falls   Lake Tahoe

EXERCISE 4 RECOGNIZING ARTICLES

Correct the errors in article usage and word form in the following paragraph. In seventeen instances you will need to add or change a word, and in four instances you will need to cross out an unnecessary article.

Influences on the Constitution

Although United States prides itself on its independences, ideas in U.S. Constitution came from many sources. The England—or more specifically, United Kingdom—had largest influence on U.S. Constitution. Taking ideas from English Bill of Rights, Americans specified that no person should be subjected to the "cruel and unusual punishment," idea based on English document called Magna Carta. Other ideas that came from English Bill of Rights include the jury trials, right to bear arms, and prohibition of excessive bail. However, many of Framers—who loved to study the history—claimed significant Dutch influence on Constitution as well.

Using Adjectives Correctly

Adjectives (words that describe nouns or pronouns) and other modifiers usually come directly before or after nouns.

Ordering Modifiers

Some modifiers need to be put in a specific order when they appear in a series.

- Articles and determiners always come first in a series of adjectives.

  the intelligent library clerk

  two clever young men

  an irritating habit
- Nouns acting as adjectives come last in a series of adjectives.

  the intelligent **library** clerk

  (Usually *library* is a noun, but in this case it is an adjective describing *clerk*.)

  an interesting **dinner** guest

  (The noun *dinner* acts as an adjective describing *guest*.)

Other types of adjectives come between these two end points, typically in the following order.

1. **Words expressing attitudes, judgments, or opinions:** tender, stern, fatherly, attractive, cruel, strong
2. **Size:** tiny, bite-sized, enormous, huge, gigantic, miniscule
3. **Shape:** oblong, cylindrical, rectangular, triangular, tall
4. **Age:** young, old, teenaged, preteen, adolescent, elderly
5. **Color:** fuschia, gold, black, violet, teal
6. **Nationality:** French, Chinese, Spanish, Nigerian
7. **Religion:** Baptist, Episcopalian, Buddhist, Muslim

Here are some examples of correctly ordered adjectives.

The <u>lovely</u> <u>triangular</u> <u>pink</u> **hat** was the talk of the tea party.

She had to smile at the <u>determined</u> <u>adolescent</u> <u>Vietnamese</u> **students.**

Has anyone seen my <u>adorable</u> <u>little</u> <u>French</u> **doll?**

Using Participles as Adjectives

Just as verb forms can act as nouns (gerunds or infinitive) or adverbs (infinitives), they can also act as adjectives. In particular, the participle verb forms, both present (-*ing* endings) and past (-*ed* endings), can communicate subtle variations in feeling.

Acting as an adjective, a present participle gives information about a noun that affects someone or something else. Talking about a *frustrating* meeting, for instance, focuses on the what caused the frustration: the *meeting*.

Acting as an adjective, however, a past participle provides information about a noun affected by someone or something else. Mentioning a *frustrated* suitor, for example, throws the focus on the person—the *suitor*—and how he or she is affected: he or she is *frustrated*.

The following word pairs give the present and past participle forms of verbs, both of which operate as adjectives.

annoying/annoyed	exhausting/exhausted
boring/bored	fascinating/fascinated
confusing/confused	frightening/frightened
depressing/depressed	interesting/interested
embarrassing/embarrassed	satisfying/satisfied
exciting/excited	surprising/surprised

EXERCISE 5 PLACING ADJECTIVES IN ORDER

Circle the correct choices in parentheses in the paragraph below.

One Big Technicality

When I was growing up, I watched (riveting law, law riveting) programs in which, inevitably, the defendant would get off on a technicality. I never knew what that meant until my mom started dating (an aging, tired; a tired, aging) defense attorney named Rich. He entertained me with (long, exciting; exciting, long) tales about how he defended his (innocent adult, adult innocent) clients simply by following the Constitution. For instance, he was able to free one (young disreputable, disreputable young) man because the local police didn't have reasonable cause to search the man's (rectangular green, green rectangular) backpack. The (young pretty, pretty young) assistant district attorney couldn't make the charges stick. Her (first memorable, memorable first) remark to Rich was that his client had been cleared "on a technicality." Rich had (automatic one, one automatic) response, however: "I guess you're right, if you consider the Constitution a technicality."

Using Prepositions Correctly

It can be difficult to determine the correct preposition to use from meaning alone. For that reason, learning correct preposition use takes time and practice. Three common prepositions, however, do allow for some guidelines.

- The preposition *at* can be used to specify a certain point in time or space.

  The game begins **at** 6:00 p.m.

  I want you to be **at** my side before we see her.
- The preposition *in* can be used to specify stretches of time or space.

  I worked as a food server **in** college.

  In the late 1990s, people worried about Y2K.
- The preposition *on* must be used with names of streets (excluding precise addresses) and with days of the week or month. *On* is also used to show an item's placement.

  I hope to work **on** Wall Street, so I put a copy of the *Wall Street Journal* **on** my desk **on** New Year's Day to remind me of my goal.

EXERCISE 6 USING PREPOSITIONS

Circle the correct prepositions in parentheses below.

Constitutional Television

I like to sit (on, in) my couch and watch my favorite political show (at, on) 8:00 p.m. (on, in) Wednesdays. I was told that if I believed I could work (at, on) Capitol Hill, it could happen. Living (at, on) my mother's house (on, in) my early twenties, though, did me no favors: (at, on) 5:00 a.m. every day, my mother would come (on, in) my room and tell me I needed to do more than stay (in, on) the house and watch what came (at, on) the television. Despite what I learned (on, in) those years, I'm happy to be out, (on, in) my own, without a television.

EDITING PRACTICE

Correct the underlined errors in the following paragraph. Cross out any unnecessary words, and write in any missing words above the mistake.

Amendments Forever Pending

More than <u>Constitutional 10,000</u> amendments have been introduced in Congress since 1789, but most have never left their congressional committees. The Eighteenth Amendment prohibiting the manufacture, import, and export of <u>alcohols</u> <u>it</u> is the only amendment to be repealed by another (the Twenty-first), which highlighted the importance of proposing and ratifying only the <u>important most</u> amendments. Because four amendments have no expiration date, <u>they still</u> technically pending. One of these, proposed by the First Congress in 1789, decided <u>setting</u> a formula for the number of members in <u>an</u> House of Representatives after <u>ten-year each</u> census. The last state to ratify this <u>it</u> did so <u>at</u> June 1792. Another pending amendment, the "Titles of Nobility Amendment," proposed <u>in</u> May 1, 1810, <u>it</u> would end the citizenship of Americans who accept "any Title of Nobility or Honour" from any foreign power. Ratified by twelve states, the last being in 1812, this <u>amendment still</u> pending.

Third is a pro-slavery proposal, which seeks <u>prohibiting</u> any <u>constitutional future</u> amendment allowing Congress <u>regulating</u> states' <u>the</u> domestic institutions. Even if ratified, <u>amendment</u> would be ineffective due to the adoption of the Thirteenth, Fourteenth, and Fifteenth Amendments. Finally, <u>child labor amendment</u> proposed by the 68th Congress <u>at</u> June 2, 1924, is now moot since <u>federal later</u> child labor laws have been upheld.

Lab Activity 52

For additional practice with ESL tips, complete Lab Activity 52 in the lab manual packaged with your textbook. If you did not receive a lab manual, you can complete this activity online at **www.ablongman.com/long.** Click on **College Resources for Writers** and then click on **Activity 52.**

PART EIGHT
Readings
for Informed Writing

Our Identities

From the time we're born, we're given labels: baby, boy or girl, child, shy, aggressive, bright, slow, kind, mean. While these labels may fit us at the time, they can never describe all of what we are. Maxine Hong Kingston and Nicolette Toussaint discuss the ways they dealt with—or were helped to deal with—trying aspects of themselves. In "Liked for Myself," Maya Angelou explores the rewards of developing one's gifts under a mentor's loving eye, and Richard Rodriguez writes in "Labor" about how people do and do not remain true to their roots. Finally, Elizabeth Austin and Michael Kinsman—in "Saving the Home from Martha Stewart" and "Respectable Addiction"—discuss the types of people we become through our choices.

Readings in This Section

Maya Angelou

Liked for Myself

A writer perhaps best known for her poetry reading at the 1993 presidential inauguration, Maya Angelou is also an actor, dancer, and singer. Using vivid images and specific language, Angelou describes her first personal encounter with Bertha Flowers, whom she considers "our side's answer to the richest white woman in town." The particulars of the visit, and its lifelong influence on Angelou, come alive in this essay.

BEFORE YOU READ

- Describe someone who expected or demanded more from you than you did from yourself at some point in your life.
- To what extent do you think that others—such as instructors, coaches, or mentors—can sometimes inspire us to achieve goals that we could not ordinarily achieve on our own? Explain.
- Describe someone you consider an exceptional person. This may be someone you know well or someone you've heard, seen, or read about. Consider what makes this person exceptional.

VOCABULARY DEVELOPMENT

Look up the following words in a dictionary and write down their meanings.

taut (paragraph 2)   inclusively (paragraph 4)
benign (paragraph 4)   clarity (paragraph 10)
infuse (paragraph 12)   boggled (paragraph 15)
sufficient (paragraph 22)   intolerant (paragraph 23)
illiteracy (paragraph 23)   cascading (paragraph 25)
sophistication (paragraph 30)

Liked for Myself

1   For nearly a year, I sopped around the house, the Store, the school and the church, like an old biscuit, dirty and inedible. Then I met, or rather got to know, the lady who threw me my first life line.

2   Mrs. Bertha Flowers was the aristocrat of Black Stamps. She had the grace of control to appear warm in the coldest weather, and on the Arkansas sum-

mer days it seemed she had a private breeze which swirled around, cooling her. She was thin without the taut look of wiry people, and her printed voile dresses and flowered hats were as right for her as denim overalls for a farmer. She was our side's answer to the richest white woman in town.

3   Her skin was a rich black that would have peeled like a plum if snagged, but then no one would have thought of getting close enough to Mrs. Flowers to ruffle her dress, let alone snag her skin. She didn't encourage familiarity. She wore gloves too.

4   I don't think I ever saw Mrs. Flowers laugh, but she smiled often. A slow widening of her thin black lips to show even, small white teeth, then the slow effortless closing. When she chose to smile on me, I always wanted to thank her. The action was so graceful and inclusively benign.

5   She was one of the few gentlewomen I have ever known, and has remained throughout my life the measure of what a human being can be. . . .

6   One summer afternoon, sweet-milk fresh in my memory, she stopped at the Store to buy provisions. Another Negro woman of her health and age would have been expected to carry the paper sacks home in one hand, but Momma said, "Sister Flowers, I'll send Bailey up to your house with these things."

7   She smiled that slow dragging smile, "Thank you, Mrs. Henderson. I'd prefer Marguerite, though." My name was beautiful when she said it. "I've been meaning to talk to her, anyway." They gave each other age-group looks. . . .

8   There was a little path beside the rocky road, and Mrs. Flowers walked in front swinging her arms and picking her way over the stones.

9   She said, without turning her head, to me, "I hear you're doing very good school work, Marguerite, but that it's all written. The teachers report that they have trouble getting you to talk in class." We passed the triangular farm on our left and the path widened to allow us to walk together. I hung back in the separate unasked and unanswerable questions.

10   "Come and walk along with me, Marguerite." I couldn't have refused even if I wanted to. She pronounced my name so nicely. Or more correctly, she spoke each word with such clarity that I was certain a foreigner who didn't understand English could have understood her.

11   "Now no one is going to make you talk—possibly no one can. But bear in mind, language is man's way of communicating with his fellow man and it is language alone which separates him from the lower animals." That was a totally new idea to me, and I would need time to think about it.

12   "Your grandmother says you read a lot. Every chance you get. That's good, but not good enough. Words mean more than what is set down on paper. It takes the human voice to infuse them with the shades of deeper meaning."

13   I memorized the part about the human voice infusing words. It seemed so valid and poetic.

14   She said she was going to give me some books and that I not only must read them, I must read them aloud. She suggested that I try to make a sentence sound in as many different ways as possible.

15   "I'll accept no excuse if you return a book to me that has been badly handled." My imagination boggled at the punishment I would deserve if in fact I did abuse a book of Mrs. Flowers'. Death would be too kind and brief.

16   The odors in the house surprised me. Somehow I had never connected Mrs. Flowers with food or eating or any other common experience of common people. There must have been an outhouse, too, but my mind never recorded it.

17   The sweet scent of vanilla had met us as she opened the door.

18   "I made tea cookies this morning. You see, I had planned to invite you for cookies and lemonade so we could have this little chat. The lemonade is in the icebox."

19   It followed that Mrs. Flowers would have ice on an ordinary day, when most families in our town bought ice late on Saturdays only a few times during the summer to be used in the wooden ice-cream freezers.

20   She took the bags from me and disappeared through the kitchen door. I looked around the room that I had never in my wildest fantasies imagined I would see. Browned photographs leered or threatened from the walls and the white, freshly done curtains pushed against themselves and against the wind. I wanted to gobble up the room entire and take it to Bailey, who would help me analyze and enjoy it.

21   "Have a seat, Marguerite. Over there by the table." She carried a platter covered with a tea towel. Although she warned that she hadn't tried her hand at baking sweets for some time, I was certain that like everything else about her the cookies would be perfect.

22   They were flat round wafers, slightly browned on the edges and butter-yellow in the center. With the cold lemonade they were sufficient for childhood's lifelong diet. Remembering my manners, I took nice little lady-like bites off the edges. She said she had made them expressly for me and that she had a few in the kitchen that I could take home to my brother. So I jammed one whole cake in my mouth and the rough crumbs scratched the insides of my jaws, and if I hadn't had to swallow, it would have been a dream come true.

23   As I ate she began the first of what we later called "my lessons in living." She said that I must always be intolerant of ignorance but understanding of illiteracy. That some people, unable to go to school, were more educated and even more intelligent than college professors. She encouraged me to listen carefully to what country people called mother wit. That in those homely sayings was couched the collective wisdom of generations.

24   When I finished the cookies she brushed off the table and brought a thick, small book from the bookcase. I had read *A Tale of Two Cities* and

found it up to my standards as a romantic novel. She opened the first page and I heard poetry for the first time in my life.

25   "It was the best of times and the worst of times . . . " Her voice slid in and curved down through and over the words. She was nearly singing. I wanted to look at the pages. Were they the same that I had read? Or were there notes, music, lined on the pages, as in a hymn book? Her sounds began cascading gently. I knew from listening to a thousand preachers that she was nearing the end of her reading, and I hadn't really heard, heard to understand, a single word.

26   "How do you like that?"

27   It occurred to me that she expected a response. The sweet vanilla flavor was still on my tongue and her reading was a wonder in my ears. I had to speak.

28   I said, "Yes, ma'am." It was the least I could do, but it was the most also.

29   "There's one more thing. Take this book of poems and memorize one for me. Next time you pay me a visit, I want you to recite."

30   I have tried often to search behind the sophistication of years for the enchantment I so easily found in those gifts. The essence escapes but its aura remains. To be allowed, no, invited, into the private lives of strangers, and to share their joys and fears, was a chance to exchange the Southern bitter wormwood for a cup of mead with Beowulf or a hot cup of tea and milk with Oliver Twist. When I said aloud, "It is a far, far better thing that I do, than I have ever done . . . " tears of love filled my eyes at my selfishness.

31   On that first day, I ran down the hill and into the road (few cars ever came along it) and had the good sense to stop running before I reached the Store.

32   I was liked, and what a difference it made. I was respected not as Mrs. Henderson's grandchild or Bailey's sister but for just being Marguerite Johnson.

33   Childhood's logic never asks to be proved (all conclusions are absolute). I didn't question why Mrs. Flowers had singled me out for attention, nor did it occur to me that Momma might have asked her to give me a little talking to. All I cared about was that she had made tea cookies for *me* and read to *me* from her favorite book. It was enough to prove that she liked me.

POST-READING EXERCISES

1. Which word on the Vocabulary Development list means "having no give or slack; tightly drawn"?

   a. boggle   b. benign

   c. taut   d. infuse

2. How does Marguerite come to spend time with Mrs. Flowers?
   a. Mrs. Flowers asks Marguerite to carry groceries home.
   b. Mrs. Flowers is Marguerite's schoolteacher.
   c. Mrs. Flowers is her mother's good friend.
   d. Mrs. Flowers lives next door to her.

3. What does Mrs. Flowers serve Marguerite?
   a. Coffee and chocolate
   b. Lemonade and tea cookies
   c. Hot tea and lemon squares
   d. Iced tea and strawberry shortcake

4. From what book does Mrs. Flowers read to Marguerite?
   a. *Oliver Twist*
   b. *Great Expectations*
   c. *David Copperfield*
   d. *A Tale of Two Cities*

5. What is one definition of the word *benign?*
   a. Of gentle disposition; gracious
   b. Harmful
   c. Of great intelligence; genius
   d. Helpful

6. What does Marguerite say in response to Mrs. Flowers's question?
   a. "No, ma'am."
   b. Nothing
   c. "Yes, ma'am."
   d. "If you please, ma'am."

7. How does Marguerite remember Mrs. Flowers?
   a. As the inspiration for the angels themselves
   b. As the measure of what a human being can be
   c. As the hand that rocked the cradle
   d. As the voice of the future

8. What does Mrs. Flowers demand of Marguerite?
   a. Read a poem.
   b. Read a poem aloud to herself.
   c. Read a poem aloud to Mrs. Flowers.
   d. Memorize and recite a poem.

9. Which word on the Vocabulary Development list means "to cause to be permeated with something"?

    a. intolerant

    b. infuse

    c. cascading

    d. sophistication

10. What does Marguerite say made "a difference" to her?

    a. Being liked for being a girl

    b. Being liked despite being related to Bailey

    c. Being liked for herself

    d. Being liked despite being related to Mrs. Henderson

Content

1. Under what circumstances does Marguerite come to know Mrs. Flowers?
2. How does Marguerite describe Mrs. Flowers?
3. What is the nature of Mrs. Flowers's actions toward Marguerite?

Style and Structure

1. What is Angelou's point in writing about Mrs. Flowers? Write her main idea in your own words.
2. What demands does Mrs. Flowers place on Marguerite? How are these significant?
3. What is Angelou's attitude toward Mrs. Flowers, even as she looks back on her childhood? How does her tone reflect this attitude?

Writing Assignments

1. Marguerite feels warmly toward Mrs. Flowers, yet their relationship is not one of two peers. *Write an essay in which you define one of the following terms:* friendship, family, *or* companion. *(You may choose another term if you prefer.)* For instance, you may write that a friend is someone who accepts you without having to, as some people feel family must. Use examples from your own experiences to illustrate your ideas.
2. Angelou writes, "I was liked, and what a difference it made." Would Mrs. Flowers have been as successful a mentor if she had not liked Marguerite? To what extent is affection necessary for successful instruction? *Write an essay explaining how affection for one's pupil is or is not important for successful teaching or*

coaching. You can consider any type of teaching: school, sports, music, church, domestic chores (housework, cooking, or yard work, for instance). Use examples from your own experiences and observations to illustrate your ideas.

3. Mrs. Flowers gives Marguerite "lessons in living." What lessons in living do you think are most important? *Write an essay explaining how a specific lesson or lessons have been particularly helpful in your life.* For instance, you might write how learning to listen before speaking helps you ask effective questions or give thoughtful responses. Use examples from your own observations and experiences to illustrate your ideas.

Elizabeth Austin

Saving the Home from Martha Stewart

A Chicago writer who considers herself an "idiot savant" when it comes to taking care of the house, Elizabeth Austin has published articles in numerous magazines, including *Nation, Newsweek*, and *Washington Monthly*. In this essay, Austin argues that mandatory home economics courses in high school would better prepare our youth for the challenges of everyday life outside of work.

BEFORE YOU READ

- How good are you at taking care of yourself, in terms of doing laundry, preparing food, and maintaining your home? Explain.
- Where have you learned the life skills—such as being able to fix a leaky pipe or sew on a button—you possess? Explain.
- How important is it for young people to be taught basic life skills such as balancing a checkbook, cooking, and fixing things around the home? Explain.

VOCABULARY DEVELOPMENT

Look up the following words in a dictionary and write down their meanings.

savant (paragraph 1)   elitism (paragraph 2)
rampant (paragraph 3)   insatiable (paragraph 5)

quixotic (paragraph 7)   mandatory (paragraph 12)

demise (paragraph 13)   inexorably (paragraph 13)

resurgence (paragraph 22)   plebeian (paragraph 23)

Saving the Home from Martha Stewart

1   I can whip up a bittersweet chocolate-and-mandarin orange cheesecake good enough to rub in your hair. . . . Yet I don't think I could plan, purchase, and prepare a week's worth of family meals or sew a simple dress if you held a gun to my head. When it comes to homemaking, I am an idiot savant. . . .

2   I'm not alone. There are millions of men and women of my generation who are missing a whole cluster of basic life skills, who simply don't know how to iron a shirt, replace a button, paint a wall, or even scrub a toilet properly. We don't have the basic competence to run our homes smoothly and efficiently, so we can't pass down those skills to the next generation. And our functional illiteracy on the domestic front is having a devastating effect on our society. With the rise of Martha Stewart and the many Martha wannabes, we've created a strange culture of domestic elitism, in which only women who have the means to hire household help have the leisure to learn household skills. So those who can least afford expensive processed foods are the least able to prepare a nutritious stew or bake a loaf of bread.

3   But there's a simple solution to all this. To fight rampant consumerism, to reduce the divorce rate, to diminish child abuse, to prevent cancer and heart disease, and to ensure domestic tranquility, this is all we have to do: Bring back home economics.

Home Wrecks

4   All right. I can hear you snickering out there. You think home ec is trivial. Home ec is stupid. Home ec is sexist.

5   Well, if that's what you believe, just take a look at the core subjects in the home economics curriculum—child development, nutrition, personal health, personal finance, and consumer protection. Publishers make millions putting out books and magazines to feed our insatiable national appetite for information on all these topics. Of the 25 books currently leading Amazon.com's sales, nine of them would fit comfortably into any basic home ec reading list.

6   Everywhere you look, you see American families desperately in need of help with the basics of daily life. Consider our national epidemic of obesity,

with 55 percent of American adults now overweight—due, in large part, to our increasing reliance on high-fat, high-sugar convenience foods. Our rapidly expanding national waistline is a major cause of heart disease and several deadly cancers. Perhaps most disturbingly, one in five children between ages six and 17 is overweight, and the number of overweight children in the United States has doubled over the past 30 years. If current trends continue, nearly half of today's children will eventually die of heart disease. Yet how many parents know the number of calories contained in a McDonald's cheeseburger Happy Meal? (It's 680, if you're interested.) And how many of those parents could tell you how many calories the average 5-year-old needs each day to stay healthy? (About 1,700.)

7   We're equally inept when it comes to balancing our checkbooks. Despite our unprecedented economic expansion, there's been an explosion of personal bankruptcy, with some 1.4 million Americans filing for bankruptcy last year alone. That figure has almost tripled over the past decade. It's no wonder this magazine has devoted years to the quixotic promotion of Cheap Chic, trying to make it fashionable to cut up our credit cards and spend less. But how can you ask uneducated consumers to content themselves with cheaper products and pass up the overpriced name brands and designer labels, when price is their only basis for judging quality?

8   These are not trivial matters. And it is criminal that we are allowing generations to grow up without the basic knowledge they need to care for themselves, their children, and their homes.

The Lost Art

9   For the first half of this century, the public schools took home economics education very seriously, at least where their female students were concerned. . . .

10   Over the years, however, home economics lost its lofty moral and political underpinnings. The idea that women would use this knowledge to begin housekeeping on a municipal scale gradually faded. Instead, home ec was viewed only as a means to teach individual students to care for their own homes and families. "Instead of 'Let's go out and help everybody,' the focus changes to 'Me and mine,' says one home economics expert. The social mission of those earlier home economists was completely lost."

Wife Ed 101

11   Then came the women's movement. And home ec didn't stand a chance. The young feminists of the early 1970s viewed home ec (with some justification) as Wife Ed 101. . . . The Dump Home Ec movement immediately caught on with school administrators, who saw a perfect opportunity to grab the moral high ground and cut costs at the same time.

12   The evaporation of home ec from the mandatory curriculum coincided with a new age in American consumerism. Shopping malls started springing up in cornfields, and a generation of middle-class Americans embraced the concept of shopping as recreation. Consumers who once limited their forays to the local department store were suddenly surrounded by a dazzling array of cute little shops selling cute little dresses. Suddenly, the solitary pursuit of home sewing didn't make sense anymore. Why invest $25 and untold hours in sewing a dress that might not turn out right? Why learn to cook when you can watch Martha? when you could probably find just what you were looking for at the local mall? And at the mall, you and your girlfriends could have lunch.

13   The demise of home sewing led inexorably to the rise of designer labels. Back in the home ec era, you never went clothes shopping without hearing some matron tsk-tsk at the price tag and say, "I could sew this myself for about five dollars." Even if a home seamstress didn't want to go to the trouble of whipping up a ball gown out of $5 worth of cheesecloth, she had the knowledge to recognize good craftsmanship. But when women forgot how to sew, they had no baseline to distinguish good-quality clothes from bad. Thus arose the designer brand, which reassured women that they were buying the good stuff (even though the label was often the only piece of quality material in the garment).

14   The rise of the service economy made it possible for young middle-class women (and men) to avoid many of the domestic tasks they never quite mastered in the first place. Thanks to frozen foods, cleaning services, and carry-out restaurants, you could survive without drafting the detailed household management plans once required of home ec students.

15   Certainly, one of the engines of this change was the increasing presence of women in the workplace. When you devote 40 or 50 hours of your week to earning wages, simple mathematics shows that you're going to have less time for housekeeping. But the change went deeper than that. In fact, American women have always worked. (Even in the hyperdomesticated 1950s, nearly half of all mothers worked outside the home.) The difference was that now neither men nor women considered homemaking to be as valuable as wage-earning. Women whose mothers had prided themselves on their shining floors and snowy linens now boasted that they hadn't cleaned their refrigerators in two years. An untidy house became a badge of honor, showing that the tenant had more important things to do in life.

Enter the Domestic Diva

16   Then came Martha Stewart.

17   In 1982, Martha Stewart launched her empire with Entertaining, a book of party recipes and menus. In and of itself, that was hardly revolutionary.

. . . But Martha was something different. Despite her slick, smug, and self-congratulatory tone, she touched a chord that resonated throughout the country. Annoying as she was, no one could doubt that Martha Stewart took homemaking very seriously indeed. And, as Martha would say, we thought that was a Good Thing. . . .

18   But the domestic diva is hardly a proponent of Cheap Chic. Just look at her own catalog, *Martha by Mail*. If you're planning a holiday meal, you might send off for her complete turkey cooking kit, which includes an instruction booklet, a 6-inch trussing needle, a spool of cotton twine, a stainless steel roasting pan and adjustable rack, a baster, a thermometer, a pastry brush, a fat separator and cheesecloth, for the low, low price of $128—plus shipping; for dessert, you can order her exclusive canvas pasty cloth, a pastry cutter, wheel and brush, two pie tins, a copper cookie cutter, and a pie basket for only $102. With her books, TV shows, and magazine, Martha Stewart has become our national home ec instructor. And we've paid her a billion dollars to do it. . . .

19   The problem is, Martha presents an unattainable goal of domestic perfection, and then makes us feel guilty when we're unable to achieve it. She tells us it's only laziness that keeps us from following in her perfectly shaped, impeccably color-coordinated footsteps. But it's ridiculous to advise suburban Americans to obtain the freshest eggs by raising their own chickens. It's almost as silly to teach us the correct way to iron the monograms on our towels (no doubt using the Martha by Mail $125 steam iron). What we really need is a good anti-Martha, someone who could promote living well while living on less. In other words, what we need is a real home ec teacher.

Home Ec—Now More Than Ever

20   In my daughter's high school, like most high schools nationwide, home ec is no longer a mandatory subject. Instead, the kids are required to take Consumer Economics. We don't even try to teach them how to produce or repair. We just teach them how to buy. "It's a very different ethic," comments historian Stage. "'Make over and make do' was the motto of home economics. Now nobody wants to do that any more." . . .

21   We just aren't willing to put energy and effort into the home front. In every decision we make, we reinforce the notion that home life always runs a distant second, or even third, to the other spheres of existence. Even in child-rearing, home always comes last. When was the last time a parent insisted that a child skip a soccer game because it conflicted with family dinnertime? . . . Domestic arts author Cheryl Mendlesson claims, "People who don't have a strong private life and a strong home cannot resist their jobs. It leaves no place where a different set of values comes into play."

Bringing It All Back Home

22   Obviously, this isn't a problem that can be solved in the classroom alone. But it seems clear that schools could fan the resurgence of interest in the domestic arts. If high schools required two years of home ec—complete with homework—for every student, many parents would get with the program. I got a personal taste of this last year, when my daughter took an elective six-week cooking class at her parochial elementary school. Inspired by her emerging interest and developing skills, I began using her as a sous-chef, assigning her to chop onions and sauté chicken strips. We probably spent more time cooking together during those six weeks than we had in the preceding 13 years, and it helped me to revive culinary skills I'd long forgotten. And I realized I'd actually save time if I made pizza at home, instead of driving to the local pizza parlor to pick up my carry-out order.

. . .

23   Parents need to demand that their school systems offer a comprehensive home ec curriculum. It's not enough to teach seventh-graders how to make chocolate chip cookies. . . . No one—male or female—should graduate from high school without demonstrating the ability to run a washing machine, fry an egg, balance a checkbook, compile a grocery list, and use a power drill. . . . And don't listen to critics who worry that such plebeian instruction will nibble away at more valuable academic classes. Our schools have made time for drug and sex education; we can find time for this too. Because, in the end, there's no place like home.

POST-READING EXERCISES

1. Which word on the Vocabulary Development list means "crude or coarse in manner or style"?

   a. inexorably   b. plebeian

   c. demise   d. resurgence

2. Which of the following does Austin *not* list as a "basic life skill"?

   a. Ironing a shirt   b. Painting a wall

   c. Replacing a light bulb   d. Scrubbing a toilet

3. Which of the following is *not* something that people buy numerous books about?

   a. Child development   b. Nutrition

   c. Personal finance   d. Personal safety

4. What benefit does knowing how to sew provide, according to Austin?

   a. Being able to recognize quality

      b. Being able to repair one's clothing

      c. Being able to create one's own style

      d. Being able to make one's own gifts

5. According to Austin, many early home economists sought to help

      a. themselves   b. their husband

      c. everybody   d. their parents

6. What is one definition of the word *quixotic?*

      a. Grossly indulgent, especially in food

      b. Completely confused

      c. Basically honest

      d. Foolishly impractical, especially in the pursuit of ideals

7. According to Austin, what concept did a new generation of middle-class Americans embrace?

      a. Shopping as recreation   b. Shopping as therapy

      c. Shopping as reward   d. Shopping as work

8. What, according to domestics arts author Cheryl Mendelsson, can people not resist if they don't have a strong private life or home?

      a. Their selfish impulses   b. Their children

      c. Their jobs   d. Their parents

9. Which word on the Vocabulary Development list means "a cessation of existence or activity"?

      a. savant   b. insatiable

      c. demise   d. rampant

10. What, according to Austin, did Martha Stewart get people to do?

      a. become gourmet cooks

      b. shop at Kmart

      c. take homemaking seriously

      d. hold themselves to a higher standard of entertaining

Content

1. What does Austin mean by "a strange culture of domestic elitism"?

2. What are some of the consequences of people not knowing how to take care of themselves?

3. What caused home ec to be dropped from curriculums?

Style and Structure

1. What is Austin's point? Rewrite her thesis in your own words.

2. What details does Austin use to illustrate her thesis?

3. What opposing arguments does Austin counter? How does she counter them?

Writing Assignments

1. Austin quotes a historian who claims that people don't want to "make over and make do," as they once did. What do you think? *Write an essay in which you argue that people are or are not willing to live a simple lifestyle.* Use examples from the essay and from your own experiences to illustrate your ideas.

2. Austin claims that people "aren't willing to put energy and effort into the home front." Is this true? *Write an essay arguing that people do or do not make their homes a priority.* Cite from Austin's essay and use examples from your own experiences and observations to illustrate your ideas.

3. Austin claims that no one should graduate from high school without certain skills. What life skills do you think are most important for people to know? *Write an essay arguing that certain life skills—such as cooking, balancing a checkbook, or being able to repair damage in your home, for instance—are particularly important for people to master.* Use examples from Austin's essay and from your experiences and observations to illustrate your ideas.

Maxine Hong Kingston

The Misery of Silence

Born and raised in the small city of Stockton, California, Maxine Hong Kingston strove to balance the Chinese and American influences in her life. Becoming not only a graduate of, but an instructor at, the University of California at Berkeley, Ms. Kingston has also gained renown from her published works, notably *The Woman Warrior: Memoirs of a Girlhood Among Ghosts*, from which this selection came, and *Tripmaster Monkey: His Fake Book* and *China Men*. In "The Misery of Silence," Kingston explores the challenge of finding her voice within two very different cultures.

BEFORE YOU READ

- How stressful is speaking out in school for you? Explain.
- At what point did speaking in school become more, or less, difficult for you? Explain.
- To what extent does your culture or upbringing influence your attitude toward speaking out in school? Explain.

VOCABULARY DEVELOPMENT

Look up the following words in a dictionary and write down their meanings.

dumbness (paragraph 1)   skittering (paragraph 1)
wince (paragraph 1)   accord (paragraph 1)
intricacies (paragraph 6)   assuredly (paragraph 6)
nonexistent (paragraph 7)   teak (paragraph 9)
ceremonial (paragraph 9)   emigrant (paragraph 12)

The Misery of Silence

1   When I went to kindergarten and had to speak English for the first time, I became silent. A dumbness—a shame—still cracks my voice in two, even when I want to say "hello" casually, or ask an easy question in front of the check-out counter, or ask directions of a bus driver. I stand frozen, or I hold up the line with the complete, grammatical sentence that comes squeaking out at impossible length. "What did you say?" says the cab driver, or "Speak up," so I have to perform again, only weaker the second time. A telephone call makes my throat bleed and takes up that day's courage. It spoils my day with self-disgust when I hear my broken voice come skittering out into the open. It makes people wince to hear it. I'm getting better, though. Recently I asked the postman for special-issue stamps; I've waited since childhood for postmen to give me some of their own accord. I am making progress, a little every day.

2   My silence was thickest—total—during the three years that I covered my school paintings with black paint. I painted layers of black over houses and flowers and suns, and when I drew on the blackboard, I put a layer of chalk on top. I was making a stage curtain, and it was the moment before the curtain parted or rose. The teachers called my parents to school, and I saw they had been saving my pictures, curling and cracking, all alike and black. The teachers pointed to the pictures and looked serious, talked seriously too, but my parents did not understand English. ("The parents and teachers of criminals were executed," said my father.) My parents took the pictures home. I spread them out (so black and full of possibilities) and pretended the curtains were swinging open, flying up, one after another, sunlight underneath, mighty operas.

3   During the first silent year I spoke to no one at school, did not ask before going to the lavatory, and flunked kindergarten. My sister also said nothing for three years, silent in the playground and silent at lunch. There were other quiet Chinese girls not of our family, but most of them got over it sooner than we did. I enjoyed the silence. At first it did not occur to me I

was supposed to talk or to pass kindergarten. I talked at home and to one or two of the Chinese kids in class. I made motions and even made some jokes. I drank out of a toy saucer when the water spilled out of the cup, and everybody laughed, pointing at me, so I did it some more. I didn't know that Americans don't drink out of saucers.

4   I liked the Negro students (Black Ghosts) best because they laughed the loudest and talked to me as if I were a daring talker too. One of the Negro girls had her mother coil braids over her ears Shanghai-style like mine; we were Shanghai twins except that she was covered with black like my paintings. Two Negro kids enrolled in Chinese school, and the teachers gave them Chinese names. Some Negro kids walked me to school and home, protecting me from the Japanese kids, who hit me and chased me and stuck gum in my ears. The Japanese kids were noisy and tough. They appeared one day in kindergarten, released from concentration camp, which was a tic-tac-toe mark, like barbed wire, on the map.

5   It was when I found out I had to talk that school became a misery, that the silence became a misery. I did not speak and felt bad each time that I did not speak. I read aloud in first grade, though, and heard the barest whisper with little squeaks come out of my throat. "Louder," said the teacher, who scared the voice away again. The other Chinese girls did not talk either, so I knew the silence had to do with being a Chinese girl.

6   Reading out loud was easier than speaking because we did not have to make up what to say, but I stopped often, and the teacher would think I'd gone quiet again. I could not understand "I." The Chinese "I" has seven strokes, intricacies. How could the American "I," assuredly wearing a hat like the Chinese, have only three strokes, the middle so straight? Was it out of politeness that this writer left off strokes the way a Chinese has to write her own name small and crooked? No, it was not politeness; "I" is a capital and "you" is lowercase. I stared at that middle line and waited so long for its black center to resolve into tight strokes and dots that I forgot to pronounce it. The other troublesome word was "here," no strong consonant to hang on to, and so flat, when "here" is two mountainous ideographs. The teacher, who had already told me every day how to read "I" and "here," put me in the low corner under the stairs again, where the noisy boys usually sat.

7   When my second grade class did a play, the whole class went to the auditorium except the Chinese girls. The teacher, lovely and Hawaiian, should have understood about us, but instead left us behind in the classroom. Our voices were too soft or nonexistent, and our parents never signed the permission slips anyway. They never signed anything unnecessary. We opened the door a crack and peeked out, but closed it again quickly. One of us (not me) won every spelling bee, though.

8   I remember telling the Hawaiian teacher, "We Chinese can't sing 'land where our fathers died.'" She argued with me about politics, while I meant because of curses. But how can I have that memory when I couldn't talk? My mother says that we, like the ghosts, have no memories.

9   After American school, we picked up our cigar boxes, in which we had arranged books, brushes, and an inkbox neatly, and went to Chinese school, from 5:00 to 7:30 P.M. There we chanted together, voices rising and falling, loud and soft, some boys shouting, everybody reading together, reciting together and not alone with one voice. When we had a memorization test, the teacher let each of us come to his desk and say the lesson to him privately, while the rest of the class practiced copying or tracing. Most of the teachers were men. The boys who were so well behaved in the American school played tricks on them and talked back to them. The girls were not mute. They screamed and yelled during recess, when there were no rules; they had fistfights. Nobody was afraid of children hurting themselves or of children hurting school property. The glass doors to the red and green balconies with the gold joy symbols were left wide open so that we could run out and climb the fire escapes. We played capture-the-flag in the auditorium, where Sun Yat-sen and Chiang Kai-shek's pictures hung at the back of the stage, the Chinese flag on their left and the American flag on their right. We climbed the teak ceremonial chairs and made flying leaps off the stage. One flag headquarters was behind the glass door and the other on stage right. Our feet drummed on the hollow stage. During recess the teachers locked themselves up in their office with the shelves of books, copybooks, inks from China. They drank tea and warmed their hands at a stove. There was no play supervision. At recess we had the school to ourselves, and also we could roam as far as we could go—downtown, Chinatown stores, home—as long as we returned before the bell rang.

10   At exactly 7:30 the teacher again picked up the brass bell that sat on his desk and swung it over our heads, while we charged down the stairs, our cheering magnified in the stairwell. Nobody had to line up.

11   Not all of the children who were silent at American school found voice at Chinese school. One new teacher said each of us had to get up and recite in front of the class, who was to listen. My sister and I had memorized the lesson perfectly. We said it to each other at home, one chanting, one listening. The teacher called on my sister to recite first. It was the first time a teacher had called on the second-born to go first. My sister was scared. She glanced at me and looked away; I looked down at my desk. I hoped that she could do it because if she could, then I would have to. She opened her mouth and a voice came out that wasn't a whisper, but it wasn't a proper voice either. I hoped that she would not cry, fear breaking up her voice like twigs underfoot. She sounded as if she were trying to sing though weeping and strangling. She did not pause or stop to end the embarrassment. She

kept going until she said the last word, and then she sat down. When it was my turn, the same voice came out, a crippled animal running on broken legs. You could hear splinters in my voice, bones rubbing jagged against one another. I was loud, though. I was glad I didn't whisper.

12   How strange that the emigrant villagers are shouters, hollering face to face. My father asks, "Why is it I can hear Chinese from blocks away? Is it that I understand the language? Or is it they talk loud?" They turn the radio up full blast to hear the operas, which do not seem to hurt their ears. And they yell over the singers that wail over the drums, everybody talking at once, big arm gestures, spit flying. You can see the disgust on American faces looking at women like that. It isn't just the loudness. It is the way Chinese sounds, ching-chong ugly, to American ears, not beautiful like Japanese sayonara words with the consonants and vowels as regular as Italian. We make guttural peasant noise and have Ton Duc Thang names you can't remember. And the Chinese can't hear Americans at all; the language is too soft and western music unhearable. I've watched a Chinese audience laugh, visit, talk-story, and holler during a piano recital, as if the musician could not hear them. A Chinese-American, somebody's son, was playing Chopin, which has no punctuation, no cymbals, no gongs. Chinese piano music is five black keys. Normal Chinese women's voices are strong and bossy. We American-Chinese girls had to whisper to make ourselves American-feminine. Apparently we whispered even more softly than the Americans. Once a year the teachers referred my sister and me to speech therapy, but our voices would straighten out, unpredictably normal, for the therapists. Some of us gave up, shook our heads, and said nothing, not one word. Some of us could not even shake our heads. At times shaking my head no is more self-assertion than I can manage. Most of us eventually found some voice, however faltering. We invented an American-feminine speaking personality.

POST-READING EXERCISES

1. Which word on the Vocabulary Development list means "to shrink back involuntarily"?

    a. teak   b. wince

    c. ceremonial   d. nonexistent

2. What happened to the writer when she went to kindergarten?

    a. She became silent.   b. She became weak.

    c. She became bold.   d. She became loud.

3. What did the black paint on the writer's paintings represent?

    a. Night   b. Fear

    c. Curtains   d. Sleep

4. What does the writer call Negro students?

    a. Night Spirits   b. Silent Strangers

    c. Dark Bodies   d. Black Ghosts

5. What is one definition of the word *skittering?*

    a. To glide or skip lightly or quickly

    b. To tap one's foot

    c. To take tiny steps

    d. To tremble as with cold

6. What two words were difficult for the writer to say or speak?

    a. *You* and *know*   b. *I* and *here*

    c. *Maxine* and *he*   d. *Teacher* and *student*

7. Which of the following does *not* describe Chinese school?

    a. Everyone chanting together

    b. Screaming and yelling girls

    c. No fear of children or property being hurt

    d. Absolute respect for the teacher

8. Which of the following is *not* one way the writer's voice sounded during a recitation in front of her class?

    a. Crippled animal running on broken legs

    b. Glass shattering

    c. Splinters in her voice

    d. Bones rubbing jagged against one another

9. Which word on the Vocabulary Development list means "lacking the human power of speech"?

    a. dumb   b. accord

    c. assured   d. intricacy

10. What term does the writer give to the voice she eventually finds?

    a. A Chinese-American talking noise

    b. A Euro-Asian communications device

    c. An American-feminine speaking personality

    d. A bicultural-woman utterance

Content

1. How does Kingston's voice affect people who hear it?

2. Why did Kingston like the Negro students?

3. Why couldn't Kingston sing "land where our fathers died"?

Style and Structure

1. What is Kingston's point? Rewrite her thesis in your own words.

2. What types of details does Kingston use to illustrate the difficulties of speaking?

3. What "effect" does Kingston write about? What are its causes?

Writing Assignments

1. Kingston vividly describes the painful sounds her voice makes when she speaks. What physical trait or habit causes you pain or discomfort? *Write an essay describing a personal weakness.* For instance, if you feel clumsy while dribbling a basketball, describe the way your fingers, hands, and body feel when you hold a basketball. Use examples from your own experiences to illustrate your ideas.

2. Kingston explores an effect—namely, the difficulty finding a voice—of growing up as part of two cultures. What is an "effect" or personal result that you have worked to bring about? *Write an essay explaining how you brought about a certain result in your life.* For instance, if you wanted to earn a promotion at work, make a sports team, or save money to purchase an expensive item, explain how you did this. Use examples from your own experiences and observations to illustrate your ideas.

3. Kingston writes of the silence of American schools and the rambunctious mood of Chinese school. How is your current school like or unlike another school you have attended? *Write an essay comparing or contrasting two schools that you have attended.* Identify at least three areas for comparison or contrast, such as student population, instructors, and course offerings. Use examples from your experiences and observations to illustrate your ideas.

Michael Kinsman

Respectable Addiction

A business writer and editor for the *San Diego Union-Tribune*, Michael Kinsman began exploring business-oriented issues when, in 1983, he realized that he was logging in more hours on the job than at home. Persuaded that others shared his work-trapped lifestyle, Kinsman began researching workaholism and other work-related habits. In "Respectable Addiction," Kinsman explores the nature of and attitudes behind what some term an addiction to work.

BEFORE YOU READ

▨ To what extent do you consider yourself a hard worker? Explain.

▨ To what extent are hard work and success linked? Explain.

▨ Do you think it's possible to work too hard? Explain.

VOCABULARY DEVELOPMENT

Look up the following words in a dictionary and write down their meanings.

devoting (paragraph 1)   perspective (paragraph 2)

dubious (paragraph 4)   adversely (paragraph 5)

lopped (paragraph 7)   constitute (paragraph 8)

attributes (paragraph 10)   outlets (paragraph 12)

era (paragraph 14)   reluctance (paragraph 17)

Respectable Addiction

1   Her workdays are typically 12 or 14 hours long and then there's the time she puts in on weekends. But don't label Colleen Peterson a workaholic. "I do work a lot and I love it," the Carmel Valley marketing consultant says. "I have a real passion for what I do. I find it very fulfilling. What's wrong with that?" Peterson is striving to build her own company and prides herself in staying one step ahead of her clients' needs. And, she doesn't feel guilty about devoting more than 40 hours a week to her job.

2   All over today's 24/7 economy, people seem to be working longer hours. Some do it because their job demands it, some do it because they think it will help them get ahead, and others do it out of fear that they will lose their job if they don't. And while most people keep their jobs in perspective with their personal lives, others cross the line and become workaholics.

3   "I think workaholism is like any other 'ism,' " says Ann Clark, whose Ann Clark Associates in San Diego administers employee assistance plans for companies nationwide. "If it begins to interfere with our social relationships or family relationships, we can probably be called workaholics."

4   Because the definition of workaholic is often vague and varies from individual to individual, no one really seems to know how many American workers qualify for this dubious title. Most estimates say that between 5 percent and 10 percent of all workers might be workaholics. "This is a respectable addiction so rates of denial are very, very high," says Clark, whose firm assists companies such as Mercy Hospital in San Diego, Sizzler

International and Mercury Insurance. "People have a lot of ways for justifying why they work so hard."

5   Sheila Arneson, coordinator of Kaiser Permanente's Employee Assistance Program in San Diego, says that while workaholism can adversely affect many aspects of an individual's life, it is not easily detected. "No one walks in the door here and says 'I'm a workaholic,'" she says. "It just doesn't work like that. People come in looking for help because they are having trouble with their spouse, or because they are having trouble with their kids or because they have money problems. Often these are just symptoms of being a workaholic."

6   American workers are more likely to become workaholics than are workers in other countries, according to a study of industrialized nations by the Organization for Economic Cooperation and Development. During a 20-year period from 1979 to 1998, the workload of Americans climbed by 61 hours per year to a total of 1,966, the highest of any industrialized country, OECD reported.

7   While the hours of U.S. workers were rising, the hours of workers in most industrialized countries were dropping. Workers in Japan, for instance, lopped 228 hours per year off their workload while workers in Germany cut 202 hours.

8   And, even if putting in extraordinary work hours doesn't constitute workaholism, employee assistance plans report seeing an increasing number of people with the symptoms of workaholism. Clark says she's witnessed a rise in workaholism in all job categories, with large gains among non-traditional workaholics such as women and those in low-paying jobs.

9   A survey of 800 senior-level executives conducted last year by Exec-U-Net, an Internet-based career information service, found that male executives typically work longer hours than female corporate officers. Yet, 52 percent of executive women with salaries in the $150,000 to $190,000 range consider themselves to be workaholics, compared with just 22 percent of men in the same salary range.

10   Dave Opton, executive director of Exec-U-Net, attributes that to women having a better sense of what constitutes a balanced lifestyle. Just working long hours isn't enough to earn the workaholic label, says Steve Heidel, a psychiatrist and president of Integrated Insights in San Diego, a provider of employee assistance plans. People go through periods of life where work projects are very important and individuals want to put in extra time to achieve their goals. "I worked 100-hour weeks when I was an intern," Heidel says. "Was I a workaholic? I don't think so. I knew it was something I had to do and wouldn't last forever."

11   That's the way Peterson sees her marketing management job. "I think there's often a one-sided definition of how hard you work that gets you called a workaholic," she says. "I don't think I am a workaholic. I live

a normal life when I'm not working. My husband encourages me in my work. When people find out how much I work, they almost feel sorry for me. They shouldn't. I feel fulfilled."

12   Kaiser Permanente believes workaholism is a big enough threat to its work force that it recently published an "Are You A Workaholic?" article in its employee newsletter. "Certainly not everyone who works long hours is an addict, but we do know that there are a number of our employees who might need help controlling their work habits," Arneson says. "It's something we know is not good for them and, ultimately, not good for our company, so we feel calling attention to it is a step toward prevention." She says that hourly workers are less likely to become workaholics, simply because of the structure they work in. "It's the white-collar, salaried work force that has more problems," Arneson said. "It's hard for them to draw barriers and just stop working. And, when they start giving up social outlets for work, that's where the problems start."

13   And, while technology probably isn't responsible for creating workaholics, it encourages them. Cell phones, pagers, e-mail, voice mail and faxes bind workers to their jobs as closely as they allow, Arneson says. "Everybody is supposed to have everything and respond instantly to any request," she says. "In addition, there is an expectation that we will do more with less, which means a lot of people wind up working longer hours to satisfy that expectation."

14   Clearly, some people work extra hours not by choice, but by fear. In an era of downsizing, some people see putting in long hours as a version of job security. Unfortunately, that might not work. "It's false economy just to think you can work longer and longer and be more efficient," Arneson says. "If you just work more, your work will suffer, and you might find yourself overwhelmed or depressed. You might even develop physical problems because you work too much. We don't want that to happen because we know that the long-term costs are much higher than if you address the problem early on. That's why we want our employees to know the danger signs. We want to stop the problem before it gets out of control."

15   Heidel of Integrated Insights is concerned that the fascination of younger generations with the get-rich-quick dot-com world might have a lasting impact on work habits. "Here are people who keep their sleeping bags at work and walk around in their pajamas," he says. "They are encouraged to live at work. Someone who is 25 might say, 'I'm 25, I can do this for a couple of years and cash in my stock options and get out.' There's a rationalization that this period will be short-lived. But when a dot-com goes bust, we'll probably see those same people going out and doing this again."

16   He also said society often views workaholism as a badge of honor. "I've heard people brag about how many hours they work," Heidel says. "I think some of these people are workaholics. But they don't admit it, they usually just say something like they work so hard because they are stimulated by their jobs."

17   The reluctance of companies to address workaholism might be attributed to a simple economic fact: it is more cost-effective to pay individuals to work longer hours than it is to add bodies to the payroll. The investment in employee benefits is the same for a person who works 40 hours per week or who works 60. "Do you ever hear of a company telling people to not work so hard?" Heidel says. "That just doesn't happen too often."

18   Clark agrees that companies should watch for signs of workaholism among their work forces, but ultimately views individuals as having responsibility for their own behavior.

19   Recognize yourself?

POST-READING EXERCISES

1. Which word on the Vocabulary Development list means "removed superfluous parts from"?

   a. attribute   b. constitute

   c. era   d. lopped

2. Typically, how many hours does Colleen Peterson—cited as an example in Kinsman's essay—work per day?

   a. 6 to 8   b. 8 to 10

   c. 10 to 12   d. 12 to 14

3. Which one of the following is *not* a reason people work long hours, according to Kinsman?

   a. Because they want to get attention

   b. Because their jobs demand it

   c. Because they think it will help them get ahead

   d. Because they fear they will lose their jobs if they don't

4. At what point are people considered workaholics?

   a. When work prevents social and family relationships

   b. When work interferes with social and family relationships

   c. When social and family relationships are all centered around work

   d. When social and family relationships survive only in the workplace

5. What is one definition of the word *dubious?*

    a. grand   b. confident

    c. doubtful   d. terrifying

6. What percentage of workers are probably workaholics?

    a. Between 5 and 10 percent

    b. Between 10 and 15 percent

    c. Between 15 and 20 percent

    d. Between 20 and 25 percent

7. Who is more likely to be a workaholic?

    a. Blue-collar, hourly workers

    b. White-collar, salaried workers

    c. Entry-level employees

    d. Management employees

8. What role has technology played in people's work habits?

    a. It makes more work.

    b. It increases pressure to stay at the office longer.

    c. It encourages them to work more.

    d. It decreases the amount of work.

9. Which word on the Vocabulary Development list means "acting against or in a contrary direction"?

    a. constitute   b. attributes

    c. devoting   d. adversely

10. To what fact might employers' reluctance to address workaholism be attributed?

    a. It is good for company morale to have hard workers.

    b. It is beneficial for people to work so hard.

    c. It is cost-effective to pay people to work longer hours.

    d. People work better when they work long hours.

Content

1. How hard do Americans work compared to people in other countries?

2. How do men and women compare in terms of being, or seeing themselves as, workaholics?

3. Why isn't working long hours enough, by itself, to constitute workaholism?

Style and Structure

1. What is Kinsman's point? Rewrite his thesis in your own words.

2. What details does Kinsman use to illustrate his thesis?

3. What details does Kinsman offer for the idea that working longer isn't good for people?

Writing Assignments

1. Kinsman writes that technology can "bind workers to their jobs." What do you think? *Write an essay in which you discuss whether or not technology is "binding," either in a personal or professional sense.* For instance, discuss how having a cell phone makes you feel as though you're never really away from work (or from friends). Use examples from your own experience to illustrate your ideas.

2. Kinsman talks about the reasons people work so hard as well as the effects of working long hours. Why do you think most people do or do not work hard? *Write an essay explaining the reasons people do or do not work hard.* You might talk about personal satisfaction, desire for greater salary, or family pressure. Use examples from your own experiences and observations to illustrate your ideas.

3. Kinsman writes about people who work twelve to fourteen hours per week, yet they don't consider themselves workaholics. What, to you, is the definition of work? *Write an essay defining the term* work. Identify at least three areas for development, such as type of activity involved, whether or not the activity is performed for an authority figure, and whether or not you are paid for the activity. Use examples from your experiences and observations to illustrate your ideas.

Richard Rodriguez

Labor

Raised in Sacramento, California, Richard Rodriguez works to weave his upbringing—as the son of Mexican immigrants—into his writing. Examining his experiences as a summer laborer working with Latinos who lacked the luxury of returning to a university in the fall, Rodriguez discovers that regardless of how similar his name or appearance is to those he works with, huge chasms of experience and privilege divide him from them.

BEFORE YOU READ

▨ What kinds of work have you done over the course of your life? Make a list of any tasks you consider "work."

▨ Of all the tasks you've performed, which types have been the most difficult? In what ways? Explain why certain tasks have proved more challenging than others.

▨ How has your attitude toward work changed over the course of your life? What experiences have influenced this attitude?

VOCABULARY DEVELOPMENT

Look up the following words in a dictionary and write down their meanings.

skepticism (paragraph 5)   expectant (paragraph 5)
bracero (paragraph 5)   exertion (paragraph 9)
savored (paragraph 9)   observant (paragraph 10)
subdued (paragraph 10)   constitute (paragraph 10)
debris (paragraph 11)   anonymous (paragraph 11)
fatalistic (paragraph 11)

Labor

1 I went to college at Stanford, attracted partly by its academic reputation, partly because it was the school rich people went to. I found myself on a campus with golden children of western America's upper middle class. Many were students both ambitious for academic success and accustomed to leisured life in the sun. In the afternoon, they lay spread out, sunbathing in front of the library, reading Swift or Engels or Beckett. Others drove by in convertibles, off to play tennis or ride horses or sail. Beach boys dressed in tank-tops and shorts were my classmates in undergraduate seminars. Tall tan girls wearing white strapless dresses sat directly in front of me in lecture rooms. I'd study them, their physical confidence. I was still recognizably kin to the boy I had been. Less tortured perhaps. But still kin. At Stanford, it's true, I began to have something like a conventional sexual life. I don't think, however, that I really believed that the women I knew found me physically appealing. I continued to stay out of the sun. I didn't linger in mirrors. And I was the student at Stanford who remembered to notice the Mexican-American janitors and gardeners working on campus.

2   It was at Stanford, one day near the end of my senior year, that a friend told me about a summer construction job he knew was available. I was quickly alert. Desire uncoiled within me. My friend said that he knew I had been looking for summer employment. He knew I needed some money. Almost apologetically he explained: It was something I probably wouldn't be interested in, but a friend of his, a contractor, needed someone for the summer to do menial jobs. There would be lots of shoveling and raking and sweeping. Nothing too hard. But nothing more interesting either. Still, the pay would be good. Did I want it? Or did I know someone who did?

3   I did. Yes, I said, surprised to hear myself say it.

4   In the weeks following, friends cautioned that I had no idea how hard physical labor really is. ("You only *think* you know what it is like to shovel for eight hours straight.") Their objections seemed to me challenges. They resolved the issue. I became happy with my plan. I decided, however, not to tell my parents. I wouldn't tell my mother because I could guess her worried reaction. I would tell my father only after the summer was over, when I could announce that, after all, I did know what "real work" is like.

5   The day I met the contractor (a Princeton graduate, it turned out), he asked me whether I had done any physical labor before. "In high school, during the summer," I lied. And although he seemed to regard me with skepticism, he decided to give me a try. Several days later, expectant, I arrived at my first construction site. I would take off my shirt to the sun. And at last grasp desired sensation. No longer afraid. At last become like a *bracero*. "We need those tree stumps out of here by tomorrow," the contractor said. I started to work.

6   I labored with excitement that first morning—and all the days after. The work was harder than I could have expected. But it was never as tedious as my friends had warned me it would be. There was too much physical pleasure in the labor. Especially early in the day, I would be most alert to the sensations of movement and straining. Beginning around seven each morning (when the air was still damp but the scent of weeds and dry earth anticipated the heat of the sun), I would feel my body resist the first thrusts of the shovel. My arms, tightened by sleep, would gradually loosen; after only several minutes, sweat would gather in beads on my forehead and then—a short while later—I would feel my chest silky with sweat in the breeze. I would return to my work. A nervous spark of pain would fly up my arm and settle to burn like an ember in the thick of my shoulder. An hour, two passed. Three. My whole body would assume regular movements; my shoveling would be described by identical, even movements. Even later in the day, my enthusiasm for primitive sensation would survive the heat and the dust and the insects prickling my back. I would strain

wildly for sensation as the day came to a close. At three-thirty, quitting time, I would stand upright and slowly let my head fall back, luxuriating in the feeling of tightness relieved.

7   Some of the men working nearby would watch me and laugh. Two or three of the older men took the trouble to teach me the right way to use a pick, the correct way to shovel. "You're doing it wrong, too fucking hard," one man scolded. Then proceeded to show me—what persons who work with their bodies all their lives quickly learn—the most economical way to use one's body in labor.

8   "Don't make your back do so much work," he instructed. I stood impatiently listening, half listening, vaguely watching, then noticed his work-thickened fingers clutching the shovel. I was annoyed. I wanted to tell him that I enjoyed shoveling the wrong way. And I didn't want to learn the right way. I wasn't afraid of back pain. I liked the way my body felt sore at the end of the day.

9   I was about to, but, as it turned out, I didn't say a thing. Rather it was at that moment I realized that I was fooling myself if I expected a few weeks of labor to gain me admission to the world of the laborer. I would not learn in three months what my father had meant by "real work." I was not bound to this job; I could imagine its rapid conclusion. For me the sensations of exertion and fatigue could be savored. For my father or uncle, working at comparable jobs when they were my age, such sensations were to be feared. Fatigue took a different toll on their bodies—and minds.

10   It was, I know, a simple insight. But it was with this realization that I took my first step that summer toward realizing something even more important about the "worker." In the company of carpenters, electricians, plumbers, and painters at lunch, I would often sit quietly, observant. I was not shy in such company. I felt easy, pleased by the knowledge that I was casually accepted, my presence taken for granted by men (exotics) who worked with their hands. Some days the younger men would talk and talk about sex, and they would howl at women who drove by in cars. Other days the talk at lunchtime was subdued; men gathered in separate groups. It depended on who was around. There were rough, good-natured workers. Others were quiet. The more I remember that summer, the more I realize that there was no single *type* of worker. I am embarrassed to say I had not expected such diversity. I certainly had not expected to meet, for example, a plumber who was an abstract painter in his off hours and admired the work of Mark Rothko. Nor did I expect so many workers with college diplomas. (They were the ones who were not surprised that I intended to enter graduate school in the fall.) I suppose what I really want to say here is painfully obvious, but I must say it nevertheless: The men of that summer were middle-class Americans. They certainly didn't constitute an oppressed society. Carefully completing their

work sheets; talking about the fortunes of local football teams; planning Las Vegas vacations; comparing the gas mileage of various makes of campers—they were not *los pobres* [the poor] my mother had spoken about.

11   On two occasions, the contractor hired a group of Mexican aliens. They were employed to cut down some trees and haul off debris. In all, there were six men of varying age. They youngest in his late twenties; the oldest (his father?) perhaps sixty years old. They came and they left in a single old truck. Anonymous men. They were never introduced to the other men at the site. Immediately upon their arrival, they would follow the contractor's directions, start working—rarely resting—seemingly driven by a fatalistic sense that work which had to be done was best done as quickly as possible.

12   I watched them sometimes. Perhaps they watched me. The only time I saw them pay me much notice was one day at lunchtime when I was laughing with the other men. The Mexicans sat apart when they ate, just as they worked by themselves. Quiet. I rarely heard them say much to each other. All I could hear were their voices calling out sharply to one another, giving directions. Otherwise, when they stood briefly resting, they talked among themselves in voices too hard to overhear.

13   The contractor knew enough Spanish, and the Mexicans—or at least the oldest of them, their spokesman—seemed to know enough English to communicate. But because I was around, the contractor decided one day to make me his translator. (He assumed I could speak Spanish.) I did what I was told. Shyly I went over to tell the Mexicans that the *patrón* wanted them to do something else before they left for the day. As I started to speak, I was afraid with my old fear that I would be unable to pronounce the Spanish words. But it was a simple instruction I had to convey. I could say it in phrases.

14   The dark sweating faces turned toward me as I spoke. They stopped their work to hear me. Each nodded in response. I stood there. I wanted to say something more. But what could I say in Spanish, even if I could have pronounced the words right? Perhaps I just wanted to engage them in small talk, to be assured of their confidence, our familiarity. I thought for a moment to ask them where in Mexico they were from. Something like that And maybe I wanted to tell them (a lie, if need be) that my parents were from the same part of Mexico.

15   I stood there.

16   Their faces watched me. The eyes of the man directly in front of me moved slowly over my shoulder, and I turned to follow his glance toward *el patrón* some distance away. For a moment I felt swept up by that glance into the Mexicans' company. But then I heard one of them returning to work. And then the others went back to work. I left them without saying anything more.

17   When they had finished, the contractor went over to pay them in cash. (He later told me that he paid them collectively—"for the job," though he

wouldn't tell me their wages. He said something quickly about the good rate of exchange "in their own country.") I can still hear the loudly confident voice he used with the Mexicans. It was the sound of the *gringo* I had heard as a very young boy. And I can still hear the quiet, indistinct sounds of the Mexican, the oldest, who replied. At hearing that voice I was sad for the Mexicans. Depressed by their vulnerability. Angry at myself. The adventure of the summer seemed suddenly ludicrous. I would not shorten the distance I felt from *los pobres* with a few weeks of physical labor. I would not become like them. They were different from me.

18   After that summer, a great deal—and not very much really—changed in my life. The curse of physical shame was broken by the sun; I was no longer ashamed of my body. No longer would I deny myself the pleasing sensations of my maleness. During those years when middle-class black Americans began to assert with pride, "Black is beautiful," I was able to regard my complexion without shame. I am today darker than I ever was as a boy. I have taken up the middle-class sport of long-distance running. Nearly every day now I run ten or fifteen miles, barely clothed, my skin exposed to the California winter rain and wind or the summer sun of late afternoon. The torso, the soccer player's calves and thighs, the arms of the twenty-year-old I never was, I possess now in my thirties. I study the youthful parody shape in the mirror: the stomach lipped tight by muscle; the shoulders rounded by chin-ups; the arms veined strong. This man. A man. I meet him. He laughs to see me, what I have become.

19   The dandy. I wear double-breasted Italian suits and custom-made English shoes. I resemble no one so much as my father—the man pictured in those honeymoon photos. At that point in life when he abandoned the dandy's posture, I assume it. At the points when my parents would not consider going on vacation, I register at the Hotel Carlyle in New York and the Plaza Athenée in Paris. I am as taken by the symbols of leisure and wealth as they were. For my parents, however, those symbols became taunts, reminders of all they could not achieve in one lifetime. For me those same symbols are reassuming reminders of public success. I tempt vulgarity to be reassured. I am filled with the gaudy delight, the monstrous grace of the *nouveau riche*.

20   In recent years I have had occasion to lecture in ghetto high schools. There I see students of remarkable style and physical grace. (One can see more dandies in such schools than one ever will find in middle-class high schools.) There is not the look of casual assurance I saw students at Stanford display. Ghetto girls mimic high-fashion models. Their dresses are of bold, forceful color; their figures elegant, long; the stance theatrical. Boys wear shirts that grip at their overdeveloped muscular bodies. (Against a powerless future, they engage images of strength.) Bad nutrition does not yet tell. Great disappointment, fatal to youth, awaits them still. For the

moment, movements in school hallways are dancelike, a procession of postures in a sexual masque. Watching them, I feel a kind of envy. I wonder how different my adolescence would have been had I been free. . . . But no, it is my parents I see—their optimism during those years when they were entertained by Italian grand opera.

21   The registration clerk in London wonders if I have just been to Switzerland. And the man who carries my luggage in New York guesses the Caribbean. My complexion becomes a mark of my leisure. Yet no one would regard my complexion the same way if I entered such hotels through the service entrance. That is only to say that my complexion assumes its significance from the context of my life. My skin, in itself, means nothing. I stress the point because I know there are people who would label me "disadvantaged" because of my color. They make the same mistake I made as a boy, when I thought a disadvantaged life was circumscribed by particular occupations. That summer I worked in the sun may have made me physically indistinguishable from the Mexicans working nearby. (My skin was actually darker because, unlike them, I worked without wearing a shirt. By late August my hands were probably as tough as theirs.) But I was not one of *los pobres*. What made me different from them was an attitude of *mind*, my imagination of myself.

22   I do not blame my mother for warning me away from the sun when I was young. In a world where her brother had become an old man in his twenties because he was dark, my complexion was something to worry about. "Don't run in the sun," she warns me today. I run. In the end, my father was right—though perhaps he did not know how right or why—to say that I would never know what real work is. I will never know what he felt at his last factory job. If tomorrow I worked at some kind of factory, it would go differently for me. My long education would favor me. I could act as a public person—able to defend my interests, to unionize, to petition, to speak up—to challenge and demand. (I will never know what real work is.) I will never know what the Mexicans knew, gathering their shovels and ladders and saws.

23   Their silence stays with me now. The wages those Mexicans received for their labor were only a measure of their disadvantaged condition. Their silence is more telling. They lack a public identity. They remain profoundly alien. Persons apart. People lacking a union obviously, people without grounds. They depend upon the relative good will or fairness of their employers each day. For such people, lacking a better alternative, it is not such an unreasonable risk.

24   Their silence stays with me. I have taken these many words to describe its impact. Only: the quiet. Something uncanny about it. Its compliance. Vulnerability. Pathos. As I heard their truck rumbling away, I shuddered, my face mirrored with sweat. I had finally come face to face with *los pobres*.

POST-READING EXERCISES

1. Which word on the Vocabulary Development list means "the remains of something broken down or destroyed"?

   a. skepticism

   b. savored

   c. anonymous

   d. debris

2. What does Rodriguez like about his job as a laborer?

   a. Being treated as an immigrant

   b. Using his body to work

   c. Getting a break from his studies

   d. Acting as a translator for the boss

3. How does Rodriguez feel when the older workers advise him on how to work?

   a. Anxious

   b. Antsy

   c. Angry

   d. Annoyed

4. What conclusion does Rodriguez draw about the men he worked with on a daily basis?

   a. They were middle-class Americans.

   b. They were from third world countries.

   c. They were exactly like he was.

   d. They were extremely unfriendly.

5. What does the word *exertion* mean?

   a. Pleasing sensation

   b. Satisfying challenge

   c. Laborious or perceptible effort

   d. Painful and humiliating work

6. What does Rodriguez want to do after he delivers the boss's instructions to the Mexican workers?

   a. Ask about their homes in Mexico.

   b. Tell them to work harder.

   c. Pretend he's the boss.

   d. Offer to do their work for them.

7. What does Rodriguez actually do after he delivers the instructions?

   a. Shakes hands with the oldest man

   b. Nothing

   c. Looks at the man's feet

   d. Smiles

8. How has Rodriguez's physical appearance changed since he was a child?

    a. Lighter skin, bleached hair

    b. Calloused hands, wrinkled face

    c. Darker skin, muscular build

    d. Gray hair, stooped posture

9. Which word on the Vocabulary Development list means "not named or identified"?

    a. savored   b. constitute

    c. anonymous   d. fatalistic

10. What does Rodriguez claim that he will never know the meaning of?

    a. Real work   b. Real fatigue

    c. Real poverty   d. Real pride

Content

1. What is Rodriguez's attitude toward physical labor at the start of his job?

2. What feelings does Rodriguez experience as a result of his brief contact with the Mexican workers?

3. What changes in Rodriguez's life after his job?

Style and Structure

1. What is Rodriguez's point? Write his argument in your own words.

2. What examples does Rodriguez use to illustrate his ideas?

3. What function does the image of a mirror serve for Rodriguez in his essay?

Writing Assignments

1. Rodriguez writes about work in his essay, comparing his experiences with his father's, among others. What, for you, constitutes "real work"? *Write an essay in which you explain what elements a job or task must have to be a form of "real work."* Use examples from your own experiences to illustrate your ideas.

2. Rodriguez writes that fatigue took a toll on "the bodies—and minds" of people who were "bound" to physical labor. What kinds of fatigue does Rodriguez mean? *Write an essay in which you define* fatigue *in terms of labor.* Explain what you mean by *labor,* and use examples from your own life for support.

3. Rodriguez writes that his "imagination of [him]self" made him different from the Mexican workers. To what extent does your idea of yourself determine who you are? *Write an essay explaining how the way you see yourself—as a student, laborer, part-time worker, or boss, perhaps—makes you what you are. For*

instance, if you wait tables now to pay rent but know that you will not have this job forever, explain how your idea of yourself in the future helps guide you to reach your goals. Use examples and illustrations from your own life to support your ideas.

Nicolette Toussaint

Hearing the Sweetest Songs

Describing herself first as a writer then as a painter and gardener, Nicolette Toussaint includes her condition as a hearing-impaired person only at the end of her list of who she is. Writing about her experiences communicating with hearing people, Toussaint argues that everyone can gain something positive from understanding how people with disabilities function.

BEFORE YOU READ

- What kinds of disabilities have you encountered, either in yourself or in others, in your life? Explain.
- What do you think most people's initial reactions to disabled people are? Why? Explain.
- To what extent does the nature of people's disabilities affect others' comfort around them? Are there some disabilities that are "easier" for people to understand or ignore? Explain.

VOCABULARY DEVELOPMENT

Look up the following words in a dictionary and write down their meanings.

pneumonia (paragraph 2)   unnerved (paragraph 4)
agitated (paragraph 4)   inquisitorial (paragraph 4)
onslaught (paragraph 4)   eccentric (paragraph 10)
mute (paragraph 12)   slapdash (paragraph 12)
capering (paragraph 13)   transcendent (paragraph 14)

Hearing the Sweetest Songs

1 Every year when I was a child, a man brought a big, black, squeaking machine to school. When he discovered I couldn't hear all his peeps and squeaks, he would get very excited. The nurse would draw a chart with a

deep canyon in it. Then I would listen to the squeaks two or three times, while the adults—who were all acting very, very nice—would watch me raise my hand. Sometimes I couldn't tell whether I heard the squeaks or just imagined them, but I liked being the center of attention.

2   My parents said I lost my hearing to pneumonia as a baby; but I knew I hadn't *lost* anything. None of my parts had dropped off. Nothing had changed: if I wanted to listen to Beethoven, I could put my head between the speakers and turn the dial up to 7 I could hear jets at the airport a block away. I could hear my mom when she was in the same room—if I wanted to. I could even hear my cat purr if I put my good ear right on top of him.

3   I wasn't aware of *not* hearing until I began to wear a hearing aid at the age of 30. It shattered my peace: shoes creaking, papers crackling, pencils tapping, phones ringing, refrigerators humming, people cracking knuckles, clearing throats and blowing noses! Cars, bikes, dogs, cats, kids all seemed to appear from nowhere and fly right at me.

4   I was constantly startled, unnerved, agitated—exhausted. I felt as though inquisitorial Nazis in an old World War II film were burning the side of my head with a merciless white spotlight. Under that onslaught, I had to break down and confess: I couldn't hear. Suddenly, I began to discover many things I couldn't do.

5   I couldn't identify sounds. One afternoon, while lying on my side watching a football game on TV, I kept hearing a noise that sounded like my cat playing with a flexible-spring doorstop. I checked, but the cat was asleep. Finally, I happened to lift my head as the noise occurred. Heard through my good ear, the metallic buzz turned out to be the referee's whistle.

6   I couldn't tell where sounds came from. I couldn't find my phone under the blizzard of papers on my desk. The more it rang, the deeper I dug. I shoveled mounds of paper onto the floor and finally had to track it down by following the cord from the wall.

7   When I lived alone, I felt helpless because I couldn't hear alarm clocks, vulnerable because I couldn't hear the front door open and frightened because I wouldn't hear a burglar until it was too late.

8   Then one day I missed a job interview because of the phone. I had gotten off the subway 20 minutes early, eager and dressed to the nines. But the address I had written down didn't exist! I must have misheard it: I searched the street, becoming overheated, late and frantic, knowing that if I confessed that I couldn't hear on the phone, I would make my odds of getting hired even worse.

9   For the first time, I felt unequal, disadvantaged and disabled. Now that I had something to compare, I knew that I *had* lost something; not just my hearing, but my independence and my sense of wholeness. I had always hated to be seen as inferior, so I never mentioned my lack of hearing. Unlike a wheelchair or a white cane, my disability doesn't announce itself. For most of my life, I chose to pass as abled, and I thought I did it quite well.

10   But after I got the hearing aid, a business friend said, "You know, Nicolette, you think you get away with not hearing, but you don't. Sometimes in meetings you answer the wrong question. People don't know you can't hear, so they think you're daydreaming, eccentric, stupid—or just plain rude. It would be better to just tell them."

11   I wondered about that then, and I still do. If I tell, I risk being seen as *un*able rather than *dis*abled. Sometimes, when I say I can't hear, the waiter will turn to my companion and say, "What does she want?" as though I have lost my power of speech.

12   If I tell, people may see *only* my disability. Once someone is labeled "deaf," "crippled," "mute" or "aged," that's too often all they are. I'm a writer, a painter, a slapdash housekeeper, a gardener who grows wondrous roses; my hearing is just part of the whole. It's a tender part, and you should handle it with care. But like most people with a disability, I don't mind if you ask about it.

13   In fact, you should ask, because it's an important part of me, something my friends see as part of my character. My friend Anne always rests a hand on my elbow in parking lots, since several times, drivers who assume that I hear them have nearly run me over. When I hold my head at a certain angle, my husband, Mason, will say, "It's a plane" or "It's a siren." And my mother loves to laugh about the things I *thought* I heard: last week I was told that "the Minotaurs in the garden are getting out of hand." I imagined capering bullmen and I was disappointed to learn that all we had in the garden were overgrown "baby tears."

14   Not hearing can be funny, or frustrating. And once in a while, it can be the cause of something truly transcendent. One morning at the shore I was listening to the ocean when Mason said, "Hear the bird?" What bird? I listened hard until I heard a faint, unbirdlike, croaking sound. If he hadn't mentioned it, I would never have noticed it. As I listened, slowly I began to hear—or perhaps imagine—a distant song. Did I *really* hear it? Or just hear in my heart when he shared with me? I don't care. Songs imagined are as sweet as songs heard, and songs shared are sweeter still.

15   That sharing is what I want for all of us. We're all just temporarily abled, and every one of us, if we live long enough, will become disabled in some way. Those of us who have gotten there first can tell you how to cope with phones and alarm clocks. About ways of holding a book, opening a door and leaning on a crutch all at the same time. And what it's like to give up in despair on Thursday, then begin all over again on Friday, because there's no other choice—and because the roses are beginning to bud in the garden.

16   These are conversations we all should have, and it's not that hard to begin. Just let me see your lips when you speak. Stay in the same room. Don't shout. And ask what you want to know.

POST-READING EXERCISES

1. Which word on the Vocabulary Development list means "haphazard" or "slip-shod"?

   a. mute   b. slapdash

   c. capering   d. eccentric

2. How did Toussaint react to the attention she received during her childhood hearing tests?

   a. She felt ashamed at not being able to hear.

   b. She enjoyed tricking the examiners.

   c. She felt confused at what was being asked of her.

   d. She liked being the center of attention.

3. What caused Toussaint's hearing loss?

   a. Pneumonia   b. Psychological trauma

   c. Scarlet fever   d. Influenza

4. How old was Toussaint when she realized she couldn't hear perfectly?

   a. 30   b. 32

   c. 18   d. 12

5. What is one definition of the word *onslaught*?

   a. An introduction

   b. An especially fierce attack

   c. An appropriate ending

   d. An interesting possibility

6. Which one of the following is *not* something Toussaint felt about living alone?

   a. Helpless   b. Vulnerable

   c. Frightened   d. Intimidated

7. What did Toussaint finally do to find her phone?

   a. Throw herself on her desk to feel it under the papers.

   b. Completely clear her desk of all papers.

   c. Track it down by following the cord from the wall.

   d. Watch the cord for vibrations.

8. What caused Toussaint to feel "unequal, disadvantaged and disabled" for the first time?

   a. Missing a job interview because of the phone

   b. Missing a flight because of an answering machine

     c. Making a mistake in a meeting because of someone's quiet voice

     d. Making a mistake in personal conversation because of background noises

9. Which word on the Vocabulary Development list means "to leap or prance about in a playful manner"?

     a. eccentric   b. capering

     c. mute   d. inquisitorial

10. How does Toussaint feel about people asking her about her hearing loss?

     a. She hates it.   b. She passionately loves it.

     c. She doesn't mind it.   d. She's embarrassed by it.

Content

1. Why does Toussaint not consider herself to have *lost* her hearing?
2. How do Toussaint's friends see her hearing loss?
3. How is Toussaint's disability different from blindness or paralysis?

Style and Structure

1. What is Toussaint's point? Rewrite her thesis in your own words.
2. What examples does Toussaint use to show that she doesn't hear perfectly?
3. What is Toussaint contrasting her experiences with? Why doesn't she include more details about the other object of contrast?

Writing Assignments

1. Toussaint writes that, as a child, she enjoyed being the center of attention during school hearing tests. To what extent, if at all, do you think people use their weaknesses for personal gain? *Write an essay explaining how people do or do not use their weaknesses—mental, physical, emotional, or professional— to their advantage.* For instance, if you've ever been ill and had someone care for you, you might have found it difficult to give up that person's care when you're well; thus, your "symptoms" may have lingered longer than if you were alone. Use examples from your own experiences and observations to illustrate your ideas.

2. Toussaint writes that, with the discovery that her hearing wasn't perfect, she began "to discover many things [she] couldn't do." To what extent does the discovery of one weakness lead to the discovery of many? *Write an essay explaining how learning something negative about yourself or someone else does or does not lead to the discovery of other negative traits.* For instance, if some-

one you trust lies to you, that breach of trust may lead you to see other faults in that person. Use examples from your own experiences and observations to illustrate your ideas.

3. Toussaint writes, "Songs imagined are as sweet as songs heard, and songs shared are sweeter still." Is she right? *Write an essay explaining how sharing experiences does or does not make them "sweeter."* Use examples from your own experiences and observations to illustrate your ideas.

Our World

In addition to the people we meet, other beings inhabit the spheres in which we dwell. In "Creatures that Haunt the America," Constance García-Barrio explores the otherworldly creatures who live in our imaginations and, perhaps, our physical worlds. In "So Tiny, So Sweet . . . So Mean" and "Caught in the Catty Corner," Richard Conniff and Nanci Hellmich write about how even the most delicate of our feathered friends and what was historically called the "gentle" sex are fiercely competitive. John McPhee describes with care two men whose lives could easily be reduced to overly simple stereotypes, and in "Poor Winnie the Pooh," Ben MacIntyre questions the efficacy of therapy in the face of anxiety or trauma. Finally, Donald Hall explains how the written words that surround us are ingested differently for different purposes.

Readings in This Section

Richard Conniff

So Tiny, So Sweet . . . So Mean

Winning the 1997 National Magazine Award for his writing in *Smithsonian,* Richard Conniff covers a wide range of subjects—wildlife, human culture, and interior design, to name some. His work has appeared in *Time, Atlantic Monthly,* the *New York Times Magazine, Worth, Architectural Digest,* and *National Geographic.* He has also written two books, *Spineless Wonders: Strange Tales from the Invertebrate World* and *Every Creeping Thing: True Tales of Faintly Repulsive Wildlife.*

BEFORE YOU READ

- Have you ever observed hummingbirds in a natural setting? Describe them.
- What impression do you have of hummingbirds? Upon what experiences are these impressions based?
- In your experience, what animals have "personalities" that do not seem to match their appearance? Explain.

VOCABULARY DEVELOPMENT

Look up the following words in a dictionary and write down their meanings.

warbler (paragraph 4)	yearningly (paragraph 4)
coruscating (paragraph 5)	fretful (7)
scrounge (paragraph 8)	nectar (paragraph 8)
iridescent (paragraph 10)	taxing (paragraph 14)
succulent (paragraph 15)	anatomically (paragraph 21)

So Tiny, So Sweet . . . So Mean

1 It wasn't quite six on a radiant Arizona morning when Marion Paton, a retired school cafeteria manager with big tinted glasses and golden hair, padded into her kitchen and glanced out the picture window. Nineteen people sitting in her backyard stared back through their binoculars. There was a fat, bearded man in a luau shirt and a hat with the brim bent up in front. There was a slight, older man, mild as a parson, with round, wire-rimmed eyeglasses and a blue zip-up jacket. There was a woman in clamdigger slacks, white socks

and a bush hat studded with birding pins. The assembled crowd was engaged in the behavior Paton calls "whooping and dooping."

2   'There's a very nice violet-crowned on number four," said a guide, "and you can really see that white breast. Oooh, oooh, it's that male rufous. Flash that tail at us again!"

3   Did Paton perhaps long for a little privacy, at least until the coffee dripped? The question astounded her. "What for?" she asked. She did not even mind the time a couple of duck blinds turned up in the yard, with television cameras trained on her house. "I love people," she said. "I love nature."

4   She wandered outside. "Canyon towhee running around by the hose," said a guide, and the binoculars whipped right. "Yellow warbler singing behind us." The crowd swiveled around. Then, one by one, the lenses came yearningly back to Paton's modest house, where feeders full of sugar water hung from the eaves. They were swarming with hummingbirds, which John James Audubon once likened to "a glittering fragment of the rainbow."

5   In fact, the tail feathers and metallic gorgets coruscating in the moist air looked more like the whole damned spectrum. But the action here was too intense for rainbow analogies: broad-taileds, Costas and calliopes jostled around every feeding hole, and other hummingbirds twittered impatiently nearby. Paton's house in the remote town of Patagonia happens to be in the middle of a major north-south flyway. It's also right next to a nature preserve. Down the road toward Nogales, Jesse Hendrix, the keeper of another unofficial hummingbird way station, boasts 10,000 hummers a day on his 150 feeders at the height of the migration, and he can run through 150 pounds of sugar a week. Paton prefers to keep things modest, with no more than eight feeders.

6   "These creatures have a following like mythical beasts," said one of the guides, a little ruefully. "There are people who don't care anything about birds, or other wildlife or nature, but they love hummingbirds. We had one woman tell us: 'I just love hummingbirds and unicorns.' And I don't think she drew a distinction between the two." The guide's name was Tom Wood. He was from the Southeastern Arizona Bird Observatory. "People come in," he continued, "and they say, 'They're so tiny, and they're so sweet,' and we'll say, 'Well, they are tiny.'" Wood trained his binoculars on a feeder. The glittering fragments of rainbow were at that moment swatting and screaming at one another in a relentless bid to get to the head of the line. "They're fighter pilots in small bodies. We've seen a bird knock another hummingbird out of the air and stab it with its bill. People still don't believe it. They think they're little fairies." He shrugged. "We're probably lucky these things aren't the size of ravens, or it would not be safe to walk in the woods."

7   Hummingbirds are among the smallest warm-blooded animals on Earth, and though it may be heresy to say so, they are also among the mean-

est. The bee hummingbird, a Cuban species, weighs less than a dime, and even middleweight species like the rufous and broad-tailed hummingbirds weigh less than a nickel. Their size makes them cute—and also dictates their fretful, bickering, high-rev way of life. A big stolid raven can store enough energy to plod through good times and bad. But even in the best of times, a hummingbird is a slave to its raging metabolism.

8   Hummingbirds get most of their energy by sipping nectar from flowers, and a typical hummingbird needs 7 to 12 calories of energy a day. This sounds idyllic, until you do the math: it's the equivalent of a 180-pound human having to scrounge up 204,300 calories a day, or about 171 pounds of hamburger. To keep itself alive, a hummingbird must manage to find as many as 1,000 flowers and drink almost twice its weight in nectar daily. It's enough to give even a very pretty little bird the personality of a junkyard dog, not to mention an urgent need to pee. A scientific paper about the rufous hummingbird includes this endearing notation: "Social behavior: None. Individual survival seems only concern."

9   One morning at the Rocky Mountain Biological Laboratory, in the village of Gothic, Colorado, a researcher named Bill Calder reached into a hardware-cloth cage and gently folded a fresh-caught rufous in the palm of one hand. "Hello, little man," he said, and to a visitor, he added, "He's straight from God-knows-where. Somewhere between Montana and Alaska." It was only mid-July, but this thumb-size bird had already flown roughly 2,000 miles north from his winter home in Mexico. With a combination of luck and cussedness, he had established a territory, defended it from rival males, put on courtship displays for passing females and mated with as many of them as possible. Now he was on the road south again.

10   "You've got to see this in the sun," Calder said. He held the bird up, and the patch of color at its throat glowed with deep, shifting reds and oranges. The throat patch, or gorget, is likely a display device for attracting females and intimidating rivals, but the iridescent colors were entirely appropriate to the rufous hummingbird's high-energy way of life. "It's like a burning coal," Calder said.

11   He took the bird inside, weighed it, crimped a tiny metal identification band on one leg, returned outdoors and set it free. He and his wife, Lorene, have been doing this for the past 30 summers at Gothic, to figure out the consequences and requirements of body size in different birds. Calder, who is a professor of biology at the University of Arizona, is a lean, energetic 65-year-old with a gray Vandyke beard, a beaky nose, and thin lips framed by deep furrows arching down from the corners of the nose. He tends to flit from subject to subject, and he is relentless about his work. The Calders' cabin at Gothic is 9,500 feet above sea level, and even in July strips of snow in the high draws still send rivulets and waterfalls down the gray flanks of the Elk Mountains. It's a good location to study hummingbirds, although

as a genus they are basically tropical. Hummingbirds are a New World family (the sunbirds of Asia and Africa are only superficially similar), and more than half the roughly 320 species live near the equator.

12   But hummingbirds are also opportunistic. They will fearlessly investigate any potential food source. This is why Calder once got kissed by a hummingbird: "I was out there working with my mouth open—was always a mouth-breather—and a hummingbird flew up to me and put her bill in, and I actually felt her tongue on my tongue."

13   Hummingbirds also routinely explore new habitats, because the cushier habitats quickly fill up with other hummingbirds. Thus some equatorial species have evolved to live high up in the Andes, and other species migrate 500 miles across the Gulf of Mexico, or down the Rocky Mountains from Alaska to Mexico. But why travel the colder mountains instead of, say, the plains? Calder indicated the swaths of yellow, violet and red wildflowers, which lay like veils across the green foothills above Gothic: "Abundant flowers in a compressed growing season," he said.

14   In fact, hummingbirds seemed to be everywhere on the slopes around the Calders' cabin. Broad-tail males perched on high branches and electric wires, each fiercely guarding a feeder or a patch of flowers. One of Calder's students found that a male broad-tail at a feeder typically flies more than 40 sorties an hour to drive off rivals. Roughly another 45 times an hour, he shoots 60 feet straight up in the air and back down in a gaudy courtship power dive, his wingtips giving off a metallic trill, urgent as a bicycle bell. This is incredibly taxing. A hummingbird's heart beats more than 1,200 times a minute in flight; his wings hum at 2,280 revolutions per minute.

15   And yet, even with a patch of succulent flowers at his feet, a male broad-tail actually eats very little for much of the day. A full belly would give him the aerodynamics of a lumbering old bomber, reducing his ability to chase rivals and display for females. So he waits till dusk, then goes on a 20-minute binge, hitting flower after flower until his crop sags and his weight balloons by a third with the fuel he needs to survive the frigid night. Then he abandons his territory and, contrary to our expectations, flies uphill. Thermal inversions make the mountains about five degrees C warmer at night than the valleys, and the males know where the warmth is. Given the speed with which small bodies lose heat (think of a spoonful of soup versus a full bowl), such subtle adaptations can save a bird's life.

16   The females, meanwhile, tough it out in the valleys with their offspring. But they've also evolved tricks for surviving harsh mountain nights. In a stand of evergreens and aspen not far from his cabin, Calder pointed out a female broad-tail's nest on a branch overhung by a higher bough in a spruce tree. The bough, he said, serves as a roof over the nest, reducing nightly heat loss. The nest itself was about the size of a baby's fist, flecked with bits of

green lichen for camouflage. The female weaves it together with spider web-
bing. Hummingbirds may also insulate their nests with down or the feath-
ery white aspen seeds that sometimes drift through the valley like a snow
flurry. But the female's last resort against cold is torpor: if she doesn't have
enough energy to get through the night, she can turn down her thermostat,
cutting her body temperature in half. In torpor, her metabolism slows two
to three times for every 10 degree C drop in temperature.

17   The female at this particular nest was a small mousy broad-tail with
mottled green back, and she welcomed her human intruders by perching
on a nearby branch, twitching her head from side to side, and screaming
chip-chip-chip. It made her visitors feel faintly ashamed, like being scolded
by a mother for waking the baby.

18   Calder backed off, and the broad-tail returned to the spruce tree in
stages, pausing in midair and glancing around, as if to make sure she was
not being followed. She began to feed, hovering in the air around the nest
with her head cocked, then zipping up, down, left and right, seizing gnats
with her bill. Despite their reputation as nectar-sippers, hummingbirds routinely get their fats and proteins by eating insects. When she'd filled her
crop, she perched on the rim of the nest, and her two nestlings rose up in a
flurry of soft feathers and gaping maws.

19   What happened next was appalling: the mother stuck her bill halfway
down one nestling's throat, as if she'd mistaken her baby for a sword-swal-
lower. Then she started jabbing up and down like a sewing machine. "That
much bill and that little chick," Calder mused. "I'm always afraid she'll over-
shoot." She was regurgitating food and literally packing it in, to get her
youngster to eight times its hatch weight in just two weeks. When she was
done, she swooped away from the nest, chip-chip-chipped some more and
hovered close enough that her human visitors could feel the turbulence
from her angry wingbeats on their faces.

20   The ancestors of hummingbirds probably started out feeding on
tiny insects around flowers, and only incidentally got their noses into
the nectar. But they took to flower-feeding like a small child to lollipops.
Hummingbirds and certain flowers have subsequently adapted in all
kinds of weird ways for the blissful moment or two when they come
together. In the Andes, for instance, certain passionflowers have developed
an elongated tube-like shape. Local hummingbirds in turn have evolved
four-inch-long swordbills for reaching deep down to the nectar at the bottom of the tube. When they finish feeding, the hummingbirds inadvertently
carry a dusting of pollen on their bills and heads and deliver it to fertilize
other passionflowers, sometimes miles away. The birds are the flowers' primary pollinators.

21   Hummingbirds have also evolved incredibly long, specialized tongues.
If you hold a hummingbird in your hand and offer it a feeder, you can

sometimes see the white flickering of the tongue entering the feeder hole just ahead of the bill. If you blow gently on the bird's head feathers as it feeds, you can actually see the tongue muscles pulsing under the translucent flesh at the back of the skull. This may seem anatomically unorthodox. The tongue itself fills the hummingbird's bill, so the muscles that support the tongue actually run back around the spinal cord, up the outside of the skull and over the top, to be anchored between the eyes. In some species, the tongue is fringed along the outer edge, which may help entangle insects. In some, the tongue ends in two troughlike channels, with which the bird draws up nectar—not by sucking but by capillary action—as the tongue flicks in and out. While the human spectators are whooping and dooping, the hummingbirds, in Calder's words, are wicking and licking.

22   So far, this is pretty straightforward. But as the relationship between flowers and hummingbirds evolved, certain mites figured out how to get in on the party. These tiny relatives of ticks and spiders eat nectar and pollen, and each mite species has evolved to feed on particular species of flowers. Getting from one flower to another can be a problem—especially given that mites are blind and may specialize on a bromeliad 100 feet up a tree in the middle of a rain forest. So the mites have evolved to use hummingbirds as their C-473.

23   Sooner or later a hummingbird will show up to feed on the flower a mite has been busy plundering. Then, according to University of Connecticut biologist Robert Colwell, who first confirmed the phenomenon, the mite sprints up the hummingbird's bill and hides in its nasal cavity. The hummingbird doesn't seem to notice the stowaway. Colwell has found as many as 10 or 15 mites per bird, and because a hummingbird typically feeds on many different flower types, the mites have at times belonged to as many as five species.

24   The mites are only along for the ride to the next preferred flower. Colwell describes them as "perpetual airline passengers that carry out all their mating and feeding in airport lounges." They apparently decide which flower is Gate 67 by the floral scent sucked in four times a second on the hummingbird's breath. Getting off at the wrong flower can mean death for the mite. But it must make its decision instantly and move quickly, because hummingbirds spend only a few seconds at any one flower.

25   Almost everything else about hummingbirds is adapted to the flowerloving life, most notably their method of flight. They need to stop and hover precisely enough to extract nectar from each flower. Relative to their size, they have the largest flight muscles of any bird, up to 30 percent of their total weight, anchored to a keelshaped sternum. They've also got twice as much heart as might be expected for their size, and a denser concentration of red blood cells for better oxygen storage. Their wings are short, and the bone structure is nearly all hand; they have an extremely short humerus,

ulna and radius, the equivalents of our upper and forearm. But unlike other birds, hummingbirds can rotate their wings in a figure eight—much as our wrist enables us to rotate a hand—due to their remarkably flexible shoulder joints.

26   When a hummingbird is hovering, its wings flap through the air horizontally, rather than up and down. As the wing sweeps toward the front, the leading edge rotates forward, for lift on the downstroke. Then, as the wing sweeps to the rear, the leading edge rotates back, for lift on the upstroke too. Other birds, with their up-and-down flapping, get lift only on the downstroke. But the hummingbird's flexibility enables it to hover, back away on the wing, even fly nearly upside down. One reason hummingbirds sometimes drive off hawks and other birds a hundred times their size is that they can outmaneuver them.

27   Hummingbirds are also smart enough to know where to fly—and where not to. One evening outside the Nordic Inn in Mount Crested Butte, a few miles down the valley from his cabin, Calder drove long stakes into the ground and set up a mist net, which is like a portable spider web, 7 feet high and 36 feet long, creating an obstacle to reaching a couple of feeders hanging from the eaves of the hotel. The Nordic has been putting out these feeders for the past 30 years, and migrating hummingbirds have come to count on the service. In spring, the hotel is one of their base camps, for forays to test if the wildflowers are blooming yet at higher elevations. If the owners forget to put out their feeders in time, the first hungry hummingbirds to arrive raise holy hell. It's a common experience among birders: hummingbirds not only get from Mexico to Alaska and back, but appear to remember flower patches and feeders on route. One biologist complained that hummingbirds continued to show up at a regular feeder site for two years after she stopped putting out the feeder.

28   "All that memory in a brain case as big as Abe Lincoln's head on a penny," Calder said. But relative to body weight, the hummingbird's brain is actually bigger than ours, and hummingbirds are also shrewd enough to adjust to changing circumstances. As Calder talked, a broad-tail came whirring in and stopped in midair to contemplate the almost invisible mist net that now separated him from his feeder. Then he flew straight up, like a helicopter, over the top, and straight down to the feeder.

29   What's more remarkable is that hummingbirds actually remember individual flowers over the course of a day. They also seem to make decisions about when to revisit a flower based on how quickly it can replenish its nectar supply. One morning back in Arizona, Susan Wethington, a Ph.D. student at the University of Arizona, set out a rack of 16 artificial flowers with differing rates of replenishment. Some stayed empty, some refilled slowly, some quickly. A black-chinned, humming through on his second visit of the day, consistently hit the fast-replenishing flowers and skipped the empties.

This sort of behavior has earned hummingbirds the reputation, among scientists, as "nature's greatest efficiency experts."

30   Hummingbirds are also smart enough not to stick exclusively to red flowers. Their legendary fondness for the color may actually be one of the great myths about how animals divvy up a resource. According to the classic ecological explanation, flowers evolving for pollination by hummingbirds tended to shift toward the red end of the color spectrum, because bees and other pollinating insects can't see red very well. But Nick Waser, an ecologist from the University of California at Riverside, whose cabin in Gothic is just up the road from Calder's, dismissed this as "a great story to teach undergraduates."

31   Studies have shown that bees are capable of seeing red (although less well than other colors), and hummingbirds can learn to respond to any color. They are not interior decorators. What they want is nectar, they want it now, and they will concentrate on whatever color flower happens to be giving it to them at the moment. Moreover, hummingbirds will visit bee flowers, and vice versa. So why do hummingbirds turn up so often on the abundance of red flowers in the American West? One possible explanation, in Waser's view, is that red may simply stand out better against a green background.

32   Specialization, said Waser, isn't what got hummingbirds where they are today, or where they are going to be. (Anna's hummingbirds have lately expanded their breeding range from California into Arizona; rufous hummingbirds have launched an invasion of the Southeastern United States.) On the contrary, hummingbirds are the ultimate opportunists.

33   "They're just such ballsy birds," Sheri Williamson was saying one afternoon outside Sierra Vista, Arizona. "There's somebody in there. You look in some other bird's eyes and it's like looking in the eyes of a cow. But hummingbirds are so aware of what's going on."

34   Williamson, who runs the Southeastern Arizona Bird Observatory with her husband, Tom Wood, was conducting her weekly hummingbird banding session at the San Pedro Riparian National Conservation Area. They had a feeder set up, enclosed in a mist-net tunnel, which was closed off at the end. Wood, a 50-year-old with a big gray beard and a contented red face, stood at a distance. When a hummingbird came to the feeder, he lumbered toward the entrance and tried to panic the bird into the netting. Sometimes it worked.

35   When Wood caught his first customer, a young black-chin female, he took her over to Williamson. After banding the bird, she wrapped it in a scrap of cloth "like a birdie burrito." The wrapping calmed the bird for her weighing and medical exam. Williamson blew on the feathers to examine the fat content beneath the tissue-thin skin. "She's already been in the first fight of her life," Williamson said, "because she's missing one of her tail

feathers." Then, the examination finished, she held her up to a feeder. "This is like juice and a cookie at the blood bank," Williamson said. "We're just trying to pay her back a bit."

36   When Williamson later held another hummingbird to the feeder, it guzzled sugar water till its crop swelled goitrously at the back of its neck. In a couple of minutes of feeding, its weight went up by a third. Williamson placed the bird in a visitor's hand to be released. It sat for a long time, unperturbed, its body thrumming, not with its heartbeat ('That's too fast for you to feel," Williamson said) but with its usual 250 breaths a minute.

37   The hummingbird blinked and looked around calmly with its glossy black eyes, lord of all it surveyed. Finally, it shuttled off in a rush, leaving behind, as a warm token of disregard, a droplet of urine in the hand that had cradled it. Williamson was ecstatic. "Aren't they just wonderful birds?" she inquired.

POST-READING EXERCISES

1. Which word on the Vocabulary Development list means "juicy" or "moist and tasty"?

   a. nectar   b. scrounge

   c. succulent   d. fretful

2. Which of the following does Conniff *not* include as a description of hummingbirds?

   a. Fragments of the rainbow

   b. Little fairies

   c. Fighter pilots in small bodies

   d. Tiny flying piranhas

3. How much energy does a typical hummingbird require each day?

   a. 7 to 12 calories   b. 7 to 12 watts

   c. 7 to 12 pounds   d. 7 to 12 ounces

4. When do hummingbirds do most of their eating?

   a. At dawn   b. At dusk

   c. All day   d. After dark

5. What does the word *taxing* mean?

   a. Placing onerous or rigorous demands on

   b. Suffering huge injuries from

   c. Relieving from pressure

   d. Forgiving from debt

6. How do bird guides respond when people say that hummingbirds are "so tiny [and] so sweet"?

   a. Well, they *are* sweet.

   b. Well, they *are* tiny.

   c. Well, you don't know what you're talking about.

   d. Well, you should observe them closely.

7. What evidence does Conniff offer to show that hummingbirds are fierce?

   a. One bird plucked another's feathers.

   b. One bird sang a threatening song to another bird.

   c. One bird raced another bird to a feeder.

   d. One bird knocked another out of the air and stabbed it with its bill.

8. Which *two* of the following does a hummingbird eat?

   a. Nectar   b. Insects

   c. Popcorn   d. Seeds

9. Which word on the Vocabulary Development list means "giving off or reflecting light in bright beams or flashes"?

   a. coruscating   b. fretful

   c. succulent   d. iridescent

10. What, according to a scientific paper, is the hummingbird's "only concern"?

   a. Survival   b. Procreation

   c. Nesting   d. Fighting

Content Questions

1. What evidence does Conniff offer to support the idea that hummingbirds are mean?

2. What other characteristics, besides ferocity, does Conniff include in his description of hummingbirds?

3. Why do hummingbirds eat so much?

Style and Structure

1. What is Conniff's point? Write his argument in your own words.

2. What examples does Conniff use to show hummingbirds' true nature?

3. What are some words or images Conniff uses to show the hummingbird's tiny size?

Writing Assignments

1. Conniff makes the point that hummingbirds are not exactly what people think they are. About what else could you say this? *Write an essay in which*

you explain how something—a car, an animal, a person, or a job, for instance— is not what it first seems to be. Use examples from your own experiences to illustrate your ideas.

2. Conniff writes that survival seems to be the hummingbird's "only concern"; thus, it eats constantly. What does survival mean for you? Is living indoors and eating regularly enough for you, or does survival include some sort of personal, academic, or professional success or recognition? *Write an essay defining the word* survival *in terms in your own life.* Use examples and illustrations from your own life to support your ideas.

3. Despite their lovely appearance, Conniff compares hummingbirds to fighter pilots, among other things. What images best describe someone you know well? *Write an essay in which you describe someone you know well.* Do your best to imitate Conniff's style of comparing one creature to others, and use examples from your own life for support.

Constance García-Barrio

Creatures That Haunt the Americas

A writer and instructor at West Chester University, West Chester, Pennsylvania, Constance García-Barrio is also multilingual, speaking English, Spanish, and Chinese. Her works have been widely published, and she is currently writing a novel. In "Creatures That Haunt the Americas," García-Barrio explores the myths and legends springing from African and other cultures, emphasizing their value for contemporary society.

BEFORE YOU READ

- What does the word *monster* bring to mind? What are your earliest impressions or imaginings of monsters?
- At what age, if ever, did you stop fearing monsters? What happened at this age to dispel your fear? Explain.
- How did you learn about monsters? To what extent were monsters, as you understood them, a possible consequence of bad behavior? Explain.

VOCABULARY DEVELOPMENT

Look up the following words in a dictionary and write down their meanings.

supernatural (paragraph 1)   mischievous (paragraph 3) looms (paragraph 4)   buxom (paragraph 5)

lair (paragraph 6)   stalk (paragraph 8)

cringe (paragraph 9)   miserly (paragraph 11)

emancipated (paragraph 11)   platoon (paragraph 12)

cache (paragraph 12)

Creatures That Haunt the Americas

1   When Africans were forced into slaving ships, the creatures, invisible, slipped in with them. A witch's brew of supernatural beings, these were creatures remembered from stories from the homeland. When Africans reached the New World, the creatures stepped ashore with them.

2   The supernatural beings made their homes in the mountains, rivers, and forests of the Americas, wherever the Africans went. The Hairy Man, for example, has the run of Georgia's woods, according to a story told by a former slave from that state. The Hairy Man is a fat, ugly little man with more hair all over than hell has devilment. Tricky as he is hairy, he can shrink or swell at will. He's afraid of dogs and is most at home near rivers. The Hairy Man spends his time capturing careless children.

3   The guije seems to be a Caribbean cousin of the Hairy Man, the way the late Cuban centenarian Esteban Montejo tells it in *The Autobiography of a Runaway Slave.* The guijes, or jigues, are mischievous little black men who wear no clothes and live near rivers. Their heads are like a frog's. Black people have a natural tendency to see them, according to Montejo. Guijes pop out of the river to admire a señorita as she bathes, especially during Holy Week. The guijes are also known to carry off children.

4   The Tunda looms large in the folklore of Esmeraldas, a predominantly black province on the northern coast of Ecuador, notes Afro-Ecuadorian writer Adalberto Ortiz. Local legend has it that in the 1530s a ship whose cargo included twenty-three enslaved blacks was traveling from Panama to Peru. As it skirted Ecuador's northern coast, the ship struck a reef. In the confusion that followed, the blacks scrambled from the vessel, swam ashore, and fought with Indians occupying the land.

5   After one especially fierce battle, dying blacks and Indians moaned so much that the noise reached hell and disturbed the devil. He decided he'd have to exterminate both sides if he wanted peace and quiet. So the devil went to Esmeraldas disguised as an African prince, Macumba. But before he could carry out his plan, a lively, buxom Esmeraldeña caught his fancy. He married her and settled down, as much as the Devil can ever settle.

6   One of the creatures born from their union is the Tunda, a deformed black woman with huge lips and clubfoot. As a child of the devil, the Tunda can't have children, so she's taken to carrying off those of black folk in Esmeraldas. The Tunda can make herself look like a member of the poten-

tial victim's family. She lures people into the forest, then stuns them by breaking wind in their faces. After this they lose their will power and are easily led to her lair, usually a place in or near water.

7   Adalberto Ortiz mentioned that there are similarities between the Tunda, a character in Afro-Colombian stories, and the Quimbungo from Bantu folklore.

8   If some creatures pursue black children, others stalk adults. The Afro-Dominican Ciguapa is a gorgeous but strange being who lives in the island's forests. She comes out at night to steal food but is never caught since she escapes by jumping from tree to tree. Her beauty has won many hearts, but she uses her magic to destroy men. Wise to her ways, they try to avoid her. But she can fool them. The Ciguapa's feet are on backward, so they think she's going when she's coming.

9   Tales of the Lobisón, or Wolfman, made many an Afro-Uruguayan peasant cringe. Legend has it that every Friday night at midnight the seventh consecutive son in a family turns into an animal. This animal has a wolf's body and a misshapen pig's head. It commits acts too horrible to tell. It has great supernatural powers, and only by wounding the Lobison and drawing its blood can it be made to return to human form.

10   The old and new worlds blend in the Lobisón legend. The story shows the influence of Bantu, European, and certain South American Indian cultures.

11   Some tales of the supernatural arose from historic events in which blacks took part. Such was the case with Spanish America's struggle for independence from Spain from 1810 to 1822. One Afro-Uruguayan story tells of a rich but miserly man who treated his slaves cruelly. Emancipated before the wars of independence, the newly freed blacks demanded money with which to start a new life. They knew their former master had gold nuggets hidden in the house. When he refused to give them anything, they killed him.

12   The money remained hidden after the murder until a platoon of black soldiers camped near the old house during the wars of independence. The location of the treasure was revealed to them by the ghost of a black who had remained with the master even after emancipation. The soldiers divided the cache, each receiving a nice sum. The ghost had waited years but finally saw that his black countrymen got the money.

13   Like the ghost who showed the soldiers the treasure, black folktales bring to light sometimes forgotten cultural treasures Africans brought to the Americas.

POST-READING EXERCISES

1. Which word on the Vocabulary Development list means "a hiding place"?
   - a. lair
   - b. stalk
   - c. cache
   - d. platoon

2. How did supernatural creatures get from Africa to the Americas?

    a. They were summoned by slaves.

    b. They rode on the backs of slave owners' horses.

    c. They were carried by women.

    d. They came on slave ships.

3. What habit do the Hairy Man and the guije share?

    a. Carrying off children

    b. Stealing corn

    c. Singing by moonlight

    d. Whispering to wild women

4. Who are the Tunda's parents?

    a. The Hairy Man and the guije

    b. The devil and a lovely Esmeraldeña

    c. Adalberto Ortiz and a Bantu woman

    d. Ciguapa and the Lobisón

5. What is one definition of the word *mischievous*?

    a. Irresponsibly playful   b. Teasingly humorous

    c. Kindly teasing   d. Unkindly joking

6. How does the Ciguapa trick people?

    a. Her head is on backward.

    b. Her feet are on backward.

    c. Her arms extend from her neck.

    d. Her feet extend from her elbows.

7. What is the only way the Lobisón can be returned to human form?

    a. By making a voodoo doll of it

    b. By capturing and killing a wolf

    c. By wounding it and drawing its blood

    d. By singing in the moonlight

8. Aside from legend, what is another source of supernatural stories?

    a. Personal fear   b. Social tension

    c. Political turmoil   d. Historic events

9. Which word on the Vocabulary Development list means "to draw in or contract one's muscles involuntarily"?

    a. stalk   b. cringe

    c. emancipated   d. looms

10. What does García-Barrio call these folktales?

    a. Imagined treasured memories

    b. Worthless, meaningless stories

    c. Silly, frightening tales

    d. Forgotten cultural treasures

Content Questions

1. What are some habits or actions that García-Barrio's creatures have in common?

2. For what reason did the devil want to "exterminate" blacks and Indians?

3. Why does the ghost reward the black soldiers with the miserly old man's gold?

Style and Structure

1. What is García-Barrio's point? Where is her thesis located? Rewrite her thesis in your own words.

2. How does García-Barrio divide and classify her subjects? What characteristics does she use?

3. What is García-Barrio's attitude toward the creatures she describes? How can you tell?

Writing Assignments

1. García-Barrio writes that "the creatures stepped ashore" with Africans who arrived in the New World. What ideas do people take with them when they begin a new part of their lives? For instance, in moving out on your own, what lessons or skills from your parents did you take with you? *Write an essay in which you divide or classify the types of information or skills you've brought with you from one experience to the next.* Be sure to include the basis for division or classification (the unifying concept), and use specific examples from your relationship with this person to illustrate your ideas.

2. García-Barrio writes that "black folktales bring to light sometimes forgotten cultural treasures Africans brought to the Americas." How are the stories from your childhood significant? *Write an essay explaining how certain stories you learned as a child were significant.* Explain, for instance, how learning that Jack from *Jack and the Beanstalk* gave away the family cow taught you to be frugal with your own resources. The stories you cite may come from books, movies, grandparents, or other sources. Use examples from your own experiences and observations to illustrate your ideas.

3. Think about things scare that people today, and compare those to García-Barrio's creatures. To what extent do you think the creatures in García-Barrio's essay, or in any folktale, simply mirror people's existing fears? In other words, do people just make up monsters that look like what they're afraid of? *Write an essay explaining how scary creatures—either in popular culture or in your family's culture—do or do not reflect people's existing fears.* Discuss, for example, how King Kong reflects people's fear of something huge, wild, and seemingly uncontrollable. Use examples from your own observations and experiences to illustrate your ideas.

Donald Hall

Four Kinds of Reading

Raising questions as to the value of reading for its own sake and the types of reading we do, Donald Hall criticizes what he labels the "piety" of reading whose purpose or value is obscure. Hall categorizes reading four ways based on purpose, process, and end result.

BEFORE YOU READ

- What is your gut reaction to the term *reading?* Upon what experiences is this reaction based?
- How much of your time do you spend reading—either for work, school, or pleasure? For what reasons do you most often read? Explain.
- To what extent is reading ever *worse* for a person than, say, watching television or playing a computer game? What must be involved in the reading process for it to be beneficial? Explain.

VOCABULARY DEVELOPMENT

Look up the following words in a dictionary and write down their meanings.

piety (paragraph 1)   aura (paragraph 2)
gentility (paragraph 2)   irrelevant (paragraph 3)
metaphor (paragraph 3)   adjacent (paragraph 4)
abstractions (paragraph 5)   embodiment (paragraph 5)
narcotic (paragraph 6)   narcolepsy (paragraph 7)
melodrama (paragraph 8)

Four Kinds of Reading

1   Everywhere one meets the idea that reading is an activity desirable in itself. It is understandable that publishers and librarians—and even writers— should promote this assumption, but it is strange that the idea should have general currency. People surround the idea of reading with piety, and do not take into account the purpose of reading or the value of what is being read. Teachers and parents praise the child who reads, and praise themselves, whether the text be *The Reader's Digest* or *Moby-Dick*. The advent of TV has increased the false values ascribed to reading, since TV provides a vulgar alternative. But this piety is silly; and most reading is no more cultural nor intellectual nor imaginative than shooting pool or watching *What's My Line*.

2   It is worth asking how the act of reading became something to value in itself, as opposed for instance to the act of conversation or the act of taking a walk. Mass literacy is a recent phenomenon, and I suggest that the aura which decorates reading is a relic of the importance of reading to our great-great-grandparents. Literacy used to be a mark of social distinction, separating a small portion of humanity from the rest. The farm laborer who was ambitious for his children did not daydream that they would become schoolteachers or doctors; he daydreamed that they would learn to read, and that a world would therefore open up to them in which they did not have to labor in the fields fourteen hours a day for six days a week in order to buy salt and cotton. On the next rank of society, ample time for reading meant that the reader was free from the necessity to spend most of his waking hours making a living. This sort of attitude shades into the contemporary man's boast of his wife's cultural activities. When he says that his wife is interested in books and music and pictures, he is not only enclosing the arts in a female world, he is saying that he is rich enough to provide her with the leisure to do nothing. Reading is an inactivity, and therefore a badge of social class. Of course, these reasons for the piety attached to reading are never acknowledged. They show themselves in the shape of our attitudes toward books; reading gives off an air of gentility.

3   It seems to me possible to name four kinds of reading, each with a characteristic manner and purpose. The first is reading for information—reading to learn about a trade, or politics, or how to accomplish something. We read a newspaper this way, or most textbooks, or directions on how to assemble a bicycle. With most of this material, the reader can learn to scan the page quickly, coming up with what he needs and ignoring what is irrelevant to him, like the rhythm of the sentence, or the play of metaphor. Courses in speed reading can help us read for this purpose, training the eye to jump quickly across the page. If we read the *New York Times* with the attention we should give a novel or a poem, we will have time for nothing else, and our mind will be cluttered with clichés and dead metaphor. Quick

eye-reading is a necessity to anyone who wants to keep up with what's happening, or learn much of what has happened in the past. The amount of reflection, which interrupts and slows down the reading, depends on the material.

4   But it is not the same activity as reading literature. There ought to be another word. If we read a work of literature properly, we read slowly, and we *hear* all the words. If our lips do not actually move, it's only laziness. The muscles in our throat move, and come together when we see the word "squeeze." We hear the sounds so accurately that if a syllable is missing in a line of poetry we hear the lack, though we may not know what we are lacking. In prose we accept the rhythms, and hear the adjacent sounds. We also register a track of feeling through the metaphors and associations of words. Careless writing prevents this sort of attention, and becomes offensive. But the great writers reward it. Only by the full exercise of our powers to receive language can we absorb their intelligence and their imagination. This kind of reading goes through the ear—though the eye takes in the print, and decodes it into sound—to the throat and the understanding, and it can never be quick. It is slow and sensual, a deep pleasure that begins with touch and ends with the sort of comprehension that we associate with dream.

5   Too many intellectuals read in order to reduce images to abstractions. One reads philosophy slowly, as if it were literature, but much time must be spent with the eyes turned away from the page, reflecting on the text. To read literature this way is to turn it into something it is not—to concepts clothed in character, or philosophy sugar-coated. I think that most literary intellectuals read this way, including brighter professors of English, with the result that they miss literature completely, and concern themselves with a minor discipline called the history of ideas. I remember a course in Chaucer at my university in which the final exam required the identification of a hundred or more fragments of Chaucer, none as long as a line. If you liked poetry, and read Chaucer through a couple of times slowly, you found yourself knowing them all. If you were a literary intellectual, well-informed about the great chain of being, chances are you had a difficult time. To read literature is to be intimately involved with the words on the page, and never to think of them as the embodiments of ideas which can be expressed in other terms. On the other hand, intellectual writing—closer to mathematics on a continuum that has at its opposite pole lyric poetry—requires intellectual reading, which is slow because it is reflective and because the reader must pause to evaluate concepts.

6   But most of the reading which is praised for itself is neither literary nor intellectual. It is narcotic. Novels, stories, and biographies—historical sagas, monthly regurgitations of book clubs, four- and five-thousand-word daydreams of the magazines—these are the opium of the suburbs. The drug is not harmful except to the addict himself, and is no more injurious to him

than Johnny Carson or a bridge club, but it is nothing to be proud of. This reading is the automated daydream, the mild trip of the housewife and the tired businessman, interested not in experience and feeling but in turning off the possibilities of experience and feeling. Great literature, if we read it well, opens us up to the world, and makes us more sensitive to it, as if we acquired eyes that could see through walls and ears that could hear the smallest sounds. But by narcotic reading, one can reduce great literature to the level of *The Valley of the Dolls.* One can read *Anna Karenina* passively and inattentively, and float down the river of lethargy as if one were reading a confession magazine: "I Spurned My Husband for a Count."

7   I think that everyone reads for narcosis occasionally, and perhaps most consistently in late adolescence, when great readers are born. I remember reading to shut the world out, away at a school where I did not want to be; I invented a word for my disease: "Bibliolepsy," on the analogy of narcolepsy. But after a while the books became a window on the world, and not a screen against it. This change doesn't always happen. I think that late adolescent narcotic reading accounts for some of the badness of English departments. As a college student, the boy loves reading and majors in English because he would be reading anyway. Deciding on a career, he takes up English teaching for the same reason. Then in graduate school he is trained to be a scholar, which is painful and irrelevant, and finds he must write papers and publish them to be a Professor—and at about this time he no longer requires reading for narcosis, and he is left with nothing but a Ph.D. and the prospect of fifty years of teaching literature; and he does not even like literature.

8   Narcotic reading survives the impact of television, because this type of reading has even less reality than melodrama; that is, the reader is in control: Once the characters reach into the reader's feelings, he is able to stop reading, or glance away, or superimpose his own daydream. The trouble with television is that it embodies its own daydream. Literature is often valued precisely because of its distance from the tangible. Some readers prefer looking into the text of a play to seeing it performed. Reading a play, it is possible to stage it oneself by an imaginative act; but it is also possible to remove it from real people. Here is Virginia Woolf, who was lavish in her praise of the act of reading, talking about reading a play rather than seeing it: "Certainly there is a good deal to be said for reading *Twelfth Night* in the book if the book can be read in a garden, with no sound but the thud of an apple falling to the earth, or of the wind ruffling the branches of the trees." She sets her own stage; the play is called *Virginia Woolf Reads Twelfth Night in a Garden.* Piety moves into narcissism, and the high metaphors of Shakespeare's lines dwindle into the flowers of an English garden; actors in ruffles wither, while the wind ruffles branches.

1968

POST-READING EXERCISES

1. Which word on the Vocabulary Development list means "not distant"?
   a. melodrama   b. embodiment
   c. narcotic   d. adjacent

2. What does TV offer that makes reading seem more attractive?
   a. A vulgar alternative
   b. Advertisements
   c. Narrow range of programming (at that time)
   d. Inactive entertainment

3. What is literacy a sign of, according to Hall?
   a. Proper eyesight and health care
   b. Good parenting
   c. Social distinction or gentility
   d. Intelligence

4. What does Hall consider the first type of reading?
   a. Reading for self-improvement
   b. Intellectual reading
   c. Reading for information
   d. Narcotic reading

5. What is one definition of the word *irrelevant?*
   a. stupid   b. boring
   c. offensive   d. inapplicable

6. Why does Hall say that "quick eye-reading" is necessary?
   a. To read for entertainment
   b. To keep up with what's happening
   c. To get good grades
   d. To impress people

7. If we read literature properly, what happens?
   a. We *hear* all the words.
   b. We *feel* all the words.
   c. We *sense* the writer's meaning.
   d. We *believe* in the writer's purpose.

8. What, according to Hall, does reading literature require?
   a. Selfless devotion to the printed word
   b. Painful denial of outside entertainment

    c. Intimate involvement with the words on the page

    d. Sensitive consideration of all possible meanings

9. Which word on the Vocabulary Development list means "a subtle sensory stimulus (as an aroma)"?

    a. melodrama   b. narcolepsy

    c. aura   d. gentility

10. Why does reading survive the impact of television?

    a. Because the reader is in control

    b. Because the reader can daydream

    c. Because the reader creates his or her own dream

    d. Because the reader is narcissistic

Content

1. How does Hall say we as a society have come to value literacy?

2. What does intellectual reading involve?

3. What is the difference in reading great literature and narcotic reading?

Style and Structure

1. What concept does Hall use by which to classify the four types of reading?

2. What kinds of examples does Hall give to illustrate each type? Based on these, which type of reading do you recognize as being part of your own reading experiences?

3. What is Hall's attitude toward contemporary reading? What kind of reading does Hall favor? How can you tell?

Writing Assignments

1. Hall writes that people are praised for reading (or praise themselves) regardless of what they read. What other habits seem to make people similarly self-congratulatory? *Write an essay in which you discuss a not necessarily positive habit that people take pride in, taking care to explain why you think people feel pride in this activity.* For instance, some people take pride in being able to drink a lot of alcohol or burp loudly. Use specific examples from your own relationship with such a person to illustrate your ideas.

2. Hall writes that "everyone reads for narcosis occasionally" and that this type of reading is "nothing to be proud of." What do you think? *Write an essay arguing that any type of reading is or is not something "to be proud of."* Explain, for instance, why reading only the sports page is or is not as good as reading English literature. Use examples from your own experiences and observations to illustrate your ideas.

3. Hall writes about the adolescent who eventually becomes a professor simply because he enjoys reading, making the process seem more a process by default than an actual choice. How often do you think people "drift" into careers? *Write an essay explaining how people do or do not make deliberate choices that direct them into their life situations.* Discuss, for example, how someone you know simply took what opportunities came her way rather than seeking out new ones and, thus, ended up with a job he or she would not have chosen. Use examples from your own observations and experiences to illustrate your ideas.

Nanci Hellmich

Caught in the Catty Corner

While nursery rhymes describe little girls as being made of sugar and spice, writer Nanci Hellmich says otherwise. Offering evidence of girls' unkindness to each other through childhood and adolescence, Hellmich points out that while girls may not be as physically aggressive as boys, girls have means of inflicting pain on each other.

 **BEFORE YOU READ**

■ To what extent do you think one gender is more unkind than the other? Explain.

■ In your experience, how do men and women differ in terms of how they treat people they don't like? Explain.

■ At what point in life, if any, do you think people are the least kind? Why? Explain.

 VOCABULARY DEVELOPMENT

Look up the following words in a dictionary and write down their meanings.

clique (paragraph 2)   phenomenon (paragraph 5)
malicious (paragraph 7)   mannerisms (paragraph 7)
covert (paragraph 12)   wield (paragraph 14)
initiate (paragraph 27)   disclosure (paragraph 28)
commandant (paragraph 36)   shunning (paragraph 37)

Caught in the Catty Corner

1 Katy Montague's seventh-grade year was a girl's worst nightmare.

2 She was excluded from parties, lunch table groups, conversations and cliques. She was teased and taunted about her looks and her glasses. She was treated this way by "the meanest people I ever met, and they were all girls," says Montague, of St. Louis.

3 "There was a lot of plotting and scheming behind people's backs. It was horrible. I don't remember anything I learned that year."

4 But there was a silver lining: She met her best friend during that trying time. "We do almost everything together. She's always there for me," says Montague, now 17.

5 Montague's experience mirrors that of millions of girls across the country as they make their way through the often painful passage of adolescence. Out of this pain often comes strength of character and genuine friendships, but while it's happening, a girl's life can be total misery. Now, some behavior experts are doing research to try to understand this phenomenon. And while they realize they may not be able to—and perhaps shouldn't—totally change it, there may be ways to help girls get through it with fewer scars.

6 Experts use the term "relational aggression" to describe the cattiness, meanness and nastiness that happens between some people but especially among girls.

7 Girls may gossip, spread malicious rumors, write nasty e-mails, give the silent treatment, exclude people from social events, betray secrets or snicker about people's clothes and mannerisms behind their backs. They may tell a girl that they're not going to be friends with her unless she does what they want.

8 "We all get angry. We all have the need to control others and our environment, and boys and girls have tendencies to do those things in different ways," says Nicki Crick, a professor of child development at the University of Minnesota–Minneapolis. She has studied relational aggression in thousands of people, from preschoolers to adults.

9 Boys and girls are equally capable of being kind or unkind, she says. "But where boys might use physical intimidation, girls will say, 'I won't be your friend anymore,' or 'I'm not going to talk to you.'"

10 Several researchers, including Crick, are trying to figure out why this happens so frequently, especially among girls from third grade to seniors in high school, when they really value close friendships.

11 This spring, several books are coming out to help parents understand the phenomenon, including *The Secret Lives of Girls; The Friendship Factor; Trust Me, Mom—Everyone Else Is Going!; Queen Bees and Wannabes; Odd Girl Out.*

12   Psychologists believe there are several explanations for some of this behavior. One may be that girls are under enormous pressure to be nice and sweet. Unlike boys, girls have few opportunities to openly express their aggression or anger, so they strike out at other girls in covert ways, says Sharon Lamb, author of *The Secret Lives of Girls* and a psychology professor at Saint Michael's College in Colchester, Vermont.

13   Some girls today work out their aggression in sports, but even there they can't be as aggressive as boys without risking criticism, she says.

14   And teen girls don't dare express their anger or aggression at boys their own age because the guys wield too much power, Lamb says. "Boys don't have a problem retaliating. They might spread a rumor that the girl's a slut."

15   Plus, boys are becoming more important to girls during adolescence. Girls evaluate each other by boys' standards, Lamb says. That makes them turn against each other and compete for boys' attention. So for these reasons, girls go after other girls. "It's like the weak fighting the weak."

16   They often tell each other their secrets, and those secrets can be used against them, Lamb says. Boys keep their secrets close to their chest.

17   Girls value relationships very highly, and when they want to hurt someone, they do it in a way that is most hurtful, says Nicole Werner, a researcher at the University of Idaho in Moscow.

18   Rachel Simmons, who interviewed 300 kids for her book, *Odd Girl Out,* says many girls say they'd rather be hit or screamed at than cut out of a clique with no warning or have a rumor started about them.

Friendships Come and Go

19   There are a couple of types of girls who frequently use relational aggression. One is a socially incompetent child who doesn't get along with her peers.

20   Another is the "Queen Bee," a nickname for the leader of cliques, Crick says. "If you ask girls if they like this person, they'll say, 'No, I hate her.' "

21   These are girls who are popular because they are dominant. They have looks, possessions and status, says Kenneth Rubin, author of *The Friendship Factor* with Andrea Thompson.

22   Queen Bees have friends because others would rather have them on their side than have them against them, he says. But their friends don't feel secure, and their friendships come and go. On the other hand, some girls are popular and have many friends because they are really decent people, he says. These are the people other kids truly want to be friends with.

23   Montague, a member of *USA Today*'s Teen Panel, says the Queen Bees consider themselves above other people and spread gossip and ruin reputations.

24   "I'm definitely afraid if I say the wrong thing with them, it'll get around," she says.

25   But there are other girls who are really involved in the community and school, and they really try to reach out and give back, she says. "They are popular because everyone knows them, and they know them for good reasons."

Children Can Figure It Out

26   As director of the Laboratory for Child and Family Relationships at the University of Maryland, Rubin has examined the importance of the friendships for hundreds of children as they make the stressful transition from elementary school to middle school.

27   In their friendships, children figure out how to get along with people, how to initiate friendships, how to walk away from relationships, and how to maintain the ones that are enjoyable and valuable, he says.

28   They learn about trust, intimacy and security. They learn they can tell their friends about things they wouldn't want anyone else to know, which is called intimate disclosure, Rubin says. They learn how they can make others feel good and secure, and they learn how others can make them feel good and secure, he says.

29   "Friendship is about having fun, enjoying each other. It's about helping, sharing and being kind. It's through friendship that you can learn to be decent," Rubin says. People who are good friends as kids become good romantic partners and good friends as adults, he says.

30   Montague says friends are crucial. "They are someone you can go to when you have a crush on a boy, and there is no one else you can tell. If you're having a bad day with your parents or at school, there is someone you can lean on."

31   Because friends are so important, it makes having trouble with them even more traumatic, experts say.

32   Lamb believes girls would have less relational aggression with other girls if they learned to be more straightforward and honest about their feelings. "In all relationships, if you get angry with people, you talk it out," she says.

And Parents Can Help

33   She recommends that parents teach their girls how to handle confrontation with dignity. They need to teach them to stand up against injustice for other people and for themselves.

34   Parents can help by giving their daughter the words to express her feelings. For example, if their daughter is teased about her clothes, the parents might suggest she say, "What you are doing is hurtful, and there is no good reason to treat me this way because clothes really don't matter."

35   Even if the daughter doesn't say the words to her tormenter, she can rehearse them in her mind and find comfort in them, Lamb says.

36   Parents also need to be good listeners and guide their children without telling them what to do, Rubin says. Parents should be a big ear, not a commandant, he says.

37   For example, if a girl says she wants to be friends with a girl who is shunning her, then the parent might ask: "Why do you want to be friends with her? What would you get out of the relationship? Is there anybody else in school whom you might be interested in being friends with?"

38   Clinical psychologist Roni Cohen-Sandler, author of *Trust Me, Mom—Everyone Else Is Going!*, says kids can learn lifelong lessons in these experiences.

39   They need to know there is meanness in the world, and they need to figure out how they are going to deal with it, she says. This prepares them for jobs where they'll confront people who are "nice and collaborative, and people who are mean and jockey for power."

40   When Montague was suffering through friendship traumas, her parents were always there for her and willing to listen, she says. One of the most valuable lessons she has learned from her experiences is the hurtfulness of gossiping and meanness. "I catch myself when I want to say something mean, and I stop because I know what it feels like to be on the other side."

POST-READING EXERCISES

1. Which word on the Vocabulary Development list means "not openly shown, engaged in, or avowed"?

   a. malicious

   b. initiate

   c. disclosure

   d. covert

2. Which of the following is *not* a way, according to Hellmich, that girls are unkind to each other?

   a. Start malicious rumors.

   b. Betray secrets.

   c. Steal another girl's boyfriend.

   d. Give the silent treatment.

3. During what years are girls most likely to be unkind to each other?

   a. Third grade to senior year in high school

   b. First through third grade

   c. Seventh through ninth grade

   d. Every year past age four

4. What is a Queen Bee in the context of this article?

   a. Someone who's popular because she gets others to do her work for her

b. Someone who's popular because she is genuinely liked

c. Someone who's popular because she's dominant

d. Someone who's popular because she's unkind

5. What is one definition of the word *wield?*

   a. To harm as with an axe

   b. To handle as a tool

   c. To flatter as with compliments

   d. To discard as garbage

6. Hellmich quotes Rachel Simmons, who claims that girls would rather be hit or screamed at than

   a. Have a popular girl ignore them.

   b. Have a boyfriend break up with them in front of their friends.

   c. Be cut out of a clique with no warning or have a rumor started about them.

   d. Run for a student office or try out for cheerleader and fail.

7. Why are the methods girls use to hurt each other so effective?

   a. Girls want to be popular.

   b. Girls value boys' good opinion.

   c. Girls value relationships.

   d. Girls want power.

8. What, according to Kenneth Rubin of the Laboratory for Child and Family Relationships at the University of Maryland, does friendship teach people?

   a. To be decent   b. To be tolerant

   c. To work together   d. To fight back

9. Which word on the Vocabulary Development list means "exaggerated or affected adherence to a particular style"?

   a. clique   b. phenomenon

   c. initiate   d. mannerisms

10. Which of the following is *not* something parents can do to help their daughters deal with unkindness?

   a. Allow them to rehearse what to say to unkind people.

   b. Listen to their daughters.

   c. Ask their daughters why they want to be friends with people who treat them unkindly.

   d. Take them shopping to lift their spirits.

Content

1. What, according to Hellmich, is "relational aggressivness"?

2. How, according to Hellmich, do boys and girls differ in their treatment of people they don't like?

3. What, according to Hellmich, are some reasons girls act so unkindly to each other?

Style and Structure

1. What is Hellmich's point? Rewrite her thesis in your own words.

2. What types of details does Hellmich use to support her thesis?

3. Which details are most convincing? Explain.

Writing Assignments

1. Hellmich writes, "Queen Bees have friends because others would rather have them on their side than have them against them." Is this true? What role, if any, do you think fear plays in friendship? *Write an essay discussing the extent to which people's fear leads them to be friends with others.* Use examples from your own experiences and observations to illustrate your ideas.

2. Psychology professor Sharon Lamb claims that girls' difficulties with each other would lessen if they learned to be "more straightforward and honest about their feelings. What role does direct communication play in resolving personal conflict? *Write an essay explaining how being direct with friends is or is not important in avoiding conflict.* Use examples from your own experiences and observations to illustrate your ideas.

3. Psychology professor Sharon Lamb claims that girls turn on each other to get boys' attention. Is this true? Is this also true for boys? *Write an essay explaining how people do or do not treat each other unkindly if they are competing for a romantic partner.* Explain, for example, competition for certain person's attention can cause—or eliminate—stress between friends. Use examples from your experiences and observations to illustrate your ideas.

Ben MacIntyre

Poor Winnie the Pooh: Not Even He Is Safe from Rampant "Therapism"

A British journalist, Ben MacIntyre has authored several books, including *The Man Who Would be King: The First American in Afghanistan* and *The Englishman's Daughter: A True Story of Love and Betrayal in World War I.* In his article "Poor Winnie the Pooh," MacIntyre explores the ways people seek comfort after trauma and the ways the "trauma industry" recommends therapy for everyone. While counseling may be the answer for some, says MacIntyre, seeking solace from other sources shouldn't be ruled out.

BEFORE YOU READ

- How do you typically deal with stress? Explain.
- What role, if any, does sharing your feelings play in helping you cope with anxiety? Explain.
- What is your attitude toward therapy or counseling? How did you develop this attitude? Explain.

VOCABULARY DEVELOPMENT

Look up the following words in a dictionary and write down their meanings.

sang-froid (paragraph 2)	sultanas (paragraph 3)
quotidian (paragraph 7)	neuroses (paragraph 7)
narcissistic (paragraph 9)	heresy (paragraph 11)
ingenious (paragraph 11)	solace (paragraph 11)
succor (paragraph 12)	ignoble (paragraph 13)

Poor Winnie the Pooh: Not Even He Is Safe From Rampant 'Therapism'

1   On the morning of July 7, I watched a commuter, who had just emerged dazed and smoke-grimed from an Underground station, being asked whether he would like to see a trauma counselor. Politely, but firmly, he declined, and staggered off. The counselor looked disappointed and mildly disapproving.

2   I cite this episode not as further evidence of British sang-froid in the face of terrorism (there are so many stiff upper lips in the media at the moment it is surprising any of us can still speak), but of something more profound. There is a widespread assumption that most people, and particularly those suffering from loss or shock, are by definition in need of psychological treatment, trauma counselling and cathartic emotional disclosure.

3   Even apparently well-adjusted creatures such as Winnie the Pooh have been hauled on to the couch. A group of Canadian psychologists recently published a paper on the hero of Hundred Acre Wood, and found that in addition to being "a bear of very little brain," Pooh is suffering from attention deficit/hyperactivity disorder, binge-eating of honey and "borderline

cognitive functioning." While not a complete fruitcake, Pooh, they concluded, is certainly a few sultanas short of a full loaf.

4   The satire was well-aimed, for Pooh is not alone. Jim Windolf, writing in the *Wall Street Journal*, studied the statistics put out by mental health agencies in the US and calculated that 77 percent of Americans are suffering (or think they are suffering) from some sort of emotional disorder. These include women depressed about their self-image, men who cannot live up to some masculine ideal and people with eating disorders and addictions ranging from cocaine to the Internet. The trauma industry has evolved an army of experts to explore feelings and vent them: "self-esteem educators," "degrieving professionals," "traumatologists" and "ventilationists," all busily identifying and measuring emotions, the better to expose them to the bracing light of day.

5   In a remarkable new book, *One Nation Under Therapy*, Christina Hoff Sommers and Sally Satel have identified the spread of what they call therapism, the growing, quasi-religious belief that humans are generally fragile and in need of psychological aid. According to the tenets of therapism, children must be protected from competition, lest their self-esteem is bruised; sharing emotions is good and reticence a sign of repression, possibly leading to post-traumatic stress disorder; normal human emotions, including grief, stress and sadness, are pathologies to be tended and cured. People who reject therapy are deemed to be in denial, and thus doubly at risk. Satel, a psychiatrist, and Sommers, a philosopher, argue that the emphasis on therapy is steadily eroding such characteristics as stoicism, self-belief and self-reliance.

6   No one would deny that psychotherapy has proved a boon to many, while doctors have developed medications for treating devastating mental illness that have transformed the lives of millions. Some therapies are not appreciated enough: in this country, counseling for bereaved children is woefully underfunded.

7   But where therapism goes too far is in the assumption that all human beings are essentially weak, unable to confront on their own the quotidian neuroses of life.

8   The therapeutic culture has reached hilarious extremes in America. Some schools have banned teachers' red marking pens in favour of lavender ink, on the grounds that red may seem too judgmental. Traditional playground games such as tag are being replaced by new, stress-free games in which no one can ever suffer from being "out" (the sort of game the England cricket team must dream about). Such thinking is swiftly spreading from the US: this month the Professional Association of Teachers in Britain proposed that the word "fail" be banned from classrooms in favour of "deferred success," so as not to undermine pupils' enthusiasm.

9   The latest research suggests that cultivating self-esteem and encouraging emotional ventilation may be detrimental to some personalities. There

is no necessary correlation between self-satisfaction and achievement, while an unmerited, narcissistic sense of self-worth has been directly linked to antisocial behaviour. For some, the suppression of feelings is not necessarily a sign of psychological frailty but the reverse, an adaptive and healthy response.

10   Conversely, being forced to discuss emotions can lead to self-pity and introspection. The expression of uninhibited emotion is fashionable, but there also is much to be said for bottling it up, for private consolation.

11   This is heresy within the trauma industry. After 9/11, the US government launched Project Liberty to encourage New Yorkers to undergo counseling: "Feel free to feel better" said the slogan. The organisers expected at least 1.5 million people to seek help, but after eight months less than one tenth of that number had turned up. With ingenious logic, some psychotherapists then claimed that the low turnout showed that New Yorkers did not know, or refused to admit, how deeply traumatised they were. It seems more likely that they had found solace elsewhere: with friends, family and within themselves.

12   Humanity is tougher, and more buoyant, than the practitioners of pop psychology would have us believe. Once it was a sign of weakness to seek therapy. Many of those touched by earlier wars simply refused to talk about the experience. Today the cultural pressure runs in the opposite direction, to the point where the person who seeks his own succor, in silence, is failing to address the inner demons.

13   There is no emotionally correct response to shock: some gain strength from airing their feelings; others do not. It is entirely right that the damaged individual should want to seek comfort through professional therapy, but equally there is nothing ignoble in walking away, like the stunned commuter at Aldgate station, and going home to have a bath, a drink and a think. He did not consider himself a victim in need of psychological help, and nor did Winnie the Pooh.

POST-READING EXERCISES

1. Which word on the Vocabulary Development list means "self-possession or imperturbability especially under strain"?

   a. sang-froid   b. sultanas

   c. heresy   d. succor

2. How does the commuter in MacIntyre's article react to the offer of counseling?

   a. Exhaustedly and slowly declining

   b. Nervously and suspiciously accepting

c. Enthusiastically and gratefully accepting

d. Politely and firmly declining

3. Which one of the following is *not* a condition that Winnie the Pooh allegedly suffers from?

    a. Attention deficit/hyperactivity disorder

    b. Binge-eating of honey

    c. Pathological friendliness

    d. Borderline cognitive functioning

4. What percentage of Americans are—or think they are—suffering from some emotional disorder?

    a. 26 percent   b. 52 percent

    c. 77 percent   d. 98 percent

5. What is one definition of the word *quotidian?*

    a. Annually   b. Daily

    c. Rarely   d. Weekly

6. Which one of the following is *not* a name for experts who explore and vent feelings?

    a. Degrieving professionals

    b. Feel-good family counselors

    c. Traumatologists

    d. Ventilationists

7. What definition of "therapism" does MacIntyre quote?

    a. A growing, quasi-religious belief that humans are generally fragile and in need of psychological aid

    b. A declining feeling that people are stronger than they realize

    c. An inconsistent, gnawing anxiety that comes with new, stressful situations

    d. The all-powerful assumption that adults are incapable of dealing with any stress without the aid of a trained professional

8. What are people who reject therapy deemed to be, according to MacIntyre?

    a. Inconsistent   b. In control

    c. Independent   d. In denial

9. Which word on the Vocabulary Development list means "dissent or deviation from a dominant theory, opinion, or practice"?

    a. solace   b. succor

    c. heresy   d. ignoble

10. What, according to MacIntyre, is the emotionally correct response to shock?

    a. Hard work   b. Pubic weeping

    c. Solitude   d. There is none.

Content

1. What "widespread assumption" does MacIntyre say his opening example illustrates?
2. Where, according to MacIntyre, does therapism go too far?
3. What does the latest research, according to MacIntyre, suggest about cultivating self-esteem and encouraging emotional ventilation?

Style and Structure

1. What is MacIntyre's point? Rewrite his thesis in your own words.
2. What types of details does MacIntyre use to illustrate his thesis?
3. What are some disorders that people fear they suffer from?

Writing Assignments

1. MacIntyre writes that therapism is based on a belief that humans are "generally fragile." To what extent are people fragile? *Write an essay in which you discuss whether or not humans are "generally fragile."* For instance, discuss how people handle crises or stressful experiences, using examples from your own experience and observations to illustrate your ideas.
2. MacIntyre quotes experts who argue that "the emphasis on therapy is steadily eroding such characteristics as stoicism, self-belief and self-reliance." What do you think? *Write an essay explaining whether or not therapy "erodes" certain positive characteristics.* Consider, for instance, how stopping to share one's feelings can delay action or bring undue stress to situations. Use examples from your own experiences and observations to illustrate your ideas.
3. MacIntyre writes about the various ways that people cope with stress, anxiety, or trauma. What, for you, is therapy? *Write an essay defining the term* therapy. Identify at least three areas for development, such as situations in which therapy is used, people who consult therapists, or effects of therapy. Use examples from your own experiences and observations to illustrate your ideas.

John McPhee

Excerpt from "The Woods in Hog Wallow"

A longtime essayist for the *New Yorker,* John McPhee covers a wide range of topics. In this section from his book *The Pine Barrens,* McPhee describes two interesting characters he meets on his travels. Fred and Bill are neighbors who, different as they are, share a common need for each other's companionship.

BEFORE YOU READ

- What does the word *neighbor* mean to you? What does the term lead you to expect of someone? Explain.
- What role do neighbors play in your life? Has this role narrowed, or expanded, as you've aged or moved to different homes? Explain.
- To what extent do you or others you know possess features or habits that someone else might find strange? Describe, for instance, an act or habit that you're accustomed to but which might surprise others.

VOCABULARY DEVELOPMENT

Look up the following words in a dictionary and write down their meanings.

dismantled (paragraph 1)   bog (paragraph 3)

bristly (paragraph 2)   poacher (paragraph 3)

gaunt (paragraph 3)   hostile (paragraph 3)

vestibule (paragraph 2)   undulating (paragraph 3)

acreage (paragraph 3)   expansively (paragraph 3)

eyelets (paragraph 3)

Excerpt from "The Woods in Hog Wallow"

1   Fred Brown's house is on an unpaved road that curves along the edge of a wide cranberry bog. What attracted me to it was the pump that stands in his yard. It was something of a wonder that I noticed the pump, because there were, among other things, eight automobiles in the yard, two of them on their sides and one of them upside down, all ten years old or older. Around the cars were old refrigerators, vacuum cleaners, partly dismantled radios, cathode-ray tubes, a short wooden ski, a large wooden mallet, dozens of cranberry picker's boxes, many tires, an orange crate dated 1946, a cord or so of firewood, mandolins, engine heads, and maybe a thousand other things. The house itself, two stories high, was covered with tarpaper that was peeling away in some places, revealing its original shingles, made of Atlantic white cedar from the stream courses of the surrounding forest. I called out to ask if anyone was home, and a voice inside called back, "Come in. Come in. Come on the hell in."

2   I walked through a vestibule that had a dirt floor, stepped up into a kitchen, and went on into another room that had several overstuffed chairs in it and a porcelain-topped table, where Fred Brown was seated, eating a

pork chop. He was dressed in a white sleeveless shirt, ankle-top shoes, and undershorts. He gave me a cheerful greeting and, without asking why I had come or what I wanted, picked up a pair of khaki trousers that had been tossed onto one of the overstuffed chairs and asked me to sit down. He set the trousers on another chair, and he apologized for being in the middle of his breakfast, explaining that he seldom drank much but the night before he had had a few drinks and this had caused his day to start slowly. "I don't know what's the matter with me, but there's got to be something the matter with me, because drink don't agree with me anymore," he said. He had a raw onion in one hand, and while he talked he shaved slices from the onion and ate them between bites of the chop. He was a muscular and well-built man, with short, bristly white hair, and he had bright, fast-moving eyes in a wide-open face. His legs were trim and strong, with large muscles in the calves. I guessed that he was about sixty, and for a man of sixty he seemed to be in remarkably good shape. He was actually seventy-nine. "My rule is: Never eat except when you're hungry," he said, and he ate another slice of the onion.

3　　In a straight-backed chair near the doorway to the kitchen sat a young man with long black hair, who wore a visored red leather cap that had darkened with age. His shirt was coarse-woven and had eyelets down a V neck that was laced with a thong. His trousers were made of canvas, and he was wearing gum boots. His arms were folded, his legs were stretched out, he had one ankle over the other, and as he sat there he appeared to be sighting carefully past his feet, as if his toes were the outer frame of a gunsight and he could see some sort of target in the floor. When I had entered, I had said hello to him, and he had nodded without looking up. He had a long, straight nose and high cheekbones, in a deeply tanned face that was, somehow, gaunt. I had no idea whether he was shy or hostile. Eventually, when I came to know him, I found him to be as shy a person as I have ever had a chance to know. His name is Bill Wasovwich, and he lives alone in a cabin about half a mile from Fred. First his father, then his mother left him when he was a young boy, and he grew up depending on the help of various people in the pines. One of them, a cranberry grower, employs him and has given him some acreage, in which Bill is building a small cranberry bog of his own, "turfing it out" by hand. When he is not working in the bogs, he goes roaming, as he puts it, setting out cross-country on long, looping journeys, hiking about thirty miles in a typical day, in search of what he calls "events"—surprising a buck, or a gray fox, or perhaps a poacher or a man with a still. Almost no one who is not native to the pines could do this, for the woods have an undulating sameness, and the understory—huckleberries, sheep laurel, sweet fern, high-bush blueberry—is often so dense that a wanderer can walk in a fairly tight circle and think that he is moving in a straight line. State forest rangers spend a good part of their time finding hikers and hunters, some of whom have vanished for days. In his long, pathless journeys, Bill always emerges from the woods near his cabin—and about when he plans to. In the fall, when thousands of hunters come into the pines, he sometimes works as a guide. In the evenings, or in the daytime when he is not working or roaming, he goes to Fred Brown's house and sits there for hours. The old man is a widower whose seven children are long since gone from Hog Wallow, and he is as expansively talkative and worldly as the young one is withdrawn and wild. Although there are fifty-three years between their ages, it is obviously fortunate for each of them to be the other's neighbor.

POST-READING EXERCISES

1. Which word on the Vocabulary Development list means "wet, spongy ground"?

   a. gaunt   b. bog

   c. acreage   d. vestibule

2. What, sitting in Fred Brown's yard, attracts McPhee to Brown's house?

   a. The pump   b. The cars

   c. The refrigerators   d. An orange crate dated 1946

3. How does Brown greet McPhee?

   a. "Get away. Get away or I'll shoot."

   b. "Open the door. Open the darn door."

   c. "What do you want? What the hell do you want?"

   d. "Come in. Come in. Come on the hell in."

4. Which of the following is Brown *not* wearing when McPhee meets him?

   a. Undershorts   b. Sleeveless shirt

   c. Ankle-top shoes   d. Knee-high socks

5. What is one definition of the word *expansively?*

   a. Characterized by low spirits, stinginess, and reluctance to talk

   b. Characterized by tension and anxiety

   c. Characterized by sleepiness and silence

   d. Characterized by high spirits, generosity, or readiness to talk

6. How does Bill Wasovwich greet McPhee?

   a. Nods without looking up

   b. Grunts without looking up

   c. Cocks his head to one side without looking up

   d. Shrugs without looking up

7. Which of the following words does *not* describe Wasovwich?

   a. Shy   b. Mute

   c. Withdrawn   d. Wild

8. What does Wasovwich go into the bogs searching for?

   a. Events   b. Incidents

   c. Occurrences   d. Happenings

9. Which word on the Vocabulary Development list means "forming or moving in waves"?

   a. bristly   b. dismantled

   c. undulating   d. eyelets

10. What conclusion does McPhee draw about Brown and Wasovwich?

    a. They are fortunate to be neighbors.

    b. They are lucky to live apart.

    c. They are more alike than they appear.

    d. They are father and son.

Content

1. Why did McPhee choose these two men, among all the people he's met, to write about?
2. What is the nature of the relationship between Brown and Wasovwich?
3. What is Bill's background? To what extent does knowing his childhood experiences help us understand him as an adult?

Style and Structure

1. What is McPhee's point? Write his main idea in your own words.
2. What details does McPhee use to describe each man? What do these details say about each?
3. What is McPhee's attitude toward these men? How can you tell?

Writing Assignments

1. Brown and Wasovwich have a close relationship, yet it doesn't easily fall under one single heading such as *friendship, neighbor,* or *companion.* What, to you, makes a friendship? *Write an essay in which you define a relationship-related term such as* friend, neighbor, family, *or* companion. *(You may choose another term if you prefer.)* For instance, you may write that a friend is someone who accepts you without having to, as some people feel family must. Use examples from your own experiences to illustrate your ideas.

2. Spending just one paragraph on each of his subjects, McPhee communicates major personality traits of each man: one is extroverted and the other shy. Who do you know that possesses one dominant personality trait? *Write an essay describing someone you know well in terms of his or her most pronounced personality trait.* You could, for example, describe how your uncle is most concerned with personal comfort or how your mother is a tireless worker. Use examples from your own experiences and observations to illustrate your ideas.

3. McPhee describes both Fred Brown and Bill Wasovwich in Brown's home, which he also describes in detail. To what extent do you think someone's home reveal that person's characteristics? *Write an essay discussing how people's homes do or do not reflect people's personalities.* For instance, you could write how your buddy's messy bedroom does *not* show his extremely organized way of thinking, or you could write about how your aunt's perfectly orderly home *is* an expression of her orderly mind. Use examples from your own observations and experiences to illustrate your ideas.

Our Values

Unless we live completely alone, we must make and endure decisions that affect not only ourselves but those around us. In "Whose Life Is It, Anyway?" and "Petty Crime, Outrageous Punishment," Mary Battiata and Carl M. Cannon pose questions about at what point we should "draw the line" in dealing with others. Similarly, Diane Ravitch's article "You Can't Say That" challenges readers to determine if it's possible to have too much of a good thing, particularly in the area of verbal sensitivity. "How to Paint a Fresco" and "How to Tell a Joke" explore the ways in which people enrich their lives, while Pat Burson's essay "A Reason to Forgive" shows the benefits of letting go of our anger, even when we've been wronged.

Readings in This Section

Mary Battiata

Whose Life Is It, Anyway?[1]

Mary Battiata, a staff writer for the *Washington Post,* addresses the issue of paying for a pet's health care even when the costs are exorbitant. For some, the term "animal rights" calls to mind a vegetarian diet and the refusal to wear leather, but in addition, we must ask ourselves how much we owe animals we care for in terms of their health.

 **BEFORE YOU READ**

- What care do you think pet owners owe their pets? Explain.
- Where do you think people should draw the line between preventive pet health care—vaccinations and flea collars—and extraordinary measures, such as resuscitation or cancer surgery? Explain.
- What rights do animals have? Do the rights vary depending on the animal? Do fish, for instance, have fewer rights than dogs because fish are less cuddly? Explain.

 **VOCABULARY DEVELOPMENT**

Look up the following words in a dictionary and write down their meanings.

stoic (paragraph 1)   enshrined (paragraph 12)
fracases (paragraph 4)   bellwether (paragraph 31)
ensconced (paragraph 29)   aggrieved (paragraph 36)
clout (paragraph 32)   distended (paragraph 48)
reproach (paragraph 2)   incision (paragraph 53)

Whose Life is it, Anyway?

1   The blood-pressure reading was fine, and now the veterinary anesthesiologist picked up a small, electric hair clipper to clear a patch of fur from my dog's foreleg, just above the paw. This was too much. Stoic through patient intake and the tightening of the blood-pressure cuff, he now turned his head toward the whirr and chick of the blades and began to quaver in a way I'd never seen.

---

[1]© 2004, The Washington Post. Excerpted with permission.

2   "He's probably just picking up on your anxiety," the vet tech said. There was reproach in her tone, but I wasn't in a position to argue. So I nodded and tried harder to act like a $1,400 veterinary brain scan under general anesthesia was no big deal.

3   But the dog knew better, and so did I. Looking down at my boon companion for more than half of my adult life, I thought, "I hope this is the right thing to be doing."

4   Bear was a mutt who looked a lot like a black Labrador, until you stood him next to one. He was 14, and he'd always been hale. He'd survived falls through pond ice, fracases with raccoons, tangles with rusted barbed wire, a tumble from a mountain catwalk, periodic midnight rambles (mostly solo and unscripted), transatlantic air travel and even a bounce off the bumper of a moving car. He could wriggle through spaces where only a pancake could fit, and he was always just as enthusiastic to be home from his travels. Nothing fazed him, except thunder and, oddly, brooms. It was part of his charm.

5   My most recent experience with major veterinary care had been way back in the '70s, when visits to the vet with the family dog never involved anything more complicated than a rabies shot or a worming pill. Back then, 10 years was old age for many dog breeds. Dog food came in huge bags at the grocery store and poured in mysterious shades of chemical orange and bright brown.

6   But now, we were uneasy pilgrims in a strange new world, where we never seemed to get out of the clinic for less than $250 and our first real sick visit cost $900, more than I'd ever spent on one doctor visit for myself.

. . .

7   In the scan room, white-coated technicians with clipboards squeaked back and forth across the gleaming white floor, noting patients' vital signs every five minutes. The center's chief, Julie Smith, one of a handful of board-certified veterinary anesthesiologists in the country, presided over this reassuring tableau with a kindly competence that generated immediate trust. Smith had spent four years in postgraduate veterinary study learning how to safely anesthetize dogs, cats, lizards, hawks. MRIs were all they did here, and they seemed to do them very well.

8   Still, I was having trouble wrapping my brain around the idea. The civilians I talked to weren't much help.

9   "An MRI for a dog?" said an acquaintance. "You're kidding, right?"

10   She shook her head. "What you need is an old-fashioned country vet," she said. She had a friend who'd had three ancient dogs, and when their time came they were "put down," and that was that.

11   "The old-fashioned kind of vet," she said firmly. "That's what you want."

12   But did I? And what did that mean, anyway? True, I'd always been a fan of the old-fashioned approach, the approach enshrined in books like James

Herriot's *All Creatures Great and Small,* where the vet is kindly and competent and does things the old-fashioned way. In principle, at least, I was as irritated as anyone by the unceasing, often pointless-seeming innovation of modern American consumer life, the incessant alarms about the dangers of this toxin or that. In fact, part of the appeal of having a dog had always been the connection it seemed to offer to a simpler way of life.

13   And now we were in the middle of a $1,400 brain scan. And if there was a brain tumor? How I would know how much medical treatment was right and how much was too much? And how much could I afford? Already we were flying on credit cards; I'd just refinanced my house to pay off debt, and now the numbers were rising again.

14   As Bear slipped off into the ether for his MRI, I was sent back to the waiting room. I was flipping through the dog magazines when a man carrying a small black-and-white Boston terrier came in the front door. They'd just driven up from North Carolina, the man said. This was the only veterinary MRI facility between home and Philadelphia, he said, and he felt very lucky to be here.

15   Me, too, I replied. We talked a little more and then fell silent.

16   In a cavernous, concrete-floored examing hall at the Leesburg campus of the Virginia-Maryland Regional College of Veterinary Medicine, a fourth-year student stood in the shadow of an enormous caramel-colored draft horse. Heather Craven, 32, was using a white plastic disposable razor to shave a small patch on the horse's neck, preparation for a catheter through which a large sack of blood would be drawn.

17   Fellow student Kelly Malec-McConnell stood nearby with a clipboard. A large, O-shaped bruise was fading from purple to dark red around her right eye. A horse she'd been treating had kicked as she'd injected an anesthetic into its leg, as part of a diagnostic test for lameness called a nerve block.

18   The emergency cases meant that a scheduled gastroscopy—in which a tiny camera on a tube is threaded through the horse's nose and into its gut—would have to be postponed. In a room across the hallway, meanwhile, a small brown horse stood passively as an X-ray machine mounted on a crane and dolly rotated around its middle. The digital images were relayed to a computer screen in the next room, where a veterinary resident inspected them for clarity. In still another room, a horse stood chewing hay and drinking water, quarantined until it excreted radioactive isotopes injected during nuclear scintigraphy, a test used to pinpoint the source of lameness.

19   Welcome to a routine (and therefore anything but routine) veterinary school clinical rotation, circa 2004—a mixture of old-fashioned bloodletting and nuclear medicine and everything in between. Craven and Malec-McConnell, rising seniors at the main veterinary campus in Blacksburg, Va., were in the final months of preparing for a career that will be expected to

embody both the veterinary profession's simpler past and its demanding, high-tech future.

20   In addition to the traditional course work—about 60 percent of it in small-animal medicine (i.e., dogs and cats)—their $200,000, four-year veterinary educations include instruction on the human-animal bond and the importance of good vet-client communication: personal touches such as sending a note when an animal in their care has died. "Even horses have gone from being farm workers to people's companions," Craven said. "That course did a good job of making it clear that the relationship has changed— that people are willing to spend the money on their animals. And they want to spend the money."

21   That recognition is one small part of a sea change that began in the late 1980s, driven by technological innovation and the rising social status of the American house pet. At the country's leading veterinary teaching hospitals, surgeons now routinely perform procedures that were unavailable to the average house pet 10 years ago: kidney transplants, cancer chemotherapy, back surgery for herniated disks, titanium hip-joint replacements, radiation treatments for goldfish, MRIs for hawks. Even treatments once reserved for very expensive animals—racehorses and champion purebred dogs—are available at the sophisticated specialty hospitals that have proliferated in the past decade and that provide a range of care previously available only at the nation's 28 veterinary school teaching hospitals.

22   "In the 1980s, pet owners began to say, 'If medical science can remove my cataracts, why can't it take out my dog's?' " says Jack Walther, head of the American Veterinary Medical Association, the profession's primary membership organization. "And the answer was, we could. We'd just never been asked."

23   Until the 1940s, and through most of its history, veterinary medicine was devoted to helping agriculture manage its food animals. The creed of veterinary medicine—to help society by helping animals (as opposed to helping animals themselves)—reflects this. Until the 1960s, most vet students were men with a background in farming or animal science. As the United States suburbanized in the 1950s, small-animal veterinary practices began to proliferate, but pet cats and dogs still spent much of their time outside. (Try to picture Lassie sprawled lengthwise on the living room couch at Timmy's house. It can't be done.) As recently as the late 1980s, most pets were treated as second-class citizens by their owners.

24   The practice of veterinary medicine reflected this lowly status. Even now, most veterinarians carry little or no malpractice insurance, because until very recently, it was impossible for a pet owner suing a vet over loss of a pet to recover anything more than the animal's replacement value. The bigger part of the vet's week was spent administering vaccines and fixing the broken bones that were a common and unremarkable fact of life in the

decades before leash laws. When a pet's medical problems became difficult or expensive to fix, the animal was "put to sleep," or euthanized.

25   "One of the most discouraging parts of my practice in the early days was having a dog come in with a simple broken leg and having the owner say, 'Well, it costs money and it's just a dog, so put him to sleep,' " says Walther, who began his practice in Nevada almost 40 years ago.

26   In the late '80s, however, pets began to fill the emotional and physical void created by rising divorce rates and growing numbers of single-person and childless households. "A pet may be the most stabilizing, permanent presence a child from a divorced home will ever experience," says Arlington vet Robert Brown.

27   Dogs and cats began to live longer, too. From 1987 to 2000, the life spans of the average dog and cat increased by more than one-third, thanks to better commercial pet foods and widespread vaccination, according to the AVMA. But longer life spans meant a jump in the incidence of the diseases of old age—cancers, organ failure, crippling arthritis and other problems. With the family pet now ensconced on the bed instead of at the far end of the yard, the medical problems were easier to spot and harder to ignore.

28   Today, many people think of their pets as members of the family, and they want them to have access to the same medical technology they do, vets say. And this is possible, thanks to the same biomedical revolution that transformed human medicine in the 1950s and '60s. According to the Food and Drug Administration, which regulates drugs for the veterinary market, the pharmaceutical industry in recent years has begun shifting its energies away from the agricultural market and toward companion animals. The number of new drugs approved for veterinary use has increased dramatically in the past decade, with special interest in drugs for behavior modification and pain relief.

29   The focus on pain medication is a particularly significant bellwether. Until very recently, desensitizing veterinary students to animal pain was an important part of their education. "When I went to vet school back in the Stone Age, we didn't really talk about pain," says Stephen F. Sundlof, director of the FDA's Center for Veterinary Medicine. "It was, 'Do the surgery, and the animals will get alone fine.' " Today, Sundlof says, there is a growing understanding of pain as a complication that impedes recovery and healing.

30   This gradual and ongoing "evolution in consciousness," says Elliott Katz, a veterinarian and founder of the advocacy group In Defense of Animals, has been spurred by the entrance of large numbers of women to the profession in the past 15 years, and by the demands of pet owners, whose economic clout is becoming a counterweight to the agribusiness interests that have traditionally underwritten much veterinary research at universities.

31   All of this has put new pressure on the ordinary neighborhood veterinary clinic. Vets, who 30 years ago needed little more than a stethoscope

and an Army surplus field X-ray machine to set up a practice, now equip their clinics with an array of expensive diagnostic equipment, from blood-analysis machines to ultrasound scanners. Even setting up a small practice costs upwards of $500,000.

32   The average veterinary bill—which has tripled in the past 10 years—reflects this. The price surge was not an accident. It is the direct result of a half-a-million-dollar study commissioned by the leading veterinary professional organizations in 1998 to figure out why veterinarians' salaries lagged far behind those in human medicine and in such professions as law and engineering. The study, by the business consulting firm KPMG, cited federal statistics showing that veterinary practice incomes had declined during the 1990s, a decade when many other professional incomes rose.

33   The study concluded that veterinarians were failing to run their practices as the demanding businesses they had become. Pressed by competition, vets were mortgaging their practices to buy expensive equipment but charging clients prices that hadn't increased much since the 1970s. The veterinary profession called the study's findings a "wake-up call" and set up a national commission dedicated to encouraging vets to concentrate harder on the bottom line.

34   These days, veterinary school graduates enter a profession more focused on management economics than ever before, and one in which ethical questions long familiar to human medicine are only now beginning to surface. Veterinary malpractice cases, once rare, are on the rise. State courts have begun awarding aggrieved pet owners sums as high as $30,000 for pain and emotional suffering, instead of limiting damages to simple replacement value of the animal, as in the past. Veterinary insurers say this change will drive up costs, but others, including some vets, say the change is inevitable and overdue. "Vets can't come into the examining room saying, 'What's wrong with your baby? What's wrong with the little boy?' and then, if they make a mistake that kills the baby, act like they broke your . . . ashtray," says Robert Newman, a California veterinary malpractice lawyer.

35   Even the nature of pet ownership itself is under review. In the past five years, more than 40 jurisdictions across North America, including the state of Rhode Island and the city of Windsor, Ontario, have approved ordinances that transform pet "owners" to "guardians," a change that proponents hope will lead to better treatment for companion animals. (Critics fear that giving vets the authority, and even the responsibility, to report animal neglect or abuse will discourage pet owners from going to the vet at all. So far, however, the debate is academic. No charges have been brought against pet owners as a result of the new wording, and Newman and other legal experts say the new language is largely toothless.)

36   The human-animal bond had been rewritten in my household the day Bear joined it. As an enthusiastic member of the roll-in-the-dead-squirrel

society, he wasn't allowed on the bed or the couch, but in all other ways he was a member of the family. The sicker he got, the more all of these philosophical questions were thrown into sharp relief. And I wasn't the only one grappling with them.

37   "Twenty years ago, if your dog had congenital heart failure or an arrhythmia, you might just be told, 'There's not much we can do,' and that was upsetting, no doubt," says Nancy Kerns, editor of the influential *Whole Dog Journal*, a national magazine. "But it's also quite upsetting to learn there are things that can be done and it's going to cost you $10,000 or $15,000 to do them. At that point, you're making serious financial decisions, and that's a lot of pressure for some people. There's so much available that it can really cause a hardship . . .

38   "You're usually in shock when the crisis has struck, and you're in crisis-management mode, and you try to do whatever you can, which you suddenly learn is a great deal."

39   The brain scan was negative, but after taking weeks to relay the radiologist's report confirming that, the neurologist no longer talked about a spinal tap. "We'll just keep him comfortable," he said. A third vet thought there might still be more diagnostic work to do—a blood culture to check for a fungal infection, for example—but this vet was in another state. I thought about piling Bear into the car, but hesitated, worried about the stress a new round of tests would inflict. And there was the cost. I knew one dog owner who'd run up a tab of $3,000 in one weekend at a university veterinary hospital, only to be given a diagnosis of "idiopathic." Translation: We don't know.

40   Bear was belatedly tested for Lyme disease, and the blood work came back positive, but the vet thought it unlikely that Lyme was the source of his problems. Antibiotics seemed to help at first, but then he deteriorated again.

41   Then events overtook us. On a Monday in early March, Bear began to run a high fever and suddenly could not take more than a few steps without help. The vet made a house call and gave an injection of a powerful antibiotic, and Bear improved for a few days. But by the end of the week, he was weak again and on Friday had to be carried to the clinic. X-rays to check for signs of cancer and other tests were inconclusive.

42   At the end of the visit, the vet proposed giving Bear an injection of one non-steroidal anti-inflammatory and a second, in pill form, to be started the next day.

43   "Um, aren't those dangerous?" I asked tentatively. I had only just heard that about the drugs' occasional side effects, and he seemed so sick. I was worried about putting more medicine on his plate.

44   "Not a problem," the vet said. "We'll only be using it for a week, and we'll be watching him closely."

45   The next day, however, the first pill caused immediate and severe gastric problems that continued through the weekend, although I stopped the pills immediately. By Monday night, Bear was panting and in pain. I called the vet clinic right before closing. How do you know when it's time to go to the dog emergency room? I asked. "Use your judgment," the vet tech said.

46   I spent Monday night lying on the floor next to Bear, spooning water into his mouth with a saucer. On Tuesday morning, the vet made another emergency house call. An appointment with an internist at a second specialty clinic for later in the week was moved up. The vet thought Bear's spleen looked distended. Have the internist check it with ultrasound, he said.

47   The spleen was fine, as it turned out, but the ultrasound revealed something much worse.

48   "Bingo," the internist said, returning to the exam room with a syringe of dark, plum-colored fluid pulled from Bear's gut. There was a hole in Bear's intestine, and the leak had caused a massive infection of the abdominal cavity. The hole had probably only opened a few days earlier. There were two options: operate immediately to close the hole and try to clean up the infection. Or, the doctor said, "I'm afraid we have to put him down."

49   Bear lay panting on the examining table between us. The doctor carefully outlined the risks and costs. The operation was major surgery. The anesthesia would be deeper and thus more dangerous than the brief sleep induced for the MRI. If Bear survived it, he would need at least two days in intensive care, followed by two weeks of convalescence and massive doses of antibiotics. The cost would be roughly $3,200.

50   I looked at Bear. Though he was clearly in pain, his head was up and he was alert. It did not seem possible to give up on him. I stroked his head one last time and gave the go-ahead. They took him off to prepare for surgery.

51   But Bear died on the operating table that night, before the surgeon made a single incision. He was weak from infection, and his heart did not tolerate the anesthesia, the vets said. For the same reason, the medicines used to stabilize adverse anesthetic reactions failed, too.

52   Shortly after they'd started the anesthesia, a nurse in surgical scrubs and a plastic shower cap had run into the little waiting room where I was staring at a fish tank. "He's having trouble with the anesthesia," she said, and asked if I would approve the use of CPR. I blinked. CPR?

53   Yes, she said. There would be a small charge for it.

54   Okay, I said, and the nurse raced out again. Much later, I wondered if what she'd really been asking was, "Is it okay to let him go?"

55   A few minutes later, the nurse came back and said Bear was gone. Doctors appeared. The emergency room vet, a woman, cried and said how sorry she was, which made me feel both better and worse, but mostly better. The internist walked me through what had happened. He took his time even though it was way past closing.

56   They'd done a quick autopsy, the internist said. The hole in Bear's gut was large enough to put your finger through. It looked as if the infection had been underway for a few days. There was no sign of cancer, or a sharp object, such as a piece of bone, that might have caused the hole. It was well below the place in the stomach where ulcerations from non-steroidal anti-inflammatories typically are seen, and, in any case, it seemed unlikely that two doses of the medicine could have been responsible. He couldn't rule it out, he said, but he really doubted it. Most likely, we'd never know what caused the hole.

57   They brought me Bear's collar and tags, and said they could make a cast of his paw print if I wanted. They explained they could dispose of the remains, or I could arrange for a cremation, in which case I'd have an urn with his ashes.

58   It occurred to me that what I'd wanted all along from veterinary medicine was the best of both worlds: the commitment, skepticism and horse sense of an old-fashioned vet, and the compassion, diagnostic smarts and philosophical approach of the new breed, vets informed by the belief that animals, in effect, were people, too.

POST-READING EXERCISES

1. Which word on the Vocabulary Development list means "a noisy brawl"?

   a. enshrined   b. stoic

   c. bellwether   d. fracases

2. What is Battiata's dog's name?

   a. Dog   b. Bear

   c. Wolf   d. Cat

3. How long has Battiata owned her dog?

   a. Half her life

   b. All her adult life

   c. All her life

   d. More than half her adult life

4. Which of the following is *not* something that Battiata's dog survived?

   a. Falls through pond ice

   b. Collisions with commuter trains

   c. Fracases with raccoons

   d. Tangles with barbed wire

5. What is one definition of the word *stoic?*

   a. Easily able to communicate one's emotions

  b. Not affected by or showing passion or feeling

  c. Concerned about the feelings of others

  d. Employed in the betterment of one's mind

6. Historically, that was the goal at veterinary medicine?

  a. To help people take care at their animals.

  b. To help animal become more like humans.

  c. To help animals help their companions.

  d. To help society by helping animals

7. Which of the following is *not* available for animal treatment?

  a. Kidney transplants   b. Botox

  c. Chemotherapy   d. Radiation

8. What helps Battiata make up her mind to have her dog undergo surgery?

  a. He was still alert.

  b. He was in pain.

  c. His condition was improving.

  d. He looked at her longingly.

9. Which word on the Vocabulary Development list means "sheltered or concealed"?

  a. clout   b. aggrieved

  c. ensconced   d. distended

10. What belief does Battiata want vets to be informed by?

  a. Animals have feelings, too

  b. Animals are more than pets.

  c. Animals are people, too.

  d. Animals need compassion.

Content

1. What issue does Battiata explore in her article?

2. What has changed in terms of the availability of care for pets?

3. What has brought about the change in pet care availability?

Style and Structure

1. What is Battiata's point? Write her argument in your own words.

2. In the past, what types of medical procedures "were reserved just for racehorses and champion purebred dogs"?

3. Though Battiata spends $1,400 on a brain scan for her dog, is she certain that she's taking the right course of action? How do you know?

Writing Assignments

1. Battiata writes that in the 1980s, "pets began to fill [an] emotional void." To what extent is this true? *Write an essay in which you explain the role or roles that you think animals play in people's lives.* For instance, if you know people whose dogs bark at strangers, you could argue that dogs can serve as burglar alarms, as well as being playmates or companions. Use examples from your own experiences to illustrate your ideas.

2. Battiata writes about paying $1,400 for a brain scan for her dog. At what point is a pet's medical care too expensive? *Write an essay discussing the point at which medical care for a pet becomes unreasonable.* Address, for instance, whether or not pets should be given organ transplants or eye surgery. Use examples from your own experiences and observations to illustrate your ideas.

3. Battiata clearly loves her dog and goes to great lengths to care for him, yet she feels some doubt about doing so. *Write an essay discussing how much people should do for the animals in their lives.* For instance, you could write about how people should do only the minimum for a pet's care and comfort, supplying food, water, and shelter. Or you could write about how the niceties—fancy collars, padded beds, expensive toys—are important in pet care. Use examples from your own observations and experiences to illustrate your ideas.

Pat Burson

A Reason to Forgive

Writing that forgiveness is something we do for ourselves, *Newsday* writer Pat Burson explores the benefits of both letting go of our anger and allowing ourselves to heal. Burson cites research that indicates that the act of forgiveness not only will improve psychological health but will improve physical health as well.

BEFORE YOU READ

- To what extent do you experience unpleasant feelings as a result of a past emotional injury? Explain.
- What kinds of emotional injuries are hardest for people to "let go"? Explain.
- What are some ways you are able to find peace after hurtful or stressful times? Explain.

VOCABULARY DEVELOPMENT

Look up the following words in a dictionary and write down their meanings.

theologians (paragraph 5)   cathartic (paragraph 10)
invigorating (paragraph 10)   martyrs (paragraph 11)
alleviate (paragraph 17)   enumerate (paragraph 19)
exact (paragraph 22)   empathy (paragraph 22)
recourse (paragraph 31)   inculcated (paragraph 33)

A Reason to Forgive

1 Victoria Ruvolo stood inside a Riverhead courtroom and gave the teenager who almost killed her a gift.

2   Her forgiveness.

3   It was an unexpected show of compassion that stunned courtroom observers witnessing the first face-to-face meeting two weeks ago between the Lake Ronkonkoma woman and Ryan Cushing, 18, of Huntington, after he'd pleaded guilty to assaulting her. He admitted tossing a 20-pound turkey out of a backseat window of a speeding car, sending it crashing through the windshield of Ruvolo's oncoming vehicle and shattering almost every bone in her face.

4   In that courtroom, victim and offender embraced for several minutes. He wept, apologized for hurting her and pleaded for her forgiveness. She held him and told him it was OK, patted his back and stroked his cheek.

5   How Ruvolo managed to forgive Cushing is an inspiration to many—and, for some, impossible to understand. But therapists and theologians say she did what we all need to do when others hurt us, we hurt them or we hurt ourselves.

6   There's really no other way, says Kathleen Griffin, author of *The Forgiveness Formula: How to Let Go of Your Pain and Move on with Life.*

7   "When writing my book," she says, "I came across astonishing examples of forgiveness: Nelson Mandela who forgave his jailers, parents whose children had been murdered, survivors of the Holocaust who had managed to forgive. It's difficult to understand how they could forgive. But what is the alternative?"

8   Forgiving someone, Griffin says, allows you to get on with your life. "When you don't forgive, it's as though you are walking around with two heavy suitcases containing all the hurt and pain. Forgiveness means putting those cases down and leaving them behind."

9   Easier said than done.

10   While forgiveness can be cathartic, holding onto anger can have its rewards. "For one thing, anger is very invigorating," says Hamilton

Beazley, author of *No Regrets: A Ten-Step Program for Living in the Present and Leaving the Past Behind*. Properly channeled, it can be inspiring. Consider Rosa Parks, whose indignation helped give momentum to the civil-rights movement.

11   "But some people enjoy being martyrs," explains Beazley, scholar-in-residence at St. Edward's University in Austin, Texas. "They like to impress people with how they have suffered." But, he adds, "you can't dwell on your past sufferings if you have forgiven."

12   For some, though, the inability to let go of an offense may stem from ignorance. "All of the major religions tell us to forgive; they don't tell us how," Beazley says. It's a process, he and others say, that can be learned, with time, courage and practice.

13   Forgiveness is a "journey in which we come to terms intellectually, emotionally and often spiritually with the perceived hurts others have inflicted on us, so the offender no longer has power to hurt us in the present," Beazley says.

14   To begin that journey, he suggests acknowledging that forgiveness is about you—not the other person.

15   "It may have a happy effect on them, no effect on them, an angry effect on them because you free them, but it has a positive effect on ourselves. Forgiveness is about us," he says.

16   In fact, unloading the guilt, resentment and anger has proven to be a key to a healthier life.

17   A surge of scientific research into forgiveness conducted since the mid-1980s has uncovered numerous physical and psychological benefits, such as helping to lower blood pressure, improve immune-system function, alleviate chronic back pain and reduce physical symptoms associated with stress, such as headaches, stomach pain and backaches.

18   Working your way toward forgiveness (and ultimately better health) could mean getting those negative feelings out of you. Some suggest writing down how you feel, either in a journal or a letter that you may not ever send. Explain what happened and what pain you suffered as a result. Such letters could even be addressed to a deceased person—or to God.

19   Therapists and researchers suggest that this can also work if you need to forgive yourself for something you've done. "After you've examined it, look at any toxic thought patterns that are keeping you from forgiving," Beazley says. "If you can enumerate them, you can talk yourself out of them."

20   But forgiveness may require examining the offense from the other's perspective, as Ruvolo has seemed to: While embracing Cushing in court, she was overheard telling the teen, "I'm going to be watching your life, and I want you to do well."

21   Empathizing with the person who hurt you is "the hardest step," says Everett Worthington, a psychology professor at Virginia Commonwealth

University and author of *Forgiving and Reconciling: Bridges to Wholeness and Hope.*

22   "Because the natural thing for people to gravitate toward when they've been hurt is justice—sometimes personal justice, which includes paying the person back or getting even, or looking for someone else to exact justice on the person," he says. "So it's really unnatural and very difficult to say, 'I'm going to think about this from the point of view of the other person.' It involves empathy, sympathy, feeling some compassion and maybe even love for the person."

23   Don't tie your willingness to forgive to the other person's response, says "energy coach" Jon Gordon, a Smithtown native living in Florida. His forthcoming book, *The 10-Minute Energy Solution,* has a section on forgiveness as a way to boost energy and overall well-being.

24   "It doesn't matter if the other person doesn't apologize," he says. "You're not forgiving them for them."

25   There is also a body of thought that forgiveness should not be given so freely—that the act should require as much effort from the offender as the victim.

26   It's not enough to say you're sorry, says Janis Abrahms Spring, author of *How Can I Forgive You? The Courage to Forgive, the Freedom Not To.* The offender should listen to the other's grievance without getting defensive, apologize genuinely for the specific offense—and then make meaningful repairs, she says.

27   Too many skirt the process, cheating themselves out of a true apology, she says, preferring instead to keep the peace or because they are so terrified of conflict or abandonment that they simply choose to let go of their anger or their hurt.

28   "Lots of people forgive too easily, and they don't process how they feel," says Spring. "They don't ask the offender to address the harm in any way."

29   Forgivness can open the door to reconciliation, says L. Gregory Jones, a theology professor and dean of the divinity school at Duke University and author of *Embodying Forgiveness: A Theological Analysis.*

30   "Reconciliation does not mean returning to a prior relationship—if there was one—but that we genuinely wish the other person well," he says. "It should be the goal, even if it seems difficult or even unimaginable at a particular point in time."

31   Prosecutors considered Ruvolo's feelings along with evaluating the evidence in the case before cutting a plea deal for Cushing to serve only six months in county jail. But her attorney, Paul Feuer of Patchogue, says she still plans to seek civil recourse for her injuries "against him and others."

32   Holding someone responsible for an offense can be healthy, as long as it aims at the other person's well-being and doesn't cross over into vengeance, Jones says. "There should be accountability," he says, "and the

person who did it should be inspired to improve his victim's circumstances in life."

An End to Myths

33   Too many believe myths about forgiveness, says Hamilton Beazley, author of *No Regrets: A Ten-Step Program for Living in the Present and Leaving the Past Behind.* Below, he attempts to debunk some of them.

Myth: To forgive, we have to excuse the offending behavior or condone it in some way.

Beazley: You can forgive without excusing the wrongdoing. You can forgive someone for a crime, for instance, and still believe that they should be sent to a penitentiary for the rest of their lives.

Myth: To forgive, we have to reconcile with the offender.

Beazley: No, we don't. Sometimes we do it because we want to, and sometimes we do it where it's strategically sensitive. For instance, at work you'll likely reconcile with your boss if you want to keep your job. Then again, you don't have to keep your job.

Myth: We should only forgive the other person if he or she deserves it.

Beazley: This is inculcated in us through the language that says, "He deserves to be forgiven," or "She doesn't deserve to be forgiven." Deserving doesn't have anything to do with the other party. Forgiving is about ourselves. We deserve it.

Myth: We only forgive in response to a request for it.

Beazley: It all comes back to forgiving for ourselves. It doesn't matter if they ask for it or not.

Myth: We forgive only on the basis of certain conditions, such as getting an apology.

Beazley: We do not need the applied permission of anybody else to forgive. Otherwise, we'd still be under their control.

Myth: Forgiveness isn't valid unless it's accepted by the other party.

Beazley: Forgiveness is a gift we make to ourselves. It's actually a gift to them, too, he adds, but they have a right to say no.

Steps Toward Forgiving

34   Forgiveness isn't an instant process but rather "takes the time it takes," says Kathleen Griffin, author of *The Forgiveness Formula: How to Let Go of Your Pain and Move on with Life.*

35   First and foremost, Griffin and others agree, forgiveness "is never about the other person who has done you harm. They may not be around to apologize, they may be dead, they may not be sorry. Forgiveness is only about you."

36   That said, if you're ready to proceed, she offers the following advice:
Go through the whole story in your head again. Imagine all the details.

Feel the emotions you went through—shout, scream or cry if you need to.

Imagine just for a moment putting all those feelings in a huge box, closing the box and walking away. How free would you feel?

Put yourself in the other person's shoes, and tell the story from his or her point of view. (This is not in any way to excuse what they did.)

Imagine a third person telling the story. How is it different from the other two versions?

Practice letting go and walking away in a beautiful place—a favorite beach or walk in the country.

POST-READING EXERCISES

1. Which word on the Vocabulary Development list means "a person who sacrifices something of great value and especially life itself for the sake of principle"?

   a. theologians   b. martyrs

   c. empathy   d. recourse

2. What, according to author Kathleen Griffin, does forgiveness allow people to do?

   a. Get even.   b. Get away from stress.

   c. Get help.   d. Get on with their lives.

3. According to the article, what can anger do for us?

   a. Inspire us.   b. Hurt us.

   c. Exhaust us.   d. Comfort us.

4. What do the major religions *not* tell people about forgiveness?

   a. Why forgiveness is important

   b. When to forgive

   c. How to forgive

   d. To what extent we should forgive

5. What is one definition of the word *enumerate?*

   a. To provide   b. To divide

   c. To measure   d. To count

6. Which of the following is *not* necessary to learn forgiveness?

   a. Time   b. Courage

   c. Energy   d. Practice

7. Which of the following is *not* a physical benefit of forgiveness?

   a. Lower blood pressure

b. Improved immune system

c. Alleviated chronic back pain

d. Decreased tooth decay

8. Why do some people "cheat themselves" out of an apology?

a. They're too proud.

b. They're rude.

c. They're afraid of conflict or abandonment.

d. They're worried about their reputation.

9. Which word on the Vocabulary Development list means "to call for forcibly or urgently and obtain"?

a. cathartic

b. invigorating

c. exact

d. empathy

10. Which of the following ailments is *not* improved by forgiveness?

a. Mental distress

b. Headaches

c. Sore throat

d. Insomnia

Content

1. What, according to university psychology professor Everett Worthington, is the hardest step in forgiveness?

2. Under what circumstances can holding someone responsible for his or her actions be harmful?

3. Who, according to writer Hamilton Beazley, deserves forgiveness?

Style and Structure

1. What is Burson's point? Rewrite her thesis in your own words.

2. What details does Burson use to show the benefits of forgiveness?

3. To what extent is forgiveness the cause or the effect in Burson's essay?

Writing Assignments

1. Burson quotes "energy coach" Jon Gordon, who claims that getting an apology has nothing to do with forgiving. What do you think? Do some wrongs warrant more action on the part of the person who performed the wrong? *Write an essay arguing whether or not receiving an apology is necessary to forgive someone.* Use examples from your own experiences and observations to illustrate your ideas.

2. According to Burson, Everett Worthington says that "it's really unnatural and very difficult to say, " 'I'm going to think about this from the point of view of the other person.' " To what extent is he right? *Write an essay explaining*

how emotionally putting oneself in another person's place is or is not difficult. Use examples from your own experiences and observations to illustrate your ideas.

3. Burson quotes several experts who offer tips for forgiving others. What works for you? *Write an essay explaining the steps you take to forgive someone.* Explain, for example, how you must wait for a few days before starting your forgiveness process to let your anger or frustration cool down. Use examples from your experiences and observations to illustrate your ideas.

Carl M. Cannon

Petty Crime, Outrageous Punishment: Why the Three-Strikes Law Doesn't Work

The White House correspondent for *National Journal,* Carl Cannon has written about national political issues for more than twenty years. He was part of the Pulitzer-winning team that covered the 1989 San Francisco earthquake, and his book *Boy Genius* about the life of Karl Rove was recently reissued. In this essay, Cannon argues that despite a need for punishment of repeat offenders, three-strikes laws go too far.

BEFORE YOU READ

- At what point, if ever, should a person be denied a chance to live in society? What crimes, if any, are so great that they require permanent punishment, such as a life sentence? Explain.

- What role do you think prior crimes should play in determining a person's punishment for a current crime? Explain.

- At what point, if ever, should a person be freed from his or her sentence, even if it's not complete? Explain.

VOCABULARY DEVELOPMENT

Look up the following words in a dictionary and write down their meanings.

heinous (paragraph 1)   recidivists (paragraph 5)
discretion (paragraph 5)   languish (paragraph 9)
abetting (paragraph 18)   aberration (paragraph 20)

pendulum (paragraph 21)   rhetoric (paragraph 26)
rescind (paragraph 27)   vindicate (paragraph 30)

Petty Crime, Outrageous Punishment: Why the Three-Strikes Law Doesn't Work

1   There was nothing honorable about it, nothing particularly heinous, either, when Leandro Andrade, a 37-year-old Army veteran with three kids and a drug habit, walked into a Kmart store in Ontario, California, stuffed five videos into his waistband and tried to leave without paying. Security guards stopped him, but two weeks later, Andrade went to another Kmart and tried to steal four more videos. The police were called, and he was tried and convicted.

2   That was ten years ago, and Leandro Andrade is still behind bars. He figures to be there a lot longer: He came out of the courtroom with a sentence of 50 years to life.

3   If you find that stunningly harsh, you're in good company. The Andrade case went all the way to the U.S. Supreme Court, where Justice David Souter wrote that the punishment was "grossly disproportionate" to the crime.

4   So why is Andrade still serving a virtual life sentence? For the same reason that, across the country, thousands of others are behind bars serving extraordinarily long terms for a variety of low-level, nonviolent crimes. It's the result of well-intentioned anti-crime laws that have gone terribly wrong.

5   Convinced that too many judges were going easy on violent recidivists, Congress enacted federal "mandatory minimum" sentences two decades ago, mainly targeting drug crimes. Throughout the 1990s, state legislatures and Congress kept upping the ante, passing new mandatory minimums, including "three strikes and you're out" laws. The upshot was a mosaic of sentencing statutes that all but eliminated judicial discretion, mercy, or even common sense.

6   Now we are living with the fallout. California came down hard on Andrade because he'd committed a petty theft in 1990 that allowed prosecutors to classify the video thefts as felonies, triggering the three-strikes law.

7   The videos that Andrade stole were kids' movies, such as *Casper* and *Snow White*—Christmas presents, he said, for nieces and nephews. A presentence report theorized he was swiping the videos to feed a heroin habit. Their retail value: $84.70 for the first batch and $68.84 for the second.

8   When Andrade's case went before the Supreme Court, a bare majority upheld his sentence. But rather than try to defend the three-strikes law, the opinion merely said the Court should not function as a super-legislature.

9   Andrade will languish in prison, then, serving a much longer state sentence for his nonviolent crimes than most first offenders or even second-timers convicted of sexual assault or manslaughter.

10   Politicians saw harsh sentences as one way to satisfy voters fed up with the rising crime rates of the '70s and '80s, and the violence associated with crack cocaine and other drugs. And most would agree that strict sentencing laws have played a key role in lowering the crime rate for violent and property crimes.

11   Last June, Florida Governor Jeb Bush celebrated his state's thirteenth straight year of declining crime rates, thanks in part to tough sentencing statutes he enacted. "If violent habitual offenders are in prison," Bush said, "they're not going to be committing crimes on innocent people."

12   California, in particular, has seen a stark drop in crime since passing its toughest-in-the-nation three-strikes law more than ten years ago. Mike Reynolds, who pushed for the legislation after his 18-year-old daughter was murdered by two career criminals, says that under three-strikes, "those who can get their lives turned around, will. Those who can't have two choices— leave California or go to prison. The one thing we cannot allow is another victim to be part of their criminal therapy."

13   But putting thousands behind bars comes at a price—a cool $750 million in California alone. That's the annual cost to the state of incarcerating the nonviolent offenders sentenced under three-strikes. Add up all the years these inmates will serve on average and, according to the Justice Policy Institute, California's taxpayers will eventually shell out more than $6 billion. For a state with a battered economy, that's a pile of money to spend on sweeping up petty crooks.

14   The law also falls hardest on minorities. African Americans are imprisoned under three-strikes at ten times the rate of whites, and Latinos at nearly double the white rate. While crime rates are higher for these minorities than for whites, the incarceration gap is disproportionately wide under three-strikes largely because of drug-related convictions.

15   Arkansas Governor Mike Huckabee is blunt when it comes to the three-strikes approach to justice: "It's the dumbest piece of public-policy legislation in a long time. We don't have a massive crime problem; we have a massive drug problem. And you don't treat that by locking drug addicts up. We're putting away people we're mad at, instead of the people we're afraid of."

16   There are some telling figures. In 1985 about 750,000 Americans were incarcerated on a variety of pending charges and convictions in federal and state prisons and local jails. The number of inmates is now about 2.1 million, of which some 440,000 were convicted on drug charges. A significant portion of the rest are there because drug addiction led them to rob and steal.

17   Early on there were signs that mandatory minimum laws—especially three-strikes statutes—had gone too far. Just a few months after Washington state passed the nation's first three-strikes law in 1993, a 29-year-old named Paul Rivers was sentenced to life for stealing $337 from an espresso

stand. Rivers had pretended he had a gun in his pocket, and the theft came after earlier convictions for second-degree robbery and assault. A prison term was appropriate. But life behind bars, without the possibility of parole? If Rivers had been packing a gun—and shot the espresso stand owner—he wouldn't have gotten any more time.

18   Just a few weeks after California's three-strikes law took effect, Brian A. Smith, a 30-year-old recovering crack addict, was charged with aiding and abetting two female shoplifters who took bed sheets from Robinsons-May department store in Los Cerritos Shopping Center. Smith got 25 years to life.

19   As a younger man, his first two strikes were for unarmed robbery and for burglarizing an unoccupied residence. Was Brian Smith really the kind of criminal whom California voters had in mind when they approved their three-strikes measure? Proponents sold the measure by saying it would keep murderers, rapists and child molesters behind bars where they belong. Instead, the law locked Smith away for his petty crime until at least 2020, and probably longer—at a cost to the state of more than $750,000.

20   His case is not an aberration. By the end of last year, 2,344 of the 7,574 three-strikers in the state's penal system got their third strike for a property offense. Scott Benscoter struck out after stealing a pair of running shoes, and is serving 25 years to life. His prior offenses were for residential burglaries that, according to the public defender's office, did not involve violence. Gregory Taylor, a homeless man in Los Angeles, was trying to jimmy a screen open to get into the kitchen of a church where he had previously been given food. But he had two prior offenses from more than a decade before: one for snatching a purse and the other for attempted robbery without a weapon. He's also doing 25 years to life.

21   One reason the pendulum has swung so far is that politicians love to get behind popular slogans, even if they lead to bad social policy.

22   Few California lawmakers, for example, could resist the "use a gun, go to prison" law, a concept so catchy that it swept the nation, and is now codified in one form or another in many state statutes and in federal law. It began as a sensible idea: Make our streets safer by discouraging drug dealers and the like from packing guns during their crimes. But the law needs to be more flexible than some rigid slogan. Ask Monica Clyburn. You can't really, because she's been in prison these past ten years. Her crime? Well, that's hard to figure out.

23   A Florida welfare mom, Clyburn accompanied her boyfriend to a pawnshop to sell his .22-caliber pistol. She provided her ID because her boyfriend didn't bring his own, and the couple got $30 for the gun. But Clyburn had a previous criminal record for minor drug charges, and when federal authorities ran a routine check of the pawnshop's records, they produced a "hit"—a felon in possession of a firearm. That's automatically 15 years in federal prison, which is exactly what Clyburn got. "I never even held the gun," she noted in an interview from prison.

24   No one is more appalled than H. Jay Stevens, the former federal public defender for the middle district of Florida. "Everyone I've described this case to says, 'This can't have happened.' [But] it's happening five days a week all over this country."

25   Several years ago, a prominent Congressman, Rep. Dan Rostenkowski of Illinois, was sent to prison on mail-fraud charges. It was only then that he learned what he'd been voting for all those years when anticrime legislation came up and he cast the safe "aye" vote. Rostenkowski told of being stunned at how many young, low-level drug offenders were doing 15- and 20-year stretches in federal prison.

26   "The waste of these lives is a loss to the entire community," Rostenkowski said. "I was swept along by the rhetoric about getting tough on crime. Frankly, I lacked both expertise and perspective on these issues."

27   Former Michigan Governor William G. Milliken signed into law his state's mandatory minimums for drug cases, but after leaving office he lobbied the state legislature to rescind them. "I have since come to realize that the provisions of the law have led to terrible injustices." Milliken wrote in 2002. Soon after, Gov. John Engler signed legislation doing away with most of Michigan's mandatory sentences.

28   On the federal level, judges have been expressing their anger with Congress for preventing them from exercising discretion and mercy. U.S. District Court Judge John S. Martin, Jr., appointed by the first President Bush, announced his retirement from the bench rather than remain part of "a sentencing system that is unnecessarily cruel and rigid."

29   While the U.S. Supreme Court has yet to strike down mandatory minimums, one justice at least has signaled his opposition to them. Justice Anthony M. Kennedy said in a speech at the 2003 American Bar Association meeting that he accepted neither the "necessity" nor "wisdom" of mandatory minimums.

30   "One day in prison is longer than almost any day you and I have had to endure," Justice Kennedy told the nation's lawyers. "When the door is locked against the prisoner, we do not think about what is behind it. To be sure, the prisoner must be punished to vindicate the law, to acknowledge the suffering of the victim, and to deter future crimes. Still, the prisoner is a person. Still, he or she is part of the family of humankind."

POST-READING EXERCISES

1. Which word on the Vocabulary Development list means "to take away or remove"?

   a. abetting   b. rescind

   c. vindicate   d. languish

2. In reaction to what did Congress enact federal "mandatory minimum" sentences?

    a. Wacky voters   b. Easy judges

    c. Repeat offenders   d. Corrupt politicians

3. Which of the following has *not* been largely eliminated by three-strikes legislation?

    a. Judicial discretion   b. Judicial mercy

    c. Judicial plea bargaining   d. Judicial common sense

4. What crimes did politicians specifically try to control with three-strikes legislation?

    a. Murders   b. Sexual assaults

    c. Thefts   d. Drug crimes

5. Who is hit hardest by three-strikes legislation?

    a. Men between the ages of 18 and 35

    b. Minorities

    c. Men who committed crimes as adolescents

    d. Gang members

6. What is one definition of the word *languish?*

    a. To relax   b. To lose weight

    c. To be or become feeble or weak d. To enjoy immensely

7. Approximately how much does it cost to keep someone in prison for life?

    a. $250,000   b. $500,000

    c. $750,000   d. $1,000,000

8. According to Cannon, what is one reason that legislation for harsh sentences passed?

    a. Catchy slogans   b. The influence of the media

    c. The power of lobbyists   d. Slick lawyers

9. Which word on the Vocabulary Development list means "to free from allegation or blame"?

    a. vindicate   b. heinous

    c. aberration   d. rhetoric

10. Of what family does Supreme Court Justice Anthony Kennedy say that prisoners are part?

    a. The family of our forefathers

    b. The family of humankind

    c. The family of the earth

    d. The family of all people

Content

1. What type of crime are nearly one-third of California's three-strikers in prison for?
2. What has happened to California's crime rate since passing the three-strikes law?
3. What two choices do people facing a "strike-out" in California face?

Style and Structure

1. What is Cannon's point? Rewrite the thesis in your own words.
2. What types of details does Cannon use to illustrate his thesis?
3. What function does the opening example serve?

Writing Assignments

1. Cannon argues that three-strikes punishment rarely fits the crime. What crimes, if any, do you think should be punished by three-strikes legislation? *Write an essay in which you argue that some crimes should be punished by three-strikes legislation.* Use examples from the essay and from your own experience to illustrate your ideas.
2. Cannon quotes Supreme Court Justice Anthony M. Kennedy, who says that one reason people favor harsh punishment is to "acknowledge the suffering" of crime victims. Does punishing the perpetrator ease a victim's pain? *Write an essay explaining how punishing the perpetrator of a crime does or does not ease the suffering of victims or their families.* You may want to consult other sources for this assignment, but do cite from Cannon's essay and use examples from your own experiences and observations to illustrate your ideas.
3. Educators nationwide worry about plagiarism. How do you think plagiarism should be punished? *Write an essay arguing that plagiarism—passing off someone else's work or ideas as your own—should be punished harshly.* You may limit your discussion to one specific level of education—such as college—or you may include different levels. You may want to consult other resources to learn about your topic, but use examples from your own experiences and observations to illustrate your ideas.

Adam Goodheart

How to Paint a Fresco

A member of the editorial board of *The American Scholar,* and a founding editor of the magazine *Civilization,* Adam Goodheart has published essays in *The Atlantic*

Monthly, The *New York Times,* and *Outside* magazine and on *Salon.com.* In "How to Paint a Fresco," he explores the trials and challenges of classical fresco painting as if they were being faced by Michelangelo and other greats today.

BEFORE YOU READ

- What do you know or imagine about the process of creating any kind of painting?
- In what types of activities is careful preparation most important? Explain.
- What are some consequences of sloppy or inadequate preparation? Explain.

VOCABULARY DEVELOPMENT

Look up the following words in a dictionary and write down their meanings.

fresco (paragraph 1)   palazzo (paragraph 1)

papal (paragraph 1)   ducal (paragraph 1)

injurious (paragraph 3)   pigments (paragraph 5)

prolong (paragraph 5)   perils (paragraph 7)

depicted (paragraph 7)   drudgery (paragraph 8)

immortality (paragraph 8)

How to Paint a Fresco

1 Although it must be painted in a very short time, a fresco will last a very long time—that is its great advantage. Many of the masterpieces of the golden age of fresco (from the 14th through the 18th centuries) are as brilliant now as when they were first painted. If you want to fresco a cathedral or palazzo today, you may have a few problems—papal and ducal commissions are scarcer than they once were, and the great Renaissance masters are no longer accepting applications for apprenticeships. Fortunately, a few of their trade secrets have come down to us through the ages.

2 **Equipment**
   Lime
   Sand
   Water
   A trowel
   Paper
   A needle

A small bag of charcoal dust
The bristles of a white hog
The hair of bears, sables, and martens
The quills of vultures, geese, hens, and doves
Ocher, burnt grapevines, lapis lazuli
Egg yolks
Goat's milk

3   **1. Preparing the wall.** Cennino Cennini, a Tuscan master, advised pupils in 1437 to "begin by decking yourselves with this attire: Enthusiasm, Reverence, Obedience, and Constancy." You'd do better to deck yourself with some old clothes, though, since the first stage of the process is quite messy. Soak the wall thoroughly and coat it with coarse plaster, two parts sand to one part lime, leaving the surface uneven. (Andrea Pozzo, a 17th-century expert, recommended hiring a professional mason to do this, since "the lime makes a foul odor, which is injurious to the head.")

4   **2. Tracing your design.** You should already have extensive drawings for your fresco—these will be much sought by scholars and collectors in centuries to come. Make a full-size sketch, on sturdy paper, of a section of the fresco that you can paint in a day. Then go over the drawing with a needle, pricking holes along every line. Lay a coat of fine plaster on a section of the wall corresponding to the location, size, and shape of the sketch, and press the sketch against the plaster. Fill a loosely woven bag with charcoal dust and strike it lightly all over the surface of the paper. Now peel the sketch off. Your design will be outlined in black dots on the wet plaster, giving you a guide for the day's work.

5   **3. Painting.** Time is of the essence: You must paint the plaster while it is wet, so that the pigments bind chemically with the lime. That gives you about six hours, although some painters had tricks to prolong drying. (Piero della Francesca packed the plaster with wet rags; problem was, this left indentations that are still visible after 500 years.) Use top-quality brushes. One 17th-century Flemish master recommended those made of "fish hair" (he probably meant seal fur), but most painters made brushes from bear, marten, or sable hairs inserted in hollow quills. Cennini suggested the bristles of a white hog for the coarser work. As for paints, every artist had his own favorite recipes, but all agreed that mineral pigments such as ocher or ground stone mixed with water were best. Avoid white lead. One 14th-century Umbrian used it to paint a nursing infant; the lime turned the white black and the milky babe into a "devilish changeling." A few pigments, such as dark blue azurite (often used for the Virgin Mary's mantle), must be mixed with egg yolk or goat's milk and added after the fresco is dry. Such colors will prove less durable.

6   Money is a consideration in choosing materials. When Michelangelo frescoed the Sistine ceiling, expenses came out of his fee, so he used cheap

blue smalt for the sky. Twenty years later, when he did the *Last Judgment,* Michelangelo used semiprecious lapis lazuli for blue, since the pope was paying for the paint. (He made up for it by using burnt grapevines for black.)

7   **4. Casualties of style.** Realism, while a worthy goal, has its perils. Spinello Aretino, a 14th-century Tuscan, is said to have painted a fresco that depicted Lucifer with such hideous accuracy that the Evil One himself came to the artist in a dream and demanded an explanation. Spinello went half-mad with fear and died shortly thereafter. On the other hand, a Florentine woodcut from 1500 depicts a painter who has portrayed the Virgin so skillfully that when he falls off the scaffold, she reaches out of the fresco and saves him.

Warning

8   Frescoing ceilings can be rough on your back. While working on the Sistine Chapel, Michelangelo wrote a poem complaining: "I've already grown a goiter at this drudgery . . . With my beard toward heaven . . . I am bent like a bow." Don't be discouraged, though. Bad posture is a small price to pay for immortality.

POST-READING EXERCISES

1. Which word on the Vocabulary Development list means "dull, irksome, and fatiguing work"?

    a. pigments   b. perils

    c. drudgery   d. immortality

2. What is the great advantage of frescoes?

    a. They are easy to paint.

    b. They last a very long time.

    c. They look much harder to do than they are.

    d. They are beautiful.

3. Which of the following is *not* a supply or piece of equipment necessary to paint frescoes?

    a. Lime   b. The bristles of a white hog

    c. Goat's milk   d. A Jersey cow's udder

4. How should one dress to paint a fresco?

    a. In old clothes   b. In comfortable clothes

    c. In layered clothing   d. In soft-soled shoes

5. What is one definition of the word *depict*?

    a. To represent by or as if by a picture

    b. To rhyme in verse

    c. To speak in verse

    d. To communicate visually

6. What should you already have before starting the fresco?

    a. Mixed paints thoroughly

    b. Purchased perfectly fluffed brushes

    c. Taken extensive notes about how to proceed

    d. Made extensive drawings

7. Why is time "of the essence"?

    a. Because no one wants to see an old fresco

    b. Because light and air can change the consistency and color of the paint

    c. Because the plaster must be wet so that the pigments bind with the lime

    d. Because slow painters earn fewer commissions

8. What does Goodheart say is "a consideration" in choosing materials?

    a. Time   b. Money

    c. Quality   d. Quantity

9. Which word on the Vocabulary Development list means "exposure to the risk of being injured, destroyed, or lost"?

    a. papal   b. ducal

    c. perils   d. palazzo

10. What physical risk does a painter run in painting a fresco?

    a. Dizziness   b. Back injury

    c. Dehydration   d. Carpal tunnel syndrome

Content

1. What does Goodheart say about many of the masterpieces of the golden age of fresco?

2. What does Goodheart say about the first step in painting a fresco?

3. What ingredients do artists agree make the best paints?

Style and Structure

1. What is Goodheart's point? Where, if at all, is it located in the essay? Rewrite his thesis in your own words.

2. How important is keeping the steps for painting a fresco in order? Explain.

3. What sources does Goodheard consult to establish his own credibility?

Writing Assignments

1. Goodheart gives the steps for painting a fresco, explaining the order and importance of each step. In what processes is order important in your life?

Write an essay explaining a process that necessarily follows a specific order. Explain, for instance, how stacking kindling and small sticks *before* lighting them is important in building a fire. Use examples from your own experiences and observations to illustrate your ideas.

2. Goodheart writes, "Money is a consideration in choosing materials" for painting a fresco. To what extent do you think money and art are connected? For instance, do you think that having more money means that people will have more art? *Write an essay explaining what you think the connection is between art and money.* Consider the role that money plays in developing art—painting, dance, or music lessons, for instance—and in acquiring it (can people without money enjoy art as much as people with money, for example?). Use examples from your own experiences and observations to illustrate your ideas.

3. Goodheart claims that realism is "a worthy goal." What are some other "worthy goals" of art? Entertainment? Protest? Inspiration? *Write an essay in which you explain what you think art should* do. For instance, if you think the best music makes people feel pain or joy, give examples of such music. Use specific examples from different art forms—paintings, poetry, music, or dance, for instance—to illustrate your ideas.

Joe Queenan

How to Tell a Joke

A former editor at *Forbes* and *Spy,* Joe Queenan has published stories in prominent magazines such as the *New Republic, Time, Newsweek,* and *Rolling Stone,* as well as essays and articles in the *Wall Street Journal* and other publications. Additionally, he has published four books and has appeared on numerous television and radio programs. In "How to Tell a Joke," Queenan offers succinct advice for getting the most from every joke.

BEFORE YOU READ

- What skills or qualities are necessary for telling a good joke? Why?
- What kills humor fastest for you? Explain.
- Who would you say is a good well-known joke teller? Explain.

VOCABULARY DEVELOPMENT

Look up the following words in a dictionary and write down their meanings.

rambling (paragraph 1)   vainly (paragraph 3)

conclave (paragraph 4)

intonations (paragraph 5)

coincidence (paragraph 10)

improvise (paragraph 12)

halfhearted (paragraph 16)

chink (paragraph 4)

stingy (paragraph 6)

kinship (paragraph 11)

marionette (paragraph 12)

How to Tell a Joke

1   Twelve years ago, I was given a magazine assignment to do a ten-minute stand-up comedy routine at New York's Improv. The results were not pretty. An effective storyteller, but a stranger to the upstanding comic arts, I devised a routine that consisted of rambling, complicated gags that made too many demands on the audience's attention. One joke involved George Armstrong Custer's refusing to share a peace pipe because he feared the effect of secondary smoke on Sioux papooses. Nobody got it.

2   The day after the story was published, Jay Leno, whose advice I had vainly sought before doing my routine, called me from an airport. A generous man, he said that I had made the classic mistake of the amateur by frantically muddying the waters. His simple advice: Keep it simple.

3   "If you just do a joke about the funny noise that potato chips make when you bite into them, you'll get more laughs. Jokes work best when they're easy to understand," Leno explained.

4   Years and years later, I am still not a good joke teller. I cannot remember jokes, I do not deliver jokes well, and I could not write a good joke if you paid me. I once addressed a conclave consisting of 400 repo men, repo wives and repo children without getting a single laugh. Luckily, I didn't have a car parked outside. Sensing that this was a serious chink in my humorist's armor, I recently began consulting with people who are good joke tellers. This is what I learned:

5   *Never tell a joke unless you've actually heard it told before.* So says Bill Scheft, head monologue writer for David Letterman. "This is the only way to know what part of the joke works best, the only way to pick up the right pauses and intonations."

6   For example: Jack Benny, who was supposed to be stingy beyond belief, famously got his biggest laugh when a holdup man said, "Your money or your life!" and Benny would pause for 45 seconds, and then say, "I'm thinking about it."

7   Other tips: *Only tell jokes in front of an audience that is already inclined to be on your side.* Or as Scheft puts it: "Don't think of a joke as an icebreaker: the ice already has to be broken and in the glass."

8   *Saturday Night Live* alumna Julia Sweeney makes another good point about the importance of not forcing things. *"Avoid announcing that the joke is going to be hysterical,"* says Sweeney. "And don't look people in the eye

afterward expecting them to be really amused. Besides that, I think it's a good idea to back off the punch line, to not oversell it. Just kind of throw it away."

9   *If you're going to tell a number of jokes, don't go with your best one first.* This is a great piece of advice that actually comes from a gifted amateur, Julian Mostel, nephew of legendary funnyman Zero Mostel. To be funny, he believes that you need to hold some material in reserve, because joke telling is a competitive art.

10   "If the waiter tells a joke, I feel that I have to top it," Mostel explains. Presumably, nobody wants to be outclassed by an annoying guy with a ponytail whose name is Todd and who will be your waiter for the evening. This is an interesting coincidence because while I have never met a funny waiter, I am the kind of person who feels that if the waiter mispronounces the house special in French, I have to mispronounce the dessert in Italian.

11   *Match your material to your audience.* "Jokes help develop kinship and affection with strangers," says my sister Eileen, one of the two best joke tellers I know. "I work in health care and I always tell this story about getting lost in a small town and asking a cop for directions and being told, 'Make a right and keep going until you get to the corner where the Laundromat used to be until it burned down.' And the punch line is: Following those directions is like trying to understand Medicare."

12   *Know the joke by heart.* Says Scheft: "Don't get halfway through the joke and start to improvise." Like, don't say, "Oh, I forgot, the guy was six-foot-seven and dressed as a marionette."

13   Other tips of a more general nature: *Don't overlook the value of a great one-liner.* They're easier to remember and can get you just as far as a joke can. For instance: "Did you hear the one about the two Frenchmen trapped on a desert island and the one offered the other a government job?"

14   Also remember: *Repeating the punch line only works if you are Jay Leno.* Explaining your joke works only if you are Johnny Carson, who loved to pretend that his material wasn't working.

15   Perhaps the most valuable piece of advice comes from Henny Youngman, the best joke teller I ever met. He told me: *Keep your jokes short, and keep them coming.* One day 20 years ago, I spent an hour and a half trying to interview him at the Friars Club. But you couldn't actually interview Youngman, because he could only speak in jokes. Trying to get him to talk like a normal person was like trying to get an Eskimo toddler to speak Farsi. So when I asked him, "Where did you grow up?" he replied, "Overseas. Like the two little ladies sitting in a room in Krakow. And the one says, 'You see what's going on in Russia?' And the other says, 'No, I live in the back; I don't see nothing.' "

16   "When you're telling a joke, you have to build up energy," says Scheft, who's been writing for Letterman now for 12 years. "You have to show peo-

ple that you're committed, that you're willing to work to make this joke suc-ceed." Beginners often make the classic mistake of telling a joke in a half-hearted way, as if it were homework. Here we come to a key point: *Don't tell a joke unless you are actually funny.* Even if you are funny, Scheft feels that it helps to "legitimize" a joke by saying that somebody famous told it to you, as in, "I was with the Pope the other day, and he passed this one along . . . "

17   When I lunched with Henny Youngman, I asked him what he thought was the single most important element in telling jokes. "Know a lot of them," he said. "Milton Berle knows a million jokes. If you knew a million jokes, you'd be funny."

18   Yes, but if I knew a million jokes, I'd have enough money to get out of the humor business.

POST-READING EXERCISES

1. Which word on the Vocabulary Development list means "a gathering of a group or association"?

    a. marionette   b. chink

    c. coincidence   d. conclave

2. What did Queenan use ineffectively in his own stand-up performance?

    a. Rambling, complicated gags

    b. Large, convoluted images

    c. Unkind, racist comments

    d. Quiet, accented speech

3. What piece of advice did comedian Jay Leno give Queenan?

    a. "Be yourself."   b. "Keep it simple."

    c. "Remember the Alamo."   d. "Don't kiss and tell."

4. Why is hearing a joke important before telling it?

    a. To make sure people can understand it

    b. To make sure you understand it

    c. To pick up the right pauses and intonations

    d. To focus on the essence of the joke

5. What is one definition of the word *coincidence?*

    a. The occurrence of seemingly connected events that happen at the same time by accident

    b. The occurrence of two or more major events in history

    c. The first meeting between two people

    d. The first impression two people make on each other

6. What does comedian Julia Sweeney say to avoid?

    a. Pretending a joke is not funny

    b. Pretending to forget a joke in mid-telling

    c. Announcing that a joke is going to be hysterical

    d. Announcing that your joke comes from another country

7. Why does Julian Mostel say not to start with your best joke?

    a. Because people need to warm up to the joke teller

    b. Because later jokes are only as good as the first one

    c. Because people may stop listening to you

    d. Because joke telling is a competitive art

8. What is the most valuable piece of advice Queenan learns?

    a. Avoid personal humor.   b. Keep it short.

    c. Stick to the point.   d. Be specific.

9. Which word on the Vocabulary Development list means "not generous or liberal"?

    a. stingy   b. kinship

    c. improvise   d. marionette

10. What is one way to "legitimize" a joke?

    a. By saying everyone who has ever heard it laughed

    b. By saying you made it up

    c. By saying someone famous told it to you

    d. By saying that telling it should be illegal

Content

1. What motivates the writer to learn about joke telling?

2. What function can jokes serve with strangers?

3. What does Henny Youngman say is the single most important element in telling jokes?

Style and Structure

1. What is Queenan's point? Rewrite his thesis in your own words.

2. To what extent is Queenan's process one that must be followed in a certain order? Explain.

3. What sources does Queenan consult to establish his own credibility?

Writing Assignments

1. Queenan passes on one person's advice not to tell a joke "unless you are actually funny." What makes a person funny? *Write an essay in which you*

explain what qualities, skills, or characteristics make a person funny. Use specific examples from people you know or have seen being funny.

2. Queenan writes that not being able to tell a joke is "a serious chink in [his] humorist's armor." How important is humor in your life? *Write an essay arguing that humor is or is not important in a specific area of your life.* Explain, for instance, how being able to make jokes when you're dealing with a disgruntled customer at work makes your job easier. Use examples from your own experiences and observations to illustrate your ideas.

3. Queenan quotes amateur humorist Julian Mostel, who says that "joke telling is a competitive art." To what extent is humor competitive? *Write an essay explaining how humor is or is not competitive.* Discuss, for example, how people "one-up" each other in social situations, or how humor can bring people together rather than divide them. Use examples from your own observations and experiences to illustrate your ideas.

Diane Ravitch

You Can't Say That

A research professor of education at New York University, Diane Ravitch has authored numerous education-oriented books, including *The Language Police: How Pressure Groups Restrict What Students Learn.* In "You Can't Say That," Ravitch argues that the cleansing of our language to avoid offense results in the homogenization of people and their forms of expression.

BEFORE YOU READ

- What kinds of language or stereotypes are most likely to offend you? Why? Explain.
- To what extent do you monitor your own language, depending on whom you speak with? Explain.
- How closely should people watch their language—both written and spoken? To what extent should some people watch their language more than others? Explain.

VOCABULARY DEVELOPMENT

Look up the following words in a dictionary and write down their meanings.

deference (paragraph 4)   stupefied (paragraph 5)

punctiliously (paragraph 6)   bowdlerizing (paragraph 6)
zeal (paragraph 7)   debacle (paragraph 8)
loom (paragraph 10)   obliterate (paragraph 10)
taboo (paragraph 11)   rousted (paragraph 13)

You Can't Say That

1   To judge by the magazines we read, the programs we watch or the music lyrics we hear, it would seem that almost anything goes, these days, when it comes to verbal expression. But that is not quite true.

2   In my book *The Language Police,* I gathered a list of more than 500 words that are routinely deleted from textbooks and tests by "bias review committees" employed by publishing companies, state education departments and the federal government. Among the forbidden words are "landlord," "cowboy," "brotherhood," "yacht," "cult" and "primitive." Such words are deleted because they are offensive to various groups—feminists, religious conservatives, multiculturalists and ethnic activists, to name a few.

3   I invited readers of the book to send me examples of language policing, and they did, by the score. A bias review committee for the state test in New Jersey rejected a short story by Langston Hughes because he used the words "Negro" and "colored person." Michigan bans a long list of topics from its state tests, including terrorism, evolution, aliens and flying saucers (which might imply evolution).

4   A textbook writer sent me the guidelines used by the Harcourt/ Steck/Vaughn company to remove photographs that might give offense. Editors must delete, the guidelines said, pictures of women with big hair or sleeveless blouses and men with dreadlocks or medallions. Photographs must not portray the soles of shoes or anyone eating with the left hand (both in deference to Muslim culture). To avoid giving offense to those who cannot afford a home computer, no one may be shown owning a home computer. To avoid offending those with strong but differing religious views, decorations for religious holidays must never appear in the background.

5   A college professor informed me that a new textbook in human development includes the following statement: "As a folksinger once sang, how many roads must an individual walk down before you can call them an adult." The professor was stupefied that someone had made the line gender-neutral and ungrammatical by rewriting Bob Dylan's folk song "Blowin' in the Wind," which had simply asked: "How many roads must a man walk down before you call him a man?"

6   While writing *The Language Police,* I could not figure out why New York State had gone so far beyond other states in punctiliously carving out almost all references to race, gender, age and ethnicity, including even weight and height. In June 2002, the state was mightily embarrassed when

reports appeared about its routine bowdlerizing on its exams of writers such as Franz Kafka and Isaac Bashevis Singer.

7   The solution to the puzzle was recently provided by Candace DeRussy, a trustee of the State University of New York. Ms. DeRussy read *The Language Police,* and she too wondered how the New York State Education Department had come to censor its regents exams with such zeal. She asked the department to explain how it decided which words to delete and how it trained its bias and sensitivity reviewers.

8   At one point, state officials said that since June 2002 (the time of the debacle) they have adhered to only one standard: "Test developers should strive to identify and eliminate language, symbols, words, phrases, and content that are generally regarded as offensive by members of racial, ethnic, gender, or other groups, except when judged to be necessary for adequate representation of the domain." Ms. DeRussy guessed (correctly) that the state was holding back the specific instructions that had emboldened the bowdlerizers. She decided to use the state's freedom-of-information law to find out more. Months later, a state official sent her the training materials for the bias and sensitivity reviewers, which included a list of words and phrases and a rationale for language policing.

9   So here is how New York made itself an international joke. The state's guidelines to language sensitivity, citing Rosalie Maggio's *The Bias-Free Wordfinder,* says: "We may not always understand why a certain word hurts. We don't have to. It is enough that someone says, 'That language doesn't respect me.' " That is, if any word or phrase is likely to give anyone offense, no matter how far-fetched, it should be deleted.

10   Next the state asked: "Is it necessary to make reference to a person's age, ancestry, disability, ethnicity, nationality, physical appearance, race, religion, sex, sexuality?" Since the answer is frequently no, nearly all references to such characteristics are eliminated. Because these matters loom large in history and literature—and because they help us to understand character, life circumstances and motives—their silent removal is bound to weaken or obliterate the reader's understanding.

11   Like every other governmental agency concerned with testing, the New York State Education Department devised its own list of taboo words. There are the usual ones that have offended feminists for a generation, like "fireman," "authoress," "handyman" and "hostess." New York exercised its leadership by discovering bias in such words as "addict" (replace with "individual with a drug addiction"); "alumna, alumnae, alumni, alumnus" (replace with "graduate or graduates"); "American" (replace with "citizen of the United States or North America"); "cancer patient" (replace with "a patient with cancer"); "city fathers" (replace with "city leaders").

12   Meanwhile, the word "elderly" should be replaced by "older adult" or "older person," if it is absolutely necessary to mention age at all. "Gentleman's agreement" must be dropped in favor of an "informal agreement."

"Ghetto" should be avoided; instead describe the social and economic circumstances of the neighborhood. "Grandfather clause" is helplessly sexist;
"retroactive coverage" is preferred instead. The term "illegal alien" must be
replaced by "undocumented worker."

13   Certain words are unacceptable under any circumstances. For example,
it is wrong to describe anyone as "illegitimate." Another word to be avoided
is "illiterate." Instead, specify whether an individual is unable to read or
write, or both. Similarly, any word that contains the three offensive letters
"m-a-n" as a prefix or a suffix must be rousted out of the language. Words
like "man-hours," "manpower," "mankind" and "manmade" are regularly
deleted. Even "penmanship," where the guilty three letters are in the middle of the word, is out.

14   New York identified as biased such male-based words as "masterpiece"
and "mastery." Among the other words singled out for extinction were *white
collar, blue collar, pink collar, teenager, senior citizen, third world, uncivilized,
underprivileged, unmarried, widow* or *widower,* and yes *man.* The goal, naturally, is to remove words that identify people by their gender, age, race,
social position or marital status.

15   Thus the great irony of bias and sensitivity reviewing. It began with the
hope of encouraging diversity, ensuring that our educational materials
would include people of different experiences and social backgrounds. It
has evolved into a bureaucratic system that removes all evidence of diversity and reduces everyone to interchangeable beings whose differences we
must not learn about—making nonsense of literature and history along the
way.

POST-READING EXERCISES

1. Which word on the Vocabulary Development list means "to omit or modify
   parts considered vulgar"?

   a. bowdlerizing   b. obliterate

   c. rousted   d. loom

2. Why are words sometimes deleted from textbooks and tests?

   a. Because they are out of date

   b. Because they are offensive

   c. Because they are poor examples of the English language

   d. Because the instructors who use the books are picky

3. Which of the following is *not* a group that bias review committees consider
   in editing books?

   a. Feminists   b. Religious conservatives

   c. Multiculturalists   d. Misogynists

4. How was a line in Bob Dylan's song "Blowin' in the Wind" rewritten?
   - a. It was made grammatically correct.
   - b. It was made religiously specific to Christianity.
   - c. It was made gender-neutral.
   - d. It was made to include children as well as adults.

5. According to Rosalie Maggio's work *The Bias-Free Wordfinder,* which of the following is true?
   - a. We must always understand why a word or term is offensive.
   - b. We may not always understand why a certain word hurts.
   - c. We will never understand why men and women offend each other.
   - d. We will never understand why racist language is still published.

6. What is one definition of the word *taboo?*
   - a. Banned on grounds of morality or taste
   - b. Approved heartily
   - c. Disapproved based on prior review
   - d. Accepted as part of a collection

7. Which of the following terms is *not* mentioned as being offensive, according to bias review committees?
   - a. Addict
   - b. Criminal
   - c. Cancer patient
   - d. Fireman

8. Which of the following terms is considered offensive, according to bias review committees?
   - a. Shipmate
   - b. Parent-teacher conference
   - c. Worker
   - d. Penmanship

9. Which word on the Vocabulary Development list means "marked by or concerned about precise accordance with the details of codes or conventions"?
   - a. stupified
   - b. zeal
   - c. punctiliously
   - d. debacle

10. What, according to Ravitch, has bias and sensitivity reviewing become?
   - a. A practice to take pride in
   - b. An effective procedure
   - c. A bureaucratic system
   - d. A negative reminder

Content

1. What are some reasons groups give for eliminating certain language?
2. What are some types of photographs eliminated?
3. What does Ravitch say the "great irony" of bias and sensitivity reviewing?

Style and Structure

1. What is Ravitch's point? Rewrite the thesis in your own words.
2. What types of details does Ravitch use to illustrate her thesis?
3. What is the writer's attitude toward her subject? How can you tell?

Writing Assignments

1. Ravitch opens her essay saying, "To judge by the magazines we read, the programs we watch or the music lyrics we hear, it would seem that almost anything goes, these days, when it comes to verbal expression." What do you think? *Write an essay in which you explain how "almost anything" is acceptable in verbal (either spoken or written) expression.* Use examples from the essay and your own experience and observations—from magazines, television, radio, or movies—to illustrate your ideas.

2. Ravitch sums up sensitivity reviewing philosophy in saying, "if any word or phrase is likely to give anyone offense, no matter how far-fetched, it should be deleted." Should it? *Write an essay agreeing or disagreeing with the idea that any potentially offensive language in any situation should be deleted.* Cite examples from Ravitch's essay and your own experiences and observations to illustrate your ideas.

3. Ravitch writes that "age, ancestry, disability, ethnicity, nationality, physical appearance, race, religion, sex, [and] sexuality . . . help us to understand character." To what extent is she right? *Write an essay explaining how knowing details about a person—such as his or her gender, race, or religion—does or does not help to understand that person's character.* For instance, knowing that a person grew up in a certain area of town might help someone understand that person's attitude —either for or against—toward law enforcement. Use examples from your experiences and observations to illustrate your ideas.

Credits

Literary Credits

Maya Angelou, from *Wouldn't Take Nothing for My Journey Now*. Copyright © 1993 by Maya Angelou. Used by permission of Random House, Inc.

Maya Angelou, from *I Know Why the Caged Bird Sings*. Copyright © 1969 and renewed 1997 by Maya Angelou. Used by permission of Random House.

Elizabeth Austin, "Saving the Home from Martha Stewart." Reprinted with permission from *The Washington Monthly*, December 1999. Copyright © 1999 by Washington Monthly Publishing, LLC, 1319 F St. NW, Suite 710, Washington, DC 20004. (202)393-5155. www.washingtonmonthly.com

Mary Battiata, from "Whose Life Is It, Anyway?" *The Washington Post Magazine*, August 29, 2004. Copyright © 2004, The Washington Post. Excerpted with permission.

Pat Burson, "A Reason to Forgive, How Letting Go of Anger Is As Good for You As It Can Be for One Who's Hurt You," *Newsday*, August 29, 2005. Copyright © 2005 Newsday, Inc. Reprinted by permission.

Carl M. Cannon, "Petty Crime, Outrageous Punishment." Reprinted with permission from the October 2005 *Reader's Digest*. Copyright © 2005 by The Reader's Digest Assn., Inc.

Richard Conniff, "So Tiny, So Sweet . . . So Mean." Originally appeared in *Smithsonian*, September 2000. Reprinted by permission of the author.

Anne Taylor Fleming, "Anywhere But Here: More Connected But More Alone" as appeared in the *Los Angeles Times*, August 8, 1999. Reprinted by permission of the author.

Constance García-Barrio, "Creatures That Haunt the Americas." Copyright

© 1989. Reprinted by permission of the author.

Adam Goodheart, "How to Paint a Fresco." First published in *Civilization*, July/August 1995. © 1995 by Adam Goodheart. By permission of The Wylie Agency.

Google™ screen shot "Google News" from http://news.google.com. Reprinted by permission of Google, Inc.

Google™ screen shot "Google Directory" from http://directory.google.com. Reprinted by permission of Google, Inc.

Donald Hall, "Four Kinds of Reading" (1968) from *To Keep Moving: Essays, 1959–1969*. Reprinted by permission of the author.

Nanci Hellmich, "Caught in the Catty Corner," *USA Today*, April 9, 2002. Copyright © USA TODAY, 2002. Reprinted with permission.

Ernest Hemingway, "Camping Out: When You Camp Out, Do It Right." Reprinted with permission of Scribner, an imprint of Simon & Schuster Adult Publishing Group, from *Ernest Hemingway: Dateline: Toronto*, edited by William White. Copyright © 1985 by Mary Hemingway, John Hemingway, Patrick Hemingway, and Gregory Hemingway.

Jamaica Kincaid, excerpt from *A Small Place*. Copyright © 1988 by Jamaica Kincaid. Reprinted by permission of Farrar, Straus and Giroux, LLC.

Maxine Hong Kingston, from *The Woman Warrior*. Copyright © 1975, 1976 by Maxine Hong Kingston. Used by permission of Alfred A. Knopf, a division of Random House, Inc.

Michael Kinsman, "Respectable Addiction: But Crossing the Line Between Worker and Workaholic Creates Its Own Set of Problems," *The San Diego Union-Tribune*, August 6,

2001. © 2001 The San-Diego Union-Tribune. Reprinted with permission.

Ted Koppel, "Take My Privacy, Please!" from *The New York Times* Op-Ed, June 13, 2005. © 2005 The New York Times Co. Reprinted by permission of The New York Times Syndication Sales Corp.

Steve Lopez, "Urban Renaissance Meets the Middle Ages," *The Los Angeles Times*, October 20, 2005. Copyright 2005, Los Angeles Times. Reprinted with permission.

Ben McIntyre, "Poor Winnie the Pooh: Not Even He Is Safe from Rampant 'Therapism'" from *The Times*, July 29, 2005. Reprinted by permission of NI Syndication Ltd.

John McPhee, excerpt from "The Woods from Hog Wallow" from *The Pine Barrens*. Copyright © 1967, 1968 by John McPhee. Reprinted by permission of Farrar, Straus and Giroux, LLC.

Robert Keith Miller, "Discrimination Is a Virtue," *Newsweek*, July 21, 1980. Reprinted by permission of the author.

Brenda Peterson, "Life Is a Musical" from *Nature and Other Mothers*. Copyright © 1992. Reprinted by permission of The Beth Vesel Literary Agency of behalf of Brenda Peterson.

James Poniewozik, "Why Reality TV Is Good For Us," *Time*, February 17, 2003. © 2003 Time Inc. Reprinted by permission.

Joe Queenan, "How to Tell a Joke." Reprinted with permission from the September 2003 *Reader's Digest*. Copyright © 2003 by The Reader's Digest Assn., Inc.

Diane Ravitch, "You Can't Say That," *The Wall Street Journal*, February 13, 2004. Reprinted by permission of The Wall Street Journal. Copyright © 2004 Dow Jones & Company, Inc. All rights reserved worldwide. License number 1437220627417.

Luis J. Rodriguez, from *Always Running—La Vida Loca, Gang Days in LA.* Copyright © 1993. Reprinted by permission of Curbstone Press.

Richard Rodriguez, "Labor." From *Hunger of Memory* by Richard Rodriguez. Reprinted by permission of David R. Godine, Publisher, Inc. Copyright © 1982 by Richard Rodriguez.

Amy Tan, "Snapshot: Lost Lives of Women." Copyright © 1991 by Amy Tan. "Snapshot: Lost Lives of Women" first appeared in *Life* Magazine, April 1991. Reprinted by permission of the author and the Sandra Dijkstra Literary Agency. Photo courtesy the author and the Sandra Dijkstra Literary Agency.

Nicolette Toussaint, "Hearing the Sweetest Songs." From *Newsweek*, May 23, 1994. © 1994 Newsweek, Inc. All rights reserved. Reprinted by permission.

Alice Walker, "Am I Blue?" from *Living by the Word: Selected Writings 1973–1987*. Copyright © 1986 by Alice Walker. Reprinted by permission of Harcourt, Inc.

http://www.how-to-box.com/boxing/book/print/8

Texas State Historical Association, *Handbook of Texas Online*, s.v. "Fisher, John King" at http://www.tsha.utexas.edu/handbook/online/articles/view/FF/ffi20.html.

Excerpted/adapted from "The First American Poem: Edgar Allan Poe's 'The Raven'" by Tony Lumpkin from the United States Naval Academy English Department, http://www.usna.edu/EnglishDept/poeperplex/ravenp.htm.

Excerpted/adapted from Tom Wilson, "A Thin Sheet over Small Water," *Fish and Game Finder Magazine*, 1996. http://www.fishandgame.com/icefish/thinsht.htm.

http://news.nationalgeographic.com/news/2004/06/0628_040628_baldeagle_2.html

http://www.sierraclub.org/john_muir_exhibit/

http://www.redlist.org/info/faq.html#examples

http://www.greenbeltmovement.org/

http://en.wikipedia.org/wiki/Idi_Amin

Michael W. Phillips, Jr., movie review of "A Farewell to Arms" from

http://goatdog.com. Copyright © 2004 Michael W. Phillips, Jr. Reprinted by permission of the author.

Excerpted/adapted from Catherine Schmidt-Jones, "Melody," Connexions Web site, March 19, 2004. http://cnx.rice.edu/content/m11647/1.4/

http://en.wikipedia.org/wiki/Mr._Potato_Head

The National Institute of Standards and Technology, www.nist.gov

Excerpted/adapted from Gift of Time Clocks Web site, http://www.giftoftimeclocks.com/en-us/pg_76.html

http://en.wikipedi.org/wiki/Glass_blowing

Excerpted/adapted from KidsAstronomy.com Web site, "Black Holes," http://www.kidsastronomy.com/black_hole.htm

Excerpted/adapted from The Vassa Network Web site, "A Brief History of Stephen Hawking,"http://vassa.net/hawking.htm

http://wn.wikipedia.org/wiki/The_Adventure_of_the_Dancing_Men

http://en.wikipedia.org/wiki/Hypnosis#Fictional_treatments

http://en.wikipedia.org/wiki/Zoo

http://en.wikipedia.org/wiki/Public_library

http://en.wikipedia.org/wiki/Andrew_Carnegie

http://hearth.com/what/historyfire.html

http://ga.water.usgs.gov/edu/waterproperties.html

http://www.usbr.gov/lc/hooverdam/educate/kidfacts.html

http://en.wikipedia.org/wiki/History_of_the_United_States_NNavy

Excerpted/adapted from Roger A. Lee, The History Guy® Web site, "World War 2: The Invasion of Normandy (1944)," http://www.historyguy.com/normandy/_links.html

http://en.wikipedia.org/wiki/Mark_twain

http://en.wikipedia.org/wiki/Sandra_Day_O%27Connor

http://www.fodors.com/miniguides/mgresults.cfm?destination=new_orleans

http://en.wikipedia.org/wiki/Space_race

http://en.wikipedia.org/wiki/Neil_Armstrong

http://en.wikipedia.org/wiki/U.S._constitution

http://www.pbs.org/wnet/colonialhouse/behind/training.html

Photo Credits

3: © David Butow/Corbis SABA; 15 © Bullit Marquez/AP Photo; 24: © DreamWorks/The Everett Collection; 67: © George Shelley/Corbis; 74: © Underwood & Underwood/Corbis; 102: © AP Photo; 113: © Paramount Pictures/Photofest; 140: © Corbis; 158: © Warner Bros./Photofest; 175: © Sven Simon/Imago/Icon SMI; 183: © AP Photo/Dave Martin; 193: © Bettmann/Corbis; 204: © Sergio Pitamitz/Corbis; 213: © A.I.P./The Kobal Collection; 229: © David Gray/Reuters/Corbis; 235: © The Everett Collection; 256: © Jeff Cadge/Getty Images; 277: © Ansel Adams Publishing Rights Trust/Corbis; 297: © ArenaPal/Topham/The Image Works; 320: © Brian Baley/Getty Images; 341: © Bettmann/Corbis; 367: © Bob Daemmrich/The Image Works; 390: © Bettmann/Corbis; 407: © Virgin (UK)/Courtesy of the Everett Collection; 432: © Leif Skoogfors/Corbis; 447: © Matthew Cavanaugh/epa/Corbis; 463: © Bettmann/Corbis; 474: © AP Photo/Journal Times/Gregory Shaver; 485: © New Line/The Everett Collection; 502: © Warner Brothers/The Everett Collection; 529: © G. Schuster/zefa/Corbis; 535: © Chris Carlson/AP Photo; 545: © Jonelle Weaver/Getty Images; 553: © Reuters/Corbis; 571: © Carolline Von Tuempling/Getty Images; 587: © AP Photo/Dale Sparks; 595: © Fitzwilliam Museum, University of Cambridge, UK/The Bridgeman Art Library; 605: © Steffen Kugler/epa/Corbis; 614: © AP Photo; 619: © Warner Bros./Photofest; 630: © Reuters/Corbis; 639: © Alan Schein/zefa/Corbis; 646: © Kelly-Mooney Photography/CORBIS; 652: © Superstock, Inc.; 658: © Robert Cameron/Getty Images; 670: © AP Photo/The Gazette/Jim Slosiarek; 679: © The Everett Collection; 690: © Susan Walsh/AP Photo; 697: © Alex Brandon/AP Photo; 707: © NASA; 713; ©The Granger Collection

Index